THE UNITED STATES AND SANTO DOMINGO,
1798-1873

A CHAPTER IN CARIBBEAN DIPLOMACY

THE WALTER HINES PAGE SCHOOL OF INTERNATIONAL RELATIONS
THE JOHNS HOPKINS UNIVERSITY

THE UNITED STATES AND SANTO DOMINGO, 1798–1873

A CHAPTER IN CARIBBEAN DIPLOMACY

BY

CHARLES CALLAN TANSILL

Albert Shaw Lecturer in Diplomatic History
The Johns Hopkins University, 1931

GLOUCESTER, MASS.

PETER SMITH

1967

PREFACE

Most of the chapters in this book were given in the form of lectures to my former students in the Graduate School of the Johns Hopkins University. The subject was suggested to me by Dr. John H. Latané, who was deeply interested in American policy in the Caribbean. I regret that his untimely demise deprived me of much valuable counsel and direction.

I owe a special debt of gratitude to Professor Allan Nevins, who gave me many suggestions of great value and who also permitted me to have access to manuscript materials that were necessary to a correct understanding of the imperialism that was so characteristic of the period immediately after the close of the Civil War. I wish also to acknowledge my indebtedness to Professor William Stull Holt, who has taken a personal interest in this study. It is entirely due to the inspiration and assistance of Professor Holt that I have been able to complete my research.

There are many other friends who have been exceedingly helpful. Mr. Reinhard Luthin has been of great assistance, and so also have been Mr. Graham C. Lovejoy, Dr. Samuel F. Bemis, Dr. J. Fred Rippy, Dr. James A. Robertson, Mr. and Mrs. B. R. Parker, Mrs. Natalia Summers, Miss Amy Holland, Miss Julia Bland, Mrs. Ernst Correll, Dr. Bernard Mayo, Mr. Samuel E. Collegeman, Mr. Willard G. Barker, Dr. and Mrs. F. L. Benton, Mr. James L. Sherwood, Mr. Rudolph J. Boehs, Colonel Alfred von Wegerer, Miss Rose Davis, Mrs. Alice Ruddy, Mrs. Mabel McCarthy, Dr. Dexter Perkins, Dr. Delos O. Kinsman, Dr. W. W. Pierson, Dr. Curtis W. Garrison, Mr. Charles Warren, and Mr. Robert Hayes.

I am glad to acknowledge the assistance of Dr. Herbert Putnam who has made available, as no one else can, the vast resources of our great national library in Washington. Mr. Martin Roberts, Superintendent of the Main Reading Room in the Library of Congress, is the friend of every scholar doing research in Washington, while Dr. Thomas P. Martin, of the Division of Manuscripts, is always ready to lend his expert assistance. To other members of the staff of the Division of Manuscripts I am under deep obligation: Mr. Vincent L. Eaton, Dr. Charles P. Powell, Mr. Donald H. Mugridge, Miss Elizabeth McPherson, Mr. John de Porry, Mr. Richard S. Ladd, Miss Cornelia W. Aldridge, Miss Dorothy S. Vastine, and Miss Stella R. Clemence.

Miss Grace Griffin and Mr. Edwin H. Pewett have placed me deeply in their debt, and Mr. Henry S. Parsons and Mr. Archibald B. Evans have made the Periodical Division of the Library of Congress an ideal corner for research. Other friends who have been of assistance are Mr. Bowen Fairfax, Dr. John S. Brooks, Mr. David C. Mearns, Mr. Verner W. Clapp and Dr. Ellery C. Stowell. I also wish to acknowledge the debt I owe to Dr. Albert K. Weinberg for his careful work as copy editor of this manuscript. After this book had approached completion, the archives in the Department of State with reference to Santo Domingo were transferred to the National Archives building. Under the able direction of Dr. R. D. W. Connor, the Archivist of the United States, a vast mass of invaluable source materials has been classified and made available to scholars. In the reference rooms of the National Archives Dr. Nelson Vance Russell has provided ideal facilities for research, and I also owe a debt of gratitude to his able assistants, Miss Elizabeth Drewry, Miss Helen Hunter, and Miss Edna Vosper.

My father and mother have greatly helped me with their much-needed advice, and my wife has not only given me the inspiration to complete this task, but at every step in the making of this book she has been my constant companion and most efficient helpmate.

CHARLES CALLAN TANSILL

Washington, D. C.

CONTENTS

CHAPTER I

THE CALL OF THE CARIBBEAN

American relations with the island of Santo Domingo began as early as the turn of the eighteenth century when venturesome Yankee skippers sailed into the Spanish Main in quest of trade.[1] Since the British islands in the Caribbean were unable to absorb the ample exports of the continental colonies, economic necessity forged colonial ties of a most cosmopolitan character. This inter-colonial trade was in direct defiance of the exclusive navigation laws of that day, but so strong were these trading instincts and so rich were the rewards from this illicit commerce that differences of race, religion, and nationality were lightly regarded. Even the many wars that vexed old Europe failed to destroy these colonial connections.

Of all the islands in the Caribbean, Santo Domingo seemed the most favored by fortune. The western half of the island had since the Peace of Ryswick (1697) belonged incontestably to France, and its fertile soil produced rich crops of coffee and sugar whose sale brought to French merchants the real wealth of the Indies. Trade with the North American colonies was of secondary importance to the planters of Haiti, but they were glad to exchange large quantities of sugar and molasses for the fish, salt meat, provisions, and Guinea blacks that were brought to them in Yankee bottoms.

The establishment of commercial relations between the British North American colonies and Haiti did not escape the watch-

[1] On the early history of Santo Domingo there is a voluminous account by P. F. X. de Charlevoix, *Histoire de l'Isle Espagnole ou de Saint Domingue* (4 vols., Amsterdam, 1730). For French commerce with Haiti see E. Levasseur, *Histoire du commerce de la France* (2 vols., Paris, 1911-1912), and P. Boissonade, *Saint-Domingue à la veille de la révolution et la question de la représentation aux États-Généraux* (Paris, 1906). For the trade between the French West Indies and the British North American colonies see Frank W. Pitman, *The Development of the British West Indies* (New Haven, 1927), chaps. ix, xii, and xiii; George L. Beer, *British Colonial Policy, 1754-1765* (N. Y., 1907), chap. vi.

ful eyes of the members of the Board of Trade at London, and instructions were promptly issued to colonial governors to forbid such intercourse. But actual prohibition of this lucrative trade was impossible.[2] Realizing this fact, the French Government in 1767 decided to make the Môle-Saint-Nicolas a free port where foreign vessels could exchange their cargoes of lumber, dyewoods, live stock, raw or tanned hides, furs, grapes, and tar for Haitian molasses and rum.[3]

This concession, however, did not go far enough to satisfy the French colonists. The chief need of the planters was an unlimited supply of cheap food for the negro slaves who tilled their fields. The Mother Country could not furnish sufficient quantities of salt meat, salt fish, rice, and flour which were the staple articles most urgently required for the proper maintenance of these slaves. In view of this situation the colonial officials in times of emergency were forced to open Haitian ports to all American provisions, and in August, 1769 American flour was formally added to the list of articles allowed to enter the Môle-Saint-Nicolas.[4]

In 1778, after France had entered into alliance with the British North American colonies which were struggling for independence, French colonial ports were opened to foreign commerce.[5] Although this ordinance of 1778 was annulled

[2] G. L. Beer, *op. cit.*, chap. vi; F. W. Pitman, *op. cit.*, chap. xiii.

[3] Hilliard d'Aubertueil, *Considérations sur l'état présent de la colonie française de Saint Domingue* (Paris, 1776), p. 286; *Lettres critiques et politiques sur les colonies et le commerce des villes maritimes de France* (Geneva, 1785), pp. 113-114; H. E. Mills, *The Early Years of the French Revolution in San Domingo* (Ithaca, 1889), p. 12. For the colonial arrêt of July 31, 1767, relative to the importation of fish into Haiti, and its renewal by the arrêt of May 19, 1775, see Archives du Ministère des Affaires Étrangères, Mémoires et Documents, Amérique, 16: 183, Library of Congress photostats.

[4] Frederick L. Nussbaum, "The French Colonial Arrêt of 1784," *South Atlantic Quarterly*, XXVII (1928), 63-64.

[5] *Lettres critiques et politiques sur les colonies et le commerce des villes maritimes de France*, p. 125; David Macpherson, *Annals of Commerce* (London, 1805), IV, 55. On the general subject of French colonial trade during the period of the American Revolution, see the "Mémoire sommaire" (1777), Arch. Aff. Étr., Mém. et Doc., Amérique, 16:213; the "Mémoire sur l'état de nos colonies et la situation actuelle de nôtre guerre avec l'Angleterre" (1780), *ibid.*, Amérique, 16:233; and the "Discours politique sur les colonies françoises," *ibid.*, 16:260.

in 1783 by a ministerial letter, it is apparent that colonial officials still permitted trade with American shippers. In the island of Martinique, Governor Damas issued a proclamation (July 23, 1783) which encouraged a limited commerce with America, and the situation at Le Cap, Haiti, is indicated in a letter to Stephen Girard from his brother who was located at that port:

Our government will not permit English flour to enter here. All other articles manufactured in New England are so abundant that this commerce presents a dull outlook.[6]

The importance of the American trade with the French West Indies is emphasized by John Adams in a letter to Robert R. Livingston on July 3, 1783. So essential is this commerce to both parties that if the "governments forbid it, it will be carried on clandestinely." [7] In France, however, the agricultural interests and the merchants around Bordeaux and Guienne were strongly in favor of the old restrictive policy, and the Ministry was slow to take any action.[8] Lafayette became the chief spokesman for America, and early in 1784 he submitted to Vergennes a memoir in which he advocated some sweeping concessions to America with reference to trade with the French West Indies.[9]

[6] W. E. Lingelbach, "England and Neutral Trade," *Military Historian and Economist*, II (1917), 155. See also George Chalmers, *Opinions on Interesting Subjects of Public Law and Commercial Policy* (London, 1784), p. 81.

[7] *The Works of John Adams* (ed. by C. F. Adams, 10 vols., Boston, 1854), VIII, 79. For the situation of the French colonies in 1783 see the memoir " Aprovisionnement des colonies françoises après la prochaine paix," Arch. Aff. Étr., Mém. et Doc., Amérique, 16:359.

[8] Vergennes to Joly de Fleury (Director General of Finances), March 13, 1783, Arch. Add. Aff. Étr., Corresp. Pol., É. U., 23:291; Texier to Vergennes, July 29, 1783, *ibid.*, É. U., 25:107.

[9] " Observations Addressed to the Count de Vergennes on the Commerce of the United States with France and the French Colonies," *Diplomatic Correspondence of the United States of America from the Treaty of Paris to the Adoption of the Present Constitution* (7 vols., Washington, 1833), I, 391-403. See also L. R. Gottschalk, " Lafayette as Commercial Expert," *American Historical Review*, XXXVI (1931), 561-570; and Albert Mathiez, "Lafayette et le commerce franco-américain à la veille de la révolution," *Annales historiques de la révolution française*, n. s. (28 vols., Paris-Reims, 1908-1936), III, 474-484. For additional material on colonial trade one can consult the memoir " Les colonies considérées relativement au commerce, January 10, 1784," Arch. Aff. Étr., Mém. et Doc., Amérique, 17:5.

After having received further advice from Barbé-Marbois and Gouverneur Morris, along with protests from the business men of Bordeaux, the French Government issued the well-known arrêt of August 30, 1784.[10] Seven free ports were now established in the French colonies in the Caribbean, three of them in Haiti—Cap Français, Port-au-Prince, and Cayes-Saint-Louis. The list of articles which were permitted to enter these ports was extended (as compared with the arrêt of 1767) by including coal, salt beef, salt fish, rice, maize, and vegetables. The entry of American flour was still prohibited, and the exports from Haiti were limited to molasses and rum.[11]

The exclusion of American flour and the regulations forbidding the export to America of cotton, coffee, and sugar evoked vehement protests from American shippers, but Jefferson wrote to James Monroe that there was little hope for the adoption of a more liberal policy:

The merchants of this country [France] are very clamorous against our admission into the West Indies and Ministers are afraid for their places.[12]

As a result of this opposition to the favors granted to American commerce by the arrêt of August 30, 1784, the French Government receded somewhat from its liberal position and imposed new and burdensome regulations upon the trade be-

[10] Marquis de Barbé-Marbois, "Mémoire sur le commerce entre la France et les États-Unis" (Philadelphia, June 2, 1783), Arch. Aff. Étr., Mém. et Doc., É. U., 14:55; Gouverneur Morris to the Marquis de Chastellux, June 17, 1784, *ibid.*, É. U., 2:120. See also the "Mémoire sur le commerce des Américains des États-Unis dans nos colonies et sur les moyens de conserver à nos négocians le commerce de nos merchandises coloniales avec l'Étranger," Arch. Aff. Étr., Mém. et Doc., Amérique, 17:14; and the "Mémoire sur le commerce des farines dans nos colonies," *ibid.*, Amérique, 17:38.

[11] "Arrêt du Conseil d'État du Roi, concernant le commerce étranger dans les Isles Françoises de l'Amérique, August 30, 1784," Arch. Aff. Étr., Mém. et Doc., Amérique, 17:53. See also Henri Sée, "Commerce between France and the United States, 1783-1784," *American Historical Review*, XXXI (1926), 732-752; David Macpherson, *Annals of Commerce*, IV, 55-56; *Recueil général des anciennes lois françaises*, A. D. 420-1789 (Paris, 1827), XXVII, 459-464.

[12] Jefferson to Monroe, February, 1785, *Writings of Thomas Jefferson* (ed. by P. L. Ford, 10 vols., N. Y., 1891-1899), IV, 31; and Jefferson, "Notes of a Conference with Vergennes, 1785," *ibid.*, IV, 130. See also Jefferson to Monroe, June 17, 1785, *Jefferson Papers*, vol. 13, MS. Library of Congress.

tween its West Indian colonies and the United States.[13] This action led to a large contraband commerce which flourished despite the elaborate precautions taken by French officials against smuggling. Commerce, like love, seemed to laugh at these government locksmiths who soon tired of their impossible task.[14]

In 1788 a new factor appeared in this difficult equation of inter-colonial trade. A serious shortage of crops in France made it next to impossible to export to Haiti the required amount of foodstuffs to maintain the large laboring population.[15] During the first three months of 1789 the town and nearby districts of Port-au-Prince were in need of some 27,000 barrels of flour for bare subsistence. From France the shipments of flour to this port dwindled to merely 5,526 barrels, and the Governor of Haiti felt constrained to issue decrees which "opened temporarily all the ports of the island to the importation of bread and foreign grain, and allowed free exportation of colonial products.[16]

[13] "Arrêt du Conseil d'État du Roi concernant les armemens de commerce pour les isles et colonies françoises," Arch. Aff. Étr., Mém. et Doc., Amérique, 17:63. For a discussion of the problem of colonial trade see the letter from Count Vergennes to M. de Bertrand, April 27, 1785, Arch. Aff. Étr., Mém. et Doc., Amérique, 17:85; and the memoir "Réfutation d'un mémoire signé de cent armateurs et négocians de Nantes contre l'admission des navires étrangères dans les colonies françaises," ibid., Amérique, 17:100. See also M. Treille, Le commerce de Nantes et la révolution (Paris, 1908); and J. de Tremaudan, "Le commerce de Nantes (XVIIᵉ et XVIIIᵉ siècles)," Revue de Bretagne, XXX (1903), 16-22.

[14] Lettres critiques et politiques sur les colonies et le commerce des villes maritimes de France, p. 113; Comte de Moustier (French Minister to the United States) to Comte de Vergennes (French Minister of Foreign Relations), February 12 and April 21, 1788, American Historical Review, VIII (1903), 724-725; Léon Deschamps, Histoire de la question coloniale en France (Paris, 1891), p. 312; David Macpherson, Annals of Commerce, IV, 55-56. With reference to trade conditions at Port-au-Prince in 1787, there is the following item in the Pennsylvania Packet and Daily Advertiser, February 17, 1787: "By a gentleman from Port au Prince we learn that a great number of American vessels are at that place taking in molasses and taffia, but so narrowly are they watched by the officers of the customs, as to render their smuggling sugar and coffee on board wholly impossible."

[15] H. Taine, The French Revolution (3 vols., N. Y., 1878-1885), I, 1-5; W. E. H. Lecky, History of England in the Eighteenth Century (N. Y., 1878-1887), V, 426-427.

[16] H. E. Mills, The Early Years of the French Revolution in San Domingo,

The immediate advantage that was taken of these emergency decrees by American shippers is indicated by the following item in the *Pennsylvania Packet and Daily Advertiser*:

Our market [at Le Cap, Haiti] is still glutted with amazing quantities of flour, and from the daily arrivals from America . . . the quantity still increases.[17]

As a result of strong pressure exerted upon the Minister of Marine by French agrarian interests, these liberal ordinances of Governor du Chilleau were annulled and the Governor himself was replaced by a new appointee who would not be so responsive to colonial demands. But the colonists were not easily cowed. In July, 1790, the General Assembly passed two laws which opened all the ports of Haiti to the free importation of provisions and of articles of "prime necessity" and set aside the restrictions against the exportation of the products of the colony. These laws were not approved by the new Governor, who took effective action by dissolving the General Assembly.[18]

The interest of the American Government in the trade with Haiti was clearly indicated by the appointment (June 7, 1790) of Sylvanus Bourne as the American consul at Cap Français.[19] Bourne arrived at this Haitian port on March 16, 1791 and presented his credentials "in due form to the Govt." But he soon found out that the French authorities in Haiti were in no hurry to recognize his official title, and he bitterly complained to the Secretary of State of their "equivocal & evasive conduct." [20] After vainly waiting some four months for official recognition which was constantly postponed on various pre-

p. 40. From a letter dated at Aux Cayes, May 6, 1789, we learn the extent of these decrees of Governor du Chilleau (Haiti) in 1789: " We have the honor to inform you that this port has been made free for the importation, by vessels of all nations, of negroes, salt provisions, flour, and every other species of merchandise hitherto prohibited." *Pennsylvania Packet and Daily Advertiser*, *July* 7, 1789.

[17] January 22, 1790.

[18] H. E. Mills, *op. cit.*, pp. 69-70; J. Garran-Coulon, *Rapport sur les troubles de Saint-Domingue* (Paris, 1798), I, 240-243, 248-268.

[19] Bourne was commissioned to " Hispaniola."

[20] Bourne to Jefferson, April 29, 1791, *Amsterdam, Consular Despatches,* vol. 1, MS. Dept. of State.

texts, Bourne concluded that his situation was so " painful " that he could no longer remain in Haiti. In the middle of July, 1791, he left Cap Français and returned to the United States, but he did not resign his commission as consul until December 28, 1791.[21]

In his despatch of April 29, 1791 to the Secretary of State, Bourne referred to the "state of politicks" in Haiti which at times excited both his "pity & Indignation." The northern and southern sections of the colony were "bitterly opposed to each other while the principles or motives which actuate each are clouded in mystic darkness." [22] In his last communication to Secretary Jefferson from Cap Français, Bourne remarked upon the hostile feeling that existed between the mulattoes and the whites. This tension was growing and it might well result in "all the horrors of a civil war." [23]

This predicted civil war in Haiti broke out with sudden fury on the night of August 22, 1791, when the enslaved

[21] Bourne to Jefferson, December 28, 1791, *Amsterdam, Consular Desp.*, vol. 1, MS. Dept. of State. The French officials in Haiti had no intention of recognizing Bourne as a consul, and M. Ternant (French Minister to the United States) wrote to the French Minister for Foreign Affairs (Montmorin), on October 24, 1791, that he regarded Jefferson's appointment of Bourne as a " forced interpretation " of the consular convention of November 14, 1788. See *Report of American Historical Association,* 1903, II, 64. Jefferson himself was fully convinced that the American Government was clearly within its rights in appointing Bourne as consul to " Hispaniola." In a letter to William Short (April 25, 1791) Jefferson remarked as follows: " I consider the consular convention [of November 14, 1788] as securing clearly our right to appoint consuls in the French colonies." He did not desire, however, to press this matter of consular appointments too far. In this letter to William Short he further observed: " Only two appointments have as yet been made (Mr. Skipwith at Martinique and Guadeloupe, and Mr. Bourne in St. Dominique), and they shall be instructed not to ask a regular Exequatur. We certainly wish to press nothing on our friends which shall be inconvenient. I shall hope that M. de Montmorin will order such attentions to be shewn these gentlemen as the patronage of commerce may call for." *Jefferson Papers,* vol. 63, MS. Library of Congress. The commerce between Haiti and the United States was a considerable item at that time. In a report to President Washington of December 23, 1791, Jefferson estimated that the exports from the United States to the French islands in the Caribbean amounted to $3,284,656, and the imports therefrom to $1,913,212. *Jefferson Papers,* vol. 68.

[22] Bourne to Jefferson, April 29, 1791, *Amsterdam, Consular Desp.,* vol. 1, MS. Dept. of State.

[23] Bourne to Jefferson, July 14, 1791, *ibid.*

blacks began to murder their masters.[24] The colonial administration quickly turned to the United States for help, and representatives were sent to Philadelphia to secure munitions of war
and provisions.[25] Ternant, the French Minister to the United
States, resented these direct appeals to the American Government, and he had grave fears of a rising spirit of independence
in Haiti. He thought that such a spirit, when viewed in connection with the inevitable increase in national power of the
United States, might constitute a real threat to French colonial
dominion in the Caribbean.[26]

These fears of Ternant were ill-grounded. On July 28, 1791,
Jefferson wrote to William Short (in Paris) and expressly
denied that the American Government had any designs upon
Haiti:

Whenever jealousies are expressed as to any supposed views of ours
on the dominion of the West Indies, you cannot go farther than the
truth in asserting that we have none. If there be one principle more
deeply rooted than any other in the mind of every American, it is—
that we should have nothing to do with conquest.[27]

Some weeks later Jefferson gave similar assurances to Ternant
as to American policy in the Caribbean, and he frankly informed the agents from Haiti that in order to secure succour
from the United States they would have to act in concert with
the French Minister.[28] This promised assistance from the
American Government was promptly extended to the colonial
administration in Haiti through payments upon the national
debt owed to France. Without this "financial assistance from
the United States it would have been almost, if not quite, impossible for the French administration to have sustained itself

[24] T. L. Stoddard, *The French Revolution in San Domingo* (N. Y., 1914),
pp. 128 ff.
[25] Charles Tarbé, *Rapport sur les troubles de Saint-Domingue* (Paris, 1791),
pp. 14 ff.; C. Tarbé, *Piéces justificatives du rapport sur les troubles de Saint-
Domingue*, Nos. 12-13, pp. 8-9; Ternant to Montmorin, September 28, 1791,
Report, American Historical Association, 1903, II, 45-51.
[26] Ternant to Montmorin, September 28, 1791, *ibid.*, 47.
[27] Jefferson to Short, July 28, 1791, *Jefferson Papers*, vol. 65, MS. Library
of Congress.
[28] Ternant to Montmorin, November 17, 1791, *Report, American Historical
Association*, 1903, II, 74-75.

in Santo Domingo during the early days of the revolution." [29]

But the United States was not the only nation to lend aid to the French colonists in Haiti. British assistance meant actual intervention by military force—intervention that resulted in little achievement and serious loss both in prestige and in man-power. The importance of this West Indian misadventure is now clearly recognized by historians, and Sir John W. Fortescue even goes so far as to maintain that the real secret of British impotence against the arms of France from 1793 to 1799 may be found in the "two fatal words, St. Domingo." [30]

Active British interest in the Haitian situation began when large numbers of French refugees sought shelter in Jamaica after the outbreak of the negro insurrection in August, 1791. In response to their entreaties for help Lord Effingham, the Governor of Jamaica, rushed supplies to Haiti, and the French planters compared this ready succour from a British colony with the seeming indifference of their native land.[31] By the terms of the decree of May 15, 1791 and the law of April 4, 1792, the National Assembly of France had endowed the mulattoes and the free negroes in Haiti with the voting franchise and with the right to sit in the colonial assemblies. This ill-considered policy enraged the planters of the colony who now looked to England as a bulwark against misguided idealism and as a means of crushing the negro revolt.[32]

On September 3, 1793 some of these dissatisfied French colonists in Haiti signed an agreement with the Governor of Jamaica whereby they formally transferred their allegiance to the British crown.[33] The Governor responded with the dis-

[29] Mary Treudley, "The United States and Santo Domingo, 1789-1866," *Journal of Race Development*, VII (1916), p. 110.

[30] Sir John W. Fortescue, *A History of the British Army* (12 vols., N. Y., 1899-1927), IV, 325.

[31] Bryan Edwards, *An Historical Survey of the French Colony in the Island of St. Domingo* (London, 1797), pp. iii-xi.

[32] T. L. Stoddard, *The French Revolution in San Domingo*, chaps. x, xiv.

[33] For the text of the agreement of September 3, 1793, see Arch. Aff. Étr., Mém. et Doc., Amérique, 14:216, 220, 297. See also J. Garran-Coulon, *Rapport sur les troubles de Saint Domingue*, IV, 128-132; Bryan Edwards, *op. cit.*, pp. 147-151; Marcus Rainsford, *An Historical Account of the Black Empire of Hayti* (London, 1805), pp. 172 ff.; A. Dalmas, *Histoire de la révolution de Saint Domingue* (2 vols., Paris, 1814), II, 230-234.

patch of a small force of British soldiers which quickly took possession of the harbor of Jérémie. It was but a short time before the great fortress of the Môle-Saint-Nicolas fell into British hands, and this success was followed by the surrender of Port-au-Prince, on June 4, 1794.[34]

The capture of Port-au-Prince marked the high tide of British good fortune in Haiti. Recession began when the mulatto general Rigaud took the offensive in the summer of 1794, and soon Léogane was in his hands. And although Toussaint failed in his assault upon Saint-Marc in September of that year, he was rapidly learning the art of war from these defeats even as the Russians learned the same lesson from the reverses they suffered at the hands of Charles XII of Sweden.[35]

In the meantime, American vessels en route to Haitian ports faced serious danger of seizure by the British fleet or by French corsairs. On May 9, 1793 the French National Convention issued a decree authorizing naval commanders to detain neutral vessels loaded with provisions and bound to enemy ports. These foodstuffs were to be bought and not confiscated, and freight

[34] Thomas Jefferson, after watching the successive military triumphs of the British forces in Haiti, became highly alarmed at the prospect of British domination of the former French colony. In a letter to James Madison on April 3, 1794, he expressed the view that the American Government would soon have to inform the British Cabinet that the French islands in the Caribbean were " to rest with France, and that we will make common cause [with France] . . . for that object." *Jefferson Papers*, vol. 97, MS. Library of Congress. Jefferson's personal feelings relative to the negro insurrection in Haiti are revealed in a letter to James Monroe, July 14, 1793: " I become daily more & more convinced that all the West India islands will remain in the hands of the people of colour & a total expulsion of the whites sooner or later take place. It is high time we should foresee the bloody scenes which our children, certainly, and possibly ourselves (south of Potomac) have to wade through, & try to avert them." *Jefferson Papers*, vol. 90.

In a public notice printed in the American press, the British Consul-General for the Middle and Southern States declared that " for the encouragement of merchants trading to the ports in the island of St. Domingo, in the possession of his Majesty's forces, assurances are given that all vessels carrying provisions thither, will, for the present, be allowed to bring away produce to the amount of their cargoes." Philadelphia *General Advertiser*, May 27, 1794.

[35] B. Edwards, *An Historical Survey of the French Colony in the Island of St. Domingo*, chap. xi; Pamphile de Lacroix, *Mémoires pour servir a l'histoire de la révolution de Saint Domingue* (2 vols., Paris, 1820), I, 298-329.

and demurrage were to be granted to the owners of the vessels.[36] On June 8, 1793 the British Government issued an Order in Council of the same tenor. In the decree of the French Convention an exception was made with reference to American vessels.[37]

In order completely to stop all trade between American ports and French ports in the Caribbean, the British Government next issued an Order in Council (November 6, 1793) directing the commanders of British war-ships to detain all ships laden with the produce of any colony belonging to France, or carrying provisions or other supplies for the use of such colony.[38] By delaying the publication of the Order in Council until late in December, 1793, the British Government made it possible for their fleet, aided by swarms of privateers, to capture some three hundred American vessels.[39]

Although under the terms of a new British Order in Council (January 8, 1794) the restrictions upon American trade with the French islands in the Caribbean were somewhat relaxed, the dangers that still attended any commercial ventures in those waters were so great that masters and mates of vessels sailing from Baltimore publicly resolved

that until the American Flag can float securely on the ocean, they will not engage to navigate our vessels.[40]

The Jay Treaty of November 19, 1794 paved the way for better relations between the United States and Great Britain, but this very fact led to difficulties with France that eventually developed into open warfare. Even before the signature of the Jay Treaty, American commerce with France had been severely injured by an embargo at Bordeaux which detained more than one hundred American vessels. This adverse action was followed by the decree of the French Directory (July 2, 1796) which set aside Franco-American treaties and provided

[36] *American State Papers, Foreign Relations* (6 vols., Wash., 1832-1839), I, 243.
[37] Samuel F. Bemis, *Jay's Treaty* (N. Y., 1924), pp. 156 ff.
[38] *American State Papers, Foreign Relations,* I, 430.
[39] Samuel F. Bemis, *A Diplomatic History of the United States* (N. Y., 1936), p. 100.
[40] Philadelphia *General Advertiser,* May 23, 1794.

that American ships should be subjected to the same rigorous treatment that was meted out to British vessels.[41]

In Haiti the agents of the French Directory (the five Civil Commissioners—Sonthonax, Roume, Leblanc, Raymond, and Giraud) were quick to carry out the wishes of France with reference to American trade, and on November 27, 1796 an order was issued to French naval commanders to seize all American ships "bound to or from British ports.[42] The disastrous effects of this order upon American commerce in the Caribbean were soon evident. In a report to the Minister of Marine (February, 1797) the Civil Commissioners remark that having found no resource

in finance, and knowing the unfriendly dispositions of the Americans, and to avoid perishing in distress, they had armed for cruizing; and that already 87 cruizers were at sea; and that for three months preceding, the administration had subsisted, and individuals been enriched, with the product of those prizes. . . . They felicitate themselves that American vessels were daily taken; and declare that they had learnt by divers persons . . . that the Americans were perfidious.[43]

In order to protect American interests in Haiti the American Government commissioned Jacob Mayer, of Pennsylvania, as American consul at Cap Français. Mayer arrived at his post about the middle of July, 1796, and his letters to Secretary Pickering are filled with descriptions of the capture of American

[41] *American State Papers, Foreign Relations,* I, 748-759; Alfred T. Mahan, *The Influence of Sea Power upon the French Revolution and Empire* (2 vols., London, 1892), II, 243; Gardner W. Allen, *Our Naval War with France* (Boston, 1909), pp. 16-40; Albert J. Beveridge, *The Life of John Marshall* (4 vols., Boston, 1916-1919), II, 223 ff. For a vast amount of valuable data bearing upon Franco-American relations from 1797 to 1800 see the new series of volumes prepared by the Office of Naval Records and Library, United States Navy Department, under the title *Naval Documents Related to the Quasi-War between the United States and France* (5 vols., Wash., 1935-1937). Hereafter cited as *Naval Documents.*

[42] *Naval Documents, February, 1797-October, 1798,* p. 3.

[43] *Actes et mémoires concernant les négociations qui ont eu lieu entre la France et les États-Unis de l'Amérique, depuis 1793, jusqu'à la conclusion de la convention du 30 Septembre, 1800* (3 vols., London, 1807), III, 384. The situation at Cap Français is indicated in a letter from that port on December 9, 1796. In this communication it is stated that there were, at the time of writing, some seventy-three American ships in that port, all of them having been seized by French privateers. Philadelphia *General Advertiser,* January 31, 1797.

vessels by French privateers. On July 17, 1797 he informed the Department of State that American trade with Haitian ports was "more precarious than ever.[44] In reply, Secretary Pickering remarked that "the atrocities and piracies which have been causelessly committed on our defenceless commerce have inflicted a wound in American Breasts which cannot soon be healed." [45] Reprisals against these lawless seizures were soon to be ordered.

By the Acts of May 28 and June 28, 1798 Congress authorized the capture of French armed vessels,[46] and the Act of June 13, 1798 suspended commercial intercourse with France and her possessions.[47] Subsequent legislation permitted American merchant vessels to carry defensive armament and to make prizes of French armed merchantmen which assumed the offensive.[48] The treaties with France were declared abrogated,[49] and a Navy Department was created.[50]

In view of this quasi-war with France, it was inevitable that many Americans should turn their thoughts toward the French colonial dominion in the Caribbean. John Quincy Adams believed that it would be expedient to have the French islands "free and independent, in close alliance and under the guarantee of the United States." [51] Alexander Hamilton was thinking

[44] Mayer to Pickering, July 17, 1797, *Cape Haitien, Consular Desp.*, vol. 1, MS. Dept. of State. See also the consular despatches from Mayer to Pickering quoted in *Naval Documents, February, 1797-October, 1798*, pp. 24-25.

[45] Pickering to Mayer, September 22, 1797, *Cape Haitien, Consular Desp.*, vol. 1, MS. Dept. of State. The terrible treatment meted out to American seamen by the masters of French privateers is given graphic description in a long narrative in *Claypoole's American Daily Advertiser* (Phila.), December 21, 1798.

[46] *United States Statutes at Large,* I, 561, 575-576. It was not long before American naval commanders (under instructions from the Secretary of the Navy) began to seize French vessels in accordance with the terms of the acts of May 28 and June 28, 1798. On July 7, 1798, Captain Stephen Decatur captured a French privateer near Egg Harbor after it had seized an American merchantman. Boston *Columbian Centinel*, July 14, 1798.

[47] *U. S. Statutes at Large,* I, 565-566.

[48] Act of June 25, 1798, *ibid.*, 572.

[49] Act of July 7, 1798, *ibid.*, 578.

[50] Act of April 30, 1798, *ibid.*, 553-554.

[51] Adams to William Vans Murray, July 14, 1798, *Writings of John Quincy Adams* (ed. by W. C. Ford, 6 vols., N. Y., 1913-1916), II, 336.

along similar lines, and in a memorandum to Oliver Wolcott
(Secretary of the Treasury) he raised the following question:

Is not the independence of the French Colonies under the Guarantee
of the United States, to be aimed at? If it is, there cannot be too much
promptness in opening negociations for the purpose.[52]

It was impossible for the Adams Administration to formulate
with any degree of speed a policy to fit the situation in the
Caribbean. Finally, on February 9, 1799, Secretary Pickering
wrote to Hamilton to seek his advice on the situation in Haiti.
Congress had just passed an act which authorized the President
to reopen trade relations with Haiti whenever he was satisfied
that American commerce would be safe in Haitian waters. The
President clearly perceived the importance of this colonial trade,
and according to Secretary Pickering, he would

undoubtedly give to the act [of February 9, 1799] as liberal a construction as will be politically expedient. Toussaint, if certain of our
commerce, will, Meyer assures me, declare the whole island of St.
Domingo independent; confident in his power to defend it, provided
we will allow of a free commercial intercourse, by which the islanders
may exchange their productions for the supplies our vessels will carry
to them. This act of independence I fully expect; & I persuade myself
that Great Britain will consent to share in it; and that Genl. Maitland
has made some arrangement with Toussaint for that purpose.[53]

Hamilton returned a prompt and cautious answer to Secretary Pickering's questions. He inclined towards the view that
it would not be advisable for the American Government to be
committed to a policy which favored Haitian independence.
There should be

no guaranty, no formal treaty—nothing that can rise up in judgment.
It will be enough to let Toussaint be assured verbally, but explicitly,
that upon his declaration of independence a commercial intercourse
will be opened.[54]

[52] Hamilton to Wolcott, June 5, 1798, *Hamilton Papers,* vol. 30, MS. Library
of Congress.
[53] Pickering to Hamilton, February 9, 1799, *ibid.,* vol. 35.
[54] Hamilton to Pickering, February 9, 1799 (this date is probably incorrect),
Works of Alexander Hamilton (ed. by J. C. Hamilton, 7 vols., N. Y., 1850-
1851), VI, 395.

Hamilton and other leaders of the Federalist party were interested in the Haitian muddle mainly from the angle of trade expansion. This economic motive is apparent in the following excerpt from a letter which Oliver Wolcott addressed to Samuel Smith:

Nothing appears to have been proposed, discussed, or settled, between the British and Toussaint, respecting the independence of the island, and with this question the United States will not interfere. Our object is to gain a trade on safe principles; questions of interior policy and government are to be settled by the people of the island, and others concerned, in their own way. . . . The object of the United States is to extend their trade and to suppress privateering.[55]

This commercial note with reference to American relations with Haiti was strongly sounded by Secretary Pickering himself in an instruction he sent to Jacob Mayer, the American consul at Cap Français:

You will take notice that the act of Congress of the last session prohibiting intercourse with France and her dominions [June 13, 1798] is limited to places *under the acknowledged power of* France, consequently if the inhabitants of St. Domingo have ceased to acknowledge that power, there will not, as I conceive, be any bar to the prompt and extensive renewal of trade between the United States and the ports of that Island. Our merchants, I understand, are already preparing to renew that commerce. . . . The putting down all privateers of the island, at least the restraining them from touching Americans, I look for as a natural consequence of the revolution. Good policy doubtless suggests to the Chiefs, and especially to the amiable and respectable Toussaint, the commander in chief, a system of peace towards Great Britain and her dependencies as well as towards the United States.[56]

If Toussaint appeared "amiable and respectable" to Secretary Pickering, it is quite obvious that to General Hédouville, the agent of the French Directory, he had a most sinister aspect. The General had landed at Le Cap [57] on April 20, 1798, and

[55] Wolcott to Smith, March 20, 1799, George Gibbs, *Memoirs of the Administrations of Washington and John Adams* (2 vols., N. Y., 1846), II, 228.

[56] Pickering to Mayer, November 30, 1798, *Cape Haitien, Consular Desp.,* vol. 1, MS. Dept. of State.

[57] Throughout this chapter the author has used the spelling Cap Français. Other spellings and names are Cap François, Cape Haytien, Cape Haitien, and Le Cap.

it was not long before he realized that Toussaint was the supreme power in the French colony. After a sojourn of some six months, he returned to France and reported that Haiti was practically independent of any outside control. The only important task before Toussaint was the defeat of the mulatto leader, Rigaud.[58]

Toussaint himself was well aware that Rigaud must be crushed before Haiti would be completely under his domination. In order to achieve this end he must court American assistance and, if possible, divert any aid to Rigaud. This would be a little difficult because Rigaud had at times favored American commerce.[59] But Toussaint had high hopes of securing American good will, and on November 6, 1798 he wrote a letter to President Adams with reference to American trade. He stated that he had noticed with the greatest surprise and sorrow that American ships had practically abandoned Haitian ports. He then hastened to offer guarantees that American commerce would be adequately protected and that the masters of American ships would receive full payment for the cargoes they brought to Haiti.[60]

Toussaint followed this overture by sending to Philadelphia in December his personal representative, Joseph Bunel, who placed before the Adams Administration the many trade advantages that would attend the reopening of American commercial relations with Haiti.[61] In response to these gestures of

[58] T. L. Stoddard, *The French Revolution in San Domingo*, chap. xxiii.

[59] In the Philadelphia *General Advertiser* of January 31, 1797, there is a brief item to the effect that Americans were "well treated" at Aux Cayes. Rigaud and his adherents were "outlawed by the Commissioners, and determined to be honest."

[60] Toussaint to Adams, November 6, 1797, *Cape Haitien, Consular Desp.*, vol. 1, MS. Dept. of State. See also "Letters of Toussaint Louverture and of Edward Stevens," *American Historical Review*, XVI (1910), 65-101.

[61] George Gibbs, *Memoirs of the Administrations of Washington and John Adams*, II, 227. Bunel was accompanied on this trip to Philadelphia by Jacob Mayer, the American consul at Cap Français. They arrived on December 19, 1798, and on December 28 the Philadelphia *General Advertiser* (or *Aurora*) spoke of Toussaint as a leader who was "beloved and respected for his talents, mild manners and good faith." With respect to Bunel and Mayer there is a sharp arraignment of their practices and a bitter attack upon their character in a letter from Edward Stevens to James Yard, August 22, 1799, *Cape Haitien,*

good will, President Adams had the Secretary of the Navy issue the following instruction to Captain John Barry:

It is very much the wish of the President, that you should take some occasion, before your return to show yourself, with the greatest part of the fleet at Cape Francois, to Genl. Toussaint, who has a great desire to see some Ships of War belonging to America—but it is not intended, that you should sacrifice any important object, to gratify this General; with whom however, if it should fall in your way, it may be well for you to cultivate a good understanding.[62]

President Adams and a large majority in both houses of Congress were favorable to a renewal of trade relations with Haiti, and under the provisions of the Act of February 9, 1799 the President was authorized to proclaim a reopening of this commerce whenever he was satisfied that the depredations committed by Haitian privateers were at an end.[63] In order to ascertain the exact state of affairs in Haiti and to learn whether it would be wise to permit American merchant ships to sail to Haitian ports, the President decided to send Edward Stevens to Cap Français to see Toussaint. Captain Thomas Tingey, of the United States Navy, was instructed to convoy to Cap Français the ship on which Mr. Stevens would sail, and in the event that he should have an interview with Toussaint the Captain was directed to "conciliate the good opinion of that General and his people." [64]

Stevens was commissioned as Consul-General to the Island of San Domingo, and he arrived at Cap Français on April 18, 1799.[65] His relations with the black dictator were friendly

---

Consular Desp., vol. 2, MS. Dept. of State: " Mayer and Bunel [are] two of the greatest scoundrels I ever knew in my Life. The former in particular is the basest and most treacherous Character I ever met with. . . . He is really a Disgrace to the American name. He is never sober after dinner; & being a weak, leaky man, he does a great Deal of mischief in his Conversations."

[62] Secretary of the Navy (Benjamin Stoddert) to Barry, January 16, 1799, *Letters to Officers of Ships of War*, vol. 1, MS. Navy Department Archives.

[63] *U. S. Statutes at Large*, I, 613-616.

[64] Stoddert to Tingey, March 16, 1799, *Letters to Officers of Ships of War*, vol. 1, MS. Navy Department Archives.

[65] The attitude of Thomas Jefferson towards the appointment of Stevens and the reopening of trade relations with Haiti is indicated in two letters which he sent to James Madison. On February 5, 1799, he informed Madison that " the

and his mission to Haiti was entirely successful. His endeavors to carry out a policy of concerted action with England relative to the commerce of Haiti are full of interest as an early exercise in Anglo-American harmony. The following chapter— The Maitland Mission—will tell the story of this important political concert.

bill for continuing the suspension of intercourse with France . . . is still before the Senate, but will pass by a very great vote. An attack is made on what is called Toussaint's clause, the object of which, as is charged by the one party and *admitted* by the other, is to facilitate the separation of the island from France. The clause will pass however, by about 19 to 8." *Jefferson Papers*, vol. 105, MS. Library of Congress. After the passage of the Act of February 9, 1799, Jefferson wrote to Madison on February 12, 1799 to advise him that " Toussaint's clause " had received the approval of both houses of Congress: " Even South Carolinians in the H. of R. voted for it. We may expect therefore black crews, & supercargoes & missionaries thence into the southern states; & when that leaven begins to work, I would gladly compound with a great part of our northern country, if they would honestly stand neuter. If this combustion can be introduced among us under any veil whatever, we have to fear it." *Ibid.*, vol. 105.

CHAPTER II

THE MAITLAND MISSION

In the previous chapter a brief allusion was made to the success that attended the intervention of the British armed forces in Haiti during the years 1793-1794. This tide of victory had rapidly receded after the capture of Tiburon in the last days of December, 1794 by the mulatto leader Rigaud. Moreover, a worse foe than either Rigaud or Toussaint stalked the British army on the island of Santo Domingo. Throughout 1795 and 1796 yellow fever exacted such a terrible toll from the British expeditionary forces that all major military offensives had to be abandoned, and the one bright spot in this long period of misfortune was the repulse of Rigaud's assault upon Léogane (March, 1796).[1]

It should be remembered, however, that notwithstanding the appalling ravages of yellow fever it is quite probable that a British force sufficiently large to conquer Haiti would have been landed at Port-au-Prince had it not been for the troublous condition of affairs that prevailed in every corner of the Caribbean. In the Windward Islands the British divided their energies in an attempt to capture Guadeloupe, Martinique, and St. Lucia, and at the same time they were faced with the additional task of suppressing revolts in their own islands of Grenada and St. Vincent. In the Leeward Islands the operations against Haiti were hindered by the serious task of coping with the rebellious Maroons in Jamaica.[2]

---

[1] Victor Schoelcher, *Vie de Toussaint-Louverture* (Paris, 1889), chaps. ix-xvii; Colonel H. de Poyen, *Histoire militaire de la révolution de Saint-Domingue* (Paris, 1899), pp. 50-57; H. Castonnet des Fosses, *La révolution de Saint-Domingue* (Paris, 1893), pp. 160-165. On January 1, 1795, out of 1,490 British troops in Haiti 738 were reported sick. During the summer of 1795 this sick roll increased. Within ten weeks after the landing in Haiti of the 81st regiment of 980 men, 630 were buried. On June 1, 1795, out of a total of 3,000 British soldiers in Haiti only 1,300 were fit for duty. B. Edwards, *An Historical Survey of the French Colony in the Island of St. Domingo*, pp. 172-173; J. W. Fortescue, *A History of the British Army*, IV, 459.

[2] J. W. Fortescue, *A History of the British Army*, IV, 350-384, 424-496.

British impotence in Haiti in 1796 led to a struggle between Toussaint and Rigaud for supremacy. Haiti, like ancient Gaul, was divided into three parts: the South was ruled by Rigaud, the West was held by the English, and the North was under the control of Toussaint. Rigaud sought to undermine the authority of Toussaint by instigating the mulattoes in Cap Français to seize Governor Laveaux and cast him into prison. But before the mulattoes could take advantage of this coup, Toussaint surrounded Cap Français with thousands of black troops. Under the threat of a general massacre, Laveaux was released and the adherents of Rigaud fled from the city. The Governor himself was so overjoyed at his escape from impending death that he invested Toussaint with the title of Lieutenant-Governor of the colony, and he promised always to follow the counsel of the black general. Such conduct spelled the "end of white prestige and the beginning of black rule." [3]

The actual establishment of this "black rule" was largely the result of the policy pursued by Sonthonax, who was the dominant member of a commission sent by the French Directory to restore the control of the Mother Country over Haiti.[4] Under the influence of this aggressive "friend of the blacks" a majority of the members of the commission favored Toussaint, whose power grew so steadily that General Desfourneaux, the commander of the French troops in the colony, wrote to the Minister of War and reported that French influence had become absolutely "nil." It was not long before the commissioners themselves admitted that the black generals treated them with indifference if not with contempt.[5]

Such treatment at the hands of Toussaint's subordinates was doubtless very annoying to the French commissioners, but it did not swerve Sonthonax from his fixed purpose of elevating

[3] Pamphile de Lacroix, *Mémoires pour servir a l'histoire de la révolution de Saint-Domingue*, I, 309.

[4] The commissioners were five in number: Sonthonax, Roume, Leblanc, Giraud, and Raymond. They arrived in Haiti in May, 1796.

[5] T. L. Stoddard, *The French Revolution in San Domingo*, pp. 260-263; V. Schoelcher, *Vie de Toussaint-Louverture*, pp. 155-169. For an adverse sidelight on the character of Sonthonax see the letter from Samuel Morris to ————, Cap Français, February 28, 1797, enclosed in the despatch from King to Pickering, July 7, 1797, *Great Britain, Desp.*, vol. 6, MS. Dept. of State.

the blacks at the expense of the mulattoes. He endeavored in every way possible to injure the cause of Rigaud, and he employed every stratagem that he knew to remove anyone who felt disposed to challenge his objectives.[6] His handling of the other commissioners was masterful. Roume stayed in Spanish Santo Domingo and was no problem. Giraud was persuaded to return to France; Raymond was too cowardly to oppose the plans of Sonthonax; and Leblanc was removed from the scene by poison. Governor Laveaux, who had become too popular with the black generals to suit Toussaint, was elected as a deputy from Santo Domingo to the French National Assembly and was thus eliminated as a possible rival.

When the wily Toussaint had no further tasks for Sonthonax to perform, he then intimated to the choleric French commissioner that it would be expedient for him to return to Paris to break down the slanders that were being levelled against the administration of affairs in Haiti. Overreached and humiliated, Sonthonax sought to delay his departure, but Toussaint insisted that he embark at once. On August 25, 1797 an ultimatum was sent to the French commissioner, who hurriedly boarded a ship in the harbor of Le Cap and sailed for France. The only person of any consequence in Haiti who could contest Toussaint's supremacy was Rigaud, and the mulatto leader was marked for early defeat.[7]

But before Toussaint could move against Rigaud he first had to undertake a campaign against the English, who still held the key positions of Jérémie, Port-au-Prince, Saint Marc, and the fortress of the Môle-Saint-Nicolas. In this struggle he was glad to have the assistance of Rigaud, and for a short while he found it expedient to make some show of deference to the new French agent, General Hédouville. The French Directory had sent Hédouville in a last attempt to bring peace

---

[6] See the letter of Rigaud to Adet (French Minister to the United States), January 11, 1797, Arch. Aff. Étr., Mém. et Doc., Amérique, 14:326.

[7] H. Pauléus Sannon, *Histoire de Toussaint-Louverture* (Port-au-Prince, 1932), chap. ii; H. C. des Fosses, *La révolution de Saint Domingue,* pp. 174-183; H. de Poyen, *Histoire militaire de la révolution de Saint Domingue,* pp. 63-64; Pamphile de Lacroix, *Mémoires pour servir a l'histoire de la révolution de Saint Domingue,* I, 320-327.

to war-torn Haiti, and he arrived at Le Cap on April 20, 1798 with a reputation as a man of superior talents. But it was soon apparent to him that his mission was well-nigh hopeless; Toussaint was too strongly intrenched in both the North and the West to be dislodged by anything less than overwhelming force. With no army under his command there was nothing he could do but work with Toussaint in a common endeavor to drive out the British. This undertaking was soon crowned with success.[8]

In 1797 the British Government had grown weary of the load of mounting expense connected with the Haitian venture. The cost of intervention in the French colony was staggering. In 1796 the annual appropriation reached £2,000,000, and for the single month of January, 1797 an indebtedness of £700,000 was incurred. Even the opulent British Treasury could not stand such a fast increasing drain.[9] In order to remedy this situation the British Secretary of War, Henry Dundas, appointed Major-General John Graves Simcoe to the command of all the British forces in Haiti. He was instructed to reduce all expenses to an annual outlay of not more than £300,000, and he was ordered to concentrate all the British troops in the fortress of the Môle-Saint-Nicolas. Simcoe himself cherished the belief that it would be possible for him to occupy the island of Tortuga near the Môle-Saint-Nicholas, and thus have a base for further operations along the Haitian coast.[10] But when he arrived at the Môle, on February 20, 1797, he discovered that his situation was too desperate to permit any offensive operations. In March, 1797 Toussaint's forces pushed the

---

[8] Antoine Michel, *La mission du General Hédouville* (Port-au-Prince, 1929), chaps. iv-v; Pamphile de Lacroix, *Mémoires pour servir a l'histoire de la révolution de Saint-Domingue,* I, 330-341; Victor Schoelcher, *Vie de Toussaint-Louverture,* pp. 220 ff.

[9] J. W. Fortescue, *A History of the British Army,* IV, 545-546; Marcus Rainsford, *An Historical Account of the Black Enpire of Haiti,* pp. 204-206.

[10] General Simcoe was a very ambitious British officer who served with ability as the commanding officer of the Queen's Rangers during the American Revolution. As the Governor of Upper Canada in 1791 he began an active campaign to restrict American expansion in the Mississippi Valley even within the limits of the Treaty of Paris, and he long toyed with the project of a neutral Indian barrier state which would achieve this purpose. For this part of his career see S. F. Bemis, *Jay's Treaty,* chap. vi.

British troops in the West back upon Port-au-Prince, and despite some small success which Simcoe was able to achieve, it was not long before the British commander realized the grave dangers that menaced his security. If the British Ministry continued to insist upon rigid economy in military expenditures in Haiti and also refused to send further reinforcements to augment the fast dwindling British army, it was useless to carry on the conflict.

In July, 1797, Simcoe returned to England with Colonel Maitland, his ablest officer, leaving Major-General Whyte to hold out as best he could against the combined attacks of Toussaint and Rigaud.[11] But Simcoe's story of the serious situation in Haiti did not cause any immediate change in the plans of the British War Office, which prepared new instructions for Major-General Nesbitt who was to be sent out in the early days of 1798. Nesbitt was directed to hold the expenditures for the "whole British Establishment in St. Domingo within the limits of £300,000 per annum." Port-au-Prince, Saint Marc, and the "dependent posts and districts" were to be evacuated, and the entire British military force was to be concentrated in the Môle-Saint-Nicholas and in Jérémie.[12]

Since it was not possible for Major-General Nesbitt to leave for Haiti immediately upon receiving these instructions from the War Office, Colonel Thomas Maitland was given a copy of them with orders to leave at once in order to prepare the way for his superior officer. He arrived at the Môle-Saint-Nicolas on March 11, 1798, and promptly reported to Secretary Dundas that the situation was even worse than he had anticipated. Toussaint had captured Mirebalais and the Grand Bois and was closely investing Port-au-Prince. Saint Marc was in danger of being taken by assault, and Irois was so closely besieged by Rigaud that it could not hold out much

---

[11] Simcoe derived no glory from his mission to Haiti. When he returned to England in the summer of 1797 he was received by the British Commander-in-Chief as " a culprit: the Minister, Dundas . . . did not choose to see him. He had even to meet . . . the charge of abandoning his post." See William R. Riddell, *Life of John Graves Simcoe* (Toronto, 1926), p. 299; and Duncan D. Scott, *John Graves Simcoe* (Toronto, 1905), chap. xii.

[12] Inst. from Dundas to Nesbitt, January 1, 1798, *Secret*, Public Record Office, London, War Office, 1/69. Hereafter referred to as W. O.

longer. In the event that Irois surrendered to Rigaud, along with the district around Jérémie, it would then become a matter for serious consideration as to "how far the retaining the Môle, as a mere Post, . . . will either be proper, honourable, or useful." A voluntary evacuation of the British posts in Haiti was much to be preferred to a "forced one." [13]

In his reports to the War Office, Maitland made no attempt to conceal his contempt for the British Commander-in-Chief in Haiti, Major-General John Whyte. Although merely a Lieutenant-Colonel, Maitland assumed a lofty tone in his communications with his superior officer, and he refused to disclose to General Whyte the instructions that the War Office had issued to Major-General Nesbitt. Nesbitt himself was detained at Madeira by serious illness, and Maitland soon dominated the scene in Haiti. When General Whyte heard of Maitland's arrival at the Môle-Saint-Nicolas, he hurriedly left Port-au-Prince and repaired to the Môle. Maitland then took over the command at Port-au-Prince, and soon began to file with the War Office a bill of complaints against the incompetent administration of General Whyte. Everything in Port-au-Prince was in a state of chaos, and the inhabitants were fearful of an early evacuation by the British troops. Maitland's first act was to issue a proclamation assuring the population of Port-au-Prince that he was determined to defend that city to the "last extremity." [14] After quieting these apprehensions, Maitland then proceeded to administer a reproof to General Whyte. On March 25, Whyte had written to Maitland to request the prompt despatch of reinforcements from Port-au-Prince to the Môle-Saint-Nicolas.[15] In his reply, Maitland bluntly declined to send "any British troops from this Place, as you have desired, untill I receive further Orders." [16] In view of the fact that Rigaud was pushing his siege of Irois, it might be necessary for Maitland to send a portion of his small force to assist the hard-pressed

---

[13] Maitland to Dundas, March 12, 1798, W. O. 1/69.

[14] Proclamation to the Inhabitants of the District of Port-au-Prince, March 21, 1798, W. O. 1/69.

[15] Whyte to Maitland, March 25, 1798, W. O. 1/69.

[16] Maitland to Whyte, March 28, 1798, W. O. 1/69. See also the Report of Lieutenant-Colonel Littlehales to Maitland, March 22, 1798, W. O. 1/69.

garrison of that fort. Because of this possibility it would be out of the question for him to send even a small detachment of troops to the Môle-Saint-Nicolas.[17]

General Whyte was quick to catch the note of command which resounded so clearly in the communications from Maitland, and he shrank from any thought of friction with his belligerent subordinate. He assured Colonel Maitland that the reasons he had assigned for his inability to send any troops to the Môle-Saint-Nicolas were "most satisfactory." He then approved the proclamation that Maitland had issued to the inhabitants of Port-au-Prince, and he commended the military dispositions that had been made with reference to the district of Arcahaye. In conclusion, General Whyte went so far as to suggest his own abdication, and he inquired whether Colonel Maitland would assume the full command of the British forces in Haiti.[18]

Such an inquiry was really superfluous. Maitland promptly informed General Whyte that he felt "no hesitation" about assuming at once the "Chief Command of the Colony." He was not one to "shrink from responsibility." [19] Indeed, even before receiving General Whyte's letter of abdication he had sent a large portion of his troops from Port-au-Prince to Jérémie, thus preparing the way for the evacuation of Port-au-Prince, Saint Marc, and L'Arcahaye in accordance with the instructions that had been issued to General Nesbitt.[20] The next item was to initiate negotiations with Toussaint relative to arranging the details of this evacuation.

[17] Maitland to Whyte, March 30, 1798, W. O. 1/69.

[18] Whyte to Maitland, March 31, 1799, W. O. 1/69. When Colonel Maitland first arrived in Haiti he had intended to communicate to General Whyte the tenor of the instructions from the War Office to Major-General Nesbitt. But when he surveyed the situation and realized that General Whyte's conduct in Haiti had been a mixture of " contradiction and apparent absurdity," he decided to withhold from the General all knowledge of the Nesbitt instructions. See Colonel Maitland to Secretary Dundas, March 18, 1798, W. O. 1/69. Also, Maitland to William Huskisson, Under-Secretary for War, April 5, 1798, in which he remarks: " To expect anything from General Whyte, or to trust anything to him, to me was impossible after seeing his positive and direct daily contradictory Conduct." W. O. 1/69.

[19] Maitland to Whyte, April 5, 1798, W. O. 1/69.

[20] Maitland to Whyte, April 4, 1798, W. O. 1/69; also Maitland to Dundas, April 5, 1798, W. O. 1/69.

On April 23, 1798 Maitland sent Major Gillespie to Toussaint with an offer that greatly attracted the black general. In order to "diminish the Misfortunes of War," the new Commander-in-Chief of the British forces was anxious to arrange for a "suspension of Arms" followed by British evacuation of Port-au-Prince, Saint Marc, and L'Arcahaye. The forts (minus the ordnance), the towns, the public works, and all private property would be left in the same condition in which they had been found. With reference to the inhabitants of these places that were about to be evacuated, Colonel Maitland expressly stipulated that Toussaint should protect and confirm them in the possession of their property.[21]

On the same day that Colonel Maitland opened communications with Toussaint, he also sent word to Major-General Whyte at the Môle-Saint-Nicolas acquainting him with this decision. In this note he included an intimation that the General should quickly fade from the picture. This was conveyed in a request (really a command) that no objection be raised against terms of settlement with Toussaint. General Whyte at once recognized that his presence in Haiti was no longer desired, and he soon sailed for England.[22]

On April 28 Toussaint sent one of his officers to arrange the terms of evacuation, which were finally agreed upon two days later.[23] Nothing remained but to embark the British

[21] Maitland to Toussaint, April 23, 1798, W. O. 1/69. See also Antoine Michel, *La mission du General Hédouville,* chap. v.

[22] Maitland to Whyte, April 23, 1798, W. O. 1/69. Colonel Maitland was very fearful that Major-General Whyte would send to Secretary Dundas a sharp attack upon the manner in which Maitland himself had handled the situation in Haiti. In order to meet this anticipated criticism, Maitland never spared an opportunity to belittle the abilities of General Whyte. It was his opinion that Whyte had left Port-au-Prince in a "most shamefull manner, and is trying to find an excuse for his own misconduct by charging me with whatever comes uppermost." Maitland to Huskisson, May 10, 1798, W. O. 1/69. See also Maitland to Dundas, May 10, 1798, W. O. 1/69.

[23] Although some authorities state that the agreement between Toussaint and Maitland relative to the evacuation of Port-au-Prince was signed on May 2, 1798, it is apparent that it was signed on April 30. In a letter to Secretary Dundas on May 10, 1798, Maitland remarks as follows: "General Toussaint immediately agreed to the last Propositions and sent to Port-au-Prince on the 28th instant a confidential Officer who having met Lieutenant Colonel Nightingall, Deputy Adjutant General, on my part, on the 30th of April the accompanying Agreement

soldiers at L'Arcahaye, Port-au-Prince, and Fort Bizoton, and transport them to Jérémie or to the Môle-Saint-Nicolas.[24] By May 10 all the details of the evacuation had been carried out and the British occupation of these important districts in Haiti was forever abandoned.

This removal of the British troops to Jérémie and to the Môle-Saint-Nicolas was in accordance with the desires of the British Cabinet, and the Duke of Portland wrote to assure Maitland (who was now addressed as Brigadier-General Maitland) that his conduct in Haiti met with the "entire approbation" of the Ministry.[25] Before he had received this letter from the Duke, Maitland had already written to Secretary Dundas to explain why he had arranged the terms of evacuation with Toussaint rather than with La Plume or with Rigaud. He had favored Toussaint because he wished to keep him, as the strongest of the three generals, at a safe distance from Jérémie. It was likely that the French agent, General Hédouville, would join with Rigaud in an attempt to crush Toussaint, and the result would be some "new scene of Bloodshed and Horror." Neither Toussaint nor Rigaud had any affection for England, and they would bend every effort to expel the remaining English troops. Toussaint would embark upon such a hostile course "with a View to gratify his ambition, Rigaud with a View . . . to reconcile himself to the Directory by whom he is outlawed."

After explaining why he had evacuated all the British posts

was mutually exchanged and ratified by both Parties." Maitland to Secretary Dundas, May 10, 1798, W. O. 1/69; Antoine Michel, *La mission du General Hédouville*, I, 162-177.

[24] Maitland to Dundas, May 10, 1798, W. O. 1/69. See also Maitland to Huskisson, May 10, 1798, W. O. 1/69. Not only did Maitland take along with him to the Môle-Saint-Nicholas all the ordnance and military stores but also " such of the Inhabitants as voluntarily wished to go, and all the Merchandise belonging to British Merchants." For other details of the evacuation see Maitland to the Duke of Portland, May 13, 1798, W. O. 1/68, and Maitland to the Gentlemen of the Privy and Superior Council, May 13, 1798, W. O. 1/68.

[25] On June 7, 1798 the Duke of Portland, through Secretary Dundas, conveyed to Maitland his " great satisfaction " at the manner in which the situation in Haiti was being handled, and he then took the occasion to inform Maitland that he had been selected as the person most qualified to execute the instructions that had been prepared for General Nesbitt. Duke of Portland to Maitland, June 7, 1798, Colonial Office 245/3. Hereafter referred to as C. O. See also Duke of Portland to Maitland, July 10, 1798, C. O. 245/3.

in Haiti with the exception of Jérémie and the Môle-Saint-Nicolas, Maitland then raised the question as to whether it would be possible to hold even these two forts in the face of attacks by Toussaint and Rigaud. Moreover, the cost of maintaining an adequate military force in Haiti would amount to at least £500,000 per annum, which was almost twice the sum allotted by the War Office. In view of this situation, Maitland then expressed a grave doubt

whether what We now hold is worth that Sum Annually as affording protection to Jamaica. . . . I confess I . . . feel myself strongly inclined to say, that on the whole, the advantage to be derived is not equal to the Expence to be incurred.[26]

With Maitland in this frame of mind it was only to be expected that he would soon initiate new negotiations with Toussaint relative to the evacuation of the Môle-Saint-Nicolas. In a letter to Lord Balcarres, Governor of Jamaica, Maitland spoke of these negotiations and stressed the importance of gaining the friendship of Toussaint, "who possesses the whole nominal, and three parts of the real strength and resources of this Country." Maitland did not have even the "most distant doubt" about Toussaint's sincerity relative to carrying out the terms of an agreement with England, and he was convinced that " under the circumstances of the case " this *rapprochement* with the Haitians would "place the security of Jamaica in a very different point of view than what it would otherwise have been in." [27]

[26] Maitland to Dundas, July 6, 1798, W. O. 1/68.

[27] Maitland to Lord Balcarres, August 31, 1798, W. O. 1/70. It is apparent that the British Ministry was deeply interested in providing for the safety of Jamaica. In the *Papers re State of St. Domingo*, by John Wigglesworth, the Commissary-General, C. O. 245/1, there is a significant sentence taken from the instructions that the Duke of Portland gave to Wigglesworth: " It cannot escape you that the first and most important . . . point to which your attention ought to be directed . . . is the security and tranquillity of Jamaica."

Although Maitland's evacuation of the Môle-Saint-Nicholas is warmly defended by Sir John W. Fortescue in his *History of the British Army*, IV, 560-563, Sir Spenser St. John, in his *Hayti or the Black Republic* (London, 1884), p. 56, takes quite a different view: " One can scarcely understand why the English gave up the mole, which a small garrison could have defended, and the importance of the position in naval warfare is indisputable. If we wanted to gain Toussaint and induce him to declare the island independent, we should have held it until that desirable event had happened."

On the morning of August 31, 1798 Toussaint paid a visit to the British camp at the Môle-Saint-Nicolas. Maitland was a diplomat as well as a soldier, and he received Toussaint with regal honors. The British troops filed by the black guest of honor in an impressive review, and then a sumptuous banquet was served. At the close of this feast the massive silver service on the table was presented to Toussaint in the name of the King of England, and other gifts were pressed upon him. With everyone in a mellow mood, Maitland thought the moment had arrived to secure the assent of Toussaint to a secret treaty which would give to the British Crown the exclusive right to control the trade of Haiti. Toussaint should proclaim himself the King of Haiti and the British Government would support his pretension by stationing in his ports a squadron of British warships.[28]

But Toussaint had not imbibed so freely that he had lost his usual cunning in statecraft. The secret treaty that he signed on August 31, 1798 gave no exclusive trade advantages to England. The parties agreed upon a policy of non-interference, both political and military, in certain territories belonging to each other. England promised to adopt a " hands off " attitude towards any part of the island of Santo Domingo under the control of Toussaint, and the black general gave a pledge that he would adopt a similar attitude towards the island of Jamaica. Maitland also promised to send to Toussaint certain supplies which would be paid for in colonial produce.[29]

---

[28] Pamphile de Lacroix, *Mémoires pour servir a l'histoire de la révolution de Saint-Domingue*, I, 346.

[29] A copy of this secret treaty of August 31, 1798 is contained in the letter from Maitland to Secretary Dundas, August 31, 1798, W. O. 1/70. In his letter to Lord Balcarres on August 31, 1798, Maitland makes the following reference to his arrangement with Toussaint: " I shall arrange the quantity of Provisions for three months this day, so that your Lordship need not act under the Convention until His Majesty's pleasure for adhering to, or breaking it off be known. But I would recommend it in the Strongest manner to your Lordship to begin a correspondence with him [Toussaint]. . . . The Quantity of provisions he will want in future is stated to be about 6000 Barrels of Flour and the same quantity of Salt Provisions annually, which he is to pay for in produce, either to the British or American Importer." W. O. 1/70. There is also a copy of the Maitland-Toussaint Treaty in the enclosures sent by Lord Grenville to Robert Liston on December 11, 1798. F. O. 115/6.

After perfecting these arrangements for the evacuation of the Môle-Saint-Nicolas, Maitland sailed for England. He clearly realized that the Haitian climate, together with the yellow fever, would continue to make serious ravages in any British army that was stationed in Santo Domingo. This climatic factor and the excessive cost of maintaining a considerable military establishment under such circumstances led him to the belief that British intervention should not again be attempted. Let the French Directory waste its military strength in Haitian misadventures!

Maitland was certain that the Haitian situation would soon resolve itself into a sanguinary struggle between Toussaint and Rigaud for supremacy. The control of France over its old colony was a thing of the past, and on August 31, 1798 Maitland expressed to Balcarres the belief that Toussaint would expel General Hédouville from Haiti in " less than a month." [30] Maitland's prediction indicates how shrewdly he had sized up the situation in Haiti. He was aware that Toussaint had kept General Hédouville informed as to the progress of the negotiations with the English, but he also realized that Toussaint had taken this step more as a gesture of good will than as a sign of subordination to the agent of the French Directory. [31]

After the British troops had finally evacuated the Môle-Saint-Nicolas and Jérémie, Toussaint thought that the time had come to force the departure of General Hédouville for France. In the early part of October, 1798, a rumor swept through the North that Hédouville was plotting to restore slavery. When a wave of resentment against the General had

[30] Maitland to Lord Balcarres, August 31, 1798, W. O. 1/70. See also Erwin Rüsch, *Die Revolution von Saint Domingue* (Hamburg, 1930), pp. 103-107.

[31] Although Toussaint had written several letters to General Hédouville during the course of the negotiations with General Maitland leading up to the agreement of April 30, 1798, it is significant that he delayed for several days the despatch of any news concerning his intention to ratify this agreement. Toussaint signified to Maitland on May 2 his approval of the agreement of April 30, but he so arranged things that Hédouville did not learn of this approval before May 6. It was then too late for Hédouville to take any adverse action. On May 6 Hédouville wrote to Toussaint to express his " astonishment " at the delay that had occurred. See A. Michel, *La mission du General Hédouville*, pp. 172-177. For a badly garbled account of the situation in Haiti at this time, see Percy Waxman, *The Black Napoleon* (N. Y. 1931), pp. 124-127.

reached its proper proportions, Toussaint suddenly approached Le Cap at the head of a large army. To Hédouville it was apparent that the negro general was in command of the situation. With a parting instruction to Rigaud to take up arms against Toussaint who had been "bought by the English, the émigrés, and the Americans," Hédouville hurriedly departed from Haiti.[32]

The stage was now all set for the war between Toussaint and Rigaud. One by one, Toussaint had pushed from the scene every possible rival but Rigaud. His cunning in statecraft had served him even better than his knowledge of military arts, and this political shrewdness was further evidenced by his overtures to England and the United States for assistance in his campaign to crush Rigaud. These overtures prepared the way for the Maitland Mission.

The diplomatic background of this mission goes back to the period of friction between France and the United States which resulted from the ratification of the Jay Treaty of November 19, 1794. It was evident to the British Foreign Secretary as early as January, 1797 that American difficulties with France might soon lead to open hostilities. In the event that these actually occurred, Lord Grenville instructed the British Minister at Washington to assure the American Government of "His Majesty's willingness to afford a naval protection to the commerce of the United States against the attacks of the common enemy." [33]

A year later, Rufus King, the American Minister at London, realized that war between France and the United States might be expected at any moment, and with this contingency in mind he wrote to the Secretary of State to advise him that the British Government would, if requested, provide convoys for American ships.[34] In subsequent despatches to Secretary Pickering, Rufus King again adverted to this question of British convoys for

---

[32] Beaubrun Ardouin, *Études sur l'histoire d'Haiti* (11 vols., Paris, 1853-1861), III, 511.

[33] Lord Grenville to Liston, January 27, 1797, *Foreign Office Transcripts* (*Henry Adams Collection*), Library of Congress.

[34] King to the Secretary of State, January 14, 1798, *Great Britain, Despatches*, vol. 6, MS. Dept. of State.

American merchant ships,[35] but President John Adams did not deem it "expedient" to make any advances to England at that time. British commercial interests would compel the British fleet to afford adequate protection to American merchantmen without any formal request from the American Government.[36]

As American relations with France became more and more strained it was inevitable that President Adams should regard with increasing favor the possibility of joint action with Great Britain against the common enemy. The British Minister believed that the Adams Administration considered a rupture with France as "almost unavoidable." Although the President and his Cabinet had no

wish for war, they do not dread it. . . . They have a very favourable idea of their public resources, and they look forward to an eventual concert and co-operation with Great Britain. This concert . . . they seem to place at a distance, partly because they do not think the public sentiments of America yet ripe for a close connection with us, and partly because they are not certain that a proposal of that sort would meet with a cordial reception in England. . . . At the same time I perceive that the American Ministers have their views fixed on the conquest of the Floridas and Louisiana for themselves and the acquisition of St. Domingo (if not of the other French Islands) by Great Britain. . . . I asked one of the ministers jocularly (taking it for granted that if they assisted us to take the French West India Islands and we assisted them to get possession of Louisiana and the Floridas, matters might be considered as pretty nearly balanced between us on that score) what return they were to make for all the care we took . . . of their shipping in every part of the world? He said that as we defended the Americans at sea they must endeavor to defend us by land.[37]

Such news from America was heartening to Lord Grenville, who would be glad to welcome America as an ally against France. Liston should assure President Adams that

any proposals for concert and co-operation will be cordially received here and this not more on account of the direct advantage, whatever it

[35] January 29 and February 7, 1798, *ibid.*
[36] Pickering to King, April 2, 1798, *Life and Correspondence of Rufus King* (6 vols., N. Y. 1894-1900), II, 296-297.
[37] Liston to Lord Grenville, May 2, 1798, Public Record Office, London, Foreign Office 5/22. Hereafter referred to as F. O.

may be, which this country may derive from them, than from the interest which we feel in contributing to enable the United States to defend themselves against the prevalence of the principles of anarchy which would inevitably follow any submission on their part to the insolence of France. . . . The conquest of Louisiana and Florida by the United States instead of being any cause of jealousy, would certainly be a matter of satisfaction to this Government, and in that state of affairs, it is also easy to see the advantage which America would derive from seeing St. Domingo in the hands of His Majesty rather than of any other European Power.[38]

However, before Liston could receive this instruction from Lord Grenville, he wrote to the Foreign Office to express his "surprise" that the leading members of the Adams Administration had suddenly

altered their ideas with regard to the Island of St. Domingo and perhaps with regard to the other possessions of the French in the West Indies. What I ventured to throw out in a former letter of the probability of their readiness to co-operate in throwing those colonies into the possession of His Majesty, I derived from the conversation I had recently had on the subject with the Secretary of State. . . . But Colonel Pickering now hints at a plan on the part of the blacks to declare themselves independent and to erect the island into a sovereign State,—to which he seems to think it would not be inconsistent with the interests of America to consent.[39]

This intimation that the American Government might look with favor upon the erection of an independent black state upon the ruins of the French colony of Haiti was highly disturbing to Lord Grenville, who confessed to Rufus King his " horror " of such a possibility.[40] There were many Americans, however, whose viewpoint was very different from that of Lord Grenville. Both John Quincy Adams and Alexander Hamilton favored the independence of the French colonies in the Caribbean "under the guarantee of the United States." [41]

---

[38] Lord Grenville to Liston, June 8, 1798, *F. O. Transcripts*, Library of Congress.
[39] Liston to Lord Grenville, June 12, 1798, Public Record Office, London, F. O. 5/22.
[40] King to the Secretary of State, July 14, 1798, *Great Britain, Desp.*, vol. 6, MS. Dept. of State.
[41] See *ante*, pp. 13-14.

That the colonists in Haiti were ready for separation from France was apparently the belief of the American consul at Cap Français, Jacob Mayer, who probably inspired Richard Yates to write to Secretary Pickering and assure him that the Haitians were ready to "acquiesce in declaring the colony independent." [42]

In September, 1798, President Adams himself inclined towards the idea of Haitian independence, and according to Mr. Liston it was the "prevailing conjecture" in the United States that

at least the largest Islands will become Independent States, and be connected with the continent by alliance and friendship rather than by subjection. To this resolution a great proportion of the inhabitants of the United States look forward with pleasure. An unrestrained commercial intercourse between this country and the West Indies opens prospects to the speculating and enterprizing that are irresistably alluring.

To President Adams it seemed that there was little likelihood that the French Government would ever regain control in Haiti, and this condition of affairs was a strong and impelling reason why the United States should enter into "some kind of agreement" with the rebellious blacks. The main reason why he had not already taken steps towards this end was his apprehension "of giving umbrage to Great Britain, who still appeared to have other views with regard to the Island." [43]

It was obvious to Liston that, despite any difference of opinion between England and America concerning the affairs of Haiti, it was greatly to the interest of his government to make some friendly advances to the Adams Administration. He did not hesitate to denounce the scandalous manner in which the British vice-admiralty courts in Haiti were condemning American shipping upon the flimsiest of pretexts,[44] and he made haste

---

[42] Yates to Pickering, April 30, 1798, *Cape Haitien, Consular Desp.,* vol. 1, MS. Dept. of State. In his letter to Lord Grenville, written on June 12, 1798, Liston remarks as follows concerning the rôle being played by the American consul, Jacob Mayer: " The idea [of independence] I suspect has been suggested by the American Consul at Cape François . . . in consequence of insinuations or overtures made him by some of the black chiefs." F. O. 5/22.

[43] Liston to Lord Grenville, September 27, 1798, F. O. 5/22.

[44] *Ibid.,* May 2, 1798.

to convey to Lord Grenville the request of Secretary Pickering for the return of some ordnance which the British had taken to Halifax when they evacuated Charleston, South Carolina, during the last days of the American Revolution.[45] Lord Grenville agreed to return this ordnance (twenty-four cannons) as a loan to the American Government,[46] but the final responsibility for the whole transaction was placed upon the shoulders of Liston who consented to execute this commission "with some anxiety of mind." [47]

These friendly gestures on the part of the British Government, together with the state of quasi-war that existed between France and America, inevitably led President Adams to think of the possibility of an alliance with Great Britain. When Mr. Liston assured him that Lord Grenville would "cordially receive" any proposal looking towards "co-operation or eventual assistance," the President answered

that he was not at the present moment prepared to go into the detail of the stipulations that might be thought expedient for the interest of the two countries, but that he would listen with attention and candour to any propositions which our government might be pleased to bring forward; and that indeed he would rather prefer that the first overtures should come from our side.[48]

Lord Grenville was just as coy as President Adams about entering into formal negotiations for a treaty of alliance between Great Britain and the United States. Mr. Liston was instructed to inform the President that in the event of an actual war between France and the United States, His Majesty's Government would "at all times be disposed to enter into any

[45] Liston to Lord Grenville, June 12, 1798, F. O. 5/22.

[46] Lord Grenville to King, September 6, 1798. Enclosed in despatch from King to Pickering, September 7, 1798, *Great Britain, Desp.*, vol. 6, MS. Dept. of State.

[47] Liston to Lord Grenville, September 27, 1798, F. O. 5/22. It is pertinent to note here that on August 16, 1798 Rufus King gave to Lord Grenville a request from the American Government to purchase 25,000 muskets, and cannon to the value of £10,000. On the following day, Lord Grenville assured King of "every facility" in the power of the British Government "in the execution" of this order. *Life and Correspondence of Rufus King,* II, 391-393. See also the letter of Liston to Sir John Wentworth, October 15, 1798, C. O. 217/69.

[48] Liston to Lord Grenville, September 27, 1798, F. O. 5/22.

concert of Measures for mutual Defence and security," but it should be clearly indicated that there was no desire on the part of the British Government to bind the United States "in a permanent system of alliance for general Purposes." [49]

After this diplomatic sparring, there was no more talk of a formal alliance between the two countries. There was, however, continued interest in some informal arrangement concerning the trade with Haiti. On December 1, 1798, Rufus King wrote to Lord Grenville to inquire about a treaty which, certain newspapers declared, had been concluded between Toussaint and General Maitland.[50] Lord Grenville referred King to Secretary Dundas who showed him the dispatches from General Maitland to the War Office and the convention of August 31, 1798. Secretary Dundas then informed King that General Maitland had, "without instruction or authority" from the War Office, signed this convention with Toussaint after he had discovered that any British conquest of Haiti was "impracticable." General Maitland also entertained the belief that Toussaint had the "most influence" and exercised the "greatest authority" of any of the leaders in Haiti. Because of his growing power and the pledge that he gave to refrain from any attack upon Jamaica, the Ministry had decided to ratify the agreement with Toussaint.

After listening to these explanations of Secretary Dundas, King hastened to the Foreign Office to see Lord Grenville. In July Grenville had expressed to King his "horror" of any idea of an independent negro state, and yet, some weeks later, a British general had signed a treaty with Toussaint whereby negro rule in Haiti was really established! Although His Lordship had little to say in answer to these criticisms, King felt certain that he did not approve of the treaty with Toussaint.[51]

King himself had grave misgivings as to the effect of this

[49] Lord Grenville to Liston, December, 1798, *F. O. Transcripts*, Library of Congress.

[50] King to Lord Grenville, December 1, 1798, *Life and Correspondence of Rufus King*, II, 474.

[51] King to the Secretary of State, December 7, 1798, *Great Britain, Desp.*, vol. 6, MS. Dept. of State.

treaty upon American trade in the Caribbean. Up to this time American merchant ships had been pillaged in Haitian waters by French corsairs, and in order to diminish these depredations the American Government had prohibited all commerce between American ports and the ports in the French colonies. This action had proved effective but it would now be undermined by the fifth article of the Maitland-Toussaint agreement, whereby supplies were to be sent from British ports to those portions of Haiti under the control of the negro general. If this article were ratified by the British Government it would result in great damage to American commerce unless it were further stipulated that

no Privateer shall be fitted out or permitted to sail from any of the Ports under the Dominion of Toussaint to cruize against the Vessels or Trade of the United States, and that no American Prize shall be received or sold in any such Ports.

King also feared that the "exclusive commerce secured to Great Britain under this Convention" would arouse the jealousy of American merchants. It would have been much more agreeable to the United States if General Maitland had established with Toussaint a truce the terms of which provided equal privileges of trade for every nation "not at war with Great Britain." [52]

Secretary Dundas was anxious to relieve the apprehensions of the American Minister. In his answering letter to King he outlined the background of the Maitland-Toussaint Treaty. He then assured the American Minister of his earnest desire to "pay all possible attention to every suggestion which coincides with your wishes, and the friendly footing on which England and America now stand with respect to each other." He was certain that there would be no difficulty in securing the adoption of the amendment which King proposed relative to the Maitland-Toussaint Treaty. [53]

Shortly after this exchange of letters between King and

---

[52] King to Dundas, December 8, 1798, W. O. 1/71.
[53] Dundas to King, December 9, 1798, W. O. 1/71. See also Lord Grenville to Liston, December 11, 1798, F. O. 115/6.

Secretary Dundas, General Maitland himself wrote to the Secretary of War to tender some advice with regard to further relations with Toussaint. The main objectives of British policy in connection with the Haitian situation should be defined as follows:

To crush if possible the french Agent, to preserve the tranquility of those who have been under the British Government, to secure the peace of the Island of Jamaica and as far as is compatible with these essential Points to throw into the channel of British Commerce as large a portion of the produce of Saint Domingo as possible.

In order to explain these objectives, General Maitland went into a discussion of the Maitland-Toussaint Treaty. He indicated the weak position of the French agent, General Hédouville, who, with "great nominal Power" in Haiti, had actually possessed but little " real Authority." Toussaint, whose abilities were not "very great," was the most powerful personage in Haiti, and although Rigaud had a much larger endowment of " cunning, subtlety and finesse " than Toussaint it was evident that both Hédouville and Rigaud were playing a losing game. But the preponderance of power possessed by Toussaint was not the only reason why he had been selected as the outstanding chief in Haiti. The "strict adherence" of the black general to his "engagements upon the evacuation of Port-au-Prince and the general disposition he had evinced to moderation and forbearance" were additional factors that had influenced General Maitland's attitude toward Toussaint. It should be clearly understood, however, that this inclination toward Toussaint was not based upon any "personal predilection for any one of the Chiefs in the Island of Saint Domingo." If Rigaud had been on a plane of equality with Toussaint he would have met with "similar treatment." In conclusion, Maitland advised the War Office to instruct any agent sent out to Haiti to keep constantly in mind the fact that he should never hold out to Toussaint "any prospect of a connection" that would make his situation a "matter of discussion when his Majesty's Ministers may think fit to treat for a general Peace." The black dictator was merely a pawn in the complicated game of politics in the Caribbean, and no British advantage should be lost through deference to mere sentiment.[54]

In another letter to Secretary Dundas some ten days later, Maitland argued against the acceptance of the amendment proposed by King to the treaty of August 31, 1798. King had stressed the importance of binding Toussaint to a pledge not to fit out privateers to prey upon American commerce. Maitland believed that there were few vessels in Toussaint's ports capable of being used as privateers, and he thought it would be most "impolitic" to admit that it was "in Toussaint's power to give either the Americans or Us the smallest annoyance by his Naval force." Such an admission would lead Toussaint to imagine that he had it in his power to do great damage to British and American commerce and he would therefore "demand some equivalent to the sacrifice he was apparently making." This " would naturally lead to much embarrassment if not to a total failure" of any mission to Haiti.

It would be best to permit Toussaint to control the coasting trade of Haiti as an apparent concession from the British and American Governments. It could then be stipulated that this trade was to be protected by British cruisers, thus obviating any necessity for Toussaint to have a fleet of his own. With respect to this trade with Haiti it was of paramount importance that a "fair understanding" be arranged with America relative to the articles that were to be imported by Toussaint. The chief Haitian imports from America would be flour and salt provisions. In such a trade British merchants could not compete, because the Americans could sell at a lower price and because "American Provisions of every kind are in higher estimation amongst the Natives of the Country than the English." British exports to Haiti would comprise all sorts of manufactured com-

[54] Maitland to Dundas, December 26, 1798, W. O. 1/70. When the British forces evacuated the Môle-Saint-Nicolas in October, 1798, some of the French émigrés carried away a few cannon and destroyed some platforms contrary to the stipulations of the treaty of August 31, 1798. When Maitland heard of these breaches of the treaty he had signed with Toussaint, he wrote to the black general (January 19, 1799) to assure him of the good faith of the British Government and of its earnest desire to " support with all possible energy " the existing friendly relations. See Maitland to Toussaint, January 19, 1799, Arch. Aff. Étr., Mém. et Doc., Amérique, 15:6.

modities, and in this regard there would be but little American competition except in "coarse muslins and Cottons either the Manufacture of India or England." Because of this possible competition in muslins and cottons it might be expedient to offer the Americans "the exclusive trade in Provisions and Flour provided she would in return concede to Us the whole of the Commerce of Manufactured Commodities of every description." [55]

These suggestions of General Maitland laid the basis of British policy concerning Haiti for the next few months. In the early part of January, 1799, Rufus King had some important conversations with several members of the British Ministry, and their viewpoint was largely that of Maitland. King frankly discussed with Lord Grenville the reasons for American interest in the erection of a stable government in Haiti. It was imperative that some step be taken to protect American commerce against the corsairs who frequented Haitian waters. The prevention of piracy in the Caribbean and the opening of the ports under Toussaint's control were two cardinal objectives in American policy. The success of such a policy largely depended upon co-operation with Great Britain.

Lord Grenville hastened to indicate his support of a policy of co-operation between America and Great Britain, and he suggested that the commerce with Haiti should be handled through a joint British-American company which would enjoy exclusive trading privileges. But King was dubious about the reception that such a suggestion would receive in America, where there had long existed a "general unpopularity of monopolies." He also doubted whether Congress had the power to create "an exclusive corporation for the purpose of trade." This reference to possible constitutional limitations aroused William Pitt to remind King that the dangers confronting America were very grave, and he thought that it would be "singular indeed, if an adequate power did not exist to guard against them." King then countered with the idea that the situation could be handled through the treaty-making power, which might negotiate treaties with Toussaint " by which it

[55] Maitland to Dundas, January 5, 1799, W. O. 1/71.

should be agreed that the Citizens of the United States and the subjects of G. Britain alone should trade to that Island." In these treaties it would be possible to include a list of regulations "to be observed by each in carrying on this trade." Such trade, of course, should be "open to all the subjects of the two countries."

Lord Grenville was quick to raise objections to any thought of opening the trade with Haiti to "all the people of the two countries." But William Pitt was not so wedded to monopoly as was Lord Grenville, and he took occasion to emphasize the importance of having England and America act in accord in this matter. King was in hearty agreement with this viewpoint, and he suggested that the British Government might send an agent to Toussaint to inform the black dictator that whatever should be arranged

between Toussaint and G. Britain should be open for the accession of the U. States, and also open to such modifications as should enable the U. States to become a party in case they decline or are unable to agree to the proposed plan.[56]

As a result of this extended discussion relative to Haitian affairs, Lord Grenville sent to King an outline of a proposed arrangement between the United States and Great Britain which he thought would be mutually advantageous.[57] All trade with those portions of Haiti under Toussaint's control should be confined to a single port of entry—Port-au-Prince. This trade should be carried on by a joint company "to be formed by the two Governments and to consist of British and American subjects." The company should be required to "furnish no manufactures but from British Territories, and no articles of Produce or live stock but from America." Any ships found trading at Haitian ports without a license from the proposed joint British-American company should be liable to seizure, and Toussaint should be pledged to discourage such illicit commerce.[58]

[56] King to the Secretary of State, January 10, 1799, *Great Britain*, *Desp.*, vol. 6, MS. Dept. of State.

[57] " Minutes " of proposed agreement between the United States and England relative to Haitian trade. W. O. 1/72, p. 1.

[58] Lord Grenville to King, January 9, 1799, enclosed in the above-cited despatch from King to the Secretary of State, January 10, 1709. While these

Without waiting to learn of King's reaction to this proposed arrangement concerning Haitian trade, the British Ministry decided to appoint Brigadier-General Maitland as a confidential agent to carry on negotiations with Toussaint and with the American Government.[59] When King was advised of this appointment he warmly urged against the issuance to General Maitland of any rigid instructions that would control his conversations with the American Government. He believed that it was

very much to be desired that every point should be left open to such practicable and safe arrangements as should be devised at Philadelphia, instead of a plan's being sent there, which with the best disposition on our part might be found impracticable, and might moreover have an unfavorable influence upon the adoption of a substitute.[60]

After Lord Grenville and Secretary Dundas had signified their agreement with this suggestion, King had an extremely satisfactory conversation with General Maitland, whom he regarded as " well chosen for the business that carries him to Philada." Maitland was convinced of the necessity for a close concert between England and America in the affair with Toussaint, and he also appeared to appreciate the force of the objections that the American Government would probably raise against the monopoly trading arrangement which Lord Grenville had outlined.[61] It is important to note, however, that

attempts were being made to establish an accord between the United States and England, the relations between the two countries were somewhat strained by the action of Captain Loring, of His Majesty's ship, *Carnatick*, in impressing certain sailors from the American ship of war, *Baltimore*. See Pickering to King, January 8, 1799, and Pickering to Liston, December 31, 1798, *Life and Correspondence of Rufus King*, II, 505-508. President Adams ascribed the incident to the fact that Captain Loring was an American Loyalist who had left his native land with greatly embittered feelings. Liston to Lord Grenville, January 16, 1799, F. O. 5/25.

[59] In his letter of January 10, 1799 to Huskisson, Maitland accepts the mission to Haiti and to America with the following reservation: " I am going on a line quite out of my beat." W. O. 1/71. On January 11, 1799, the War Office ordered Lieutenant-Colonel Harcourt to proceed at once to Haiti to ratify the treaty of August 31, 1798 between Maitland and Toussaint.

[60] King to the Secretary of State, January 16, 1799. *Great Britain Desp.*, vol. 6, MS. Dept. of State.

[61] *Ibid.*, January 25, 1799. See also King to Maitland, January 27, 1799, *Life and Correspondence of Rufus King*, II, 529-530.

General Maitland carried with him on his trip to America a copy of Lord Grenville's proposed agreement for limiting trade with Haiti to a joint British-American company which would enjoy exclusive commercial privileges. Moreover, he was instructed to refer to the terms of this proposed agreement as a means of guidance during the negotiations with American statesmen.

The instructions entrusted to General Maitland were very comprehensive. The first objective of the British War Office in sending Maitland to Philadelphia was to guard the British

Colonial Possessions against the danger with which they are threatened by the present political and military state of Saint Domingo, . . . and the next (a consequence and a principal security to the former) is to exclude other Nations (the United States excepted) from participating in any Commercial advantages that can be derived from an intercourse with that Island.

The danger to be apprehended from

the state of Saint Domingo, may be considered in two distinct points of view. 1st. As arising from the possibility of an open attack being made from that Island upon any of the Possessions either of this Country or America. 2d. As likely to be produced by the example and description of the Military Authority existing in Saint Domingo, upon every Country of which the principal population consists in Slaves, assisted by means of influence and seduction that will be most actively exerted among such Slaves in the British Colonies and the Southern States of America, unless the utmost precautions are taken on the one hand, by . . . destroying the authority of France in Saint Domingo, and . . . by placing all Intercourse with that Island under . . . severe checks and controul.

In order to preclude any possibility of an armed expedition leaving Haiti, it was essential that Toussaint should " bind himself in the strongest manner not to fit out any Expedition, or to give any assistance or countenance to any hostile operations against the Territories of His Majesty or the United States." In the matter of trade with Toussaint it was important, during the negotiations with the United States, to follow as far as possible the suggestions advanced by Lord Grenville in his outline of a proposed commercial arrangement.[62] It was possible that Toussaint would strongly object to placing the control of the coasting trade under an agent of the British-American company. In this event General Maitland was to be guided by his own discretion, but he should be careful not to make any arrangement that would serve as a cover to " illicit intercourse with the parts of the Island not subject to General Toussaint."

The British Ministry was especially hopeful that the American Government would look with favor upon the proposal to restrict all trade with Haiti to a joint British-American company. If mere " commercial advantages were the only or principal object in view," the British Government would never consider giving such exclusive privileges to any trading company. The main reason behind such a proposal was effectively to control the unsettled situation in Haiti. To procure the acquiescence of America upon this point was regarded as one of the " most essential parts " of the program entrusted to General Maitland. He was warned against being swayed by any " secondary or slight difficulties " raised by American negotiators in this regard, and he was to agree to amendments only upon the " fullest conviction" that American opposition to a trading monopoly was adamant.

It was also of the " utmost importance " to secure an agreement whereby all trade with Toussaint should be confined to one port—Port-au-Prince. The advantages of such an arrangement were so obvious that the Ministry insisted that no deviation from this instruction be permitted.

In his negotiations with the American Government, General Maitland was to insist that all commerce with Haiti be controlled by agreements concluded between England and Toussaint. If Toussaint should refuse to accede to these British proposals, America should " engage not to form any separate Commercial Agreement, and as far as it may be practicable not to suffer any supplies whatever to be sent to him from the

[62] For a copy of this outline of Lord Grenville relative to British-American trade with Haiti, see W. O. 1/72, p. 1.

United States, without the consent and concurrence of His Majesty's Government." [63]

While General Maitland was en route to America with these far-reaching instructions, Toussaint himself had opened relations with the American Government. In a letter of November 6, 1798, the black dictator had assured President Adams that American commerce in Haitian ports under his control would be adequately protected,[64] and he had followed this gesture of friendship by sending to America in December, 1798 his personal representative, Joseph Bunel.[65] According to Liston, Bunel was a " man of no parts and of mean character." [66] He owed his position in the Haitian Government to the fact that he had married a negro woman who was a " particular favourite and constant counsellor of Toussaint." [67]

Liston believed that these overtures from Toussaint were well received by the American Government. Bunel soon dined with Secretary Pickering, and before long was honored by an invitation to visit the President. His conversations with American statesmen were not without effect for we find Alexander Hamilton urging Secretary Pickering to open commercial relations with Haiti,[68] and on February 9, 1799 the President approved an Act of Congress which authorized him to renew this trade whenever he was satisfied that American merchant ships were safe from depredations by privateers.[69]

In the opinion of Liston, President Adams approved this Act of February 9, 1799 only after he was satisfied that the British Government would take no offence at such action. General Maitland's evacuation of Haiti had been followed by

[63] War Office to Maitland, January 26, 1799, W. O. 1/71. See also Lord Grenville to Liston, January 19, 1799, F. O. 115/7.

[64] Toussaint to Adams, November 6, 1798, *Cape Haitien, Consular Desp.,* vol. 1, MS. Dept. of State.

[65] George Gibbs, *Memoirs of the Administrations of Washington and Adams,* II, 227.

[66] This low estimate of the character of Bunel was confirmed by Edward Stevens, who regarded him as a " great scoundrel." See Stevens to James Yard, *Cape Haitien, Consular Desp.,* vol. 2, MS. Dept. of State.

[67] Liston to Lord Grenville, January 31, 1799, F. O. 5/25.

[68] Hamilton to Pickering, February 9, 1799, *Works of Alexander Hamilton,* VI, 395.

[69] *U. S. Statutes at Large,* I, 613-616.

strong rumors in the British press that hinted at some secret understanding between Maitland and Toussaint relative to a recognition of Haitian independence. The American Government had been influenced by these rumors and was taking a realistic view of the situation. Secretary Pickering was in favor of allowing Toussaint to carry on trade relations with " all the world " but he was convinced that it would be a mistake to permit the black general to have any ships under his own control. He should be forbidden to send out "a single boat, unless with a view to go from one part of the island to another." [70]

In the early part of March, 1799, Liston received from Lord Grenville a copy of the treaty concluded on August 31, 1798 between General Maitland and Toussaint. The fears of some American statesmen that this secret treaty had included a provision giving exclusive concessions to British trade were now dispelled.[71] Secretary Pickering received " with much pleasure " these assurances about the real purport of the Maitland-Toussaint negotiations, and preparations were hurriedly made to send Edward Stevens to talk with Toussaint about opportunities for American trade. Inasmuch as Congress had made no appropriation to pay the expenses of the Stevens mission, Secretary Pickering authorized Mr. Stevens to load on the vessel carrying him to Cap Français a large cargo of provisions which would be sold to Toussaint. The profits resulting from this transaction would be used to defray the expenses incurred by Stevens.[72]

---

[70] Liston to Lord Grenville, February 18, 1799, F. O. 5/25.

[71] On March 16, 1799 Secretary Stoddert wrote to Samuel Smith, in Baltimore, to convey the following assurance: " The Treaty between Tousant and the British amounts to no more than a Truce for the War. Stevens is not to treat with a British Agent—& is to do no more than to make a Bargain for our Trade during the War with Toussant." General Letter Book, MS. Navy Department Archives.

[72] Liston to Lord Grenville, March 12, 1799, F. O. 5/25. The fact that Stevens had been authorized to carry to Cap Français a large cargo of provisions to sell to Toussaint on government account aroused a great deal of hostile feeling in Philadelphia. In a letter from Secretary Stoddert to Secretary Pickering, dated March 8, 1799, there is the following illustrative comment: " Mr. Harrison who mixes a good deal with the Merchants, called at my office this morning to tell me there was great clamour at the Coffee House & generally all over the City— on acct. of the Vessel to carry Doct Stevens being permitted to take provisions.

By the middle of March, 1799 Stevens was ready to sail for Haiti, and Secretary Stoddert instructed Captain Thomas Tingey to convoy the ship bearing the American envoy as far as the harbor of Cap Français. Captain Tingey could then remain outside the harbor for a day or two in order to give Mr. Stevens " an opportunity to influence Tousant " to extend an invitation to the Captain to enter Cap Français. If Toussaint should make this friendly advance, the Captain was to conduct himself with " prudence and good sense." It was the policy of the Administration to " conciliate the good opinion of that General, and his people," and Captain Tingey should bear this fact in mind.[73]

It was the expectation of Secretary Pickering that Stevens would have no trouble in securing a pledge from Toussaint to put an end to all attacks upon American shipping in the waters adjacent to the ports under his control. Upon receiving this assurance, President Adams would proclaim a reopening of trade relations with Haiti. By the first week in May, 1799 all negotiations would be completed, and commerce between Haiti and the United States would be placed upon a secure basis.[74]

All these preparations for a renewal of commercial relations with Haiti had been completed and Stevens had actually sailed for Cap Français before General Maitland arrived at Philadelphia on April 2, 1799. After a rapid survey of the situation he wrote to Secretary Dundas in none too hopeful a tone. It was apparent to him that the views of the British Ministry and those of the American Government were

extremely different. Our Policy is to protect, theirs to destroy the

. . . It is said that the Prest. has no power to do this." *Timothy Pickering Papers*, MS. Massachusetts Historical Society.

[73] Stoddert to Tingey, March 16, 1799, *Letters to Officers of Ships of War*, vol. 1, MS. Navy Department Archives. It is pertinent to note that Toussaint apparently was in no mood to meet Captain Tingey, who finally left Cap Français without any opportunity to " conciliate the good opinion " of the black commander-in-chief. See Tingey to Stoddert, April 21, 1799, *Tingey Letter Book*, MS. Navy Department Archives.

[74] Pickering to Stephen Higginson, March 15, 1799, *Domestic Letters, 1798-1799*, vol. 11, MS. Dept. of State.

present Colonial System. Our Views only go to a partial, theirs to a compleat opening of the Saint Domingo Market. We are willing to submit to a temporary Evil to avoid a greater; they see no Evil and some of them much good in the present situation of Saint Domingo.

With such fundamental differences of view regarding Toussaint and Haiti, it did not seem very likely that the American Government would " cordially enter " into the agreement that had been outlined by the British Ministry. But inasmuch as the British naval blockade of Haitian ports could not be disregarded, it was possible that this fact would induce the Adams Administration to give reluctant consent to a system of " restricted intercourse " with Toussaint. It was obvious, however, that the American Government would never agree to the formation of a British-American trading company with exclusive privileges.

General Maitland still nursed a hope that Secretary Pickering and President Adams would favor a policy of co-operation with Great Britain in Haitian affairs, and if they could be brought to this point of view it would be possible to send a vessel to Cap Français to instruct Stevens and Lieutenant-Colonel Harcourt to " stay all proceedings " until a final agreement had been reached. It was fortunate that the American Government was still seeking some solution for the unsettled situation in Haiti, and General Maitland believed that notwithstanding the many obstacles that lay in his path he would make a partial success of his mission. But this optimism was tempered with a contempt for the American people and their institutions. To him it appeared that America was in a most

deplorable state of National debility. The Executive Government without energy; the People without the smallest feeling of National honour, all occupied in accumulating Money and he not only the best, but the ablest Man who gets the most, tho' possibly in the unfairest Manner. From such a Government and such a People, We can expect nothing either vigorous or beyond the narrow limits of their paltry views of their immediate Interest. War they will never declare, and insult they will ever submit to.[75]

[75] Maitland to Dundas, April 3, 1799, W. O. 1/71.

Maitland's open distaste for everything American was not lessened by the discovery that Secretary Pickering was a shrewd bargainer.[76]   After some extended conversations with the American Secretary of State, General Maitland and Liston submitted a detailed " Sketch of Proposed Regulations " relative to trade relations with Haiti.[77]   Although several important amendments were made by the American Government, these regulations outlined a policy relative to Haitian affairs that was largely adopted by both Great Britain and the United States.

[76] The negotiations with Liston and Brigadier-General Maitland were carried on entirely by Secretary Pickering. President Adams was away on a visit to Quincy, Massachusetts, and he entrusted to the Secretary of State this whole matter of Haitian trade. See Adams to Pickering, April 13, 1799, *Misc. Letters, January-June, 1799*, MS. Dept. of State.

[77] " Sketch of Proposed Regulations " presented by General Maitland and Robert Liston, April 11, 1799, W. O. 1/71:

" 1. The whole Trade of the Island of Saint Domingo to be for the present at least confined to one Port viz., Port-au-Prince.

" 2. That an Agent for each of the Governments [of Great Britain and America] shall reside at the specified Port, and shall have the exclusive management of the Coasting Trade, which they shall carry on by means of Boats of the Country to a sufficient extent for the supply of the different Ports of the Island which are under the command of General Toussaint and for bringing back the produce of these ports to Port-au-Prince.

" 3. That all Vessels trading from America to Saint Domingo shall be furnished with Passports of a description to be hereafter settled, respectively signed by the President of the United States and His Majesty's Plenipotentiary to America. That all Vessels trading from Saint Domingo shall have Passports signed by the Resident Agents of the two Nations at Saint Domingo.

" 4. That all Manufactured Commodities be furnished exclusively from the British Dominions, all Articles of produce (Lumber, Live Stock, etc.) from the territories of the United States.

" 5. Should General Toussaint violate on his side the Conditions of the Arrangement with respect to either Country, the whole shall be suspended, and neither the Subjects of Great Britain, nor of the United States shall be at liberty from thence forward to carry on trade to the Port agreed upon—much less to the other Ports of Saint Domingo.

" 6. No intercourse shall be opened with those ports of the Island, which are not subject to General Toussaint, and no extension or change shall take place, in the present Arrangement without the joint consent of the Governments of Great Britain and America.

" 7. The Article binding General Toussaint to prohibit the equipment of Privateers, and the annoying of the British or American Trade, by armed Ships sailing from any of the Ports that are subject to him, to be drawn up in the strongest terms, and to be extended as far as possible."

There were several items in this list of "Proposed Regulations" which did not meet with the approval of Secretary Pickering.   On April 13, 1799, he handed to General Maitland and Mr. Liston an extended commentary which covered every phase of British-American trade with Haiti.   Some of his remarks were so cogent that they were promptly agreed to by the British negotiators.   With reference to article one, he indicated his assent to the belief that it was within the " *power* of the President of the United States to declare *one* or *more* ports in St. Domingo open to Commerce of the United States." He then made it clear, however, that before the Chief Executive could take such action he must first be certain that the opening of Haitian trade would be " consistent with the Interest of the United States."

In connection with article two of the proposed regulations he expressed the view that the Consul-General of the United States in Haiti had ample authority to co-operate with the British agent at Port-au-Prince in devising plans for the control of the coasting trade.   If necessary, he could also issue passports to American ships engaged in commerce with Haiti.   But before any agreement was reached with reference to such measures it would behoove the American Government to give careful consideration to the question as to how this restrictive policy would affect American interests.   If American exports to Haiti were confined to one port of entry it would be evident that the market at that port would soon be glutted and prices for American products would fall " below the prime cost."   It would also be true that American ships would have to remain at this one port until provision was made for the trans-shipment of their cargoes to the other Haitian ports.   This would result in such a delay at Port-au-Prince that the bottoms of these American vessels would be " ruined by worms, the perishable goods on board be injured or lost and the Crews be unnecessarily exposed to destruction by the diseases of the Country."

It should also be remembered that there was not sufficient

Mercantile Capital at any one port equal to the purchase of their Cargoes: and consequently, the Master and Supercargoes must either embark themselves in the Coasting Vessels, to be their own factors at the other Ports or they must employ factors of the Island whom generally they would not know, and whom they could not safely trust; incurring a certain and considerable loss by Commissions alone.

After this preliminary criticism of the regulations proposed by General Maitland and Liston with regard to Haitian commerce, Secretary Pickering pointed out the numerous dangers that might result from an undue development of the coasting trade of Haiti. Even though this trade were carried on under the strict supervision of resident American and British agents, there was still a possibility that within a short time Toussaint would have a fleet that would constitute a real threat to all foreign shipping.

With regard to the passport system as outlined in article three of the proposed regulations, Secretary Pickering was equally critical. Such a system would require all American ships trading to Haiti to obtain passports from the British Minister to the United States, but all British vessels, whether from Europe or from the British colonies in America, could engage in commerce to Haiti without the worry and delay of obtaining passports. The British defense of this passport system was that it would prevent the danger of "*french principles* and *French emissaries* penetrating the British West India Colonies, and the Southern parts of the United States, where the Slaves form a great Mass of the population." If this argument was valid the question then immediately arose as to why all British vessels, including those from the British West Indies, were permitted to go to Haiti without the "least restraint" being imposed upon them.

Article four of the proposed regulations was especially distasteful to Secretary Pickering. Under its terms all manufactured commodities were to be furnished " exclusively from the British Dominions," while all articles of produce like lumber and live stock were to be furnished by the United States. To the Secretary of State it seemed that these restrictions were repugnant to the " Commercial Ideas and Policy of the United States." American commerce included the productions and manufactures of

many foreign Countries, as well as numerous Articles of the growth and manufacture of the United States. If all foreign productions and all Manufactures, domestic as well as foreign, were to be excluded from our Commerce with Saint Domingo, it would very sensibly affect many branches of our foreign Trade, and very injuriously narrow the limits of our intercourse with that Island. . . . Is there not, also, in this proposition, a want of reciprocity? While all Manufactured Commodities are to be furnished *exclusively* from the British Dominions, it is not proposed that all Articles of produce (lumber, live stock etc.) should be furnished exclusively from the territories of the United States. Thus, besides that the British Continental Colonies may export their own lumber, live stock, etc., both these and the Colonies in the Islands, may carry every species of the produce of the United States to St. Domingo.

In connection with articles five, six, and seven of the proposed regulations, Secretary Pickering was of the opinion that no difficulty would arise with regard to their adoption. It was wise to remember, however, that in the exercise of the treaty-making power the President would have to act in conjunction with the Senate, and the Senate would not convene until December of that year (1799).[78]

To the British negotiators (Maitland and Liston) these detailed comments of Secretary Pickering appeared to indicate an inclination towards the belief that Haitian independence was inevitable. Indeed, General Maitland assured Secretary Dundas that the instructions that were given to Edward Stevens were so worded as to incite Toussaint " to declare the Island independent." [79] Stevens himself had deprecated the idea of Haitian independence, but he believed that it was inevitable and that therefore nothing remained for the American Government but to take " advantage of the event with as little hazard as possible to the Southern parts of the Union." [80]

With special reference to this question of Haitian independence it is interesting to note the divergent views of Secretary Pickering and of President Adams. Although the Secretary of

---

[78] " Observations by Secretary Pickering on the ' Sketch of Proposed Regulations ' for controlling the trade of the Island of Saint Domingo," April 13, 1799, W. O. 1/71.

[79] Maitland to Dundas, April 20, 1799, W. O. 1/71.

[80] Liston to Lord Grenville, March 30, 1799, F. O. 5/25.

State looked with some favor upon the erection of an independent government in the island of San Domingo, President Adams felt that the independence of the French colonies in the Caribbean was " the worst and most dangerous condition they can be in, for the United States." [81]

In the formulation of the policy of the United States concerning Haiti, Secretary Pickering was largely left to his own devices. President Adams was in Quincy, Massachusetts during the negotiations with General Maitland and Liston, and he approved the steps taken by the Secretary of State. In the conduct of these negotiations Secretary Pickering enjoyed a definite advantage over the British negotiators. Before General Maitland had reached Philadelphia Stevens was already en route for Haiti, and there was a distinct possibility that he might be able to conclude with Toussaint a convention which would give to the United States some exclusive trade privileges. This fact gave serious concern to Maitland and Liston, and it helped to strengthen their decision to cast aside their instructions and rapidly reach an accord with the American Government. It was not long before a compromise was arranged and some basic principles were adopted.[82]

[81] Adams to Pickering, April 17, 1799, *Life and Works of John Adams*, VIII, 634.

[82] This compromise was entitled " Points on which there is an understanding between the Governments of Great Britain and the United States of America in consequence of the foregoing proposed regulations." It embodied the following items:

" 1. It is understood that Great Britain and the United States have a common interest in preventing the dissemination of dangerous principles among the slaves of their respective countries; and that they will mutually and sincerely attend to that interest, to guard both against the danger here alluded to in consequence of the proposed intercourse with St. Domingo.

" 2. That any infringement of the contemplated regulations which may be agreed upon with Toussaint, and which will constitute the basis of the determination of the two nations, respectively, to open a commercial intercourse with St. Domingo, or any hostility commenced, or manifestly intended, on his part, against either, shall lead to an immediate suspension of intercourse with that island, on the part of both nations, while the laws of the United States authorize such a suspension on their part.

" 3. That it is the interest of both nations to induce General Toussaint to refuse an asylum to any French armed vessels in the ports of St. Domingo:

After some further discussion, Secretary Pickering and the British negotiators worked out a list of regulations which General Maitland should propose to Toussaint. If the black dictator accepted these regulations it was to be understood that both Great Britain and the United States would be bound thereby.[83]

such an asylum being deemed incompatible with the safety of the proposed commercial intercourse.

" 4. That it is the positive object of both nations by pacific arrangements to put an end, *in toto*, or as nearly as possible, to all maritime operation or exertion of any kind in the island of St. Domingo.

" 5. That the American Consul-General in that island shall be instructed to assist in carrying into effect the proposed regulations.

" 6. That no commercial vessel of either nation shall be permitted to enter the port or ports to be opened, as before proposed, until the day to be fixed according to the fifth article of the regulations to be proposed to General Toussaint.

" 7. As the present political state of St. Domingo is subject to constant change and fluctuation, and as even its situation at the moment is not perfectly ascertained, it is understood that the whole of the present arrangement shall be open to such future discussion and decision as the nature of the case, in the opinion of the respective governments, may demand."

See W. O. 1/71; and letter of President Adams to Secretary Pickering, May 1, 1799, *Works of John Adams,* VIII, 639-640.

[83] " Heads of Regulations to be proposed by Brigr. General Maitland to Genl. Toussaint to be established by the Authority of the latter; and to which it is understood that the American Government will assent:

" 1st. That one or two Ports of entry be established in the Island of Saint Domingo, to which all British & American Vessels trading to that Island, shall be obliged to go, under penalty of seizure. That if one Port only be established, the Cape is to be the exclusive Port: If two ports of entry be allowed; they shall be the Cape and Port au Prince. It is however understood that a latitude exists to fix upon any other Port in preference to Port au Prince, if it should be clearly proved that a benefit will accrue to either Party by so doing.

" 2nd. That the Agents of the two Nations, with the consent of General Toussaint shall have respectively a latitude to grant to Vessels, after entering as stated above, passports which shall enable them to proceed from the Port or Ports of entry to other Ports in the Island, where they may find a Market, and receive their returns.

" 3rd. That no Frenchman or Foreigner be permitted to take his Passage on board of any British or American Vessel bound to Saint Domingo, without having a Passport from an Authority which will be satisfactory to General Toussaint.

" 4th. That no French or foreign Passenger be taken on board any British or American Vessel returning from Saint Domingo without a Passport from the principal Agent of each Nation.

" 5th. That a day be fixed on to open the Port or Ports of entry, so as to enable Vessels of both Nations to arrive as nearly as possible at the same time.

" 6th. That the vessels of the two Nations shall for the present be allowed

As one reads over these regulations that General Maitland and Mr. Liston agreed to, it is evident that Secretary Pickering gained a distinct victory. The British negotiators were forced to abandon the articles that the War Office and Foreign Office had strongly insisted upon, and they discovered that it was expedient to compromise on other items of less importance. After such a brilliant performance it was only to be expected that President Adams would express his " fullest approbation " of the course followed by Secretary Pickering.[84]

In a letter to Secretary Dundas, April 20, 1799, General Maitland gave a résumé of his conversations with Secretary Pickering and Secretary Wolcott, and he then explained why he and Mr. Liston finally consented to an agreement which ran so counter to their instructions:

Had the Negotiation been at a stand on all sides it might have been both prudent and fitting to have delayed proceedings till We received further Instructions from home; but as the American Government was actually negotiating [with Toussaint through Edward Stevens], as they were expecting with the utmost impatience the result of that Negotiation; We conceived it our duty to come to a temporary Arrangement as close as We could to the Spirit of the Views of His Majesty's Ministers. . . . We witheld entering into written discussions upon any of the points, as it could do no good, and might tend to a lengthened literary correspondence, which must have widened any difference, but never could have brought Us nearer on the occasion.[85]

to carry to Saint Domingo every species of Merchandize and produce; but it is well understood, that both Governments will as soon as may be confer and endeavour to agree upon terms for regulating their future trade, with that Island.

" 7th. That the Vessels of the two Nations shall be restricted to carry on trade with St. Domingo directly to and from their own possessions.

" Philadelphia, April 20, 1799." See W. O. 1/71.

[84] Adams to Pickering, May 1, 1799, *Works of John Adams,* VIII, 639-640. Before General Maitland had landed in Philadelphia to begin his negotiations with the American Government, the British Ministry had already abandoned hope of securing the consent of the American Government to the organization of a British-American company with exclusive rights to trade with Haiti. But they were particularly anxious to win American acceptance of the articles which restricted this Haitian trade to one port, made provision for an elaborate passport system to control all contact with Haiti, and limited American exports to live stock and provisions. On all these points the British negotiators had to recede.

[85] Maitland to Dundas, April 20, 1799, W. O. 1/71.

In a private letter to Secretary Dundas (April 20, 1799), General Maitland vented his spleen upon America. His personal pride was deeply hurt by the fact that Secretary Pickering had insisted upon compliance with American desires, and his comments upon American habitudes of thought are far from complimentary. Although he had been in America only a few weeks he was certain that his opinions, if not " perfectly founded," were " pretty near the truth." He greatly feared that the line of conduct which Liston seemed

inclined to pursue here and the Government at home wishes to adopt, will never answer any good end, or tend in the smallest degree to forward the views for which it is adopted—it appears to me that we wish by conciliation on our part to lead the Americans into war with France, and into a closer connection with us. Allowing that we should derive an advantage from either or both of those, still I venture to say that by conciliation you will never effect it. If the manner is all that is meant to be conciliatory, . . . it can be of no avail, . . . and will only lead on their part to the expectation of further concessions.

. . . I will venture to assert, there is but one principle which actuates either the Government or the People of America, viz., the narrowest view of Commercial benefit: now as the balance of their trade with Great Britain amounts on an average to three Millions Sterling in our favour, and as the balance in favour of America, in the other parts of Europe, in great part goes to cover the balance due to Us; it is by no means astonishing they should look at a Nation which carries on so beneficial a Commerce; with the strongest Eye of envy and jealousy. . . . Our Naval supremacy added to this and the whole tinctured with a recollection of the calamities of last War, are the sole grounds on which this opinion of Us is formed.

. . . Their only mode of viewing or arguing any point is merely on the score of Profit and loss, to every other feeling they are perfectly dead, and if one half per Cent could be gained by making even the most disgraceful Peace, it would be impossible for the Government to carry on the War for a Moment if so inclined.[86]

In his letter to Secretary Grenville (April 20, 1799), Liston does not take such a pessimistic view of the situation. It seemed to him that the agreement which he and General Maitland had just concluded with Secretary Pickering was of dis-

[86] Maitland to Dundas, April 20, 1799, *Private*, W. O. 1/71.

tinct value to Great Britain. By accepting a compromise the British Government secured the

aid of America in establishing restrictive regulations; which if we stood alone we could not effectually enforce. We draw the Government of the United States closer to Great Britain, and give consistency to measures which tend to widen their breach with France. We obtain essential though not exclusive advantages of commerce, which must add to the strength and promote the general prosperity of the Empire. This reasoning appears to me solid and conclusive.[87]

Two days after coming to an agreement with General Maitland and Liston relative to the situation in Haiti, Secretary Pickering wrote to King, in London, to acquaint him with the result of the negotiations. In conclusion he repudiated all thought that the American Government had in any way intrigued with Great Britain in order to induce Toussaint to issue a declaration of independence. While it was not denied that the Department of State had " strong expectations " that Toussaint would soon sever all connections with France, it was vehemently asserted that any such action was not " owing to the intrigues, nor the advice, nor even the suggestion of the United States." [88]

Secretary Pickering also wrote to Edward Stevens, in Haiti, to explain the purport of the agreement with General Maitland and Liston. From the viewpoint of the American Government it appeared that this arrangement with Great Britain would open a " lucrative trade to St. Domingo." The continuance and expansion of that trade would rest " chiefly on the Naval superiority of Great Britain." It was obvious, then, that the United States was bound " by a direct regard to our commercial interests, and considerations of political safety against what may justly be called a common enemy, to act in perfect concert with Great Britain in all this business respecting St. Domingo." [89]

[87] Liston to Lord Grenville, April 20, 1799, *Foreign Office Transcripts*, MS. Library of Congress.

[88] Pickering to King, April 22, 1799, *Life and Correspondence of Rufus King*, III, 5-7.

[89] Pickering to Stevens, April 20, 1799, *Cape Haitien, Consular Desp.*, vol. 1, MS. Dept. of State.

In the meantime, Stevens had landed at Cap Français (April 18, 1799) and was soon given an audience with Toussaint. The Haitian dictator was delighted with the supply of provisions that Stevens had brought along with him because at that moment the inhabitants of Cap Français had been reduced " to the extremest Distress " by the British blockade.[90] Partly as a result of these much needed supplies, but more on account of the personal charm of Stevens, the relations between the new American Consul-General and Toussaint grew quite friendly. When Stevens first arrived at Cap Français, Toussaint was engaged in negotiations with Lieutenant-Colonel Harcourt with reference to the ratification of the Maitland-Toussaint Treaty of August 31, 1798.[91] Stevens was fearful that the British Government was endeavoring to gain exclusive

[90] Secretary Pickering had two reasons for permitting Mr. Stevens to carry as cargo on the *Kingston* some supplies for Toussaint. It was through the sale of the provisions that the cost of the Stevens mission was to be defrayed. Secretary Pickering also wished to give to Toussaint some " visible evidence " and an " earnest of further supplies, when his total suppression of privateering should enable the President of the United States to open the trade of the island." Without this " immediate supply and proof to the Senses of the uninformed blacks," he feared that the " main object of the law, the securing of a full commerce with Saint Domingo," would be " put in jeopardy." Pickering to President Adams, February 20, 1799, *Cape Haitien, Consular Desp.,* vol. 1, MS. Dept. of State. The fact that Stevens was about to carry a cargo of provisions on the *Kingston* raised a storm of disapproval in certain mercantile circles in Philadelphia, and this was increased when Jacob Mayer, the American consul at Cape Haitien, sent to some friends in Philadelphia an invoice of the *Kingston's* cargo. Stoddert to Pickering, March 8, 1799, *Pickering Papers*, MS. Massachusetts Historical Society; and Stevens to Yard, August 22, and 24, 1799, *Cape Haitien, Consular Desp.,* vol. 1, MS. Dept. of State. Although Mayer was the American consul at Cap Français, he did not hesitate to plot behind the back of Stevens. As soon as he reached Haiti he wrote " circular Letters thro' the whole Colony, informing the Planters that certain Speculators had come out with large sums of money in the *Kingston* to buy up their produce; and advising them not to sell, as the Ports would undoubtedly be opened; and they would then get what price they pleased. In this he was seconded by his Coadjutor Bunel. The immediate effect of this plot was to raise the Price of all Kinds of Produce immensely." Mr. Mayer then went so far as to insinuate that " the President & Mr. Pickering were concerned in the *Kingston's* Cargo." Stevens to Yard, August 22 and August 24, 1799, *ibid.*

[91] Harcourt to Toussaint, April 20 and 24, 1799, Arch. Aff. Étr., Mém. et Doc., Amérique, 15:7, 9. Harcourt was interested also in securing a pledge from Toussaint that both American and British ships would be safe from attack and confiscation in the Haitian waters under Toussaint's control.

trading privileges with Haiti, and therefore he sent to Toussaint a strong letter urging him to postpone the negotiations with Harcourt until he was acquainted with the attitude of the Adams Administration relative to trade. After receiving this letter from Stevens, Toussaint journeyed at once to Cap Français to discuss the situation with the American representative.[92]

Under the expert handling of Stevens, Toussaint became quite tractable, and he soon announced his willingness to protect American commerce. Privateers were to be recalled and their commissions would not be renewed. The property of American citizens would no longer be seized by any Haitians under the control of Toussaint, and all future transactions would be conducted " on the principles of Equity." The armed vessels of the United States, both public and private, as well as merchant ships, would be permitted to enter the ports of Haiti, and would " in all Respects " be received and treated as " Friends." A proclamation setting forth these facts would be published immediately, and all vessels belonging to American citizens, captured and carried into Haitian ports after this proclamation was issued, would be released at once.

After securing all these concessions from Toussaint, Stevens was certain that the " Depredations, Aggressions, and Hostilities, which occasioned the Restraints and Prohibitions of commercial intercourse between this Colony, and the United States, will not continue in future and that the Trade may of course be renewed with the utmost safety." In order that American commercial interests should be safeguarded and promoted it was expedient to reopen this trade with Haiti " as quickly as possible." [93]

[92] According to General Maitland, Stevens soon gained an ascendancy over Toussaint: " On reaching Saint Domingo I soon found, that in Consequence of the Arrival of Mr. Stevens, Toussaint had closed with the American propositions, and had witheld coming into any positive Agreement with Colonel Harcourt, though at first, previous to the Arrival of the American Consul, he had entered into all our views, and shewn much anxiety to conclude the business on our own terms." Maitland to Admiral Sir Hyde Parker, May 31, 1799, W. O. 1/71.

[93] Stevens to Pickering, May 3, 1799, *Cape Haitien, Consular Desp.,* vol. 1, MS. Dept. of State.

Flushed with this signal success as a negotiator, Stevens was inclined to be somewhat generous towards the British. He prevented Roume (the agent of the French Directory) from including in the proclamation concerning Haitian commerce " some insolent and offensive expressions with regard to the English," and he persuaded Toussaint to renew the negotiations with the representative of the British Government. In the discussions that ensued with Lieutenant-Colonel Harcourt, Stevens took a prominent part, and he endeavored to " demonstrate to Toussaint the necessity of making Great Britain a party in the business." When the black general demurred at the proposal to admit British shipping to the ports under his control, Stevens suggested that any difficulties with France in this regard could be obviated by allowing British ships to enter " under the American flag."

Toussaint, however, was none too friendly to the British. He resented the fact that the British Ministry had postponed for many months any attempt to secure the ratification of the Maitland-Toussaint Treaty of August 31, 1798. In this convention General Maitland had promised him some supplies from Jamaica, but these had never arrived. Moreover, the conduct of the British war-ships in Haitian waters had been " extremely hostile and disrespectful." [94]

Toussaint was still in this anti-British mood when General Maitland arrived at Cap Français on May 14. Remaining on board the British frigate *Camilla,* he sent word to Toussaint that he would appreciate the opportunity of an interview with him at the Môle-Saint-Nicolas.[95] He also informed Edward Stevens that there were " particular reasons " why he could not land at Cap Français, and he invited the American Consul-General to come on board the *Camilla* to discuss the terms of a proposed arrangement relative to Dominican affairs. Stevens promptly accepted this invitation, and after a consultation with

[94] Liston to Lord Grenville, May 29, 1799, F. O. 5/25.
[95] Maitland to Toussaint, May 14, 1799, Arch. Aff. Étr., Mém. et Doc., Amérique, 15:11. Inasmuch as the agent of the French Directory, M. Roume, was still at Cap Français, it would have been embarrassing for Toussaint to meet General Maitland at that port.

General Maitland he decided to accompany the British agent to Gonaives.[96]

Upon arriving at Gonaives, General Maitland wrote to Toussaint to inquire about the negotiations that had been carried on with Stevens. He assumed, of course, that British commerce would be placed on the same footing as American. This being true, he was ready to conclude an armistice with Toussaint which would extend to certain American and British vessels the right to enter specified Haitian ports. If Toussaint was not ready to agree to this parity between British and American commerce the existing blockade of all Haitian ports by British cruisers would continue, and in spite of the friendly relations between the United States and Great Britain no American ships would be permitted to land cargoes.[97]

Although General Maitland remained on the *Camilla*, Stevens went on shore at Gonaives and put pressure upon Toussaint in favor of an arrangement that would satisfy British demands. In response to the efforts of the American Consul-General, Toussaint (on May 22) promised to prevent any attacks by Haitian troops upon any part of the United States or upon any British possessions in the Caribbean. He also agreed to surrender all vessels (American or British) that might be captured and brought into Haitian ports by French privateers whether " of St. Domingo or belonging to any other Island." Finally, he gave his consent to an understanding that the only two ports of entry in Haiti should be Cap Français and Port-au-Prince.[98]

But this agreement of May 22, 1799 was only the outline of a more comprehensive convention which Maitland and Stevens now pushed to completion. It was necessary to give more ample expression to the desires of both the British and the American Governments for the suppression of all privateering in Haitian waters. General Maitland himself was also eager

---

[96] Maitland to Stevens, May 14, 1799, *Cape Haitien, Consular Desp.*, vol. 1, MS. Dept. of State.

[97] Maitland to Toussaint, May 20, 1799, Arch. Aff. Étr., Mém et Doc., Amérique, 15:12.

[98] For the text of this agreement of May 22, 1799 see *Cape Haitien, Consular Desp.*, vol. 1, MS. Dept. of State.

to include an article whereby the vessels of the two nations should be placed " on the same Footing in every Point." [99]

After further consultation between Stevens and General Maitland, it was agreed that Cap Français and Port-au-Prince should be opened to British-American commerce on August 1, 1799.[100] This understanding having been arrived at, General Maitland sailed for Jamaica to discuss matters of urgent importance with the Governor. He had been advised by Stevens of a projected attack by Rigaud upon the coast of that island, and he was anxious to forestall it.[101]

It is apparent that the relations between Maitland and Stevens were quite friendly. There was no friction about the procedure to be followed in carrying out the instructions they had both received relative to the negotiations with Toussaint, and it was fortunate that in some regards these instructions accorded with the views of the black general. He was in favor of restricting the commerce of Haiti to two ports of entry, and he raised no difficulty about the establishment of a passport system that would control the coasting trade between other ports that were under his control.[102]

Notwithstanding this conciliatory attitude on the part of Toussaint, General Maitland was distinctly skeptical about the advantages that would attend the reopening of the commerce of Haiti:

In a Commercial point of view, I have no hesitation in saying that in the present situation of that Island it is impossible to reap any permanent Commercial benefit by any Intercourse we may open with it.

[99] Maitland to Stevens, May 23, 1799, *ibid.*

[100] Maitland to Pickering, May 23, 1799, *ibid.*

[101] Stevens to Maitland, May 23, 1799, *ibid.* See also W. O. 1/71, where this letter from Stevens to Maitland is dated May 24, 1799.

[102] Maitland to Liston, May 23, 1799, W. O. 1/71. See also Maitland to Stevens, May 23, 1799, *Cape Haitien, Consular Desp.*, vol. 1, MS. Dept. of State. In a letter from Secretary Pickering to President Adams, May 29, 1799, the Secretary remarks: " It is remarkable, that General Toussaint should desire the ports of Cape Francois and Port au Prince, alone to be opened to our commerce in the first instance, and that our vessels should there receive passports to go to the other ports, within Toussaint's jurisdiction. This is precisely the arrangement formed here with Genl. Maitland." *Domestic Letters*, vol. 11, MS. Dept. of State.

The Nature of all property there is so extremely precarious, the Nature of the Government, (if it can be so called,) so extremely fluctuating and uncertain, and the Views of the Administration so deeply rooted, that I can see no possibility of any British Merchant investing any part of his Capital with common prudence in any Speculation that relates to it. Indeed I am clearly of opinion that whatever benefit is to be derived by this Intercourse will entirely rest with the Americans. . . . Without Capital, without principle, trading in small Vessels, and always in the desperate Speculation of having nothing to lose, and everything to gain, they will undoubtedly run every risk and most probably in many instances will succeed.[103]

In a letter to Liston (in Philadelphia), Maitland continues his lament about American lack of character and the manner in which the American Government had bungled the situation:

It is infinitely to be regretted that in consequence of the American interference we have been obliged to open anything like a general intercourse with Toussaint's part of the Island. Any general commercial benefit arising to the Country under his dominion is a thing he has by no means Comprehension to understand, any private advantage that would have arisen by supplying him simply with provisions, was an arrangement, which exactly suited the Calibre of his Understanding, but placed as we were with the certainty that the Americans would open a general intercourse, whether we wished it or not, . . . I cannot help thinking that it . . . was both prudent and fitting to make the Arrangement and give it a fair trial. In this view of the Subject you will perceive the necessity of making the American Government aware, that our continuing or breaking off such an Arrangement must entirely depend on future Occurrences. . . . That the Americans will derive almost the whole of the commercial Benefit . . . I am perfectly clear.[104]

There is little doubt that Stevens was a much better diplomat than General Maitland. It took him but a short time to gain an astonishing mastery over Toussaint, and it was only through Stevens's gift of persuasion that the black general consented to carry on negotiations with the British envoy. The British Government had unwisely permitted the terms of the secret treaty of August 31, 1798 to become public, and the British press had freely commented upon the Haitian situation. In Haiti the

---

[103] Maitland to Parker, May 31, 1799, W. O. 1/71.
[104] Maitland to Liston, June 3, 1799, W. O. 1/71.

news of this Maitland-Toussaint Treaty had been used by the enemies of Toussaint as a means of embarrassing his relations with the agent of the French Directory. The black dictator was not ready to break all bonds with France, and he flatly refused to receive Colonel Grant as a resident British agent.[105]

Maitland finally consented to an arrangement whereby Stevens would "superintend" British commerce with Haiti until Toussaint was ready to admit a British agent.[106] After this compromise had been agreed upon, the negotiations between Maitland and Toussaint were quickly concluded, and on June 13, 1799 another secret treaty was signed. Although Edward Stevens did not place his signature upon this treaty, it was clearly understood by all parties that the American Government would be bound by its articles. First of all, the treaty provided for the suspension of all hostilities between Great Britain and that portion of Haiti which was under the control of Toussaint. General Maitland promised that no British forces would attack the territories governed by Toussaint, and the black general gave a similar pledge with reference to any expeditions aimed at British or American possessions.[107]

[105] General Maitland appreciated the difficulties of Toussaint's position and did not insist upon Colonel Grant's reception. In a letter to Lord Balcarres, dated June 1, 1799, Maitland explains the situation: "A difficulty has been made by Toussaint on the subject of receiving Colonel Grant as Agent to reside in St. Domingo. . . . I have not been able as yet to get the better of this difficulty and had the objection to Colonel Grant rested upon any captious Principle, or any apparent opposition to the views of Government I should certainly have considered this difficulty as Paramount; but the Case is so much the reverse and the reasons which he assigns for this refusal . . . so likely to be of a Nature to impress themselves most strongly on his mind, that I cannot help feeling that they are stated fairly and exactly as he thinks on the occasion. It is no Objection either to Colonel Grant in person, or to the thing, but both his Agents in France and the French Directory have set out in French on one side and in English on the other, all the foolish paragraphs that have appeared in the Newspapers relative to Grant's Appointment, and his feeling undoubtedly is, that receiving Grant . . . would be an immediate and virtual declaration of Alliance with us, and Independence of France, before he has arranged his means to come to such a Measure." W. O. 1/71.

[106] Stevens to Pickering, June 23, 1799, *Cape Haitien, Consular Desp.,* vol. 1, MS. Dept. of State.

[107] The text of this convention of June 13, 1799 may be found in W. O. 1/71, and in Arch. Aff. Étr., Mém. et Doc., Amérique, 15:14. See also Stevens to Pickering, June 23, 1799, *Cape Haitien, Consular Desp.,* vol. 1, MS. Dept. of State.

The principal object of these negotiations with Toussaint was to secure some measure of protection against the attacks of French corsairs upon British and American commerce. The Haitian dictator readily agreed to take immediate action in this regard, and he was also willing to promise that he would stop any further sale of the prizes taken by such corsairs.

The commerce with Haiti was to be limited to the ports of Cap Français and Port-au-Prince, and General Maitland gave a pledge that British and American ships engaged in this commerce would not be molested by British cruisers if they were not carrying contraband of war. American and British merchant ships would be permitted to carry on a coasting trade between Haitian ports upon the issuance of the proper passports by the resident agents of the two powers. British merchantmen would be allowed to enter Haitian ports if they flew " Flags of Truce," and " on Condition that they wear no Colours in Port."

After signing this convention of June 13, 1799, General Maitland then wrote a long letter to Colonel Grant (the British agent who was to carry out the terms of the treaty) and explained its terms. Although he believed that it would not " suit the Character of the British Nation to enter into any further agreement with a Person of Toussaint's description," yet it should be noted that the black general had scrupulously carried out the conditions laid down in the treaty of August 31, 1798. But even though Toussaint had up to the present time fulfilled all treaty obligations, Colonel Grant should take great care to prevent any possibility that Haitian territory would be used as a base of operations against British possessions in the Caribbean. He should also keep a most careful watch upon the size of Toussaint's fleet of coasting vessels.[108] It would be highly dangerous to permit this fleet to serve as the nursery for a formidable Haitian navy. Through a judicious use of the passport system a check could be devised for the

[108] The Haitian vessels which were permitted to engage in the coasting trade were described as " boats belonging to the Government of the Island, not private property, and they have no Commissions for capturing vessels of any Nation whatsoever."

effective control of the growth of Toussaint's naval forces, and this same system could also be used to advantage in preventing the emigration of Haitian undesirables.

The principal object of the negotiations with Toussaint was to make adequate provision for the safety of the island of Jamaica. Thanks to the convention of June 13, 1799 there was no longer any danger from armed expeditions sailing from Haiti, but it should be kept in mind that this freedom from attack was partly due to the unsettled conditions that prevailed in the former French colony. This state of chaos was of distinct advantage to British interests in the Caribbean, and Colonel Grant should endeavor to " prevent any amicable arrangement taking place between Rigaud and Toussaint." With Toussaint involved in serious difficulties with both Rigaud and the agent of the French Directory, there was every reason to suppose that he would continue to court the favor of the British and the Americans.

To Maitland it seemed very clear that as far as British interests were concerned it would be better for Toussaint to remain " in rebellion against the Directory than in any other Character." But in the event that this state of rebellion could not long endure, and if the French Directory began to gain " an ascendancy in the Island," then Colonel Grant should urge Toussaint to issue a declaration of independence. He was not, however, to hold out to Toussaint " the smallest appearance of any further protection, or countenance from our Government."

Finally, Colonel Grant was instructed by General Maitland to

act hand in hand with the American Consul General. You are to consult with him, upon every occasion, and in all your transactions with General Toussaint, you are previously to concert with him the line of conduct fitting to adopt for the interest of the two Nations.[109]

After issuing these detailed instructions to Colonel Grant, General Maitland wrote to Lord Balcarres, the Governor of Jamaica, and gave him a résumé of the situation in Haiti.

[109] Maitland to Grant, June 17, 1799, *Secret*, W. O. 1/71.

There was no doubt in his mind that the convention of June 13 would add to the political security of British possessions in the Caribbean, but from a commercial viewpoint the opening of Haitian ports would mean little to British merchants. There was so much uncertainty about the progress of affairs in Haiti that it would probably be expedient for Lord Balcarres to permit merely a very restricted trade with the ports under Toussaint's control. It should be expected, of course, that American trade with Haiti would gain by leaps and bounds,

for their Government possesses no means of restricting it, and it exactly suits the speculative Character of the American Merchant. It is for them however to attend to their own interests, as it is for us not to follow them in a speculation which without giving any additional political security might tend to disappointment and possibly eventually to the loss of the very political good we are looking to.

In conclusion, General Maitland urged Lord Balcarres to send at once to Haiti a supply of provisions, and he expressed the view that the fate of Toussaint's cause " undoubtedly in a considerable degree depends upon their arrival." [110] On the same day (June 17) he sent a second letter to Lord Balcarres in which he also requested that Toussaint be supplied with one hundred barrels of gunpowder, two hundred stand of arms, " and a few Flints." These, he was sure, would be of " infinite use " to the black general.[111]

While General Maitland and Edward Stevens were busily

---

[110] Maitland to Lord Balcarres, June 17, 1799, W. O. 1/71.

[111] *Ibid.* On June 20 Maitland again wrote to Lord Balcarres to inform him that he had just learned that Toussaint was " in a situation extremely unpleasant. Rigaud is already in motion and has put to death a very considerable number of White Inhabitants both at Jeremie and Aux Cayes, and universally to a man at Petit Goaves. . . . I find Toussaint is in very great want indeed of Provisions so much so that his Troops are at a stand for want of them. . . . The whole aspect of things here, shews the crisis of this Island to be at hand, and at present though the chances are in Toussaint's favour, still there is not anything like certainty. . . . Every hour convinces me more of the propriety of my advice to Your Lordship of not opening the Ports generally to English Vessels even after the first of August." W. O. 1/71. Maitland also wrote to Admiral Sir Hyde Parker on June 20, 1799 and urged that provisions be sent at once to Toussaint and that the ports under Rigaud's control be subjected to the " strictest blockade." W. O. 1/71.

negotiating with Toussaint in Haiti, Secretary Pickering wrote a letter of inquiry to President Adams in which he frankly asked the following question: "Whether if the British commerce with St. Domingo be excluded, it will be ' expedient and consistent with the interest of the United States, to remit and discontinue ' the existing ' restraints and prohibitions ' on the commerce of the United States? " In other words, Secretary Pickering sought to ascertain what policy President Adams wished to follow in the event that Toussaint refused to negotiate with General Maitland on the basis of the terms that had been agreed upon by both the British and American Governments.[112]

In his answering letter of June 15, President Adams refused to give a " definitive opinion " on this tangled topic. He thought it would be wise to wait for

further information. I am afraid that the jealousy and avidity of the English will do an Injury to themselves as well as to us. But We cannot help it. My opinion is, that if the Powers of St. Domingo will not admit British Ships of War or Commerce into their Ports, the British Government ought to be contented with sufficient assurances of the Neutrality of that Island . . . and not insist on defeating the Connection between the United States & St. Domingo. It is my earnest desire, however, to do nothing without the Consent, Concert and Co-operation of the British Government in this Case. They are so deeply interested, that they ought to be consulted, and the Commerce of the Island is not worth to us, the Risque of any dispute with them.[113]

To President Adams it seemed apparent that harmony with England was of far greater importance to America than trade with Haiti. With this viewpoint in mind he wrote to Secretary

[112] Pickering to Adams, June 5, 1799, *Cape Haitien, Consular Desp.,* vol. 1, MS. Dept. of State.

[113] Adams to Pickering, June 15, 1799, *Misc. Letters, January-June, 1799,* MS. Dept. of State. In a letter to Secretary Stoddert, dated June 7, 1799, President Adams expressed himself in a similar vein: " We shall do nothing with St. Domingo until we hear again from Stevens. . . . We can do nothing but in concert with Maitland, and what his reception may be is uncertain. The English, in my opinion, have made much mischief for themselves as well as for us in that island. The hopes of our merchants, of great profit from the trade, will be found too sanguine, and the evils in store seem not to be foreseen." *Works of John Adams,* VIII, 655.

Pickering and freely commented on the difficult situation that seemed to confront General Maitland and Stevens:

If the British Merchant Vessells are to enter the Ports of Cape Francois and Port au Prince, under a Flagg of Truce, and ours do not: and if an Agent from the British Government is not Admitted, while one from the U. S. is, this will render it more necessary for us to be particularly delicate and complaisant towards the English and our Consuls and Merchants and Marines ought to have this Duty carefully inculcated upon them. A good understanding with the English is of more importance to us than the trade of St. Domingo.[114]

In a third letter to Secretary Pickering, President Adams once more refers to the necessity of acting in concert with the British Government with regard to trade relations with Toussaint. His attitude in this matter was very clearly defined:

Harmony with the English, in all this Business of St. Domingo is the thing I have most at heart. The Result of the whole is in my mind problematical and precarious. Toussaint has evidently puzzled himself, the French Government, the English Cabinet and the Administration of the United States. All the rest of the World knows as little what to do with him as he knows what to do with himself. His example may be followed by all the Islands French English Dutch and Spanish and all will be one day played off against the U. S. by European Powers.[115]

These letters reveal President Adams as a political realist of much the same stripe as General Maitland. Sentiment for Toussaint should not lead American foreign policy into dangerous friction with Great Britain. For the present, co-operation with Great Britain in the Caribbean was prescribed by wise statesmanship. For the future, watchful waiting would disclose the path best suited to American advancement.[116]

---

[114] Adams to Pickering, June 29, 1799, *Misc. Letters, January-June, 1799,* MS. Dept. of State.

[115] Adams to Pickering, July 2, 1799, *Misc. Letters, July-December, 1799,* MS. Dept. of State.

[116] In a despatch to Lord Grenville, on February 18, 1799, Liston gives an interesting viewpoint with reference to the political ideas of President Adams: "Mr. Adams from the time of his being placed at the head of the Administration of this Country has uniformly endeavoured to strengthen and increase its political connections in Europe, and has combated on all occasions the erroneous and impracticable theory maintained by some speculators here, that America is sufficient to herself, is independent of the rest of the world, and ought to reject foreign treaties and negotiations of every sort." F. O. 5/25.

CHAPTER III

JEFFERSON ANTICIPATES THE TERM
REALPOLITIK

As a result of the treaty of June 13, 1799 between Toussaint and General Maitland, President Adams issued a proclamation (June 26, 1799) which lifted the embargo that had been imposed upon American trade with Haiti.[1] On this same day a circular was sent by the Secretary of the Treasury to all collectors of customs in the United States with reference to the regulations that would govern this commerce.[2] It had been the understanding of Secretary Pickering that two ports in Haiti (Cap Français and Port-au-Prince) would be opened to British and American trade on August 1, and the Navy Department took the precaution of rushing war-ships to the Haitian coast so as to protect American interests.[3]

For some strange reason, Stevens suddenly got it into his head that the Haitian ports were not to be opened on August 1. This date, he believed, merely fixed the time when British and American ships should set sail for Haiti. Not wishing to quarrel with the American Consul-General, General Maitland acquiesced in this viewpoint, and the admiral in charge of the British fleet was so notified.[4] In America, however, this stand of Stevens created much " astonishment," and Secretary

[1] Proclamation of President Adams, June 26, 1799, *Misc. Letters, January-June, 1799*, MS. Dept. of State.

[2] Circular to Collectors of Customs from the Secretary of the Treasury, June 26, 1799, *ibid.*

[3] Stoddert to Captain Patrick Fletcher, June 25, 1799, *Letters to Officers of Ships of War*, MS. Navy Department Archives; Stoddert to Captain George Little, *Letter Book, 1799-1807*, MS. Navy Department Archives; Stoddert to Captain Silas Talbot, July 27, 1799, *Letters to Officers of Ships of War*, MS. Navy Department Archives. In this letter to Captain Talbot, Secretary Stoddert emphasizes the importance of cultivating a " Good Understanding with General Toussaint & the people of the Island by rendering them Friendly Offices whenever the occasion may be presented."

[4] Maitland to Liston, July 2, 1799, *Pickering Papers*, MS. Massachusetts Historical Society.

Pickering turned to Liston for assistance. There was only one course open to Mr. Liston, and he took prompt action. An explanatory letter was hurriedly despatched to Admiral Sir Hyde Parker, and serious difficulties with the American Government were thus averted.[5]

This renewal of trade with Haiti was of great advantage to Toussaint in his struggle with Rigaud for supremacy. It was to be a bitter contest with all the horrors of a war of extermination. According to Edward Stevens, the army of Rigaud was " well fed, well clothed, and well paid." The trade he had carried on with the other islands in the Caribbean, and with America, had supplied him with " plenty of Provisions, Clothing, and Ammunition." His infantry was well disciplined and his cavalry was the best in Haiti. Altogether, his army numbered some fifty-five thousand troops who were inured to war.

Toussaint, on the other hand, was faced with severe handicaps in this approaching conflict with Rigaud. His army was " in want of every Thing." There was but little ammunition and only a " few Military Stores." Until some expected supplies from Jamaica arrived it would be impossible to undertake any offensive operations. With reference to the outcome of the contest between Toussaint and Rigaud, Stevens was certain that the former would win. Such an issue would be of great assistance to American interests, and it seemed evident to the American Consul-General that Toussaint should be supported by " every legal Measure." [6]

This friendly attitude on the part of Mr. Stevens led Toussaint to write to President Adams and request that some American war-ships be sent to Haitian waters for the purpose of blockading the coasts and ports under the control of Rigaud.[7] Stevens himself then wrote to Secretary Pickering in warm praise of Toussaint. He had the

most perfect Confidence in the Attachment of Toussaint to the Government of the U. S. and in his sincere Desire to establish a beneficial and

[5] Liston to Lord Grenville, August 2, 1799, F. O. 5/25.
[6] Stevens to Pickering, June 24, 1799, *Cape Haitien, Consular Desp.*, vol. 1, MS. Dept. of State.
[7] Toussaint to Adams, August 14, 1799, *ibid.*

permanent Commerce between the two Countries. As to the Property and Persons of American Citizens I consider them as perfectly secure.[8]

To Toussaint, Stevens wrote in a similar vein. He assured him that the American Government had an " exalted opinion " of his character, and he was certain that it was the " unequivocal desire " of the Adams Administration to " maintain the Harmony which Subsists between the two Countries." [9]

These expressions of good faith and friendship between Toussaint and the representatives of the American Government were distinctly lacking in the relations that existed between the negro leader and the agents of Great Britain. Lord Balcarras (Governor of Jamaica) and Admiral Sir Hyde Parker were not entirely convinced that it was good policy to maintain intimate relations with Toussaint, and these suspicions were reciprocated by the black dictator.[10]

It is also true, however, that at times Toussaint even entertained suspicions of Stevens. In the early part of January, 1800, the American Consul-General discovered that the mind of Toussaint had suddenly turned " much soured " against him. But the plots of " designing Intriguers " were soon broken down by the magnetic American who drew from Toussaint a declaration that the persons and properties of American citizens should " at all Times, and under all Circumstances be considered as sacred." [11]

But Stevens's return to favor was not due wholly to his pleasing personality. Toussaint was astute enough to perceive that the American Consul-General would be very useful to him in his dealings with the British agents in the Caribbean.

[8] Stevens to Pickering, October 26, 1799, *ibid.*

[9] Stevens to Toussaint, November 15, 1799, *Cape Haitien, Consular Desp.,* vol. 2, MS. Dept. of State. As a token of his good will towards the United States Toussaint, at the request of Stevens, lowered the tariff duties which had just been fixed by the agent of the French Directory (Roume). Stevens to Pickering, December 1, 1799, *ibid.* In a despatch which he sent to Pickering on December 2, 1799, Stevens expressed the opinion that in the future, American property would be exempt from " arbitrary Requisitions." *Ibid.*

[10] Cathcart to Maitland, August 22, 1799, and Cathcart to Lord Balcarras, October 2 and December 21, 1799, C. O. 245/1.

[11] Stevens to Pickering, January 16, 1800, *Cape Haitien, Consular Desp.,* vol. 2, MS. Dept. of State.

British forbearance was essential to the success of Toussaint's plans for crushing Rigaud, and, when Admiral Parker seized six of the black general's armed vessels that were about to institute a blockade of Jacmel, the situation looked desperate. Stevens immediately wrote to Secretary Pickering with reference to Admiral Parker's action, and Pickering discussed the matter with Mr. Liston, the British Minister, who informed Lord Grenville about the " serious consequences " that might attend further seizures by the British fleet.[12]

The Adams Administration now decided upon open co-operation with Toussaint, and American war-ships began to capture vessels en route to the ports controlled by Rigaud. Captain Christopher Perry, of the frigate *General Greene,* received orders to " assist in securing the Convoy against the Boats of Rigaud," and to " intercept them as much as possible." With regard to Toussaint the orders were couched in a different key. Captain Perry was to be careful not to take any action that would " disturb the Harmony " that existed between Toussaint " and the People of the United States." [13]

As a result of these orders to American naval commanders an open warfare was carried on against the shipping bound to Rigaud's ports. The mulatto general was in desperate straits, and Edward Stevens was confident that within a short time the whole colony would be under the domination of Toussaint. This would mean that every connection with France would " soon be broken off " and that independence would be formally declared.[14]

The complete defeat of Rigaud's armed forces was ensured when American naval officers were no longer content to blockade Jacmel but adopted the more positive strategy of bombarding the forts that guarded its entrance. Successive broadsides from the frigate *General Greene* quickly dismantled the forts and caused their evacuation. Just before Jacmel was taken by the black troops of Toussaint on March 11, 1800, a handful

[12] Liston to Lord Grenville, February 6, 1800, F. O. 5/29.

[13] Captain Silas Talbot to Captain Christopher Raymond Perry, January 18, 1800, *Court Martial Records, 1799-1805,* vol. 1, MS. Navy Department Archives.

[14] Stevens to Pickering, February 13, 1800, *Cape Haitien, Consular Desp.,* vol. 2, MS. Dept. of State.

of the élite corps of Rigaud's army cut their way through the besieging cordon and made their way to safety.[15]

The capture of Jacmel paved the way for a complete victory for Toussaint's troops in the south. The black general was fully aware of the importance of American co-operation in the attack upon Rigaud's stronghold, and he expressed in extravagant terms his appreciation for this assistance.[16] In this regard the following letter from Toussaint to Edward Stevens is typical:

> I could not be more grateful to you than I am for all the trouble to which you have gone with regard to Commodore Silas Talbot, in order to persuade him to give me succor with ships. . . . It affords me renewed pleasure in offering you my thanks, to tell you how glad I am and how I appreciate the signal and important services which the Commander of the United States frigate *General Green*, . . . has rendered me. . . . He has contributed not a little to the success by his cruise, every effort being made by him to aid me in the taking of Jacmel.[17]

With Jacmel in his hands, Toussaint now proceeded to take action against the agent of the French Directory (Roume). The agent was invited to help in the campaign waged against Rigaud, and when he refused he was placed in prison to keep

[15] T. L. Stoddard, *The French Revolution in San Domingo*, pp. 279-281; P. de Lacroix, *Mémoires pour servir a l'histoire de la révolution de Saint-Domingue*, I, 373-394; H. C. des Fosses, *La révolution de Saint-Domingue*, pp. 194-214. In a private letter to Secretary Pickering, dated March 19, 1800, Edward Stevens remarks as follows: " In a Letter I received from the Genl. in Chief yesterday, he writes me that this important place [Jacmel] was evacuated on the Night of the 10th Inst." *Cape Haitien, Consular Desp.*, vol. 2, MS. Dept. of State.

[16] The following excerpt from a letter written by an officer on board the *General Greene* will give an idea of Toussaint's reaction to this help from the American naval forces: " It is impossible for me to describe to you the manner in which Toussaint expressed his gratitude to Capt. Perry on the occasion." *Connecticut Courant*, June 2, 1800.

[17] Toussaint to Stevens, March 16, 1800, *Cape Haitien, Consular Desp.*, vol. 2, MS. Dept. of State. The extent of the close co-operation between the American naval forces and the Toussaint Government is indicated in a letter from Captain Talbot to Edward Stevens of March 28, 1800 in which he indicates his willingness to make a pretended seizure of Haitian vessels and convoy them to Jacmel to prevent interference by British war-ships. *Ibid.* Captain Perry, of the *General Greene*, was so anxious to please Toussaint that he disregarded orders from his superior officer. See Captain Talbot to Secretary Stoddert, April 26, 1800. *Court Martial Records, 1799-1805*, vol. 1, MS. Navy Department Archives.

him from physical violence at the hands of belligerent blacks. A few days in the durance vile of a Haitian prison led Roume to promise full co-operation with Toussaint, but his offer of assistance came too late, and Toussaint decided that in order to prevent any intrigues that might be hatched against his administration it would be expedient to keep the agent in close confinement.[18] Another spell of imprisonment once more broke Roume's spirit, and, by the end of April, 1800, he was ready to comply with Toussaint's demand that a formal authorization be given to occupy Spanish Santo Domingo, which had been ceded to France under the provisions of the Treaty of Bâle (1795).

Toussaint's plans for the domination of the entire island of Santo Domingo received a temporary setback from the arrival of commissioners from France with instructions to mediate a truce between Toussaint and Rigaud. They were shown scant respect by the black dictator who promptly shipped one of the commissioners back to France. The campaign against Rigaud was pushed with such renewed vigor that the mulatto general was finally driven from the island in the last days of July, and on August 1, 1800 Toussaint made a triumphal entry into Les Cayes.[19]

During the entire period of the campaign against Rigaud, Toussaint continued to rely upon American co-operation, and his relations with the Adams Administration were of the most cordial nature. In the instructions which Secretary Stoddert gave to Captain Alexander Murray, who was about to proceed to Haitian waters, there is a sentence which illustrates these friendly feelings:

You cannot be too attentive to the cultivation of a good understanding, between Genl. Toussaint & the people under his command.[20]

---

[18] Stevens to Pickering, April 19, 24 and 27, 1800, *Cape Haitien, Consular Desp.*, vol. 2, MS. Dept. of State.

[19] In a despatch to Secretary John Marshall, dated August 14, 1800, Edward Stevens makes the following comment: " The War in the South has at last terminated, and tranquility is once more restored to the whole of that extensive Department." *Ibid.*

[20] Stoddert to Murray, May 13, 1800, *Letters to Officers of Ships of War, 1799-1800*, vol. 3, MS. Navy Department Archives. The attitude of President

But this high temperature of cordial friendship went down several degrees after Toussaint made himself master of all Haiti and then set out to add Spanish Santo Domingo to his dominions. In December, 1800, just before Toussaint's armies began their march against the Spanish portion of the island, a new arrêt was issued which imposed heavy tariff duties on imports and exports. Despite the vehement protests of Edward Stevens, these onerous duties were allowed to remain in effect. It was obvious to the American Consul-General that this action would bear heavily upon American business interests in Haiti, but Toussaint refused to repeal these new duties. With Rigaud a fugitive in foreign lands, and with the entire island of Santo Domingo under his secure control, it seemed to the black general that American good will no longer had to be courted so ardently. He still wished American ships to frequent his ports but considered that he was now in a position to sell his favors more dearly.[21] In this regard he dismally failed to read the signs of the times: America had reached the parting of the ways and was fast marching down the road to friendship with France. This friendship meant coolness towards England and covert hostility towards the black government of Haiti.

On September 30, 1800, by the treaty of Morfontaine, France and America put an end to the quarrel which had resulted in a state of quasi-warfare injurious to both nations. The law prohibiting intercourse with France and her colonies would expire on March 3, 1801 by its own limitation. Under the provisions of this act, President Adams had developed his co-operative policy with England and with Toussaint.[22] There was little likelihood that the Jefferson Administration would follow a similar course. As early as November, 1800 certain

Adams towards Toussaint is revealed in an instruction from Charles Lee, Secretary of State *ad interim*, to Edward Stevens on May 21, 1800: "It gives the President much satisfaction to learn that General Toussaint continues in his friendly dispositions to the United States." *Inst. to Ministers, 1798-1800,* vol. 5, MS. Dept. of State.

[21] Henry Hammond to Secretary Marshall, December 23, 1800; Stevens to Marshall, January 10, 1801, *Cape Haitien, Consular Desp.,* vol. 2, MS. Dept. of State.

[22] Edward Thornton to Lord Grenville, Washington, January 16, 1801, *Henry Adams Transcripts,* MS. Library of Congress.

difficulties between England and America had already developed, and these boded ill for any continuance of the close concert that had existed between the two powers. In May, 1800 President Adams had issued a proclamation permitting American ships to trade with the port of Jacmel on condition that they first put into either Cap Français or Port-au-Prince and secure passports signed by the American and British consuls residing in those towns. Edward Robinson, the British agent at Port-au-Prince, had not received any instructions from London which authorized trade relations with Jacmel, and, misinterpreting the spirit of the Maitland-Toussaint Treaty of June 13, 1799, he refused to issue passports to American ships bound to that port. As a result of his ill-advised action American vessels were seized by British war-ships, and protests began to pour into the Department of State at Washington.[23]

The new British Minister to Washington, Edward Thornton, immediately wrote to Lord Balcarres, at Kingston, to advise him that the proclamation issued by President Adams opening Jacmel to American trade was entirely legal and in " strict conformity " with the treaty of June 13, 1799.[24] He also wrote to Edward Corbet, the British agent in Haiti, in order to set him right as to the proper interpretation of the Maitland-Toussaint Treaty.[25] But the seizures of American ships by British cruisers continued, and the smooth course of Anglo-American relations became vexed by this treatment. Under President Adams it might have been possible to remedy this situation and restore the cordial spirit that formerly prevailed in British and American official circles. With Jefferson as President after March 4, 1801, it was soon apparent that the new Administration would make no overtures to England for a revival of the Maitland-Toussaint Treaty. That convention found little favor in the eyes of either President Jefferson or Secretary Madison.

In January, 1801 a Frenchman by the name of Dambrugeac arrived in Philadelphia from Haiti, and soon he was closeted

[23] Liston to Lord Grenville, November 4, 1801, F. O. 5/29.
[24] Thornton to Lord Balcarres, April 17, 1801, C. O. 137/105.
[25] Thornton to Corbet, May 18, 19, 1801, C. O. 137/106.

with Jefferson, the recently elected President of the United States. It is probable that he discussed in great detail the Haitian situation with the incoming President, and helped to form his opinions as to the best policy to pursue. At any rate, as soon as he took office on March 4, 1801, Jefferson began a close study of all the correspondence in the Department of State relative to Santo Domingo, and when Edward Thornton, the British Minister, called to see him on March 11, his mind was already made up as to what line he should follow. It was his belief that the two " essential objects " of the Maitland-Toussaint Treaty were " the establishment of a free and open trade for the subjects of the two countries, and the prevention of all maritime exertion on the part of the Negroes." With reference to these objectives he wished to say that they met with his entire approval, but beyond these two points he " considered it necessary to establish a system of perfect neutrality."

Jefferson then remarked that the correspondence of Edward Stevens seemed to him to exhibit " undoubted proofs of his too great bias in favour of England." For this reason Stevens would be recalled and another agent would be sent to Santo Domingo who would maintain a more " even course " with regard to relations with England and France.

Mr. Thornton was fearful that this decision of President Jefferson was dictated by some " lurking ill-will " towards England, and this suspicion put him on guard in his relations with the new Administration.[26] He was especially anxious to avoid any friction concerning the trade with the ports in the southern part of Haiti, and he requested Secretary Madison to see to it that American vessels stopped at Cap Français or Port-au-Prince and secured passports before sailing south. He was distinctly surprised when the Secretary of State refused to take such action. From his conversation with President Jefferson on March 11, he had understood that the new Administration was quite willing to carry out this regulation. Madison's refusal to do so indicated to him that

under these circumstances the trade between the United States and

[26] Thornton to Lord Grenville, March 28, 1801, *Henry Adams Transcripts*, MS. Library of Congress.

Hispaniola becomes in fact, as far as the interference of the Government is concerned, independent of General Maitland's Convention with Toussaint, and returns to the footing on which it stood before the late rupture with France. And it is on this account there is room to apprehend that, unless His Majesty's pleasure can soon be learnt, the harmony of the two countries may suffer some interruption.[27]

If Thornton could have heard the conversations between President Jefferson and Louis Pichon, the French chargé d'affaires at Washington, he would have been even more convinced that the existing harmony between England and the United States might " suffer some interruption." Jefferson was bent on reversing the policy of co-operation with England pursued by the Adams Administration in connection with Haitian affairs. He had little regard for Toussaint, and he was entirely willing for France to regain her lost colony.

In June, 1801 Pichon made a visit to New York to survey the situation with reference to American trade with Haiti, and he was annoyed because the masters of the ships which arrived daily from the Caribbean insisted upon maintaining " an absolute silence on affairs in Haiti." This attitude was probably the result of the influence of Edward Stevens who was the instrument employed by the Adams Administration to carry out the hostile projects that had been aimed at Santo Domingo. Pichon did learn, however, that Toussaint was laying his plans for declaring Haiti an independent state. The recent treaty of friendship between France and America, and the changed

[27] Thornton to Lord Hawkesbury, June 2, 1801, F. O. 5/32. In a letter to Edward Corbet of June 18, 1801, Thornton gives a pertinent paragraph on the position taken by Secretary Madison with reference to Haitian trade: " You are not, perhaps, aware that the late Administration of the United States, was enabled to engage in *an understanding* with His Majesty's Government relative to the terms of General Maitland's Convention, by the Clause of an Act of Congress, which, while it prohibited the General Intercourse with France and her Dependencies, authorized the President to renew it with any portion of the French Dominions, if he should deem it for the interests of the United States. The Law in question expired by its own limitation on the 3rd of March, . . . and the Convention with France, recently ratified, brings back the Commercial Relations between the United States and her Dependencies, to their ordinary Channel. However, therefore, the present Government of the United States might be disposed to adhere to the terms of the regulation with Toussaint, the President cannot enforce by an active inter-position the observance of them." C. O. 137/107.

situation in Europe, had affected Toussaint's plans, but merely by way of postponing them.[28]

On July 11, Pichon had an interview with Secretary Madison who informed the French chargé that with reference to trade with Haiti the new Administration had adopted a policy of " taking things just as they were without pretending to judge them." He could rest assured that nothing would be done which would affect the rights or prerogatives of France in her former colony, but he should also realize that the American Government did not wish to get into difficulties with Toussaint. Although neither the United States nor Great Britain wished to see Toussaint set up an independent government in Haiti, it seemed very likely that the black general had ambitions in that regard.[29]

Pichon was not completely satisfied with these reserved remarks of Madison. After waiting some nine days he made an informal call on President Jefferson. The President was in an expansive mood and it was not long before the subject of Santo Domingo came into the conversation. Pichon complained that he had not been able to glean from the guarded language of Secretary Madison whether the Administration favored the ambitions of Toussaint. He was at once assured by the Chief Executive that the plans of Toussaint would receive no support from the present American Government. It should be kept in mind, however, that the trade between the United States and Santo Domingo was a lucrative one which could not easily be abandoned. Pichon readily admitted this fact and merely pressed for a reassurance that the far-reaching projects of Toussaint were not looked upon with approval by the Administration. Jefferson then repeated his disinclination to lend any assistance to Toussaint. Pichon adroitly followed this statement with a direct question that went into the pith of the issue: Would the United States act jointly with France in order that French supremacy over Santo Domingo could be restored? Jefferson replied without evasion that the American

[28] Pichon to the Minister of Marine and Colonies, June 3, 1801, *French State Papers, 1798-1802*, vol. 1, *Henry Adams Transcripts*, MS. Library of Congress.
[29] Pichon to Talleyrand, July 20, 1801, Arch. Aff. Étr., É.U., Pol. Corresp., 53:169-174.

Government would take joint measures with France in this Haitian situation, but in order that

this concert may be complete and effective you must [first] make peace with England; then nothing would be easier than to furnish your army and fleet with everything, and to reduce Toussaint to starvation.[30]

As to English policy in Haiti, Jefferson was certain that the British Cabinet would participate in

a concert to suppress this rebellion, and independently of her fears for her own colonies . . . she is observing like us how St. Domingo is becoming another Algiers in the seas of America."

Some weeks later, Pichon wrote to the Minister of Marine and Colonies in the same key. He thought it would not be difficult to secure the co-operation of Great Britain in certain measures against Toussaint because British officials in the Caribbean were aware of the dangers of an independent black government in Haiti. It was also very likely that Toussaint himself now harbored definite suspicions about the real attitude of England and America towards a negro dictator who might grow too strong for their liking.[31]

These suspicions were in part engendered by the prompt action of the Jefferson Administration in recalling Edward Stevens from Haiti. Stevens stood very close to Toussaint who often looked to him for sage counsel. Moreover, Stevens was a brilliant man with a keen perception of political realities. His successor was a pedestrian person of modest pretensions. Tobias Lear had at one time served as a secretary to George Washington, and he was generally regarded as a man " of mild temper and moderate manners." [32] Stevens had been commissioned as Consul-General to the " Island of San Domingo." On March 31, 1801, Lear was given a similar commission, but, thanks to the intervention of Pichon, this commission was suppressed, and on May 11 he was commissioned merely as " General Commercial Agent to the Island of San Domingo."

---

[30] Pichon to Talleyrand, July 22, 1801, Arch. Aff. Étr., É. U., 53:177-184.

[31] Pichon to the Minister of Marine and Colonies, September 5, 1801, *French State Papers, Henry Adams Transcripts*, vol. 1, MS. Library of Congress.

[32] Thornton to Corbet, May 18, 1801, C. O. 137/106.

He arrived at Cap Français on July 4, 1801, and was met by Edward Stevens who showed him " every mark of polite attention." He was then introduced to Toussaint, whose power was fast reaching its peak. The black dictator was just about to proclaim a constitution which named him governor for life over the island of Santo Domingo with the power to choose his successor.[33] He definitely felt that this high office bestowed upon him some of that divinity that hedges in a king, and he adopted certain regal characteristics. He wished to deal directly with other sovereigns, and he showed sharp irritation when his letters to Napoleon were invariably answered by the Minister of Marine and Colonies. Upon one occasion his temper burst all bounds, and, tossing aside unopened one of these communications from the Minister of Marine, he murmured scornfully: " *Ministre! . . . valet!* " [34]

It was into this explosive atmosphere that Lear suddenly made his appearance, and when Toussaint learned that the new American Commercial Agent brought with him no personal letter from President Jefferson, he at once broke out with recriminations. The scene that followed is well told by Lear in his despatch to Secretary Madison:

On my arrival I delivered your letter to Dr. Stevens. . . . He went with me to General Toussaint Louverture, to whom he introduced me as the person who was to succeed him in his Office. I handed my Commission to the General, who asked me if I had not a letter for him from the President, or from the Government. I told him I had not, and explained the reason, as not being customary in missions of this kind, where I should be introduced by my Predecessor and exhibit my commission as an evidence of my appointment. He immediately returned my Commission without opening it, expressing his disappointment and disgust in strong terms, saying that his colour was the cause of his being neglected, and not thought worthy of the usual attentions. I explained to him, with temper and candour, the nature of the appointment as not requiring those particular introductions which are given to

---

[33] V. Schoelcher, *Vie de Toussaint-Louverture*, chap. xxv; Percy Waxman, *The Black Napoleon*, chap. xii; Spenser St. John, *Hayti or the Black Republic*, pp. 63 ff.

[34] P. de Lacroix, *Mémoires pour servir a l'histoire de la révolution de Saint-Domingue*, II, 52.

Diplomatic characters. . . . He became more cool—said he would consider the matter, and desired me to see him at 9 o'clock the next morning. I went accordingly. . . . He repeated the observations which he had made the Evening before, and added, that it must hurt him in the eyes of his Chief Officers, when it was found that he was not . . . worthy of having a letter from the President. . . . I gave the same explanations wh. I had offered before. He appeared to be hurt; but after some further conversation, said that, notwithstanding the mortification he felt, he would give an evidence of his sincere desire to preserve harmony . . . with the United States, by receiving me.[35]

Toussaint's disappointment in not receiving a personal letter from President Jefferson did not blind him to the importance of preserving friendly relations with the United States. His dream of Haitian independence could be realized only through the assistance he derived from commerce with the United States. Munitions of war could best be secured from America, and General Hédouville reported to Napoleon on November 15, 1800 that from the port of New York alone some " twenty-five thousand muskets, sixteen pieces of artillery, and an immense amount of war *matériel* had already started for San Domingo." [36]

In view of this dependence upon the United States for essential war supplies, Toussaint was anxious to court further

[35] Lear to Madison, July 17, 1801, *Cape Haitien, Consular Desp.*, vol. 3, MS. Dept. of State. The story of Toussaint's pique because he did not receive a personal letter from President Jefferson was soon known to the British Minister at Washington who promptly repeated it in a despatch to Lord Hawkesbury: " The new American consul General Mr. Lear arrived sometime ago at Cap. François, and has succeeded to the duties of his office. But I learn from a quarter which may be depended on, that it required all the personal influence of his predecessor, Mr. Stevens, to induce the Negro General to receive him. Independently of the apprehensions which Toussaint entertained of Mr. Jefferson's predilection for the French, and of the danger which threatens his power from the renewed connexion between the United States and France, he regarded the recall of Mr. Stevens as a personal insult offered to himself. He knew, he said, Mr. Stevens to be a good man. How then could the President be good, whose first act was that of removing him? Another circumstance particularly displeasing to Toussaint, was the arrival of Mr. Lear without the slightest communication of his mission or any credential addressed to himself: and he observed, that perhaps Mr. Jefferson might learn who he was and what character he bore, from the new Constitution which had just been adopted." Thornton to Lord Hawkesbury, September 19, 1801, F. O. 5/32.

[36] T. L. Stoddard, *The French Revolution in San Domingo*, p. 301.

American favor, and Bartholomew Dandridge, the American consul at Aux Cayes, reported that " all the officers of Administration seem to be sensible of the importance of a friendly intercourse with the United States & strongly express a Desire for its continuance." [37] Lear, who was close to Toussaint at Cap Français, soon recognized that Toussaint was an " extraordinary man " who was " adored by all the Inhabitants of all colours." He also assured Secretary Madison that the black dictator was showing every disposition to " promote our intercourse." [38] A few weeks later, Toussaint had conclusively shown that he was quite cordial to American interests in Haiti, and his " declarations of a determination to do justice " were " very strong." It was also true that recently he had " given better proofs than declarations " of his intention to foster friendly relations with America.[39]

In his relations with British officials, Toussaint was equally cordial. This fact led the British Minister at Philadelphia to hope that with " prudent and conciliatory management " Toussaint might be

brought to enforce on the American Merchantmen the strict observance of the Convention made with General Maitland, towards the support of which no active co-operation is to be looked for from this Government, and which cannot be departed from without endangering the tranquillity of the relations that subsist at present between all the parties concerned.[40]

These increasingly intimate relations between Toussaint and British officials in the Caribbean led to the conclusion on November 16, 1801 of a convention between Joseph Bunel, acting for Toussaint, and Edward Corbet, the agent for " British Affairs in Saint Domingo." This treaty was to be considered as a " sequel to, and an Explanation of the Secret Convention entered into between . . . General T. Maitland and Toussaint Louverture . . . the 13th June 1799." According to its terms

---

[37] Dandridge to Madison, July 23, 1801, *Cape Haitien, Consular Desp.,* vol. 3, MS. Dept. of State.

[38] Lear to Madison, July 20, 1801, *ibid.*

[39] Lear to Madison, August 30, 1801, *ibid.*

[40] Thornton to Lord Hawkesbury, September 10, 1801, F. O. 5/32.

Toussaint agreed to grant protection to the French refugees from Santo Domingo who were now resident in Jamaica, and to assist in their " reinstatement " to their properties in the former French colony. The Governor of Jamaica was given the right to appoint agents to reside in the ports in the island of Santo Domingo which were open to trade, and protection was extended to British merchants and their properties in the island. Provision was also made for a coasting trade which would proceed from Cap Français and Port-au-Prince to other ports now open to commerce.[41]

These earnest efforts of Toussaint to conciliate Great Britain and America were all in vain. Jefferson was committed to a policy of co-operation with France against the black dictator, and the Department of State permitted our official relations with Santo Domingo to decline to a vanishing point. The significance of this official silence was not lost upon Lear, who wrote to Madison to complain that for months there had not been

a single line of intercourse between the Government of the U. S. and this—not a single line of communication from my Government (on which head I have been often questioned; and have been obliged to exercise my utmost ingenuity to parry the question)—no public Ships or Vessels of the U. S. on the coasts or in the harbours as heretofore.[42]

Toussaint's growing anxiety about the intentions of the American Government was well founded. Jefferson had little liking for the negro dictator, and he had no scruples about laying plans for his destruction. If Napoleon wished to restore the French empire in the Caribbean he would have no more sincere well-wisher than Jefferson, who failed to see that these French colonial possessions in the old Spanish Main were linked inextricably to Louisiana. In the event that a French armada crushed Toussaint it would not be long before a formidable French military establishment was set up in the Mississippi Valley.

[41] There is a copy of this convention of November 16, 1801 in W. O. 1/71.
[42] Lear to Madison, November 9, 1801, *Cape Haitien, Consular Desp.,* vol. 3, MS. Dept. of State.

It seems quite likely that Napoleon's interest in Louisiana was commercial rather than political; it would serve admirably as an abundant granary for Santo Domingo.[43] The former prosperity of the French colony of Haiti would probably return under efficient French rule,[44] and in 1800 Napoleon decided to send an expedition which would lay the basis for the new administration. In taking this step he was somewhat influenced by the group of ruined Haitian planters who constantly clamored for action against Toussaint, and it is probable that Josephine herself, a Creole by birth, helped to awaken Napoleon's interest in projects in the Caribbean.[45]

At any rate, on November 4, 1800 Napoleon warned Toussaint against any interference in Spanish Santo Domingo,[46] and some months later he instructed the Minister of Marine and Colonies to prepare a comprehensive report on all French colonial possessions.[47] The preliminaries of the Treaty of Amiens were signed on October 1, 1801, and instructions were hurriedly prepared directing General Leclerc to lead a large expedition against Toussaint.[48] In the French Foreign Office the despatches from Pichon at Washington were carefully studied, and not only were some of the suggestions of President Jefferson adopted, but even the very language he used in his conversations with the French chargé was here employed. In

[43] Elijah W. Lyon, *Louisiana in French Diplomacy, 1759-1804* (Norman, Oklahoma, 1934), p. 96. For a different viewpoint see F. P. Renaut, *La question de la Louisiane, 1796-1806* (Paris, 1918), p. 23; Raymond Guyot, *Le Directoire et la paix de l'Europe des traités de Bâle à deuxième coalition, 1795-1799* (Paris, 1911), pp. 233-237; André Fugier, *Napoléon et l'Espagne* (Paris, 1930), I, 27; and Mildred S. Fletcher, "Louisiana as a Factor in French Diplomacy from 1763 to 1800," *Mississippi Valley Historical Review,* XVII (1930), 367.

[44] The trade between Haiti and France had been a most lucrative one. In 1788 the exportations from Haiti to France were valued at 461,348,678 livres, and its imports from France reached a total of 255,372,282 livres. See Ludovic Sciout, "La révolution à Saint Domingue, les commissaires Sonthonax et Polverel," *Revue des questions historiques,* LXIV (1898), 399.

[45] F. P. Renaut, *La question de la Louisiane,* p. 88.

[46] Napoleon to Toussaint, November 4, 1800, *Correspondance de Napoléon Ier* (32 vols., Paris, 1853-1870), VI, 497. It should be remembered that Spanish Santo Domingo was ceded to France by Spain under the terms of the Treaty of Bâle in 1795.

[47] Napoleon to Forfait, August 22, 1801, *ibid.,* VII, 230.

[48] Napoleon to Berthier, October 8, 1801, *ibid.,* VII, 279-280.

Talleyrand's instructions to Otto, at the Court of St. James, it was assumed that the British Government was in favor of a punitive expedition against Toussaint. Details of the French expedition to Santo Domingo were freely supplied to the British Foreign Secretary, and a request was made that instructions be sent to the Governor of Jamaica to supply provisions to the French fleet. Leclerc was to be regarded as heading a crusade against barbarous blacks that were a growing menace to all whites, whether European or American. With reference to American assistance there was no doubt in Napoleon's mind, and he expressed his interpretation of Jefferson's talks with Pichon in the following graphic sentence: " Jefferson has promised that the instant the French army arrives all measures will be taken to reduce Toussaint to starvation and to aid the army." [49]

It is interesting to note that in the instructions which Napoleon drew up for Leclerc's guidance, he was specifically directed to admit American commerce to Santo Domingo during the operations against Toussaint. But after the island was completely under his control, measures should then be taken by Leclerc to admit only French ships and " the old regulations of the period before the revolution shall again be put into force." [50] If Jefferson had known of these instructions and of the real purpose behind the Leclerc expedition he would have taken immediate steps to reverse his friendly policy toward France. As it was, his program of co-operation with Napoleon had dangerous implications for America, and had it not been for the valor and military skill of Toussaint, together with the decimation of Leclerc's legions by the yellow fever, both Louisiana and Santo Domingo would soon have been French.[51]

[49] Carl L. Lokke, " Jefferson and the Leclerc Expedition," *American Historical Review*, XXXIII (1928), 326-328; Gustav Roloff, *Die Kolonialpolitik Napoleons I* (Leipzig, 1899), pp. 244 ff.; Henry Adams, *History of the United States of America during the First Administration of Thomas Jefferson* (2 vols., N. Y., 1898), I, 287 ff.

[50] Gustav Roloff, *Die Kolonialpolitik Napoleons I*, p. 254.

[51] It is of importance to note that, as far as Louisiana was concerned, the only reason why General Victor did not occupy it early in 1803 was that the fleet on which he was to have sailed was ice-bound in Dutch harbors. In this regard,

In Washington, Secretary Madison was eagerly awaiting news of the arrival of General Leclerc in Santo Domingo. On January 8, 1802 he wrote to Tobias Lear and gave him several instructions which would serve as a guide to American policy. He should be careful to avoid " any steps that would controvert or offend the authority of the French Republic over St. Domingo or have the appearance of intermeddling in any manner in its affairs." It was also desirable " on the part of the United States to avoid every unnecessary irritation or umbrage to the people of the Island." With special reference to the functions of American commercial agents on the island of Santo Domingo, Secretary Madison indicated that they should continue to look after American interests only as long as their lives were not endangered by the disturbed condition of affairs which would follow the landing of Leclerc's army.[52]

It was soon apparent to Pichon, the French chargé, that the Administration's friendly attitude toward France boded ill for Toussaint. In January, 1802, he learned that Tobias Lear, at Cap Français, had presented " an address of felicitation " to Toussaint, and that this action on the part of the American Commercial Agent had not met with the approval of the Department of State.[53] Encouraged by this stand taken by Secretary Madison, Pichon requested copies of the instructions that Secretary Pickering had given to Edward Stevens with reference to his mission to Haiti during the Adams administration. He wished also to secure copies of the " propositions " that had been discussed in Philadelphia between General Maitland and Secretary Pickering. Without any hesitation the Department of State gave these important documents to Pichon, who promptly forwarded them to Talleyrand.[54]

Professor E. W. Lyon, in his monograph *Louisiana in French Diplomacy, 1759-1804*, pp. 139-140, remarks: " It is very probable that the ice of the Netherlands in the winter of 1803 rendered the United States a favor comparable . . . to that which the Channel winds have often bestowed on the British Isles. Had it not been for the ice of January and February, Victor would have sailed for Louisiana, and the effective military occupation of New Orleans might have changed the subsequent destiny of the Mississippi Valley."

[52] Madison to Lear, January 8, 1802, *Cape Haitien, Consular Desp.*, vol. 4, MS. Dept. of State.

[53] Pichon to Talleyrand, January 2, 1802, Arch. Aff. Étr., É.-U., 54:17.

[54] Pichon to Talleyrand, February 14, 1802, *ibid.*, 54:65-67.

But these gestures of friendship were ill repaid by General Leclerc, who occupied Cap Français on February 6, 1802. In the harbor there were some twenty American merchant ships with cargoes of provisions which were badly needed by the French troops. In a very abrupt manner, General Leclerc sought to secure these American cargoes at a bargain price, but he soon found that these Yankee shipmasters were not easily bullied. After some unsuccessful dickering with them he complained to the Minister of Marine and Colonies that they were avaricious " Jews with whom it is impossible to deal." [55]

General Leclerc then turned to Tobias Lear for assistance. He recognized Lear as the Commercial Agent of the United States at Cap Français and thereby established a precedent. Since 1791 the French Government had refused to recognize American consuls or commercial agents in their colonies, and this action by Leclerc seemed to indicate a new official attitude.[56] But these friendly relations were seriously disturbed by the difficulties that Leclerc had with the American shipmasters at Cap Français. Believing that the terms set by these American skippers for their cargoes of provisions were " most extravagant," Leclerc informed Tobias Lear that he was " determined to make an offer, fixing the prices from wh. he wd. not deviate: adding that if these were not complied with, he wd. not permit the Vessels to unload, or depart." When Lear strongly argued in favor of " liberty of commerce," Leclerc merely replied that he would be justified " by the law of nations, in taking Vessels & Cargoes, and accountg. for them to the Govt. of the U. S." [57]

Finally, Leclerc lost his patience and not only seized American cargoes but placed some American shipmasters in jail. Such conduct naturally aroused a bitter feeling between the Americans at Cap Français and the French officials who showed scant regard for American rights, and Lear felt constrained to write to General Boyer to call his attention to the serious situation that existed:

[55] General Leclerc to Minister of Marine and Colonies, February 9, 1802, *French State Papers, Henry Adams Transcripts*, vol. 1, MS. Library of Congress.

[56] Lear to Robert R. Livingston, March 5, 1802, Arch. Aff. Étr., É.-U., 54:187.

[57] Lear to Madison, February 28, 1802, *Cape Haitien, Consular Desp.*, vol. 3, MS. Dept. of State.

It is with extreme regret . . . that I have observed for some time past, an increasing animosity between some of the Citizens of our Respective nations in this City. . . . The general censure which has been attached to the American Character, makes it highly necessary that the Citizens of the United States, resorting hither, should know upon what ground they stand, whether as friends and allies of the French Republic, or as Citizens of a Nation who now are, or expect to be in a state of hostility.[58]

In America the story of Leclerc's high-handed actions aroused widespread indignation, but, in Washington, President Jefferson assured Pichon that the American Government would recognize " in their full vigor " the regulations that had been adopted by French officials in Santo Domingo.[59] In much the same key an assurance was given to Admiral Villaret that

the United States will not fail to manifest on this occasion, the full respect which is due to the authority of the French Republic and to the regulations adopted by it, as necessary to give tranquillity and happiness to a portion of its dominions so much distinguished by past calamities. Should any American Citizens therefore be allured into illicit Commerce of any kind with that Island, they will contravene the purposes of their own Government.[60]

In Paris, however, American rights were strongly defended by Livingston who sent a vehement protest to Talleyrand with regard to actions of General Leclerc in Santo Domingo. Livingston had just learned from

private advices from St. Domingo, that General Le Clerc had, on the 21st February, notified the Agent for Commercial Relations of the United States, that he intended to take all the cargoes of American

---

[58] Lear to Boyer, March 15, 1802, *ibid.*, vol. 4.

[59] Pichon to Talleyrand, March 22, 1802, Arch. Aff. Étr., É.-U., 54:221-228. In a note from Thomas Sumter, Secretary of the American Legation in Paris, to the French Minister of Foreign Relations, the French Government was given an assurance that all the regulations that had been adopted relative to Santo Domingo would " receive from the United States, the respect which is due to the authority under which it is made." *Ibid.*, 54:381.

[60] Thomas Sumter to Villaret, March 25, 1802, *ibid.*, 54:380. See also Secretary Madison's warm denial that any American citizen had engaged in " commerce of any sort with Toussaint and his adherents " after the arrival of Leclerc's fleet. *Writings of James Madison* (ed. by G. Hunt., 9 vols., N. Y., 1900-1910), VI, 458.

Vessels at a price fixed by himself, much below what they were disposed to sell them at and to pay for them one fifth in money & the remainder in bills upon Paris. And that upon their refusing to accept this offer, he declared he would put them in requisition.

I make no remarks, Sir, on this act of violence exercised . . . in time of peace upon an allied nation, . . . except to observe, that bills upon Paris can never be of much value . . . while so many of these bills, already accepted, are dishonored by non-payment.[61]

In Santo Domingo, Lear reflected the wishes of the Administration, and his attitude towards General Leclerc was most conciliatory. In a letter to John E. Caldwell, who had been commissioned by the Department of State as a commercial agent to the " Island of San Domingo," Lear remarked:

It is particularly the wish of the President, that no just ground or specious pretext may be left for complaint, or suspicion on the part of the French Republic of a want of due respect for its authority in the Governmt. of the U. States.[62]

After this letter of advice to Caldwell with reference to a proper regard for French authority in Santo Domingo, Lear wrote to Secretary Madison and voiced a warning against American malcontents who tried to raise a clamor against French administration in that island. He was convinced that a " great proportion " of the difficulties that had arisen between Americans and French officials in Haitian ports was really the result of

the imprudence, not to say outrage, of our Countrymen; not only the Captns. but others residing here; particularly a Mr. Myers, of restless memory, who was most intimately and warmly attached to the Chiefs here before the arrival of the French, and who has execrated them (The French) . . . ever since their arrival. I am told he embarked for the U. States a few days ago, in a moment of violent passion, and intends, I have no doubt to sound the tocsin in the U. S. but so contemptible is his personal character that he will not be attended to by any one.[63]

[61] Livingston to Talleyrand, March 27, 1802, Arch. Aff. Étr., É.-U., 54:246.
[62] Lear to Caldwell, March 28, 1802, *Cape Haitien, Consular Desp.,* vol. 4, MS. Dept. of State.
[63] Lear to Madison, April 8, 1802, *ibid.* Some American newspapers, like the *Aurora,* were strongly pro-French and reflected that bias. On March 29, 1802

However, all these efforts of Lear to earn the good will of General Leclerc were in vain. On April 10, the General suddenly informed Lear that he would no longer recognize him " as a public character from the United States," and that therefore Lear could no longer exercise " the functions of commercial Agent in the Island." He admitted that when he first arrived in Santo Domingo with the French military forces he had been so " much engaged in a variety of important objects " that he had recognized Lear " without reflection " upon all the issues involved. He then went on to accuse Lear of having written to the United States to warn American citizens against frequenting Haitian ports because their cargoes would be settled in bills on Paris which " would never be paid."

Although Lear hotly protested against these charges and assured General Leclerc that they were a " base calumny and a scandelous falsehood," the General held firm and Lear's tenure of office as " Commercial Agent " was brought to an abrupt close.[64]

After having received this rebuff from General Leclerc, Lear despatched a letter to the General protesting sharply against the imprisonment of Captains Rodgers and Davidson. French officials in Santo Domingo should realize that the American Government would

not see with indifference its Citizens treated with undeserved indig-

the *Aurora* came out with a counterblast against all critics of French policy in Santo Domingo. With reference to the attitude of the Adams Administration concerning Santo Domingo, the *Aurora* declared: " Our readers may be assured that we have for two years been in possession of a knowledge of such *facts* concerning the transactions of the late administration of St. Domingo as must one day consign them to eternal infamy."

[64] Lear to Madison, April 11, 1802, *ibid.* On Leclerc's refusal to continue to recognize Lear as the American Commercial Agent the Philadelphia *Aurora*, May 15, 1802, remarked as follows: " The refusal of general Leclerc to acknowledge Mr. Lear as consul of the United States . . . need excite no surprise whatever—it is well known that the French government never acknowledged a consul from any country to their colonies, that in Adet's time he refused an authority which was sought for an American consul to reside there. Lear was never acknowledged by an efficient agent of France, but by the hypocrite Toussaint." From an opposite viewpoint see the note of protest sent by Livingston to Talleyrand, on June 15, 1802, with reference to the refusal of Leclerc to recognize Lear as the American Commercial Agent. Arch. Aff. Étr., É.-U., 54:375-378.

nity, or unjustifiable cruelty. . . . I again repeat, that Captain Rodgers holds a commission in the navy of the United States; but whether this will have any effect or not I am unable to say. As to Captain Davidson, his character as a man of uprightness and prudence, so far as I have learnt it, should shield him from treatment of this nature. . . . What offences these gentlemen may have committed to deserve such punishment is not within the field of conjecture. Worse could not be inflicted on criminals convicted of the blackest crimes before their execution.[65]

General Leclerc's reply cited complaints of so frivolous a nature against Captain Rodgers and Captain Davidson that Lear must have been amazed at such impudence: Captain Rodgers had spread in the United States false reports concerning the French army in Santo Domingo, and Captain Davidson had bestowed upon his ship a name which was most displeasing to General Leclerc.[66]

Secretary Madison promptly filed a complaint with Pichon, the French chargé, against the imprisonment of Captains Rodgers and Davidson,[67] and Pichon at once wrote to Talleyrand that he regarded General Leclerc's conduct in this respect as " impossible to justify." [68] He also sent a protest to General Leclerc himself in which he pointed out that his action against Captain Rodgers was without any legal justification. With reference to the charge against Captain Davidson, he reminded the General that even though the Captain had given his ship a name that was obnoxious to French officials this act did not in itself constitute a crime.[69]

Leclerc did not relish these criticisms from Pichon. In a letter to the Minister of Marine and Colonies he bitterly complained that he was " not at all satisfied with Citizen Pichon "

[65] Lear to Leclerc, April 14, 1802, Arch. Aff. Étr., É.-U., 54:463-464.

[66] Leclerc to Lear, April 19, 1802, *ibid.*, 54:564. In a letter written in Cap Français on April 14, 1802 and published in the Philadelphia *Aurora* on May 11, 1802, there is a pertinent paragraph: " Captain Rogers of Baltimore, and Davidson of Philadelphia, have both been put in prison; the former it is supposed has said something against the government since his arrival, and the latter is suspected for being concerned in a ship with Toussaint, which vessel is now in the harbour of Cape-François, with Toussaint's figure for a head."

[67] Madison to Pichon, May 6, 1802, Arch. Aff. Étr., É.-U., 54:310.

[68] Pichon to Talleyrand, May 7, 1802, *ibid.*, 54:304-306.

[69] Pichon to Leclerc, May 7, 1802, *ibid.*, 54:35-36.

who apparently welcomed " all the false reports " which spiteful tongues in the United States spread broadcast about the French Administration in Santo Domingo. In his correspondence with Leclerc, Pichon did little else than to dilate upon the injuries that had been " inflicted upon Americans" by the French military authorities, and this emphasis was regarded by Leclerc as distinctly " improper." [70]

Pichon's protests, no matter how unwelcome, must have made some impression upon Leclerc, who finally released both Captain Rodgers and Captain Davidson.[71] But before the news of their release reached Paris, Livingston sent a letter to Talleyrand in which he recounted the imprisonment of these two Americans by Leclerc for " imaginary crimes." He had been instructed by the Department of State to

apply to the justice . . . of France, for the immediate release of these persons; and such satisfaction as shall compensate their suffering, and the United States for the indignity offered them in the person of their Citizens.[72]

In his reply, Talleyrand was as astute as usual. He was certain that Leclerc was well aware that the French Government strongly desired to maintain friendly relations with the United States and therefore would undertake no measures against American citizens without some justification. It was well known that the successive steps taken by General Leclerc to establish his administration in Santo Domingo had resulted in a very extensive trade with America that was still flourishing. Although the full details concerning the imprisonment of Captains Rodgers and Davidson were not yet available, it was

[70] Leclerc to Minister of Marine and Colonies, May 6, 1802, *French State Papers*, vol. 1, *Henry Adams Transcripts*, MS. Library of Congress. See also Henry Adams, *Historical Essays* (N. Y., 1891), pp. 140-141; and Gustav Roloff, *Die Kolonialpolitik Napoleons I*, pp. 100-102.

[71] Pichon to Talleyrand, June 3, 1802, Arch. Aff. Étr., É.-U., 54:357-358. As soon as he reached Baltimore, Captain Rodgers sent a strong letter to Secretary Madison in which he set forth the " unjust, insulting and cruel treatment " that had been " wantonly exercised " by the Leclerc Administration with respect to him and Captain Davidson. Rodgers to Madison, June, 1802, *Cape Haitien, Consular Desp.*, vol. 4, MS. Dept. of State. See also Charles O. Paullin, *Commodore John Rodgers* (Cleveland, 1911), chap. iv.

[72] Livingston to Talleyrand, July 19, 1802, Arch. Aff. Étr., É.-U., 54:461-462.

obvious that this action on the part of General Leclerc must have been based upon purely personal grounds.[73]

After waiting several months, Livingston received from Secretary Madison copies of a deposition made by Captain Davidson with reference to his imprisonment by General Leclerc, and a letter from Pichon to Leclerc protesting against such action. Armed with these documents Livingston, on October 18, 1802, called at the Ministry of Foreign Relations to see Talleyrand. The treatment he was accorded by the cynical and contemptuous Minister is clearly indicated in the following note of protest which the indignant Livingston addressed the following day to Talleyrand:

I did myself the honor yesterday to wait upon you with a view to obtain an audience on the subject of several matters interesting to the government of the United States. . . . It is with regret, Sir, that I find myself reduced to the necessity of transacting this business and all other in future with your office by notes only—till I receive specific instructions from the United States on the subject of the indignity offered them in my person yesterday. When in violation of the establish'd Rules of your office, four different gentlemen who arrived after me, were admitted to an audience while I remained waiting.[74]

At about the same time that Talleyrand was wounding the sensitive feelings of the American Minister by refusing to grant him an audience at the Foreign Office, he was also censuring the French chargé in Washington for the manner in which Madison's complaints about the expulsion of Lear had been handled. In reply, Pichon told how he had been at Madison's house when Lear was present, and he described how the Commercial Agent had read aloud the peremptory letter he had received from General Leclerc. A rumor was then spread abroad that Pichon himself had connived at the im-

---

[73] Talleyrand to Livingston, July 29, 1802, Arch. Aff. Étr., É.-U., 54:468-469.

[74] Livingston to Talleyrand, October 19, 1802, *ibid.,* 55:33, 37. It is worth while to note that on February 23, 1803 Secretary of State Madison once more instructed Livingston to endeavor to obtain from the French Government some satisfaction for the " outrages " committed upon Captains Rodgers and Davidson in Santo Domingo. *American State Papers, Foreign Relations*, II, 537. This instruction was repeated in Madison's note to Livingston, May 25, 1803, but without avail. See *Writings of James Madison*, VII, 47.

prisonment of Captain Rodgers, and it was necessary that he take steps to break down such a canard. It was possible, of course, that he had acted in this regard with " too much heat," but it had seemed to him that circumstances required the despatch of a strong protest to General Leclerc.[75]

Two days later, Pichon sent a second letter to Talleyrand in which he again tried to make clear the reasons that lay behind the correspondence he had had with General Leclerc. To him it appeared obvious that if the American Government had broken off relations with Toussaint the result would have been to give the English a free hand in the colony. It was probably true that Americans were desirous of breaking down the monopoly enjoyed by European nations in trading with their colonies in the Caribbean, but it was quite natural that they should entertain such feelings. This very fact made it important for France to interest Americans in helping to maintain the French colonial empire, and it was most essential that America should not be pushed into the friendly arms of England.[76]

These discussions of Leclerc's conduct in Santo Domingo were soon brought to a close by the swift course of events in that island. After a series of bloody encounters, the French troops finally crushed the resistance of Toussaint and his generals. Dessalines, Christophe, Maurepas, Laplume, and other black leaders took service in Leclerc's army, but Toussaint was marked for destruction. After being lured into French hands by a dishonorable strategem, he was hustled aboard a frigate and sent to die in a French fortress along the Swiss frontier. But this triumph of French arms and French guile was short-lived. The yellow fever came as a belated but terribly effective ally of the black armies, and by November 1, 1802 Leclerc and his legions were wiped out. Santo Domingo was lost forever to France.[77]

---

[75] Pichon to Talleyrand, October 14, 1802, Arch. Aff. Étr., É.-U., 55:8-12.

[76] Pichon to Talleyrand, October 16, 1802, *ibid.*, 55:29-32.

[77] V. Schoelcher, *Vie de Toussaint-Louverture*, chap. xxvii; H. de Poyen, *Histoire militaire de la révolution de Saint Domingue*, pp. 212-215; Gustav Roloff, *Die Kolonialpolitik Napoleons I*, pp. 95-96.

But the French Government refused to take a realistic view of the situation, and General Rochambeau maintained for a while in Santo Domingo a régime at whose record of bloodshed and wanton massacre historians still shudder. Although the struggle of the remnants of Leclerc's armies to regain control of the island was a hopeless one, many French officials still cherished a belief that the negroes would finally be subdued and that Santo Domingo would be restored to the French colonial dominion. In America, however, serious doubts about the stability of General Rochambeau's administration began to circulate, and in December, 1802 news arrived that forced loans had been levied upon American merchants. Those who opposed such exactions were placed in prison, and thus American citizens were exposed to fresh indignities without much hope that the French Government would intervene in their behalf.[78]

One of the best ways to meet protests against these infractions of the rights of American citizens was to file prior protests against the sale by American merchants of munitions to the rebellious blacks of Santo Domingo. On March 20, 1803, Talleyrand despatched a note to Livingston in which a complaint was voiced that American ships were carrying arms to ports in Santo Domingo that were under the control of the rebels. The Minister of Foreign Relations had secured his information relative to this alleged traffic in arms from the Minister of Marine and Colonies who stated that these American " merchants of death " were mostly located in Philadelphia.

Livingston was very painfully surprised to read such unfounded accusations, and he immediately attempted to refute them. It was incredible that American shipmasters would risk a long trip to Haitian waters to supply arms to impoverished blacks who could not furnish return cargoes. As to the charge that a subscription had been opened in Philadelphia for the support of these rebellious Haitians, Livingston hurriedly adduced two reasons to show the unreliability of such a report:

1st, because the Quakers who are the great patrons of the blacks are

---

[78] Pichon to Talleyrand, January 23, 1803, Arch. Aff. Étr., É.-U., 55:188-191.

by their tenets forbidden to contribute money to the support of any war however justifiable even to the defence of their own persons and country. 2nd, because no letters published or private . . . make any mention of such subscription. The Minister of Exterior Relations is too well acquainted with the nature of these publications in America not to know that they scarce suffer any transaction however uninteresting to escape their notice, and that an act of this kind could hardly fail to attract their attention.[79]

Some weeks later, Pichon himself sent to Talleyrand a similar denial that munitions of war were being sent from America to Haitian ports. If such shipments were actually reaching the rebellious blacks, it was more than likely that they were coming from adjacent islands.[80] After a lengthy investigation into the question of a subscription in Philadelphia for the benefit of Haitian rebels, Pichon came to the conclusion that the whole story was purely " imaginary." [81]

But these strong assurances from Livingston and Pichon were not meant to imply that there was no trade of any kind between American merchants and rebellious Haitians. American ships continued to visit ports under control of these rebels and freely supplied them with provisions. This fact led to some " very animated conversations " between Pichon and Secretary Madison. When the French chargé chided the Secretary of State for permitting this traffic, Madison replied that the American Government could not be required by France to enforce its own municipal law. From the viewpoint of international law, the Government of France had no more right to ask President Jefferson to prohibit this commerce than the Government of Great Britain would have in asking the President to stop American trade with ports that a British fleet was blockading.[82]

After some further conversations with Secretary Madison, Pichon recommended to Talleyrand that American trade with Santo Domingo be allowed. It would occur despite any attempt

[79] Livingston to Talleyrand, March 21, 1803, *ibid.*, 55:347-348.
[80] Pichon to Talleyrand, May 24, 1803, *ibid.*, 55:432-436.
[81] Pichon to Talleyrand, May 28, 1803, *ibid.*, 55:446-449.
[82] Pichon to Talleyrand, January 17, 1804, *ibid.*, 56:289-294. See also Madison's instruction to Livingston of January 31, 1804, *Instructions to Ministers*, vol. 6, MS. Dept. of State.

at strict regulation, and these restrictions would only cause serious friction without any compensating advantages.[83] But despite this recommendation to Talleyrand, Pichon sent to Secretary Madison a long note in which he vigorously protested against the growing traffic in arms between American and Haitian ports.[84]

In answer to this note of protest from Pichon, Secretary Madison sent an instruction to Livingston in Paris in which he pointed out that the United States were " bound by the law of Nations to nothing further than to leave their offending citizens to the consequence of an illicit trade." The American Government, however, was ready to make a deal in this matter now under dispute. If France would agree to permit the trade with Santo Domingo in all articles other than contraband on condition that America would agree to prohibit the shipment of contraband articles, a satisfactory arrangement could be agreed upon. But if this course should be considered objectionable, the same object might be obtained

by a tacit understanding between the two Governments. . . . Altho' a legal regulation on our part cannot be absolutely promised, yet with a candid explanation of this constitutional circumstance, there can be little risk . . . that the Legislative authority here would interpose its sanction.[85]

Madison was especially anxious to come to some agreement with the French Government because French corsairs, with their headquarters on the island of Cuba, had established a paper blockade of Haitian ports and were seizing American ships en route to them. As these depredations increased, American shipmasters began to equip their vessels with defensive armament, and this action led Pichon to send another note of protest to the Department of State. It was his opinion that American citizens by arming their merchant ships bound for Haitian ports were really carrying on

a private and piratical war against a Power with which the United

[83] Pichon to Talleyrand, February 9, 1804, Arch. Aff. Étr., É.-U., 56:362-364.
[84] Pichon to Madison, March 9, 1804, *ibid.*, 56:412.
[85] Madison to Livingston, March 31, 1804, *Inst. to Ministers*, vol. 6, MS. Dept. of State.

States are at peace. The undersigned would be wanting in his duty if he did not . . . call the attention of Mr. Madison to the disagreeable reflections which the French Government would have a right to make, if the silence of the local authorities, respecting acts of this nature, should be imitated by the Government of the United States. The French Government certainly could not see, without a profound regret, that, after having given to the United States the most marked proofs of the desire to place the good understanding of the two nations upon the most immoveable foundations . . . individual interests should now be permitted to compromise this good understanding.[86]

Through Livingston, the American Government gave a long and cogent answer to French complaints against American trade with Santo Domingo. The depredations of French corsairs upon American commerce were alluded to, and reference was made to the necessity of arming American merchantmen to repel these attacks. The French Government was not

ignorant of the influence that the Commercial cities have upon the politicks of the United States & how difficult it will be to prevent their forcing the Government into measures which may be considered as unfriendly to France, tho' in fact they may be only those of legitimate defence against plunderers that the Government of France cannot but disavow. Be assured, Sir, that nothing would be more painful to the President of the United States than to be compelled to recur to measures which might weaken the friendship & confidence that at present so happily connect France & the United States.

The principal source of this evil arises from the present State of St. Domingo: This Island has always been supplied from the United States with provisions during a war even while it was Subject to the Govt. of France; its wants continue the Same, & they are as usual Supplied from the United States. The interests of France concur with those of America in encouraging this trade, Since without it, all the Commerce of the Island would naturally fall into the hands of a rival nation & not only add to their wealth but give them a controuling interest in the politicks of the Island.

If France looks forward to a reconquest of that Island, it is to her Interest as far as possible to preserve the inhabitants from sinking into a State of barbarism which it would undoubtedly do if it were possible to deprive them of all commerce. . . .

[86] Pichon to Madison, May 7, 1804, Arch. Aff. Étr., É.-U., 57:9-12; *American State Papers, Foreign Relations*, II, 607.

Various interests then concur to induce the Government of France to encourage the Commerce between the United States & St. Domingo in every article but that which consists in contraband of war; These France may justly intercept & punish the infractors of the law of nations by the forfeiture of the articles. Some Idea appears to have been entertained, by the *chargé des affairs* of France in the United States, that their Government Should go further than the law of nations requires, & put restrictions upon the Commerce in Such articles. But Sir, you will readily See the delicacy of Such a procedure during a State of War.

In conclusion, Livingston placed before the French Government the proposal to permit American trade with Santo Domingo on condition that the American Government take steps to prevent the shipment of articles of contraband.[87]

Talleyrand had promised Livingston that he would discuss with Napoleon the whole question of American trade with Santo Domingo.[88] Before he had received instructions from the Emperor in this regard, he wrote to Livingston and suggested that the American Minister take the matter up with the Minister of Marine and Colonies.[89] Talleyrand himself then addressed a note to the Minister of Marine and reviewed the history of French depredations upon American commerce with the resulting American practice of placing armament upon their merchant vessels. The only way out of these growing difficulties was to conclude as soon as possible an arrangement with the United States that would be mutually satisfactory.[90]

In accordance with the suggestion of Talleyrand, Livingston wrote to the Minister of Marine and Colonies in defense of American trade with Santo Domingo. It should be apparent, he thought, that the United States could really take the position that Santo Domingo was an independent state and that therefore all commerce with her was perfectly legitimate. Friendship for France prevented any such stand by the Ameri-

[87] Livingston to Talleyrand, June 27, 1804, Arch. Aff. Étr., É.-U., 57:144-146.
[88] Livingston to Madison, June 22, 1804, *France, Desp.*, vol. 9, MS. Dept. of State.
[89] Talleyrand to Livingston, July 8, 1804, Arch. Aff. Étr., É.-U., 57:163.
[90] Talleyrand to Minister of Marine and Colonies, August 24, 1804, *ibid.*, Supplement, 2:201.

can Government, but it should be clearly realized by French officials that any prohibition of American commerce with Santo Domingo would give Great Britain exclusive trade advantages with that island.[91]

After waiting a few days Livingston talked the situation over with the Minister of Marine and Colonies, who reported that he had had several conversations with Napoleon on this matter of trade with Santo Domingo. The Emperor believed that it was not necessary to have any formal arrangement with America regarding commerce in the Caribbean. Instead, he thought it would be best for France merely to " connive " at American trade relations with the revolted blacks in Haiti. As a further concession to America he would also send " strict orders " to " restrain " the depredations of French corsairs who were using the island of Cuba as a base of operations. When Livingston inquired when these orders would be issued, the Minister of Marine refused to name any specific date. It was evident to the American Minister that Napoleon might promise what he had little intention of fulfilling. Moreover, according to Livingston, " the Emperor's head " was filled with his " new dignity and they are all occupied, to the very great dissatisfaction of the nation, with arrangements for the organization of the new court and the coronation." [92]

After waiting several weeks for the Emperor to take some action, Livingston wrote to Talleyrand and complained once more about the attacks of French privateers upon American shipping.[93] Talleyrand, thoroughly tired of American protests, returned a prompt and acid answer. He pointed out how American shipmasters, without any authorization from the American Government, had placed armament upon merchant ships for the purpose of protecting an illicit trade with Santo Domingo. Inasmuch as such action was in direct violation of international law it was somewhat surprising to have the American Government complain about the counter-measures which French colonial officials had been forced to adopt.[94]

[91] Livingston to Minister of Marine and Colonies, July 10, 1804, *France, Desp.*, vol. 9, MS. Dept. of State.
[92] Livingston to Madison, July 25, 1804, *ibid.*
[93] Livingston to Talleyrand, August 25, 1804, *ibid.*
[94] Talleyrand to Livingston, August 28, 1804, Arch. Aff. Étr., É.-U., 57:246.

This tart note from Talleyrand gave pause to any further notes from Livingston concerning the depredations of French corsairs. In a despatch to Madison (August 29), Livingston mentioned that Talleyrand's note contained "a certain degree of asperity," and he thought it best to let things rest for a while in order that French officials might "cool a little."[95] Even as late as October 10, he still found that in the French Foreign Office there was "too much sensibility on the subject of St. Domingo to press the business closely."[96]

This "sensibility" on the part of the French Foreign Office was far more feigned than felt. Instead of feeling outraged at American impudence, Talleyrand was swinging round in favor of concessions to America. In his note of June 27, Livingston had renewed an old request that the French Government permit the residence of American commercial agents in the French colonies in the Caribbean. Although on previous occasions this request had been consistently denied, it was now obvious to the French Minister of Foreign Relations that some change in policy was expedient. In the archives of the French Foreign Office there is an undated memorandum, probably drawn up by Talleyrand, which deals with this question of American commercial agents, and there is also an official minute which records Napoleon's rejection of this suggestion.[97]

Even though the Emperor was opposed to the right of residence for American commercial agents in French colonies, he was open to other suggestions concerning the need for concessions to America. In July he had informed the Minister of Marine and Colonies that he was ready to "connive" at American trade with Santo Domingo, and in view of this conciliatory attitude the Foreign Office now drew up a carefully reasoned memorandum for his consideration. It indicated how the American Government had not only refused to prohibit the commerce between the United States and the ports of Santo Domingo, but had even permitted American shipmasters to arm their vessels so as to prevent their capture by French cor-

[95] Livingston to Madison, August 29, 1804, *France, Desp.*, vol. 9, MS. Dept. of State.
[96] Livingston to Madison, October 10, 1804, *ibid.*
[97] See Arch. Aff. Étr., É.-U., 57:351-352.

sairs. This passive policy of the Jefferson Administration had resulted in a state of quasi-warfare in the Caribbean which might lead to grave consequences. In order to avoid these, Livingston had proposed an arrangement which would admit American commerce to Santo Domingo in return for a prohibition of the export of war munitions from America. In ordinary circumstances no attention should be paid to such a suggestion, but with a large portion of Santo Domingo in revolt against the Mother Country it was probably wise to permit American trade with at least those portions of the island still loyal to France. If this were not done, it was quite likely that American assistance would be extended to the black generals who were now aiming at erecting an independent state.[98]

This report seems to have made some impression upon Napoleon, who at length agreed to the residence of American commercial agents in Santo Domingo " during the continuance of the war." The Emperor also sent word to Livingston that he would give the " most precise orders " on the subject of depredations upon American commerce.[99]

In Washington this conciliatory spirit of Napoleon was matched by a similar mood on the part of President Jefferson. In October John Quincy Adams found that the President was anxious to stop all American trade with Santo Domingo,[100] and on November 8 Congress received a message from the Chief Executive which indicated the dangers involved in a commerce that required merchant ships to be heavily armed in order that it might be successful.[101]

It was evident that the Administration was laying plans either to restrict or, if possible, to prohibit altogether any American trade with Santo Domingo. On January 3 Albert

[98] " Report to His Imperial Majesty," September 5, 1804, *ibid.*, Suppl., 2:205-207.

[99] Livingston to Madison, October 23, 1804, *France, Desp.*, vol. 9, MS. Dept. of State.

[100] John Quincy Adams, *Memoirs,* I, 314.

[101] James D. Richardson, *Compilation of Messages and Papers of the Presidents* (10 vols., Wash., 1896-1899), I, 369-373. At this same time, November 10, 1804, Secretary Madison instructed Armstrong, the American Minister at Paris, to conclude an arrangement with France whereby " innocent commerce " with Santo Domingo would be sanctioned. See *Inst. to Ministers*, vol. 6, MS. Dept. of State.

Gallatin wrote to Senator S. L. Mitchell and expressed the view that American commerce with the revolted blacks of Santo Domingo was " illicit " and was being carried on in a " manner contrary to the law of nations." [102] Other prominent members of the Democratic party were equally averse to trade relations with blacks who had slain their masters in a struggle for independence. Senator James Jackson announced that he was willing to go " whole lengths " in support of Jefferson's restrictive policy. He not only wished to " prohibit the trade of St. Domingo," but he was also of the belief that the " usurped government of that unfortunate island must be destroyed." John Breckinridge thought that " sound policy " required the American Government to restrain all American citizens from trading with Santo Domingo, while John W. Eppes was moved to remark that " he would venture to pledge the Treasury of the United States that the Negro government should be destroyed." [103]

With important legislators in this frame of mind it was not long before a bill was introduced into Congress which provided that no vessel owned in whole, or in part, by any citizen or citizens of the United States should receive a clearance for any island in the West Indies without a bond being given by the owner that the armament on board the vessel would be used merely for defense in case of involuntary hostility. Senator Logan, of Pennsylvania, promptly moved an amendment which would prohibit all commerce, armed or unarmed, with Santo Domingo. This amendment was defeated only by the casting vote of Vice-President Burr, and the bill became a law on March 3, 1805.[104]

In a note of instruction to James Monroe, March 6, 1805,

[102] Gallatin to Mitchell, January 3, 1805, *Writings of Albert Gallatin* (3 vols., Phila., 1879), I, 220-223.

[103] William Plumer, *Memorandum of Proceedings in the United States Senate, 1803-1807* (ed. by E. S. Brown, N. Y., 1923), pp. 243-245. Talleyrand was quick to catch this conciliatory spirit on the part of the Administration. See Talleyrand to the Minister of Marine and Colonies, January 6, 1805, Arch. Aff. Étr., É.-U., 58:3.

[104] Act of March 3, 1805, *U. S. Statutes at Large*, II, 342-343. Also, Henry Adams, *History of the United States of America during the Second Administration of Thomas Jefferson* (2 vols., N. Y., 1890), I, 88.

Secretary Madison gave the following explanation with reference to the Act of March 3, 1805:

This Act was occasioned by the abuse made of . . . armaments in forcing a trade, even in contraband of war, with the Island of St. Domingo; and by the representations made on the subject of that trade by the French Chargé des Affaires and Minister here, and by the British Minister with respect to abuses which had resulted or might result from such armaments. . . . The Act, in substituting a security against the unlawful use of the armaments in place of an absolute prohibition of them, is not only consistent with the obligations of a neutral nation, but conformable to the laws . . . of Great Britain and France themselves.[105]

It was soon discovered by the Administration that the new legislation which was designed to restrict the armed commerce to Santo Domingo was not very effective. In May, 1805, a large fleet of American vessels engaged in the trade of Santo Domingo returned to New York where a very elaborate banquet was given in honor of their safe and lucrative voyage. Important public men like Rufus King and Samuel G. Ogden were present, and a large number of interesting toasts were given. Number nine of these toasts was especially significant:

To the Government of Haiti, founded on the only legitimate basis of all authority—the people's choice. May it be as durable as its principles are pure.[106]

According to information sent to Talleyrand, the fleet of armed vessels proceeding from American ports to Santo Domingo was equal in strength to the naval forces that President Jefferson sent to the Mediterranean to wage war against the Barbary pirates. There is little wonder that French officials became highly incensed at this news,[107] and on June 6, 1805

[105] Madison to Monroe, March 6, 1805, *Writings of James Madison*, VII, 171.

[106] Rey [the French Commercial Agent in New York] to Talleyrand, June 15, 1805, Arch. Aff. Étr., É.-U., 58:175.

[107] Talleyrand was indignant when he heard of this dinner in New York and of the toasts that were drunk. In a letter to Armstrong, the American Minister at Paris, he remarked as follows: " It is impossible that the Government of the United States should longer shut its eyes upon the communications of their commerce with St. Domingo. The adventures for that island are making with a scandalous publicity. They are supported by armed vessels. At their return, feasts are given in order to vaunt the success of their speculations; . . . and in

General Ferrand, with headquarters at Santo Domingo City, issued some very sweeping decrees which he hoped would suppress entirely this " execrable commerce." [108] Secretary Madison was seriously concerned over the operation of these decrees, and he instructed General John Armstrong, at Paris, to make representations to Talleyrand with reference to them. There was no " reason to believe that under the decree of Genl. Ferrand any of our Citizens have been put to death; but it seems certain that they have suffered the indignity and the outrage of corporal punishment." [109]

But Talleyrand was in no mood to conciliate America. On July 5 he instructed General Turreau, at Washington, to demand the prohibition of all American trade with Santo Domingo,[110] and this decision to put pressure upon the Jefferson Administration was greatly strengthened by the following note that he received from the Emperor:

The despatch from Washington has fixed my attention. I request you to send a note to the American minister accredited to me. . . . You will declare to him that it is time for this thing to stop; that it is shameful in the Americans to provide supplies for brigands and to take part in a commerce so scandalous; that I will declare a good prize everything which shall enter or leave the ports of St. Domingo; and that I can no longer see with indifference the armaments evidently directed against France which the American government allows to be made in its ports.[111]

Although Armstrong on August 11 addressed to Talleyrand a friendly note which enclosed a copy of the Act of March 3, 1805 regulating the armed commerce with Santo Domingo,[112] the Minister of Foreign Relations refused to be placated and

the midst of an immense concourse . . . the principles of the Government of Hayti are celebrated, and . . . vows are made for its duration." *American State Papers, Foreign Relations*, II, 726.

[108] *Ibid.*, II, 728-730.

[109] Madison to Armstrong, June 6, 1805, *Writings of James Madison*, VII, 189.

[110] Talleyrand to Turreau, July 5, 1805, Arch. Aff. Étr., É.-U., 58:188-189.

[111] Napoleon to Talleyrand, August 10, 1805, quoted in Henry Adams, *History of the United States of America during the Second Administration of Thomas Jefferson*, I, 89.

[112] Armstrong to Talleyrand, August 11, 1805, Arch. Aff. Étr., É.-U., Suppl., 5:178.

in reply sent a communication which strongly sounded a note
of menace. After a short reference to the banquet which had
been given in New York City in honor of the shipmasters who
had returned from a successful voyage to Santo Domingo, he
asked a very direct question: " How can the Federal Government tolerate that the rebels of this colony should continue to
receive from America succors against the parent country? "
Without much worry as to what answer the American Government would give to this inquiry, Talleyrand closed his note
with the following challenge:

As the seriousness of the facts which occasion this complaint obliges
His Majesty to consider as good prize everything which shall enter
the part of St. Domingo occupied by the rebels, and everything coming
out, he persuades himself that the Government of the United States
will take on its part, against this commerce at once illicit and contrary
to all the principles of the law of nations, all the repressive and
authoritative measures proper to put an end to it. This system of
impunity and tolerance can no longer continue, and His Majesty is
convinced that your Government will think it due from its frankness
promptly to put an end to it.[113]

At Washington, General Turreau echoed this trenchant language of the Minister of Foreign Affairs. To him it was amazing that Americans would send supplies to the rebellious blacks
of Santo Domingo who were nothing more than the " refuse
of nature." He was confident, however, that the Government
of the United States would take " the most prompt, as well as
the most effectual prohibitory measures " to put an end to this
commerce.[114]

Jefferson, with his eye upon West Florida, which he hoped
to secure through Napoleon's assistance, was eager to follow
the promptings of Talleyrand. Also, coming from the South,
he could never forget the fact that the rebellious Haitians were
blacks who had murdered their masters. Recognition of a successful negro revolution was a dangerous precedent for the
American Government to establish in view of the large slave
population south of the Potomac. It would be better to repress

[113] Talleyrand to Armstrong, August 16, 1805, *American State Papers, Foreign
Relations*, II, 727.

[114] Turreau to Madison, October 14, 1805, *ibid.*, II, 725-726.

than to spread this spirit of revolt among the blacks, and Jefferson pushed through Congress the Act of February 28, 1806. Under its terms all intercourse between the United States and those portions of Santo Domingo not under the control of France was suspended.[115]

To Henry Adams it seemed that this Act of February 28, 1806 violated the principles of international law, sacrificed the interests of Northern commerce, strained the powers of the Constitution as formerly construed by the party of State-rights, and, taken in all its relations, might claim distinction among the most disgraceful statutes ever enacted by the United States government.[116]

Although this criticism by America's most eminent historian is too vehement to be accepted without some qualification, yet there is little doubt that constitutional scruples had little weight with Jefferson when he was faced with pressing political problems. In his anxiety to take possession of West Florida he was willing to go to great lengths to court the favor of Napoleon. He was certain that the Emperor could win the instant acquiescence of Charles IV of Spain to American annexation of West Florida by a brief note of suggestion. To secure that brief note, Jefferson was willing to be a pupil of Machiavelli and, for the time being, to sacrifice the hard-won independence of Haitian blacks along with his own political principles. But his lust for land was in vain. Napoleon was many lessons ahead of Machiavelli in the art of statecraft, and when it came to devious political deals he was far too subtle for the Sage of Monticello. Although Jefferson sponsored a third Act of Congress (February 24, 1807) to control American trade with Santo Domingo,[117] Napoleon still withheld his support from any American scheme to absorb West Florida. It was only when the French Emperor was deeply involved in his last great struggle against England and other European powers that the meek Madison, now President, moved into West Florida and seized possession of a prize that had long beckoned to his official predecessor. There was no longer any need to conciliate France, and American trade with Santo Domingo could follow the ancient law of supply and demand.

[115] *U. S. Statutes at Large*, II, 351-352.
[116] Henry Adams, *op. cit.*, I, 142.   [117] *U. S. Statutes at Large*, II, 351-352.

CHAPTER IV

———— ◦

AMERICA DRAWS THE COLOR LINE IN ITS POLICY OF RECOGNITION

When the French military forces in Santo Domingo heard on November 2, 1802 that General Leclerc had succumbed to malaria fever, they clearly realized that in one sense the demise of their leader was timely: it certainly saved him from the anguish of witnessing the final collapse of the military organization he had so proudly brought to the island some few months before. But even before his death there had been many signs of approaching disaster. The malaria, the yellow fever, and the tropical climate were an unholy trinity that stalked through French Santo Domingo and caused Leclerc's legions to disappear at the rate of one hundred a day. Seeing this rapid destruction of the French forces, the black generals who had taken service under Leclerc grew restive, and on October 10 Clervaux suddenly revolted. Christophe and Dessalines soon followed suit, and by the middle of November, 1802 a large portion of Haiti was once more under black control.[1]

Rochambeau, the new Governor-General of Santo Domingo, took active measures to stem this tide of revolution, and for a while he was somewhat successful. He recaptured some of the lost territory in the North and West, and in the spring of 1803 his " ultimate triumph grew clearer with every day." [2] But the relations between Great Britain and France grew more and more strained during this same period, and on May 12, 1803 the Peace of Amiens was broken by open warfare. With a British fleet blockading the ports of Santo Domingo, there was little opportunity for Rochambeau to secure the supplies which

[1] Lieutenant-Colonel H. de Poyen, *Histoire militaire de la révolution de Saint-Domingue*, pp. 273-297, 303-320; H. C. des Fosses, *La révolution de Saint-Domingue*, pp. 321-335.

[2] T. L. Stoddard, *The French Revolution in San Domingo*, p. 347; G. Roloff, *Die Kolonialpolitik Napoleons I*, pp. 134-150.

were necessary for his military campaigns. On November 10, 1803 he sailed out of Le Cap (Cap Français) and surrendered to the British admiral who was investing that port. Some two weeks later (November 28) the Môle-Saint-Nicolas was evacuated by the French troops, and French Santo Domingo passed under the control of Dessalines, who formally proclaimed the independence of the island (December, 1803). In October, 1804, Dessalines pushed his black rivals aside and crowned himself emperor in apparent imitation of Napoleon. This act of self-investiture was the symbol of the birth of a new nation.[3]

In October, 1806 the brief rule of Dessalines was terminated by his assassination, and for a while Santo Domingo was divided into five independent governments. In the Spanish portion of the island the French Government continued to maintain itself until it was driven out in 1809 by the combined efforts of the native inhabitants and an English expeditionary force. After the ejection of the French, the inhabitants accepted the rule of Spain until in 1821 a republic was proclaimed. In the western part of the island there were numerous divisions of authority. No less than four independent rulers raised their standards: Henry Christophe in the north, Pétion in the west, Rigaud in the south, and Goman in the extreme west of the southern department. But Rigaud and Goman soon passed off the scene, leaving Christophe and Pétion to carry on a contest for supremacy until the death of Pétion in 1818, and the suicide of Christophe in 1820 prepared the way for Boyer to seize control of the whole island in 1822.[4]

American relations with the mulatto leader Pétion followed a smoother course than those with Christophe. In November, 1813 William Taylor was received by Pétion " in the most courteous and polite manner," and a note was sent to Taylor in which he was formally acknowledged as the Commercial Agent of the United States. After these arrangements had been completed, Taylor inquired whether American vessels of war and

---

[3] H. C. des Fosses, *La révolution de Saint-Domingue*, pp. 334-346.
[4] Sir Spenser St. John, *Hayti or the Black Republic* (London, 1884), chap. iii; Sir J. Basket, *History of the Island of St. Domingo from Its First Discovery by Columbus to the Present Period* (London, 1818), chaps. xi-xii.

privateers could enter Haitian harbors, whereupon Pétion remarked that the ports under his control were at all times open to American war-ships of all descriptions, where they would be allowed to

refit and procure supplies, but not to make sales of prizes, as that would be deviating from that strict neutrality, the observance of which at this particular time He conceives to be all Important to the interest and welfare of Hayti.[5]

Some months later, Taylor wrote to Monroe that the " conduct of Pétion to our Privateers is *barely friendly*, in a very recent instance it was extremely vexatious." [6] As the years passed on, Taylor became increasingly disillusioned with reference to Pétion's alleged good qualities. Thus, on January 19, 1817, he wrote to Monroe in order to disclose his final estimate of the mulatto executive:

I was for a long time a friend of Petion because I believed him honest, humane, and benevolent. I now entertain a very different opinion of him. Believe me, he has thus long imposed upon the world, by *appearances,* owing to the want of time, or opp'y to observe him well by those who have visited the Island.[7]

Even if Pétion did not live up to Taylor's expectations his attitude towards the United States was far more friendly than

[5] Taylor to Monroe, December 10, 1813, *Cape Haitien, Consular Desp.,* vol. 4, MS. Dept. of State.
[6] Taylor to Monroe, August 30, 1814, *ibid.,* vol. 5.
[7] Taylor to Monroe, January 19, 1817, *ibid.* The general estimates of Pétion are slightly at variance. According to Sir Spenser St. John, he was not a great man but rather one " who sincerely loved his country, and devoted his energies to govern it well; but he was feeble in his measures, and from love of popularity allowed every kind of abuse to flourish in the financial administration." *Hayti or the Black Republic,* p. 80. Samuel Hazard, in his *Santo Domingo Past and Present,* p. 161, expresses the opinion that Pétion, " although much beloved by his people, seems to have been too mild and gentle a man to rule over such a peculiar population; and the inhabitants, especially the cultivators, had, under him, sunk into such a state of idleness and sloth, that the island suffered much in its commerce and products." A similar opinion is voiced by Charles Mackenzie, who was sent to Haiti in 1826 as British Consul-General. He believed that the " great objects of Pétion's life appear to have been the consolidation and improvement of the republic, and the subversion of the authority of his Northern rival. Though declaiming in favor of industry, he protected idleness: instead of resolutely punishing disorder, he palliated crime." *Notes on Haiti* (2 vols., London, 1830), II, 76.

that of Christophe, who revelled in his rôle of Black Majesty in North Haiti. If we could believe the facile Baron de Vastey, who was Chancellor of Christophe's kingdom and Field Marshal of the armed hosts of Haiti, the character of Christophe was much like that of Sir Galahad. Like other eminent men he was " a great admirer of truth, and an enemy to falsehood and flattery," while his " principles of honour and integrity " were lofty and invariable.[8] Unfortunately, contemporary Americans would not have recognized this portrait, and in the copious correspondence in the Department of State there are many documents which seem to indicate that Christophe, for all his royal robes, still had his early outlook of stable-boy.[9]

In 1810, Christophe sent to certain merchants in Baltimore, Messrs. von Kapff and Brune, coffee and bills of exchange amounting to $130,681.83. For reasons best known to themselves, these merchants failed to purchase and send to Christophe the articles he desired in exchange for his products. When these goods failed to arrive in Haiti, Christophe could have sued in American courts for damages, but that procedure would have consumed more time and effort than he cared to expend. Besides, that would be an undignified course for royalty to pursue! Of what use were kingly prerogatives if they could not be invoked at the sovereign's convenience? With supreme contempt for any untoward consequences, Christophe, on October 8, 1810, appointed Messrs. Dodge, Marple, French,

---

[8] Baron de Vastey, *An Essay on the Causes of the Revolution and Civil Wars of Hayti* (Exeter, 1823), p. 113.

[9] For recent colorful interpretations of Christophe see Blair Niles, *Black Haiti* (N. Y., 1926), and John W. Vandercook, *Black Majesty* (N. Y., 1928). Charles Mackenzie, the British Consul-General in Haiti, supplies a portrait of Christophe which is quite different from that of Baron de Vastey. Mackenzie believed that during the early part of Christophe's reign he was " mild, forbearing, and humane; but afterwards his nature seemed to have been completely changed, and he indulged in whatever his uncontrolled passions suggested—and they suggested almost every act that can violate the charities of life." *Notes on Haiti*, pp. 160-161. Sir Spenser St. John, in his *Hayti or the Black Republic*, p. 81, observes as follows: " Christophe was no doubt a very remarkable man, with indomitable energy, who saw the necessity of developing his country, but whose despotic nature cared not for the means, so that the ends were attained." According to Samuel Hazard, *Santo Domingo Past and Present* (N. Y., 1873), p. 162, Christophe became " one of the greatest of human monsters."

Myers, and O'Brien to act as special commissioners for the purpose of examining the books and accounts of American merchants living in Gonaives and Cape Henry. After this examination had been completed, another decree was issued on January 3, 1811. This second decree fixed the amount due to Christophe from Messrs. von Kapff and Brune at $124,955.19. Inasmuch as the examination into the books of the American merchants had disclosed the fact that there was on hand, in money, merchandise, and debts, the sum of $132,428.52, nothing was easier than to sequester enough of these assets to pay the amount due Christophe from von Kapff and Brune, namely, $124,955.19. Thus on April 27, 1811 the American merchants residing at Cape Henry and Gonaives were ordered

to pay into the Treasury of the capital, the sums sequestrated in their hands for the property of the Government fraudulently detained in the United States, according to the terms of the general order of the army, of the 3d of January, of the current year, 1811. This payment must be made within 24 hours at furthest.[10]

In defense of this summary procedure Christophe, in his order of January 3, 1811, inserted the following paragraph:

Seeing that not only the articles . . . have been detained in the United States by the said von Kapff and Brune and McFaden, but that the said funds have been unjustly withheld to this day, notwithstanding the many fruitless steps that his Most Serene Highness has taken, especially the useless mission of Mr. Marple, merchant of this city, a citizen of the United States, empowered to act on this business; thinking it just to use the means which are in his power, to repossess himself of this property, especially where it is thus fraudulently withheld in contempt of all that is sacred among men, His Most Serene Highness has decided on the following measure, repugnant alike to his feelings and policy, but which is the sole resource left him for the recovery of the property of the State.[11]

This confiscation of American property by Christophe became known as the "great sequestration of 1811," and the

---

[10] *House Ex. Doc.* No. 36, 27 Cong., 3 sess., p. 36.
[11] *Ibid.*, p. 35. In the Department of State, *Cape Haitien, Consular Desp.*, vols. 3-8, MS. Library of Congress, there is an immense amount of manuscript material on American claims against Haiti.

American Government was appealed to for redress. There were, however, other claims against the black government of Haiti, for under both Toussaint and Dessalines American citizens had been plundered. In order to arrive at some understanding with the government of Christophe relative to these claims, the American Secretary of State, James Monroe, wrote to Septimus Tyler on December 20, 1816 to announce that President Madison had decided to appoint him to the office of Commercial Agent at " Cape François, in the island of St. Domingo." He was instructed to make inquiries as to the amount of duties " payable by our vessels and those of other nations; to the illegal seizures of American vessels and merchandise; and to the treatment experienced by our citizens in the ports under the jurisdiction of General Christophe." [12] Such a mission would require some show of force, and consequently Tyler was to be transported to Cap Français in a vessel of war.

On January 29, 1817 he was given further instructions with reference to American claims. Upon his arrival in the island he was to lose no time in remonstrating against the " unjust " seizures of Christophe. He was also to inform King Henry that if he had

confided in persons in this country who betrayed the trust reposed in them, by embezzling or withholding his property, it surely afforded no ground for him to extort indemnity from unoffending citizens, who resorted to his ports with commercial views. The courts of the United States, in such cases, were open to him for redress, and through them he should have sought it.[13]

In preparing for this mission of Septimus Tyler to Christophe, great care had been observed in phrasing his credentials in order that the black government could have no basis for any claim of American recognition. He was to act merely as Commercial Agent at Cap Français and therefore was not accredited to the government of Christophe. As it happened, Christophe

[12] *Ho. Ex. Doc.* No. 36, 27 Cong., 3 sess., p. 114.
[13] Monroe to Tyler, January 29, 1817, *Desp. to Consuls*, vol. 1, MS. Dept. of State.

had recently rechristened Cap Français, and also the island of Santo Domingo itself. At the time of Tyler's arrival Cap Français had been styled Cape Henry, and Santo Domingo had been changed to the old Indian name of Haiti. These recent changes served as an excellent subterfuge for refusing to receive Tyler as Commercial Agent. On August 1, 1817, Count de Limonade, Minister of Foreign Affairs, addressed a formal note to Baron Dupuy in which he explained the reasons why Tyler could not be received. It was a note quite as tart as the Count's name. First of all, the Count was greatly surprised to discover that Tyler carried no letter of credence, but instead a " *simple certificat couché dans des termes inusitées, inadmissibles, et de plus renfermant les mots de Cap François et d'Isle de Saint Domingue.*" These particular expressions the Count considered quite " improper and injurious to the Government of His Majesty." And furthermore, in spite of the desire of King Henry to see firmly established both amicable and commercial relations with the United States, it would be impossible for the King to receive Mr. Tyler as Commercial Agent in the absence of credentials, " *authentiques en bonne et due forme, que l'accréditent suffisament auprès du Gouvernement d'Haïti.*" Therefore, inasmuch as Mr. Tyler had ignored the established diplomatic forms always observed in the King's realm, he was to be advised of this fact and also to be given the opportunity of perusing a copy of the royal declaration of November 20, 1816.[14]

The transparent quality of these evasions on the part of Christophe was very evident to the American Government, and consequently another effort was made to satisfy the sensibilities of Black Majesty and at the same time to secure some promise of redress for American claimants. In February, 1818 William Taylor, who for several years had been the American Commercial Agent at Port-au-Prince, was appointed as Commercial Agent to Cape Henry. In the instructions from John

---

[14] Comte de Limonade to Baron de Dupuy, Sécrétaire Interprète du Roi, August 1, 1817, *Ho. Ex. Doc.* No. 36, 27 Cong., 3 sess., p. 117. For the correspondence of Tyler with the Secretary of State, see *Cape Haitien, Consular Desp.*, vol. 5, MS. Dept. of State.

Quincy Adams, Secretary of State, Mr. Taylor was advised that since objections had been made to the admission of Tyler

on acount of the name of the island, and the alleged royal title of the chief, it will be proper if possible, to avoid their recurrence. For this purpose, it is proposed that, upon your arrival, Captain Reed should land with you, and present you personally as the agent of the United States. You will be careful to observe all suitable respect to the existing authority.

In case, however, a formal acknowledgment of the Government of Christophe by that of the United States

be insisted upon as the condition of your admission, you will declare your incompetency to agree to such a condition, and will proceed in the ship, and return in her to the United States.[15]

Taylor arrived at Cape Henry on April 22, 1818, and on the following day was introduced to Baron Dupuy as the Commercial Agent from the United States. On April 24, he made an informal call upon the Baron and informed him of the anxious desire of the President of the United States that there should be " a good understanding between the two Governments, and a free, friendly, and unrestrained intercourse between the citizens of the United States and the subjects of Hayti." Dupuy was greatly pleased with such friendly sentiments and was relieved to find that in Mr. Taylor's commission there was no repetition of the " exceptionable words " contained in the commission of Mr. Tyler.[16]

On April 25, Dupuy called upon Mr. Taylor to express his " great desire " that the American Commercial Agent be received by Christophe in his " official character." He had been summoned to Christophe's palace at Sans Souci, and upon his return on the 27th he would acquaint Taylor with the disposition of His Majesty. On the appointed day Taylor waited upon the Baron and was informed that the King had decided to refuse to recognize the American Commercial Agent

---

[15] Adams to Taylor, February, 1818, *Desp. to Consuls*, vol. 2, MS. Dept. of State.
[16] Taylor to Adams, May 30, 1818, *Ho. Ex. Doc.* No. 36, 27 Cong., 3 sess., pp. 118-119.

because of the " informal " character of his appointment. When Taylor remarked that such an objection was obviated because of his formal introduction by Captain Reed of the U. S. S. S. *Hornet,* the Baron smiled a knowing smile and said that the introduction

ought to have been supported . . . by the usual and customary documents, the absence of which rendered the introduction through Captain Reed a species of deception, the object of which his Majesty the King could not readily comprehend, and had therefore passed it over in silence.[17]

Later on that evening, Taylor received a copy of the formal note from the ever punctilious Count de Limonade in which regret was expressed that once more the Government of the United States had ignored the accepted usage of nations in the matter of diplomatic communications.[18] With the receipt of this impudently correct note, relations between the United States and the government of King Christophe came to an abrupt end. On the evening of October 20, 1820, in the face of a serious revolt among his troops, Christophe committed suicide, and inasmuch as his rival Pétion had already died in 1818, the two conflicting jurisdictions in Haiti were now brought

[17] Taylor to John Quincy Adams, May 30, 1818, *ibid.,* pp. 119-120. Already on May 5 Taylor had written to Adams from Port-au-Prince announcing that he had not been received because of the " informality " of his appointment. See *Cape Haitien, Consular Desp.,* vol. 5, MS. Dept. of State.

[18] *Ho. Ex. Doc.* No. 36, 27 Cong., 3 sess., pp. 120-121. Dr. H. M. Wriston, in his admirable study of *Executive Agents in American Foreign Relations* (Baltimore, 1929), p. 432, with reference to the refusal of the Haitian authorities to receive either Tyler or Taylor as commercial agents, remarks as follows: " The real fact was that Taylor and Tyler came on missions that were unwelcome. If they had come to do something which Christophe desired, no difficulty would have been made about credentials. But he wished to escape diplomatic pressure for payment and took refuge in impossible demands—impossible because they would have involved recognition of a government which did not meet the standards required of independent states." With reference to Christophe's attitude toward Americans, there is an interesting but incorrect statement in Dr. Mary Treudley, " The United States and Santo Domingo," *Journal of Race Development,* VII (1916), 222. See also the account in *Niles' Register,* XIV, 263, in which Christophe's action in refusing to receive American commercial agents is attributed to his unwillingness to pay the large American claims against his government.

under the control of one ruler, Jean Pierre Boyer.[19] But Boyer was not content to be merely the ruler of united Haiti. In the autumn of 1821, the inhabitants of the eastern part of the island of Santo Domingo, the old Spanish Santo Domingo, successfully revolted against Spanish authority and proclaimed their independence. This was an opportunity that Boyer was too keen to overlook. An invasion of Spanish Santo Domingo would formerly have meant a war against the Mother Country, Spain, but now that the Dominicans had proclaimed their independence there was no danger of European complications. Boyer hurriedly mobilized his troops and crossed the Dominican frontiers without opposition, and in February, 1822 he was formally acknowledged as the ruler over the entire island of Santo Domingo.[20]

The American Government was quick to take advantage of the political changes in Santo Domingo. On January 30, 1821, shortly after the death of Christophe, John Quincy Adams instructed Edward Wyer to proceed to the island and endeavour to effect some arrangement relative to American claims against the black government. Although Wyer was unable to secure any promise of redress for these claimants, Boyer did indicate more friendly feeling towards the United States than did his predecessor Christophe.[21] In the spring of 1820 Andrew Armstrong had been received by Boyer as Commercial Agent at Port-au-Prince, and Wyer reported to Secre-

[19] For an interesting and valuable account of Santo Domingo in the early years of Boyer's rule see the two volumes by the former British consul, Charles Mackenzie, *Notes on Haiti*. With reference to the relations between Christophe and Americans resident in Haiti, Mackenzie relates the following anecdote: "A ludicrous story is told of an American captain who had been brought before him [Christophe] for some violation of law and who, indignant at the rating he received, and ignorant of his Majesty's accomplishments, muttered to himself a wish that he had the sable king at Charleston. Henry quietly asked him, ' How much do you think I should fetch: ' The offender was dismissed, nor do I believe that any further notice was taken of his irreverent remark." I, 161-162.

[20] Samuel Hazard, *Santo Domingo Past and Present*, pp. 162-163. S. St. John, *Hayti or the Black Republic*, pp. 80 ff.

[21] Adams to Wyer, January 30, 1821, *Ho. Ex. Doc.* No. 36, 27 Cong., 3 sess., pp. 121-122. See letter from Boyer to Wyer, March 21, 1821, *Special Agents Series*, MS. Dept. of State. The despatches from Wyer to Adams relative to his mission are also contained in the *Special Agents Series*.

tary Adams that Armstrong was very much respected in Haiti and stood " very high with the President Boyer." [22]

In the following year (1821) W. D. Robinson, who was at Port-au-Prince to present certain claims of Commodore Lewis, expressed the opinion that Boyer and his Secretary-General

were anxious to cultivate the good will of our government, and I feel confident that if our cabinet were to offer to acknowledge the independence of Hayti, or to make a commercial treaty with them, we might make our own terms and receive satisfaction for all claims.[23]

It is apparent that the régime of President Boyer was a stimulant to American trade with Haiti. In 1822 the value of American exports to Haiti was equivalent to the combined exports to Russia, Prussia, Sweden, Denmark, and Ireland.[24] In view of these lucrative economic ties that bound the United States to Haiti, President Boyer had hopes that the American Government would extend recognition to his administration. His formal application for political recognition was referred to the Senate of the United States by President Monroe with the following comments:

[22] Wyer to Adams, March 12, 1821, *Special Agents Series*, MS. Dept. of State. The reports of Armstrong to the Department of State are contained in *Cape Haitien, Consular Desp.*, vol. 5.

[23] *House Doc.* No. 36, 27 Cong., 3 sess., p. 29. President Boyer was very anxious to encourage the immigration of negroes into Haiti. Even before his term as President, Boyer had witnessed the attempts of Dessalines to attract American negroes to Haiti, and he doubtless knew of the efforts of the Maryland Haytian Society in the same direction. See *The Writings of James Monroe*, IV, 186, and *Niles' Register*, XIX, 415. In 1824 Boyer sent Jonathan Granville to New York with a plan to pay the passage of negro immigrants to Haiti. These immigrants were to be given financial aid in addition to farm lands when they arrived in Haiti. According to Benjamin P. Hunt, *Remarks on Hayti as a Place of Settlement for Afric-Americans* (Phila., 1860), some thirteen thousand black immigrants were brought to Haiti as a result of President Boyer's project. See also *Biographie de Jonathan Granville* (Paris, 1873). There was strong opposition in the South to this negro immigration to Haiti. Southern planters could never forget the terrible massacres that followed the negro revolt in Haiti, and they were fearful that any close connection between American negroes and the blacks of Santo Domingo might lead to uprisings throughout the Southern states. It happened that this plan of President Boyer was not very successful. Many American negroes soon became dissatisfied with conditions in Haiti and returned to the United States.

[24] *Niles' Register*, XX, 49.

In adverting to the political state of St. Domingo I have to observe that the whole island is now united under one Government under a constitution which retains the sovereignty in the hands of the people of color. . . .   The establishment of a Government of people of color in the island on the principles above stated evinces distinctly the idea of a separate interest and a distrust of other nations. . . .   To what extent that spirit may be indulged or to what purposes applied our experience has yet been too limited to enable us to form a just estimate.   These are inquiries more peculiarly interesting to the neighboring islands.   They nevertheless deserve the attention of the United States.[25]

After this non-committal message from the President to the Senate, the question of Haitian recognition came before the President's Cabinet for discussion. When the subject had been carefully canvassed it was decided by the Cabinet that recognition of the Boyer Administration in Haiti should not be granted.[26]

The attitude of Congress towards Haitian recognition was an unfavorable one, and representatives from the South were particularly vehement in their opposition. Their opportunity for denunciation came in 1825-1826 when it was proposed that the American Government send delegates to an inter-American congress that was to be held at Panama in the summer of 1826. One of the subjects to be discussed at this forthcoming congress was the political status of Haiti. Such an item in the agenda of the conference was bound to evoke the deep resentment of Southern Senators, and Mr. Hayne, of South Carolina, waxed eloquent in his opposition:

With nothing connected with slavery can we consent to treat with other nations, and, least of all ought we to touch the question of the independence of Hayti in conjunction with Revolutionary governments, whose own history affords an example scarcely less fatal to our repose. . . . Our policy with regard to Hayti is plain. We never can acknowledge her independence.[27]

Senator Benton, of Missouri, was equally hostile to any

[25] Message of President Monroe to the Senate, February 25, 1823, J. D. Richardson, *Messages and Papers of the Presidents*, II, 204-205.
[26] John Quincy Adams, *Memoirs*, VI, 233.
[27] *Register of Debates in Congress*, 19 Cong., 1 sess., p. 166.

thought of Haitian recognition. American policy towards that government had been fixed for more than thirty years. Although we had commercial relations with the blacks of that island, we had not established any diplomatic posts there:

We purchase coffee from her, and pay her for it; but we interchange no consuls or ministers. . . . And why? Because the peace of eleven states will not permit the fruits of a successful negro insurrection to be exhibited among them. . . . It will not permit the fact to be seen, and told, that for the murder of their masters and mistresses, they are to find friends among the white people of these United States.[28]

European powers, however, were not as cautious as the United States in the matter of according recognition to the Government of Haiti. On July 11, 1825 President Boyer, after lengthy negotiations, accepted certain proposals of the French Government whereby recognition was extended to Haiti on the express condition that French nationals should pay only half of the regular customs duties levied on imports and exports, and that one hundred and fifty millions of francs be paid as an indemnity in five equal installments, beginning on December 31, 1825.[29] The British Government showed a similar disposition to recognize the government of President Boyer, and on May 24, 1826 a British Consul-General, Charles Mackenzie, landed at Port-au-Prince to begin his official duties.

It was during this third decade of the 19th century that American trade with Santo Domingo began to appear as a con-

---

[28] *Ibid.,* p. 330. President Boyer was so angry at the attitude of the American Government that he refused to permit Armstrong to continue to fulfill the duties of Commercial Agent at Port-au-Prince. Just before Secretary Adams appointed Francis M. Dimond as the new Commercial Agent at that port, he expressed the view that such an appointment "must be of an informal commercial agency, and with a probable prospect of not being recognized; as they had refused to act upon representations of our last commercial agent, Andrew Armstrong, on the ground that we declined to recognize the Haytian government as sovereign and independent." John Quincy Adams, *Memoirs,* VII, 441. Armstrong left Port-au-Prince in April, 1827, and Dimond did not arrive there to take up his duties until September, 1828. He remained at his post until April 1, 1837.

[29] M. Wallez, *Précis historique des négociations entre la France et Saint-Domingue* (Paris, 1826), pp. 43-89; H. C. des Fosses, *La révolution de Saint-Domingue,* pp. 362-365; Charles Mackenzie, *Notes on Haiti,* II, 86 ff.

siderable item. Perhaps it was this fact that led Henry Clay in 1825 to express the opinion that " the independence of the Haytian government must shortly be recognized." [30] After 1830 the development of the movement for the abolition of slavery led to an increased interest in the recognition of Haiti, and petitions to this effect began to pour in upon Congress. During the winter of 1838-1839 more than two hundred petitions requesting Haitian recognition were received by the House of Representatives, and in the succeeding sessions of Congress they continued in large numbers.[31] In 1843 John Quincy Adams, while serving as a member of the House Committee on Foreign Affairs, offered a resolution " that a Consul ought to be forthwith appointed to the republic of Hayti to prosecute the claims of our citizens." Although there were three other members of the committee from the North, the vote of Adams was the only one cast in favor of the resolution.[32]

This American prejudice against any political relations with the island of Santo Domingo was destined to be greatly lessened after 1844, when the inhabitants of Spanish Santo Domingo

---

[30] John Q. Adams, *Memoirs*, VI, 530.

[31] Adelaide R. Hasse, *Index to the United States Documents Relating to Foreign Affairs, 1828-1861* (3 vols., Washington, 1914-1921), I, 720-721.

[32] The following short table will give some indication of the importance of the trade between Haiti and the United States during the decade 1821-1831:

Years	American imports from Haiti	American exports to Haiti
1821	$2,246,257	$2,270,601
1824	2,247,235	2,365,155
1828	2,163,585	1,332,711
1831	1,580,578	1,318,375

See Timothy Pitkin, *Statistical View of the Commerce of the United States of America* (New Haven, 1835), p. 219. In 1822, it was estimated that the exports of the United States to Haiti were as large as the combined exports to Russia, Prussia, Sweden, Denmark, and Ireland, and that more shipping entered the ports of the United States from Haiti than from any other country except England, the British American colonies, and Cuba. See *Niles' Register*, XXVII, 31. Charles Mackenzie, in his *Notes on Hayti*, II, app., note kk, gives the following table relative to the commerce of certain nations with Haiti:

Year	Vessels	Tonnage	Nation
1825	374	39,199	United States
	78	11,952	Great Britain
	16	1,195	Colombia
	65	11,136	France
	17	3,185	Germany

rose in revolt against Haitian misrule and proclaimed the independence of the Dominican Republic.[33] At first the Dominicans did not seek American assistance. Since the revolutionary leaders apparently believed that France would be more sympathetic towards their aspirations than would any other nation, in 1843 some sort of an informal arrangement was entered into whereby the French Government was to co-operate with the insurgents. The price of such aid was to be either Samaná Bay as a French naval base or the extension of a French protectorate over Santo Domingo. A French fleet under Rear-Admiral Moges arrived very opportunely for the revolutionists, but fear of British opposition finally prevented the French agents from carrying out their program.[34]

[33] The ease with which the people of Spanish Santo Domingo threw off the Haitian yoke is indicated by the small number of Dominican casualties in the battles with the Haitian armed forces. In the manuscript *Journal of a Mission to Santo Domingo, 1846*, kept by Lieutenant David D. Porter, there is the following pertinent passage: " History does not record any battles where the disparity of force was so great, and where the weaker party met with . . . so little loss to themselves: in two great battles where the enemy lost over a thousand men, the Dominicans lost but three." Duke University Library.

[34] Although the responsible authorities at the Quai d'Orsay were not interested in establishing a French protectorate over the Dominican Republic, French agents in the island of Santo Domingo were active in promoting such a scheme. In 1841 Levasseur, the French Consul-General at Port-au-Prince, urged his government to seize Samaná Bay as a compensation for the failure of the Haitian Administration to carry out the terms of their treaties with France. In 1843 these French agents were in close concert with the Dominicans who were plotting a revolution against Haiti, and Admiral Moges even went so far as to aid the Dominicans in a naval engagement with Haitian warships. Outstanding Dominican leaders like Pedro Santana and Buenaventura Baez were ready to accept a French protectorate over the Dominican Republic, and the revolutionary Junta in charge of Dominican affairs was anxious for a treaty of friendship and alliance with France in return for commercial concessions and a cession of Samaná Bay which could be developed into a French naval base. But the Guizot Government thought that a successful revolution on the part of the Dominicans would seriously diminish Haitian resources and would therefore render Haiti incapable of meeting her financial obligations to France. Moreover, Guizot feared that any aggressive French policy in Santo Domingo would give umbrage to England. Later French governments had similar fears, and this fact accounts for the policy of non-intervention which they adopted.

In France there were certain publicists like Pelletier de Saint Rémy and Gustave d'Alaux who endeavored to stir up public sentiment in favor of a more positive policy regarding intervention in Santo Domingo. Saint Rémy published in Paris in 1846 a volume entitled *Étude et solution nouvelle de la question haïtienne*, in which he strongly argues for the cession of Samaná Bay to France

After vainly seeking European assistance, President Santana, of the new Dominican Republic, sent Dr. José M. Caminero as a special envoy to the United States in order to establish closer relations with the American Government.[35] On January 6, 1845, Caminero had an interview with John C. Calhoun, the American Secretary of State, who promptly made extensive inquiries as to the real situation in Santo Domingo. Two days later, Caminero sent a lengthy reply to Calhoun's queries. After discussing the events leading up to the revolution against black misrule, Caminero set forth the political, social, and economic aspects of Dominican life. The reins of government were held by the educated and prosperous minority which was largely white. The population was now some two hundred thousand persons; half of these were whites, and, of the other half, two-thirds were mulattoes. A considerable number of these mulattoes were landed proprietors. Others practiced the mechanic arts or profitable professions. The territory of the republic was exceedingly fertile, and there were large mineral deposits of gold, copper, iron, and coal. All that was needed to accomplish the complete regeneration of Santo Domingo was the recognition of the present government by the leading world powers.[36]

On February 21, 1845, Calhoun wrote to Caminero to advise him that his memoir had been read with great interest by President Tyler. It was, however, the practice of the American Government, before it recognized the independence of any new state, to

appoint a commissioner to proceed to the country and to investigate and report his opinion on all the facts and circumstances on which it is deemed necessary to be informed before a decision is made.[37]

(pp. 242-402), and some years later Gustave d'Alaux, in the *Revue des deux mondes,* XIX, 211 ff., does the same.

On these French schemes in Santo Domingo see Dexter Perkins, *The Monroe Doctrine, 1826-1867* (Baltimore, 1933), pp. 253-262; B. C. Clark, *Remarks upon the United States Intervention in Hayti* (Boston, 1853), pp. 18-21; Sumner Welles, *Naboth's Vineyard* (2 vols., N. Y., 1928), I, 67 ff.

[35] Santana to President Tyler, December 5, 1844, *Dominican Republic, Notes from,* vol. 1, MS. Dept. of State.

[36] *Sen. Ex. Doc.* No. 16, 41 Cong., 3 sess., pp. 27 ff.

[37] *Special Missions,* vol. 1, MS. Dept. of State.

On the following day, Calhoun sent instructions to John Hogan to proceed at once to Santo Domingo and report on the following points:

1. The extent and limits of the territory over which the Dominican government claims and exercises jurisdiction. 2. The character and composition of its population. 3. The number, discipline, and equipment of the troops. 4. The aggregate population of the country, and the proportions of European, African, and mixed races. 5. The financial system and resources of the republic.[38]

Mr. Hogan left for Santo Domingo immediately, and when he arrived he addressed some questionnaires to Tomás Bobadilla, the Dominican Minister of Foreign Affairs,[39] and to two American citizens there, Abner Burbank and Francis Harrison. Bobadilla spared no effort to make his report a careful and complete one. If rich natural resources were an argument in favor of recognition, then it was obvious that such action could not long be delayed. The territory of the Dominican Republic, it appeared, abounded " in gold mines, copper, silver, iron, quicksilver, sulphur, stone, coal, gypsum, salt, and other productions of nature." The government was beneficient, the climate salubrious, and the people " mild, docile, religious to a considerable degree, . . . with all the qualities requisite to form an excellent nation." [40]

The separate reports of Francis Harrison and Abner Burbank confirmed the glowing account of Bobadilla, and Harrison hinted that recognition might lead the Government of the Dominican Republic to grant to the United States some port which would serve as a naval station.[41]

On the basis of these answers to his questions, Hogan made his report to the Department of State. In his opinion the island was of " inestimable value," and it had " one of the most admirable positions which the world can exhibit for a com-

---

[38] Calhoun to Hogan, February 22, 1845, *ibid.*
[39] Hogan to Bobadilla, June 12, 1845, *Special Agents Series,* vol. 13, MS. Dept. of State.
[40] Bobadilla to Hogan, June 19, 1845, *ibid.*
[41] Harrison to Hogan, June 26, 1845, July 4, 1845, and Burbank to Hogan, June 24, 1845, *ibid.*

mercial emporium." He was particularly impressed with its vast and secure bays, which " would afford shelter for the congregated navies of the world." All that would be required to restore the island to " its former grandeur, is that it should maintain its present independent character."

Thanks to the ingratiating manner of Hogan,

no apprehension need be entertained but that our country will enjoy a large proportion of the respect and good feelings of the government and people of Dominica, and participate freely in every commercial privilege which may be granted to any other.

In conclusion, Hogan stated that he had

no doubt that the republic of Dominica, if not interfered with by foreign influence, has the entire capacity to maintain its independence, and even to extend its sovereignty, ere long, over the entire island.[42]

It is obvious that when Secretary Calhoun sent his instructions to Hogan (February 22, 1845) he understood that this special agent of the Department of State could not return to America in time to report to the Tyler Administration. Hogan's report was addressed to the new Secretary of State, James Buchanan, and was received by the Department of State on October 4, 1845. Both President Polk and Secretary Buchanan appreciated the work accomplished by Hogan, but conditions in the Caribbean changed so rapidly that it was thought expedient to send another special agent to the Dominican Republic. The new mission was entrusted to a young naval lieutenant, David D. Porter, who arrived at his destination in May, 1846.

President Santana expressed " much surprise " upon learning that Lieutenant Porter was a special agent of the United States. He immediately referred to the recent visit of Mr. Hogan and frankly informed Lieutenant Porter that the Dominican Government was now waiting " with the expectation of a recognition

---

[42] Hogan to Buchanan, received at Dept. of State on October 4, 1845, *ibid.* It is interesting to note that during the years 1844 to 1846 there was a strong party in the Dominican Republic that favored a Spanish protectorate. The versatile Baez sometimes inclined towards Spain and at other times towards France. *Documentos Relativos à la Cuestión de Santo Domingo. Sometidos al Congreso de los Diputados*, Ministerio del Estado (Madrid, 1865), pp. 4-14.

of their Independence." The Lieutenant did his best to soften their disappointment, and "with the usual compliments" that envoys give to rulers whom they visit, he set about his task of gathering information about the resources and stability of the Dominican Republic.

President Santana promised to extend to Lieutenant Porter every facility for travelling over the island. The Lieutenant soon discovered that these facilities were primitive indeed, and his travelogue, if it had been published, would not have induced many visitors to follow his route. Samaná Bay appealed to him strongly as an important location for a naval base, but his enthusiasm from the viewpoint of naval advantage was tempered by his realism as to the discomforts that would have to be faced by any Americans stationed near this body of water:

> With all the delights of Samana are mixed up many of the discomforts of life. It abounds with all kinds of venomous reptiles. The air at night is filled with poisonous flies; and mosquitoes drive one almost mad.

He was convinced that the Dominicans were "much better fitted by intellect" to administer the affairs of state than the Haitians, and he wondered why they should have submitted for such a long period to the iron rule of the black generals. He then gave an interesting picture of French intrigue in Santo Domingo, and he told of the efforts of French agents to induce the Dominicans to revolt against Haitian misrule and place themselves under the protection of France.

As far as the constitution of the Dominican Republic was concerned he believed that

> it might as well never been adopted, excepting that the day is not far distant when the rights it bequeaths to the people may be given to them. At present, the article 210 gives the President authority to do as he pleases; and I have known instances where the most flagrant abuses of power have occurred, where none were absolutely necessary. These cases however, are few, and President Santana feels little disposed to take advantage of that article of the Constitution.

It was still uncertain whether the Dominican Republic would "ever attain to any eminence in the scale of nations." Although the government was "too young, yet, to form an opinion," it should be kept in mind that the Dominican people had "struggled for three years with little apparent disorder; and with means inadequate to overthrow their enemy."

After this survey of political conditions in the Dominican Republic, Lieutenant Porter discussed the rich natural resources which seemed to abound in the island. There was little doubt that they would yield handsome returns if properly developed.[43]

The outbreak of the Mexican War in May, 1846 prevented any further action with reference to Santo Domingo until fear of foreign intrigues drove the American Government to make a thorough canvass of the situation. In February, 1846 a squadron of Spanish war-ships cruised for a time in Dominican waters, and, encouraged by this gesture, the Dominican Government appointed in April of that year a commission to visit Spain, France, and England in order to ascertain the attitude of those powers relative to intervention in Santo Domingo.[44]

President Polk became increasingly alarmed over the possibility of European control over Santo Domingo. The report of Lieutenant Porter in the early summer of 1846 had indicated the dire distress of many of the inhabitants of the Dominican Republic, but it had also referred to rich natural resources that could be developed by foreign capital. It seemed certain to Polk that European powers were only seeking an opportunity to declare a protectorate over the Dominican Republic. In order that he might keep a watchful eye on any such movements, he appointed Francis Harrison as Commercial Agent to that government.

Harrison arrived at Porto Plata on February 18, 1847, and soon found it possible to make a trip over the island. In his

---

[43] David D. Porter, *Journal of a Mission to Santo Domingo, 1846.* This manuscript journal of Lieutenant Porter is now in the Duke University Library. There is no copy available in the archives of the Department of State. In his article entitled "Secret Missions to San Domingo," in the *North American Review*, CXXVIII, 616-630, Admiral Porter refers to this journal: "On my return home in the *Porpoise* from Porto Plata, I made a full report in duplicate—one for the State and the other for the Navy Department—but both of these disappeared from the departments prior to the breaking out of our civil war in 1861."

[44] Sumner Welles, *Naboth's Vineyard,* I, 74 ff.

letters to the Secretary of State, James Buchanan, he sets forth in detail the condition of affairs. With respect to foreign interference, he discovered that there was a strong French interest in the republic. As a result, the French navy was unusually active in Dominican waters. Indeed, in the last four months of the year 1846 French officers had made " extensive surveys of Samana Bay," and at times there were " as many as six vessels of war employed in that service." [45]

Harrison's tenure as Commercial Agent was cut short by a fatal attack of yellow fever, and Jonathan Elliot was appointed to fill the vacancy. In the meantime, in August, 1848, President Santana resigned his office and was succeeded by General Manuel Jiménez. The new President was not long in discovering that his executive duties seriously interfered with his pleasures. There was only one recourse left for a true sportsman. His whole time was soon

spent in cleaning, training, and fighting cocks, it being frequently necessary to send acts of Congress and other official papers to the cockpit for his approval and signature.[46]

In American history there have been certain chief executives who have sought sportive pleasures to lighten their heavy burdens, and it has even been stated that in his younger days Andrew Jackson was fond of fighting cocks. It has also been stated, however, that when a foreign foe was at the gates Jackson was eagerly awaiting it. Apparently President Jiménez was not made of this sterner stuff, for in March, 1849, when a Haitian army crossed the Dominican frontier, there was an evident lack of presidential leadership, and the " greatest consternation and alarm " arose in the Dominican Republic. Some Dominicans, like Buenaventura Baez, saw safety in French intervention. Many others soon became converted to the same idea, and on April 19 the Dominican Congress met in secret session and adopted a resolution requesting the French Government to declare a protectorate over the Dominican Republic.

[45] Harrison to Buchanan, March 31, 1847, *Santo Domingo, Consular Desp.*, vol. 1, MS. Dept. of State.

[46] Benjamin E. Green to Clayton, September 27, 1849, *Secret Service*, MS. Dept. of State.

In return for assistance against the Haitian invaders, France was to receive Samaná Bay.[47]

The former President, General Pedro Santana, was known to favor Spanish protection, while according to some reports the British consul, Sir Robert Schomburgk, was busily engaged in announcing the advantages of British control. President Jiménez, however, turned to the United States, and in a private interview with the American Commercial Agent, Jonathan Elliot, he inquired whether the Dominicans could " annex themselves " to the great American republic of the North.[48] It was high time for the American Government to bestir itself.

John M. Clayton, the American Secretary of State, seemed especially fearful of British designs, and therefore on June 4, 1849 he sent to George Bancroft, American Minister at London, the following cipher instruction:

> The Department has been informed, not officially, but from a reliable source, that the British government has a Commissioner accredited to the Government of the Dominican Republic who is charged to obtain by negotiation the cession to Great Britain of the Bay of Samana; that there is a draft of a Treaty by which England pledges herself to recognize the independence of that Republic in consideration of the grant. . . . The intelligence relates to a subject obviously too important to admit of any delay in attempting to ascertain its authenticity. You will consequently endeavor to inform yourself in regard to it.[49]

On June 29, 1849, Bancroft replied in a despatch which discounted these fears of the Secretary of State. He was certain that it was

[47] Green to Clayton, August 27, September 27, October 24, 1849, *ibid*. With reference to this international rivalry in Santo Domingo, Ussher, the British consul at Port-au-Prince, wrote to Palmerston on May 30, 1849 as follows: " Mr. Raybaud communicated to me a few days ago a letter from Place, the French Consul at St. Domingo, in which the latter states that the Dominican Govt. alarmed at the rapid approach of the Haytian Army proposed to place the Republic under the protection of France and to hoist the French Flag. Raybaud states that he gave positive orders to Place to refuse this proposition. It is then stated . . . that Sir Robert Schomburgk immediately offered to the Dominican Govt. the protection of Great Britain." F. O. 35/36, No. 22.

[48] Elliot to Clayton, May 2, 1849, *Santo Domingo, Consular Desp.*, vol. 1, MS. Dept. of State.

[49] Clayton to Bancroft, June 4, 1849, *Clayton Papers*, vol. 5, MS. Library of Congress. It is interesting to note that this cipher instruction is not contained in the official files in the Department of State.

no part of British policy to increase their possessions in the West India Islands. Having abrogated slavery, and having also abrogated the differential duty in favor of sugar produced by free labor, the British Government cares very little for new acquisitions in that quarter; and if it could make them, would not know what to do with them. In a particular manner, any attempt to appropriate a part of St. Domingo would arouse the jealousy of the French. Still more, the House of Commons, which makes and unmakes, and controls Ministries, would not approve any such encroachment. A just sentiment that we should be discontented by the alleged design, would weigh greatly with the Ministry; for be assured, American diplomacy, if conducted with a knowledge of the nature of this Government, with firmness, and with care to avoid wounding national pride, has great influence in its deliberations. These are my views. I have made inquiries among those likely to be well informed, and find them confirmed.[50]

But before Clayton could receive Bancroft's reassuring despatch of June 29, he had already on June 13 appointed Benjamin E. Green as a special agent to visit Santo Domingo and report upon the situation. After advising Green of the reported intention of Great Britain to secure the cession of the Bay of Samaná as a naval base, Clayton instructed him as follows:

You will endeavor to ascertain the truth of the reports relative to the cession of the Bay of Samana, and if you should find that the Dominican Government has gone too far to recede, you will then communicate to the Department the terms of the cession and the purposes of Great Britain in acquiring it, so far as they may be within your reach. If the cession should not have been completed, you will endeavor to defeat it by strenuous yet respectful representations to the Minister for Foreign Affairs, the President, or other persons in high office in that Republic.

When Mr. Green had expended his best efforts to defeat British intrigues, he was then to make a careful study of the condition of affairs in the Dominican Republic, and if his observations

should confirm the statements of Messrs. Hogan and Porter in regard to their competency to discharge the duties of an independent state,

---

[50] Bancroft to Clayton, June 29, *England, Desp.*, vol. 59, MS. Dept. of State.

the President will now be inclined to give a public acknowledgment of this on the part of this government. . . . If your inquiries and reflections upon these points should have a favorable issue, you will then sound the Dominican Minister for Foreign Affairs upon the subject of concluding a treaty with the United States.

After the signature of this convention, Mr. Green was next to ascertain the

disposition of that government to grant to us a site on the coast of the Bay of Samana, suitable as a stopping place for the United States steamers, and as a place of deposit for coal to be used by them. If this grant should not be refused, you will then ascertain upon what terms it may be obtained.[51]

From the tenor of these instructions it is evident that Green was not only entrusted with the duty of defeating foreign schemes for securing Samaná Bay but was further expected to prepare the Dominican Government to cede this very bay to the United States. This task, it would seem, required such high talents that its accomplishment should have been regarded by Green as worthy of all his efforts. Green, however, looked upon the cession of Samaná Bay to the United States as only one important item in his program. He had carefully noted how certain canny Americans had grown rich by inducing the Government of Mexico to grant them wide acres in return for introducing colonists into the unsettled portions of Texas. He had also observed with interest how these same colonists had waxed strong under the lax rule of Mexico and had gained their independence after a brief struggle. He would now apply the same process to the unoccupied lands of the Dominican Republic.

According to the New York *Daily Tribune*, Green's project was decidedly grandiose and included the granting to the Dominican Government of a

[51] Clayton to Green, June 13, 1849, *Special Missions*, vol. 1, MS. Dept. of State. After Green had left for Santo Domingo, Secretary Clayton decided that " the application of the Dominican authorities for the protection of France, which must have been made from a dread of further invasions on the part of the Haytians, would seem to indicate that the independence of the Republic is not established with such firmness as to warrant us in concluding a treaty with them." See *Sen. Ex. Doc.* No. 12, 33 Cong., 1 sess., and *Special Missions*, vol. 1, MS. Dept. of State.

considerable loan of money, one or two steamers, and the advantages of a regular postal communication with the United States, in consideration of which, the Greens and their associates were to be allowed to introduce American colonists, who shall carry on mining, the cutting of dyewoods and other precious trees, and agriculture, and enjoy certain peculiar privileges, among the rest that of a *separate military organization with their own officers*.[52]

When Green arrived in the Dominican Republic towards the latter part of August, 1849, he found that President Jiménez had hurriedly forsaken his onerous post as chief executive. The new President, Buenaventura Baez, unlike his predecessor in office, was an active intriguer of sinister talents, who for several decades was one of the outstanding figures in Dominican politics. He was the son of " an old Spaniard by a woman of color " and had the obvious advantage of a European education.[53] Slight of stature, with long prominent nose, bright furtive eyes that saw through political complications as well as they read the desires of Dominicans, and with dark curly hair that extended down his cheeks in modish Burnsides, President Baez was a " dandy " in politics who could charm by his suavity and impress by his ready grasp of realities.

It was well recognized in Santo Domingo that Baez favored a French protectorate, and Green soon discovered that his chief duties would be to counteract these pro-French tendencies. His instructions had indicated England as the nation most closely to be watched, but the English consul, Sir Robert Schomburgk, tried to quiet these fears and assured him that Lord Palmerston did not believe that " British interests and commerce were sufficiently involved " to warrant intervention in the Dominican Republic. Green, however, still retained a suspicion that the English consul attached " very great im-

---

[52] September 5, 1854.   Italics are the author's.

[53] Green to Clayton, September 27, 1849, *Secret Service*, MS. Dept. of State. In a genealogical list given in the New York *Evening Post* of September 2, 1854, with reference to the background of leading Dominican politicians, the following item is given in connection with Baez: " Bonaventura Baez, founder of the political existence of the Dominicans, is a descendant of African blood in both lines. His mother is dead; she was a slave to his father."

portance to Samana, so much so as may hereafter cause his government to covet its possession." [54]

From the American point of view the situation in the Caribbean was seriously involved. In accordance with the Monroe Doctrine it was the desire of the American Government constantly to diminish European control and steadily to magnify American influence in that region. The European idea of a balance of power had never been entertained by American statesmen, and the fundamental concept of " America before all " found a ready spokesman in the person of Green. During the first week in October, 1849 he had a long interview with Manuel Del Monte, the Dominican Minister of Foreign Relations, and lost no time in stressing the dangers of European protection. Only a cursory glance at the backward condition of European possessions in the West Indies should be convincing proof of the utter failure of European imperialism.

During his frequent conversations with the Minister of Foreign Relations, Green made no attempt to portray the evident advantages of American protection; he would let the warm fancy of the Minister fill in the picture as he wished. And it must have been a pleasant vista that rose before Del Monte's eyes, for he promptly inquired whether it would be possible for the United States to " take them under its protection, or what they would prefer, annex them." [55]

Green was hoist on his own petard. His ardent denunciation of European intrigues had led the Foreign Minister to suspect that the American Government was ready to proclaim a protectorate over the Dominican Republic. Weary of European indecision, the Dominican Government was now ready to accept annexation to the United States, but Green had to shatter this hope by confessing that he had no instructions that contemplated such a contingency. [56] He softened the blow, however,

[54] Green to Clayton, September 27, 1849, *Secret Service*, MS. Dept. of State. In a letter of August 27, 1849, Green wrote to Clayton that it was his impression that " both England and France desire above all things to get possession of Samana; and that this Government will not hesitate to grant it for a term of years or in perpetuity to whichever will negotiate and guaranty a Treaty of peace with Hayti." *Ibid*.

[55] Green to Clayton, October 6, 1849, *ibid*.

[56] *Ibid*.

by stating that under certain circumstances he was empowered to extend recognition to the Dominican Republic. Encouraged by this new gesture of friendship, and hoping that the American Government had sent new instructions, the Minister of Foreign Relations, on January 24, 1850, addressed a note to Mr. Green in which American intervention was again requested.

For a second time Green was forced to reply that he had no instructions that would warrant any promise of protection or intervention.[57] But the Dominican Government refused to abandon hope of American aid, and on February 18, 1850 President Baez sought the counsel of Mr. Green. The Haitian Emperor, Faustin, was making dire threats against the Dominican Republic. Could the American Government be relied upon to teach this belligerent black a much needed lesson in the blessings of peace? But Green could only repeat his familiar formula about the lack of specific instructions to cover such a case, whereupon the Dominican Government, on February 22, 1850, addressed identical notes to the representatives of the United States, France, and England, requesting joint intervention and mediation. The matter thus became an international affair, and for the next two years these three powers exerted pressure upon the Emperor of Haiti in favor of a conciliatory policy towards the Dominican Republic.[58]

[57] Green to Del Monte, January 24, 1850, *Secret Service*, MS. Dept. of State.
[58] On the general question of mediation by the three powers between Haiti and the Dominican Republic, see John Bassett Moore, *Digest of International Law* (8 vols., Wash., 1906), VI, 509-514; Mary Treudley, " The United States and Santo Domingo," in *The Journal of Race Development*, VII (1916), 236 ff.; F. L. Paxson, "A Tripartite Intervention in Hayti," in *University of Colorado Studies*, I, 323-330; B. C. Clark, *Remarks upon the United States Intervention in Hayti*, pp. 4 ff.

CHAPTER V

BLACK MAJESTY LAUGHS AT DIPLOMACY

From a close study of the records in the British Foreign Office it would appear that Great Britain took the lead in trying to effect peace between Haiti and the Dominican Republic. In the latter part of the year 1848 Thomas R. Ussher, the British consul at Port-au-Prince, frequently warned Lord Palmerston, the British Foreign Secretary, of the belligerent attitude of the Haitian Emperor, Faustin, with reference to the Dominican Republic. The Haitian Government had steadily refused to recognize the independence of the Dominican Republic and was contemplating a formidable invasion that was designed to restore Haitian control over the whole island of Santo Domingo. Palmerston distinctly deprecated this warlike policy and he repeatedly instructed Ussher to offer mediation to the contending parties. Thus, as early as December 13, 1848, we find him instructing Ussher to dissuade the Emperor " from his projected Invasion of the Dominican Territory."

On January 23, 1849, Ussher wrote to Palmerston to describe the reaction of the Haitian Government to his note of protest. General Dufrêne, the Haitian Foreign Secretary, appeared " thunderstruck " when he was informed of Palmerston's instructions, and he assured Ussher that

Her Majesty's Government must be imperfectly informed respecting the question, and the peculiar position of the President, who, he said, dared not, even were he so inclined, to recognize the independence of the Dominicans, after having sworn to maintain the Integrity of the Territory. President Soulouque having expressed a desire to see me, I waited upon him and repeated to him verbally the views of Her Majesty's Government, their anxious desire to avert a sanguinary war, and their offer to mediate. . . . He assured me that he would endeavour to effect his object without bloodshed if possible, and appeared more confident of success than ever. . . . I then, according to Your Lordship's desire, suggested to him the probability of the Dominicans receiving assistance from Europe, which might turn the scale against him. He smiled and said that he had already been apprised of such a project, and added that nothing would serve his cause more effectually than the landing of Foreign troops in Hayti, as, in such a case, the Nation would rise to a man to support him.[1]

With reference to the projected invasion of the Dominican Republic, Ussher reported that the Emperor did not speak of any "immediate intentions" of carrying out such a plan, and the prevailing opinion in Haiti was that he would "defer it sine die." But in the event that the Emperor did actually launch such an invasion of neighboring territory, Ussher had little faith in any "Foreign mediation." He was of the impression, however, that there was

greater confidence felt in the British Government; but in this matter I entertain great doubts of our being able to prevail upon the Haytian Government to abandon their long cherished desire to unite under one Flag, as formerly, the entire Island of St. Domingo.[2]

On January 16, 1849, after reading Ussher's despatch of November 28, 1848, Palmerston again repeated these pacific counsels. He was to omit no opportunity to urge the Emperor of Haiti to come to

a friendly understanding with the Dominicans instead of waging against them a War, which, from difference of Race and Language and opinions would become a war of extermination, and would soon attract the attention, and might possibly engage the sympathies of other Powers. You will add that H. M. Govt. would feel great pleasure if it should be in their power to assist in bringing about a good understanding between the People of the two portions of the Island.[3]

But despite the intransigent attitude of the Emperor Faustin, the warning words of Palmerston seemed to have some effect upon the dusky potentate, for on May 30, 1849 Ussher was able to report assurance that there would be no attack upon the

---

[1] Ussher to Palmerston, January 23, 1849, F. O. 35/36.
[2] Ibid.
[3] Palmerston to Ussher, January 16, 1849, ibid. It is interesting to note that in the early part of this correspondence between Ussher and Palmerston the Emperor Faustin is usually referred to by the title of "President."

Dominican Republic in the near future.[4] The Emperor, however, still cherished feelings of sharp hostility against the
Dominicans, and Ussher was unable to persuade him to come to

an amicable arrangement with his neighbors. He appears determined
to listen to no arrangement which is not based on their return to their
allegiance. It is however probable that there will be a long suspension
of hostilities.[5]

At the same time that Palmerston was endeavoring to arrange
a peaceful settlement of Dominican difficulties through the
efforts of Consul Ussher, he did not fail to draft similar instructions for the direction of Robert H. Schomburgk, the
British consul at Santo Domingo City. On March 28, 1849
Schomburgk wrote to Palmerston to request instructions relative to the situation in the Dominican Republic. First, he
desired to know what attitude he should take with reference
to the establishment of a French protectorate over the Dominican Republic. In this case, Palmerston instructed him " to
remain passive " until he received " further Instructions." It
would be expedient, however, for Schomburgk to " shew to
the Dominicans that it is more for their interest and advantage
to remain independent; or even to come to some arrangement
with the Haytians . . . than to become annexed to the Territory
of any European Power." Schomburgk had next inquired
whether, in the event of a Haitian invasion of the Dominican
Republic, it would be proper for him to " plead with the Commander of the Haytian Forces for a cessation of Hostilities."
In answer to this queston, Palmerston assured him that such
a plea would be " quite proper." Finally, Palmerston instructed Schomburgk to offer British mediation whenever any
opportunity arose.[6]

[4] In 1930 the distinguished Haitian publicist, Abel-Nicolas Léger, brought
out a valuable *Histoire diplomatique d'Haiti* which treats in detail the relations
between Haiti and the Dominican Republic during the fifties. It also gives
considerable space to the attempts of foreign powers to secure Faustin's recognition of Dominican independence. For a contemporary estimate of Faustin see
Gustave d'Alaux (Maxime Raybaud), *L'Empereur Soulouque et son empire*
(Paris, 1856).
[5] Ussher to Palmerston, May 30, 1849, F. O. 35/36.
[6] Palmerston to Schomburgk, June 8, 1849, F. O. 23/2.

In a second instruction of this same date, June 8, 1849, Palmerston discussed the question of the extension of a British protectorate over the Dominican Republic. In a despatch of April 10, 1849, Schomburgk had stated that a " Majority of the Members of the Government " desired to place the republic under the protection of Great Britain, and the British consul was anxious to ascertain Lord Palmerston's views in this regard. In reply, Palmerston informed Schomburgk that Her Majesty's Government

would not be disposed to engage in the complicated Responsibilities which would attach to a compliance with this Request of the Dominicans to be placed under the Protectorship of Great Britain. In fact it would seem that the real meaning of the application is that Great Britain should send military assistance to enable the Dominicans to defend themselves against the Haitians: But however much Her Majesty's Govt. may wish that the manly Efforts of the Dominicans to maintain their Independence may be attended with Success, yet no British Interest of sufficient Magnitude is involved in the Issue of the Contest between them and the Haitians to justify Her M's Govt. in incurring the Expenditure of British Money, and the Loss of British Life which might attend the active Interference of Great Britain in the Contest between the two Republicks.[7]

While the British Government did not wish to assume the responsibilities of a protectorate over the Dominican Republic, it was none the less active in trying to promote peace on the island of Santo Domingo. When Palmerston received word

[7] Palmerston to Schomburgk, June 8, 1849, F. O. 23/2. On this same day, June 8, 1849, Lord Palmerston sent the following instruction to Lord Normandy, the British Ambassador at Paris: " I have the honor to instruct Your Excellency to inform the French Government that while the Fate of War between the Haitians and the Dominicans was still uncertain, warmest applications were made to the British Consul at St. Domingo by many Persons of Influence in the Republic for British Assistance, and that the Dominican Republic might be taken under the formal Protectorship of Great Britain. Sir Robert Schomburgk, well knowing the Opinions and Policy of Her Majesty's Government on such Matters, at once explained to the Parties who had made such Communications to him, that the British Government had no desire to acquire any Footing or Authority in the Territory of the Dominican Republic, and that on the contrary it was the Wish of Her Majesty's Government that the Dominican Republic should continue a separate and entirely independent State." F. O. 27/836, No. 268.

from Ussher relative to the refusal of the Emperor Faustin to agree to an amicable arrangement with the Dominicans, he immediately repeated to the British consul at Port-au-Prince his former instruction " to omit no opportunity of urging the President to take that Course." [8]   And this is the burden of Palmerston's instructions throughout the year 1849 and during the early months of 1850. Thus, on March 12, 1850 we find the Foreign Secretary writing to Acting-Consul Wyke, at Port-au-Prince, to " continue to use every Argument to induce the Emperor to abstain from a renewed attack upon the Dominican Republic." [9]   It was inevitable, therefore, that the British Government should look with approval upon any favorable manifestations on the part of the United States in regard to joint mediation between Haiti and the Dominican Republic. And this manifestation was soon to come.

When Green was sent to the Dominican Republic in June, 1849, he was not limited to negotiations with that country but was also empowered to visit Port-au-Prince and discuss with the Haitian Government the question of long pending claims. He was informed that the American Government had for many years refused to recognize the black government in Haiti, and that there was no present intention

materially to depart from this policy. As the interests of our citizens resorting thither, however, require more efficient protection than can be bestowed by the unrecognized commercial agents of the United States in Hayti, it is hoped that some compromise may be effected with that government, by means of which, without incurring any obligation to receive a diplomatic agent or Consul from them, we might obtain the substantial benefits of a full recognition of that government.

After discussing this question of partial recognition, Secretary Clayton proceeded to raise the closely related topic of American claims against Haiti. Most of these claims had been

long pending and are of undoubted merit. The aggrieved parties, however, can never hope for redress without a resort to force so long as this government may deem it expedient to adhere to the punctilio in

---

[8] Palmerston to Ussher, July 21, 1849, F. O. 35/36.
[9] Palmerston to Wyke, March 12, 1850, F. O. 35/38.

regard to recognizing that of Hayti, which has hitherto been paramount in our councils. It is believed, however, that the Haytian Government would be satisfied with a partial recognition and that this might conduce to the adjustment and payment of the claims adverted to. Without therefore, in the outset allowing it to be known that you are an agent of this government, you will sound the Haytien authorities upon this subject. Ask, if the United States were to send an agent duly empowered to negotiate upon the subject of the claims of their citizens against the Haytien Government, whether that government would receive him respectfully and would treat with him. If you should get a satisfactory answer to this question, you may inform the Minister for Foreign Affairs that you have been appointed and authorized for that purpose.[10]

On February 16, 1850, Secretary Clayton sent new instructions to Green with reference both to the Dominican Republic and to Haiti. In regard to Haiti, Green was to proceed to Port-au-Prince and press the matter of American claims against the Haitian Government. In case the Emperor Faustin should refuse to give adequate consideration to these claims, Green was then

to intimate to the Haitian authorities that this government will not view with indifference any further incursions on their part into the territories of the Dominican Republic for warlike or predatory purposes. You will endeavor to bring your correspondence to a speedy close in order that you may embark for the United States in the same vessel of war which will take you to Port au Prince.[11]

It is apparent that these instructions of February 16, 1850 were decidedly more threatening than those of June 13, 1849. Clayton was fast losing patience with the Haitian Government for its failure to make some provision for the payment of American claims.[12] If the Emperor Faustin would only cease his preparations for war against the Dominican Republic he

---

[10] Clayton to Green, June 13, 1849, *Special Missions*, vol. 1, MS. Dept. of State.

[11] Clayton to Green, February 16, 1850, *ibid.*

[12] Bulwer to Palmerston, March 2, 1850, F. O. 5/512. It should also be noted that the American Government had a just cause for complaint against the Haitian tariff, which discriminated against American goods. See George Usher to Clayton, *Port-au-Prince, Consular Desp., 1850-1857*, MS. Dept. of State.

would have ample revenues for the satisfaction of all these obligations. Perhaps joint mediation or intervention in the threatened struggle between Haiti and the Dominican Republic would be the best means of instructing the black emperor in the principles of international law! With this end in view, on March 1, 1850 Clayton had a conversation with Sir Henry Bulwer, the British Minister at Washington, during the course of which he discussed the state of affairs in the island of Santo Domingo. He assured Bulwer that the American Government had " no intention to take the Dominicans under their protection," but he added that the wars between the Haitians and Dominicans were " bloody and cruel " and that the white people in the United States " felt for the white people engaged in these struggles." Then Clayton made a most important suggestion; one that marked his readiness to act in concert with European powers even in the disposition of problems that pertained to the American Hemisphere. He avowed to Bulwer that with reference to the difficulties between Haiti and the Dominican Republic

he should be very happy if the United States, Great Britain, and France, could be brought to act unitedly together for the purpose of procuring a permanent cessation of hostilities between the two races.[18]

During the interval that elapsed between Clayton's suggestion and the reply of the British Foreign Secretary, the American Secretary of State and the British Minister gave extended consideration to the situation in Santo Domingo, and Bulwer reported to Lord Palmerston the substance of some of these conversations. With reference to the mission of Green to Santo Domingo, Clayton informed Bulwer that the American Government had

various claims against the latter, and that Mr. Green had been ordered to present himself in a vessel of war at the seat of the Haitian Government and there to demand the immediate settlement of the claims in question. If these claims were settled Mr. Clayton said that then the American Government had nothing more to observe. In the opposite case, however, he was charged to inform the Government of

[18] Bulwer to Palmerston, March 2, 1850, F. O. 5/512.

Hayti that the American Government would not tolerate its squandering the money away in war which ought to applied to its creditors.[14]

While Sir Henry Bulwer saw "nothing in Clayton's remarks" that might lead him to believe that the American Government was "going into any hostilities against Hayti," yet he could not help thinking that

if Great Britain and France have the intention of interfering in the quarrel of the Haytians and Dominicans in conjunction with the United States it would be well to do so before the United States had any separate cause of quarrel with Hayti.

Lord Palmerston was entirely agreeable to Clayton's suggestion of March 1, and on May 11, 1850 Sir Henry Bulwer wrote to the American Secretary of State in order to assure him of the "willingness" of both the British and the French Government to co-operate with the American Government " for the purpose of arresting the conflict between the different races in St. Domingo." To the British Government it seemed that the

best course to pursue in order to effect the said purpose is to instruct the Representatives of England, France and the United States at Haiti to make a joint and concurrent representation to the Haitian Government in order to induce them to consent to a Treaty of peace and friendship with the Dominican Republic.[15]

Clayton answered this note by informing Sir Henry that the diplomatic correspondence relative to the Dominican difficulties would be submitted to the United States Senate as soon as Green returned from his special mission. There would also be sent to the Senate the nomination of a chargé d'affaires to the Dominican Republic. If this nomination should be confirmed by the Senate, then the President would be ready to proceed in unison with France and England.[16]

[14] Bulwer to Palmerston, April 29, 1850, F. O. 5/512.

[15] Bulwer to Clayton, May 11, 1850, *British Legation, Notes from*, vol. 27, MS. Dept. of State. It is important to note that in his instruction to Lord Normandy, at Paris, June 8, 1849, Lord Palmerston announced that " Her Majesty's Government would be ready to co-operate with the Government of France in the Employment of good offices for the Purpose of inducing the Haitians to desist from further attacks upon the Dominicans." F. O. 27/836, No. 268.

[16] Clayton to Bulwer, May 20, 1850, *Great Britain, Notes to*, vol. 7, MS. Dept. of State.

The British Government, feeling that Clayton would soon act with reference to this nomination, sent instructions to Pro-Consul Wyke, at Port-au-Prince, to place himself " immediately in communication with the Representatives" of France and the United States, and to use his "best endeavours in conjunction with them to put an end to the conflict between the Republics of Haiti and San Domingo." [17]

In the meantime Secretary of State Clayton was apparently desirous of securing legislative approval of the despatch of a special agent to the island of Santo Domingo with instructions that would threaten war against the Haitian Government if it persisted in ignoring American claims. On July 3, 1850 Isaac Holmes, of South Carolina, introduced in the House of Representatives a resolution directing the Committee on Foreign Affairs to " inquire into, and report upon, the expediency of placing at the disposal of the President so much of the naval force of the United States as may be necessary to enforce the payment of the just claims of citizens of the United States against Hayti." The resolution was objected to and was not received.[18]

Five days later Senator Foote, of Mississippi, submitted a similar resolution directing the Committee on Foreign Relations to

inquire into the expediency of appointing a special agent or commissioner of the United States to reside near the Government of the Dominican Republic; and also as to the expediency of placing at the disposal of the President a competent naval force for the purpose of coercing the payment of just claims of citizens of the United States against Hayti.[19]

In the Senate there was a discussion relative to the passage of such a resolution, and Daniel Webster raised a question as to its expediency. Such a resolution opened " a very broad question relating to the expediency and propriety of enforcing the payment of private debts by public force." He had no objection to the appointment of a special agent to the Domini-

[17] Palmerston to Wyke, June 13, 1850, F. O. 35/38.
[18] Cong. Globe, 31 Cong., 1 sess., p. 1331.
[19] Ibid., p. 1329.

can Republic, but he did have his doubts about any action that would " put an armed force at the disposition of the President to compel the performance of stipulations entered into with American citizens." He would prefer that the resolution " lie over " until the following day.[20]

On July 9, 1850 President Taylor died, and John M. Clayton promptly submitted his resignation as Secretary of State. This turn of events had an immediate effect upon the efforts of the United States, France, and Great Britain to effect joint mediation between Haiti and the Dominican Republic. Clayton had evidently been preparing the way for speedy and decisive action on the part of the American Government, and it would seem that there was a definite connection between his desires in that regard and the introduction of the resolutions of Mr. Holmes and Mr. Foote. Webster, it will be remembered, was in favor of moving with distinct deliberation in the matter of coercing the Haitian Government, and when he succeeded Clayton as Secretary of State, on July 22, 1850, it was patent that he would not be hurried into taking any action.

Meanwhile, the British and French consuls at Port-au-Prince had received their instructions to act jointly with the American representative for the purpose of restraining the warlike activities of the Emperor Faustin. In the first part of May, 1850 they requested Green to co-operate with them in putting pressure upon the Haitian Government, but the American agent refused to participate in any such joint action and instead, on May 8, 1850, addressed a note to the Duke de Tiburon in which he strongly protested against any continuance of hostilities against the Dominican Republic. He informed the Haitian Government that the United States had a

direct interest in the termination of hostilities; various citizens of the United States have large claims against Hayti, many of which are of long standing. The Government of Hayti is not now able, if disposed, to pay the full amount justly due, and each new military expedition by exhausting its resources diminishes its security for some ultimate and tardy reparation to the American claimants. . . . The Government

[20] *Ibid.*

of the United States has therefore instructed me to make known to the Haytian authorities its desire for the pacification of the Island, and that it will not view with indifference any further incursions from this part into the Territories of the Dominican Republic.[21]

But if Green was loath to act in conjunction with the French and British representatives at Port-au-Prince in the matter of a joint note to the Emperor Faustin protesting against any renewal of hostilities against the Dominican Republic, such was not the case with the American Commercial Agent at Port-au-Prince, George Usher. On June 16, 1850 Usher received a note from Jonathan Elliot, the American Commercial Agent at Santo Domingo City, requesting him to present a sealed protest to Faustin against any further hostilities with the Dominican Republic.[22] Before taking any action in regard to this protest, Usher consulted with the consuls of Great Britain and France and discovered that they had received similar notes of protest from the British and French representatives in Santo Domingo City. After taking the whole question under careful consideration, it was finally decided not to present these notes of protest from the British, French, and American representatives in Santo Domingo City, but instead to present a joint note of protest signed only by the representatives of these three powers at Port-au-Prince. On June 18 Messrs. Wyke and Raybaud, the British and French consuls, and Usher, the American Commercial Agent, signed a joint note requesting the Emperor to consent to an immediate armistice:

The undersigned hasten to inform the Emperor that their Govern-

[21] Green to the Duke de Tiburon, May 8, 1850, *British Legation, Notes from*, vol. 27, MS. Dept. of State. With respect to the submission of Green's note to the Duke de Tiburon, George Usher wrote to Secretary Clayton on May 13, 1850 as follows: " Immediately before leaving, Mr. Green informed this Government of the disposition of the Government of the U. States in relation to the contentions now existing between the East and West parts of this Island. The effect that this information has had on the Emperor and his advisors has not yet appeared. . . . This timely visit of an American fleet has produced most beneficial effects by showing to these people that our Government will protect its citizens and their property." *Port-au-Prince, Consular Desp., 1850-1857*, MS. Dept. of State.

[22] The text of Elliot's note of protest is contained in the despatch from Usher to Secretary Clayton of June 28, 1850, *ibid.*

ments wish that he may renounce all intentions of the invasion of the part of the Island heretofore belonging to Spain which has constituted itself into a separate state. That, acknowledging the act which has been for a long time accomplished, His Majesty will determine to conclude a treaty of peace and friendship with the Dominican Republic.[23]

In the face of this united pressure, the Haitian Government gave way and agreed to a truce which was to last until September 30. In granting this concession, however, the Haitian Minister of Foreign Affairs made it very clear that Haiti did not consent to any recognition of the independence of the Dominican Republic.[24]

The readiness displayed by the American Commercial Agent at Port-au-Prince to co-operate with the French and British consuls in exerting pressure upon the Emperor Faustin must have been pleasing to the British Minister at Washington, Sir Henry Bulwer. It did not, however, keep him from expressing his surprise that Green, the special agent of the Department of State, had refused to take any part in this co-operative policy. During one of his frequent conversations with Clayton, the American Secretary of State, Sir Henry asked

how it was that his Agent, Mr. Green, should have interfered alone to prevent the Government of Haiti from pursuing hostilities against the Dominican Government, after he [Mr. Clayton] had invited the Governments of England and France to co-operate with that of the United States for this purpose?

Clayton replied that Green had been acting upon instructions that " he had received previous to the triple engagement." He further informed Sir Henry that Green had been instructed to warn the Haitian Government that the United States would

---

[23] The text of this joint note of June 18, 1850 is contained in the despatch of Usher, the American Commercial Agent, to Secretary Clayton on June 28, 1850, *Port-au-Prince, Consular Desp., 1850-1857*, MS. Dept. of State. In this same despatch Usher explains as follows why he signed the joint note of June 18: " I felt reluctant to take any active interest in this matter, but the cause of humanity prevailed. And the dread of American power, now entertained by these people, seemed to render it necessary, to insure success of so desirable an object, that the name of the United States should appear in the paper."

[24] Abel-Nicolas Léger, *Histoire diplomatique d'Haiti*, pp. 276-277.

not "view with indifference any further incursions" from Haiti into the Dominican Republic, especially when these incursions cost large sums of money that could be better spent in paying the claims of American citizens. Indeed, said Clayton, the Haitians had gone from bad to worse, for now they had acquired the habit of seizing American ships "and selling them in order to obtain money to carry on their war of extermination against the neighboring state."[25]

Although Clayton's explanations to Sir Henry Bulwer were reassuring, yet the British Minister thought it best to send an official letter to the new Secretary of State, Daniel Webster, in order to give to his protest against Green's actions a formal character. Therefore, on August 17, 1850, he sent to the Department of State a note in which he described the want of co-operation in the matter of mediation between Haiti and the Dominican Republic. He then urged that instructions be sent to the United States agent in Santo Domingo directing him to act in concert with the British and French agents.[26]

On the following day, Bulwer wrote to Palmerston that Webster "seemed to think that the joint mediation was the plan to pursue," and that he would soon be able to give the matter the consideration it deserved. With the Secretary of State committed to the plan of joint mediation, the next thing to do was to put pressure upon the agents of the three mediating powers in Santo Domingo in order to compel them to act in unison. From a review of their conduct it appeared to Sir Henry that these agents had distinctly indicated a reluctance

[25] Bulwer to Palmerston, August 6, 1850, F. O. 5/514. Ussher, the British consul at Port-au-Prince, indignantly denied this charge of Clayton with reference to Haitian seizures of American ships, and he assured Lord Palmerston that there was "not the slightest foundation" for such an accusation. The Haitian Government, he was certain, had "not seized and sold any American Vessel, nor the Vessel of any other Nation to enable them to carry on the Dominican War or for any other purpose." Ussher to Palmerston, October 22, 1850, F. O. 35/38, No. 36. From the records in the Department of State, it would appear that Clayton was entirely justified in his accusations. Just before he sent his instructions of June 13, 1849 to Green, the Haitian Government had seized the American schooner, *Samuel Noyes*, on the flimsiest of pretexts. See *Special Missions*, vol. 1, MS. Dept. of State.

[26] Bulwer to Webster, August 17, 1850, *British Legation, Notes from*, vol. 27, MS. Dept. of State.

" to act together from an idea very possibly that they thus sacrifice a portion of their individual importance." Therefore, it seemed expedient for both the French and British Governments to send their Ministers in Washington full powers

to come to some understanding with Mr. Webster as to the manner in which the Agents of the three Countries should interpose, and the result of this common understanding should be transmitted to the several Agents in question with orders that they attend thereto.[27]

On August 20, 1850, Webster wrote to Bulwer to explain that the reason why Mr. Green had refused co-operation with the British and French agents was the lack of specific instructions to that effect. The British note suggesting joint mediation had been dated May 11, 1850, and thus it had been impossible for the American Government to send instructions to Green in time for joint mediation in the first part of May.[28]

But this explanation did not entirely satisfy Sir Henry Bulwer, who complained to Palmerston that

Mr. Webster seems to lose sight of one fact, namely, that the note of mine to which he refers as dated the 11th of May, and which, consequently, could not have been known to Mr. Green when he wrote to the Government of Hayti on May the 8th, was, as appears on the face of it, the consequence of a suggestion made by Mr. Clayton himself some time previously; of this suggestion Mr. Green need not have been ignorant, but he seems to have been so. The difference, however, between the expressed wishes of the United States' Government and the conduct of its agent having received an explanation, ceases to be of importance; and it appears likely from Mr. Webster's present note that this Government will, ere long, be prepared to act efficiently with the Governments of Great Britain and France for the purpose of bringing about a peace between Haiti and the Dominican republic.[29]

On September 23, 1850, Bulwer wrote to Palmerston to advise him that he had recently informed Webster that both

[27] Bulwer to Palmerston, August 18, 1850, F. O. 5/514.
[28] Webster to Bulwer, August 20, 1850, *British Legation, Notes to*, vol. 7, MS. Dept. of State. See also Webster to Bois-le-Comte, August 24, 1850, *France, Notes to*, vol. 6, MS. Dept. of State. Ernest André Olivier Sain de Bois-le-Comte was the French Minister at Washington.
[29] Bulwer to Palmerston, August 24, 1850, F. O. 5/514.

the Governments of Great Britain and France were anxious that the proposed plan for joint mediation between Haiti and the Dominican Republic be " at once carried into effect." In reply, Webster had stated that

he would name an agent to St. Domingo directly the Senate had adjourned; and that if M. Bois-le-Comte and myself could then suggest to him any plan of instructions that we would be disposed to give to the English and French agents, he would be disposed to give the same to the agent of the United States.[30]

On this same day, Bulwer wrote a second despatch to Palmerston in which he discussed in detail the dangers of the imperialistic spirit of Young America. Already, on August 6, 1850, Bulwer had asked Clayton if he " knew anything of Green's project of establishing an American colony in the neighbourhood of the great harbour of Samana ? " Clayton, however, immediately assured him that " Mr. Green had received no sort of instructions whatsoever on this subject, and that whatever he had done with respect to it he had done without authority." [31]

It seems very likely that Bulwer received further intimations that Green, the American agent, had far-reaching plans for securing control of the island of Santo Domingo, for on September 23, 1850 he expressed his fears as to American policy. Palmerston had discounted these fears with reference to Haiti because he greatly doubted that the American Union would ever admit a state " which like Hayti contains a population chiefly composed of free blacks." Bulwer agreed with Palmerston in that regard, but he believed that this race prejudice failed to furnish " any security for Hayti." The events which would probably occur

with respect to Hayti, if the attention of these people were once directed in that quarter, are likely to be something similar to those which occurred in other cases of the same kind, and one especially which bears to it some sort of analogy. A few American adventurers settled in Texas. They soon raised the banner of Texian independence.

[30] Bulwer to Palmerston, September 23, 1850, F. O. 5/515.
[31] Bulwer to Palmerston, August 6, 1850, F. O. 5/514.

They wrested the Country of which they had become the occupants, from Mexican rule. Then succeeded the annexation of Texas to the United States.

Therefore, if Haiti should become an object of serious attention for any set of adventurers,

as furnishing the means of plunder, or as offering an easy gratification to the constant ardour which prevails throughout this land for action and acquisition, such adventurers will look out for some pretext under cover of which their worst motives may be concealed, and their objects followed up. To assist Whites against blacks would be a pretext of this kind, and excite a feeling something like that which was formerly excited by the instance of affording assistance to Americans against Mexicans.

There was already a sort of

vague idea which has been shadowed out in Pamphlets, appears at times in different portions of the public Press, and in the conversations of members of Congress, that the Island in which Hayti and St. Domingo are situated, must become in some way or other attached to this Empire. But the idea has as yet no fixed or concentrated point.[32]

As the autumn of 1850 approached, Bulwer became convinced that it would probably be necessary for the Governments of Great Britain, France, and the United States to send instructions to their respective agents in the island of Santo Domingo which would distinctly contemplate the employment of force in order to compel the Haitian Government to accept mediation. In a letter to Webster, October 14, 1850, Bulwer set forth his new attitude relative to the settlement of Dominican difficulties. Some months previous it had seemed to him

that it would be sufficient for the three Governments simply to urge upon the Government of Hayti, the advisability of adopting a truce of ten years, if it could not be prevailed upon to consent to the establishment of peace upon more permanent foundations; and I imagined that such advice given conjointly by the three Governments of the United States, France and Great Britain, would at once have been attended to. By information which I have received since the period to which I refer, it would appear that the Government of Hayti had

[32] Bulwer to Palmerston, September 23, 1850, F. O. 5/515.

already rejected the counsels I then suggested; and having this morning had an interview with M. Bois-le-Comte, I am now able to make to you the inclosed proposal which is in conformity with instructions which reached me from Her Majesty's Government by the last packet, and similar to one which Her Majesty's Ambassador at Paris has been instructed to make to the Govt. of France.

The enclosed proposal for joint action in mediating between Haiti and the Dominican Republic read as follows:

The undersigned has the honour to propose, as a means of stopping the barbarous war which now threatens the island, divided under the Governments of Hayti and Saint Domingo, that the consuls of the United States, France and Great Britain, in that Island, should be instructed to demand jointly from the Emperor of Hayti, a formal agreement to a truce of ten years; and the Emperor should be informed that in case he does not consent to this, the three powers will oppose by force any renewal of hostilities on his part against the Dominicans. The Undersigned has the honour to add that it appears to Viscount Palmerston, that a truce of such duration would practically have the same effect as a definitive Peace, while it would not involve that formal acknowledgment of the independence of the Dominican Republic which it seems that the Emperor Soulouque is unwilling to consent to.[33]

After waiting some weeks for an answer which never came, Sir Henry Bulwer decided to go to Boston and see Webster personally. On November 15, 1850, he wrote to Palmerston and recounted the substance of several of his conversations with the American Secretary of State. By way of explaining the reason for not having promptly answered Bulwer's note of October 14, Webster stated that he had been

very unwell and occupied with other affairs, but that he had obtained from the President permission to name an accredited agent from the United States to the Dominican Government, and that this would be done directly he returned to Washington, and that he should then endeavour to make the instructions given to the said agent as conformable as possible to those which Mr. Bois-le-Comte and myself might deem ourselves authorized to send to the agents of France and

[33] Bulwer to Webster, October 14, 1850, enclosed in the despatch of Bulwer to Palmerston, December 8, 1850, F. O. 5/515.

Great Britain at Hayti and St. Domingo, but that he did not know whether he could pledge the United States Government to adopt any measures of coercion towards the Emperor should he not attend to the friendly remonstrances. Mr. Webster added that he would think over this point and see me about it in Washington.[34]

Three days later, Bulwer wrote to Palmerston and expressed his dissatisfaction at the "long delays" of the American Government in taking any effective action with reference to joint mediation. The only consolation he could extract from the situation was his conviction that

the United States Government cannot now take any more active part in this question than the other Governments of France and England; which from the manner in which Mr. Clayton first spoke to me on this subject might, I think, have been the case had we refused to co-operate with him on his proposal to effect a peace.[35]

On December 2, 1850 President Fillmore sent his first annual message to Congress, and in one paragraph he directly referred to the Dominican imbroglio and the necessity for some speedy adjustment:

The relations between those parts of the island of St. Domingo which were formerly colonies of Spain and France, respectively, are still in an unsettled condition. The proximity of that island to the United States and the delicate questions involved in the existing controversy there render it desirable that it should be permanently and speedily adjusted. The interests of humanity and of general commerce also demand this, and as intimations of the same sentiment have been received from other governments, it is hoped that some plan may soon be devised to effect the object in a manner likely to give general satisfaction. The Government of the United States will not fail, by the exercise of all proper friendly offices, to do all in its power to put an end to the destructive war which has raged between the different parts of the island and to secure to them both the benefits of peace and commerce.[36]

A few days after the President's message had been sent to

[34] Bulwer to Palmerston, November 15, 1850, F. O. 5/515.
[35] Bulwer to Palmerston, November 18, 1850, *Secret and Confidential*, F. O. 5/515.
[36] J. D. Richardson, *Messages and Papers of the Presidents*, V, 83.

Congress, Bulwer wrote a long despatch to Palmerston in which he discussed the implications of that executive communication. He also gave a résumé of his latest conversations with Webster, who had recently promised him that

in the course of the ensuing week an agent will be named by the United States Government to St. Domingo and sent forthwith. He added that the forms of this Government were more popular than those of France and Great Britain, and that consequently he could not speak in the President's name, nor the President himself speak of employing coercive measures, which indicate more or less a state of war, and which could only be ordered or commenced by Congress; but that he should be willing to go as far with us as the forms of the United States Government allow, and finally I fixed that he should receive M. Bois-le-Comte and myself the day after tomorrow at twelve o'clock, in order that we might come if possible to some definite understanding on this question.[37]

Bulwer, however, far from satisfied with the procrastinating policy of the United States, on December 8 sent a second despatch to Palmerston, of a confidential nature, in the course of which he expressed his misgivings as to some ulterior motives on the part of the American Government. It was difficult for him to account for the

singular conduct of the United States Government with respect to its joint interference with Great Britain and France in the quarrel between the Haytian and Dominican Governments; Mr. Clayton having first suggested such joint interference, and neither himself nor Mr. Webster having since taken the first step towards it, viz., that of naming an accredited agent to those parts. One mode however of accounting for this inconsistency would be to suppose that General Taylor entertained, at one time, the idea of interfering himself in favour of the Dominicans; and that in order to lessen the effect that such interference might produce upon European Powers, the late Secretary of State, had thrown out, carelessly as it were, and without any intention that it should be formally taken up, the proposition of a general intervention. It is to be remembered that at the period to which I allude, there was an American naval force cruising off the Haytian coast. If the foregoing supposition be true, it will in some

[37] Bulwer to Palmerston, December 8, 1850, F. O. 5/515.

degree explain that sort of procrastination and incertitude which has followed the prompt acquiescence of Great Britain and France in Mr. Clayton's suggestion.[38]

But notwithstanding these suspicions, Sir Henry Bulwer now thought that the " more recent delays" on the part of the American Government were somewhat due to " Mr. Webster's absence and illness," and he expressed the opinion that the Secretary of State would be " inclined to act fairly, as far as he has the power, in conformity with the views expressed by his predecessor and himself."

On December 10, 1850 Bulwer and Bois-le-Comte had an interview with Webster relative to joint mediation, and Bulwer reported to Palmerston that it was, " upon the whole," satisfactory.[39] Some ten days later, Bulwer wrote to Webster and enclosed a copy of the letter of instructions to the British consul at Port-au-Prince with reference to mediation between Haiti and the Dominican Republic. According to the terms of this letter, the main purpose of joint mediation was to secure

a settled peace upon a fair and durable basis, or a lengthened truce upon reasonable conditions.   Whichever of these is most feasible you may consider the best; I do not therefore enter into any discussion as to their relative merits.[40]

In order to attain such an objective, it was requisite that the agents of the three mediating powers work in complete harmony " so that no person within the governments of Hayti or

[38] Bulwer to Palmerston, December 8, 1850, *Secret and Confidential*, F. O. 5/515. On January 27, 1851 Bulwer wrote to Palmerston a despatch which confirmed these early suspicions of Clayton. He stated that " Mr. Calderon informed me the other day that Mr. Clayton had told him at one time that the United States's Government did intend to interfere in the quarrel between the Haytians and Dominicans in favor of the latter, and put down completely the black population of Hayti, in which enterprise he said that he should meet with no opposition from France or England. . . . It would appear from all this that the late Secretary of State . . . had further plans than he disclosed and that if Her Majesty's Government had not responded to his invitation . . . he would have lent the assistance of the United States alone to St. Domingo." F. O. 5/527.

[39] Bulwer to Palmerston, December 16, 1850, F. O. 5/515.

[40] Bulwer to Webster, December 21, 1850, *British Legation, Notes from*, vol. 27, MS. Dept. of State.

St. Domingo should imagine there is an English policy, or an American policy, or a French policy to be pursued in this matter."

In the event that the Emperor of Haiti refused to adopt the suggestions of the three agents, they were then to threaten him with the " determination " of the mediating powers to have their terms accepted " in the main," or at least to prevent any recurrence of the war between Haiti and the Dominican Republic " until other terms have been substituted by the mediating powers in lieu thereof."

It was important, however, for the British agent to understand that the measures of coercion which Her Majesty's Government and that of France were willing to adopt were for the present confined " to a blockade of the Ports of Hayti such as Port au Prince, Jacmel, Aux Cayes, Gonaives etc.," but if it should appear that a blockade would not be effective in securing the objective of the mediating powers, then the menace of further force should be made in such vague terms as would not commit Her Majesty's Government to employ force until it should be known what species of force would be necessary.[41]

Even after Webster had received Bulwer's letter of December 21, it was nearly a month before a new special agent was chosen to visit Santo Domingo. This agent was Robert M. Walsh, whose despatches to the Department of State have a rhythm and sparkle unusual in official documents.[42] Finally, on January 18, 1851, Webster completed the instructions to Walsh, and they clearly reveal his attempt to follow as closely as possible the instructions of Sir Henry Bulwer to the British agent in Haiti. Immediately upon arriving at Port-au-Prince, Walsh was to

seek a conference with Mr. Usher and the consul of France upon the subject of your mission, and particularly with a view of inducing the

[41] Bulwer to Ussher, December 21, 1850, enclosed in Bulwer's despatch to Palmerston, December 30, 1850, F. O. 5/515.

[42] In a despatch to Palmerston of January 13, 1851, Bulwer states that Webster had confided to him that he " had appointed Mr. Slocum, a Gentleman of great respectability and well acquainted with the Spanish language, to proceed to St. Domingo." F. O. 5/527.

Emperor Soulouque to consent to a lengthened truce, or a permanent peace with the Dominicans. As in co-operating for this end the three governments are actuated by philanthropic views, to which they believe any material interests which all or either may have in question are quite subordinate, you will endeavor, in all your communications with your colleagues, and with either the Dominican or the Haytian governments, to keep your mind free from any prejudice resulting from color or forms of government.

After Walsh had held "free and full conferences" with his colleagues and had "ascertained the reciprocal claims of the parties to the war," if the Emperor Soulouque still insisted upon maintaining a belligerent attitude the American agent was to join with the agents of the other two parties in a solemn protest against such imperial obstinacy. If this remonstrance should prove unavailing, then Walsh was to inform the Emperor that he would give immediate notice to his government, in order that the President, with the concurrence of Congress, might adopt such measures, in co-operation with the Governments of England and France, as may cause the intervention of the three powers to be respected.[43]

Walsh reached Port-au-Prince on February 2, 1851, and his troubles began at once. His first night in the Haitian capital was

one map of misery in recollection, for, in addition to the flies and the fleas and the mosquitoes and bugs, with a huge black spider sprawling along the wall, that, hushed in grim repose, awaited its coming prey, there was a perpetual crowing of cocks, as if the demons wanted, like the Western imitation of Chanticleer, to take the sun in and make him rise before his time, intermingled with the perpetual roar of amorous donkeys, whose sentimental strains in the streets were the very reverse of those of Philomela warbling 'mid the leaves.[44]

On February 4 Walsh was received by an extremely eloquent Haitian nobleman, who was no less a personage than the Duke de Tiburon. Walsh was agreeably surprised by the

[43] Webster to Walsh, January 18, 1851, *Special Missions*, vol. 1, MS. Dept. of State. Also, *Sen. Ex. Doc.* No. 113, 32 Cong., 1 sess., pp. 3-4.

[44] Robert M. Walsh, "My Mission to San Domingo," *Lippincott's Magazine*, VII (1871), 294-295.

Minister's "appearance and manners, and cultivated intelligence," but the Emperor Faustin was "stout and short, and very black, with an unpleasant expression, and a carriage that does not grace a throne." Moreover, he was "ignorant in the extreme," though of late he had made some small progress in the mysteries of reading and writing.[45]

It seemed obvious to Walsh that the "logic of force" was the "only kind" that the Haitian Government was disposed to respect. Thus after a lengthy conversation with the British and French agents at Port-au-Prince, the American agent had an interview with the Duke de Tiburon during which he spoke his mind with crisp decisiveness. The Duke should understand that in international law the principle was fully established that the

actual possession of independence for a reasonable time, entitles a nation to be acknowledged as sovereign. This is a principle which the American world especially has consecrated, and must ever uphold. It is the sole foundation, in fact, of the independence of Hayti herself, and to attack it in any way is to strike at the very root of her own institutions. The best interests of the empire demand the recognition of Dominican independence, which would give it a useful neighbor instead of a turbulent province or a determined foe. . . . In every point of view, therefore, the government of the United States entertained the conviction that it was incumbent upon the emperor to recognize the independence of Saint Domingo, and I earnestly hoped that his Majesty would consent to do so without further delay.[46]

While Walsh was delivering this little speech to the Duke de Tiburon, he accompanied it with harsh words and with harsh looks, for "you were not thought in earnest unless you looked a little fierce." [47] But the Duke refused to be frightened. Instead of acquiescing in the American demands, he entered into an elaborate account of the geography and past history of the island, and after having completely exhausted the patience of the American agent with irrelevant details, he concluded with the argument that

[45] Walsh to Webster, February 5, 1851, *Secret Service*, MS. Dept. of State.
[46] Walsh to Webster, February 14, 1851, *ibid.*
[47] R. M. Walsh, *op. cit.*, p. 297.

nature had designed the whole island to be under one and the same government; and in the second place, the Constitution of 1816 had proclaimed it to be one and indivisible, and this Constitution the Emperor was obliged to maintain.

Although it was difficult to reply " gravely to such logic as this," Walsh made a brave attempt to hold his temper and continue the conversation. He endeavored to prove to the dubious Duke that the

designs of nature, even when unmistakable, were not necessarily good titles in law, and that the proclamation, as a fact, of what did not exist, by no means called it into being; for the constitution of which the minister spoke, was promulgated long before any junction of the different parts of the island had been effected.[48]

The Duke, however, remained unconvinced by such cogent reasoning, and it was necessary to try the effects of concerted pressure. Therefore, on February 11, 1851, Walsh, Raybaud, the Consul-General of France, and Ussher, the consul of Great Britain at Port-au-Prince, sent a joint note in which they requested a

categorical answer to the following proposition: *A definitive treaty of peace,* or a truce of ten years, between the empire of Hayti and the Dominican Republic.[49]

After a week had passed, the agents of the three mediating powers called upon the Duke de Tiburon in order to ascertain the nature of the reply to their note of February 11. Once more the loquacious and plausible Duke pleaded that constitutional limitations rendered it impossible for the Emperor to consent to the independence of the Dominican Republic. To the importunate agents this argument seemed to border on the ludicrous, and Walsh thought that

it required some command of countenance upon the part of his grace of Tiburon, to insist upon the incompetency of the emperor to conclude a peace, knowing as he well does that the latter can do and does do whatever he pleases, and that scarcely a day goes by without his vio-

[48] Walsh to Webster, February 14, 1851, *Secret Service,* MS. Dept. of State.
[49] This note is enclosed in Walsh's despatch to Webster of February 14, 1851.

lating the sacred instrument invoked, for the nonce, to prevent him from performing an act to which he is averse.[50]

The Duke, however, was a stickler for adherence to constitutional forms, and he assured the three agents that no " positive answer " could be made to their joint note until the last of March, for the Senate would have to be specially convened in order to consider this question. Indeed, he could not even promise with any certainty that both the Senate and the Emperor could settle so thorny a problem to the satisfaction of the three powers.

While matters stood in this twilight zone of indecision, the ulterior motives of the Haitian Government were revealed to the three agents by the indiscreet admissions of the private secretary to the Emperor. It was the old, old case of " *veritas in vino.*" The private secretary had freely indulged in certain liquid delights on board a French sloop-of-war lying in the harbor of Port-au-Prince, and, having grown unwise with his wine, he

very candidly informed the officers that his master would let the plenipotentiaries, as he styled them, amuse themselves for a while with speeches and notes, but would eventually get rid of them without committing himself in the least.[51]

On February 21, 1851, the Haitian Minister of Foreign Relations addressed to the three agents a note in which he advised them of the appointment of four commissioners who were to conduct all negotiations relative to a cessation of hostilities against the Dominican Republic.[52] Three days later, a second note was sent to the agents in which formal inquiry was made with reference to " the motives of the three powers in wishing to secure the tranquillity of the island by a treaty of peace, or at least by a truce of ten years." [53]

On March 4, 1851, the three agents signed a note which

[50] Walsh to Webster, March 3, 1851, *Secret Service*, MS. Dept. of State.
[51] *Ibid.*
[52] L. Dufrêne to Walsh, Raybaud, and Ussher, February 21, 1851, enclosed in despatch of Walsh to Webster, March 3, 1851, *ibid.*
[53] Dufrêne to Walsh, Raybaud, and Ussher, February 24, 1851, *Secret Service*, MS. Dept. of State.

strongly defended the right of the Dominican Republic to be regarded as an independent state and sharply attacked the alleged right of the Haitian Government to compel the Dominicans to return to their former allegiance.[54] On March 6, the agents of the three powers met the four Haitian commissioners and presented the note of March 4. After this ceremony of presentation, arguments were presented by each group with special regard to peace with the Dominican Republic. The Haitians, being anxious to reinforce their arguments with an impressive personal appearance, had fitted themselves in " gorgeous toggery, with embroidered collars above their ears and polished leather, *splendidior vitro*, on their feet, when the heat was such that one wanted, like Sydney Smith, to take off one's flesh and sit on one's bones."

These arguments, however, were in such

ludicrous harmony with the toilettes that the old weeping philosopher himself would have felt tempted to cry on the wrong side of his mouth.   A marvellous discussion it was, to be sure, leading precisely to what the imperial 'possum desired—viz., nothing at all.   We had but a single interview with our embroidered and polished friends, that being quite sufficient to show that, in Shelley's phrase, they were ' pinnacled deep in the intense inane,' like the stars with whose glittering counterfeits their breasts were so studded.[55]

On March 24, 1851, Walsh sent a note to the Haitian Minister of Foreign Relations in which he stressed the necessity of a speedy answer to the note of the agents of the three mediating powers requesting a cessation of hostilities. He also warned the Haitian Government

for the last time, in the most earnest and emphatic manner, against any attack upon the Dominican republic.[56]

In explanation of the tone of menace contained in this note of March 24, Walsh remarked that the only chance to bring about mediation between Haiti and the Dominican Republic

---

[54] Enclosed in Walsh's despatch to Webster, March 16, 1851, *ibid.*

[55] R. M. Walsh, *op. cit.*, p. 297.

[56] Walsh to the Minister of Foreign Relations, March 24, 1851, enclosed in Walsh's despatch to Webster, March 31, 1851, *Secret Service*, MS. Dept. of State.

was through the adoption of a policy of "intimidation."
Moreover, his colleagues, before his arrival, had already

menaced coercive action, and if I had allowed it to be suspected that
there was not a perfect agreement between their governments and that
of the United States in regard to the ulterior measures, all hope of a
favorable result would have been crushed.[57]

On April 10, 1851, Walsh wrote a most colorful despatch
to Webster which is filled with details concerning the comic
opera aspects of Haitian rule. Port-au-Prince was filled with the
martial display of "nearly five hundred Generals," while
myriads of mere colonels thronged the streets. These distinguished personages had been summoned to the capital for the
double purpose of ascertaining their views relative to the war
with the Dominican Republic, and of presenting them with
the decorations that had just arrived from the shops of Paris.
So numerous were these badges of distinction that " a Haytian
without a decoration is very rare as well as a very unhappy
individual, at least among the inhabitants of the towns. In
the country, however, a banana is generally regarded with more
interest and admiration than even the grand cross of St. Faustin." In fact, the whole social fabric in Haiti was an absurd
caricature of civilization, and nothing saved the Haitians from
being infinitely ridiculous but the fact that their fearful
atrocities made them often supremely disgusting.[58]
On April 19, 1851, the Haitian Government sent its formal
answer to the note of the agents of the three mediating powers
relative to arranging with the Dominican Government a
" definitive treaty of peace, or a truce of ten years." First of
all, it would be impossible for the Government of Haiti to

[57] Walsh to Webster, March 31, 1851, *loc. cit.* When Bulwer heard in February, 1851 that Raybaud and Ussher had already in December, 1850 " obtained
by means of coercion" an arrangement between Haiti and the Dominican Republic without waiting for the arrival of the American agent, he was distinctly
disturbed and informed Palmerston that he considered Ussher's conduct as
" very extraordinary." He was considerably relieved when the Haitian Government failed to answer this joint note of the British and French agents and thus
made it possible for the three agents to act in concert in February, 1851. Bulwer
to Palmerston, February 24, 1851, F. O. 5/527.
[58] Walsh to Webster, April 10, 1851, *Secret Service*, MS. Dept. of State.

negotiate a definitive treaty of peace with the Dominican Republic for the excellent reason that such a procedure would violate articles 1, 4, and 116 of the Haitian constitution. A truce of ten years would be equivalent to a treaty of peace and therefore would also be unconstitutional. However, in order that the Emperor Faustin might clearly indicate his passion for peace, the Haitian Government was willing to continue the existing truce between Haiti and the Dominican Republic. And in addition to this pacific gesture, the Emperor was further desirous of settling all points of difference by the appointment of deputies empowered to negotiate a satisfactory arrangement with deputies appointed by the Dominican Government.[59] These direct negotiations could only proceed on the basis of an explicit acknowledgment on the part of the Dominican Government of the sovereignty of the Emperor Faustin over the whole island.

It was evident that the agents of the mediating powers could never accept such a settlement of Dominican difficulties. But inasmuch as the tenor of the Haitian note was pacific, and since there appeared an " evident desire " on the part of that government for peace, the French and British consuls did not feel justified in renewing official menaces " similar to that of the 21st of December last." They were confirmed in this attitude when Ussher obtained from the Emperor Faustin the most " positive assurances " that he had no intention of renewing hostilities against the Dominican Republic.[60]

Walsh believed that the Emperor was " pretty well satisfied of the impossibility of ever getting possession of the ' eastern part of the island,' " and he thought that there was little likelihood of any new invasion. Therefore, Walsh did consider that the joint efforts of the mediating powers had been productive of some good. But he was convinced that the only way to compel the Emperor to sign a formal treaty of peace was to send an adequate force with definite coercive powers. Until such action was taken, the Emperor would continue to

[59] Dufrêne to the allied agents, April 19, 1851, *ibid.*

[60] Ussher to Bulwer, April 25, 1851, enclosed in Bulwer's despatch to Palmerston, May 21, 1851, F. O. 5/528.

assume all the airs of a hero setting at defiance the world in arms, to the infinite admiration of the mass of his subjects, and will have a plausible excuse for keeping up the immense army in which he beholds his glory and his strength.[61]

Walsh was deeply disappointed that the French and British agents did not resort to actual coercive measures against the Emperor of Haiti, and he was never able to

throw off a suspicion that Soulouque had secret intimations that the former giant [France] at least, had no intention to resort to *voies de fait*. He would hardly have been so obstinate and so valorous if he had really believed in the menaced blow, especially as the only man-of-war in the harbor during the negotiations was the little steamer which was to play yacht for the Frenchman, and which did not look very mischievous to the naked eye.[62]

On May 1, 1851 Walsh, considering that he had fulfilled his instructions to the best of his ability, decided to leave Haiti for the Dominican Republic.[63] When he arrived at Santo Domingo City he had an interview with President Baez, who greatly regretted that the agents of the three mediating powers had not been able to secure a definitive peace between Haiti and the Dominican Republic. Perhaps this lack of executive appreciation caused a certain distaste in Walsh's mind, for he reported that his interview at the presidential palace failed to imbue him with the feeling

which, according to Carlyle, puts even the haughtiest featherheads on their marrow-bones when in the presence of a true kind of men. . . .

---

[61] Walsh to Webster, April 23, 1851, *Secret Service*, MS. Dept. of State.

[62] R. M. Walsh, *op. cit.*, p. 307.

[63] In a despatch to Daniel Webster, Secretary of State, the American Commercial Agent at Port-au-Prince, George Usher, on May 4, 1851 comments as follows upon the results of the Walsh mission: " I have the honor to inform you, that Mr. Walsh, Special Agent, left this port on the first Inst. for St. Domingo City without, as he informed me, having succeeded in the object of his mission here. . . . As I remarked in my despatch No. 15, no object of moment to which these people are opposed, can be accomplished without the presence of a Naval force to give visible importance to the agent employed to effect it." Usher did admit, however, that American commerce " with the Island is now prosperous; our vessels and citizens enjoying generally all the privileges and advantages accorded to those of other nations." *Port-au-Prince, Consular Desp., 1850-1857,* MS. Dept. of State.

No halo was reflected upon his brow from his luminousness within, any more than from his yellowness without, for he is a bright mulatto, a sort of *guinea* nigger, whose skin might have been the result of a goldbeater's skill.[64]

After Walsh had paid a short visit to the Dominican Repub-lic, both he and Raybaud, the French agent, sailed for the United States. Shortly after they arrived, Bulwer sought them out and had conversations with them. He found Raybaud to be a man of " some ability," but possessed of " a sort of na-tional hatred against the Haytians and all his opinions are evidently coloured by the sentiment." [65] Upon Walsh he placed a higher estimate. The American agent was

decidedly an able man, and though imbued with the feelings towards the Negro Race more or less natural to a Virginian, looks at matters more cooly. They both represent the country to be in a miserable state, and consider that the Emperor would at once yield to any request of the three Powers, if he did not consider that by delays he should be able to evade their demands.[66]

While Bulwer was trying to formulate some new plan to solve the Dominican difficulties, he received instructions from Palmerston, dated May 29 and May 30, 1851, which not only invited the American Government to join in a proposal to the Emperor Faustin to " give twelve months notice to the three mediating Powers before commencing hostilities against the Dominicans," but also requested American co-operation with Great Britain and France " in the measures which the latter Powers agreed to adopt against the Emperor Soulouque in case he should attack the Dominicans." [67]

Although Bulwer promised at once to discuss these pro-posals with Webster, he frankly expressed his doubts as to the advantages to be gained thereby. To his mind it seemed essential to secure either " a definite peace, or a long truce,"

[64] R. M. Walsh, *op. cit.*, p. 307.

[65] In 1856, Raybaud brought out an interesting volume entitled *L'Empereur Soulouque* in which he discussed the political, social, religious, and economic conditions in Haiti.

[66] Bulwer to Palmerston, July 7, 1851, *Secret and Confidential*, F. O. 5/529.

[67] Bulwer to Palmerston, June 30, 1851, F. O. 5/529.

and he believed that a " truce of merely short duration . . .
would still leave the end which is most desirable to attain,
unaccomplished."

On June 22, 1851, Bulwer addressed two notes to Webster
in which he informed the Secretary of State of the desire of
the British Government for American co-operation in the matter of a joint note to the Emperor Soulouque requesting a
notice of twelve months to the three powers before commencing
hostilities against the Dominican Republic. He also proposed
to the American Government a joint policy with reference to
adopting coercive measures against the Haitian Emperor in
case he resumed offensive operations against the Dominicans.[68]

After a lapse of nearly two weeks, Webster replied that with
reference to the proposal concerning the notice of twelve months
to be given by the Emperor of Haiti before commencing hostilities against the Dominican Republic, the President of the
United States had received such a suggestion " favorably," and
that in this regard a co-operative policy would be resumed by
the United States just as soon as they should have " a suitable
agent for the purpose at Port au Prince." With reference to
coercive measures against the Haitians, the President " entirely
concurred " in the " expediency of the measures which it
proposes." However, the

naval commanders of the United States could not be ordered to
co-operate with those of Great Britain and France for such a purpose,
without the authority of Congress. For this authority the President
will apply at its next session, if meanwhile an accommodation should
not take place between the contending parties in St. Domingo.[69]

Meanwhile, Bulwer began to grow increasingly anxious
about the designs of American filibusters against Haiti. He
had learned that in the vicinity of New York there were some
2,500 adventurers who were ready to go to the Dominican
Republic as colonists, but who were really military " auxili-
aries." Therefore, he lost no time in writing, on July 2, 1851,

[68] Bulwer to Webster, June 22, 1851, enclosed in despatch of Bulwer to
Palmerston, July 7, 1851, F. O. 5/529.
[69] Webster to Bulwer, July 5, 1851, *ibid.*

to the British consul to advise him to warn the Haitian Emperor in unmistakable terms that " a war on his part is in reality out of the question; and if he cannot make war is it not desirable that he should make peace? " [70]

The Emperor, however, responded by showing further symptoms of belligerency. He disdained any answer to the joint note of the British and French consuls with reference to a notice of twelve months before resuming hostilities against the Dominican Republic, but in order to show his peaceful intentions he sent one of his many generals into Dominican territory to proclaim a truce. This individual was perhaps merely maladroit, for he announced the tidings of peace

in so belligerent a way that the inhabitants fell upon him and drove him back. On his return to the capital the emperor took hold of him, and, to prove his pacific propensities and good faith, had him summarily shot.[71]

Furthermore, on July 14, 1851 the Haitian Minister of Foreign Affairs warmly assured the French and British consuls that the Emperor was decidedly averse to war. The consuls, however, thinking that he protested entirely too much to be trusted, on July 24 addressed the Emperor a note which again warned him that the

inevitable consequence of any hostile demonstration of aggressive action against the Dominicans would be the immediate blockade of all the ports of the Empire.[72]

[70] Bulwer to Ussher, July 2, 1851, enclosed in Bulwer to Palmerston, July 16, 1851, F. O. 5/529. With reference to the danger from filibuster attacks against Haiti, Bulwer enclosed a clipping from the New York *Herald* of July, 1851 which heartily endorsed aggressive measures: " The condition of Dominica is such as to give ample encouragement to every emigrant. The government have already offered to every settler a handsome bounty in the shape of land, and should any one be called into active service, he would be liberally rewarded for his aid in protecting the country from an invasion. . . . The cause should not be allowed to rest under discussion. Action is required."

[71] R. M. Walsh, *op. cit.*, p. 305.

[72] Thos. R. Ussher and E. Wiet to Soulouque, July 24, 1851, enclosed in a note from Crampton to William Hunter, *British Legation, Notes from*, vol. 28, MS. Dept. of State. One of the reasons why Faustin was not disposed to take these British and French remonstrances seriously was that he had high hopes of

But the Emperor was inclined to make light of this note of menace, and preparations for an invasion of the Dominican Republic were continued. Whereupon the French and British consuls, on August 9, requested the commanders of the French and British war vessels at Port-au-Prince to

proceed to Cape Haytien for the purpose of checking by their presence the movements of the Emperor, as well as to prevent, if necessary, the Haytian Fleet from conveying troops and stores to the Eastern part of the Island.[73]

After the English fleet reached Cape Haitien, a severe storm drove one of the Haitian vessels upon a reef. It was finally pulled from this precarious position by the British ship *Devastation*, but not before a cargo of munitions of war had to be removed in order to lighten the ship. It was thus very clear that the Haitian Government was ready for war. When Ussher was informed of these facts he called to see the Emperor at Cape Haitien, and upon his arrival he was chided by the Minister of Foreign Relations for the " threatening note " of July 24. When he replied that the discovery of munitions of war on board the Haitian ship had clearly indicated warlike intentions on the part of the Emperor, the Minister of Foreign Relations tried to explain that these were only such stores " as were required for the fleet." Ussher refused to believe that such a large store was necessary for a mere peace footing, and he informed the Minister that

a speedy change in British policy. A Haitian agent, Seguy Villevaleix, was sent to London for the express purpose of persuading Palmerston to reverse his position. In a letter to Palmerston of July 28, 1851, Villevaleix endeavors to point out how essential it is for the whole island of Santo Domingo to be under one government. For Haiti this unity of administration is " *une question de vie ou de mort.*" He then requested the good offices of England for the purpose of arranging a conference between Haitian and Dominican commissioners who would meet in order to arrange for the reincorporation of the Dominican Republic into the Haitian state.

Lord Palmerston, however, bluntly rejected this suggestion, and informed Villevaleix that the British Government was not disposed to permit " *la race noire d'Haiti de subjuguer le peuple dominicain d'origine espagnole.*" After this rejoinder the mission of Villevaleix came to an abrupt end. See Abel-Nicolas Léger, *Histoire diplomatique d'Haiti*, pp. 282 ff.

[73] Ussher to Palmerston, August 25, 1851, F. O. 35/41.

the Squadron now assembled would not leave the Haytian Waters until the Government had entered into some engagement with the three Powers which would satisfy them that the War should not be renewed between the two States.[74]

Up to this time Ussher had tried in every way to give the Emperor the benefit of the doubt, but he could no longer close his eyes

to the fact that the Emperor has been trifling with us and trying to deceive me. I am credibly informed that he fully intended on this occasion to invade the Dominican Territory, notwithstanding his pacific assurances, and that he has only been stopped by the opportune arrival of our Ships.

It was apparent to the British Government that the Emperor would respect only a continued threat of intervention on the part of the three mediating powers. Thus, in order to preserve unity of action, John F. Crampton, the British Minister at Washington, addressed a note to William Hunter, the acting Secretary of State, in which he requested that instructions be sent to American naval commanders in the Caribbean to co-operate as far as possible with the representatives of England and France.

The American Government was entirely willing to adopt this suggestion, and on September 4, 1851 Crampton was informed that the President had issued orders to the commanding officer of the Home Squadron to co-operate with the officers of Great Britain and France

in any measures short of actual coercion consistent with the views of this Government as conveyed in the instructions from this Department to its special agent in St. Domingo, and subsequently communicated to the British and French legations in this city.[75]

This order was really the last positive step taken by the American Government in carrying out the policy of joint mediation which had been inaugurated by Secretary Clayton. It

[74] *Ibid.*

[75] W. S. Derrick to Crampton, September 4, 1851, *Great Britain, Notes to,* vol. 7, MS. Dept. of State.

was assumed that the truce that had been effected between Haiti and the Dominican Republic would lead to eventual amicable relations between these hitherto warring neighbors, and President Fillmore, in his message to Congress of December 2, 1851, expressed the hope that the present peaceful relations rested " upon a durable basis." [76]

[76] J. D. Richardson, *Messages and Papers of the Presidents*, V, 122. It is somewhat remarkable that Whig Secretaries of State like Clayton and Webster were willing to enter into concert with European powers to propose mediation to an American nation like Haiti. This fact clearly indicated that the Whig Administration was not much concerned about any close adherence to the principles of the Monroe Doctrine. In December, 1845, President Polk had sent a message to Congress strongly reaffirming these principles and condemning the " purely advisory policy which France and England had pursued in Texas; he would not concede any right of interference whatsoever." Dexter Perkins, *The Monroe Doctrine, 1826-1867*, p. 90.

CHAPTER VI

A CONSULAR TEMPEST IN A DOMINICAN TEAPOT

After the policy of joint mediation had been abandoned in 1852, it was not long before suspicions of French designs in the Caribbean were noised about, and, according to some rumors, the French Government was about to secure a cession of Samaná Bay from the Dominican Republic in return for support against a projected invasion from Haiti.[1] When the American Secretary of State, Edward Everett, inquired of the French Minister at Washington whether this story was true, M. de Sartiges replied that it "might" be founded "in fact." This cryptic answer was quite alarming to Everett, who deeply deplored any disturbance of the balance of power in the Caribbean. Immediately after this conversation with M. de Sartiges, Everett wrote to Rives, the American Minister at Paris, and expressed the opposition of the American Government to any French scheme to acquire Samaná Bay. He also took occasion to elaborate upon the unselfish and disinterested attitude the American Government had always displayed with reference to the Caribbean:

The policy pursued by the United States in this respect has been wholly disinterested. It has been, no doubt, in our power, to obtain

---

[1] As a sample of the rumors concerning French intrigue in the Caribbean, the following despatch from the American Commercial Agent at Port-au-Prince is illustrative: "About three weeks since a French War Steamer arrived from St. Domingo City, having on board the French Consul and a commissioner from the Dominican Republic. . . . The object of the Dominican Commissioner was to ascertain the views of the Emperor and if possible arrange the differences existing between the two parts of the Island. . . . Tomorrow, without having been successful, . . . he will leave in the same steamer for St. Domingo City, and will be accompanied by the French Consul who told me last evening at the Palace, that he was instructed by his Government to conclude a treaty of Commerce between France and the Dominicans. The spacious Bay of Samana, in the Northeast part of this Island, may get fully under the control of France." Usher to Webster, April 25, 1852, *Port-au-Prince, Consular Desp.,* MS. Dept. of State.

a permanent foothold in Dominica; and we have as much need of a naval station at Samana as any European power could possibly have. It has, however, been the steady rule of our policy to avoid, as far as possible, all disturbance of the existing political relations of the West Indies.[2]

Some three weeks later, on January 3, 1853, Everett wrote to John P. Kennedy, the Secretary of the Navy, and requested that he

direct some vessel belonging to the home Squadron to visit the Eastern end of the island and look into the ports of St. Domingo with a view to communicate with our Consul there, and gather such information as he may possess and then pass round to the bay of Samana.[3]

On the following day, Kennedy wrote to Everett to inform him that Commander James T. Gerry would proceed at once to Santo Domingo " for the purpose of obtaining the information desired by the President."[4] There is no record, however, of any report submitted by Gerry in this regard. But on January 25, 1853 Everett received from Rives, the American Minister at Paris, a long despatch that must have banished any fears of aggression by France. On January 5 Rives had an interview with the Minister of Foreign Affairs, who assured him that the rumored occupation of Samaná Bay by a French squadron was nothing more than " a fable [*une histoire*] from beginning to end." Moreover, the French Minister of the Marine had informed the Minister of Foreign Affairs that

not a single French vessel of war was at Samana or in its neighborhood at the time of the reported occupation, and that no orders or instructions, certainly had issued from his Department authorizing such a proceeding.[5]

[2] Everett to Rives, December 17, 1852, *France, Inst.*, vol. 15, MS. Dept. of State.

[3] Everett to Kennedy, January 3, 1853, *Domestic Letters*, vol. 14, MS. Dept. of State.

[4] Kennedy to Everett, January 4, 1853, *Misc. Letters, January-February, 1853*, MS. Dept. of State.

[5] Rives to Everett, January 6, 1853, *France, Desp.*, vol. 34, MS. Dept. of State. On January 13, 1853 Rives wrote to Everett in a somewhat troubled spirit concerning possible French designs upon Samaná Bay, and these doubts about French policy in Santo Domingo are again expressed in his despatch to Everett on January 20, 1853. *Ibid.*

Everett could now retire from the office of Secretary of State, on March 4, 1853, with few apprehensions as to French designs upon Santo Domingo. On the very day, however, that his successor, William L. Marcy, assumed office, the American Commercial Agent at Santo Domingo City, Jonathan Elliot, wrote to the Department of State to sound a new warning against Gallic intrigue. The French Consul-General, Raybaud, was expected to arrive soon in the island, and it was believed that

one of his principal objects is to make a secret Treaty of Alliance with this Government, as it is well known here that they have requested a military force from France, the greater part of which is to be placed at Samana.[6]

Notwithstanding this impending danger, the Commercial Agent was not of the opinion that the situation called for the despatch of any more special agents to Santo Domingo. It was Elliot's view that such representatives as Hogan, Green, and Walsh had done " no good, but to the contrary a great deal of injury to our interests." In order to negotiate successfully with the Dominicans it was " necessary to have a thorough knowledge of them." [7] While a certain modicum of modesty prevented Elliot from proclaiming his own peculiar fitness for the task of dealing with Dominican diplomats, he apparently felt certain that Marcy could read between the lines and recognize evident ability.

On May 3, 1853 he again advised the Secretary of State as to plots that were being hatched on the island, and upon this occasion it was the wily Spaniard who would bear watching. On April 25 a Spanish war-ship had entered the harbor of San Domingo City, and the commander had spent four days in close conference with the Dominican authorities. Although the whole matter had been kept very secret, it was suspected that Spain was endeavouring to effect an alliance with the Dominican Government for the purpose of protecting them against the Haitians, and " more particularly to prevent any

[6] Elliot to the Secretary of State, March 7, 1853, *Santo Domingo, Consular Desp.*, vol. 1, MS. Dept. of State.
[7] *Ibid.*

large emigration to this part of the Island from the United States."

Elliot, however, felt somewhat reassured when President Santana informed him that he intended to " send a mission to Washington to obtain the recognition of this Republic and to make a Treaty." When asked to express his opinion as to the wisdom of such a step, Elliot advised Santana to defer for some months such action, for " the United States Government having recently changed its officers, were very much occupied at the present time." [8]

On November 27, 1853, Elliot sounded another alarm against a French scheme to overthrow President Santana and restore to power former President Baez, who " most cordially hates Americans and all that is American and is purely a Frenchman in his heart." [9] But even before the receipt of this warning missive, Secretary Marcy had decided to send a special agent to the Dominican Republic to report upon conditions. Apparently, he had not been impressed with Elliot's words of warning against the blunders of executive agents upon former occasions. In the first week of November, 1853, he addressed instructions to General William L. Cazneau which directed Cazneau to repair at once to Santo Domingo and investigate " the present condition of the Dominican Republic, particularly in regard to its relations with the Empire of Hayti." It was important for Cazneau to " ascertain the relative strength of the two states in order to form a correct judgment of the probable result of renewed hostilities." Also, did the Dominican Republic have " the ability to sustain itself as an independent State?" Had its independent status been recognized by any European nations? [10]

[8] *Ibid.*, May 3, 1853.

[9] *Ibid.*, November 27, 1853.

[10] Marcy to Cazneau, November 2, 1853, *Special Missions*, vol. 3, MS. Dept. of State. In 1853 R. A. Parrish, Jr., of Philadelphia, submitted to the Department of State a long " memorial " on the " Goldfields of Santo Domingo." He was certain that Santo Domingo was " unquestionably destined to stand foremost amidst all the Gold producing regions of the Globe. Within five days distance of New York, this inestimable formation—easy of access, & easy of acquisition—is at this moment, idly awaiting for its development, the advent of the people of ' the States.' " *Misc. Papers* (unbound), MS. Dept. of State.

Cazneau was a colorful personality who was destined, during the next two decades, to act as a sort of "contact man" between the United States and the Dominican Republic. At the time of his appointment in November, 1853 he had already enjoyed a varied career. Born and educated in Boston, he was, like many other men of Northern birth, attracted by the lure of easy fortunes in land speculations in Texas. After participating in the stirring events leading up to the independence of Texas he settled in Eagle Pass, where, according to his enemies, he began to study the shortest ways to wealth. These detractors would also have us believe that the General soon became so unpopular that he was glad to flee to a more hospitable climate.[11] Later, in some unknown manner, he attracted the attention of William L. Marcy, the American Secretary of State, who came to regard him as the one best fitted to act as special agent to the Dominican Republic. In Santo Domingo Cazneau discovered a virgin field so abundant in promise that he soon decided to make his permanent home in the island.

In his first despatch to Marcy, on January 23, 1854, Cazneau argued strongly for the establishment of closer relations between the United States and the Dominican Republic. None of the American powers had given "this sister republic the just and politic support of a friendly recognition, which leaves it dependent upon the good-will of France and England for even the temporary relief of the existing truce with Hayti." Ignored by the United States, while recognized and protected by Europe, the Dominican Republic had no choice "but to submit to the requirements of European policy."[12]

The recent elevation of General Santana to the presidency of the republic appeared to usher in a new era. The predecessor of General Santana in the presidential office had been Buenaventura Baez, who had made no attempt to "conceal his repugnance to the introduction of American settlers nor his predilections for Europe." Santana, however, was a man of

---

[11] *Report of the U. S. Senate Select Committee on the Memorial of David Hatch, Sen. Report* No. 234, 41 Cong., 2 sess., pp. 22-23, 178-179. Also Sumner Welles, *Naboth's Vineyard*, I, 137 ff.; H. Handelmann, *Geschichte der Insel Hayti* (Kiel, 1860), pp. 185 ff.

[12] Cazneau to Marcy, January 23, 1854, *Special Service*, MS. Dept. of State.

liberal views, a statesman who appreciated the importance of American friendship. Although there still existed in the minds of many Dominicans a vague dread of the " real intentions of the United States," yet these doubts could be dissipated by an active and friendly policy on the part of the American Government. After mature consideration, Cazneau was certain that " the present is a most propitious time for establishing mutually advantageous relations between our own and the Dominican people." [13]

When Cazneau returned to the United States he not only reported to Secretary Marcy with reference to the political considerations that pointed towards closer relations between the United States and the Dominican Republic, but he also stressed the rich natural resources of the island that awaited American development. So warm was his advocacy of American political and economic penetration into the Caribbean that imperialists at once took heart and began to support his program. Although Secretary Marcy was somewhat dubious about the alleged benefits of closer relations between the United States and the Dominican Republic, two other members of President Pierce's Cabinet, Jefferson Davis, the Secretary of War, and James Guthrie, the Secretary of the Treasury, strongly urged the President to take some positive action.[14] As a result of this pressure, Marcy finally decided to send Cazneau back to the Dominican Republic with the draft of a treaty that he was instructed to negotiate. In the instructions controlling this negotiation he was informed that the strongest inducement which would lead the United States to recognize the Government of the Dominican Republic was the

acquirement of the advantages which the United States expect to derive from the possession and control of the tract of country on Samana Bay for the limited purposes mentioned in Article XXVII. . . . It is not proposed that the Territory to be leased be large. A mile square would probably afford all the conveniences which the United States seek to obtain. It is deemed quite important that you should

[13] Cazneau to Marcy, February 12 and July 24, 1854, *ibid.*
[14] William L. Cazneau, *To the American Press: the Dominican Negotiacions* (Santo Domingo, 1870), p. 4. Also D. D. Porter, *op. cit.*, p. 626.

obtain along with the grant of possession of the premises, all the rights of authority and control over it proposed in the article relating to the subject. An essential curtailment of them would render the acquisition of such a place much less valuable—and without authority to protect persons and property there the possession would not be worth having. Such a place in the occupancy of the United States, constantly resorted to by our steamers and other vessels, could not fail to give stability to the Dominican Republic.[15]

In order to further the plans of the Administration, Senator Stephen A. Douglas introduced into the Senate (on May 23, 1854) a resolution requiring the Committee on Foreign Relations to "inquire into the expediency of recognizing the independence of the Republic of Dominica, and of opening diplomatic intercourse with the same." [16]

This resolution aroused the sharp opposition of the anti-slavery leaders in Congress, who believed that recognition would be but a prelude to annexation. Charles Sumner was particularly disturbed over the implications of this move on the part of Senator Douglas, and on June 17, 1854 he wrote to John Bigelow that he had not been out of his seat during the morning sessions of the Senate for fear "that the resolution might be sprung upon us." In the event that it did come before the Senate, Sumner intended to move an amendment by adding " and Haiti." He was certain that Southern antipathy towards the recognition of the black empire would defeat the resolution with such an amendment tacked on.[17]

The Douglas resolution, however, never came up for a vote, and it is extremely doubtful whether it could have secured a majority in its favor. The opposition press, led by the New York *Tribune* and the New York *Evening Post*, was waging a bitter and effective fight against either the recognition of the Dominican Republic or the acquisition of Samaná Bay. When Cazneau arrived in the Dominican Republic in January, 1854, on his first mission, the New York *Evening Post* carried the

---

[15] Marcy to Cazneau, June 17, 1854, *Special Service*, MS. Dept. of State.

[16] *Cong. Globe*, 33 Cong., 1 sess., p. 1280.

[17] John Bigelow, *Retrospections of an Active Life* (2 vols., N. Y., 1909-1910), I, 160.

following paragraph written by John Bigelow, who was then visiting the island of St. Thomas:

Mr. Cazneau the husband of 'Cora Montgomery,' sailed hence recently for the city of St. Domingo, under a commission from Mr. Marcy. His wife, who is already somewhat famous as a filibustera, had preceded him to his post of observation a month or more. What the precise nature of their mission is, he did not know himself when here, his wife having his commission in her possession, but it is inferred from her statements, made in St. Domingo shortly after her arrival, that they are to make arrangements for the annexation of the eastern part of Hayti to the United States. . . . She has not hesitated to assure the people of St. Domingo, that the country would belong to the United States in six months.[18]

On May 24, 1854, the New York *Evening Post* returned to the attack and printed an explanatory item with reference to Mrs. Cazneau, whom it regarded as the moving spirit in the plan to secure Samaná Bay:

It may be well for the public to know something more of this commissioner. It is no other than the redoubtable and immaculate Cora Montgomery, alias Mrs. Storm, formerly editress of the *Sun,* and companion-in-arms of Beach the elder, with whom she visited Cuba and other foreign parts in times gone by. At the close of that engagement, she became a follower of the American army in the Mexican war, where she may have had the good fortune to make the acquaintance of Brigadier-General Pierce, and produce an impression of which this appointment is one of the fruits.

After thus disposing of Mrs. Cazneau, the *Evening Post* on the following day paid its respects to General Cazneau.[19] The General at once replied by charging that the *Evening Post* was

working in concert with Faustin, the negro Emperor of Hayti, for the destruction of the white population of that island. I charge it—in its capacity of organ and co-laborer of the negro party—of murder and desolation in Hayti, with habitually garbling and suppressing important truths, in order to prevent the American people from turning their

[18] February 21, 1854. For other articles of John Bigelow on Haiti, see New York *Evening Post*, July 6, July 12, July 15, September 26, and October 4, 1854.
[19] New York *Evening Post*, May 25, 1854.

attention and sympathy to the noble struggle of the Dominicans for freedom and self-government.[20]

In support of Cazneau's character, Thomas J. Green rushed into print with a statement concerning the General's service in Texas. Mr. Green had served with General Cazneau both in the field and in the Congress of the late Republic of Texas, and knew

that a more bold, honorable, high-minded and energetic man did not serve in her cause. His constituents have given many public testimonials of their appreciation of his talents and integrity. In this all the Texas delegation in Congress—with the exception of one personal enemy—will fully concur, and we can refer with confidence to ex-President Burnet, Lamar and Jones, and to every other gentleman of distinction in the state.

General Cazneau held an honorable commission under the first Presidential government of Texas, and from President Lamar's administration he was our active and efficient Quartermaster-General, up to the disbandment of the army. Subsequently, for nine successive popular elections, he beat all opposition at the capital of the state for Congress, the convention, the legislature, and general of the Western Brigade, and finally retired without a single defeat, with increased popularity.[21]

This strong defence of Cazneau's career in Texas did not convert the editor of the *Evening Post* to a new appreciation of the purity of the General's motives in the Dominican Republic. The policy of opposition to the Administration's Dominican schemes was vigorously continued, and the attack was finally focussed on the supposed desire of the Secretary of State to extend recognition to the Dominican Republic. In an attempt to forestall any such action, the New York *Evening Post* published on September 2, 1854 an extended " genealogy of the political authorities of St. Domingo." This genealogy was particularly effective in showing that the Dominican

[20] *Ibid.*, May 31, 1854.
[21] *Ibid.*, May 31, 1854. In an editorial comment upon Cazneau's letter of May 31, the New York *Evening Post* of the same date (May 31) observes: " Mr. Cazneau knows . . . that in all Dominica, with a population of from seventy-five to a hundred thousand, there are not two hundred and fifty whites, all told, sailors and diplomats included."

leaders were all either negroes or mulattoes, and that the pure white population of the Dominican Republic was almost a negative quantity. It was shrewdly surmised that Southern statesmen would not be quick to extend any privileges to a government based upon negro or mulatto supremacy, especially when this government controlled part of an island in seas adjacent to the Southern states of the American Union.

This genealogy printed in the *Evening Post* is too detailed for reproduction here, but the following excerpts will indicate its character:

Pedro Santana, President of the Republic. His father was an old resident of Hincke, and was a mulatto and slave of Don Miguel de la Cayo.

The Minister Miguel Bartedo; mulatto on his father's side.

The Minister Aba al Fau and his brothers are all mulattoes.

General Antonio Duverger is a mulatto.

General Moreno, black.

General Aranjo, black.

General Juan Rosa, mulatto.

General Bernadino, black.

General Ramon Meya, mulatto, from both lines.

General Pedro Florentino, black.

General Mejias, colored.

General Ramon Vido, mulatto.

General Contrera, African blood, both lines.

General Sandavar, mulatto.[22]

[22] *Ibid.*, September 2, 1854. It has already been indicated, *ante*, p. 79, n. 1, that John Bigelow paid a visit to the island of Santo Domingo during the year 1854. While in Santo Domingo City he learned of Cazneau's mission to secure Samaná Bay. When he also discovered that Mrs. Cazneau was a Roman Catholic, he became convinced that the Papacy was working in concert with Mrs. Cazneau in order to further American imperialism. Many years later, in a letter to his friend Charles Sumner, he confessed to a belief that political Romanism was the motive force that was pushing America into the Caribbean. He thought it would be well worth while to inquire whether the " Catholic Church is not at the bottom of these intrigues for the annexation of St. Domingo to the U. S. Soulouque, the old Emperor of Hayti, had a quarrel with the pope about the right of investiture and about naming black priests, etc., the precise tenor of which I have forgotten, and as a consequence Soulouque was not in favor at Rome. A man by the name of Walsh, son of our former Minister to Paris, and a Catholic, went out there once as a commissioner under Fillmore, and insulted Soulouque by going to court in a sack coat, and in connexion with the repre-

This persistent opposition to the plans of the Administration with reference to securing Samaná Bay, or at least to establishing closer relations with the Dominican Republic, materially helped to mobilize public sentiment in the North against American expansion in the Caribbean. And in addition to this growing hostility at home, the Administration was also going to face even more effective opposition from France, Great Britain, and Spain. With Great Britain, in particular, American relations had become so strained that war might well have been the issue. The " fisheries dispute " that had arisen out of varying interpretations of the Treaty of 1818 had grown so acute that in April, 1854 James Buchanan, the American Minister at London, lived in daily fear that a " collision " would take place between " Her Majesty's Cruisers and our Fishing vessels." Such a collision would " electrify our whole population " and thus produce an open conflict.[23]

Rivalry in Central America was another source of grave misunderstanding. The Clayton-Bulwer Treaty of April, 1850 had merely opened a Pandora's box of mounting difficulties that, during the middle fifties, caused a crisis in Anglo-American relations.[24] Moreover, British public opinion was piqued because of American sympathy for Russia during the Crimean War. The British public has always regarded its antagonists in every war as vicious barbarians who are trying to pull down

sentatives of France and England undertook to bully Soulouque into an abandonment of the war in which he had engaged with St. Domingo. He was succeeded by Cazneau at St. Domingo as the representative of the Church and an anti-Haytian policy, and the latter has proved irrepressible. I can imagine that the Roman church would prefer that the island should be under our control than under that of a refractory Catholic power. I should not wonder if the Romish interest had a great deal to do with the pressure making upon our Government for the annexation of islands in the West Indies." Bigelow to Sumner, February 22, 1871, *Sumner Papers*, MS. Harvard College Library.

[23] Buchanan to Marcy, April 14, 1854, *England, Desp.*, vol. 65, MS. Dept. of State. See also Charles C. Tansill, *The Canadian Reciprocity Treaty of 1854* (Balto., 1922), pp. 39 ff.

[24] Mary W. Williams, *Anglo-American Isthmian Diplomacy* (Wash., 1916); H. B. Learned, " William L. Marcy," in *American Secretaries of State and Their Diplomacy* (10 vols., N. Y., 1927-1929), vol. 6; F. A. Golder, " Russian-American Relations During the Crimean War," *American Historical Review*, XXXI (1925), 462 ff.

the structure of civilization and therefore deserve no consideration from any quarter. Whether against Napoleon, Czar Nicholas, or Kaiser Wilhelm, the charge has been of the same tenor, and America has been sharply condemned because she did not see through British eyes. In 1854, the British viewed the Crimean War as a conflict in which the British people had a large interest. From the viewpoint of the British Liberals, it was a " war to promote progress and free principles." For these reasons they regarded with " embittered feelings the news that ' their cousins on the other side of the Atlantic' sympathize with Russia." [25]

These points of friction were all of a serious nature and might in time lead to open conflict, but in 1854 both Great Britain and France had to strain every resource to cope with Russia in the Crimea. To American imperialists it seemed a most opportune moment for America to push her schemes for aggrandizement. Not only was the Pierce Administration desirous of securing a naval station in the Dominican Republic, but it also cherished the more ambitious design of acquiring the island of Cuba. For several decades American Secretaries of State had formulated schemes for its annexation, but the disinclination of Spain to part with this rich colony, the outspoken opposition of France and Great Britain, and the unfriendly attitude of anti-imperialists in the United States had constituted an impenetrable barrier to American advance in this direction.[26] Imperialism, however, became increasingly popular in the late forties and early fifties, and even some of the important Whigs caught the fever. Thus we find John M. Clayton, the Secretary of State under President Taylor, writing to his Democratic friend, James Buchanan, as follows:

What will you give me to recall Romulus Saunders from Spain? Speak out—do not be bashful. Shall I try to buy Cuba after you have

[25] Buchanan to John W. Forney, December 14, 1854, *The Works of James Buchanan* (ed. by J. B. Moore, 12 vols., Phila., 1908-1911), IX, 284; also Buchanan to Marcy, November 21 and December 15, 1854, *England, Desp.*, vol. 66, MS. Dept. of State.

[26] James M. Callahan, *Cuba and International Relations* (Baltimore, 1899), chaps. 1-10; F. E. Chadwick, *The Relations of the United States and Spain* (N. Y., 1909), chaps. 10-13.

made such a botch of that business? Do you wish like Sancho to have an island? [27]

Clayton was evidently making an effort at badinage, but Buchanan's reply was distinctly serious and reveals his viewpoint:

We must have Cuba. We can't do without Cuba and above all we must not suffer its transfer to Great Britain. We shall acquire it by a coup d'état at some propitious moment which from the present state of Europe may not be far distant.[28]

This was the gospel of "Young America," and, with the inauguration of Franklin Pierce as President, the expansionist desires seemed to have an excellent chance of realization. The principal diplomatic posts abroad "were filled with a view to the manipulation of affairs to secure the purchase of Cuba," [29] and "at no time in American history did the pro-slavery leaders feel themselves more firmly seated." [30] It might well be the "propitious moment" for Buchanan's anticipated "coup d'état." Marcy, the Secretary of State, did not believe that England would take any active steps to prevent the cession of Cuba to the United States. Of the attitude of the French Government, indeed, he was somewhat doubtful,[31] but at any rate both these powers were now engaged in the Crimean War, which for some time would absorb most of their energies.

In this connection it is interesting to note that, some months before the outbreak of the Crimean War, Marcy wrote instructions which must have been based upon the expectation of such a conflict and the consequent inability of France and England to intervene in behalf of Spain. On April 3, 1854 Marcy instructed Soulé, the American Minister at Madrid, to "enter into a convention or treaty for the purchase of Cuba," and, if the Spanish Government was not willing to consider the cession of Cuba, then Soulé was to direct his efforts

---

[27] Clayton to Buchanan, April 14, 1849, *Clayton Papers*, MS. Library of Congress.
[28] Buchanan to Clayton, April 17, 1849, *ibid*.
[29] J. M. Callahan, *op. cit.*, p. 259.
[30] F. E. Chadwick, *op. cit.*, p. 251.
[31] Marcy to Soulé, August 16, 1854, *Spain, Inst.*, vol. 15, MS. Dept. of State.

to the next more desirable object which is to detach that island from the Spanish dominion and from all dependence on any European power.[32]

Soulé's undiplomatic actions in Spain did not advance the plans of the Pierce Administration with regard to Cuba, and when Soulé, in conjunction with John Y. Mason, the American Minister to France, and James Buchanan, the American Minister to England, held a conference in Ostend and at Aix-la-Chapelle during the second and third weeks of October, 1854, this fact increased European suspicion of American policy in the Caribbean. And it is against such a background of uncertainty and hostility that Cazneau's mission to the Dominican Republic in the summer of 1854 must be viewed.

Cazneau arrived in Santo Domingo City on July 17, 1854, and a week later he reported to Secretary Marcy that the

only possible obstacle to the early and complete success of my mission is a vague dread of the real intention of the United States. . . . Europeans here labor incessantly to instill into the Dominicans a belief that their domain will be seized, the native whites set aside, and the blacks enslaved if Americans gain a foothold.[33]

It was apparent that the only possible chance for the success of the Cazneau mission was, first of all, to banish this " vague dread " that many Dominicans entertained towards the " real intentions of the United States." If Cazneau was to secure the consent of the Dominican Government to the cession of Samaná Bay to the United States, he would certainly have to employ to good effect those chief attributes of a skillful diplomatist, " patience and penetration." These excellent qualities Cazneau

---

[32] Marcy to Soulé, April 3, 1854, *Confidential, Spain, Inst.*, vol. 15, MS. Dept. of State. For an informative account of the events leading up to the Ostend Manifesto, see H. B. Learned, " William L. Marcy," in *American Secretaries of State and Their Diplomacy*, VI, 185 ff. On the foreign policy of the Pierce Administration with reference to Cuba, see chapters xlvi, xlviii, and lii in the scholarly and interesting *Life of Franklin Pierce* by Professor Roy F. Nichols (Phila., 1921). With reference to the Ostend Manifesto and the dubious activities of Pierre Soulé, there is a detailed and authoritative volume by Professor Amos A. Ettinger, *The Mission to Spain of Pierre Soulé* (New Haven, 1932).

[33] Cazneau to Marcy, July 24, 1854, *Special Service*, MS. Dept. of State.

had in sufficient measure, but his negotiations were jeopardized from the very start by the rashness of a young captain of the Engineer Corps of the United States Army, who was under orders to survey the Bay of Samaná and select the best site for a naval station. This youthful officer was none other than George Brinton McClellan, who manifested an overwhelming desire for speedy accomplishment that contrasts strangely with the temporizing policy that characterized his record during the American Civil War. Cazneau had advised him that it would be expedient to secure the express consent of the Dominican Government before any surveys should be made of Samaná Bay. McClellan, however, was impatient to begin his duties, and on July 19, 1854, two days after his arrival in Santo Domingo City, he sent a note to Cazneau in which he protested against any delay in making his survey. The flagship *Columbia* was " short of provisions," and inclement weather might be expected at any time. It really mattered very little whether the Dominican Government gave or withheld its consent to the survey. The main thing was to act at once, and, if the Dominican authorities finally extended permission to go ahead with the work, the results of the survey would enable Cazneau to conclude his negotiations

definitely and understandingly: as a matter of course no terms can be agreed upon until the examination has determined what we need. Should the Dominican Govt. eventually refuse to grant the desired privileges, the advantages of our going to Samana at once, with or without permission to make the examination, will naturally suggest themselves to you.[34]

McClellan had served in the Mexican War and had thoroughly learned the efficacy of force in international relations. Force was especially important when dealing with the backward peoples in southern latitudes, and it seemed very natural to McClellan to disregard the feelings of nations too weak to command international respect.[35] Cazneau, lately from Texas,

[34] McClellan to Cazneau, July 19, 1854, *McClellan Papers*, second series, vol. 3, MS. Library of Congress.
[35] On August 27, 1854 and September 30, 1854, McClellan submitted to Jefferson Davis, Secretary of War, two reports relative to his surveys along the

felt much the same way about it, but he had a far better appreciation of all the factors involved in the situation. America would by no means have a free hand in the Caribbean. Both France and England were nervously anxious to prevent American expansion into the West Indies, and they would endeavour in every way to prevent the consummation of American plans. Secrecy was essential to American success, and not only must Dominican sensibilities be courted, but foreign representatives in Santo Domingo must not suspect American desires and, by effective protests, thwart them. In the preceding year, the Secretary of State, Edward Everett, had protested against rumored French designs in Santo Domingo, and had adverted to the necessity of maintaining the status quo in the Caribbean. Foreign nations must still be led to believe that America's attitude was disinterested, and when they were presented with a *fait accompli* it would be difficult for them to alter the new order of things.

As soon as Cazneau received McClellan's note of July 19, he replied in a note of warning. He was well aware of the inconveniences of delay at this time, but an immediate survey of Samaná Bay

> would be wrongly interpreted as an intention to take high-handed possession of the country, and I am satisfied would arouse suspicions and create impediments which would greatly embarrass my negociations, and which we are most desirous of avoiding.

Moreover, there was no necessity for undue haste. The Dominican Government was ready to extend permission for the survey within a very short time, and Cazneau thought it would be obviously the best procedure to " sacrifice a few days time " rather than " hazard the confidence and good-will of this government and people." [36]

But Cazneau's counsel was unavailing. McClellan's desire for prompt action was shared by Commander Newton of the flagship *Columbia*, who wrote to Cazneau on July 20 and

island of Santo Domingo. His report of August 27 indicates the advantage of a naval base at Samaná Bay. See *Sen. Ex. Doc.* No. 17, 41 Cong., 3 sess., pp. 70-77.

[36] Cazneau to McClellan, July 19, 1854, *McClellan Papers, loc. cit.*

announced his intention of proceeding immediately to Samaná Bay. Once again the American Commissioner stressed the necessity for delay,[37] but Newton was contemptuous of the devious ways of diplomacy, and the *Columbia* weighed anchor for Samaná. On August 3, 1854, McClellan sent a note to Cazneau in order to inform him that the survey was nearly completed and that

the position selected for a coal depot etc., will require at least two square miles of land, and perhaps somewhat more; it will also be necessary to obtain the use and control of the *Levantado bays,* at the entrance of the Bay. There are five of these bays—two large and three very small ones. The place selected for a depot is the harbour of the ' Carenero Chico.' [38]

Three days later, Cazneau informed McClellan that he would strive to secure the Carenero Chico, and that he had high hopes of success if " nothing occurs to excite the jealousies of this suspicious people." But knowing the dispositions of leading Dominicans to look askance at concessions to foreign governments, he was still of the opinion that the way in which the survey had been conducted was enough to cause serious trouble, and he hoped that McClellan had acted with " extreme precaution." [39]

In a despatch to Secretary Marcy, dated August 8, 1854, Cazneau voiced the opinion that McClellan's hasty action in pushing the survey of Samaná Bay without first waiting for the American Commissioner to disarm the fears of the Dominican Government was highly inexpedient:

Our most reliable friends here regret with me the premature demonstration in Samana Bay, as the report reached here immediately overland and the Anti-American party raised the absurd cry that the United States intended to take the country, and that Genl. Santana was conspiring to betray the colored population into slavery. It was desirable to prepare the way before any movement was made by us which could in any manner be perverted to excite popular opposition.[40]

[37] Cazneau to Marcy, July 24, 1854, *Special Service*, MS. Dept. of State.
[38] *McClellan Papers, loc. cit.*
[39] Cazneau to McClellan, August 6, 1854, *ibid.*
[40] Cazneau to Marcy, August 8, 1854, *Special Service*, MS. Dept. of State.

As a prophet of evil tidings, Cazneau was infallible. Shortly after Captain McClellan had commenced his surveying operations, one of the members of the Dominican Cabinet informed Sir Robert Schomburgk, the British consul, that one of the articles in the projected treaty with the United States bestowed upon American citizens the right to " establish two or more depots within the Dominican Republic for warehousing coals for the steamers that in future were to touch here in their voyage to or from the Isthmus."

Schomburgk immediately drew the Minister's attention to the fact that under the regulations

which already existed in the Dominican Republic respecting foreign commerce, any person had the right to establish Coal depots in the Ports of Santo Domingo, or in any other one open to Commerce. There was therefore no necessity to introduce such an article into the treaty, which it was very obvious aimed at a firm footing.

Schomburgk had also received intimations that

a large body of American emigrants will be thrown into the Republic to sink the natural Character of the Dominicans. For such a plan speculations have already been set on foot in the United States.

In view of these circumstances Schomburgk expressed to Lord Clarendon, the British Foreign Secretary, the opinion that " the presence of a couple of English or French Men of war would inspire much confidence at this moment, and prevent the realization of the American projects." [41]

Schomburgk next secured an interview with President Santana and two of his Cabinet, and acquainted them with the fact that, because of the " friendly disposition " now shown by the Emperor Soulouque towards the Dominicans, it was hoped by both the British and French Governments that " an early adjustment of their difficulties " could be effected. A vigorous protest was then filed against " any stipulations or agreement which would give to the United States a coal depot," and finally the British consul confided his fears that " at the moment this treaty had entered into force, Santo Domingo

[41] Schomburgk to Lord Clarendon, August 7, 1854, Confidential, F. O. 23/19, No. 38.

would be overrun with American adventurers, and the Dominican Nationality sunk in the mass of the new Settlers." [42]

President Santana did not commit himself at this interview, but it was apparent to everyone that the Dominican Government was still fearful of invasions by Haitian armies and therefore was inclined to give some heed to protests from the mediating powers, Great Britain and France.

Cazneau, however, endeavored to allay all these fears that had been conjured up by the British consul, and his efforts met with such success that on September 7, 1854 the Dominican Minister of Foreign Relations, J. N. Tejera, called upon Cazneau to inform him that

President Santana finally accepted slight changes in Article 28 of the treaty relative to the grant of an appropriate site for the Government of the United States to establish in the Bay of Samana a coaling station for mail steamers.

Once again, however, Sir Robert Schomburgk interposed. On the morning of September 8 he paid a visit to the Dominican Foreign Office, accompanied by M. Darasse, the French consul, and a joint protest was filed against any grant to the United States " even though it were only for one inch of land." [43]

But these strong protests did not yield the prompt results hoped for by the British consul, who wrote to Lord Clarendon, on September 20, 1854, to inform him of the Dominican situation. He had made a special visit to Samaná Bay to investigate the proceedings of Captain McClellan and had discovered that it was an open secret that part of the bay was to be sold to the United States. He had also learned that McClellan was particularly interested in the Carenero Chico, which possessed " all that can be desired for the establishment of a Depot."

When Schomburgk returned from this visit to Samaná Bay he found out that the Dominican Congress had adjourned and

[42] Schomburgk to Lord Clarendon, August 22, 1854, F. O. 23/19, No. 40. See also Cazneau to Marcy, August 19, 1854, *Special Service*, MS. Dept. of State. In the New York *Evening Post* of August 31, 1854 there is an extended and trenchant attack upon the Cazneau mission, with a good guess as to the objects which the Pierce Administration hoped to gain thereby. See also New York *Evening Post*, September 15 and October 9, 1854.

[43] Tejera to Cazneau, September 28, 1854, *Special Service*, MS. Dept. of State.

that President Santana had refrained from presenting to it the treaty that was being negotiated with the United States. It was also hinted that General Cazneau had

disbursed considerable sums of money to gain advocates for his scheme among the Government members; and the large quantity of new American coin now afloat, renders such a supposition probable. Everything is tending to a military despotism, induced and promoted by General Cazneau who figured already in such a capacity in Texas.

At about this same time rumors reached Schomburgk to the effect that President Santana was contemplating a coup d'état by which he would overthrow the Dominican constitution and assume dictatorial powers, in this way making it possible for him to push through the treaty with the United States. Thoroughly alarmed at the situation, the British consul had an interview with Santana during which he voiced all his fears and requested that the President give him " verbal assurances " to quiet them. He received, however, only " evasive and unsatisfactory answers."

When Schomburgk saw that he could make very little impression upon Santana by indicating the dangers of American imperialism, he then changed his tactics and declared that he would claim

in the name of Her Majesty for Great Britain any Privileges that might be granted to the United States which the Treaty between her and the Dominion Republic did not already confer.[44]

On the same day that Schomburgk wrote his despatch to Lord Clarendon, he also sent to Mr. Crampton, the British Minister at Washington, a long report of General Cazneau's activities in the Dominican Republic. After discussing the attempts of the American Commissioner to secure a naval base in Samaná Bay, he frankly admits that he had

used, in connection with my Colleague the Consul of France at this Republic, every effort to prevent the realization of such a scheme, which, if effected, could only prove injurious to the interests of Her Majesty's Government.[45]

[44] Schomburgk to Lord Clarendon, September 20, 1854, F. O. 23/19, No. 43.
[45] Schomburgk to Crampton, September 20, 1854, enclosed in despatch from Crampton to Lord Clarendon, October 23, 1854, F. O. 5/599.

But before Mr. Crampton received this communication from Schomburgk, he had already discussed with Marcy, the American Secretary of State, the question of the Cazneau mission to the Dominican Republic, and in a despatch to Lord Clarendon, dated October 9, 1854, he expressed his views as to American policy. First of all he had inquired of Marcy whether there was any truth in the rumor that

certain American ships of war had been sent to Samaná in San Domingo, with a view of obtaining the permission of the Dominican Government to establish there a naval rendezvous, as a convenient place for the Retreat, in case of need, of a force about to invade Cuba, or for effecting repairs to such force, and that a large additional American Force might shortly be expected at Samaná to take coal from the Bay and erect a fort there.

Marcy's reply to this inquiry was not very satisfactory. He informed Crampton that he had

no knowledge of the conclusion of any Treaty of the sort I had described:— that he *believed* a desire existed of obtaining a coal depot in some part of the Island of San Domingo, and this, he hoped, would give no umbrage to anybody, and was very necessary for the United States, who had a number of steamers continually passing to and from in the West Indies.

Crampton then remarked that Marcy

must not be surprised if the arrival at San Domingo of an American Plenipotentiary, accompanied by Ships of War, excited some attention on the part of Her Majesty's Government, and I recalled to his recollection the strong impression which had been produced about two years ago in the United States by the mere report of the presence of a French Man of War in the Bay of Samaná, to the Commander of which was attributed the very intention now attributed to the Plenipotentiary sent by the United States, namely, to obtain permanent possession of that Bay as a Naval Station.

Moreover, it seemed to Crampton that

the selection of the Plenipotentiary employed by the American Government in the matter was not calculated to calm any apprehension which might now be felt by the Spanish Government, for General Cazneau's views were well known, and those of his Lady, by whom he was accompanied, were very notoriously in favor of the annexation by any means of Cuba to the United States.[46]

At the mention of the name of Mrs. Cazneau, Secretary Marcy smilingly observed:

I assure you, Mr. Crampton, I have had no dealings of any sort with that Lady. [47]

Meanwhile, in spite of British and French opposition, Cazneau went ahead and concluded with the Dominican Republic a treaty of amity and commerce. This treaty was signed on October 5, 1854, and it did not include any provision for the acquisition by the United States of a naval base in Samaná Bay. But notwithstanding this fact, the French and British consuls bent all their efforts to defeat it. On the same day that this treaty was concluded, the British consul wrote a despatch to Lord Clarendon to acknowledge the receipt of instructions which authorized him to claim for Her Majesty's Government all the privileges that were accorded by the Dominican Government to the United States. He then observed that the Dominican Congress had been summoned to meet in extraordinary session on November 1, but that it was

not expected that the requisite Number for a majority will meet, consequently it is conjected that President Santana will take this circumstance as his reason for declaring the urgency of directing the affairs of the Republic without a Congress merely assisted by a Council of State.[48]

Two days later, October 7, Schomburgk addressed an " immediate and confidential " despatch to Lord Clarendon which outlined a very bold measure of retaliation against American intrigue. It was apparent to the British consul that " corrup-

[46] With reference to Mrs. Cazneau, Crampton remarked as follows: " Mrs. Cazneau . . . is an Irish lady who, under the name of Corah Montgomery, founded and for a long time edited at New York a newspaper in the Spanish language called ' La Verdad,' devoted to what is called the Filibustero Party, and which was clandestinely introduced into the Island of Cuba with a view to excite discontent and insurrection against the Spanish Government." Crampton to Lord Clarendon, October 9, 1854, *ibid*.

[47] Crampton to Lord Clarendon, *ibid*.

[48] Schomburgk to Lord Clarendon, October 5, 1854, F. O. 23/19, No. 49.

tion and bribery have rendered the persons in power blind to their own interest." Therefore, other measures than " mere reasoning with the President and his Ministers must be taken to prevent the Settlement of the Americans here." The best way to cope with this situation was for the British Government to instruct Mr. Schomburgk to go on board a British ship of war and proceed to Samaná Bay. After arriving there it would be a simple matter to take possession of Fort Cacao. Such an act of force would be welcomed by a strong party in the Dominican Republic who were only awaiting a favorable opportunity to declare themselves against the " corrupted Ministry of Santana." [49]

While waiting for instructions from Lord Clarendon in regard to taking possession of Fort Cacao, Schomburgk spared no effort to bring about the failure of the Cazneau mission. On October 20, 1854 Lavastida, the Dominican Minister of Finance, called to see the British consul, and during the course of the conversation Schomburgk stated that he had learned from good authority that the Dominican Government had concluded two conventions with the United States. One of these was " a plain Treaty, on the same basis as those of Great Britain and France," but the other convention contained " a conditional concession to the United States of a part of Samana."

Lavastida very emphatically denied that this second convention concerning Samaná Bay was of the nature of a " Treaty Stipulation." It was

merely a note from the Minister of Foreign Affairs of the Dominican Republic to the Plenipotentiary of the United States, stating the Dominican Government did not wish to reject entirely the possibility of granting hereafter to the United States the concessions demanded by Article 28, if such seem advantageous to the Republic as per example in case that England and France should withdraw from the Mediation, or find it impossible to procure from the Emperor of Hayti, peace or a long truce for this Republic.[50]

At the conclusion of this conversation between Lavastida

---

[49] Schomburgk to Lord Clarendon, October 7, 1854, *ibid.*, No. 50.
[50] Schomburgk to Lord Clarendon, October 21, 1854, *ibid.*, No. 52.

and Sir Robert Schomburgk, the British consul expressed his disappointment that this diplomatic note with reference to Samaná Bay had been sent to Mr. Cazneau. It appeared to him that such a procedure left "the door open for American intrigues." There was, however, help at hand for the British consul. Shortly after Schomburgk's meeting with Lavastida, there arrived at Santo Domingo City M. Raybaud, the French chargé d'affaires and consul-general at Port-au-Prince. Raybaud at once assured Schomburgk that "something ought to be done to destroy the influence of the Americans," and he promised his cordial co-operation in such an undertaking.

About this same time Schomburgk received instructions from Lord Clarendon, dated September 29, directing him to express surprise at the course followed by the Dominican Government. In compliance with these instructions, on October 28 Schomburgk addressed the following note to the Dominican Minister of Foreign Relations:

I am instructed by the Earl of Clarendon . . . to inform the Dominican Government that Her Majesty's Government learns with surprise that notwithstanding the advice offered by the Representatives of the mediating Powers, . . . the President has thought proper to negociate a treaty with the United States by which both the safety and welfare of the Republic will be greatly and immediately endangered. England and France have on more than one occasion interfered to uphold the independence of the Dominican Republic when that independence was threatened by a neighboring Power and they have a right to expect that the arrangements contemplated by this treaty should not have been made without their knowledge and sanction, particularly with a power which has hitherto refused to acknowledge the independence of the Dominican Republic.[51]

This united opposition on the part of Sir Robert Schomburgk and M. Raybaud was increasingly effective in developing hostility among Dominicans to any treaty with the United States.[52]

[51] Schomburgk to the Dominican Minister of Foreign Relations, October 28, 1854, *Special Agents Series*, vol. 19, MS. Dept. of State.

[52] According to a letter printed in the New York *Evening Post* on October 25, 1854, Sir Robert Schomburgk told the members of the Dominican Congress "not to treat with the United States, or England and France would set the

As this anti-American movement began to gather strength, Cazneau tried to counteract it by every device he could make use of, but all to no purpose. At length, thoroughly aroused by what he considered to be unfair tactics, he addressed to Sir Robert Schomburgk and Raybaud the following letter of protest:

The Undersigned Commissioner Plenipotentiary of the United States of America near this government, having good reason to know that the Agents of France and England have by various means— aided by the menacing display of an armed force before this Capital— overawed and controlled the free action of the Dominican Republic in its relations with the United States, hereby protests in the name of his country, against this breach of honorable faith towards his government and against this unwarranted encroachment upon the sovereign rights of an independent American power.[53]

This note of protest availed Cazneau but very little. In a despatch to Lord Clarendon, dated November 22, 1854, Schomburgk observed that Cazneau had taken great umbrage at the arrival of several French ships of war. This, he thought, was unnecessary in view of the fact that the United States had recently stationed a large naval force in Dominican waters. Also, the French and British consuls had good reason to summon this imposing squadron of war-ships because they had learned from " good sources " that Mr. and Mrs. Cazneau had " employed every intrigue, to induce the Dominican Government to rid themselves of the mediation, and to throw themselves for support into the arms of the United States." As for Cazneau's note of protest, it was only what could be expected of " a person of little education, and of much less experience in the transaction of questions of National importance." [54]

Haytian negroes upon them—or rather, he said, the negro army was forty thousand strong, and would not leave a drop of white blood on the island, if European influence did not hold them back."

[53] Cazneau to the British and French consuls, November 17, 1854, enclosed in Cazneau's despatch to Marcy, November 23, 1854, *Special Service*, MS. Dept. of State.

[54] Schomburgk to Lord Clarendon, November 22, 1854, F. O. 23/19, No. 60. It is pertinent here to note that in his letter of November 17, 1854 General

On the following day, November 23, 1854, Schomburgk wrote to Mr. Crampton, at Washington, to advise him of Cazneau's actions. The American Commissioner had just addressed a note to the Dominican Minister of Foreign Relations in which he announced that " for the present " he withdrew " from the ulterior action of the Dominican Government the Treaty of recognition and amity now pending between the Governments of our respective Nations." [55]

The Dominican Minister refused to accede to Cazneau's request to return the treaty of October 5, 1854, and the Dominican Congress appointed a committee to report upon it. At this juncture the British consul threw his whole influence to secure objectionable amendments to the treaty, and thus destroy any chance of its ratification by the American Senate. His efforts in this regard were described as follows in his despatch to Lord Clarendon of December 18, 1854:

I used whatever influence I possessed with a great number of the members, in order to draw their attention to the humiliating clause of Article 3, by which nine-tenths of their population were rendered liable to arrest and imprisonment, should they, as per example, land in Charleston in South Carolina.

In the Dominican Congress the leading rôle in opposition to the treaty was taken by Theodore Heneken, an Englishman by birth who had settled in the Dominican Republic and had risen to prominence in Dominican public life. Heneken was made chairman of the committee of the Dominican Congress which was to report upon the American treaty, and when this report was submitted it contained a suggestion which so modified Article 3 that " the same rights and privileges which American Citizens would enjoy on their arrival here throughout the Dominican Republic, should equally be conferred upon

Cazneau based his opposition to the obstructive policy of France and England upon the principles of the Monroe Doctrine. Although not mentioned by name, the " principles of 1823," as enunciated in 1845 by President Polk, were the guiding stars upon which General Cazneau relied. Schomburgk had already, on July 20, 1852 and December 31, 1853, referred to the " Monroe principle." See Dexter Perkins, *The Monroe Doctrine, 1826-1867*, pp. 269-271.

[55] Schomburgk to Crampton, November 23, 1854, F. O. 5/600.

Dominican citizens, without distinction of race or colour, throughout the States composing the Union." [56]

It was obvious to Cazneau that such an amendment would be extremely distasteful to the Southern states of the American Union and that no treaty with such an amendment would be ratified by the United States. Therefore on December 4 Cazneau again wrote to the Dominican Minister of Foreign Relations to inform him that the American treaty should be regarded as withdrawn from further consideration.[57] As on a previous occasion, the Dominican Government refused to heed this request, and the Dominican Congress proceeded unanimously to approve the report of the Heneken Committee. Next they rejected the American treaty as submitted, and they approved it only with the suggested amendments which were known to be objectionable to the American Government.

Not content with having defeated every attempt on the part of Cazneau to secure a concession in Samaná Bay or even to negotiate an acceptable treaty of amity and commerce with the Dominican Republic, Schomburgk and Raybaud went so far as to send to President Santana, on December 14, 1854, an ultimatum which forbade the Dominican Government to consent to any alienation of Dominican territory, or to make any contract or engagement for the acceptance of a subsidy, or to enter into any treaty to hypothecate any branch of Dominican revenue.[58]

While the Dominican Government was considering what answer to give to this latest note of the British and French consuls, Cazneau was endeavoring to soothe his wounded feelings by sharp denunciations of certain Dominicans who ap-

[56] Schomburgk to Lord Clarendon, December 7 and December 18, 1854, F. O. 23/19, Nos. 60 and 61.

[57] Cazneau to the Minister of Foreign Relations, December 4, 1854, *Special Service*, MS. Dept. of State. See also New York *Evening Post*, December 27, 1854.

[58] This note is contained in the despatch of Schomburgk to Crampton, December 16, 1854, F. O. 5/619. With reference to the policy pursued by British and French agents in the Dominican Republic, Dexter Perkins, *The Monroe Doctrine, 1826-1867*, p. 272, remarks: ". . . it is curious that the Pierce administration never gave vent to the resentment which it must have felt at the policy of France and England in the Dominican republic."

peared to be wholly under the control of foreign influences. In his note of December 4, 1854, withdrawing the American treaty from the consideration of the Dominican Congress, he had sounded a note of menace. The Dominican Government, he asserted, must be aware of the fact that the United States, under the law of nations, had the right " to enforce by all the means in its Power, the satisfaction and redress " which they would be forced to " demand for the singular equivocations and repeated injustices practised towards our Citizens and Government by the Dominican Executive."

When Cazneau made other strong remonstrances against the action of the Dominican Government in regard to the American treaty, some Dominican officials, and both the French and British consuls, interpreted his words as a threat that the United States was prepared to repeat at Santo Domingo City the procedure that had been followed at Greytown, Nicaragua. In that case the American sloop-of-war *Cyane* had redressed American injuries by bombarding Greytown and thus destroying it, and this action had been justified by both the American Secretary of the Navy and the Secretary of State. Inasmuch as the Greytown incident had happened only a few months previously, it remained a constant reminder to the foreign consuls and to the Dominican authorities of the disposition of the American Government to insist upon the prompt recognition of what were regarded as American rights.[59]

It was only to be expected, therefore, that Cazneau's threats should be very seriously considered, and Schomburgk immediately informed Rear-Admiral Fanshawe

of the State of Affairs, especially with regard to the general apprehensions entertained here, that a Naval Force from the United States will make its appearance to force the Treaty upon them, or to take vengeance of imaginary insults.[60]

A few days later, December 21, Schomburgk and Raybaud

[59] With reference to the Greytown incident see M. W. Williams, *Anglo-American Isthmian Diplomacy*, chap. vi. Also J. B. Moore, *Digest of International Law*, II, 414-417.

[60] Schomburgk to Lord Clarendon, December 18, 1854, F. O. 23/19, No. 61. Also Schomburgk to Crampton, December 16, 1854, F. O. 5/619.

became so concerned over the possibility of a punitive American expedition visiting Santo Domingo City that they wrote to the commanders of the French and British fleets in West Indian waters to send at once a " force of sufficient strength " to protect French and British interests. In the event that no English or French naval force, equal or superior to that of the United States, could be sent in time to the Dominican Republic, an appeal could then be issued by the Dominican Government to the consuls of England and France requesting protection against the Americans. The consuls would then permit the Dominicans

to hoist the colours of England and France jointly and of their own free will on their battlements, to grant them provisional protection, as far as the moral impression of the emblems of England and France can afford them a safeguard.[61]

In taking this determined stand against what was believed to be the aggressive spirit informing American foreign policy under Secretary Marcy, Sir Robert Schomburgk admitted to Lord Clarendon that he had largely followed the lead of M. Raybaud, the French Consul-General at Port-au-Prince. When Raybaud visited Santo Domingo City for the express purpose of defeating the American treaty of October 5, 1854, Schomburgk readily recognized that Raybaud had such a commanding influence over many of the leading Dominicans that

it would be much more advantageous for the realization of our mutual object, [to leave] to him exclusively the intercourse and management between the Executive and his Ministers reserving to myself a cordial co-operation, and giving advice to some of the Members of the Legislature over whom I knew to possess influence. I should do an injustice to Mr. Raybaud if I hesitated in pronouncing that the favourable result, we have hitherto effected, is mainly to be ascribed to him.[62]

---

[61] Schomburgk to Lord Clarendon, December 21, 1854, F. O. 23/19, No. 64. It is important to note that as early as April 22, 1854 the French Secretary of Foreign Affairs expressed to the American Minister at Paris his disapproval of the activities of the French agent in the Dominican Republic.

[62] Schomburgk to Lord Clarendon, December 21, 1854, *ibid*. In this despatch to Lord Clarendon, Schomburgk clearly indicates that the French Consul-General

On February 15, 1855, Lord Clarendon responded to this hysterical despatch of Schomburgk by giving him a lesson in the principles of British foreign policy. If an American squadron should attack Santo Domingo City in the presence of French and British squadrons, it would be necessary for the British and French consuls to proceed with

caution in requiring the intervention of the Naval Forces of Your respective Countries, as much will depend upon the cause alleged by the United States for the hostile demonstration. The real cause of such a demonstration would probably be to compel the Dominicans to agree to a Treaty that is obnoxious to them, and that they have rejected; but even if this were openly avowed, England and France would have no right to interfere, nor are they bound by any Treaty engagement to protect Santo Domingo from foreign aggression. It might be expedient to prevent the perpetration of an Act of gross injustice, to protect a weak state against a powerful assailant, and not to allow the United States to acquire by force, that which they had been unable to obtain by peaceful means. Nevertheless, as no abstract right exists, and England and France are under no obligations, it would not be prudent to leave the question of peace or War with the United States in the hands of yourself and your French Colleague, by authorizing you to act upon what may appear expedient, unless the two Governments were in full possession of all the circumstances preceding and attending the contemplated attack.

. . . If no allusion should be made to the Treaty by the Naval Commander of the United States, and if he should confine himself to demanding redress for grievances, real or imaginary, of Citizens of the United States, it does not appear to Her Majesty's Government that the Intervention of the Consuls of England and France would be justifiable beyond offering themselves as Mediators, and Protesting against any injury being done to English and French Subjects.

I have to add that the Government of France, to whom I have communicated your Despatch, have expressed their entire concurrence in the opinions which I have stated above, and by which you will be guided in this matter.[63]

was anxious to bring about a joint protectorate by France and England over the entire island of Santo Domingo. In time this joint protectorate would " resolve itself into two Separate ones "—France would control Haiti and England the Dominican Republic.

[63] Lord Clarendon to Schomburgk, February 15, 1855, F. O. 23/21, No. 10.

Lord Clarendon, it would appear, was sincerely anxious to avoid friction with the United States, and in January, 1855, during a conversation with James Buchanan, the American Minister at London, he emphasized that it was the earnest desire of the British Government to " cultivate the most friendly relations with the United States." Buchanan, however, was somewhat doubtful about British good will towards the United States. Thus by way of controverting Clarendon's statement, he referred

to the recent conduct of the British and French Consuls acting in concert to prevent the United States from concluding a Treaty of Commerce with the Dominican Republic; and observed that on all occasions in which the United States were interested, the officials of the two Governments appeared "to hunt in couples," and to be ever ready to do us injury.

To this criticism Lord Clarendon replied

that there had been too much of this—it was all wrong, and he would take care that for the future we should have no cause to complain on this account.[64]

But whatever the future would hold, it was certain that for the present the plans of the American Government with reference to Samaná Bay, or even with regard to a treaty of amity and commerce with the Dominican Republic, were completely defeated through the opposition of Schomburgk and Raybaud. On December 18, 1854 Secretary Marcy instructed Cazneau to return to the United States by the " earliest conveyance," [65] and he repeated this instruction on January 12 and on February 3, 1855. Cazneau, however, remained in Santo Domingo for some months longer, vainly hoping to circumvent European opposition. Finally, on June 9, 1855, he wrote to

[64] Buchanan to Marcy, January 19, 1855, *England, Desp.*, vol. 66, MS. Dept. of State.

[65] Marcy to Cazneau, December 18, 1854, *Special Missions*, vol. 3, MS. Dept. of State. It should be remembered that Cazneau's letter of November 17, 1854 to the British and French representatives in the Dominican Republic was the " first diplomatic protest based upon the claims of the Monroe Doctrine." In view of this fact, it is somewhat difficult to understand the basis for Marcy's recall of Cazneau. See Dexter Perkins, *op. cit.*, p. 273.

Marcy and ascribed his failure to the "dictatorial intervention of the agents of France and England." It was his reasoned conviction that those two nations were "undoubtedly co-operating with Hayti and the negro party headed by Baez to extinguish the Dominican Republic and convert the whole island into an African dependency." [66] Thus ended the Cazneau mission, but for the next decade and a half this colorful adventurer figures prominently in all the relations between the United States and the Dominican Republic.

On October 5, 1855, Secretary Marcy wrote to Jonathan Elliot, the American Commercial Agent at Santo Domingo City, and instructed him to send to the Department of State a copy of the amendments which the Dominican Government had proposed relative to the treaty of October 5, 1854. Cazneau had neglected to transmit an exact copy of these desired changes, but he had intimated something of their character. If the amendments were of the character that Cazneau had hinted, no treaty could now be negotiated, but if the Dominican Government would recede from these proposed amendments it would be perfectly proper for Elliot to conclude a treaty on the basis of the rejected treaty of October 5. If the Dominican Government should prefer to substitute some other site for that of Samaná Bay, the United States "would treat for it after making a survey of the same." [67]

On October 9, 1855, Marcy again wrote to Elliot to instruct him with reference to the amendment proposed by the Dominican Government relative to Article 3 of the treaty of October 5, 1854. It would appear that this amendment proposed

to place Dominicans in the United States, of all complexions, on the same footing as citizens of the United States. This is not to be entertained, it being contrary to the feeling of a large proportion of our citizens. . . . The safety and peace of the Southern States require

---

[66] Cazneau to Marcy, June 9, 1855, *Special Service*, MS. Dept. of State.

[67] Marcy to Elliot, October 5, 1855, *ibid.* In December, 1855 the Emperor of Haiti led an army against the Dominican Republic but was "most shamefully beaten." This fact led him to assent to negotiations looking toward a truce with the Dominican Government. Joseph N. Lewis to Marcy, March 1, 1856, *Port-au-Prince, Consular Desp.*, vol. 3, MS. Dept. of State.

this exclusion, and it is hoped the Dominican Government will appreciate this necessity.[68]

A treaty of amity, commerce, navigation, and extradition was finally signed on March 8, 1856, but it did not transfer any territory bordering on the Bay of Samaná. European opposition had been too strong to admit of any such action. President Santana, however, remained very friendly to the United States and the American Commercial Agent was of the opinion that the cession could be arranged " a little later." Indeed, it could be effected at once if the United States would " protect the Republic from the consequences." [69]

Marcy, however, had no desire to adopt an aggressive policy that would again invite the sharp opposition of the European powers and thus re-enact the Cazneau episode. Besides, the suspicions of European statesmen had recently been kindled by the publication, in the spring of 1855, of the report of the Ostend Conference, which had been signed on October 18, 1854 by Soulé, Buchanan, and Mason.[70] From many quarters there had come bitter denunciation of the " stand and deliver " tenor of this Ostend Manifesto. In Europe it was regarded by some statesmen as an indication of impatient imperialism, and the Spanish Government was awakened to the necessity of straining every effort to conserve the last remnants of her colonial empire. In December, 1855, there arrived in the Dominican Republic a new Spanish chargé d'affaires and consul, Sr. Segovia, who promptly announced that

a war between the United States and Spain is indispensable this year, and it will better suit Spain to meet the Americans here as the field of battle, instead of Cuba.[71]

From the moment of his arrival in Santo Domingo City, Segovia bent every effort to thwart American expansion. Soon

---

[68] Marcy to Elliot, October 9, 1855, *Special Service*, MS. Dept. of State.

[69] Elliot to Marcy, March 22, 1856, *ibid.*

[69] Elliot to Marcy, March 22, 1856, *ibid.* The treaty of March 8, 1856 was never ratified by the United States. It too closely resembled the treaty of October 5, 1854. See *Unperfected Treaties,* MS. Dept. of State.

[70] *Ho. Ex. Doc.* No. 93, 33 Cong., 2 sess.

[71] Pereira to the Secretary of State, August 7, 1856, *Santo Domingo, Consular Desp.*, vol. 2, MS. Dept. of State.

he gained such prestige that Elliot, the American Commercial Agent, anxiously strove to counteract his efforts and to induce the American Government to adopt a more positive policy in Santo Domingo. He was certain that

we can have a naval station where we chose on our own terms and in case of necessity, depend on assistance from these people—if we only take some interest in them.[72]

Fearful that any delay in reopening negotiations might defeat American hopes of securing Samaná, Elliot left Santo Domingo City on August 2, 1856 and took passage for the United States. On September 10 he was in Washington, and on that day he wrote to the Secretary of State that he was

authorized to offer to the United States Government not only any location in the Bay of Samana for their purposes, but the coal mines in that harbor, and any other commercial advantages they require— but on the condition that the United States will guard them against any of the consequences thereof. . . . Give me powers—let Commodore Paulding go with me, with two vessels of war, and at this moment I can accomplish all that may be desired.[73]

Elliot's efforts were, however, all in vain. Immediately after he left for the United States, the anti-American party in the Dominican Republic, led by the Spanish Consul-General, Segovia, redoubled their efforts to restore their leader, the former President, Buenaventura Baez, to power. Some months previously, President Santana had resigned the executive office and had been succeeded by General Mota, the former Vice-President. It was upon General Mota, therefore, that increasing pressure was brought to bear in favor of the return of Baez. At the suggestion of Segovia, General Mota wrote to General Santana and advised that a reconciliation be effected with Baez. Santana at once gave his assent to the return of Baez, and he confirmed this position by resigning as commander-in-chief of the Dominican army.

Santana was enough of a statesman to understand the necessity of bowing to superior force. In the face of strong

[72] Elliot to Marcy, July 9, 1856, *ibid.*
[73] Elliot to Marcy, September 10, 1856, *ibid.*

European opposition he had inclined towards a policy of intimate friendship with the United States, but it had finally been
revealed to him in an unmistakable manner that American
support was a most uncertain quantity. Neither President Pierce
nor Secretary Marcy was ready for active intervention in
Santo Domingo and Santana at length perceived how patheti-
cally unwise his policy had been. It was no wonder that he
sharply criticized his own futile leadership:

This is what I am reduced to after having signed the American
Treaty, and what have I gained with the friendship of the United
States? Not even a vessel of war to investigate matters, and Baez
once here, adieu to all American projects or conventions.[74]

The way was now prepared for the restoration of Baez. It
was arranged that he should return as Vice-President, and then
President Mota was to resign and thus permit the accession of
Baez. This program was duly carried out in October, 1856, and
at once the new Administration exhibited the most rancorous
hostility towards the United States. On the night of October 11,
a mob assembled before the American agency in Santo Domingo
City for the express purpose of "pulling down the flagstaff
and National Sign," and it was only with great difficulty that
they were dissuaded from such action.[75] In the following month
only the timely aid of Captain Dunlop, of the British steam
frigate *Tartar,* saved the lives of the acting American Commercial Agent and his family. Almost every night the streets
of Santo Domingo City resounded with the cries of "down
with the Yankees, down with the Eagle," and the American
flag was openly tramped upon.[76]

As the months passed the situation grew steadily worse. In
March, 1857, the American Commercial Agent reported that
in Santo Domingo there was no justice to be had in the courts

for strangers and more particularly Americans—they are all a corrupt,
swindling set. . . . Some steps should immediately be taken by the
Government, for since they see that no notice has been taken of the

[74] Pereira to Marcy, August 7, 1856, *ibid.*
[75] Pereira to Marcy, October 30 and November 22, 1856, *ibid.*
[76] Pereira to Marcy, November 22, 1856, *ibid.*

gross insults offered to our flag, the Consulate and citizens of the United States . . . they become more emboldened and there is no safety here for either our Citizens or their property.[77]

In November, Elliot informed Secretary Cass that the antipathy to Americans was so marked in Santo Domingo City that their lives were in the " greatest danger," and that he had been warned " not to go unarmed or go out at night." [78] In April, 1858, a prominent Dominican official attempted to assassinate the wife of the American Commercial Agent. When a protest was lodged with the Minister of Justice against this reprehensible action, the wife of the Minister launched such a " tirade of abuse " at the American agent that he was " glad to retreat." [79]

Fortunately for the United States, the Baez régime, which was responsible for the hostile attitude towards all Americans, was soon to pass away. Baez had been placed in power largely through the leadership of the Spanish Consul-General, Segovia, and the anti-American party in Santo Domingo drew its inspiration from him. To their dismay, Segovia was recalled by the Spanish Government because his actions had given umbrage to France and England. Deprived of such an artful and aggressive leader, the Baez faction was soon faced with open revolution in Santo Domingo. After a siege of many months Santo Domingo City was starved into submission, and through the mediation of Commodore John M. McIntosh, of the U. S. S. S. *Colorado,* a capitulation was signed on June 12, 1858. Under its terms President Baez consented to resign his office, and General Santana promised to refrain from imposing condign punishment upon the followers of the fallen president. Inasmuch as General Santana had been the leader of the opposition against President Baez, it was inevitable that he should succeed to the presidential office. He was formally inaugurated on January 31, 1859, and a friendly attitude towards the United States was again manifest. On March 21, 1859, the American Commercial Agent at Santo Domingo City wrote to Secretary

[77] Elliot to the Secretary of State, March 9, 1857, *ibid.*
[78] Elliot to Cass, November 7, 1857, *ibid.*
[79] Elliot to Cass, April 21, 1858, *ibid.*

Cass to inform him that "the time has arrived when we can have a good station for our Navy and depots for our steamers in these waters." [80] He also intimated to the Secretary of State that it would be far wiser to authorize the Commercial Agent to conduct negotiations for naval depots than to appoint a special agent for that purpose. Such a matter would have to be handled with skill and despatch, and Elliot believed that he himself had an abundance of both these qualities.

Secretary Cass, however, did not appear to recognize the self-advertised merits of the complacent Commercial Agent, and on April 7, 1859, he appointed General William L. Cazneau as a special agent to the Dominican Republic. Since his stormy service in Santo Domingo in 1854-1855, Cazneau had been careful to keep in touch with conditions in the island, and if Cass desired to inaugurate a bold and imperialistic policy no better choice could have been made. The immediate events leading up to his appointment are interestingly told by Cazneau's wife in a little brochure entitled *Our Winter Eden:*

Our government temporarily abandoned the plan of a naval station in the West Indies, but General Cazneau never lost sight of it for a single month. He and many leading Dominicans were mutually pledged not to rest until they had planted an anchor of hope and peace for the Republic, by creating at Samana a free and neutral port, somewhat on the municipal and commercial basis of St. Thomas. The plan was submitted to President Buchanan, with the concurrence of several eminent Dominicans, but he postponed action, even while he endorsed the idea. A boding fear of a disruption of the Union chilled his heart against everything that could possibly lead to any foreign entanglement. I was twice present in the library of the White House, when the project of a free port at Samana was explained and defended by General Cazneau. It was discussed in a spirit of private and personal confidence, quite apart from any present thought of making it a national measure. On the last occasion, Mr. Cass, the Secretary of State, came in as we were about taking leave, and the President detained us, to mention to him General Cazneau's views of securing a new American trade centre, in the shape of a free port at Samana bay.

[80] Elliot to Cass, March 21, 1859, *Santo Domingo, Consular Desp.,* vol. 3, MS. Dept. of State.

" In the way of a private enterprise, or a national measure? " asked Secretary Cass, after a few sentences of explanations.

" It is feasible in either way, or in both conjointly," replied Cazneau, " and with or without aid of my government I shall continue to work for its accomplishment."

" Do you intend returning to Santo Domingo on this business? " asked the Secretary, in a tone I thought slightly tinged with surprise or disapproval.

" Certainly; my passage is already engaged, and I shall remain there until Samana is a free port, or the Dominican Republic is reduced to a Spanish dependency."

I shall never forget the incredulous glance and smile with which President Buchanan replied

" A new Spanish colony to flank Cuba? We can scarcely admit such a possibility."

" It is more than possible, Mr. President; I know that something like it is planned at Santo Domingo, if Washington seconds the motion of Madrid," said Cazneau, rather stiffly.

" Can you seriously believe," said the President, still smiling incredulously, " that Spain dreams of appropriating the Dominican Republic? "

" I am firmly convinced that Spain has all the cards in hand at this moment," was the decided answer. " Whether she plays them or not, depends on how the game is likely to be accepted at Washington."

. . . On taking leave . . . Secretary Cass invited Cazneau to call at the State Department at a certain hour in the morning. The visit was duly made, and the result of this interview was, that Cazneau accepted an appointment as Special Agent of the United States, to watch and report the course of political events in Santo Domingo, but with the understanding that the question of a naval depot at Samana should be kept in silent abeyance until the sectional differences at home had time to reach a peaceful solution.

Meanwhile private enterprise was in no wise to be invoked in aid of Cazneau's darling scheme of a free port—free to all nations and forever neutral of war—in the matchless bay of Samana. This was an error on both sides, and a source of life-long regret to Cazneau.[81]

The actual instructions to Cazneau directed him to make himself acquainted with the

state of the Country, and from time to time transmit all such useful information as you may collect to this Department. You are especially

[81] Pp. 118-121.

desired to report upon the situation and probable stability of the government, upon the prospects of the trade and productions of the Country, upon the security and protection of foreigners and particularly of American citizens, and whether there is any special subject which demands the interposition of this government.[82]

On June 19, 1859, Cazneau wrote a long and enthusiastic letter to Cass from Santo Domingo City. After a careful survey of the possibilities of the island it was evident to Cazneau that there was

not a fruit or vegetable in general use, or a plant of commercial value now cultivated on our continent anywhere between the Equator and the Arctic Circle, which cannot be raised with facility and profit either on the fertile table lands of La Vega or in the surrounding vallies.

In this same letter Cazneau made a strong plea for the establishment of a free port along the coast of the Dominican territory that bordered on Haiti. There were good harbors at both ends of this depopulated border land, but one of them demanded

special attention as being that Bay of Mancenille of which I have already spoken as the key of La Vega and a standing menace to Dominican independence. Commercially and politically it would be an excellent site for a free, neutral port if Hayti and her European allies would consent to such an arrangement. . . . By this formal declaration of free trade and strict neutrality, this frontier port and territory would be placed under the protection of all the maritime powers.[83]

On October 17, 1859, Cazneau wrote to Cass to announce the opening of the port of Samaná to American commerce,[84] and two months later he pointed out the anxious desire of the Dominican Cabinet for American recognition and the price they were willing to pay for it. Should the United States be willing to recognize the Dominican Republic it would then be possible for Cazneau to negotiate a treaty that would

[82] Cass to Cazneau, April 7, 1859, *Special Missions*, vol. 3, MS. Dept. of State.

[83] Cazneau to Cass, June 19, 1859, *Special Service*, MS. Dept. of State.

[84] *Ibid.*

hold all the resources of the Dominican territory invitingly open to American enterprise. Without straining its stipulations beyond what is already conceded by the laws, or has been heretofore granted to other nations, the vast national capabilities of this country could be made almost as free to our people as if it were their own soil.[85]

The longer that Cazneau resided in Santo Domingo the more he became impressed with the rich natural resources of the island and the opportunities for profitable investment by Americans. On February 22, 1860, he informed Cass that he believed

it highly probable that American interests to the amount of a milion dollars will be within a year permanently invested by American capitalists and settlers in what is now the wildest and least valued section of the Dominican Republic.[86]

These representations of Cazneau made such a definite impression upon Secretary Cass that he wrote to the special agent to assure him that the " subject of a Treaty with the Dominican Republic . . . is now under the consideration of the President." [87]

Encouraged by this evidence of executive interest, Cazneau spared no effort to promote friendly relations between the United States and the Dominican Republic. On May 12, 1860, he sent an interesting despatch relative to the opening of Samaná as a port of entry, and he took the opportunity to advise Cass that it would be possible for the American Government " at any time it chose to negociate for it," to obtain the Bay of Samaná " for a coal depot and mail or naval station." [88]

There was another way in which Cazneau could excite the American Government to take a more lively interest in Santo Domingo—by indicating the pressing danger of a Spanish protectorate. As early as March 4, 1860, he warned Cass that the Spanish Government was making plans for the absorption of its former colony,[89] and in a lengthy despatch of July 31,

---

[85] Cazneau to Cass, December 13, 1859, *ibid.*

[86] *Ibid.*

[87] Cass to Cazneau, March 30, 1860, *Special Missions*, vol. 2, MS. Dept. of State.

[88] Special Service, MS. Dept. of State.

[89] *Ibid.*

1860 he declared that it was common knowledge in Santo Domingo that some sort of an understanding had been arranged with Spain. He felt certain, however, that President Santana would make even at this late hour a strong effort to maintain the republican independence of the Dominicans were he fortified by a timely recognition and some public demonstration of kindly interest on the part of the United States.[90]

Although the maintenance of the Monroe Doctrine was directly involved in the matter of preventing a Spanish protectorate over Santo Domingo, yet both President Buchanan and Secretary Cass seemed so occupied with the domestic situation in the United States that there was but little attention directed towards the Caribbean. Indeed, not a single instruction was sent to Cazneau indicating the attitude of the Administration with reference to any extension of Spanish sovereignty in that area.[91] On October 13, 1860, Cazneau informed Cass that a Spanish protectorate over the Dominican Republic had become " an admitted fact," and that the policy of the Spanish officials had begun " to operate seriously on American interests."[92] But even this alarming statement failed to elicit any response from Cass, and American interests in the island were consigned to the tender mercies of a régime that had given unmistakable evidence of deep-seated hostility towards everything American.

[90] Cazneau to Cass, July 31, 1860, *ibid.*

[91] H. M. Wriston, *Executive Agents in American Foreign Relations*, p. 458.

[92] *Special Service*, MS. Dept. of State. In the spring of 1859 the relations between Spain and the Dominican Republic became increasingly intimate, and in May President Santana sent General Felipe Alfau to Madrid to arrange for a " close understanding." Munitions of war, some money, and military advisers from the Spanish army were sent to the Dominican Republic to help defend it against threatened Haitian aggression. In November, 1860 Francisco Serrano, the Captain-General of Cuba, forwarded to Madrid a definite project which looked either toward annexation or to a protectorate. On March 18, 1861 President Santana proclaimed the reannexation of the Dominican Republic to Spain. See *Documentos Relativos à la Cuestión de Santo Domingo*, pp. 22-35.

CHAPTER VII

SEWARD AND SANTO DOMINGO

When Seward entered upon his duties as Secretary of State he was firmly convinced that the Union could best be saved by a vigorous policy that would involve the United States in armed conflict with European powers and thereby evoke a passionate patriotism that would once more weld into one the fragments of the American State. It was this belief that led to the well-known " Thoughts for the President's Consideration " of April 1, 1861, which advised President Lincoln to adopt the following aggressive attitude:

I would demand explanations from Spain and France, categorically at once. I would seek explanations from Great Britain and Russia, and send agents into Canada, Mexico, and Central America to rouse a vigorous continental spirit of independence on this continent against European intervention.[1]

Seward had heard that Spain and France were desirous of intervening in Mexico, and he had been definitely informed of Spanish designs in Santo Domingo. In view of this situation, he would have the American executive demand the proper explanations from those two nations, and if their answers

---

[1] J. G. Nicolay and John Hay, *Abraham Lincoln, a History* (10 vols., N. Y., 1890), III, 445-447; Frederic Bancroft, *The Life of William H. Seward* (2 vols., N. Y., 1900), II, 132 ff.; Ephraim D. Adams, *Great Britain and the American Civil War* (2 vols., N. Y., 1925), vol. 1, chap. 4. Professor N. W. Stephenson, in his brilliant biography *Lincoln* (Indianapolis, 1924), pp. 157-158, holds that Seward's desire for " an instant, predatory, foreign war " was motivated by the belief that the consequence of such a war would be expansion southward. The possibility of such expansion would be a potent lure to Southern imperialists and thus prove an effective check to the secession movement. The exalted mood which Seward felt in the spring of 1861 is well illustrated by the following excerpt from a despatch sent by the Russian Minister at Washington, Stoeckl, to Prime Minister Gorchakov on May 23, 1861: " As to Mr. Seward . . . he labors under a complete ignorance of international questions; at the same time his self-conceit is such that he refuses to listen to anyone. His arrogance does more harm to the Administration than the ineptitude of his colleagues." Central Archive, Moscow, Foreign Affairs, 49:974, Library of Congress photostats.

were not satisfactory, he would then suggest to the President that he " convene Congress and declare war against them."

On the following day, April 1, Secretary Seward sent a note to Tassara, the Spanish Minister at Washington, which was nothing less than a challenge to the Spanish Government relative to its program in Santo Domingo. After adverting to the reported action of Spanish officials with reference to the subversion of the Dominican Republic, Seward concluded with a paragraph that fairly bristled with menace:

I am directed to inform you and the government of her Catholic Majesty, in a direct manner, that, if they [the reported actions of the Spanish officers] shall be found to have received at any time the sanction of that government, the President will be obliged to regard them as manifesting an unfriendly spirit towards the United States, and to meet the further prosecution of enterprises of that kind in regard to either the Dominican Republic or any part of the American continent or islands, with a prompt, persistent, and if possible, effective resistance.[2]

On this same day Seward also drafted instructions for a special agent who was to replace William L. Cazneau in the Dominican Republic. This agent was to inform himself of

occurrences there as they pass and to communicate to this Department, from time to time, whatever it may seem to you important that this Government should know. It is uncertain what will be the actual condition of political affairs on your arrival. You may find the Republican authorities still existing there, or you may find there a Spanish Protectorate or some other form of foreign domination. . . . While you are not expected to deny or conceal the fact that the Government of the United States has cherished a friendly regard for the Dominican Republic and does not look with favor upon the reported intention of Spanish subjects from Cuba for its subversion, nevertheless if you should find that that Government has given place to another you will refrain from any active participation offensive or disrespectful to the new authorities existing there, but will on the contrary, demean yourself in all respects in full obedience to the laws and institutions of the country.[3]

---

[2] Seward to Tassara, April 2, 1861, *Spanish Legation, Notes to*, vol. 7, MS. Dept. of State.

[3] Seward to ————, April 2, 1861, *Special Missions*, vol. 2, MS. Dept. of State. This challenging spirit so strongly voiced by Seward was reflected in

Seward, however, soon realized that the increasing serious-ness of the domestic situation would render it necessary for him to recede from this advanced position. President Lincoln was too wise to adopt Seward's policy of saving the Union at the expense of a foreign war, and it daily grew more doubtful whether the element in the South loyal to the federal compact was anything more than a mere minority. Realizing that it was best to proceed with caution, Seward finally cancelled the instructions of April 2, providing for a new special agent to the Dominican Republic. In August, 1861 Seward informed Schurz, the American Minister at Madrid, that it had been de-cided to submit the whole question of the subversion of the Dominican Republic to " the consideration of Congress at its next regular session." [4] Such a decision was merely " Seward's graceful way of escape from making good the threats of a few months before." [5]

Throughout the next four years, Seward was careful to refrain from making any further threats against Spanish inter-vention in Santo Domingo, and American business interests soon found it advantageous to come to an understanding with the Spanish officials resident in the island. To certain American adventurers it seemed quite possible to capitalize the dire woes that had descended upon the United States during the American Civil War. There should be many peaceful spirits who would welcome escape from this turmoil, and what adjacent country offered a surer haven of refuge or richer opportunities than did Santo Domingo. As early as 1860 there were some Americans who had already felt the call of the tropics. Thus we find in that year W. S. Courtney publishing in New York City an interesting travel-book which he entitled *The Gold Fields of St. Domingo.* If Americans had braved the dangers of western wilds and the storms and fevers of ocean voyages in their

the note that William Preston, the American Minister at Madrid, addressed to the Spanish Foreign Office—a note that was based squarely upon the principles of the Monroe Doctrine. April 12, 1861, *Spain, Desp.*, vol. 42, MS. Dept. of State. See also the note of Horatio Perry to the Spanish Foreign Office, June 19, 1861, *Spain, Desp.*, vol. 43, MS. Dept. of State.

[4] Seward to Schurz, August 14, 1861, *Spain, Inst.*, vol. 15, MS. Dept. of State.

[5] Frederic Bancroft, *Life of William H. Seward*, II, 159.

quest for the gold of distant California, why would they not rush post-haste to Santo Domingo where the whole island " is one immense gold field from one extremity to the other? " Moreover, a plentiful gold supply was only one of the myriad advantages that the island offered There were many valleys with " fabulously rich savannahs," while the high lands of the interior were ideal for grazing purposes. The climate was unique. During the warm, bright days a land breeze tempered the vertical rays of the sun, while at night air currents from the sea brought refreshing slumber even to the most confirmed insomniac. Of course, there were sinister rumors to the effect that yellow fever took its toll of victims, but this was largely hearsay. If one would only observe certain precautions, such as keeping out of the noon-day sun unless protected by a sun-shade, and refraining from eating fruits in the afternoon and evening, there was little danger of an attack of the fever. But even in case one did contract this over-advertised ailment, the " timely administration of anything that will quicken the action of the biliary and gastric processes will speedily carry it off." Finally, with reference to the dread hurricanes that were supposed to scourge the coasts of Santo Domingo, it should be realized that such storms come only at one time of the day, namely, " between sun set and sun rise." [6]

From the perusal of these inspired pages it was only too apparent that the wealth of the Indies was available to any American with sufficient capital and energy to travel to Santo Domingo. Impressed with the opportunities that beckoned to settlers from the United States, General William L. Cazneau devoted his ample talents to organizing, on October 1, 1862, the " American West India Company," with a capital stock of $1,000,000.[7] This stock was divided into 10,000 shares of

[6] W. S. Courtney, *The Gold Fields of St. Domingo* (N. Y., 1860), pp. 8-9, 11, 19, 74-75, 86-87, 123. In this same year James Redpath brought out a *Guide to Hayti* (Boston, 1860), describing in great detail the opportunities which awaited the immigrant to that country.

[7] Cazneau and Fabens had made a last desperate attempt to secure concessions from the Dominican Government just prior to the proclamation that announced the extinction of the Dominican Republic and the restoration of Spanish rule (March 18, 1861). This venture of the two American fortune hunters is disclosed in a letter from Ricart y Torres, the Dominican Minister of Finance, to

$100 each, " all of which was paid in for real estate, rights and privileges in Santo Domingo." The trustees of the company were listed as Hiram Ketchum, N. Y., William L. Cazneau, Santo Domingo City, Richard Kimball, N. Y., George F. Dunning, Supt. of United States Assay Office, and Joseph W. Fabens, N. Y. It was entirely fitting that one with the name of Hiram Ketchum was made president of this company, while Colonel Fabens was appointed secretary, George F. Dunning was given the office of treasurer, and Joseph W. Currier was selected as assistant treasurer. In their prospectus issued in 1862 they clearly indicate their holdings in Santo Domingo and their program:

It is proposed to commence operations in the Island of Santo Domingo. The fertility of the soil, productiveness of the mines, and great wealth in forest woods of the Island, are unrivalled on the globe. . . . The Company have already secured . . . a clear and undisputable title to some of the most inviting districts upon the Island. . . . They are sole owners, by purchase, of the townships of Azomante and Palenque. . . . Palenque is situated on the south side of the Island about twelve miles west of the capital. It has the best harbor on the south coast. . . . Its position is unrivalled for healthfulness of climate, beauty of scenery, and fertility of soil. . . . It is the purpose of the

Francisco Serrano, the Captain-General of Cuba. It bears the date of March 7, 1861, and refers to the visit of a certain American who had recently arrived in Santo Domingo City. The object of his visit was at first supposed to have some bearing on the question of the removal of guano from the island of Alta Vela, but Ricart soon discovered that it was of far greater significance than that. This strange gentleman, together with " General Cazneau and Colonel Fabens (other strangers, both Americans), spoke with me first, and later proposed in a conference which they had with the President of the Republic, the following points:
" 1. To grant a loan to the Government of 500,000 pesos, bearing a small rate of interest and running for a long term, which amount would naturally be placed at the disposal of the Republic.
" 2. To establish a current of immigration which would people the Peninsula of Samana, the cost of which they themselves would bear.
" 3. In return for these advantages . . . they request the exclusive privilege of opening up the navigation of the Yuna and Yaque Rivers (the two principal rivers of the island) ; permission to establish a shipyard to be built by immigrants; the right of exploitation of the coal and all other mines in the Republic, and a concession of some leagues of agricultural land along the banks of the Yuna and Yaque rivers for the purpose of establishing agricultural colonies." For this letter see José de la Gándara y Navarro, *Anexión y Guerra de Santo Domingo* (2 vols., Madrid, 1884), I, 153-155.

Company to have their lands surveyed into suitable lots and homesteads for distribution among actual settlers and members of the Company at a small advance on cost. Each share of stock will be represented by, and redeemable in, twenty acres of land, or a lot of ten thousand square feet in the town of Azomante or Palenque. It will thus be seen that the stock represents a positive and sufficient value, without taking into account the mining, manufacturing, and commercial advantages held by the Company.[8]

In a circular letter sent out by Hiram Ketchum on March 8, 1863, numerous other inducements are held out to prospective settlers. Thus " no taxes will be levied on the lands of settlers introduced under the auspices of the Company, for ten years next succeeding their arrival in the country." Moreover, " ready-made houses, mechanical implements, seeds, cattle and personal effects " would be admitted free of duty.[9]

This rosy recital of the advantages offered to American immigrants should have been sufficient to convince even the most dubious. But the American West India Company went even further, and soon it began to publish letters from satisfied settlers. The following communication from F. H. Dupont, of Rouse's Point, New York, is typical:

We are all well satisfied. We like the country better every day. . . . Let a northern farmer come here and cultivate the land properly and he can't help getting rich in a short time even with a small capital to begin with.[10]

These circular letters of the company were read with growing interest by many Americans, and, in order to confirm the favorable impression they were intended to create, Colonel Fabens, who served as secretary of the company, took his facile pen in hand and wrote glowing reports of the undeveloped riches of Santo Domingo. In 1863 Fabens read before the American Geographical and Statistical Society of New York a colorful paper on the *Resources of Santo Domingo*. After dilating upon the vast mineral wealth in the island and the

---

[8] There is a copy of this prospectus in the New York Public Library.

[9] See pamphlet literature on Santo Domingo in the New York Public Library.

[10] This letter is dated May 13, 1863 and is contained in the literature of the company now in the possession of the New York Public Library.

agricultural possibilities that could be realized by American farmers, he discussed at length the political aspects of the situation. The Dominican people had been sorely tried since they had achieved their independence in 1844. After looking in vain to Europe and the United States for protection against the belligerent Haitians, they had finally turned to their old Mother Country, Spain, for assistance. They had heard with " lively pleasure " of the regeneration of Spain. They had heard of her " railways and steamships, of her encouragement of popular education, of the repeal or relaxation of her old oppressive laws regulating commerce and industry," and " they asked to be participants in the benefits of her liberal enlightened policy." With " very natural feelings of pride " Young Spain had accepted the responsibility of raising the Dominicans to higher levels. She had already undertaken to build new roads and establish postal communications, and she had promised to lower import duties and repeal altogether the duties on exports. But, most important of all from the viewpoint of Americans, the Spanish officials in Santo Domingo had adopted a policy of direct encouragement to immigrants from the United States.[11]

In this same year, 1863, Fabens made another effort to acquaint Americans with the many opportunities that awaited them in Santo Domingo. In an interesting and highly colored travel-book, entitled *In the Tropics,* he attempted to portray scenes that would take one back to days in ancient Arcady.[12] To Americans who had grown weary of the long northern winters and yearned to see nature in her more bountiful moods, these enthusiastic descriptions of Dominican life proved distinctly alluring. The American West India Company began active operations and settlers took passage for this new Isle of the Blest. But soon certain reports less tinged with rose began to reach the United States. On April 6, 1863 William G. Jaeger, the American Commercial Agent at Santo Domingo City, wrote to the Department of State in a very discouraging tone. Some twelve or fifteen American settlers had recently arrived in the Dominican Republic under the auspices of

[11] (N. Y., 1863).   [12] (N. Y., 1863).

Col. J. W. Fabens, (of Greytown fame), and William L. Cazneau (formerly United States especial agent of this City). They all intend to return to the United States by the first conveyance, cursing in their tears, the "West India Company" of Fabens and Cazneau, and more particularly the Spaniards in St. Domingo.[13]

In July, 1863, Jaeger was equally melancholy. Of the last lot of emigrants sent out by the West India Company, some fourteen in all, nine had died, "two went home, and the rest with those who came before are down with the fever, and not expected to live." [14]

In the following month, August, 1863, a formidable insurrection broke out against the so-called "beneficent rule" of Young Spain in Santo Domingo, and this unsettled condition of affairs continued until in July, 1865, when the Spanish armies evacuated the island.[15] Such being the case, it was apparent that the grandiose schemes of the American West India Company would come to naught. Indeed, so forgetful were the Spaniards of the fine phrases forged for their edification by Fabens in his pamphlets and addresses that they even destroyed the splendid estate of that bosom friend of Fabens, General William L. Cazneau, the most active promoter of American emigration to Santo Domingo.[16]

On September 14, 1863 the Dominican insurgents proclaimed the restoration of the Dominican Republic, and General José Salcedo was chosen as President of the Provisional Government. One of the first acts of the new government was to prepare instructions for William Clark, who was to be sent as a special agent to the United States to solicit assistance.[17] But inasmuch

[13] Jaeger to Seward, April 6, 1863, *Santo Domingo, Consular Desp.*, vol. 4, MS. Dept. of State.

[14] Jaeger to Seward, July 2, 1863, *ibid.*

[15] The standard account of Spanish intervention in the Dominican Republic is that of General José de la Gándara y Navarro, *Anexión y Guerra de Santo Domingo.* See also *Documentos Relativos a la Cuestión de Santo Domingo, remitidos al Congreso de los Diputados por el Ministerio de la Guerra* (Madrid, 1865).

[16] Jaeger to Seward, December 27, 1863, *Santo Domingo, Consular Desp.*, vol. 4, MS. Dept. of State.

[17] Clark was instructed that one of his "principal objects ought to be to engage, through your friends and the public Press, the good will and feelings

as Seward was determined to maintain a neutral attitude towards the contending parties in Santo Domingo this special mission was doomed to failure. But not dismayed by this lack of American response, the Dominican Government very promptly sent another agent to Washington to open negotiations with the American Government. On February 1, 1864 Pablo Pujol wrote to Seward to acquaint him with the fact that he had arrived in Washington " with full powers " to treat with the American Government relative to a common understanding. In conclusion, he requested Seward to " grant an interview, indicating the day and hour for the purpose." [18]

Receiving no answer from the Secretary of State, Pujol on February 6, 1864 wrote a second note to Seward. He was not

unaware of the line of conduct which the Cabinet of Washington has traced for itself in respect to its international relations, during the existence of the civil war, which . . . afflicts for the time this prosperous country. But in addressing to the Secretary his said note, he promised himself that it would at any rate procure for him some reply by which the undersigned might show to his Government that it had not been altogether a barren and idle step to recur in its day of trial to the source of liberty in the New World. But notwithstanding the Secretary of the Undersigned attended on the 4th at the Department in expectation of the hoped for reply, because that was the day of admission for the purpose, and despite his having obtained in a manner which was seemingly effective, the attainment of access to the Secretary, he obtained neither the one thing or the other, but the conviction only that the Secretary was not disposed to acknowledge the Undersigned as Commissioner of the Dominican Republic.

This distinct rebuff to the Dominican Commissioner would have been sufficient to discourage most men, but Pujol still hoped that Secretary Seward might alter his attitude. For this reason he entered into a long discussion of the propriety of receiving representatives of unrecognized governments, and cited in detail the practice of European Governments in accord-

of the American Government and the People in our behalf and in favor of the Dominican cause." November 26, 1863, *Santo Domingo, Reports, September 28, 1859–July 31, 1871,* MS. Dept. of State.

[18] Pujol to Seward, February 1, 1864, *Dominican Republic, Notes from,* vol. 1, MS. Dept. of State.

ing receptions to the diplomatic agents of the Southern Con-
federacy.[19] Such arguments, however, were far from convincing
to Seward, who continued to pursue a non-committal course.
In view of the fact that he had vigorously protested against
the reception of the Confederate agents by the British Government, it was hardly likely that he would now change his principles merely to favor the cause of the insurgent Dominicans.[20]
Indeed, he made the proposals of the Dominican agent the
occasion to draft instructions to Koerner, the American Minister
at Madrid, in which the recognition policy of the United States
is clearly stated:

The revolutionists in the island [Santo Domingo] have, in various
forms and through several channels, appealed to this government for
recognition, for aid, and for sympathy. Pursuing the policy we have
too ineffectually insisted upon at the hands of other nations, we have
not received any agents of the revolution, even informally, nor have we
in any way responded to them, while we have given instructions to
the ministerial officers to see that the neutrality laws of the United
States are regularly maintained and enforced.[21]

Deprived of American assistance, the Dominican Provisional
Government endeavoured to effect peace by coming to terms
with the Spanish military authorities. But these efforts were
fruitless, and certain Dominican generals seized upon these
negotiations as an indication of undue familiarity on the part
of General Salcedo with the Spanish Captain-General, José de
la Gándara y Navarro. It was not long before Salcedo was
removed by assassination, and in March, 1865 General Pedro
Antonio Pimentel was installed as the new president of the
Dominican Republic. But Pimentel himself was soon forced to
vacate the presidential office in favor of another of the numerous Dominican generals, José Maria Cabral.[22]

[19] Pujol to Seward, February 6, 1864, *ibid.*

[20] E. D. Adams, *Great Britain and the American Civil War*, I, 105 ff.

[21] Seward to Koerner, March 12, 1864, *Diplomatic Correspondence*, 1864,
pt. 4, p. 12.

[22] With reference to the relations between the Dominican generals and the
Spanish military authorities, see José de la Gándara y Navarro, *Anexión y
Guerra de Santo Domingo*. For the Dominican side, see Gregorio Luperón,
Notas Autobiográficas y Apuntes Históricos sobre la República Dominicana
(2 vols., Ponce, 1896).

The latest incumbent of the executive office was a " warm friend of America," and the American Commercial Agent, Paul T. Jones, confessed to Seward that he had a high personal regard for Cabral. In view of the existing situation, Jones thought it highly expedient to commence negotiations for securing Samaná Bay as a naval station. If Secretary Seward desired such a station, Jones was certain that " it could easily be obtained." It would appear that Samaná abounded in valuable timber and coal, and from its commanding location it was the " Key of the West Indies." [23]

But Jones was not destined to acquire fame by negotiating a treaty for the cession of Samaná Bay to the United States. In the Dominican Republic the office of president was of such uncertain tenure that it was difficult to conclude any negotiations that lasted more than a few months. No sooner did Cabral assume the executive duties than malcontents intrigued against him, and it was not long before the state of affairs compelled him to give way before the most talented adventurer in Dominican politics, Buenaventura Baez. During the period of Spanish occupation Baez had lived in Europe, where he enjoyed a liberal subsidy from the Spanish Crown and was even raised to the honorary rank of Field Marshal in the Spanish army. After the outbreak of the insurrection in Santo Domingo against Spanish rule, Baez resigned his commission as Field Marshal and laid plans to return to the island, where his abilities were all too well recognized. Light on his life in Europe during the Spanish occupation of the Dominican Republic is cast by an interesting letter from Gustavus Koerner, the American Minister at Madrid, to Carl Schurz, part of which is as follows:

General Baez I know well. While my family was at one time absent from Madrid for some five or six weeks I took my meals at the Prince's Hotel where he was then living, and as he was looked upon as a diplomatic character, they assigned him a regular seat at my left. He is a man, as the French would say, *bien rusé*, educated partly in France, with European manners, and well calculated to deceive, if he wants to.

---

[23] Jones to Seward, August 14 and September 25, 1865, *Santo Domingo, Consular Desp.*, vol. 5, MS. Dept. of State.

I could never find out from him whether he had had a hand in the annexation in the first place. He did not join the insurgents, and became so suspected by the liberals, that he had to leave and went to France, long in fact before the insurrection commenced. He was in Madrid, it was said, for the purpose of advising the Spaniards how to administer the country, and probably wanted employment, that is, before the troubles broke out in open war. He declared himself neutral to me, that is, after the fighting had commenced, and must have satisfied the Spaniards that he rather favored them, or else they would have quickly sent him away from Madrid.[24]

In the autumn of 1865 it became apparent to Dominican politicians that General Cabral would soon be forced to make as hurried an exit from the presidential office as had his predecessor, General Pimentel. The prestige of the former chief executive, Buenaventura Baez, now conveniently living on the neighboring island of Curaçao, was rapidly growing, and by November first it had reached such proportions that Cabral addressed a petition to Baez requesting him to hasten to the Dominican Republic, where "a general popular movement" had proclaimed him President.[25] Baez immediately wrote to express his appreciation of such a compliment, but he desired that some formal manifestation of popular sentiment be exhibited.[26] In order to satisfy this condition the Dominican National Assembly, on November 14, 1865, issued a decree which nominated Baez as President of the Republic, and appointed a committee to wait upon him at Curaçao and escort him back to Santo Domingo City.[27] On December 8 he was inaugurated for the third time as chief executive of the Dominican Republic.

While this movement in favor of Baez was gathering strength, Mrs. Cora Montgomery Cazneau, wife of General W. L. Cazneau, wrote to Secretary James Harlan with reference to the establishment of a "free zone" on the island of Santo

---

[24] Koerner to Schurz, January 17, 1870, *Schurz Papers*, MS. Library of Congress.

[25] Cabral to Baez, November 1, 1865, *Report of the United States Commission of Inquiry to Santo Domingo* (Wash., 1871), pp. 152-153.

[26] Baez to Cabral, November 5, 1865, *ibid.*, p. 153.

[27] J. B. Curiel to Baez, November 16, 1865, *ibid.*, p. 154.

Domingo. Her project was very similar to that advocated by her husband in 1859-1860, and she requested Secretary Harlan to place her letter before Secretary Seward. The most pertinent paragraphs in her letter are as follows:

In the winter of 1859-60, while W. L. Cazneau was acting as Special Agent of the United States near the Dominican Government, the majority of the senate and cabinet of that republic had many anxious, though unofficial, consultations as to the means of escaping from the projected submission to Spain, . . . and from the union with Hayti and the supremacy of the negro race. To prevent these evils the men who at this moment control the action of the Dominican Republic, eagerly acceded to this *projet*:

" 1. In consideration of amity, recognition, etc., the Dominican Republic would cede to the United States a naval station on the Bay of Manzanill at the northwest corner of her limits—the Bay to be made neutral of war forever to all nations.

" 2. That a belt of free and neutral territory seven (or nine) leagues wide should be drawn across the island from sea to sea, including the Bay of Manzanill on the North and embracing the disputed frontier villages, which ' Banda Neutral ' should be open to colonization for all citizens of nations at peace with both republics, and have all its ports free and neutral of war—with municipal independence."

Mrs. Cazneau then expressed the opinion that the Dominican Government would now be ready to accede to this same proposal if it could be

prepared at Washington—*privately and at once*—and sent without delay to Port au Prince for ratification.[28]

Secretary Harlan promptly forwarded this letter to Secretary Seward, who was deeply impressed with the project set forth by Mrs. Cazneau. Before taking any action in this matter Seward thought it best to take a cruise in the Caribbean in order to survey the situation with his own eyes. He soon announced to his fellow Cabinet members that he wished to make the trip in order to enjoy a much needed rest, but Gideon Welles, the Secretary of the Navy, regarded such talk as " ri-

[28] Cora Montgomery Cazneau to James Harlan (Secretary of the Interior), September 6, 1865, *Seward Papers*, MS. Auburn, N. Y.

diculous." [29] It was evident that the Secretary of State had some ulterior motive, but no one was able to penetrate his plans.

On December 26, 1865, Welles noted in his *Diary* that at the Cabinet meeting on that day Seward

had a long story about Mrs. Cazneau and St. Domingo. I judge from his own statement or manner of stating, and from his omission to read Mrs. C's communication, that he has committed some mistakes which he does not wish to become public.[30]

In view of the sharp opposition expressed by European governments in past years relative to the acquisition of an American naval base in the Dominican Republic, it was expedient for Seward to keep the project of Mrs. Cazneau as secret as possible. On January 9, 1866 he visited the Danish island of St. Thomas, and on January 14 he arrived at Santo Domingo City. He was immediately greeted by General Cazneau whose zealous attention to the wants of the Secretary of State is acidly described by Davis Hatch:

Mr. Cazneau was on the watch, and managed to get him [Seward] to his house before I or any other citizen of the United States knew of his arrival. His motives in his cunning management to have him quite to himself were readily understood. Having always publicly vilified and traduced him, it would not suit him to have any one else present in his conferences with him. As Mr. Seward was in the city but a few hours, he succeeded in preventing any other citizen seeing him.[31]

In order to further his many pet projects it was necessary for Cazneau to convince Baez that the American Secretary of State still reposed confidence in the former special agent of the American Government. After Baez saw the exclusive way in which General Cazneau shepherded Seward around the streets of Santo Domingo City, it was only natural that any lingering doubts of his should have been dispelled. During the short time that Seward remained in the Dominican capital he was

[29] Gideon Welles, *Diary*, II, 409.   [30] *Ibid.*, 404.
[31] *Report of the Select Committee of the Senate on the Memorial of Davis Hatch*, Sen. Rep. No. 234, 41 Cong., 2 sess. (Wash., 1870), p. 126. Hereafter cited as the *Hatch Report*.

accorded a public reception by the Dominican President, who seemed to make a favorable impression upon the American visitors.[32] After an exchange of courtesies, Seward discussed the recognition policy of the United States with reference to new governments in the Western Hemisphere. Thanks to the American founding fathers, there had been erected in the northern part of the American continent a republic with broad foundations. Indeed, this American state had grown to be an imposing, possibly

a majestic empire. Like every other structure of large proportions, it requires outward buttresses. Those buttresses will arise in the development of civilization in this hemisphere. They will consist of republics like our own, founded in adjacent countries and islands upon the principle of the equal rights of men. . . . We desire those buttresses to be multiplied, and strengthened, as fast as it can be done, without the exercise of fraud or force on our own part. . . . We have, therefore, no choice but to recognize the Republic of Dominica, as soon as it shall afford the necessary guaranty of its own stability.[33]

On January 28, 1866 Seward returned to Washington, and on the following day Cazneau addressed him a letter from Santo Domingo in which he described several interviews he had recently had with President Baez. It was his opinion that Baez was a " statesman " who was very anxious to carry out Seward's suggestions relative to cultivating more intimate connections with the United States. Also, the new president had avowed his intention to stimulate " American enterprise." [34] This should be welcome news to American investors!

In the first week in February, 1866 President Baez, evidently encouraged by Seward's visit, wrote a personal letter to Presi-

[32] Frederick Seward, in his *Seward at Washington* (N. Y., 1891), p. 310, remarks that President Baez was " a man of medium height and prepossessing appearance."

[33] Frederick Seward, *op. cit.*, p. 311. According to the correspondent of the New York *Herald*, on February 5, 1886, Seward complimented President Baez on his excellent administration of affairs in the Dominican Republic: " Your policy seems to have been eminently judicious. I trust it will prove as successful as it was manifestly wise."

[34] Cazneau to Seward, January 29, 1866, *Santo Domingo, Consular Desp.*, vol. 5, MS. Dept. of State.

dent Johnson which was a plea for friendship and recognition. After referring to the reorganization of the Dominican Republic that followed the withdrawal of the Spanish military forces, Baez expressed the hope that the

Republic of the United States and its Government will be pleased to see the reorganization of this country, and will contribute powerfully to place this small American State in the congress of free nations, by strengthening its good and cordial relations with it. The Dominican Republic confides in the consideration of the Great Powers, like the United States, that has put into practice the most elevated principles of justice and humanity, to assist in perfecting its internal progress, and securing foreign peace. My efforts will be great to deserve that consideration for my country, with which I am identified, and to perpetuate the friendship which must be the inevitable result. I pray the Almighty to have Your Excellency in his holy keeping.[35]

A week before Baez wrote this letter to President Johnson, the American Chief Executive had already decided to recognize the Dominican Republic. On January 30, 1866, Johnson sent a message to both the Senate and House of Representatives in which he expressed the belief that " the commercial interests of our country would be promoted by a formal recognition of the independence of the Dominican Republic." Therefore he nominated General Cazneau as the United States Commissioner and Consul-General to Dominica, and requested the appropriation of the requisite salary for that position.[36] But

[35] Baez to Johnson, February 6, 1866, *Santo Domingo, Reports, 1859-1871*, MS. Dept. of State.

[36] J. D. Richardson, *Messages and Papers of the Presidents*, VI, 377. The attitude of the Haitian Government towards President Baez of the Dominican Republic, and also towards General Cazneau, the bosom friend of Baez, is well indicated in the following despatch of H. E. Peck, the American consul at Port-au-Prince, to the Department of State on April 20, 1866. According to Peck, the Haitian Government had for some time, " but especially since the appointment of Gen. Cazneau as U. S. Commissioner in St. Domingo, evinced, at first suspicion, and later, actual hatred of Pres. Biaz. . . . In a recent informal conversation with the Minister of Foreign Affairs, after drawing from him what I regarded as an admission that his government had taken alarm at the appointment of Gen. Cazneau, regarding it as a sign that Pres. Biaz was proposing to renew the old Samana negotiations with us, I ventured to repeat to him some of the statements made by Mr. Seward to me during his late visit here. The main points of these statements, as I communicated them to the Minister were nearly

before Cazneau could be informed of his nomination, he had written an interesting letter to Seward, on April 11, 1866, in which he disclosed how President Baez had honored him with an " accurate and confidential exposition " of his plan of policy. Friendship with the United States was to be the basic fact in the foreign relations of the Dominican Republic.[37] The statement in President Johnson's message to Congress of January 30 with reference to the recognition of the Baez Government was followed in the Dominican Republic by

mining and other concessions of great value to several of our citizens. It would hardly be too strong an expression to say that this opportune act has sealed the destiny of the Dominican Republic as an American state. . . . Several competent engineers are already at work in behalf of numerous capitalists in the United States, exploring the mineral districts, examining road-ways etc. It would not surprise me to see a million of dollars invested by American citizens under the liberal mining and colonization laws of this Republic before the close of the current year.[38]

as follows: (1) . . . The present administration is of the opinion that no privilege, here or elsewhere, can be of such value that it would be worth while to get it by force. . . . (2) As to the appointment of Gen. Cazneau, it was not made with reference to the acquisition by us of territory. . . . Gen. C. was, it must be acknowledged, the cheerful agent of the Buchanan administration in the Samana affair. But time has radically changed his political views. He is now in full accord with the Anti Slavery policy of our government and no longer believes that territorial enlargement is essential to the development of any of our institutions." See *Hayti, Consular Desp.*, vol. 2, MS. Dept. of State.

[37] In a confidential communication to Lord Clarendon of June 6, 1866 Sir Spenser St. John, the British representative at Port-au-Prince, commented upon a recent conversation he had had with Peck, the American consul. Peck told how he had tried to quiet Haitian fears of General Cazneau by assuring the Foreign Office that Cazneau's " views had been greatly modified by recent events." He then concluded his conversation with St. John with the following significant words: " I will not hide from you that Mr. Seward said to me when he visited Port au Prince: ' We want a Naval Station in the West Indies, and we must and will have one.' " F. O. 115/450.

[38] Cazneau to Seward, April 11, 1866, *Santo Domingo, Consular Desp.*, vol. 5, MS. Dept. of State. On April 9, 1866, Mrs. Cora Montgomery Cazneau wrote to Frederick Seward in much the same tenor. President Baez had turned out to be " pretty soundly American." The chief difficulty in cementing friendly relations between the United States and the Dominican Republic had long been the low caliber of the American consular agents. These agents seemed always to be chosen for their " superior powers of intemperance." But in spite of the maladroit conduct of American officials the relations between the two countries

On April 16, 1866, Seward wrote to Cazneau to inform him of his nomination as Commissioner and Consul-General to the Dominican Republic, but he took care to remark that the " Senate has not yet confirmed the nomination." [39] As it happened, the Senate continued to withhold its consent to the nomination of Cazneau, and the reason for this action was indicated by Davis Hatch in his testimony before the Select Committee of the Senate in 1870. According to this testimony, it would appear that Cazneau took Seward under his wing the moment that the Secretary of State landed in Santo Domingo City on January 14, 1866. This awakened the suspicions of Hatch and led him to write to a friend in Washington with reference to Cazneau's

character and antecedents, his unpopularity with his countrymen by his selfish and mischievous course.

This letter was then handed to

Mr. Seward, and he handed it to Mr. Sumner, with the remark that Mr. Cazneau had deceived him. Further inquiry was made, which resulted in his being dropped.[40]

But despite the fact that the Senate refused to confirm the nomination of Cazneau, this indefatigable individual continued to advise Secretary Seward with reference to the situation in the Dominican Republic. In March, 1866, there were numerous indications that the administration of President Baez was not

were daily growing more intimate. " Every vessel brings in parties from the United States in quest of mines, etc. President Baez receives them cordially and whoever brings a fair show of responsibility is sure of getting the right to do something. Our people will open up a second California here within two years, and those who make fortunes here may thank Mr. Seward's visit and President Johnson's message about the Dominican republic for it, for they opened the hearts and the souls of the Dominicans." *Seward Papers*, MS. Auburn, N. Y.

[39] Seward to Cazneau, April 16, 1866, *Dominica, Inst.*, vol. 1, MS. Dept. of State. It is interesting to note that, notwithstanding the intimate association between President Baez and General Cazneau, there was also a close concert between Baez and the French consul at Santo Domingo City. When Baez was overthrown by the revolution in the last week in May, he immediately sought sanctuary in the house of the French consul and remained there until he was given permission to go into exile. See David Leon (British consul at Santo Domingo City) to Lord Clarendon, June 9, 1866, F. O. 115/451.

[40] *Hatch Report*, p. 126.

receiving popular support, and on the night of May 28-29 he was forced to vacate the presidential office.[41] His enemies had busily circulated charges that he had " treated the Republic as his private patrimony " and had used its resources for " his individual interest." General Cazneau does not attempt to refute this grave charge against President Baez, but he does go into considerable detail with reference to the friendly interest that the Dominican Chief Executive had recently evinced in

[41] On February 28, 1866 Paul T. Jones, the American Commercial Agent at Santo Domingo City, reported to Seward that there was a " strong undercurrent setting against the government," and on March 7 he advised the Secretary of State that both the French and the British consuls at Santo Domingo City regarded the Baez Government as " unstable." The French consul had even remarked to Mr. Jones that " no one save Mr. Baez knows what he's about." *Santo Domingo, Consular Desp.*, vol. 5, MS. Dept. of State.

It is important here to note another scheme for joint mediation on the part of the United States, England, and France with reference to the unfriendly relations that existed between the Dominican Republic and Haiti. On June 16, 1866 Lord Clarendon wrote to Sir Frederick Bruce, at Washington, to advise him that Charles Francis Adams had recently suggested that the troubles between the two states on the island of Santo Domingo might be adjusted by the joint action of England and the United States. Lord Clarendon immediately consulted with the Haitian Minister at London with regard to mediation on the part of England, France, and the United States, and found him quite receptive. Clarendon then instructed Mr. Bruce to take the matter up with Secretary Seward. Lord Clarendon to Sir Frederick Bruce, June 16, 1866, F. O. 115/451, No. 204. Lord Cowley, at Paris, hastened to broach this question of mediation to the French Secretary of Foreign Affairs, who " expressed his readiness to co-operate with H. M. Govt. and with that of the United States with the object of placing the relations between Haiti and Santo Domingo upon a better footing." Cowley to Clarendon, Paris, June 22, 1866, F. O. 115/451, enclosed in No. 211. On July 10, 1866 Sir Frederick Bruce wrote a note to Secretary Seward and inquired whether the American Government was " inclined to take part in the mediation in concert with France and Great Britain." Bruce to Seward, July 10, 1866, F. O. 5/1066, enclosed in No. 239. On the following day, Seward replied that the President of the United States entirely concurred " in the sentiments of His Majesty's Government and of the French Government upon this subject, which you have communicated to me, and . . . he would have been prepared to express that concurrence in some practical form . . . if the conditions of both of those Republics had undergone no change since his attention was first called to the subject. A revolution, however, has now occurred in St. Domingo, and no permanent Govt. or Administration has yet been established there. Under these circumstances the President thinks that it has become necessary to await a re-organization of the Govt. in that part of the Island. When that re-organization shall occur, the President will with pleasure recur to the subject, if a necessity for good offices . . . shall seem to exist." Seward to Bruce, July 11, 1866, F. O. 5/1066, enclosed in No. 239.

connection with schemes for American economic penetration of the island. It was Cazneau's firm belief that President Baez had "earnestly labored to bring the vast natural wealth of this soil into the sphere of American enterprise." Despite the fact that the American Government had not seen fit to recognize the Dominican Government, President Baez had never faltered in his determination to plant and to fortify

a strong American interest on this soil. In the absence of any accredited representative of the United States with whom he could frankly confer, he repeatedly sent for me to explain, and impress upon me, the course to be pursued for the protection of the extensive and varied rights which Americans have latterly acquired here by purchase and concession.[42]

After General Cazneau had discussed at length the merits of the Baez administration from the viewpoint of the American investor, he confided to Seward that the new Dominican government of General Cabral had extended to him the "strongest assurances of favor and protection for American trade and enterprise," and he felt that these assurances were "sincere." In view of this friendly attitude, the American Government sent J. Somers Smith as the new Commercial Agent at Santo Domingo City, while on September 17, 1866 the Dominican Government was formally recognized by issuance of an exequatur to a Dominican Consul-General to be located in New York City.[43] In August, 1866, shortly after the arrival of Smith at Santo Domingo City, President Cabral called to pay his respects, and according to Smith the following conversation took place:

"General, what is the state of your country?" Said he, "We are very poor indeed, and I do not know what we can do. Can you give us any assistance, consul?" "Well," said I, "perhaps we might. What do you want?" Said he, "I cannot tell exactly." Said I, "Send

---

[42] Cazneau to Seward, June 10, 1866, *Santo Domingo, Consular Desp.*, vol. 5, MS. Dept. of State. The reason why President Baez made General Cazneau his close companion was not merely that both of them were interested in Dominican public lands and mining properties, but also that the American Commercial Agent at Santo Domingo City, Paul T. Jones, was personally hostile to the Dominican Chief Executive.

[43] J. B. Moore, *Digest of International Law*, I, 107.

over your minister of finance to me." The minister of finance came the
following day, and I asked him, "What do you want?" He said,
"We want about a million." Said I, "What can you give us as
indemnity? We cannot agree to give money without getting something
for it." He said, "We have coal mines at Samana." "Oh," said I,
"we have plenty of coal in the United States; we want something better
than that. What do you think of Samana Bay as a naval station?"
He thought it might be brought about.[44]

Encouraged by this conversation, José G. Garcia, the Dominican Secretary of Foreign Relations, wrote to Seward on
November 8, 1866 to request an advance of a million dollars
"in the character of a loan on just, equitable, and reasonable
conditions." In addition to this loan the Dominican Government was anxious to secure from the United States, "on
credit," a "number of pieces of heavy artillery sufficient to
meet the necessity she has for them, because all those are
broken up which were in her strong places before the Spanish
rule." [45]

On the same day the American Commercial Agent, J. Somers
Smith, wrote to Seward in a similar vein. The Dominican
Government had requested him to address Seward relative to
a loan of "one or two millions of dollars," part of which
would be used to bolster up the depreciated paper currency of
the republic. Furthermore, the Dominican Government was
desirous of "purchasing 10,000 stand of approved arms—100
pieces of cannon, including some field pieces, and a few heavy
guns for fortifications, and a small steam propeller for packet
or other service." [46]

In return for this assistance the Dominican Government
would extend to the American Government the "use of the
coal mines at Samana, and the keys called 'Levantado' and
'Carenero' for such purposes and for such time as may be
agreed upon, if satisfactory arrangements can be concluded."
It was the opinion of Smith that the possession of these keys

[44] *Hatch Report*, p. 159.

[45] Garcia to Seward, November 8, 1866, *Santo Domingo, Reports, 1859-1871*,
MS. Dept. of State.

[46] Smith to Seward, November 8, 1866, *Santo Domingo, Consular Desp.*, vol.
5, MS. Dept. of State.

at the entrance to the Bay of Samaná would be of great value if the American Government desired a naval station on the island of Santo Domingo. During the period of Spanish occupation, 1861-1865, the Lavantado key was used for their naval headquarters, while the Carenero key served as a coal depot.

Upon the receipt of both of these communications from Santo Domingo, Seward began to evince a most anxious desire to secure Samaná as a naval base. On December 3, 1866, Stanton sent a note to Gideon Welles requesting that he come at once to the War Department to have a conference with Stanton and Seward. When Welles reached the department, Seward began to discuss the importance of acquiring Samaná Bay. According to the *Diary* of Welles, Seward questioned him with reference to his power to purchase or lease the Bay. Whereupon Welles

told him we leased for coaling and supply stations, but this was done prudently, carefully, and at little cost; that I was not aware of any statutory permission, etc. etc. Stanton was confident I had the power. He got the laws, read something indefinite, thought it sufficient. I did not. Told them if such a purchase was to be made it would be best to go at once to the Senate. Seward doubted. Stanton objected to going to the Senate first. The result was, the subject was postponed until Cabinet-meeting to-morrow.

On the following day the question came up before the Cabinet for discussion:

Seward and Stanton pressed it strongly, and all favored it. I stated the objections: first, that it is very sickly; second, that it lies off the direct route to Aspinwall,—the bay itself being thirty miles deep; third, but few inhabitants and no market; fourth, the condition of the Treasury. McCulloch said he thought it best to purchase, and the President favored it.[47]

After receiving this authorization from the President and the support of the majority of the Cabinet, Seward at once began an active campaign to secure Samaná. On December 5, he wrote to J. Somers Smith to acknowledge the despatch of November 8 and to advise him that the whole question of

[47] Gideon Welles, *Diary*, II, 630-631.

Samaná Bay should be treated in a most "confidential manner." [48] He then decided to approach Thaddeus Stevens, the aggressive leader of the Republican party in the House of Representatives, and endeavour to secure his approval of an appropriation designed to facilitate the leasing of Samaná Bay. The very fact that Seward would seek to enlist the aid of Stevens in the Dominican venture shows how deeply interested he was in the project. The campaign of 1866 was just over, and it had resulted in one of the most partisan plebiscites in American history. While the campaign was in operation Stevens had not hesitated to abuse the President and Cabinet in that scurrilous language of which he was so fond and so unsparing. If he deemed Johnson no better than a scheming, Southern traitor, his opinion of the Cabinet was equally low, and he frequently voiced his contempt of "the jesuitism, the imbecility, the impudence and vacillation shown by the Cabinet ministers." [49] Seward, in particular, was denounced as Johnson's "chief clown." [50] And when the Radicals had carried the elections by a large majority, he hurried to Washington in order to convince the members of Congress that this recent mandate from the people meant that Congressional leadership was to be substituted for presidential ineptitude. In part, it was a program of petty spite and gross misrepresentation, and it caused Johnson to abandon his conciliatory attitude that had already found expression in the draft of a message to Congress, and instead to meet that body with a message that breathed "futile and bitter defiance." [51]

It was because of this apparent hostility between Stevens and Seward that great curiosity was excited one morning in the reporters' gallery, and on the floor of the House of Representatives,

by the sudden appearance of Secretary Seward, who walked down the main aisle to the seat of Thaddeus Stevens, greeted him and sat down for a chat. As Stevens was the especial leader of the opponents of the

---

[48] Seward to Smith, December 5, 1866, *Confidential, Dominica, Inst. to Consuls*, vol. 9, MS. Dept. of State.

[49] New York *Herald*, September 4, 1866.

[50] *Ibid.*, September 29, 1866.

[51] Howard K. Beale, *The Critical Year* (N. Y., 1930), pp. 402-403.

President, the evident cordiality and confidence between him and Seward was an enigma to both sides of the House. It grew more puzzling, when Stevens went to dine and spend the evening with Seward, and a day or two after proposed an extra appropriation, " for special service," to be expended under direction of the Secretary of State.[52]

The pact between Seward and Stevens became obvious on December 13, 1866, when the " deficiency bill" was before the House of Representatives for consideration: Among the many items in the bill was one which read as follows:

Department of State. To supply a deficiency in the appropriation for the contingent expenses of foreign intercourse for the fiscal year ending June 30, 1867, $250,000.[53]

As soon as the item was read, Glenni W. Scofield, of Pennsylvania, moved to strike it out. But no sooner had Scofield spoken when Thaddeus Stevens arose and announced his intention to explain the reason for the appropriation:

When this appropriation was requested by the Secretary of State, being a larger amount than that Department ever asked for before . . . , I did not feel disposed to recommend it either to the committee or to the House without knowing the reason for it. Not being very well, I requested the Secretary of State, he being a young man [laughter], to call and explain it to me, which he did with great courtesy. And I may as well say to the gentlemen now, for they may want to know, that we did not talk about anything except this appropriation. [Laughter.] He convinced me not only that this sum was wanted for

[52] F. W. Seward, *Seward at Washington*, p. 344. The Washington correspondent of the New York *Tribune* wrote the following paragraph to his paper on December 7, 1866: " It is stated here that last evening Secretary Seward called on Mr. Thaddeus Stevens, at his rooms, and had a long private interview with him. The statement causes a good deal of comment here, and much speculation is rife to know what it all meant. The above gentlemen have not been on friendly relations with each other for several years."

[53] *Cong. Globe*, 39 Cong., 2 sess., p. 112. With reference to this appropriation, Sir Frederick Bruce wrote to Lord Stanley and remarked: " Before the Xmas recess, Congress had appropriated a sum of $250,000 to the service of the State Department on the demand of Mr. Stevens, and in the present temper of that body, it is highly improbable that they would have placed that sum at Mr. Stevens's disposal, had it not been for some secret purpose of general interest." January 8, 1867, *Confidential*, F. O. 5/1104, No. 8.

useful purposes, but that it would finally be found to be too small. . . .
I feel it due to the administration of that Department to go as far as
may be prudent in voting the appropriations asked for it; and however
I may differ politically with the head of that Department, I cannot
allow myself to be influenced by such considerations in acting upon a
question of this kind.[54]

On December 15 Seward sent his carriage for Gideon
Welles, and, when the latter arrived at Seward's residence, the
Secretary of State entered into a long discussion relative to
the purchase of Samaná Bay. According to Welles, Seward

detailed his operations, how he had seen, *first,* Thad Stevens, *then*
Fessenden, *then* Grimes, and had got each of them enlisted. I told him
that the more I had examined the question, the more disinclined I was
to purchase, especially at the price he named—two millions. I thought
if it was decided we should obtain the Bay, it could be procured for half
that sum. He said he did not doubt it, but then we ought to be liberal
and not take advantage of a poor, weak neighbor who was in need.
The two Senators and Stevens, he says, are zealous for the purchase
and at the price mentioned.[55]

Seward paid little attention to the objections of Secretary
Welles. He had already secured the support of the President
and the majority of his Cabinet, and had induced Congress to
agree to a deficiency appropriation. Therefore on December 17,
1866 he issued the following instructions to his son, Frederick
W. Seward, who was to undertake the mission to the Dominican
Republic for the purpose of securing Samaná. He was given
full power to

conclude a convention with the Dominican Republic for the cession or
lease of certain territory of that Republic to the United States for the
consideration of not more than two millions of dollars, payable one
half in cash and the other half in arms and munitions of war. . . . It
is expected that if the cession should be made, it will be in full
sovereignty to the United States. This would of course be preferable
to a lease. If, however, you should not be able to obtain the sovereignty,
you may stipulate for a lease for the term of thirty years. In that event

[54] *Cong. Globe,* 39 Cong., 2 sess., p. 113.
[55] Gideon Welles, *Diary,* II, 642-643.

the sum of ten thousand dollars may be made payable on the ratification of the Convention by that government and a rent of twelve thousand dollars payable annually during the lease in gold or in munitions at the option of that government. . . . Of course, before you make any proposition in writing, it would be advisable for you to have a conference with the Minister for Foreign Affairs in the course of which you may intimate that if our wishes shall be acceded to, we will be willing to pay a part of the consideration at once.[56]

On the following day, December 18, the Samaná cession was formally discussed at a Cabinet meeting, and, when Welles repeated his objections to the cession, Seward " was a little annoyed." The objections of Welles had but little weight, and he noted in his *Diary* that " the project goes on." [57]

This special mission to the Dominican Republic, however, seemed ill-starred from the moment it was organized. After Seward had appointed his son Frederick as the special agent to conduct the negotiations for the cession of Samaná Bay to the United States, he requested Vice-Admiral David D. Porter to accompany the mission in an advisory capacity. In the spring of 1846 Porter, then a lieutenant in the American Navy, had been appointed by President Polk as an executive agent to investigate conditions in the Dominican Republic, and after a careful canvass of the situation he had turned into the Department of State a complete and valuable report. In view of this service, and also because of Porter's evident abilities, Seward thought that he would prove an excellent aide to the Assistant Secretary of State on this new mission to Santo Domingo. But difficulties seemed to arise at the very outset of the mission. After Seward and Porter had embarked on the U. S. S. S. *Gettysburg*, at Annapolis, and weighed anchor for the Caribbean, " the pilot ran the ship hard and fast on an oyster-bank; the wind came out strongly from the north, and in a few hours a man could walk all around her." Porter then telegraphed for the U. S. S. S. *Don*, into which the members of the mission were transferred, but the winds and waves off Cape Hatteras were so furious that the ship nearly foundered and

[56] W. H. Seward to F. W. Seward, December 17, 1866, *Special Missions*, vol. 2, MS. Dept. of State.
[57] Gideon Welles, *Diary*, p. 644.

was fortunate to be able to return to Hampton Roads. By this time the *Gettysburg* had gotten clear of the oyster-bank near Annapolis, and on January 6, 1867 the mission again sailed for Santo Domingo.[58] On January 19 the *Gettysburg* anchored in the harbor of Santo Domingo City, and on the following morning Frederick W. Seward and Vice-Admiral Porter had a long interview with José Garcia, the Minister of Foreign Relations, and with President Cabral.

In a letter to the Secretary of State, January 20, 1867, Frederick W. Seward described this first interview with the Dominican officials. After explaining why the American Government was disinclined to grant a loan to the Dominican Republic, Seward adverted to the advantages that would accrue to both countries through either a lease or a sale to the United States of the territory adjacent to the Bay of Samaná. In doing so he referred to

the purchase of Louisiana from France, of Florida from Spain, and of various territories from Mexico, and the leases of several naval coal stations in different parts of the world, as being in accordance with the traditional usages and policy of the United States and as having been productive only of friendship and mutual advantages to the respective nations concerned. On the other hand, events in Mexico, in Hayti, and elsewhere, indicated but too plainly how difficult it is to preserve independent sovereignty and peaceable relations between two nations, one of whom occupies the attitude of a creditor and the other that of a debtor.[59]

President Cabral and the members of the Dominican Ministry listened " courteously and attentively " to the explanations of Frederick Seward and then requested " time for further consideration of the subject." During the course of later con-

---

[58] Vice-Admiral David D. Porter, "Secret Missions to San Domingo," in *North American Review*, CXXVIII (1879), 629. In the *Diary* of Gideon Welles there is an interesting paragraph concerning Vice-Admiral Porter and the mission to Santo Domingo. On December 17, 1866 he recorded that Porter concurred with him in objecting to Samaná Bay as a naval base, except that Porter adduced " the further objectionable facts that the entrance is difficult and the bay easily blockaded. At first he was very decided against going, but after an interview with Seward he changed his mind." II, 643-644.

[59] F. W. Seward to W. H. Seward, January 20, 1867, *Special Missions*, vol. 1, MS. Dept. of State.

ferences the Dominican officials expressed a desire to reach some agreement relative to granting to the American Government a naval base at Samaná Bay, but objection was made " to an absolute sale of territory" as violating the constitution of the republic. The proposal was then made by the Dominicans that a lease be drawn up with reference to the Levantado key which commanded the entrance to the Bay of Samaná, and the use of the adjacent waters together with certain specified privileges on the mainland of the peninsula.[60]

Frederick Seward, however, thought that such proposals could not be entertained because the Levantado key and the adjacent waters were commanded by the heights of the peninsula. Moreover, it was doubtful whether these particular waters embraced sufficient space for naval uses. After carefully considering these adverse points, Frederick Seward formally declined the Dominican proposals and frankly informed the Dominican officials that the United States wished

no place at all, unless it is one over which we shall have absolute control while we own it, one which is large enough for our uses, and one which we can hold, fortify and maintain against all enemies.[61]

[60] F. W. Seward to W. H. Seward, January 22, 1867, *Special Agents*, vol. 1, MS. Dept. of State.

[61] F. W. Seward to W. H. Seward, January 22, 1867, *ibid*. In a despatch from F. W. Seward to W. H. Seward of January 23, 1867, there was enclosed a memorandum which presented the proposals of the Dominican Government. They were as follows: " 1. The lease of the waters of Samana to be possessed conjointly with the Dominican Republic. 2. The formation of shipyards on the Peninsula. 3. The United States will furnish the Dominican Republic the means of defence from the Bay, in order to maintain the convention. 4. The lease of Cayo Levantado and the Cayo Carenero, on the above conditions, for which concession the United States will pay the Dominican Republic the sum of ....after the exchange of ratifications." The following replies of Frederick Seward were appended to this Dominican memorandum: " 1. This cannot be accepted. It is contrary to what has now become an established principle in the foreign policy of the United States, viz., to avoid entangling alliances. 2. Shipyards would be worse than useless to the United States if they could not be protected and defended by United States fortifications. 3. The United States by having possession of the peninsula could fortify it and thus defend it far more effectually than by mere assistance. 4. The cayos alone would not have sufficient extent, strength, or safety." In declining these proposals of the Dominican Government, Frederick Seward was largely guided by the advice of Vice-Admiral Porter, whose " judgment, tact, and thorough knowledge of the country and the people " are warmly praised in the official despatches.

He then endeavoured to indicate the many advantages that would accrue to the Dominican Republic from the cession of Samaná Bay to the United States, such as the

increase of commerce and of emigration; the increase of the value of property, the impetus likely to be given to the development of the mineral and other resources of the country, and the additional strength, stability and peace which would be imparted to that Republic.

Such arguments, however, were in vain. The recent Spanish occupation had created a strong distrust of foreign powers, and it was precisely this feeling that had led to the insertion in the Dominican constitution of an article which expressly forbade any alienation of the national territory. It was apparent, therefore, to Frederick Seward that no further progress could be made in the matter of securing Samaná Bay for the United States. Thus there was nothing left but to return to the United States.[62] On February 8 Frederick Seward, accompanied by his father, called to see Gideon Welles in order to acquaint him with the negative results of the mission. Welles was delighted to hear of Frederick Seward's failure, and he confided to his *Diary* that there was really no reason to pay for a Caribbean naval base when in case of necessity the American navy could " capture without difficulty one or more of these islands." [63]

According to a magazine article by Vice-Admiral Porter, the Dominican officials treated both him and Frederick Seward with the " greatest courtesy," and when the mission left for the United States " tears stood in the eyes of the administration at the thought of so much specie being carried away which ought to have belonged to them." [64] The Dominican treasury was just about as bare as old Mother Hubbard's cupboard, and consequently it was not long before J. Somers Smith, the American Commercial Agent, was writing to Frederick Seward, at Washington, that he felt confident " that the deficiency of funds to carry on the government " would compel President

---

[62] The real purpose of the visit of Frederick Seward to the Dominican Republic was quickly ascertained by David Leon, the British consul at Santo Domingo City, who promptly reported the facts to Lord Stanley. Leon to Lord Stanley, February 8, 1867, F. O. 115/462.

[63] III, 40.   [64] D. D. Porter, *op. cit.*, p. 629.

Cabral " to accede to the offers of the United States." If the American Government still desired the cession of Samaná Bay it would be wise to empower the Commercial Agent to reopen negotiations, because Dominican necessities would soon force that government to seek American assistance.[65]

Frederick Seward was so much impressed with the statements in Smith's despatch that he at once prepared some special instructions empowering the Commercial Agent to reopen the negotiations for either a cession of Samaná Bay to the United States or at the very least a long-time lease of the territory in question. If the Dominican officials raised objections to the cession of Samaná on the ground that it would violate their constitution, Smith should then suggest the expediency of an amendment to their frame of government. If they flatly re-

[65] Smith to F. W. Seward, February 8, 1867, *Santo Domingo, Consular Desp.,* vol. 5, MS. Dept. of State. Just at this time when the American Government was bending every effort to secure Samaná Bay, the British Government had this same project under consideration. On February 23, 1867 Theodore Farrington, the British vice-consul at Porto Plata, Dominican Republic, wrote to Lord Stanley to advise him that President Cabral was in desperate financial straits and badly needed funds to carry on his government. Some Dominican officials had intimated to Farrington that " the President with the Consent of Congress would transfer to him Samana, not only the Bay but the Land about 32 miles long and 10 miles wide, for fifty years for £30,000 under certain specified conditions." Farrington inquired of Lord Stanley whether he should go ahead with this proposition. F. O. 23/56. In the British Foreign Office there is a memorandum on this project which reads as follows: " There can be no doubt that it would be an advantageous thing if the Samana Harbour and District were in an Englishman's hands, but I [Lord Stanley] apprehend that he could not hoist the British Flag as a token of Brit. Sovereignty, and that it would not be desirable for H. M. GT. to do at this moment the very thing we are fearful of the United States doing, namely openly to purchase it. If, as a mercantile scheme, Mr. Farrington should like to enter into it, there might be no objection." F. O. 23/56.

Lord Stanley finally decided to send Farrington's project to both the Admiralty and the Colonial Offices with " an expression of doubt on my part whether it is desirable to enter into any such enterprise." On March 22, 1867 the Admiralty reported that " having considered the question, they have not any wish, as far as naval interests are concerned, that Her Majesty's Government should take any steps to acquire a footing in the Island of San Domingo." A week later (March 29, 1867) the Colonial Office expressed a similar opinion to Lord Stanley: " I am directed by His Grace to state that he entirely concurs with Lord Stanley in thinking that Her Majesty's Government should on no account be party to an enterprise of this kind. [Signed by] Frederic Rogers." F. O. 23/56.

jected this possibility it might be best to go ahead and secure a ninety-nine-year lease on Samaná Bay and adjacent lands. But in any event it was imperative to secure from the Dominican Government the right to display the American flag and to erect fortifications on any land acquired, whether through cession or by lease.

For the outright cession of Samaná Bay and adjacent territory to the United States the Commercial Agent was authorized to offer " not more than two millions of dollars, payable one half in cash and the other half in arms and munitions of war, or instead, if desired, a steam war vessel." For the lease of this same territory it would be proper to offer " not more than one million dollars payable in like manner." Finally, in the event that a treaty was signed providing for the cession of Samaná Bay to the United States, it would be possible for the American Government to advance to the Dominican authorities the sum of seventy-five thousand dollars immediately after the instrument was formally ratified. In the event that a convention was signed which merely provided for a long-time lease of this territory, the American Government would advance only the small sum of twenty-five thousand dollars. And even this tiny advance payment to the Dominican Government could not be made until after the ratification of the treaty which contained the lease.[66]

[66] F. W. Seward to Smith, February 26, 1867, *Special Missions*, vol. 2, MS. Dept. of State. In the first article of the draft treaty sent to Smith, it is provided that the Dominican Republic cede " in full sovereignty to the United States the territory known as the peninsula of Samana on the island of St. Domingo, the Bay of Samana, and the keys known as ' Levantado ' and ' Carenero,' with all the rights and appurtenances thereto belonging as they have heretofore belonged to the government of that Republic. The territory hereby ceded is understood to extend from west to east thirty-two miles and to be eleven miles across at its greatest breadth." On March 7, 1867 Elwood Cooper wrote to Thaddeus Stevens, who had already shown an interest in the Dominican question, and stressed the importance of Samaná Bay as a naval station. He also enclosed a clipping from the *Opinion Nationale* of Paris which indicated the uneasiness felt in France relative to the cession of Samaná Bay to the United States. The following excerpt from the clipping is illustrative: " If the United States become masters of the bay of Samana it is evident that they will occupy a preponderating position in the Antilles, and will be able to set themselves up as the sovereign arbiter of the destinies of that archipelago. We are not enemies of the United States, and we have given striking and constant proofs

In spite of the high hopes of Smith that the frenzied finances of the Dominican Republic would compel the existing government to accept whatever terms the United States thought it best to offer, the Dominican officials seemed in no hurry to begin negotiations after the American Commercial Agent informed them that he had received full powers from the Department of State. President Cabral, it appeared, was in favor of postponing the question for a while from fear that " it might make a pretext for a revolutionary movement." [67]

When the American Secretary of State learned of this reluctance on the part of the Dominican Government to treat for either the lease or sale of Samaná Bay, he at once instructed Smith that there

would be an inconvenience in leaving the proposals of this Government longer open to be accepted or rejected by the Government of Dominica. In the event, therefore, that when this dispatch shall come to your hands, the Dominican government shall not have decided to accept the proposal of the United States in one of the forms in which it is expressed, you will desist from further prosecution of the business, and will give notice to the President that the proposals of the United States are no longer in force.[68]

Seward was very wise in refusing to continue the negotiations for Samaná notwithstanding the optimistic reports of the American Commercial Agent. It was soon apparent that the opposition to any sale or lease of Samaná was far stronger than Smith had realized. On May 31, 1867 there was held a secret session of the Dominican Congress at which the whole matter of granting a naval base to the United States was thoroughly discussed, and the Congress agreed to resolutions which denounced any attempt to amend the Dominican con-

of this fact. But we cannot bring our sympathy up to that point at which it would turn into a blind condescension for ambitious schemes, and menace the legitimate and secular rights of Europe as well as the interests of those nationalities which have already been formed." *Stevens Papers*, vol. 9, MS. Library of Congress.

[67] Smith to F. W. Seward, April 8, 1867, *Santo Domingo, Consular Desp.*, vol. 5, MS. Dept. of State.

[68] W. H. Seward to Smith, May 8, 1867, *Special Missions*, vol. 2, MS. Dept. of State.

stitution so as to permit a sale of the national territory.[69]

Such proceedings were not lost even upon Smith, who returned to the Department of State on June 8, 1867 his power to open negotiations for Samaná Bay. In acknowledging the return by Smith of his power to treat with the Dominican Government for the cession or lease to the United States of a naval base, Seward expressed his regret that there should linger in the minds of any Dominican officials a suspicion of the motives of the American Government, which was really " incapable of entertaining an ungenerous thought or design against the Republic." [70] Moreover, these groundless suspicions, and the consequent refusal on the part of the Dominican Government to discuss the cession of Samaná Bay, had caused the American Government to open

parallel negotiations in other quarters. There is good reason to expect that they will be successful and thus the chief want of the United States be supplied. Those collateral proceedings would not have been adopted if there had been a reasonable prospect of an acceptance of the offer made to Dominica.

The " parallel negotiations " to which Seward referred were those with Denmark concerning the acquisition of the Danish West Indies. The statement that " those collateral proceedings would not have been adopted if there had been a reasonable prospect of an acceptance of the offer made to Dominica " is interesting if true. Ever since January, 1865 Seward had been dickering with the Danish Government with reference to the purchase of the Danish colonies in the Caribbean, and throughout 1866 and the early months of 1867 this interest had steadily increased. At the very time in January, 1867 that Frederick Seward was on his way to Santo Domingo to secure the cession of Samaná Bay, the Secretary of State was urging the Danish Government to accept the proposals of the American Government relative to the purchase of the Danish West Indies. On February 26, 1867 Frederick Seward had sent instructions to J. Somers Smith to open negotiations for the cession or lease

[69] See *El Monitor* (Santo Domingo City), June 8, 1867.

[70] W. H. Seward to Smith, July 1, 1867, *Confidential, Special Missions*, vol. 2, MS. Dept. of State.

of Samaná Bay, but that did not mean that the negotiations for the Danish West Indies had been called off. The failure of the Dominican negotiations was not known to the Department of State until after the middle of April, and yet Seward in the latter part of March was again pressing the Danish Government to come to an agreement with the United States in regard to the Virgin Islands. As a matter of fact, Seward was really anxious to have several naval bases in the Caribbean, and, shortly after he had received the despatch from J. Somers Smith informing him of the refusal of the Dominican Government to cede or lease Samaná Bay to the United States, he decided to send George Bancroft on a special mission to Spain to purchase the islands of Culebra and Culebrita. Indeed, so strong and so apparent was this desire on the part of the Secretary of State to add to the insular possessions of the United States that Gideon Welles was of the opinion that Seward had become " almost a monomaniac on the subject of territorial acquisition." [71]

Whether or not this is an overstatement of the case, it is certain that Seward did not for a moment lose his interest in the Dominican Republic. He welcomed any news from the Caribbean, and for that reason the literary adventurer, Fabens, felt at perfect liberty to correspond with the Secretary of State, and incidentally to endeavour to further the projects that he and Cazneau were pushing in the Dominican Republic. On October 2, 1867, he addressed a letter to Seward in which he assured him that if the American Government was still desirous of securing Samaná Bay there was now no " serious obstacle in the way." He had recently returned to New York after a visit to the island, and he did not think it would be difficult " to persuade the Govt. of Santo Domingo to comply with the wishes of the people in this matter." It seemed to Mr. Fabens, however, that the best place for a naval station was at the Bay of Monte Christo. The town and adjacent country were " wonderfully healthful." In fact, so obvious were the many advantages that this site offered that Fabens grew ecstatic when he considered them. Should the American

[71] *Diary*, III, 125.

Government succeed in establishing a naval base at Monte Christo, he was certain that it would prove "the gateway through which, under the protecting folds of the Stars and Stripes, a stream of emigration would set into this beautiful valley of the Yague, making of Santo Domingo the garden of America." [72]

A few days after Fabens wrote this letter to Secretary Seward, J. Somers Smith also wrote from Santo Domingo City to inform Frederick Seward that he had been talking with several influential Dominicans who believed that a lease of Samaná Bay could be secured if the United States would pay a bonus sufficient to redeem the currency, and an annual rent. The amount of the rent was not discussed, but the reason for such a payment was that it could not be absorbed in a lump by avaricious politicians and therefore would be of lasting benefit to the republic. [73] In reply to this indefinite overture, Frederick Seward instructed Smith to the effect that the American Government had no intention of renewing "the proposition for the purchase of Samaná." [74]

But before Smith could receive this discouraging instruction, he had had further conversations with certain Dominicans, the chief of whom was Fiallo, formerly a Secretary of the Treasury, and a nephew of President Cabral. Fiallo was particularly interested in ascertaining whether the American Government,

---

[72] Fabens to W. H. Seward, October 2, 1867, *Misc. Letters, October, 1867*, pt. 1, MS. Dept. of State. This ecstasy over the superlative advantages of the Bay of Monte Christo for a naval station was partly caused by the economic interests of Fabens and General Cazneau in that district. At this time these resourceful adventurers had decided that the outstanding need in the Dominican Republic was a better system of transportation. In order to meet this need, Fabens and Cazneau imported some thirty camels and set them to work in the Monte Christo area. For a while Fabens was most enthusiastic over the prospect of better transportation facilities through the employment of camels, and on July 8, 1867 he wrote to Cazneau in the following lyric vein: "I am awestruck with the brilliant prospect." *Fabens Papers*, cited in the thesis of Mr. Graham Lovejoy, "The Relations of the United States and the Dominican Republic during the Administration of President Grant," MS. Columbia University Library.

[73] Smith to F. W. Seward, October 8, 1867, *Santo Domingo, Consular Desp.*, vol. 5, MS. Dept. of State.

[74] F. W. Seward to Smith, October 28, 1867, *Desp. to Consuls*, vol. 47, MS. Dept. of State.

in case it secured a lease of Samaná Bay, would protect the Dominican Republic against any invasions from Haiti. In this regard Smith could not hold out any promise of a formal protective pact, but he did assure Fiallo that the Dominican Government could count upon the "moral support" of the United States.[75]

Some two weeks later, Smith again wrote to the Secretary of State to announce not only that the district called "the Cibao" was in favor of the lease, but also that the Southern and Eastern provinces were of like mind. Moreover, such important personages as Generals Luperón and Pimentel had signified their approval of the lease. Therefore, there was nothing left to do but arrange the terms of the instrument of conveyance. Fiallo thought that it should run for twenty-five years, and the United States was to "have the control and jurisdiction of the entire Peninsula, keys, waters and public property, the use of the mines, and everything as contained in the proposal made by Hon. F. W. Seward in January last." For these privileges the United States was to pay $2,100,000, but only the sum of two million dollars was to appear in the terms of the convention; the remaining one hundred thousand dollars were desired for "special purposes." The payments for the lease were to be arranged as follows: $500,000 upon ratification of the treaty, $500,000 one year later, $900,000—or $300,000 a year for three years after that date—, and finally the sum of $100,000 at the end of five years.[76]

On December 16, 1867 Smith wrote to Secretary Seward a letter in which he rehearsed a recent conversation with President Cabral relative to the expediency of sending a Dominican commissioner to the United States to negotiate for the lease of Samaná.[77] On the following day he addressed to Seward a letter formally introducing Pujol as the agent of the Dominican Government entrusted with the mission of arranging terms with the American Government.[78]

[75] Smith to W. H. Seward, November 8, 1867, *Santo Domingo, Consular Desp.*, vol. 5, MS. Dept. of State.

[76] Smith to Seward, November 20, 1867, *ibid.*

[77] Smith to Seward, December 16, 1867, *ibid.*

[78] Smith to Seward, December 17, 1867, *ibid.*

As soon as this action on the part of the Dominican Government became known in Santo Domingo City, General Cazneau, who continued to advise Seward on Dominican matters, wrote to the Secretary of State to assure him that public opinion in the Dominican Republic

no longer opposes the cession you proposed, and whatever Don Pablo Pujol engages at Washington will be honorably and promptly sustained at Santo Domingo. The way has never before been so completely open for the accomplishment of your wishes. It now rests with you and the President alone to conclude a treaty as beneficial to this republic as it will be popular with our people and honorable to the enlightened statesmanship that creates this new landmark in American history.[79]

In the meantime, on December 13 Seward had written a long instruction to J. Somers Smith which dealt in detail with the different aspects of the Samaná lease. It was unfortunate that the policy of the Dominican Government had been so vacillating with reference to granting to the United States the use of Samaná Bay as a naval base:

We have from that Government an explicit refusal to negotiate. We have before us a treaty by which the Dominican Republic has entered into a very extraordinary agreement with Hayti, binding the former to the latter virtually to refuse the proposal of the United States. We have, moreover, a proclamation issued by President Cabral declaring that the Government will not upon any terms transfer the Peninsula of Samana to the United States. In view of such formal and solemn proceedings of the Dominican Government it would be incompatible with the self-respect of this Government to entertain the questions which Mr. Fiallo has raised without being first furnished with authentic evidence of powers of negotiation conferred upon him by the Government of the Dominican Republic.

But even in the event that these objections could be waived and Mr. Fiallo be invested with full powers to treat with the American Government, Seward still deemed it his duty to instruct Smith

that the United States could not now negotiate for a lease of Samana for a term of years; because, first, the United States could not consent

<hr/>

[79] Cazneau to Seward, December 18, 1867, *ibid*.

to be a tenant to any foreign power; because, second, the United States could not consent to lay a foundation for ulterior controversy with the Dominican Republic by taking a lease for years of a possession which it would be inconvenient for them to relinquish at the end of the stipulated term.[80]

Before this instruction reached Mr. Smith the Dominican Government had already decided to send Pablo Pujol to the United States to negotiate for the lease of Samaná, and on January 8, 1868 the Dominican commissioner wrote to Seward to announce his arrival in Washington.[81] According to Pujol, the Dominican Government was willing to lease to the United States the peninsula and bay of Samaná, together with the keys and ports of the peninsula except those "which lie on the Southern Shore up to a mile of distance from it." The lease was to run for a term of "twenty to fifty years, with perfect and exclusive sovereignty and jurisdiction through that time over the territories and waters above mentioned." The United States was also to have the right

to cut, use, and carry away building timber, to mine, use, and carry away mineral coal, and any other mineral which may be found in the leased territory during the time agreed upon, it being understood in relation to minerals that on their extraction the Dominican Republic shall be paid according to the mining laws now in force; and to use and occupy all the public grounds, places, establishments, that may be found in the leased territory. The Dominican Government will retain the free use of the waters of the Bay.

For this leased territory the American Government was to

[80] Seward to Smith, December 13, 1867, *Special Missions*, vol. 2, MS. Dept. of State.

[81] On January 11, 1868 the New York *Tribune* observed that "the feeling in Congress and outside seems to be almost unanimous in favor of rejecting the St. Thomas treaty, and substituting Samana. The Dominican Commissioner is said to have made a favorable impression here in regard to the value of Samana to the United States."

On January 6, 1868, Seward wrote to General N. P. Banks a letter introducing General Pablo Pujol as "the plenipotentiary" of the Dominican Republic. As General Banks was the chairman of the Committee on Foreign Affairs of the House of Representatives, there was pressing need of a conference between him and the Dominican representative. See the *Nathaniel P. Banks Papers*, MS. Essex Institute, Salem, Massachusetts.

pay to the Dominican Republic the sum of one million dollars down, and three hundred thousand dollars in coin every year during the term of the lease. In addition, the American Government was to furnish six one-hundred-pound guns and other fixtures.

Immediately after the signature of this lease the American Government was to send a vessel "with the amount which they are to pay down, and which shall be delivered to the Government of the Dominican Republic with the securities which may be deemed necessary, until the approval of the convention by the Legislative Body."

As a protective measure, the United States was to

engage in the most solemn manner to sustain the autonomy and integrity of the territory of the Dominican Republic if in consequence of this act of leasing, any difficulties should be superinduced with any foreign nation.

Finally, it was provided that Dominican nationals should have the right to "possess every kind of property in the leased territory, preserving their citizenship." [82]

On January 10, 1868, Seward wrote a long note to Pujol in which he discussed the history of the negotiations for Samaná Bay since November, 1866. With reference to the proposals advanced by Pujol, Seward was willing to accept the description of the leased territory that was set forth in Pujol's letter of January 8. But in regard to the conditions and terms of the lease, Seward insisted that the United States must have

a cession in fee simple, or if that shall be incompatible with the Constitution of the Dominican Republic, then a lease with unqualified and unrestricted sovereignty and property, both of domain and dominion, over the land and waters to be ceded for the term of nine hundred and ninety-nine years, leaving however to the Dominican Government the

[82] Pujol to Seward, January 8-9, 1868, *Dominican Republic, Notes from*, vol. 2, MS. Dept. of State. In the New York *Tribune* of January 3, 1868, notice is given of the projected visit of Pujol to the United States. According to the *Tribune's* special correspondent at Havana, Pujol "will endeavor to close the Bay of Samana negotiation upon the basis of $300,000 annual rent for the term of 99 years." It would seem that the correspondent had secured "inside information" concerning the terms of the proposed convention with the United States.

privilege of free access through the Bay of Samana to the ports and keys which lie on the southern shore of the Bay, and within a mile from that shore.

The article in the Dominican *projet* which called for the payment by the American Government of one million dollars down and a yearly rent of three hundred thousand dollars for a short-time lease of Samaná Bay was entirely " inadmissible." In the instructions that Seward had prepared for his son Frederick Seward on December 17, 1866, it was provided that in the event of a lease of Samaná Bay he was to offer the sum of ten thousand dollars down upon the ratification of the convention by the Dominican Government, and a rent of " twelve thousand dollars payable annually during the lease in gold or in munitions at the option of that government." On February 26, 1867, Frederick Seward had sent instructions to J. Somers Smith, the American Commercial Agent at Santo Domingo City, authorizing him to negotiate for either a cession or a lease of Samaná Bay to the United States. In the event of a lease he was empowered to offer " not more than one million dollars, payable one half in cash and the other half in arms and munitions of war." This sum of one million dollars was to constitute the only financial obligation on the part of the American Government, and there was to be no annual rent. It would be out of the question for the American Government to meet the present demands of the Dominican Republic.

It was also impossible for the American Government to send to the Dominican Republic, " immediately after the conclusion of the convention for leasing," the " amount which they are to pay down." Whatever purchase money the United States agreed to pay was to be paid " at the Treasury of the United States, and whatever armament they may agree to furnish shall be furnished within the United States."

Finally, it was to be clearly understood by the Dominican Government that the United States could not enter into any engagement " to sustain the autonomy and integrity of the territory of the Dominican Republic." Since the adoption by the United States of a

constitutional form of Government they have never entered into any treaty of alliance, offensive or defensive, with any foreign power. They cannot depart from this policy on the present occasion, although they cherish a sincere sympathy and earnest desire for the welfare and stability of the Dominican Republic.[83]

On January 18, 1868, Pujol wrote to Seward to announce his willingness to accept certain amendments to his *projet*. It would be perfectly agreeable to the Dominican Government to have the term of the lease fixed at ninety-nine years instead of from twenty to fifty years, and in lieu of a payment of one million dollars down and an annual rent of three hundred thousand dollars for a lease of Samaná Bay, the Dominican Government would now be willing to accept as full payment the sum of two million dollars in gold. With reference to a guarantee of the independence of the Dominican Republic the Dominican envoy suggested the following alternative proposition:

Whatever difficulty may arise in the future between the United States of North America and the Dominican Republic in the fulfillment of this treaty, or of any other nature it may be, shall be determined by the Supreme Court of the United States to which end the Dominican Republic will delegate to it full powers by submitting to its arbitrament any differences which it may in the future have with any foreign nation whatever, provided always that such may lend its acceptance of such

---

[83] Seward to Pujol, January 10, 1868, *Dominican Legation, Notes to*, vol. 1, MS. Dept. of State. On January 11, 1868, Seward made an official report to President Johnson in which he expressed the opinion that it was " inexpedient " to conclude a convention with the Dominican Republic for the acquisition of Samaná Bay " without first consulting the Senate of the United States thereupon. While the Secretary of State is of opinion that it would be for the interest of the United States, in a political view, to obtain the cession not only of St. Thomas and St. John but also of Samana, he is nevertheless bound to consider that the Senate may not regard the acquisition of both or either of those territories as urgently expedient at the present time. . . . Considering the two projects in the aspect of such a competition as had been indicated, the Secretary is of opinion that the Islands of St. Thomas and St. John, upon the terms stipulated in the Treaty now before the Senate, offer advantages to the United States superior to those which Samana offers upon the terms proposed by the Dominican Republic." *Report Book, December 5, 1864–May 15, 1868*, vol. 9, MS. Dept. of State. There is no record in the Department of State of any formal reference to the Senate of the draft of the Dominican treaty, or of any consultations with members of the Senate concerning this draft treaty.

arbitrament; the Republic of the United States of North America engaging in such cases to lend effective and impartial co-operation, that in this manner arrangements may be made in conformity with law and equity.[84]

In his reply of January 20, 1868, Seward indicated that while he was ready to reduce the term of the lease of Samaná Bay from nine hundred and ninety-nine years to ninety-nine years, he could not consider any other form of payment than " one million dollars down, and one million dollars in munitions of war, both payable and deliverable in the United States." With reference to submitting disputes to the Supreme Court of the United States it needed only to be said that such a procedure would be " incompatible with the Constitution of the United States." [85]

It is apparent from the above quotation that Seward considered the ninety-nine year lease of Samaná Bay as equivalent to a cession, and therefore was willing to pay handsomely for it. But the Dominican envoy was strongly opposed to the mode of payment. The Dominican Republic, with less than three hundred thousand inhabitants, did not need one million dollars in munitions of war. A compromise might be arranged by paying to the Dominican Government the sum of $1,500,000 in gold, and $500,000 in armaments, munitions, clothing for troops, one or two vessels, printing presses, etc. Pujol was particularly anxious that the sum of two hundred thousand dollars be paid to the Dominican Government immediately after the approval by the American Senate, " without waiting for the ratification by the constitutional authorities of Santo Domingo." [86] The purpose of such a fund can easily be imagined!

On January 28, 1868, Seward gave his final answer to the Dominican propositions. With reference to the equivalents requested by the Dominican envoy for the lease of Samaná

---

[84] Pujol to Seward, January 18, 1868, *Dominican Republic, Notes from*, vol. 1, MS. Dept. of State.

[85] Seward to Pujol, January 20, 1868, *Dominican Legation, Notes to*, vol. 1, MS. Dept. of State.

[86] Pujol to Seward, January 25, 1868, *Dominican Republic, Notes from*, vol. 2, MS. Dept. of State.

Bay, it was to be remembered that in the event the American Government took over the lease it would have to pay several million dollars in order to fortify the lands adjacent to the bay and thus render it available as a naval base. Moreover, since the initiation of the negotiations with the Dominican Government there had been other negotiations with the Danish Government for the annexation of the Danish West Indies. These latter negotiations would have been " discontinued if the Dominican Republic had avowed a change of its determination in regard to Samana." With the Dominican Government showing a resolute determination neither to sell nor lease Samaná to the United States, it was necessary for the United States to look elsewhere for a naval base. Thus finally, on October 24, 1867, a treaty was signed with Denmark providing for the cession of the Danish West Indies. The acquisition of these islands had lessened the need for the lease of Samaná Bay; therefore, it was now considered inexpedient to make any change in the terms offered by the United States, namely, one million dollars down and one million dollars in munitions of war. Seward was willing, however, to

present to the consideration of the Senate the desire of General Pujol that in view of the political situation of the Dominican Republic an advance payment of two hundred thousand dollars be made without waiting for ratification by the Constitutional authorities of the Dominican Government.[87]

---

[87] Seward to Pujol, January 28, 1868, *Dominican Legation, Notes to,* vol. 1, MS. Dept. of State. It is very apparent that the British Government was fully acquainted with every detail of the negotiations between the United States and the Dominican Republic with reference to the sale or lease of Samaná Bay On December 8, 1867 David Leon, the British consul at Santo Domingo City, wrote to Lord Stanley and expressed the fear that the serious financial depression in the Dominican Republic might lead President Cabral to sell or lease to the United States some portion of Dominican territory. The idea of leasing Samaná Bay to the United States had gained " so much ground " that " several secret meetings of Members of Congress " had been held in order to discuss the matter. Leon had called on President Cabral, who discounted the rumors about leasing Samaná Bay to the United States, but nevertheless the British consul was afraid that " the exhausted state of the public Treasury, and the disturbances caused by Mr. Baez's party," might bring about the eventual transfer of Samaná Bay to the American Government. Leon to Lord Stanley, December 8, 1867, F. O. 23/56, No. 16. Some ten days later Leon wrote to Lord Stanley to inform

A few days later Seward received from Pujol a note in which he signified his readiness to approve a treaty

in the terms laid down in the minute which the Secretary thought proper to address to the Undersigned under date of the 20th of last month.[88]

Unfortunately, however, just when Pujol and Secretary Seward were in agreement as to the bases of a treaty between the United States and the Dominican Republic, a revolution broke out against the rule of President Cabral, and in January, 1868 he had to relinquish the presidential office. There was nothing left for Pujol to do but write to Secretary Seward on March 6, 1868 and announce the termination of his mission. He also requested the Secretary of State to " cause the suspension by the Senate of the recognition of the Treaty which the undersigned had the honor of adjusting with Seward." [89]

him that the matter of the sale or lease of Samaná Bay to the United States had taken a more serious turn, and that in the Dominican Congress there had been " stormy and alarming sessions " in this regard. Angered by this show of Congressional opposition, President Cabral dissolved the Dominican Legislature and assumed dictatorial powers. He was now in favor of some concessions to the American Government with reference to Samaná Bay and had despatched Pablo Pujol to Washington to initiate negotiations looking towards some settlement of this question. Leon to Lord Stanley, December 19, 1867, F. O. 23/56, No. 17.

The French consul at Santo Domingo City now inquired of Leon whether he would co-operate with him in sending a joint protest to the Dominican Government with regard to the sale or lease of Samaná Bay to the United States. Leon referred the matter to the British Foreign Office for answer, and, on January 17, 1868, Lord Stanley instructed him " carefully to abstain from taking part in any such Protest." Stanley to Leon, January 17, 1868, F. O. 23/57, No. 1. On April 8, 1868, Leon suggested to Lord Stanley the " advantages which would accrue to British commercial interests should they lease Samana." *Confidential*, F. O. 23/57. Leon's despatch was at once turned over to E. Hammond, in the British Foreign Office, for a critical opinion on the suggestion that it contained, and Hammond gave the following advice: "As to Samana, unless the Harbour would be useful for Postal purposes, I should be indisposed to meddle with it, with a view to acquiring influence, and property there. I do not think good generally comes from such proceedings." Remarks of E. H. Hammond, April 30, 1868, on Leon's despatch of April 8, 1868, F. O. 23/57.

Finally, on May 16, 1868, Lord Stanley wrote to Leon to instruct him that " Her Majesty's Government are not prepared to take any steps with regard to Samana as suggested in that [April 8, 1868] despatch." F. O. 23/57, No. 4.

[88] Pujol to Seward, February 4, 1868, *Dominican Republic, Notes from*, vol. 1, MS. Dept. of State.

[89] Pujol to Seward, March 6, 1868, *ibid.*

The Cabral Government had staked everything on the success of the Pujol mission to the United States, and when the weeks passed without the receipt of any favorable news from Washington with reference to the lease of Samaná Bay, the supporters of the existing administration abandoned all hope of resisting the advance of the revolutionary armies.[90] In February, 1868 a Provisional Government was set up in Santo Domingo City, and soon it was rumored that Buenaventura Baez, now conveniently residing at Curaçao, would be invited to return as President of the Dominican Republic. From the viewpoint of political experience Baez would, it seemed, prove an able executive, and it was undeniable that he had certain dubious talents. Indeed, he greatly resembled that colorful Mexican adventurer, General Lopez de Santa Anna, who, like some great jack-in-the-box, would upon occasion frighten many Mexicans into instant awe and then be found out for what he was and be securely fastened down until national curiosity needed another thrill.

Baez was now an old hand at this presidential game and he had grown weary of hurried flights from his native land. In order to make his position more secure he thought it would be best to court the friendship of the United States, and therefore, while he was an exile at Curaçao, he began his advances to J. Somers Smith, the American Commercial Agent at Santo Domingo City. Hardly had the Cabral Government fallen when Ramirez Baez, the Minister of Foreign Relations in the Provisional Government, called to see Smith to assure him that a great change had come over the former Dominican President, Buenaventura Baez. Previously he had regarded the best solution for Dominican troubles to be nothing less than annexation to some European power. But now the spirit of political prescience had descended upon the homesick exile, who clearly saw that it was requisite to cultivate the

most intimate relations with the United States, as it is very evident that in the course of a few years, this Island, with Cuba and Puerto Rico, are destined to become a part of the great Republic.

[90] Smith to Seward, February 7, 1868, *Santo Domingo, Consular Desp.*, vol. 5, MS. Dept. of State.

It would also appear that Baez was ready to promise that as soon as he was installed as President of the Dominican Republic he would be " prepared to lease Samana, should the United States still be disposed to treat on that subject." [91]

On March 18, 1868, Smith again wrote to Seward to inform him of the necessity on the part of the Dominican Republic of negotiating with the United States for a lease of Samaná Bay, and he requested that full powers be sent him in order that he might conclude a treaty to that end.[92] On March 29 Buenaventura Baez landed at Santo Domingo City, and Smith lost no time in ascertaining his views with reference to Samaná. When Smith indicated the unwillingness of the American Government to accept a mere lease of Samaná Bay, Baez expressed the opinion that the Dominican constitution could be so amended as to permit a sale of the territory to the United States. To Smith it seemed evident that Baez would be disposed to adopt toward the American Government a more friendly attitude than any preceding administration.[93]

It is very likely, of course, that this friendly disposition was partly induced by the efforts of that choice pair of American imperialists, Colonel Fabens and General Cazneau. Despite the swiftly changing fortunes of the Dominican Republic, these adventurers had retained an invincible belief in the rich opportunities that awaited American development. They soon discovered in President Baez a kindred spirit who regarded patriotism in terms of pecuniary profits, and they made haste to form an unholy trinity that had few qualms as to how low they might have to stoop to conquer. On April 18, 1868, Cazneau wrote a long note to Seward in which he advised him of the mission of Colonel Fabens to Washington to inform the American Government of the anxious desire of Baez to co-operate to the fullest extent with the United States. In fact, many prominent Dominicans had assured Cazneau " of their disposition to merge the destinies of this republic into those of the United States."

[91] Smith to Seward, March 8, 1868, *ibid.*
[92] Smith to Seward, March 18, 1868, *ibid.*
[93] Smith to Seward, April 8, 1868, *ibid.*

With reference to the personality and capacity of Baez, the letter of General Cazneau is warmly enthusiastic. The man and the hour had met, and so convinced was General Cazneau of the transcendent abilities of Baez that he was strongly urging him to assume dictatorial powers and proceed at once to the regeneration of the Dominican Republic. In the closing paragraph of his letter, Cazneau comes to the kernel of his communication—the profits that awaited American exploitation. Baez, who was soon to be inaugurated as President of the Dominican Republic, would

welcome and encourage American enterprise of every description. Knowing as I do, that this island possesses a great gold bearing territory which the introduction of American skill and capital is sure to develop speedily, I am fully convinced that if the negotiation above alluded to is carried out with Mr. Baez, and the protection of our flag extended over any portion of this country, it will not only be hailed with joy and gratitude here, but will give to our country a new and extended field for enterprise, and a very prolific source of national wealth.[94]

On the same day that General Cazneau addressed this letter to Seward, Gautier, the Dominican Secretary of Foreign Relations, entrusted Colonel Fabens with instructions that governed his mission to the United States. First it was clearly indicated that the Dominican Government was desirous of securing information as to the exact relations between the Government of President Cabral and the United States. It was impossible to learn from the archives available in Santo Domingo City anything definite about the results of Pujol's mission in the early part of 1868. Therefore Fabens was to " insinuate " himself into the favor of Seward and not only acquaint him with conditions in Santo Domingo but also elicit from the Secretary of State " everything which may have passed in respect of the mission of Pujol, about which the public has been so much occupied, and of which the Government has not had any reliable narrative." He was also " to contradict in becoming manner any injurious or calumnious imputation which the enemies of the existing order of things may publish." [95]

[94] Cazneau to Seward, April 18, 1868, *Dominican Republic, Notes from*, vol. 2, MS. Dept. of State.

[95] Gautier to Fabens, April 18, 1868, *ibid.*

On May 5, 1868 Fabens wrote to Seward from New York to announce his arrival in the United States, and to inform him that he would soon be in Washington for the purpose of delivering some important documents from the Dominican Government. In accordance with this promise, Fabens called at the Department and left the following memorandum which President Baez had addressed to him on April 2, 1868:

At the moment of your departure for the United States I have thought proper to address to you these lines—This country needs the importation of every class of the elements of civilization whether coming from America or from Europe, and it cannot be otherwise. The solemn engagements which every man who respects himself contracts on accepting the delicate mission of guiding a nation, demand these with greater urgency in the difficult situation in which this unfortunate country now finds itself. Assure your friends, or countrymen who may desire to come to this Republic upon any enterprise whether agricultural, telegraphic, or other pursuits which may tend to develop the spirit of industry, which has so much fallen off, that I will receive them with all kindness, and will protect them with all my power.[96]

Such a memorandum was nothing else than an invitation to American capitalists to initiate in the Dominican Republic a program of economic imperialism—a program clearly foreshadowed in 1862-1863 in the circulars of the American West India Company. Not only would American investors supply the much needed capital for Dominican development, but these economic ties might well lead to political ones of an intimate nature.

After Fabens had arrived in Washington it was assumed in Santo Domingo City that the most cordial relations had been established with the American Government, and Felix Delmonte, the Minister of Justice and Public Instruction, called to

---

[96] Baez to Fabens, April 2, 1868, *ibid.* Before coming to Washington, Fabens talked with General Banks on May 8, at the home of Dr. Samuel G. Howe. *Banks Papers*, MS. Essex Institute. On June 5 Fabens wrote again to Seward to assure him that "commercial prospects" in the Dominican Republic were "flattering." He was confident that the mere "unfolding of our flag upon the island" would be sufficient to carry all these enterprises "to a brilliant success." This consummation, it was hoped, would be realized under the "official auspices" of Seward himself. *Seward Papers*, MS. Auburn, N. Y.

see J. Somers Smith on very important business. President Baez, it appeared, was now ready to " accept the proposal made by the Hon. F. W. Seward when here in the ' Gettysburg,' for the purchase of the Peninsula and the bay of Samana." Mr. Smith was thrilled at this information and he gave assurance to Delmonte that, if he would secure from President Baez a formal instruction to this effect, then some action could immediately be taken. In fact, so interested was he in capitalizing this opportunity that he offered to send his son, E. P. Smith, as a special messenger to Washington, " and if the United States acceded, to return immediately, if possible in a man of war with a convention drawn up, and a sum, say, of one hundred thousand dollars to be paid on the ratification here." Delmonte promised to return on the following day (May 9, 1868) with the desired letter from Baez, but an unkind fate thwarted this carefully laid plan. The steamer for the United States was not expected to call at Santo Domingo City until May 10, but for some unforeseen reason it arrived early on the morning of the 9th and remained only a short time. It was too much to expect that the rusty wheels of Dominican administration could be speeded up to meet such an emergency, and the whole project fell through.[97] But not for long.

On June 19, Smith again wrote to Seward to advise him that on the preceding day Delmonte had paid him a visit for the purpose of renewing the proposal of May 8. President Baez was anxious to sell to the United States the peninsula and bay of Samaná for two millions of dollars in gold, one million in gold coin, and the other million " in effects, gold valuation." In the event the American Government accepted this proposal, Baez desired that a full power to negotiate be sent at once to Smith along with three vessels of war which would be used to sustain the Baez Government "until the country would settle down after the sale is perfected."[98]

[97] Smith to Seward, May 18, 1868, *Santo Domingo, Consular Desp.*, vol. 5, MS. Dept. of State. The interview between Smith and Delmonte took place on May 8, 1868.

[98] Smith to Seward, June 19, 1868, *ibid.* There was a growing public interest in the acquisition of Samaná which was reflected in the daily press. The New York *Tribune* was filled with items concerning Santo Domingo, the following

Seward, however, was not as anxious for the purchase as he had been in the spring of 1866. The long and bitter fight with reference to the impeachment of President Johnson was just over. The treaty with Denmark for the purchase of the Virgin Islands (signed on October 24, 1867) was still slumbering in the Senate Foreign Relations Committee with no immediate prospect of ratification, while the treaty for the purchase of Alaska (March 30, 1867) had caused Seward no end of trouble. Although this treaty had been ratified by the Senate on April 9, 1867, the heirs of Benjamin Perkins had managed to prevent for a number of months any appropriation by the House of Representatives to pay for Alaska, and it was during the spring and early summer of 1868 that Seward was engaged in employing " all sorts of means " to secure a majority in Congress with reference to the passage of the appropriation bill of $7,200,000.[99] It was no wonder that he was hesitant in regard to the purchase of Samana Bay,[100] and in an instruction to Smith, dated July 8, 1868, he hinted at existing difficulties in that regard. After instructing Smith to advise President Baez that his proposition " will be held under consideration," Seward delivered a homily on the element of uncertainty that is usually involved in diplomatic transactions. He pointed out the fact that " national transactions, however desirable and however important, sometimes depend upon occasion quite as much

one, of June 29, 1868, being typical: " Under the constitution [Dominican] it is impossible to sell Samana, although the Government is hard pressed for money. Jesserun has been empowered to raise a loan of $1,000,000 in Europe on the security of the mines. A New York steamship king has offered a large rent for Samana as a steamer station, and will pay a year's rent in advance. . . . The International Mail Steamship Company offers a rent of $100,000 for the bay and peninsula of Samana, with the privilege of working the mines on royalty, if acceptable, Samana to remain a free port under the protection of all the maritime powers."

[99] See F. A. Golder, " The Purchase of Alaska," *American Historical Review*, XXVI (1920), 421 ff.; and William A. Dunning, " Paying for Alaska," *Political Science Quarterly*, XXVII (1912), 385 ff.

[100] During the summer of 1868, there was an unending stream of newspaper criticism against colonial expansion. The following excerpt from the New York *Tribune*, July 16, 1868, is typical: " Gentlemen who want to sell us Northern Mexico, Lower California, St. Thomas, St. Jan, Bay of Samana, and other knickknacks, understand once for all, that both Houses of Congress must assent or there is no valid trade. We have debt enough, and none too much gold."

as they do upon the merit of the policy involved." This was particularly true at that time, for a " conjuncture exists in the United States which seems to render it improbable that a negotiation for the purchase of Samana can be opened within the present summer." [101]

Before this negative instruction reached Smith in Santo Domingo City, he wrote to Seward on July 18, 1868 to inform him that on the preceding day he had had an interview with President Baez in the course of which the Dominican executive again referred to the sale of Samaná Bay to the United States, and upon this occasion he assured Smith that if the American Government would give him " moral and material support " he would at once " acquiesce with the views of the United States, and Samaná could be taken possession of and the question of money would be an after consideration." But in case the American Government refused any assistance, then a similar proposal would be made to England, France, or Spain.[102]

When Smith received Seward's instruction of July 8 he ignored the last paragraph, which informed him that the Samaná negotiation would not be reopened in the near future, and instead he seemed to focus his attention upon Seward's casual statement that the matter would be " held under consideration." President Baez, to whom Smith had read Seward's instruction, appeared also to have high hopes that the American Government would take immediate steps to secure Samaná Bay. Smith assured Secretary Seward that the negotiation

[101] Seward to Smith, July 8, 1868, *Desp. to Consuls*, vol. 47, MS. Dept. of State.

[102] Smith to Seward, July 18, 1868, *Santo Domingo, Consular Desp.*, vol. 5, MS. Dept. of State. Although the New York *Tribune* was generally opposed to a policy of colonial expansion, at times it seemed quite impressed with the opportunities that beckoned from Santo Domingo to American capitalists. On August 8, 1868 the following interesting item was published: " President Baez is signalizing his administration by a most liberal and progressive policy. . . . There is no doubt that he has the warm support of every man of intelligence and enterprise in the country. . . . The great mineral resources of Santo Domingo are well known to those conversant with the history of the country. Not to speak of the gold, . . . there is a copper region on the river Haina . . . which is said to be quite as promising as the celebrated copper district . . . of Cuba."

would be kept very secret, and that so far only President Baez, Delmonte, and the American Commercial Agent were privy to the whole affair. It had been stated in New York newspapers that the Dominican Government had a special agent in the United States who was authorized to negotiate for Samaná Bay, but Smith assured Seward that these rumors were without foundation. Indeed, he had been informed by Minister Delmonte himself that the Dominican Government had " no official Commissioner nor Agent in the United States, and no one has any *authority whatever* to act for it." [103]

Seward was much surprised to learn that the Dominican Government had informed Smith that there was no special agent representing that government in the United States. As early as September 8, 1868, he had written to Smith advising him that " Colonel Fabens had been for three months in the United States, representing himself as the confidential agent of Mr. Baez to treat concerning Samana." When Smith received this instruction he at once discussed the matter with Delmonte, who again assured him that Fabens had " no *official* position, nor authority whatever " from the Dominican Government, and President Baez himself denied " most emphatically " that Fabens had been authorized to treat for the purchase of Samaná Bay.[104]

What these assurances were worth may be seen from the fact that on April 18, 1868 Gautier, the Dominican Minister of Foreign Relations, had sent Colonel Fabens to the United States on a special mission which had for its object the establishment of closer relations between the two governments. One of the most available means for bringing the two nations into more intimate contact was the cession of Samaná Bay to the United States, and Fabens spared no effort to accomplish this

[103] Smith to Seward, August 18, 1868, *ibid.*

[104] Smith to Seward, October 19 and 24, 1868, *ibid.* On October 19, 1868 Fabens wrote to Seward to advise him of an early departure for the Dominican Republic. If there was any message " of a confidential nature " that the Secretary of State desired to send to President Baez he would be glad to deliver it in person. Also, in the event that " any developments of an interesting nature occur " in Santo Domingo, Mr. Fabens would not fail to get in touch with the Department of State. *Seward Papers*, MS. Auburn, N. Y.

transfer. In July, 1868 he arranged personal interviews with the leading members of the American Congress, during which he strongly stressed the advisability of annexing the Dominican Republic to the United States. The most important member of the House of Representatives to win over was Thaddeus Stevens, who had exerted his decisive influence in favor of a special appropriation for the special mission of Frederick W. Seward to Santo Domingo in December-January, 1866-1867. In view of such a favorable precedent Fabens concentrated his attention upon Stevens, and he apparently gained a favorable hearing for his Dominican projects. On July 25, 1868 he sent Stevens the following letter:

I regret exceedingly to hear of your continued illness, and sincerely hope that you may recover your health during the recess. If you feel strong enough in the course of the day to send the Samana resolution to any friend in the House who will offer it for you, I think it will be passed. All the members with whom I have spoken are favorable.

In this letter to Stevens there was enclosed the following resolution, which evidently Fabens thought was perfectly acceptable to the magisterial member from Pennsylvania:

WHEREAS, the West India Islands naturally gravitate towards the United States, and ought to be included, when practicable, in the commercial and political systems of this Republic, therefore,

Resolved, that the West India Islands, or such of them as may from time to time desire to be annexed to the United States, ought to be and will be received; provided always that no proceeding shall, in that case, be adopted which shall be inconsistent with a proper regard to national economy or shall involve war, or any breach of international law.

Along with this letter and resolution there was also enclosed a long memorandum which indicated the many advantages that would accrue to the United States from the acquisition of Samaná Bay.[105] Not only would Samaná Bay be of great value

---

[105] In the New York *Tribune*, August 13, 1868, there is a record of an interview between Thaddeus Stevens and Simon Stevens just before Stevens died. In the course of this interview Stevens spoke as follows of Seward: " His purchase of Alaska was the biggest thing in his life, and if he could have purchased Samana it would have been the crowning event of his whole career."

to the United States as a naval base, but there were adjacent deposits of coal which would greatly add to its general importance. Moreover, Fabens believed that it

could be had now at one half less than its real value. I suppose it would not cost one-fifth of Alaska; and to my mind would be much more valuable. At any rate let our negotiators examine the subject and decide.[106]

Unfortunately for the plans of Fabens, the continued illness of Thaddeus Stevens resulted in his death on August 11, 1868, and Fabens was forced to look elsewhere for his support. He had always been careful to maintain friendly relations with Seward. Therefore, on August 14, 1868 he wrote to the Secretary of State and enclosed a copy of a contract that had just been executed between him and the Dominican Government for an " exploration and a Geological and Mineralogical examination of the different provinces and districts of the Dominican Republic." For the expert services of Fabens the Dominican Government was willing to pay liberally in the form of certain concessions. In Seward's opinion, the contract seemed to be

a fair one and yet one which is marked with sagacious liberality on the part of the Dominican Government. If its provisions should be executed it cannot be doubted that the results would be useful, not only to the Dominican Government, but also to commerce and civilization generally. It is especially gratifying to see that citizens of the United States take so deep an interest in developing the resources of a sister Republic.[107]

In his reply of September 5, 1868, Fabens first thanked Seward for his friendly interest and then adduced some evidence of the prosperous condition of affairs in the Dominican Republic. Finally, he added a bit of information which clearly showed the confidence that President Baez reposed in him and how close their relations really were. On August 18 he had received a letter from Gautier, the Dominican Minister of

[106] Fabens to Stevens, July 25, 1868, *Stevens Papers*, vol. 12, MS. Library of Congress.
[107] Seward to Fabens, August 19, 1868, *Domestic Letters*, vol. 79, MS. Dept. of State.

Foreign Relations, in which he had been instructed to "seek a suitable occasion to congratulate President Johnson, in the name of President Baez, on the triumph of constitutional principles shown in the result of the recent impeachment." [108] How the shade of Thaddeus Stevens must have raged!

President Baez, however, was not content to seek fulfillment of his schemes merely through Fabens. At times he was glad to avail himself of the services of Smith, the American Commercial Agent. On August 31, 1868, Seward had written to Smith to inform him that the question of the cession of Samaná Bay to the United States was involved in "complications so numerous and so grave" that the Secretary of State did not think it would be "prudent to open a discussion upon it in the absence of Congress from the seat of government." [109] When Smith received this instruction, towards the middle of October, he lost no time in communicating its contents to the Dominican Government. Both Delmonte and President Baez were of the opinion that a mere cession of Samaná Bay would no longer suffice to settle the rapidly increasing difficulties in the Dominican situation. In July, 1868 Fabens had been assiduously working for Dominican annexation to the United States, and now the Dominican Government, despite the discouraging instruction from Seward of August 31, decided to appeal to the Secretary of State on the basis of the Fabens program.

After two interviews with Smith, President Baez and Delmonte expressed a wish that the American Government would

publish a declaration placing the Dominican Republic under the protection of the United States, and sustain the proclamation by sending vessels of war to take possession of Samana and Manzanilla bays, and in fact, any other points that a military necessity may require.

In case the United States took this course, the Dominican Republic would immediately "apply for admission into the Union, which is the fervent wish of a large portion of the

[108] Fabens to Seward, September 5, 1868, *Dominican Republic, Notes from*, vol. 1, MS. Dept. of State.

[109] Seward to Smith, August 31, 1868, *Desp. to Consuls*, vol. 47, MS. Dept. of State.

inhabitants." In short, the American Government was now invited "to take this Republic under protection and pave the way for annexation by Mr. Baez, who, although President by name, is virtually clothed with Dictatorial Powers." [110]

From these manoeuvres of President Baez, it was quite evident that he had lost all faith in the validity of republican government in Santo Domingo and was anxious to exchange turbulent independence for the security of American protection. Under an American régime there would still be ample opportunity for political careers, while American capital would probably be ready to develop Dominican resources in a way that would bring definite economic advantage to certain canny Dominican politicians. With these ideas in mind, Baez now persuaded Smith to send his son, Eugene Smith, to the United States to place before Seward the numerous favorable aspects of Dominican annexation.[111] But before the younger Smith could arrive in the United States Seward, on November 17, 1868, sent a detailed instruction to the American Commercial Agent

[110] Smith to Seward, October 24, 1868, *Santo Domingo, Consular Desp.*, vol. 5, MS. Dept. of State. President Baez reposed great confidence in the ability of J. W. Fabens to sell Samaná Bay to the United States, and many influential Dominicans believed that the sale would soon be effected. On August 22, 1868 the Dominican correspondent of the New York *Times* telegraphed the following item to his paper: "Another hope for Mr. Baez is the sale of Samana to the United States for $2,000,000. Col. Fabens, who is now in Washington, is said to be the agent of Baez for that purpose, and, in fact, it is asserted that the bargain is already closed between Fabens and Mr. Seward."

[111] Smith to Seward, November 9, 1868, *ibid.* See also the instructions of J. Somers Smith to his son Eugene Smith, November 9, 1868, *ibid.* In the *Senate Report* No. 234, 41 Cong., 2 sess. (the so-called *Hatch Report*), p. 158, Smith gives further evidence concerning the mission of his son Eugene to Washington: "Mr. Baez sent for me in November; he used to send for me three or four times a day. I went to see him at his request about the 8th or 10th of November, 1868, and he said, 'I want you to do something for me.' I asked him, 'What is it?' He said: 'Will you send word for me to the United States? I want to send a proposition to your government.' I said to him, 'Make it out; send Delmonte to me; let me know the nature of it, and I will send my son home with it. But, Mr. Baez, as he is going home on your account, you will have to bear the expense.' Mr. Baez said: 'Consul, we are very poor; I have not got a dollar; but after the business is finished, if you are at any expense, which you will be, of course, I will pay you.' I said: 'I cannot say whether my government will be willing to pay your messenger; but I will see what I can do.' I went to see a friend and said to him: 'I want a

in which he discussed the whole question from its many angles. With reference to the issuance by the American Government of a proclamation which would place the Dominican Republic under the protection of the United States, President Baez should be advised that such a proclamation would really amount to " an act of war, and that, as such, it transcends the power of the Executive Government, and falls within the exclusive province of Congress." It would be equivalent to an act of war because it would be taking sides against the party of opposition in the Dominican Republic, which had voiced strong objections to any alienation of the national territory. In submitting such a transaction to the judgment of mankind,

it would be difficult to distinguish it from the attempt which was made during our recent civil war by Spain to re-annex the Dominican Republic to her own dominion by means of an illegal arrangement made between the Spanish Government and Santa Anna, then President of the Dominican Republic. . . . To establish the protectorate in St. Domingo would be virtual annexation by act of war, and not by the consent and agreement of the people of the Dominican Republic. . . . Nevertheless, the subject is a very important one, and I reserve further consideration of it until Congress shall have assembled which will be on the first Monday in December.[112]

It is doubtless very true that when Seward wrote this instruction of November 17, he regarded the question of Dominican annexation as a " very important one," and, after the arrival of Eugene Smith with instructions from Baez to arrange the details of such a transfer with the American Secretary of State, there were no longer any qualms in Seward's mind as to the proper course to pursue. He promptly laid the whole matter before President Johnson and easily succeeded in securing his

thousand dollars to send my son home with a proposition to the United States government.' He told me, ' You can have anything you want.' I told my son to get ready to take the proposition to the United States.'. . . My son came home; and he was the cause of the paragraph in President Johnson's message of December, 1868, . . . stating that the time had arrived when it was necessary to look into the affairs of San Domingo."

[112] Seward to Smith, November 17, 1868, *Desp. to Consuls*, vol. 53, MS. Dept. of State.

approval of annexation. Therefore on December 9, 1868, in the President's fourth annual message to Congress, there was included the following paragraph concerning the Dominican situation:

It can not be long before it will become necessary for this Government to lend some effective aid to the solution of the political and social problems which are continually kept before the world by the two Republics of the island of St. Domingo, and which are now disclosing themselves more distinctly than heretofore in the island of Cuba. The subject is commended to your consideration with all the more earnestness because I am satisfied that the time has arrived when even so direct a proceeding as a proposition for an annexation of the two Republics of the island of St. Domingo would not only receive the consent of the people interested, but would also give satisfaction to all other foreign nations.[113]

Two days later, December 11, the question of Dominican annexation came before the President's Cabinet, and the following excerpt from the *Diary* of Welles is illustrative:

Seward read a proposition to the effect that San Domingo wished to come under the protection of the United States. In the present condition of the country there can be little done. Radical partyism must have its insane, shallow run. The real interests of the country are neglected, and it would be unwise to attempt to consider the subject now, if ever.[114]

Apparently the Cabinet did not formally pass upon the subject of Dominican annexation, but this fact did not lessen Seward's enthusiasm for a project that was continually being brought to his attention by the American Commercial Agent at Santo Domingo City. On December 10, 1868, Smith wrote to inform Seward that President Baez had written letters to "different authorities throughout the Republic on the question of seeking the protection of the United States," and had received replies which indicated that such a course would be "very popular in all parts of the country." Baez, therefore,

---

[113] J. D. Richardson, *Messages and Papers of the Presidents*, VI, 689.
[114] III, 480.

was " most anxious " that the proposals made through Eugene Smith be immediately accepted by the United States and that three vessels of war be despatched to the island.[115]

A few days later, December 19, Smith wrote to acknowledge receipt of Seward's instruction of November 17, in which objection had been raised to presidential annexation of Santo Domingo as a measure which would invade the war powers of Congress. Baez was anxious to meet this objection by proving that the majority of Dominicans were heartily in favor of annexation, and he was willing to have a plebiscite upon this question. But before such action could be taken it would be advisable for the American Government to decide upon extending American protection to the Dominican Republic, and " at the same time send out to this city a vessel of war with a convention and the sum of three hundred thousand dollars." Should this course be adopted the American Government could " take possession of Samaná, and in a little while the people will apply for annexation." But in the event that the United States was not ready for measures looking towards annexation, President Baez was then in favor of the purchase of Samaná on the same terms that were offered by Frederick W. Seward in January, 1867.[116]

In Santo Domingo the position of President Baez was constantly being undermined by revolutionary elements, and this fact led him to press more and more strongly for American intervention. On December 22, Delmonte called to see Smith and inquired what would be the attitude of the American Commercial Agent if the different Dominican provinces " should hoist the American flag, and proclaim by acclamation that they placed themselves under the government of the United States." So strong had this desire for annexation to the United States developed throughout the Dominican Republic that Delmonte believed that President Baez, " even if disposed, could scarcely restrain a movement, which may occur at any time."

[115] Smith to Seward, December 10, 1868, *Santo Domingo, Consular Desp.*, vol. 5, MS. Dept. of State.
[116] Smith to Seward, December 19, 1868, *ibid.*

Smith did his best to control such outspoken ardor for American protection, but it was difficult to repel these fervent advances. On January 2, 1869, Delmonte again called and endeavoured to convince Smith that the present moment was most propitious for annexation because the unanimous desire of the Dominicans to merge their destinies with that of the United States would effectually silence any European opposition.[117]

In the early part of January, 1869, a copy of President Johnson's message to Congress of December 9, 1868 reached Santo Domingo City, and at once President Baez redoubled his efforts to bring about annexation. It was patent that the President of the United States was favorable to such a measure, and Baez lost no time in expressing his gratitude for such political clairvoyance. In a confidential letter to President Johnson of January 8, 1869, Baez remarked in part as follows:

The Government of the Dominican Republic feels ineffable satisfaction at the ideas expressed by Your Excellency, in your last Message to Congress, in relation to the great political measure that ought to be adopted immediately by the Cabinet at Washington, in reference to the future of Santo Domingo. We have the honor to say to Your Excellency that the sentiments of a Nation were never so well interpreted as they were on that occasion, by Your Excellency; and that such are the sentiments of an immense majority of the inhabitants of our Country, which has been depleted too long by the oppression of anarchy.[118]

This overture for annexation was sent to the United States at once in the hope that everything could be arranged while the Johnson Administration was still in office. Louis P. Augenard, an American citizen, was selected as the person best fitted to handle this matter, and he was requested to explain to Secretary Seward " the real situation of this country." [119]

Fabens, of course, was not to be neglected, and Gautier, the Dominican Minister of Foreign Relations, requested him to proceed to Washington and present to Seward an official

[117] Smith to Seward, January 9, 1869, *ibid.*, vol. 6.

[118] Baez to Johnson, January 8, 1869, *Dominican Republic, Notes from*, vol. 2, MS. Dept. of State.

[119] Gautier to Seward, January 8, 1869, *ibid.*

instruction relative to the extension of American protection over the Dominican Republic.[120]

In the meantime Fabens, living temporarily in New York City, was made suspicious concerning the good faith of both Secretary Seward and the Dominican Government. On January 2 Jasper K. Herbert wrote to General Butler with regard to a rumor that the American Government had recently disbursed about $100,000 in " partial pay't for St. Thomas & Samana." Fabens was particularly anxious to ascertain whether this rumor was true and whether such payments were " on private account or for the Govt's." Both Fabens and Herbert had heard that

the Sec. of State is in it. If it is Gov't account we are all right; if not we want to know who are in it. Mr. F. is the associate of some parties who are already in St. D. or have an agent there & he fears an attempt to " sell him out." [121]

General Butler quickly learned from Secretary Seward that " the Government would not purchase either St. Thomas or Samana." If any payments had been made they were on " private account," and the Department of State was not involved in any way.[122] But before this letter could reach New York Fabens had already paid a hurried visit to Washington to see General Butler. Reassured as to the Dominican situation, he immediately wrote to C. K. Garrison who was closely associated with him in the Samaná Bay venture. He had talked matters over with General Butler, who admitted the " great importance " and inviting nature of the whole Dominican project but who very cannily inquired as to " his share of the scheme." When Fabens quickly explained that this pecuniary angle of the enterprise could be " arranged " in a " satisfactory manner," the General displayed further interest and agreed to support a resolution in Congress favoring the extension of American protection over the Dominican Republic.

[120] Fabens to Seward, January 11, 1869, *Dominican Republic, ibid.*
[121] Herbert to Butler, January 2, 1869, *B. F. Butler Papers*, MS. Library of Congress.
[122] Butler to Herbert, January 6, 1869, *ibid.*

The opportunity to derive some substantial financial advantage from this scheme of Dominican annexation appealed so strongly to General Butler that he contrived a long interview with Secretary Seward, who promised to " dispatch a national ship to Santo Domingo " to assist these importunate imperialists. The promptness of this offer from Seward was a little disconcerting to Butler, who advised Fabens to conclude all negotiations for the lease of Samaná Bay " prior to the arrival " of this American ship of war. Inasmuch as this lease or purchase of Samaná Bay was to be the private affair of the Samaná Bay Company, it would be expedient to have available at once the first installment of the total sum agreed upon. And as for Congressional action upon the resolution making the Dominican Republic a protectorate of the United States, Butler promised to talk with such bosom friends as Washburne, Schenck, and Logan, who would see that there was no delay in passing it.

Fabens was jubilant over the attitude of Secretary Seward, who was " well pleased " with the " shape the affair has taken " and who would do all he could " to advance " the " interests " of the Samaná Bay group.[123]

Before any resolution providing for the extension of American protection over the Dominican Republic could be introduced in the House of Representatives it was necessary to have indubitable evidence that the Dominican Government desired such action. Fortunately, Fabens had just received the instruction from Gautier, the Dominican Secretary of Foreign Relations, requesting American protection, and he immediately wrote to Secretary Seward and to General Butler advising them of this fact.[124] The next step was taken on January 12, 1869

[123] Fabens to C. K. Garrison, January 6, 1869, *Fabens Papers,* MS. in possession of Mr. Graham C. Lovejoy. Garrison was a very wealthy resident of New York who was interested in some steamship lines to South America. He was on intimate terms with General Butler and upon occasion was glad to extend favors to him. See James H. Young to Butler, February 10, 1869, and Butler to Garrison, February 15, 1869, *Butler Papers.*

[124] Fabens to Seward, January 11, 1869, *Dominican Republic, Notes from,* vol. 2, MS. Dept. of State, and Fabens to Butler, January 11, 1869, *Butler Papers.* The power of Butler in the House of Representatives at this period is well illustrated by the following letter from George L. Boutwell, of Massa-

by General Nathaniel P. Banks, chairman of the House Committee on Foreign Affairs, who reported a resolution which expressly authorized the President

to extend to the Governments and people of the republics of Hayti and San Domingo the protection of the United States, for the purpose of assisting them to establish permanent republican institutions whenever those Governments, or either of them, shall apply to the United States for its protection, or whenever the President shall be satisfied that the Government and the people of those republics desire or voluntarily consent to the protection of this Government: *Provided*, that the President shall communicate to the two Houses of Congress immediate information of any action which the Government of the United States may take upon this subject: *And provided also*, That no action which may call for or require any appropriation of money from the Treasury of the United States shall be authorized or commenced under the authority of this resolution without the previous consent of Congress.[125]

In support of this resolution Banks explained that it was based upon the theory that " the two republics of Haiti and San Domingo desire the action here recommended." For that reason it was expressly stated in the resolution that unless they should voluntarily consent to this action no further steps would be taken in the matter. Banks then went on to say that the resolution in question did not contemplate " a protectorate in the European sense, according to which the protecting Government interferes with or controls or is in some degree responsible for the Government that is protected." Under the resolution he had just introduced nothing more would be required

than that the United States shall, perhaps, send a vessel of war to that island, and in case of any interruption of the public peace, or any violent proceedings against the Government, to advise those parties attempting revolution that it would be better for them and their country

chusetts, who was quick to apologize for certain sarcastic remarks he had uttered against Butler during a heated debate: " In the remarks to you yesterday I said, under the excitement of the moment, what my judgment disapproves. With my regret therefore I trust you will regard what was said as not said." *Butler Papers*. Boutwell was one of the important Radicals in Congress and later was Secretary of the Treasury in the Grant Administration.

[125] *Cong. Globe*, 40 Cong., 3 sess., p. 317.

to wait until the regular period of election should occur before they proceed against the Government.

When Representative Woodward, of Pennsylvania, inquired whether this would not be the first step in the formation of an entangling alliance, Banks assured him that it was " not an initiatory step to anything except the maintenance of good government in the Island of San Domingo by the people of the island." Delano, of Ohio, then interposed to ask whether there was any precedent for such a resolution, whereupon Banks admitted that there was " no precedent for the proposed action." He declared, however, that we were " in an age when new action is required, and this is one of the instances." Finally Representative Ferriss, of New York, requested information as to whether the Committee on Foreign Affairs regarded this resolution " as a step to the ultimate annexation of these islands to the United States as a part of our territory? " Without any hesitation, Banks replied that " the committee had no such idea." [126]

After a short discussion the question was postponed until the following day, when an extended debate was held on the subject of the resolution. Some members, like Judd, of Illinois, were anxious to know whether the Department of State could furnish any light upon the necessity for the extension of American protection over Haiti and the Dominican Republic, but it was apparent that the chairman of the Committee on Foreign Affairs did not feel at liberty to make any disclosures in that regard. Such a hesitancy was all the more marked when it was realized that the whole basis of the resolution was a supposed desire on the part of the people of both Haiti and the Dominican Republic for American protection.

During this rather extended debate on January 13 Delano was one of the most vehement opponents of the resolution, and to his mind it seemed very probable that the American protection called for in future emergencies in the island of Santo Domingo might well be equivalent to actual warfare. The history of Haiti was one long record of rebellions. Such being

[126] *Ibid.*, pp. 333-335.

the case, why was it necessary for America to become embroiled in such constant friction? If, on the other hand, we should, from time to time, find certain nations " ripe for our institutions and ready for our plan of government," then let us

incorporate them and protect them afterward. But to go out as a protector of other nations who are struggling among themselves for self-government is to adopt a policy which will end in the overthrow of our institutions and in ruin to our nation.[127]

After the opponents of the resolution had the floor for some time, Maynard, of Tennessee, rose to remind his colleagues that according to the Monroe Doctrine the United States had a special interest in safeguarding the republican institutions of our Latin-American neighbors. The pending resolution was entirely consistent with American policy, and a precisely similar line of action had been taken by the American Government in its support of the Juarez Government during the entire period of our Civil War. Such arguments, however, were in vain, for the resolution was tabled by an overwhelming vote of 126 yeas, 36 nays.[128]

But despite such a legislative rebuff, the question of Dominican annexation was not definitively settled. On January 26, 1869 Seward received a note from Louis P. Augenard, who had been sent by the Dominican Government to the United States as a special agent to further the plans of Baez.[129] Three days later Nathaniel P. Banks wrote to Seward with reference to conditions in Haiti and Santo Domingo, and the Secretary of State hastened to advise the chairman of the House Committee on Foreign Affairs of the arrival of the Dominican

[127] *Ibid.*, p. 337.

[128] *Ibid.*, p. 340. On January 18, 1869 J. W. Fabens wrote to General Banks to inquire as to the possibility of the " protectorate resolution " being passed at a later date: " Mr. Seward observed to me on the day after the vote on the ' Protectorate Resolution ' in the House that he thought the matter could yet be carried during the present session. What is your opinion on this subject? Can I be of any service to you in Washington? Please advise me frankly. The affairs are fully ripe in St. Domingo and it is a pity that it should drag here." *Banks Papers*, MS. Essex Institute, Salem, Mass.

[129] Augenard to Seward, January 26, 1869, *Dominican Republic, Notes from*, vol. 2, MS. Dept. of State.

agent, Augenard. In a reply of the same date, Seward informed the chairman that

the opinion expressed by the President that those Republics are not unprepared for a direct proposition of annexation was inferred from the nature of the propositions which had been received at this Department before the meeting of Congress, but which expressed or implied some limitation or condition of military aid or pecuniary equivalent. Within the present week, however, a reliable and confidential proposition comes from the Dominican Republic which proposes immediate annexation, waives all preliminary stipulations, and addresses itself simply to the discretion and friendship of the United States. An agent from St. Domingo awaits the action of the Government. I am obliged to ask that this communication, although it is official, may for the present be regarded as entirely confidential.[130]

In this communication to Banks, Seward was emphasizing the question of Dominican annexation to the United States. In the resolution introduced by Banks on January 12, provision had been made simply to assist the people of Haiti and Santo Domingo in the establishment of " permanent republican institutions," and Banks himself had explicitly stated that the members of the House Committee on Foreign Affairs had no idea that American protection would lead to Dominican annexation to the United States. But now, in view of the insistent requests from the Baez Government that the American Government formally annex the Dominican Republic, it would be necessary for the Committee on Foreign Affairs to report an unambiguous resolution to that effect. Banks, of course, could not stultify himself by reversing his attitude of January 12 and 13, when he was on record as opposing such action. Thus on

[130] Seward to Banks, January 29, 1869, *Domestic Letters*, vol. 80, MS. Dept. of State. In the *Diary* of Gideon Welles, III, 516, there is the following entry under the date of January 29: " He [Seward] says there is an authorized agent here from San Domingo who wishes that country to be annexed to the United States, on whatever terms we please."

On this same date, January 29, there is also a letter from Seward to Banks enclosing a copy of the constitution of the Dominican Republic. Inasmuch as it was the only copy available in the Department of State, Seward requested General Banks to return it after he had " made sufficient use of it." *Banks Papers*.

February 1, 1869 Orth, of Indiana, introduced a resolution which provided that

the territory belonging to the Dominican Republic shall, upon the application of the Government and people of said republic, be admitted into the Union as a territory of the United States, to be called the Territory of San Domingo, upon the conditions and in the manner following: first, the people of that republic shall adopt a republican form of territorial government by deputies in convention assembled for that purpose; second, such action by the people shall be with the consent and cooperation of the existing Government of said republic; third, such form of government shall thereafter be submitted to the Congress of the United States for their approval; fourth, the admission of said territory shall be made with a view to an ultimate establishment of a State government republican in form in and over the said territory in conformity to the Constitution of the United States and with the approval of Congress.[131]

It is significant that this resolution provides for the formal annexation of the Dominican Republic and for its eventual incorporation into the American Union. In many of the leading newspapers of that day it was stated that not only were the Government and the people of the Dominican Republic anxious to come under the control of the American Government, but that this same desire was also in evidence in Haiti. Seward himself gave currency to this idea, and in a report that he made to President Johnson, on January 30, 1869, he voiced the opinion that Haiti was ready for annexation to the United States. After discussing the negotiations between the United States and the Dominican Republic with reference to Samaná Bay, he remarked:

Similar propositions for the cession of naval stations which would give a commanding influence in the Republic of Hayti have within the last year been received by the Executive of the United States, and, for sufficient reasons, rejected. The continual presence of visitors in the United States eminent for their influence and authority in the Dominican Republic and in the Republic of Hayti, who have pressed the public mind with arguments and persuasion for the extension of a protectorate as an expedient of annexation of each of those republics, and also for

[131] *Cong. Globe*, 40 Cong., 3 sess., p. 769.

their annexation itself, is universally stated by the public press without contradiction. These historical statements are abundantly sustained by documents which remain in the archives of this Department. It will readily be understood, however, that those documents have emanated from official persons who are in the employment either of the Foreign Governments concerned, or of the Government of the United States; and as such, they were necessarily written under the seal of confidence.[132]

It is true that President Salnave had offered to the United States the Môle-Saint-Nicolas as a naval station, but he had required in exchange that the American Government assume the debt due from Haiti to France and also enter into an offensive and defensive alliance with the Government of Haiti.[133] These were impossible conditions and were not seriously considered by Seward. They mark, however, the limit of the concessions that President Salnave was willing to offer to the United States, and, despite Seward's statement as above quoted, there was little sentiment in Haiti in favor of downright annexation to the United States.[134]

On February 1, 1869 Orth presented his resolution providing for the annexation of the Dominican Republic, and he took occasion to inform the House that this resolution had "the approbation of a large majority of the Committee on Foreign Affairs." But notwithstanding such strong support, the resolution was defeated on the very day it was introduced by a vote of 110 yeas, 63 nays.[135] This vote, of course, was much closer than the one on General Banks's resolution, and it clearly showed that a large number of the members of the House of Representatives were more favorable to annexation than to a mere protective policy.

On February 4 Joseph Medill, of the Chicago *Tribune*, wrote

---

[132] Seward to Johnson, January 30, 1869, *Report Book, May 15, 1868–January 15, 1872*, vol. 10, MS. Dept. of State.

[133] Hollister to Seward, August 10, 1868, *Haiti, Consular Desp.*, vol. 3, MS. Dept. of State.

[134] The attitude of the Haitian Government with reference to annexation is clearly shown in a despatch from Hollister to Seward, January 26, 1869, in which he discusses the political situation in Haiti and concludes with the statement: "It seems that a protectorate is out of the question." *Ibid.*

[135] *Cong. Globe*, 40 Cong., 3 sess., p. 769.

to General Banks to indicate his warm personal endorsement of an annexation policy:

> Your "protectorate" proposition was received with "shouts of laughter" by the people. But the annexation idea is a horse of a different color and sets people to thinking. . . . Go ahead with the negotiation. It is a magnificent Island, and in our hands would be worth untold millions to commerce.[136]

On the following day Seward wrote to the American Commercial Agent in Santo Domingo City and explained the reasons for the adverse action on the part of Congress. First, it seemed to him that such action was largely due

> to the fact that the movers of the resolutions proceeded upon information which is regarded by the Executive Department as confidential and therefore was not in possession of the House of Representatives. That information however is regarded by the Executive as confidential not upon any considerations affecting the Government of the United States, but upon considerations of propriety and delicacy towards the Government and people of Dominica. Secondly, such proceedings as are indicated by the resolutions upon which the House of Representatives were engaged are regarded by a part of Congress and the American people as being inconvenient in the present juncture of our domestic affairs, while on the other hand, those proceedings are believed to be in harmony with the general sentiments and expectations of the people and Government of the United States.[137]

Seward also wrote to General Banks to inform him that

> important despatches touching a subject which has been before the House of Representatives, have this day been received from the City of St. Domingo. These despatches Mr. Seward would like to show to General Banks or to any other member of the Committee on Foreign Relations who may do him the honor to call here in the course of tomorrow.[138]

---

[136] *Banks Papers,* MS. Essex Institute, Salem, Mass.

[137] Seward to Smith, February 5, 1869, *Special Missions,* vol. 2, MS. Dept. of State.

[138] Seward to Banks, February 5, 1869, *Report Book, May 15, 1868–January 15, 1872,* vol. 10, MS. Dept. of State.

One of the most important topics with which the Committee on Foreign Affairs of the House of Representatives had been occupied in connection with the proposed annexation of the Dominican Republic was the matter of the national debt of the little republic. In a conversation with two members of the Foreign Affairs Committee (Orth and Cullom) on the morning of February 6, Seward had assured them that this debt was really " nominal," and did not exceed " a half a million of dollars." Seward, however, did not have any documentary evidence to prove this assertion, and the members of the committee had to accept it on faith. Some hours later, however, this evidence came into the possession of Seward, who immediately communicated it to General Banks.[139]

At the same time that Seward was sending this information to General Banks, Colonel Fabens was writing to Banks along similar lines. He hastened to correct the false statements in the public press relative to the public debt of the Dominican Republic, and he could state " with authority that the total indebtedness of the Republic, including the paper currency in circulation on the 1st January 1869 did not exceed $500,000." [140]

General Banks must have been impressed with the assurances of Fabens, and he apparently became a convert to the cause of annexation. This much can be inferred from the following letter from Fabens to Banks, of February 18, 1869:

Your letter of yesterday is admirable and fully covers the case. It will enable me to place matters in such a light before the people and government of Santo Domingo that I anticipate no difficulty in a speedy and satisfactory solution of the question. I enclose herewith some photographs of prominent edifices in Santo Domingo City, a letter from a newspaper correspondent (not furnished to the press) and a letter from President Baez to me, both of which will give you further insight into the character of the man. . . . Please bear in mind the copies of U. S. and State Constitutions, which you kindly promised to forward to me, and with my most cordial acknowledgments of the deep interest which you have manifested in the welfare of the Dominican Republic.[141]

---

[139] *Ibid.*, February 6, 1869.
[140] Fabens to Banks, February 6, 1869, *Banks Papers.*
[141] *Ibid.*, February 18, 1869.

It is very apparent from the foregoing letter that the friends of Dominican annexation were not unduly dismayed by the adverse vote in Congress on the Orth resolution, and they merely bided their time until the accession of General Grant to the presidency seemed to spell the certain success of their efforts.

In the meantime, Seward had set out on another adventure in Caribbean diplomacy which ended as dismally as the Dominican enterprise. In his desire to secure a naval base somewhere in the old Spanish Main he opened negotiations with several countries whose possessions he desired. These negotiations, however, were closely related one to the other, and at times they began immediately after the failure of diplomatic efforts in an adjacent quarter. Activity was one of the principal canons in Seward's credo, and if his plans did not usually command success it was not through lack of energy and persistence.

In the spring of 1867 Seward was engaged in negotiations with the Dominican Republic for the lease of Samaná Bay, but by the first week in May it was apparent that the Cabral Government was fearful of coming to any agreement with the United States because of popular hostility to such a measure. Therefore, on May 8, 1867 Seward instructed the American Commercial Agent at Santo Domingo City to terminate the negotiations for Samaná Bay.[142] It was advisable to look elsewhere for the acquisition of a naval base, and this was all the more important since Denmark continued to pursue a policy of studied delay with reference to the cession of the Danish West Indies to the United States. Perhaps Spain might be more acquiescent!

---

[142] See *ante,* pp. 244-245. In the *Diary* of Gideon Welles, under date of May 15, 1867, there is the following entry regarding the islands of Culebra and Culebrita: "Returning from the Department this P. M., I met Seward, who was going with his sons to call on me. . . . Some New-Yorker has informed him of an uninhabited island, called Snake Island, near St. Thomas, which has a capacious and excellent harbor. . . . The island, he says, is low and well timbered. . . . I advised . . . that his New York friend should resume possession and that we would defend him in his rights. If Spain should claim jurisdiction, we must adjust the matter with her. I told him I much preferred this to buying St. Thomas." III, 94.

With this idea in mind Seward now turned to George Bancroft, who was about to leave for Berlin as the American Minister to Prussia, and instructed him to approach the Spanish Government with reference to the cession of the islands of Culebra and Culebrita off the coast of Porto Rico. As is well known, Bancroft received this appointment to Berlin largely as a reward for the service he had rendered to President Johnson by writing the first message that Johnson sent to Congress, on December 5, 1865.[143]

Bancroft's appointment was made in May, 1867, and in the last week of that month Seward gave him instructions to proceed to Madrid in order that he might give his

unofficial and informal attention to a discussion of the subject [of the cession of the islands of Culebra and Culebrita] between Mr. Hale, our Representative at Madrid, and the Spanish Government. For this purpose you will place all the papers in Mr. Hale's hands, including this instruction; and leaving to him the official conduct of the matter, you will render him such advice, assistance and co-operation, unofficially, as you may be able to give. It will be important that the following suggestions be observed by Mr. Hale and yourself, namely: 1st. The proceeding on our part should be for the present entirely confidential. 2nd. It is tentative only, and no arrangement is to be definitely entered into without instructions from this Department. 3rd. Mr. Hale will be informed that the parallel negotiations referred to relate to the peninsula of Samana in St. Domingo, and to the Danish West India Islands, St. Thomas and St. John. . . . 4th. The parallel negotiations just referred to, one or both of them, may take such a turn as to render it desirable and even necessary on our part to desist from the proposition to Spain for the purchase of Culebra and Culebrita. 5th. I think that it may with safety and propriety be said to Spain that the occupation of a suitable naval station in the West Indies by the United States instead of being injurious to the safety and prestige of Spain would operate to relieve many jealousies that are unavoidable while the United States are practically unrepresented in that quarter.[144]

[143] William A. Dunning, " More Light on Andrew Johnson," *American Historical Review*, XI (1906), 574 ff.

[144] Seward to Bancroft, May 29, 1867, *Prussia, Inst.*, vol. 14, MS. Dept. of State. See also M. A. DeWolfe Howe, *Life and Letters of George Bancroft*, II,

On May 29, 1867 Seward wrote an instruction to John P. Hale, at Madrid, informing him of the desire of the United States to acquire the islands of Culebra and Culebrita, and of the rôle that Bancroft was to play in the conduct of the negotiations. He was then directed to " pursue the matter vigorously but discreetly." [145]

Some six weeks later, Hale wrote to Seward to inform him that no proposal had been made to the Spanish Government because he was " decidedly of opinion " that any offer made at this time to purchase the islands of Culebra and Culebrita would meet with an " unequivocal refusal." In this respect Bancroft entirely agreed with him.[146]

Bancroft himself wrote to Seward on July 12 that Hale was " decided in the opinion that the indications are not favorable " and " that no overture should be made at the present moment." After a thorough canvass of the political situation in Spain, Bancroft came to the same conclusion and expressed the opinion that the " Minister who should attempt " any alienation of the Spanish domain would " involve himself in conflict with all the parties and all the factions around him, and would certainly go down." [147]

On August 8 Seward wrote to Bancroft that " the Department acquiesces in your conclusion that the present is not a propitious moment for instituting formal application " for the

---

167-168. In the Department of State there is a " Memorandum " which sets forth the gist of a conversation between Seward and the Spanish Minister at Washington in regard to the cession of the islands of Culebra and Culebrita. Seward, apparently, did most of the talking, and at the end of his interview he remarked: " The President would be pleased if her Catholic Majesty would take the subject into consideration and inform us whether the *projet* of a cession of those islands, in sovereignty, to the United States, for the purposes aforesaid, is deemed advisable, and upon what terms of compensation. If fair and reasonable terms could be accepted by Spain, the United States would cheerfully agree to consider the cession, under the circumstances, as a manifestation of international friendship." *Spain, Inst.*, vol. 16, MS. Dept. of State.

[145] Seward to Hale, May 29, 1867, *Spain, Inst.*, vol. 16, MS. Dept. of State.
[146] Hale to Seward, July 15, 1867, *Spain, Desp.*, vol. 50, MS. Dept. of State.
[147] Bancroft to Seward, July 12, 1867, *Prussia, Desp.*, vol. 14, MS. Dept. of State.

islands of Culebra and Culebrita.[148] Two days later a similar message was sent to Hale at Madrid, thus marking the definite defeat of one of Seward's schemes for expansion in the Caribbean.[149]

---

[148] Seward to Bancroft, August 8, 1867, *Prussia, Inst.*, vol. 14, MS. Dept. of State.

[149] Seward to Hale, August 10, 1867, *Spain, Inst.*, vol. 15, MS. Dept. of State. On February 8, 1867, Seward concluded a treaty with the Dominican Republic which was agreed to by the American Senate on March 20, 1867, and ratified by the President on July 31. It was a treaty of amity, commerce, navigation, and extradition, and it merely followed a familiar pattern. There was no mention of the proposed cession of Samaná Bay to the United States, and the matter of Dominican annexation to the United States was left unnoticed. The treaty was a routine affair with little significance.

CHAPTER VIII

JEREMIAH BLACK LEARNS THAT DIPLOMACY IS THE "CRAFT SINISTER"

Of all the many ramifications of Seward's Dominican policy there was none so filled with human interest as the so-called "Alta Vela Affair." There were few contemporaries who took a middle ground in their discussions of this question: either President Johnson and Secretary Seward were pilloried as arrant knaves who sacrificed national interests for personal considerations, or they were warmly praised as pure-souled statesmen who stood firm against the insistent demands of venal politicians. Even today, the biographers of Andrew Johnson have only eulogistic phrases for the President's position in this Alta Vela imbroglio. One of the ablest of this group, in his colorful volume *The Age of Hate,* devotes a few pages to the course followed by President Johnson in dealing with the questions that arose in connection with American claims to this tiny Caribbean island, and then he takes occasion to pay a fervid tribute to the lofty integrity of Lincoln's successor:

If there be in the record of any President of the United States, a finer illustration of calm courage and of devotion to a rigorous conception of duty than the foregoing, it has not been brought to public attention. Andrew Johnson's conduct in the Alta Vela case approached closely to Immanuel Kant's categorical imperative.[1]

This is high praise from a good source, and there is little doubt that when Andrew Johnson finally selected the path he was to follow in the settlement of any disputed question, he was not likely to be diverted by any adverse advice. But it is also true that firm resolution and categorical imperatives are not always the handmaids of justice. One may adopt a certain line of policy because of personal preferences as well as through righteous motives, and in the "Alta Vela Affair"

[1] George F. Milton, *The Age of Hate* (N. Y., 1930), pp. 583-539.

it seems clear that President Johnson made but a feeble attempt to think the matter through; it was far easier to follow the counsel of Secretary Seward. Such an attitude of mind was typical of Johnson. During his term as President there were numerous instances when quick decision and immediate action would have confounded his opponents. But he never capitalized these opportunities. Indeed, as Professor Beale shrewdly remarks: " In most matters Johnson lacked assurance, sought advice, hesitated in full realization of his own shortcomings." [2]

This natural hesitancy in taking a firm stand upon questions that arose during his administration is particularly evident in matters of foreign policy. To anyone who has carefully studied the diplomatic problems of the period from 1865 to 1869, it is apparent that the President paid scant attention to the conduct of foreign relations. In the large collection of Johnson manuscripts in the Library of Congress, there is hardly a volume in which there is even a short reference to the many questions that grew out of our intercourse with other nations. The voluminous records in the Department of State are equally devoid of indications of executive interest in foreign affairs. The truth is that Secretary Seward ran the Department of State much as he pleased. If he even went so far as to propose to the French Government a joint expedition to punish belligerent Koreans, this far-flung venture evoked no criticism from the acquiescent occupant of the White House.[3] In the matter of the purchase of Alaska, in the conduct of relations with France with reference to Mexico, in every question that related to the Caribbean, Seward had a free hand. Indeed, it is hardly likely that President Johnson ever gave any thought to placing obstacles in Seward's way. The Secretary of State had earned many laurels by the skillful manner in which he had handled the numerous serious problems that arose during the Civil War. And not only did the President have great respect for Seward's ability as a diplomat, but, like Lincoln, he

[2] H. K. Beale, *The Critical Year,* p. 11.
[3] Tyler Dennett, " Seward's Far Eastern Policy," *American Historical Review,* XXVIII (1922), 45-62.

warmed towards a strong man who laughed at dangers, personal or political, or who smiled when disaster dogged his footsteps. Thus there is in the *Diary* of Colonel William G. Moore, Johnson's private secretary, the following illustrative entry:

For Seward the President entertains a most sincere and friendly feeling. He seemed to be a perplexing study to the President, who never ceased to wonder at the Secretary's equanimity under all circumstances. . . . The President considers Mr. Seward a man of great firmness, of pure and lofty patriotism, of extraordinary ability and most generous emotions.[4]

It is probably true, therefore, that in the matter of Alta Vela the President adhered to a fixed rule that he was never to thwart his great Secretary of State in the conduct of foreign relations. Seward had outlined a definite procedure to follow, and Johnson, having neither time nor desire to make an independent judgment, refused to hamper the Secretary of State in his course. He did, in this Alta Vela question, indicate some doubt as to the justice of Seward's actions by never formally supporting the Secretary's contentions, but a do-nothing attitude was a great advantage to the Secretary of State and it indicated the appalling dependence of the President upon the counsel of his most astute adviser.

In order to understand this Alta Vela affair it is necessary to make a short reference to the history of American agriculture during the middle decades of the nineteenth century. Soil exhaustion was a factor with which many farmers in the East and South had to contend, and it was soon recognized that one of the best fertilizing agents then available was guano. The principal source of this fertilizer was a group of islands (Chincha Islands) off the coast of Peru, but monopoly prices made guano too expensive for the average American farmer, and a search was made for other sources of supply. It was not long before guano was discovered on some of the smaller islands in the Caribbean. The pressing need for cheap fertilizers in the American seaboard states led to a growing in-

[4] *Diary of William G. Moore,* May 7, 1867, MS. Library of Congress.

terest in the acquisition of these islands. In response to this
popular demand, a law was enacted by Congress (August 18,
1856) to legalize the claims of American citizens to unoccupied
islands with guano deposits.[5] Under the provisions of this
act, whenever any American citizen chanced to discover a deposit of guano on any island, rock, or key

not within the lawful jurisdiction of any other Government, and not
occupied by the citizens of any other Government, and takes peaceable
possession thereof, and occupies the same, such island, rock, or key
may, at the discretion of the President, be considered as appertaining
to the United States.

As soon as practicable, the claimant should give notice to
the Department of State of such discovery and occupation,

describing the island, rock, or key, and the latitude and longitude
thereof, as near as may be, and showing that such possession was taken
in the name of the United States; and shall furnish satisfactory evidence to the State Department that such island, rock or key was not
at the time of discovery thereof, or of the taking possession and
occupation thereof by the claimants, in the possession or occupation of
any other Government.

After these conditions had been complied with by the dis-
coverer, he might be allowed, at the pleasure of Congress, the
" exclusive right of occupying such islands, rocks, or keys, for
the purpose of obtaining guano, and of selling and delivering
the same to citizens of the United States." [6]

This act led to great activity on the part of many enter-
prising Americans who scoured the southern seas in search
of uninhabited guano islands. One of these was a certain
Captain S. R. Kimball, in command of the schooner *Boston,* of
Baltimore, owned by Messrs. Patterson and Murguiendo of
that city, who, on February 23, 1860, landed and took possession of the little island of Alta Vela off the coast of Santo
Domingo. On May 14, 1860, Messrs. Patterson and Murgui-

[5] Roy F. Nichols, "Latin American Guano Diplomacy," *Modern Hispanic
America* (ed. by A. C. Wilgus, Wash., 1933), pp. 517-543.

[6] *U. S. Statutes at Large,* XI, 119-120. Also, *Sen. Ex. Doc.* No. 25, 34 Cong.,
3 sess., and *Sen. Ex. Doc.* No. 10, 36 Cong., 2 sess.

endo wrote to Lewis Cass, the Secretary of State, to announce
the occupation of the island, and on July 16 they forwarded
to the Department of State an affidavit of Captain Kimball
relative to taking possession of the island.[7]

In the ordinary course of events it is more than likely that
Messrs. Patterson and Murguiendo [8] would have had their claim
to Alta Vela confirmed by the Department of State, and that
they would have been protected from interference by citizens
of other nations. It happened, however, that their claim arose
in the last days of the do-nothing Buchanan Administration.
Buchanan and Cass were more absorbed in the threatening
domestic situation than in the conduct of foreign relations,
even to the extent of almost abdicating American rights in
the Caribbean. William L. Cazneau, the special agent of the
Department of State in the Dominican Republic, sent warning
after warning to Cass about the encroachments of Spain upon
the sovereignty of the little republic, but to no avail. Spain,
therefore, pushed her plans for restoring her control over
the Dominican Republic, and American rights were given short
shrift.

On April 8, 1860, a Spanish war-ship stopped at Alta Vela
to inquire as to American purposes on the island. The American workmen replied that they were removing guano. This
answer seemed to satisfy the Spanish officer in charge of the
landing party, and no attempt was made to interfere with the
workmen. Some months later, on September 4, the Dominican
schooner *Merced* visited Alta Vela, and, after it was ascertained
what the Americans were doing, a request was made for a
sample of the guano that was being shipped to the United
States. When this request had been complied with, the schooner
left for the Dominican Republic.[9]

After this sample was analyzed by the Spanish agents in
Santo Domingo and its value as a high-grade fertilizer was
confirmed, it was at once decided that the profits from the sale
of guano should be turned into Spanish pockets rather than

[7] *Sen. Ex. Doc.* No. 38, 40 Cong. 2 sess., pp. 2-3, 27, 30-31.
[8] There are variant spellings of this name—Murguiendo and Murguiondo.
[9] *Sen. Ex. Doc.* No. 38, 40 Cong. 2 sess., pp. 31-32.

American. On the eve of a civil war, the American Government would not be in a position to resent in an effective way any violation of American rights in the Dominican Republic; thus it would be an easy and profitable task to dispossess the American owners of Alta Vela. With this end in view, a Dominican official was sent in the early part of October, 1860 to the island with instructions to order the Americans to withdraw at once. When, very naturally, they refused to do this, the matter was then discussed between Mr. Cazneau, the special agent of the American Government in the Dominican Republic, and the Dominican Secretary for Foreign Affairs. The Minister insisted that Alta Vela, "though never occupied or used in any manner" by the Dominicans, had always been considered as " an appanage of the republic."

Cazneau also took care to point out that the island had been merely a " desert sandspit which the whole world had previously neglected " until the " money and industry of the citizens of the United States had developed in it an unexpected capacity to yield profits." After this explanation the Dominican Cabinet manifested " a more amicable disposition," but Cazneau soon noted that " these friendly assurances were immediately followed by counter-indications from the Spanish officers, deputed from Madrid to govern this government." He was fearful, therefore, that there was " imminent danger that American interests at Alta Vela may be destroyed." [10]

These fears were soon realized, for on October 23, 1860 two Dominican ships, the *Merced* and the *Degalo,* anchored off Alta Vela and ordered the Americans to abandon their works and leave the island. Troops were then landed, the equipment for removing guano was placed on the Dominican vessels, and the workmen were made prisoners. Four days later the ships reached Santo Domingo City, where, without more ado, the Americans were turned over, with all their effects, to the American Commercial Agent. [11]

On January 8, 1861, Abraham B. Patterson and Prudence de Murguiendo wrote to Jeremiah S. Black, the American Sec-

---

[10] Cazneau to Cass, October 13, 1860, *Special Service,* MS. Dept. of State.
[11] Cazneau to Cass, November 17, 1860, *ibid.*

retary of State, to file a strong protest against the action of the Dominican Government.[12] A week later, Secretary Black wrote to assure them that the American Government was "entirely disposed" to protect them in the enjoyment of any rights they had legally acquired to the guano on the island of Alta Vela. But inasmuch

as the Dominican Republic is understood to claim jurisdiction over Alta Vela—a claim which another applicant was informed in June last, might probably be asserted on account of the position of the island—the Department deems it proper, before taking other steps in the matter, to address a communication to its special agent, Mr. Cazneau, with instructions to ascertain from the Dominican government the grounds on which its claim to the island is based.[13]

On January 15, Secretary Black wrote to Cazneau to direct the attention of the Dominican Government to the expulsion of the Americans from Alta Vela, and to "learn particularly the grounds upon which they claim jurisdiction of the island, in order that this government may know what measures are necessary to protect the interests of our citizens in that quarter."[14]

More than a month later, Cazneau wrote a long and interesting despatch to Secretary Black in which he discussed from every angle the question of the expulsion of the American workmen from the island. Alta Vela was a small

desert cay, lying, according to some charts, more than five leagues . . . to the southward of that "border belt" which has been completely desolated by the wars between the Dominican and Haytien Republics. Neither government permits the citizens of the other to live on this frontier, and a long margin of the main land nearest to Altavela cay is a depopulated waste, without settled inhabitants, without cultivation, and in point of actual fact without a government.

The Dominican government claims this depopulated district because it is within the line of the old Spanish colony, which now constitutes

---

[12] *Sen. Ex. Doc.* No. 38, 40 Cong., 2 sess., pp. 35-38.

[13] Black to Patterson and Murguiendo, January 14, 1861, *ibid.*, pp. 47-48.

[14] Black to Cazneau, January 15, 1861, *Special Missions*, vol. 2, MS. Dept. of State. See also Roy F. Nichols, "Jeremiah Sullivan Black," in *American Secretaries of State and Their Diplomacy*, VI, 397.

the territory of this republic. By a law of 1855 it is defined as a portion of the province of Azua, together with the adjacent islets, Beata and Altavela, which are there named as dependencies of that province. Except, however, in the descent of the war schooner Merced on the American guano diggers, last October, I cannot ascertain that this republic has ever exercised the sovereign duties of protection or government on either Beata or Altavela since it has been a nation.

. . . The American explorers had, in their repeated visits to the cay, always found it desolate, unused, and, to all appearances, outside of that care and charge which is the usual evidence of settled jurisdiction with any recognized government. . . . As the government of Hayti, which exercises the only visible jurisdiction in that neighborhood . . ., permitted the guano company to continue their business without remonstrance, . . . they seemed entitled to consider themselves tenants-at-will of the government of Hayti, rather than trespassers on the soil and sovereignty of the Dominican Republic.[15]

When Cazneau remonstrated against the summary manner in which the Americans had been removed from Alta Vela he was never able to obtain a " lucid and satisfactory answer from any of the Dominican officials."

Since the Buchanan administration came to an end before the receipt of this long despatch from Cazneau, it was impossible for Secretary Black to take any effective action for the protection of the rights of the American claimants to the island of Alta Vela. But after March 4, 1861, when Black no longer held the office of Secretary of State, he was engaged by Messrs. Patterson and Murguiendo as their counsel, and on March 27 he wrote a letter to Secretary Seward in which he made a very cogent argument in favor of his clients. In his opinion,

the prompt interposition of this Government for the restoration of Messrs. Patterson and Murguiondo, of Baltimore, to the possession of the Island of Alta Vela is clearly demanded by all the circumstances of the case. Those gentlemen discovered the deposits of guano on the island. It was barren, destitute of water, and worthless for everything but the guano. . . . It had never been inhabited or occupied for any purpose. Neither the Dominican government nor any other had ever exercised or claimed authority or jurisdiction over it. The discovery of

---

[15] Cazneau to Black, February 19, 1861, *Special Service*, MS. Dept. of State.

the guano upon it by Patterson and Murguiondo brought them within the spirit and letter of the act of Congress of 23rd August, 1856. They took and kept possession of it. They filed in the State Department the evidence of their discovery and possession. The proper record was made up, and the proper certificate issued. They were in every way by the law of nations and by the municipal law of the United States entitled to be protected by the power of this government.

. . . The reasons why it is absolutely necessary for the United States to see that the Dominican government is compelled to make restitution are too obvious to require even presentation. . . . The character of our government at home and abroad would suffer very seriously by a failure to perform its full duty in this case. Such a failure would be at once ascribed to our domestic troubles. I need not say how important it is just at the present time to avoid any act or omission which might imply a confession of weakness.[16]

As already indicated in the previous chapter, it was just at this time that Seward was contemplating drastic action against Spain for its agency in overturning the Dominican Republic, and of course it was Spain who was responsible for the expulsion of the Americans from the island of Alta Vela. Therefore, if Lincoln had not interposed and modified Seward's policy, it is quite possible that, as a result of American intervention in Santo Domingo, the American claimants to Alta Vela would have been restored to possession.[17] Seward, however, soon realized the wisdom of Lincoln's suggestions in regard to maintaining friendly relations with European powers, and during the continuance of the Civil War there was thus no chance whatever for pressure being exerted upon Spain in behalf of Messrs. Patterson and Murguiendo.

After the close of the Civil War the Spanish Government, because of a revolution in Santo Domingo against Spanish rule and because of the probability of American pressure, withdrew its armed forces from the island of Santo Domingo, and the Dominican Republic was re-established. There was now an excellent opportunity for Seward to restore Messrs. Patterson and Murguiendo to their rights in Alta Vela, for the

[16] Black to Seward, March 27, 1861, *Guano Papers*, MS. Dept. of State.
[17] See *ante*, pp. 213-215.

Dominican Government was in no position to withstand any demands of the United States. However, in the late fall of 1865 Seward became very much interested in pushing his ambitious plans for American expansion in the Caribbean, and in December 1865-January 1866 he made a voyage to that region in order to look over the islands best fitted for naval bases. When he arrived in Santo Domingo City he was at once taken under the wing of the former special agent of the State Department, William L. Cazneau, who expatiated at great length upon the advantages of a closer connection between the United States and the Dominican Republic. Seward was impressed with this discourse, and it was not long before he was negotiating with the Dominican Government for a lease of Samaná Bay.[18] Under these circumstances it was not likely that he would press upon the attention of the Dominican Government the claim of Messrs. Patterson and Murguiendo. Indeed, he frankly admitted in his report to the President, dated April 12, 1868, that while he was conducting these negotiations during the first half of the year 1867 he had refused on the " grounds of inexpediency " to support this claim to the island of Alta Vela.[19]

In this connection Seward makes a statement that is decidedly disingenuous. He speaks of this negotiation for Samaná Bay as having failed " during the summer of 1867." This would lead to the inference that after the summer of 1867 the Secretary of State would have felt perfectly free to push the Alta Vela claim. As a matter of fact Seward continued to be vitally interested in securing Samaná Bay, and in the spring of 1868, just before he submitted his report to the President, he had been actively negotiating with an accredited agent of the Dominican Government for a lease of this harbor. And even after this negotiation came to naught, Seward retained such a strong interest in acquiring Samaná Bay that he caused President Johnson to insert in his annual Congressional message of 1868 a suggestion that the Dominican Republic be annexed to the United States.[20] From this short

[18] See *ante,* pp. 226-241.
[19] *Sen. Ex. Doc.* No. 38, 40 Cong. 2 sess., p. 9.
[20] See *ante,* pp. 269-270.

survey of Seward's policy it is very apparent that throughout the administration of President Johnson the Secretary of State believed it to be highly expedient to cultivate the most friendly relations with the Dominican Government in order to accomplish his ends. In the pursuit of these ends it did not greatly matter if certain American claims were disregarded; national needs were of more importance than securing justice for a few American claimants.

Of course these facts were not suspected by Jeremiah Black, who, as the counsel of Patterson and Murguiendo, repeatedly wrote to Seward with reference to the rights of his clients. Thus, on April 3, 1866, Black wrote to the Secretary of State as follows:

In our conversation of yesterday I called your attention to the claim of Messrs. Patterson and Murguiondo of Baltimore, for the guano island of Alta Vela. You will find the fact established by the papers on file that the Island in question was discovered by Messrs. Patterson and Murguiondo. They took possession of it and occupied it under the act of Congress. . . . The claimants were detruded from the possession wrongfully and are entitled to restitution. . . . I wrote to the Department on the 27th of March a statement of the material facts which I suppose to be on file. . . . You then thought it right to postpone the consideration of the subject or at least to decline any forcible interference on account of our conditions with reference to the Southern insurrection. This morning the President proclaims that we have peace in all our borders. Let me hope that this will be accompanied with justice and right to our citizens.[21]

Seward paid little attention to this request, and on October

[21] Black to Seward, April 3, 1866, *Guano Papers*, MS. Dept. of State. The close connection between Seward's desire to secure Samaná Bay and his apathy concerning the rights of the American claimants to the island of Alta Vela is interestingly illustrated in a letter from P. H. Sullivan to Chauncey Black of August 26, 1867: " It is stated in our Baltimore papers that President Cabral of Dominica, has sent an Ambassador to this country to close the negotiation for the sale to us for $5,000,000 of Samana Bay. Whether this be true or not I cannot say, but I am sure there is enough in it to involve our interest very seriously one way or the other, and I trust you will take the rumor enough to heart to cause you to find out all about it, and work the matter to our advantage if possible." *Jeremiah S. Black Papers*, MS. Library of Congress.

17, 1866 Black wrote to the Department of State for the
purpose of again calling attention

to the claim of Patterson and Murguiondo of Baltimore to the Island
of Alta Vela. They discovered it and took legal possession of it under
the act of Congress relating to Guano Islands. They were forcibly
removed from it by the Dominican authorities, who had no more right
to it than the Emperor of China or the King of Dahomey. The faith
of the United States is pledged to restore my clients; and I am sure
that you will do what is proper to give them the justice which up to
this time they have not received.[22]

Since this communication to Seward received as little notice
as the previous one, it was necessary to send a series of letters
to the State Department in which stronger and stronger emphasis was placed upon the great injury that was being visited
upon the American claimants by the procrastination of the
American Government. These communications are sometimes
signed by Jeremiah S. Black, while at other times they have
the general signature of Black, Lamon and Company, the law
firm that was handling the interests of Patterson and Murguiendo. In this law firm, besides J. S. Black and Ward H. Lamon,
there was the irrepressible Chauncey F. Black, J. S. Black's
able son.

In the *Black Papers* in the Library of Congress there is a
large collection of letters from the American claimants of
Alta Vela. Some of these are from Patterson and Murguiendo,
but the larger number comes from one P. H. Sullivan, who
had a financial interest in their claim. The letters from Sullivan are very insistent, and sometimes to the point, as for
example his note of June 2, 1867 to Chauncey Black:

Why in the hell don't you write me and keep me in spirits, for I
am very much depressed? [23]

A few days later, Sullivan wrote to the law firm of Black,
Lamon and Company to warn them of a new development
that boded ill for the Baltimore claimants to Alta Vela. Sullivan had just learned from G. E. White, the agent of Thomas

---

[22] Black to Seward, October 17, 1866, *Guano Papers*, MS. Dept. of State.
[23] Sullivan to C. F. Black, June 2, 1867, vol. 46, *Black Papers*.

A. R. Webster and Company, of New York, that his company had just received a letter from Seward

in which he says that the title to the island of Alta Vela is *entirely in the Dominican Government, and that no other government or party have any lawful claim to it.* They assert that this letter was received by Webster and Company before any Guano was removed from the Island, and that that was the inducement to go to work there.

I cannot credit such a story, as it would involve Mr. Seward in an act of duplicity of which I could not think him capable. In any event it is something for you to go upon, and it will afford you an opportunity of asking or even *demanding* an explanation. This New York firm seems very secure in their position, as I learn they are now trying to charter a vessel to take a cargo to England by way of experiment.[24]

After the receipt of this letter, it was arranged by Black, Lamon and Company that Colonel Lamon should go at once to interview Seward in this connection. On June 15, Sullivan wrote to Chauncey Black to request some information as to the

result of Col. Lamon's interview with Seward, which you said would take place yesterday. If Mr. S. be really guilty of the duplicity with which he is charged, he ought to be drummed out of the State department to the tune of the rogue's march.[25]

Seward's answer was by way of a memorandum prepared by E. Peshine Smith, Examiner of Claims in the Department of State, and filed under the date of June 17, 1867. It took Smith only a very little while to arrive at the conclusion that Messrs. Patterson and Murguiendo had no semblance of a title to the island of Alta Vela. He placed great store by a decision of Lord Stowell in the case of the *Anna,* which dealt with the title to certain small islands off the mouth of the Mississippi River. In this case there was no doubt in the mind of the learned English jurist that these islands belonged, by virtue of their location, to the United States. Otherwise,

any other power might occupy them. . . . What a thorn this would be in the side of America! . . . The possibility of such consequence is

---

[24] Sullivan to Black, Lamon and Company, June 7, 1867, *ibid.*
[25] Sullivan to C. F. Black, June 15, 1867, *ibid.*

enough to expose the fallacy of any arguments which are addressed to show that these islands are not to be considered as part of the territory of America.

Smith then referred to a case given in Halleck's *International Law,* with reference to islands that lie near the coasts of different countries. Such islands, says Halleck,

if in the vicinity of the mainland, are regarded as dependencies, unless some one else has acquired title to them by virtue of discovery, colonization, purchase, conquest, or some recognized mode of territorial acquisition. The ownership and occupation of the mainland includes the adjacent islands, even though no positive acts of ownership may have been exercised over them.

These authorities had great weight with Smith, and in line with their opinions he believed it would be impossible

to fix a precise limit within which the right of jurisdiction from military considerations can be confined. . . . I do not know the distance of Alta Vela from the mainland nor from Beata, which lies between. I gather, however, that there is no question of the jurisdiction of the Dominican Republic now, and of either that or Hayti for many years past, over Beata. Alta Vela, judging from the charts, is near enough to Beata to be deemed an appendage to it, and so an appendage to the mainland, upon the principle that its occupation by strangers would menace the security of both.[26]

According to Seward, Judge Black knew nothing of the preparation of Smith's "report," and thus he continued to write to the President about the claim of his clients. The injury from which they suffered

was committed more than seven years ago. They demanded the intervention of their own government immediately afterwards. They, however, consented not to press the subject at the time, lest it might aggravate the troubles of the country. . . . Since the war the Department of State has exhibited so strong an inclination to do nothing,

[26] *Sen. Ex. Doc.* No. 38, 40 Cong. 2 sess., pp. 51-53. It is important to note that E. Peshine Smith, who made this report to Secretary Seward upon the claim of Patterson and Murguiendo to Alta Vela, was formerly employed by Thurlow Weed as editor of the Albany *Evening Journal.* See New York *Daily Tribune,* October 23, 1882.

that the sufferers are compelled at last to think of looking elsewhere for a remedy. . . . Patterson and Murguiendo embarked their all in this enterprise; it was an enterprise not only lawful but laudable; they went into it under a solemn promise of protection; they were shamelessly robbed by men who had no color of right, and who acted without the show of excuse.

. . . What is now asked is, that you send a vessel to Alta Vela, and put Messrs. Patterson and Murguiendo into possession. This is the short and simple way of dealing with the business.[27]

Jeremiah Black was further stirred up when his son Chauncey received another letter from P. H. Sullivan, of Baltimore, which recounted the activities of Thomas A. R. Webster and Company of New York. In a conversation with Mr. Sullivan, Webster said very

positively that the letter from Mr. Seward to them is now in their hands—that it was written about eighteen months since—that it is signed by Mr. Seward in his own name as Secretary of State—that he argues the question and claims that the title to Alta Vela rests entirely in the Dominican Government, and that he officially advises them how to proceed in their business so as not to impair the force of their contract with the Dominicans. . . . Now this makes patent one of two facts, either that he or Seward is the d—dest liar on the face of the earth.[28]

About this same time, Black also received a memorandum from the Department of State simply stating that, on July 18, the President had accepted " the conclusions of a report made by the Bureau of Claims on the subject of the island in question." This memorandum was not signed or otherwise authenticated. How, when, where, or by whom it was made does not appear. It represents that the President accepted certain conclusions of a " report " made to him, but neither the text of the report nor that of the conclusions is given. It did not say what was the subject-matter of the report. It did mention

---

[27] J. S. Black to Johnson, July 22, 1867, *Sen. Ex. Doc.* No. 38, 40 Cong., 2 sess., pp. 53-54.

[28] Sullivan to C. F. Black, July 24, 1867, *Black Papers,* vol. 46. This new firm, which was working the guano deposits on Alta Vela and in which Thurlow Weed had a financial interest, was known as Root, Webster, Clark and Company.

the island of Alta Vela, and therefore Jeremiah Black inquired of the President whether this " memorandum " discussed the geography, the political jurisdiction, the commercial products of it, or did it investigate the rights of the American owners? If it was upon the latter question, did it conclude that the owners might be plundered by foreigners, or that they ought to be protected according to law? . . . Even the vague and indefinite statement of the memorandum that you accepted some conclusion of some report concerning the island of Alta Vela, is not true in point of fact. I bring no charges of wilful falsehood against anybody, nor do I know what was the nature of the misapprehension which caused the memorandum to be made. But the fact is not truly stated; my contradiction rests on these grounds:

1st. The memorandum says that you " accepted the conclusion " on the 18th of July. Only one day afterwards, namely, on the 19th of that month, I presented to you a memorial on the case, and explained it somewhat at large. You had then manifestly never heard of the matter before; it was entirely new to you.

2nd. After I got this memorandum I told you of it, and you said emphatically that it never could have been officially before you in such a way as to make any impression upon your mind.

3rd. It is morally impossible that you, with the facts of the case before you, could have done otherwise than order the restitution of the island to its owners. You are wholly incapable of sanctioning, directly or indirectly, a naked robbery like this.[29]

After one reads the above letter, it seems manifest that Seward was conducting himself in a very ambiguous manner. Johnson was certain to have remembered if such a report had been " accepted " by him, and his assurance to Black of the contrary would seem to indicate that Seward was resorting to bare-faced lying in order to gain his ends.

This letter of Judge Black to the President was not without some effect, for Seward now called upon E. Peshine Smith,

[29] J. S. Black to Johnson, August 7, 1867, *Sen. Ex. Doc.* No. 38, 40 Cong., 2 sess., pp. 55-56. It is interesting to note that on August 12, 1867 Judge Black received a letter from Mr. Patterson of the firm of Patterson and Murguiendo to the effect that he had been approached by a " respectable party " in Baltimore who offered to send down an armed force to repossess the island of Alta Vela if a " fair interest in the Guano " on the island could be offered in exchange for this assistance. *Black Papers*, vol. 46.

the Examiner of Claims, to make a supplemental report on the title of Patterson and Murguiendo to the island of Alta Vela. Such a report was submitted to Seward on September 19, 1867 and was of much the same tenor as the report of June 17. Once again Smith comes to the conclusion that any islands adjacent to the coast of any country are regarded as a part of the mainland:

Take the recent case of the cession of Alaska and with it the long chain of Aleutian islands, running some fifteen hundred miles into the ocean. These are separated from each other by much larger distances than three miles; but does anybody suppose that the title of Russia to one of them, which may always have been uninhabited, was impaired by that circumstance?

There is one consideration suggested by Judge Black deserving of some thought. It is that Beata (the island between Alta Vela and the mainland) was at the time of the taking possession of Alta Vela by his clients, occupied by *Haytian* fishermen. That Hayti was therefore the de facto possessor of Beata and that the acquiescence of Hayti in the American occupation of Alta Vela is to preclude the Dominicans when they subsequently repossessed themselves of Beata, even if the temporary possession of Beata by Hayti was wrongful.

. . . The argument, I suppose, must be intended to have this effect. Conceding for the moment that Alta Vela is to be regarded as appurtenant to Beata; then Beata practically was under the jurisdiction of Hayti, not St. Domingo. Hayti had or had not the right to object to American occupation of Alta Vela, Dominica had none.

The answer is to come down to the region of real estate law—that the plaintiff in ejectment must recover on the strength of his own title, not on the weakness of his adversaries. Before the claimants could entitle themselves to any protection under our Guano Island Act . . . they were bound to show that the island was not " within the lawful jurisdiction of any other government." This is the condition precedent, and the jurisdiction of Hayti is as fatal to the claim as that of Dominica.

. . . The strong probability is that neither government attached much importance to a desolate key destitute of wood and water, and only resorted to occasionally by fishermen. This kind of occupation was enough, for an island of that character, to take it out of the category of land without any proprietor and open to the first occupant.[30]

---

[30] Smith to Seward, September 19, 1867, *Guano Papers*, MS. Dept. of State.

In these opinions of E. Peshine Smith, special emphasis is placed upon the contention that where adjacent islands are necessary to the security and protection of the mainland the title to these islands naturally inheres in the country owning the mainland. This is true even if the island is beyond " cannon-shot of the shore " and is rocky and desolate. The controlling question is whether it is " capable of being made auxiliary to operations of naval war."

In supporting this contention Smith quotes freely from an opinion of Lord Stowell in the case *Anna* and from Halleck's volume on *International Law*. He does not quote the passage from Henry Wheaton's *Elements of International Law* which deals with this subject as follows:

The maritime territory of every State extends to the ports, harbors, bays, mouths of rivers, and adjacent parts of the sea inclosed by headlands, belonging to the same State. The general usage of nations superadds to this extent of territorial jurisdiction a distance of a marine league, or as far as a cannon-shot will reach from the shore along all the coasts of the State. . . . The term " coasts " includes the natural appendages of the territory which rise out of the water, although these islands are not of sufficient firmness to be inhabited or fortified. . . . The rule of law on this subject is *Terrae dominium finitur, ubi finitur armorum vis;* and since the introduction of fire-arms, that distance has usually been recognized to be about three miles from the shore.[81]

This view of Henry Wheaton received subsequent confirmation in the writings of the eminent British jurist, Sir Robert Phillimore:

Though the open sea be thus incapable of being subject of the rights of property, or jurisdiction, yet reason, practice, and authority have firmly settled that a different rule is applicable to *certain portions* of the sea. And first with respect to that portion of the sea which washes the coast of an independent State. Various claims have been made, and various opinions pronounced, at different epochs of history, as to the extent to which territorial property and jurisdiction may be extended. But the rule of law may be now considered as fairly established— namely, that this absolute property and jurisdiction does not extend,

[81] Ed. by Richard Henry Dana (London, 1866), pp. 255-256.

unless by the specific provisions of a Treaty or an unquestioned usage, beyond a marine league (being three miles), or the distance of a canon-shot from the shore at low tide.[32]

It is also very possible that Smith was not aware of the fact that in August, 1852 Daniel Webster, as Secretary of State, had a correspondence with the Peruvian Government relative to the ownership of the Lobos Islands. In this correspondence, Webster distinctly argued that, as the ordinary jurisdiction of a state extends only three miles from the coast, the Lobos Islands could not be claimed by Peru on the simple ground of contiguity.[33]

But more than that, Smith chose to disregard the action of the Department of State in two important cases involving title to certain guano islands. The first case was with respect to Aves or Bird Island, on which guano had been discovered by American citizens in 1854. When American citizens proceeded to take possession of the island and remove the guano, the Government of Venezuela sent an armed force to expel them. The American Government at once objected to this procedure and presented to Venezuela a claim for damages. The dispute was finally settled in 1859 by a treaty which bound the Government of Venezuela to pay $130,000 to indemnify the claimants for their losses while the American Government agreed to make no further claim to the island.[34]

The other pertinent case which Smith purposely overlooked in his opinions was that which dealt with the claim to Navassa Island. This island lies some thirty miles from the coast of Haiti, and in 1857 one Peter Duncan, an American citizen, wrote to the Secretary of State and claimed that he landed upon it and found it uninhabited. In accordance with the Act of August 18, 1856, he informed the Department of State of his discovery and requested a certificate of title showing that all the conditions set forth in the Act had been complied with.

[32] *Commentaries upon International Law* (London, 1871), I, 235.

[33] Webster to Osma (Peruvian Minister), August 21, 1852, *Sen. Ex. Doc.* No. 109, 32 Cong., 1 sess., p. 12.

[34] *Sen. Ex. Doc.* No. 25, 34 Cong., 3 sess.; *Sen. Ex. Doc.* No. 10, 36 Cong., 2 sess. The full correspondence in this case may be found in the *Guano Papers*, MS. Dept. of State.

The Secretary of State regarded this claim as perfectly valid, and when Duncan assigned his rights to Edward K. Cooper, the American Government took prompt measures to protect these rights against any interference by armed forces from Haiti. The Haitian Government entered a vigorous protest against the claim of Cooper, arguing that the island of Navassa had not only been for many decades a rendezvous for Haitian fishermen but had always been regarded as a dependency of Haiti. Little heed, however, was paid to these protests, and American war-ships were sent to uphold the rights of the American claimant. This action is all the more significant when it is realized that it was authorized by the slow-moving President Buchanan and the Secretary of State, Lewis Cass.[35]

It was very clear to every competent observer of that period that Secretary Seward, on the basis of these two precedents, could adopt a very firm policy towards the Dominican Government and demand either that the rights of Patterson and Murguiendo be respected or that a large indemnity be paid for the damages they had sustained. In case the Dominican Government hesitated about the payment of a large indemnity, he could then seize Samaná Bay as a reprisal. This would put an end to the protracted and futile negotiations he had been carrying on with the Dominican Government for a lease of this bay, and he could appeal to Congress for an appropriation to satisfy the claim of Patterson and Murguiendo.

This procedure was warmly pressed by P. H. Sullivan in his letters to Chauncey Black. In a communication of November 27, 1867, he complained that Seward lacked initiative in such a matter:

Lord! but I am getting sick of Mr. S's trifling . . . when he can get Samana bay and all the rest of Dominica (and Hayti too) if the skulking coward would only for once be bold.[36]

---

[35] In the *Guano Papers* in the Department of State there is a large amount of correspondence with reference to Navassa Island. See also *Sen. Rep.* No. 379, 35 Cong., 2 sess., and *Sen. Ex. Doc.* No. 37, 36 Cong., 1 sess. For an exhaustive and scholarly account of this question, see Roy F. Nichols, "Navassa: A Forgotten Acquisition," *American Historical Review*, XXXVIII (1933), 505-510.

[36] Sullivan to C. F. Black, November 27, 1867, *Black Papers*, vol. 47.

Shortly afterwards he returns to this same theme:

Now, about those Danish West India Islands. What have hurricanes and earthquakes left of them? . . . If we buy St. Thomas and St. Johns, with all their poverty . . . do we not assume a protectorate over as heterogeneous a mass of humanity as might be found in any quarter of this side of—you know where, but if we get Samana by seizure as indemnity for damages, do we do anything but get a naval station, without reference to the internal state of the island, and at the same time obtain a coaling depot right at hand which would put to shame some of the finest properties in the Cumberland region? [37]

There was little chance, however, that Secretary Seward would adopt so bold a policy as was outlined in these letters, and this is especially apparent when one recalls that the Secretary was none too friendly to the claim of Patterson and Murguiendo. Indeed there is some evidence that Seward's son Frederick Seward, who held the position of Assistant Secretary of State, adopted devious devices to discredit the claim of these Baltimore merchants. In this regard there is a pertinent letter from Prudence Murguiendo to Chauncey Black in which a definite charge is lodged against both Sewards:

You will perhaps recollect that Mr. S. (Fred Seward Esq.), did state to your Father that he had sent or requested Com. Porter to stop at Alta Vela, and report to him (F. S.) whether or not there was guano on the Island; that he did report, stating that there was no guano on the Island, which naturally induced your Father to slacken his efforts in our behalf. We found, on investigation, that he, Com. Porter, only passed within six miles of the Island. These facts, my dear Chauncey, show evidence of interest against us, for had he (Mr. F. S.) not been identified with our opponents, he would not have had a cause to make false statements to you or to your Father. Therefore, I take the liberty of requesting what may have been forgot, but which certainly bears much interest on our behalf. These things should be known by the President, and he with his good judgment will readily see that there is *some object* which keeps the Secty- of State from granting us justice. Consider therefore, these points, and give us your decision. I *beg* of you that you will come on tomorrow night, and spend Sunday with us. . . .

Another promise made to your Father by the Scty. of State when he

[37] Sullivan to C. F. Black, December 10, 1867, *Black Papers*, vol. 47.

saw him this past summer, was to the effect, when he asked him for the Island, Mr. S. replied: " Its the Island you want is it? I thought you wanted damages. The Island is yours and you shall have it." [38]

Murguiendo now wrote to a Mr. John F. Coyle, of Washington, who was closely associated with the firm of Black, Lamon and Company, and asked his assistance in securing justice for his claim. On December 20, 1867, Coyle replied in a letter filled with sage counsel. He had talked the matter over with Jeremiah Black, who had requested him to arrange for an interview with President Johnson. He did so at once, and Judge Black obtained from Johnson

the assurance that he should have the case taken up and immediate action on it. I am opposed to going to Congress for that is an interminable tribunal, unless you give *all* of it away to sharks. I think however that it is well to use that *intention* as it may induce Seward to act. He is not anxious to have his correspondence overhauled, and I so told the President. Judge Black, from whom you have heard, feels very much encouraged by the positive assurance of the President. I am not unmindful of the importance of the matter, and rarely see the President without jogging his memory and pitching into Seward.[39]

Judge Black evidently came from this interview with the feeling that President Johnson was anxious to have justice done and would not support Seward in any dubious practices. Chauncey Black, now believing that Seward was in a difficult position, decided to write the President a letter which would show how Seward was very prone to sacrifice the interests of American claimants in order to promote his diplomatic schemes. The letter is long and vitriolic, as the following excerpts will indicate:

Late intelligence, part of it public and part of it private, makes it necessary for me to renew my solicitations on the subject of Alta Vela with increased earnestness. A new company has been formed in New York on the basis of the pretended lease to Webster and Company, for the purpose of plundering that Island of its guano. In one day alone they chartered *ten* vessels to go there and carry away the property

[38] Murguiendo to C. F. Black, December 6, 1867, *ibid.*
[39] Coyle to Murguiendo, December 20, 1867, *ibid.*

which as clearly belongs to our clients as do the boots on their feet or the coats on their backs. . . . We are told by persons who have investigated the matter in St. Domingo, that Cabral (who was President several days ago), and other officials of that country are largely interested in the stock of the new company.

The Havana despatches of Tuesday convey a piece of information which is startling to men who have already suffered so much from the unexplained "political reasons" of an officer whose duty it was to do them exact justice according to law and vindicate the honor of his country independent of any and all other considerations. We are told by this news that a Commissioner is on his way from St. Domingo to treat with us for the transfer of Samana Bay. We have long known (or *thought* we knew) that Mr. Seward awaited the accession to power of Baez, the revolutionist, when he fully expected the Commissioner who is now heralded by the telegraph. His present intention is to purchase Samana at any cost. To effect it he will relinquish all claim to this "appendage to the United States," and he will engage that the United States shall forget that its flag was torn down by an armed force, that its territory was invaded, and that its citizens were first plundered and then imprisoned. He will agree that so much of the public law of the world as applies to this case shall be ignored and that the Act of Congress shall be quietly suspended. . . . He will not only do nothing to redress our injuries, but he will stipulate to assist in the final consummation of the robbery. It may be said that these remarks are founded upon a bare supposition and can have no reasonable foundation. But in reply I ask what may not be expected from a Secretary who deliberately put his official hand to a naked untruth? He promises you to report the facts and correspondence relating to this claim. . . . Be assured, Mr. President, you will never learn the facts of a case from him, or be permitted to apply the law with his consent.[40]

Three days after Chauncey Black wrote this letter to the President, it was decided by the firm of Black, Lamon and Company that it would be expedient for Judge Black, Chauncey Black, and John F. Coyle to visit the Chief Executive and discuss the matter with him in person. When they called at the White House, Coyle informed President Johnson that it was getting more and more difficult to restrain Patterson and

[40] C. F. Black to Johnson, December 26, 1867, *Johnson Papers*, vol. 127, MS. Library of Congress.

Murguiendo from placing the question of Alta Vela before Congress. When Johnson assured Coyle that he had requested Seward to produce all the papers in the case, Coyle warned him that all the papers would not be sent him by Seward. Coyle then requested the President to permit the firm of Black, Lamon and Company to examine these papers when they had been produced by the Secretary of State, and he was promised that this request would be acceded to.

As a result of this interview with the President, Judge Black was " full of confidence " with reference to a favorable disposition of the Alta Vela case, but Coyle expressed to Murguiendo the fear that they would all be " sold out to purchase *Samana*—Nous verrons." [41]

This news was none too reassuring to Patterson and Murguiendo who now, through the law firm of Black, Lamon and Company, put their claim before certain Republican Senators so effectively that on January 13, 1868 a resolution was adopted which requested the President to furnish all the correspondence relating to Alta Vela. In compliance with this resolution, Seward on February 12, 1868 sent to President Johnson the file in the Department of State supposedly containing all the letters in question. The file was then sent to the Senate and published as a government document. [42]

Immediately after the publication of this document, J. W. Shaffer, who was associated with the law firm of Black, Lamon and Company in pleading for the rights of Patterson and Murguiendo, discovered that Secretary Seward had failed to include in the file which he sent to President Johnson some very important and pertinent documents: (1) The first despatch from General W. L. Cazneau to the Department of State recounting injuries inflicted upon Americans on the island of Alta Vela. (2) A despatch from the American consul at

---

[41] Coyle to Sullivan and Murguiendo, December 29, 1867, *Black Papers,* vol. 47. On January 10, 1868 the Washington *Daily National Intelligencer* remarked: " If this palpable wrong is still unatoned for [wrong to Patterson and Murguiendo], we do not see upon what principle of national honor . . . we can go to buying and selling with the Government of St. Domingo until it has restored that island [Alta Vela] to our jurisdiction."

[42] *Sen. Ex. Doc.* No. 38, 40 Cong., 2 sess.

Porto Rico. (3) Patterson's private report to Seward on the condition of affairs on Alta Vela. (4) The correspondence of Root, Webster and Clark showing the financial interest of Thurlow Weed in the guano taken from Alta Vela.[43]

The fact that Seward would have the audacity to suppress these pertinent documents was disheartening to Patterson and Murguiendo, and P. H. Sullivan wrote a despairing letter to Chauncey Black in which he expressed the fear that "if we don't look out, we are up a spout certain." [44]

With regard to the relations between "big business" and Alta Vela, there had long been a definite suspicion that Seward's intimate friend and political henchman, Thurlow Weed, had a large interest in this firm of Webster and Company that was removing the guano from Alta Vela. This suspicion was voiced as early as October 12, 1867, in the following letter from P. H. Sullivan to Black, Lamon and Company:

We have reports here that the New York parties are now removing from Alta Vela 2,000 tons of guano per month, and we shall be exhausted in time unless the government will interpose in behalf of us—the legal owners. Why this delay? . . . Mr. Seward has been the guest of Thurlow Weed, and the former gentleman has left for his residence at Auburn. When you reflect upon the fact that Mr. Weed is in the interest of the New York bucaneers, I am sure this fact will not be held in light esteem by you.[45]

The interest of Thurlow Weed in the guano on Alta Vela was soon a topic of general conversation in the larger cities in the East, and the more that Judge Black and his son reflected upon the situation, the more they became convinced that Seward was sacrificing their clients not only for the sake of his diplomatic scheme to secure Samaná Bay but also to line the pockets of his friend Weed. It is no wonder that their anger mounted daily, nor is it strange that finally they lost patience with the procrastinating attitude of President Johnson and sharply broke with him.

[43] William N. Brigance, *Jeremiah Sullivan Black* (Phila., 1934), p. 192.
[44] Sullivan to C. F. Black, February 20, 1868, *Black Papers*, vol. 48.
[45] *Black Papers*, vol. 47. See also W. N. Brigance, *Jeremiah S. Black*, p. 191; Gideon Welles, *Diary*, III, 305-306, 318.

On March 6, 1868, the firm of Black, Lamon and Company addressed another letter to the President in which they called attention to the manner in which their clients were being plundered:

We are daily receiving the most imploring letters from our clients in the Alta Vela case. The rate at which they are daily being robbed of their property by the company which holds possession of the island under the auspices of Mr. Seward is appalling to them and to us. . . . In the meantime the spring trade is coming and will soon be going. If after that we should get possession, we must wait another year before we can realize even a part of the profits which St. Domingo, Thurlow Weed and Co., are now industriously putting into their pockets.

. . . It is useless to say to a magistrate, mentally and morally organized as you are, that all the world would applaud an act which rights a national wrong and accords private justice. . . . If your character is preeminent for one thing above another, it is for your stern and inflexible sense of justice. To this we must, and do now, address our appeal.[46]

Along with this letter, the firm of Black, Lamon and Company sent as enclosures a memorial from Patterson and Murguiendo; a formal memorandum setting forth the former practice of the Department of State with reference to guano islands; and a draft of a proposed order placing the island of Alta Vela once more in possession of the Baltimore claimants.

As President Johnson still delayed taking action in this case, a new development arose that had far-reaching consequences. On February 24, 1868 the House of Representatives agreed to a resolution of impeachment against the President, and it was apparent that the impeachment trial would soon take place. It was advisable for the Chief Executive to employ eminent counsel for his defence, and his choice fell upon Judge Black himself, who had not only written some of Johnson's ablest veto messages but also the President's third annual message to Congress.[47]

---

[46] Black, Lamon and Company to Johnson, March 6, 1868, *Johnson Papers*, vol. 134.

[47] William A. Dunning, "More Light on Andrew Johnson," *American Historical Review*, XI (1906), 574 ff.

Seward was quick to see danger in such an appointment. He strongly opposed the selection of Black as one of the associate counsel, but in this case his advice was rejected, and the appointment was made.[48]

One of the members of the Cabinet who supported the selection of Black as one of the President's counsel was Gideon Welles, the Secretary of the Navy. In his *Diary,* under the date of March 9, 1868, Welles makes the following interesting entry:

I called on the President this morning and informed him I had reflected much on the subject of his counsel, and although there was opposition to Black, it appeared to me he ought not to give way to it, provided B. had his confidence. He thanked me and said the retention of Black was not an open question and he had so informed Mr. Seward who called last evening and wished to dissuade him. The President attributed the hostility of Seward to the fact that Black had been opposed to Seward in the Alta Vela matter. I have understood that Thurlow Weed was interested in that question, and his interest in that questionable transaction was in consequence of his intimacy and well-known influence with the Secretary of State, and I so informed the President. For a little matter, Seward has manifested the deepest anxiety in the Alta Vela business. I do not think he had any pecuniary interest in it, but he is solicitous for his friend Weed, who has.[49]

Although Seward was defeated in this matter of the selection of Judge Black as one of Johnson's associate counsel, the victory of the Black faction was soon nullified by the precipitancy of Chauncey Black. For some time Chauncey Black had played with the idea that one of the most effective ways of forcing President Johnson to take some decisive action with reference to Alta Vela was that of securing favorable opinions from leading Republican Senators and Representatives. Associated with him in this dubious scheme were C. H. Winder and J.

[48] Seward was not the only one of Johnson's close friends to oppose the appointment of Black as one of the associate counsel. On March 1, 1868, Thomas Ewing wrote to Johnson and urged him not to employ Black: " He is known as a violent man—has talents but no discretion and he would in the heat of his nature sacrifice your cause rather than omit saying a bitter thing." *Johnson Papers,* vol. 133.

[49] III, 305-306.

W. Shaffer, who, as early as February 28, were sounding out certain Republican Senators.[50] On March 9, unknown to Judge Black, Shaffer went to Benjamin Butler, under whom he had served during the Civil War as an aid-de-camp, and secured a letter from that gentleman which read as follows:

I am clearly of the opinion that under the claim of the United States, its citizens have the exclusive right to take guano from Alta Vela. I have never been able to understand why the Executive did not long since assert the rights of the government, and sustain the rightful claims of its citizens to the possession of the island in the most forcible manner consistent with the dignity and honor of the nation.[51]

Shaffer then repaired to the office of Representative John A. Logan, who wrote under Butler's signature: "I concur in the opinion above expressed by General Butler." Shaffer then approached Representative James A. Garfield, who consented to add underneath Logan's signature the following words: "And I, J. A. Garfield."

After Shaffer had secured these signatures he returned to the office of Black, Lamon and Company and showed them to Chauncey Black, who, on March 10, addressed President Johnson as follows:

I enclose you an expression of opinion on the claim to Alta Vela by Gen'l. Butler, Gen. Logan, and Gen. Garfield. It so happened that these gentlemen have long understood this case and appreciated the scandalous attitude in which Mr. Seward's management has placed the Government. I do not think there is a member of the American Congress who would not express the same opinion were he put in possession of the facts. I do not expect the views of these gentlemen to materially affect your judgment. I merely submit them to show that men of all

---

[50] Winder to Murguiendo, February 28, 1868, Black Papers, vol. 48. It seems quite probable that the idea of securing the opinions of important members of Congress upon the question of Alta Vela was a suggestion of Patterson and Murguiendo. In this above-cited letter from Winder to Murguiendo, there is a pertinent passage: "We are now engaged in the very suggestion you have made —Shaffer will try to get the expression [of Republican Senators] of opinions favorable to the claim. We cannot of course expect to get them to ask a favor of Johnson."

[51] Proceedings in the Trial of Andrew Johnson (Wash., 1868), p. 613. The full text of the letter is given in the Cong. Globe, 40 Cong., 2 sess., p. 2338.

classes and all parties are scandalized by the shameful wrongs which the Government as well as our clients have been made to suffer in the history of this affair.[52]

On this same day, Chauncey Black wrote a letter to P. H. Sullivan, in Baltimore, which would indicate that he believed the President would soon respond to the pressure that was being exerted upon him. Thus:

The President seems not to doubt the justice of our claim, but it requires an awful pressure to make him act in the present ticklish condition of affairs. Shaffer yesterday laid the foundation for getting the names of a lot of radical congressmen to a letter already signed by Ben Butler. With this we cannot fail. Mr. Dawson had a highly satisfactory interview yesterday and Sim Johnson is now with him. I have indicated the kind of orders we want, and am sure we will have them tomorrow or next day.[53]

On the following day Chauncey Black again wrote Sullivan to advise him that the

President is studying Alta Vela. I put in radical endorsements last night. Sim J. saw him yesterday. He said it was a clear case. Father is now with him.[54]

On March 12, Chauncey Black wrote Johnson another letter in which he begged that some decision be made forthwith in regard to Alta Vela, and he closed with the warning that he could not " suffer Mr. Seward's corrupt combination to prevail finally over the rights which the laws of our country and of the world have given us." [55]

After waiting two days for the ever hesitant President to take some action, Judge Black himself decided to make one

---

[52] C. F. Black to Johnson, March 10, 1868, *Johnson Papers*, vol. 134.

[53] C. F. Black to Sullivan, March 10, 1868, *Black Papers*, vol. 48. With regard to this letter, which Colonel J. W. Shaffer secured with the Congressional endorsements, Jeremiah Black, in a letter to General Garfield on April 28, 1868, remarks: " I knew nothing about the paper until it went into the hands of the President. I never in my life spoke to any of the signers about the case except to you and not to you until after the date of the paper." *Garfield Papers*, MS. Library of Congress.

[54] C. F. Black to Sullivan, March 11, 1868, *Black Papers*, vol. 48.

[55] C. F. Black to Johnson, March 12, 1868, *Johnson Papers*, vol. 134.

more attempt to convince Johnson that it was imperatively necessary to decide one way or the other. His son Chauncey, in the meantime, had secured not only the endorsements of Logan and Garfield to the Butler letter, but also those of Thaddeus Stevens, John A. Bingham, James G. Blaine, J. K. Moorehead, and W. K. Koontz. Thus, four of the seven managers of the forthcoming impeachment trial were warning President Johnson that it would be just and expedient for him to favor the clients of Judge Black. But this was not all the ammunition that Black had in reserve for this occasion. He had secured a letter signed by the entire Maryland delegation in Congress which favored the claim of Patterson and Murguiendo, and in addition the Maryland House of Delegates had passed on March 9, 1868, by a unanimous vote, a resolution which vigorously upheld the rights of the Baltimore claimants.[56]

Armed with these strong arguments, Black was now ready for an ultimatum. In justice to him it should be understood that he had not sponsored the scheme of securing the signatures of the Radical Representatives in order to put pressure upon President Johnson, but when that step had once been taken he appeared to accept it as a possible means to defeat an unrighteous scheme of Secretary Seward.

On March 14, 1868 Black wrote Johnson a letter that clearly marked the parting of the ways: a policy of delay could no longer be countenanced. Pertinent portions of this important communication are as follows:

Mr. S. Johnson has induced me to believe that I may have misunderstood your attitude in the Alta Vela case, and I think you did not rightly apprehend mine. A refusal on your part to do the owners of

[56] Maryland House of Delegates, *Journal*, pp. 709-710. The vote was 48 ayes to 0 nays. E. C. Reeves makes a statement that Ben Butler was financially interested in Alta Vela and that Jeremiah Black was a counsel for Butler. L. P. Stryker, *Andrew Johnson*, pp. 829 ff. Stryker himself speaks of Butler's private vessel that was ready to visit Alta Vela. There seems to be little basis for these statements. George F. Milton, *The Age of Hate*, p. 535, believes that Butler was assigned some interest in Alta Vela by Black, Lamon and Company. He remarks about an assignment from Patterson and Murguiendo to Black, Lamon and Company for " one and one-half per cent on all their rights . . . on island of Alta Vela (March 6, 1868)." He is incorrect in both the date (really March 3) and the amount of assignment."

that Island the plain and manifest justice which they claim and which by law they are entitled to, must drive them into measures which would make it impossible for me to aid you in any way or any manner. It literally compels me to decline acting as your counsel, not because I am unwilling to continue but because I cannot. This is no reason why you should do what they request. If you will consider the subject at all, Mr. S. Johnson and Mr. C. F. Black will satisfy you:

1. That the Dominicans had and pretended to have no claim upon the Island.

2. That Mr. Seward in plain and shameless violation of his duty to the American owners set up a claim for the Dominicans which they did not assert for themselves.

3. That this claim so set up by Mr. Seward is destitute of all reason, right, truth or fairness—a series of paltry quibbles which the State Department under Marcy and Cass had pronounced in other cases to be not only inadmissible but insulting.

4. That every man who has looked into this subject has come to the same conclusion namely, that Patterson and Murguiendo were in possession under the act of 1856, and were entitled under that act and by the public law of the world to the protection of their government to keep them in their possession or restore them in case they were turned out by mere wrong doers.

. . . In order that you may understand it please to hear these gentlemen. It will be a great relief to me to have it settled either or any way. Let me assure you further that no matter what you may determine it will make no change in my personal feelings to you, nor will it diminish my wish for your future prosperity and success.

Please don't understand me as making any condition. I am so connected with this business that as long as it is pending I cannot desert my robbed and ruined clients. I am compelled to take the misfortune of your adverse action or inaction coupled with the superadded calamity of retiring from the impeachment case. I am perfectly sure this will not influence you for I don't want any decision in the case that is not founded in your sense of right and justice and duty to the law of the land.[57]

Four days later Judge Black called to see Gideon Welles, who gives the gist of their conversation in his *Diary:*

Judge Jere Black called on me this morning and had a strange talk about Alta Vela. Represents Seward as behaving badly and to the dis-

[57] J. S. Black to Johnson, March 14, 1868, *Johnson Papers*, vol. 134.

credit of the country in that matter. Told him I knew little of it, that I had been the confidant of neither party. Black inquired in regard to the naval vessels—whether there was not one or more at St. Thomas which could be ordered to protect American interests, which Seward was abandoning. . . . I remarked that nothing would be done, of course, until Seward returned, as it was a subject within his Department, and he had studied it thoroughly, whatever might be his views. This, I saw, did not suit Black.[58]

On the morning of March 19, Judge Black and Chauncey Black called to see Welles and inquired

if the President had given me any orders in relation to Alta Vela. I told him no order had been received. He inquired if I had seen the President since his and my interview yesterday. I replied that I had, but nothing had been said to me concerning Alta Vela. Black expressed astonishment, appeared vexed, said the President could not go on in this way, yet he was sorry to leave him just at this time. I remarked that he would not. But he turned short and left. An hour or two after, S. Johnson, who writes for the *Intelligencer,* but who is a special friend and admirer of Black's, called on me in alarm on account of a disagreement between the President and Black. Says the President has not kept his word with Black, and the latter has told him so. He says Black will not go on with the trial if the Alta Vela matter is not arranged. I discredited this and so told Johnson.[59]

As soon as Judge Black and his son left the office of Gideon Welles, they began the preparation of a letter to President Johnson which Judge Black sent him that afternoon. It was a letter of withdrawal from service as one of Johnson's associate counsel because of the President's refusal to take any positive stand in the Alta Vela case.[60] The following excerpts will indicate its tenor:

---

[58] III, 316.   [59] *Ibid.*, pp. 317-318.

[60] Professor Roy F. Nichols, in his abbreviated sketch of " Jeremiah Sullivan Black " for the *Dictionary of American Biography*, II, 312, expresses the view that Black " withdrew in a fit of pique because Johnson would not overrule Seward for one of his clients." This seems hardly an adequate explanation. One of Andrew Johnson's most scholarly biographers, St. George L. Sioussat, " Andrew Johnson," *Dictionary of American Biography*, X, 88, is equally uncomplimentary.

Your determination to determine nothing for the relief of the owners of Alta Vela makes it impossible for me to serve you longer as counsel in the impeachment case. They cannot allow their rights to be trifled with and I cannot advise them to submit in silence to the outrage perpetrated upon them. They must seek elsewhere for the justice which you deny them.

I am sure you will admit that I have never urged this upon your attention until you had a full opportunity of examining it, nor asked you for a decision until you expressed the opinion that the title was just and legal. Mr. Seward's little finger it appears, is thicker than the loins of the law. He, and the thieves whose interests he has guarded so faithfully, are welcome to the short-lived victory they have won.

My retirement from your cause will not probably diminish the chances of its success. . . . But to me it is cause of sincere grief that I cannot aid in the struggle you are making for truth, justice, and the constitution of your country. . . . I hope you see plainly that I have adopted the only possible mode of relieving myself from embarrassments and complications which would be wholly unendurable if I did not get rid of them in some way.[61]

But despite this very decisive letter, there was at least one mutual friend of Judge Black and of President Johnson who endeavored to bridge the gap that was fast widening between them. Thus, on March 22, Simeon Johnson wrote a long letter to the President in which he strongly argued the case of Judge Black as against Secretary Seward. In a conversation with Judge Black, he had been informed that there was " no earthly reason " why the President should not " immediately act," and that his refusal to do so could be interpreted only as evidence of an unfriendly feeling for Black himself. Simeon Johnson had then reminded Black of the

peculiar condition of the Presidency, and the disposition to seize upon anything to color the proceedings before the Senate and satisfy the country. He answered that the managers and confessed leaders of impeachment had expressed the opinion that the President should use *any force* at his command to put his clients in possession of the Island. . . . He is deeply incensed at " Mr. Seward's craftiness," and as he believes, " dishonest behaviour." Just here is the evil of the matter, for

[61] J. S. Black to Johnson, March 19, 1868, *Johnson Papers*, vol. 135.

it does appear to me that Mr. Seward acted very badly in setting up a claim to the island which the Dominican Government wholly neglected to do. This feature of the case has served to intensify the mortification of Judge Black. Undoubtedly it is justice that he asks.[62]

Simeon Johnson was not the only one who thought that the clients of Judge Black had been denied simple justice with reference to the non-enforcement of their claim to Alta Vela. On March 18, 1868, the Maryland Senate approved by a unanimous vote a resolution requesting the President to give "immediate and efficient protection" to Patterson and Murguiendo in pursuit of their rights in the island of Alta Vela, and to compel at once the Government of Santo Domingo not only to forgo their claim to the island but also to make "ample atonement" for the gross insult they had offered to the American flag.[63] On March 27 the Pennsylvania Senate approved a similar resolution, while on April 8 the Pennsylvania House of Representatives concurred in this action.[64]

Indeed, President Johnson himself had very decided doubts as to the justice of Seward's policy and it was only his abject dependence upon the Secretary of State that kept him from intervening on behalf of Patterson and Murguiendo. Thus, he admitted to Gideon Welles that

as regarded Alta Vela, he had not decided against Black's clients; he had thought there might be merit, or the color of merit, in the claim. The Secretary of State, whose special duty it was to look into the question, had investigated it and was against Black, whether rightfully or wrongfully he could not say. The whole subject, however, had been called for by Congress, and at this time and under present circumstances he could not take any step, nor was he inclined to make himself a party in the matter.[65]

This admission is particularly significant, for it indicates

---

[62] Simeon Johnson to Johnson, March 22, 1868, *ibid.*

[63] Maryland Senate, *Journal*, March 18, 1868, pp. 532-533. Also *Laws of the State of Maryland* (Annapolis, 1868), pp. 983-984.

[64] Pennsylvania Senate, *Journal*, March 27, 1868, p. 770; Pennsylvania House of Representatives, April 8, 1868, *Journal*, pp. 1128-1129. Also, *Laws of the General Assembly of the State of Pennsylvania* (Harrisburg, 1868), pp. 1178-1179.

[65] Gideon Welles, *Diary*, III, 322-323.

that even after Black had withdrawn as one of Johnson's associate counsel, the President was still undecided as to the merits of the Alta Vela case, and purposely refrained from coming to any decision. It is no wonder that Judge Black lost patience with such an attitude!

But whatever the merits of the case, it was soon apparent to the country at large that Judge Black had had some disagreement with the President, and the press was filled with speculations concerning it. On March 24 the Baltimore *Sun* reported that the cause of the breach was the President's refusal to " order a vessel of war to proceed to and take possession of the Island of Alta Vela." The following day, the New York *Tribune* published an explanation from Judge Black in which he stated that his retirement from the impeachment trial had nothing to do with any quarrel with the President relative to the line of defence to be pursued during the trial. He had retired because, after the President had promised to settle the Alta Vela dispute, Seward " interfered and prevented such a settlement." [66]

To the New York *Herald* it was apparent that Black had retired from the case because he had been denied justice for his clients through the devious practices of Seward and Thurlow Weed. The island of Alta Vela had been discovered by certain citizens of Baltimore who had taken effective possession of it under the Act of 1856. When they started to ship guano to the United States at a nice profit, the politicians in Santo Domingo soon

got wind of it, and finding there was money in the enterprise, forcibly expelled these intruders and took possession of the island in the name of said republic. . . . It appears, too, that they secured a recognition of their claim to the island from Mr. Seward, on the basis of a compromise that an American company should have the privilege of working out that guano. Next, it appears that the company installed under this privilege were Mr. Thurlow Weed and company, and that they have found the guano of Alta Vela as profitable as a first class whiskey speculation. . . . This is a curious case and evidently a big job, or Thurlow Weed would not be in it.[67]

[66] March 25, 1868. [67] March 26, 1868.

As the discussion with reference to Judge Black's retirement grew more and more heated, the Judge himself thought it worth while to write a personal letter to Representative James A. Garfield in order to give the complete background of the Alta Vela affair. After discussing the discovery and settlement of the island, Judge Black examined with care the tortuous policy followed by Secretary Seward:

Many guano deposits were held and worked by Americans under the principles of public law before 1856, and many more have since been taken. We have now fifty-eight in all. In no case, except the present one, has any department of the Government shown the least hesitation about enforcing the rights of the owners. Now let us assume for one moment that St. Domingo had a title, did she not lose all right to assert it by encouraging the occupants to spend their money, time and labor on the island in the belief that the title was their own? . . . Mr. Seward asserts that the sufferers in this case are not entitled either to restitution of the property, or to the damages for the losses inflicted upon them. . . . He is either ignorant that law and common interests required the Dominicans to give warning of their title, or else he acts in total disregard of the obvious principle. On the one supposition he is mentally, and on the other he is morally, unfit for his place.

. . . Mr. Seward sent me a "memorandum," that the President had "accepted the conclusion" of a report said to have been made by somebody in the Department. Although this was senseless on its face, it was easy to see that it would be used at some future time to prove an adjudication by the President against us, for the "memorandum" could be applied to any report which might afterwards be got up. But I happened by mere accident to know that, in point of fact, the case never had been submitted to the President in any shape, and that he knew nothing of it. The President when interrogated on the subject, averred that the "memorandum" was wholly untrue.

. . . Perhaps diplomacy is a business in which a man is not required to be perfectly honest. It may be that some allowance ought to be made for the tricks of the trade. But surely it is discreditable to the United States that they should have a Secretary whose principles are so loose that he volunteers the influence of his office to defeat justice, and employs his time in making false defences for foreigners who have wronged and dishonored the nation.[68]

[68] The complete text of the Black letter to James A. Garfield may be found in the Baltimore *American and Commercial Advertiser*, April 6, 1868, or in the Philadelphia *Daily News*, April 9, 1868.

In commenting upon this letter from Judge Black, the Baltimore *American and Commercial Advertiser,* which was certainly not friendly to Black himself, had the following to say:

We have not that respect for Mr. Black which would lead us to condemn any one on his representation, but in this case there is to be said that his testimony of Mr. Seward's tricky character is but a repetition of what has often been recorded by those brought into personal or political contact with him.[69]

Judge Black had a facile pen as well as an active brain, and his communications to the press evoked widespread favorable comment. There was abroad in the land a deep suspicion that Seward's character was not above reproach, and in the summer of 1868 there were many persons who held the belief that the Secretary of State had realized large dividends from his diplomacy. This was particularly true with reference to Seward's activities in regard to the ratification of the treaty for the purchase of Alaska—activities which induced the House of Representatives to vote the purchase money only after some of its more important members had been bribed by funds from the Russian Minister. Although this fact could not be established by the investigating committee of the House of Representatives, yet a large number of persons refused to accept this official whitewash, and modern research has conclusively shown that if Seward was not personally corrupt he was none the less a bold and adroit liar.[70]

President Johnson, however, although he had indisputable evidence of Seward's mendacious qualities,[71] retained the most friendly feelings for his Secretary of State and " did all in his power to put him in a favorable view before the public." [72]

[69] April 6, 1868.

[70] W. A. Dunning, " Paying for Alaska," *Political Science Quarterly,* XXVII (1912), pp. 385 ff.; Frank A. Golder, " The Purchase of Alaska," *American Historical Review,* XXV (1920), pp. 411-425.

[71] In Professor Dunning's article, which is cited above, it is clearly demonstrated that either Seward lied to Johnson concerning the bribing of members of Congress or he lied to the Congressional investigating committee, when he denied such bribing.

[72] *Small Diary of William G. Moore,* August 14, 1867, MS. Library of Congress.

And after the retirement of Judge Black, which was caused by Seward's sinuous policy, Johnson turned the vials of his wrath against his former counsel and denounced him for an ingrate. Thus, on April 12, 1868 Colonel William G. Moore, Johnson's private secretary, made the following revealing entry in his *Diary:*

Entering his office, he brought me the paper to show that the case as submitted by Black was endorsed by 4 of the members of the Senate, headed by Ben Butler, and that too, subsequently to their appointment to conduct the case against himself. The letter of Butler, was I think, headed March 9, and was addressed to G. W. Shaffer, strongly favoring the claim and expressing surprise that the Union had not long since taken measures to vindicate the rights of its citizens. Pinned to the letter with the expression of a simple concurrence in its views, were the names of Logan, Stevens, Bingham, J. G. Blaine and W. H. Koontz. Thus 4 of the 7 men selected by the Senate to prosecute me came to ask me in February to prosecute an award, doubtless that they might secure . . . a half million or it may be a million of dollars. The whole land seems to be rank with corruption. *Judge Black won't do.*[73]

This passage evidently indicates either that Johnson was woefully ignorant of the fact that the Senate had nothing to do with the selection by the House of Representatives of Butler, Bingham, Logan, and Stevens to serve as four of the seven managers of the impeachment, or else that Colonel Moore incorrectly quotes the President. That the claim of Judge Black's clients was not a spurious one is attested by the fact that Johnson himself was not able to make up his mind one way or the other.

On May 7, 1868 the President, in his conversation with Colonel Moore, recounted to him an incident that is full of interest:

The President told me also what before I did not know, that Chauncey Black married a daughter of J. L. Dawson. The President said she came to see him one day and asked him all about the incidents that had occurred growing out the Alta Vela matter. " She approached me," said the President, " as though I were her friend, and when I told her

[73] *Large Diary of William G. Moore*, April 7, 1868—June 22, 1870, MS. Library of Congress.

of the facts, she said earnestly: They have done wrong and I am glad to know all about it. Chauncey has an interest in the claim and I wanted to know his prospects." She thanked the President very kindly and retired.[74]

In this particular case the wife of Chauncey Black had very little influence on her husband, for in his subsequent correspondence there is not a single hint that he regretted the stand that he had taken. Indeed, as we go into the evidence we shall find it quite otherwise.

As the trial of President Johnson progressed, it was inevitable that some discussion of the Alta Vela matter would arise. Finally, on April 24, Thomas A. R. Nelson, one of Johnson's counsel, brought the matter directly before the Senate when he objected to certain references that had been made in regard to the reasons for Judge Black's decision to retire from the trial. Nelson gave a short history of the Alta Vela case, and then adverted to the action of Messrs. Butler, Logan, Bingham, and Stevens in signing or endorsing a letter which denounced the President for not actively intervening in behalf of the clients of Judge Black. Was it not clear that this action had been taken for the express purpose of exerting pressure upon the President in behalf of these clients? The House of Representatives had voted for the impeachment of the President on February 24, while Butler's letter to Colonel J. W. Shaffer was dated March 9. What could have been the purpose of this gentleman in adopting such an unusual procedure?

Of course it was not Nelson's desire to

censure Judge Black or make any reflection upon or imputation against any of the honorable Managers. The island of Alta Vela, or the claim for damages, is said to amount in value to more than a million dollars, and it is quite likely that an extensive speculation is on foot. I have no reason to charge that any of the Managers are engaged in it, and presume that the letters were signed, as such communications are often signed by members of Congress, through the importunity of friends. Judge Black no doubt thought it was his duty to other clients to press this claim; but how did the President view it? . . . If the President went to war with a weak and feeble Power to gain the island, it would

[74] *Ibid.*

seem that he had done so in fear of the Managers and in the fear of losing the highly valued services of Judge Black. If he failed to do the thing which he was called upon to do by his eminent and distinguished counsel, there was danger that he would exasperate Judge Black and his friends, and their influence would be turned against him on the trial. . . . He was between Scylla and Charybdis. . . . And he acted like a noble-hearted man, as he is. . . . He was determined not to do an act which he believed to be wrong. . . . He was determined not . . . to be used as an instrument in the hands of anybody . . . to carry on a speculation which he believed might be carried on with dishonor to the Government.[75]

It would be difficult to imagine a more ridiculous statement than the foregoing, and it certainly does not reflect any credit upon the intelligence of Nelson. It was arrant nonsense to declare that effective pressure upon the Dominican Government to restore the island of Alta Vela to Patterson and Murguiendo would result in an unjust war upon a " weak and feeble Power." There was no more danger of a war with the Dominican Republic in this case than there was with the Government of Haiti in the case of the island of Navassa (1858-1859). And the fact that a weak nation authorizes an invasion of American rights is no reason to forbid an immediate intervention for the protection of those rights. Also, the insinuation that the Alta Vela matter was simply a big speculation that would redound only to the advantage of certain Congressmen is an insult to American claimants who had too long been defrauded of their just dues.

On April 28 Butler, in the course of his argument in favor of the impeachment of the President, took time to answer some of the insinuations made by Nelson. First of all, he showed that his interest in the Alta Vela matter preceded by many months his letter to Colonel J. W. Shaffer:

Some time in the summer of 1867, being in waiting on other business in the office of the Attorney General, Mr. Stanbery, I was present at an argument by Judge Black in behalf of the American citizens claiming an interest in that island. I there, for the first time, learned the facts agreed and in dispute concerning it by listening to and incidentally

[75] *Proceedings in the Trial of Andrew Johnson*, pp. 613-614.

taking a part, on being appealed to, in the discussion. In February last my attention was next drawn to the matter of the spoliation and imprisonment of American citizens upon the island of Alta Vela by an inquiry of a personal friend, Colonel Shaffer, if I had any acquaintance with the question, and if so, would give him my opinion as a lawyer upon the merits of the controversy. To serve a friend simply, upon recollection of the discussion with the Attorney General, I gave him such " opinion," the rough draft of which I hold in my hand, which is without date, and which, being copied, I signed and placed in his hands. This I believe to have been in the early part of February; certainly before the act was committed by Andrew Johnson which brought on this impeachment. From that time until I saw my " opinion " published in the New York *Herald,* purporting to come from President Johnson, I never saw it or communicated with either of the gentlemen whose names appear in the counsel's statement attached thereto. . . . Mr. Black [76] made a copy of my " opinion," and afterwards at his convenience procured a member of Congress, a personal friend of his, one of the signers, to get the names of other members of Congress, two of whom happened to be Managers of the impeachment. This was done by a separate application to each without any concert of action whatever, or knowledge or belief that the paper was to be used in any way or for any purpose other than the expression of their opinions upon the subject matter.

Butler then produced an affidavit of Chauncey Black which corroborated the version he had just given of the rôle he had played in this Alta Vela affair. After denying that he had any " knowledge of or interest, directly or indirectly, in any claim whatever arising in any manner out of the island of Alta Vela other than as above stated," Butler finally observed:

There is another deliberate falsehood in the thrice reiterated statement that these signatures were procured and sent to him [President Johnson] for the purpose of intimidating him into doing any act after he was impeached, the propriety and legality of which was contrary to his judgment, when, in truth and in fact, the signatures were procured and sent to him in order, as he averred, to sustain him in doing what he himself declared was just and legal in the premises, and which he intended to do.[77]

[76] Chauncey Black, Judge Black's son.
[77] *Proceedings in the Trial of Andrew Johnson,* pp. 696 ff.

Nelson answered that his whole purpose in referring to the Butler letter was merely to show that the President had been placed " in a dilemma such as no man under accusation had ever been placed in before," and to indicate that this correspondence had taken place " after the articles of impeachment had been agreed upon." He had attempted to treat Butler with " civility and kindness," but that gentleman had " made imputations upon me which I hurl back with indignation and with scorn—undeserved imputations." [78]

He then asked permission to place the Butler correspondence before the Senate. Butler objected to this procedure until he was satisfied that his letters had not been " mutilated." On the following day Nelson was given permission to read only those parts of the Butler letters that related to the dates when they were sent. The only date found in this correspondence was March 9, and this fact did not accord with Butler's claim that he had written his letter to Colonel J. W. Shaffer " in the early part of February." [79]

Senator Sumner soon countered (on April 30) with a motion to the effect that " Mr. Nelson, one of the counsel of the President, had justly deserved the disapprobation of the Senate " because he had used " disorderly words " with the intention of provoking a duel. But this was going a little too far even for the partisan Senate, and the motion was laid on the table by a vote of 35 to 10. [80]

The struggle over Alta Vela was transferred to the House of Representatives when James Brooks, of New York, introduced a resolution providing that Stevens, Butler, Logan, and Bingham be called before the House to explain why they had signed or endorsed the letter from Butler to Colonel Shaffer. Representative Brooks believed that this letter, with the endorsements, had been secured for the express purpose of exerting pressure upon President Johnson in behalf of Patterson and Murguiendo.

The vote on this resolution was 25 yeas to 52 nays, with

[78] *Ibid.*, pp. 700-710.
[79] *Ibid.*, pp. 709-710.
[80] *Ibid.*, pp. 727-728.

109 not voting.[81] Inasmuch as a quorum was lacking, Brooks on the following day (May 1) submitted a new resolution closely modelled upon the one he had previously introduced.[82] Although this had no chance of passing the House of Representatives, it did serve the purpose of eliciting statements from some of the members who had endorsed the Butler letter. Representative Logan at once arose to repel the " villainous attack " that had been made upon him, and he forthwith gave his version as to the endorsement he had placed upon the Butler letter. He wished to make it very clear that there was

no claim in this Alta Vela matter against this Government for one cent. . . . The statement is not true that we recommended a claim. I will not say that the statement was made knowing it was untrue. But it has been thrown before the country in a light to induce people to believe that we signed a recommendation for a claim. . . . What did we sign? A mere opinion as to the right of this Government to protect its citizens in taking guano from the island of Alta Vela. That is all there is in it. . . . So far as regards signing this letter with the view to its going before the President of the United States, I deny it. . . . After this letter was brought out before the Senate by Mr. Nelson I sent for Mr. Black. . . . I asked Mr. Black why he had sent that letter to the President? Mr. Black told me that he had done it without the knowledge of his father or of anybody else; but that the President had told him and his father over and over again that he would make the order they desired; he had promised to make such an order. . . . Mr. Black tells me that Mr. Johnson suggested to him to get the names of some members of Congress to a paper in order to authorize him to do this thing, and at the suggestion of the President, Mr. Black came here and got Mr. Garfield and others to sign it. That is what Mr. Black told me,

---

[81] *Cong. Globe*, 40 Cong., 2 sess., pp. 2333-2334. In support of his resolution Brooks remarked: " The Butler letters were calculated to have upon his [President Johnson's] mind either the influence of intimidation or the influence of persuasion, or some other influence to be properly described by some stronger word than ' persuasion.' They were calculated to have such an influence over him as powerfully to control his action, or to threaten to control it, in the matter of this Alta Vela claim. The claim is very large, of vast magnitude, amounting to more than a million dollars, as some say to two or three millions." *Cong. Globe*, 40 Cong., 2 sess., p. 2344.

[82] This second resolution was promptly laid on the table, on May 1, 1868. *Cong. Globe*, 40 Cong., 2 sess., p. 2348.

and I guess it is the fact. And the very minute he gets the names of these men to that paper, what does he do? He turns round and puts you forward as a catspaw in order to say to the country that these men are trying to influence him and publish the letter.[83]

Butler's explanation of his writing the letter to Colonel Shaffer was quite similar to the one he had made in the Senate. All that he had asked

was that the President should protect American citizens in their rights. . . . Do they say it was to make war on Dominica? Pooh! We make war on Dominica! Shoot off a twenty-four pounder at a pig-sty?[84]

In the Butler manuscripts in the Library of Congress there is a letter to the chief clerk of the Senate requesting the papers that had been filed by Nelson. This letter is dated April 29, 1868. On May 18 the chief clerk of the Senate wrote to Butler requesting the return of the file of letters that had been sent to him.[85] It is apparent, therefore, that he had in his possession the letter he had written to Colonel Shaffer on March 9, 1868, and it is obvious why he passed quickly over the question of its *date*.

Following Logan, Representative Garfield rose to give his explanation as to his reason for endorsing the Butler letter to Colonel Shaffer. Either Chauncey Black or Colonel Shaffer had shown him

an opinion written by General Butler and approved by General Logan, and asked me whether I felt at liberty to sign it. I glanced hastily over it and was of the opinion, as I still am, that it was good law, and I signed the paper. I cannot fix the date of that, but I am quite confident *it was as* [86] *early as, perhaps before, the 1st of March.* . . . Some days

---

[83] *Cong. Globe*, 40 Cong., 2 sess., pp. 2341 ff. In the affidavit made by Chauncey Black with regard to securing the endorsements to the Butler letter on March 9, there is the following significant statement: "Learning from a mutual friend that it would be desirable for the President to receive the recommendations of other members of Congress, I carried a copy of the opinion to the House of Representatives and procured the signatures of some of my personal friends and asked them to procure the signatures of others which were attached to the copy." *Ibid.*, p. 2343.

[84] *Ibid.*, p. 2344.

[85] *Butler Papers*, MS. Library of Congress.

[86] Italics are the author's.

after that . . . a copy of that paper . . . was brought to this House. Colonel Shaffer and Mr. Black, I think, were here together, and they, not having the privilege of the floor, asked me if I would not hand that to two or three gentlemen for their signatures. I went to the gentleman from Ohio (Mr. Bingham), a prominent man, and occupying a seat near the front, where the paper was given to me, I asked him to sign it. "What is it," he said, in his apparently rather petulant way. I replied, " It is an opinion of General Butler in favor of asserting the right of some American citizens to a certain island." " Oh," said he, " you mean that Alta Vela matter; I do not know much about it." I let the paper lie on his table.

Probably in five minutes from that time I passed by there and said, " Bingham, have you signed that paper? " " Well, is it all right? " said he. " I think it is; I signed it myself," I replied; and then he signed his name. . . . I also passed the paper to Mr. Stevens, who was sitting . . . at the Clerk's desk. I said, " This is an opinion of General Butler, Mr. Stevens, with regard to the claim of some of our citizens to an island." "Well," said he, " I know something about that; I think Seward has acted like a rascal," or some remark like that, and he signed the paper. That accounts for the signatures of the two managers; and so far from there being any concert of action, any purpose in that signing except such as appears on a hundred papers that are on the desks of members every month, I am perfectly clear . . . that those two gentlemen had no notion whatever, any more than I had or any other man had, that they were a party to any scheme.[87]

It would certainly seem that all these gentlemen protest their innocence a little too vehemently to carry complete conviction. There was hardly any point in securing the Butler letter of March 9, 1868 and the subsequent endorsements upon it unless through this means certain pressure could be exerted upon President Johnson in behalf of Judge Black's clients.[88]

[87] *Cong. Globe,* 40 Cong., 2 sess., pp. 2345-2346. With reference to the resolution introduced by Brooks, of New York, it is worth while to note that there was sharp enmity between Brooks and Butler. In the Butler manuscripts there is a letter to Butler telling him how Brooks was using his franking privilege to promote his private business interests. In reply Butler observed: " Thanks for your evidence of the Villainy of Brooks. I will keep it for use." J. P. Johnson to Butler, May 6, 1868; Butler to Johnson, May 7, 1868, *Butler Papers.*

[88] On April 28, 1868 Jeremiah Black himself wrote a long letter to President Johnson with reference to the Alta Vela affair. After calling attention to the

None of the Radicals in the House of Representatives was so blind that he could not surmise what use would be made of this document. The firm of Black, Lamon and Company had long been interested in Alta Vela and for years had been requesting the President to take action in favor of their clients. This was common knowledge at that time. Also, the President was empowered by the act of 1856 to take action in their behalf. Therefore, it was the President, and he alone, who

---

" wrongs " they had suffered, he observed: " For some time past you have been well posted on the merits of this case. You are quite aware that American citizens on the island of Alta Vela, in pursuit of their lawful business . . ., were lawlessly captured, imprisoned, robbed and ruined. You never suggested a possible justification of this outrage, nor did you ever, to my knowledge, utter a word in excuse of the secretary, who has for years been hindering the justice which his duty bound him to promote. It is necessary ' to stir up your pure mind by way of remembrance,' for I am assured that Mr. Seward is plying his arts with more assiduity than ever. Your White House reporter for the Baltimore *Sun* and New York *World* is manifestly under his influence, and the publisher of the *Commercial Advertiser* is known to be his *alter ego*. Through them he makes certain statements by which he expects to operate indirectly on you.

" He tries to make the impression without asserting it as a fact that some understanding existed between me and your radical opponents in the House of Representatives, whose names are appended to the written opinion in favor of my clients. In truth I knew nothing of that paper until after it went into your hands, heard nothing about it, had no communication with the signers, direct or indirect, verbally or in writing. I saw the paper first when you yourself showed it to me. I was not aware that the Maryland delegation in Congress had expressed their opinion until I saw it among the records long after it was filed. Nor did I know that the subject was before the legislatures of Maryland, Pennsylvania, and New Jersey until after the resolutions upon it had been unanimously passed by those bodies.

" Mr. Seward, through his New York organ, broadly asserts that I, while Secretary of State, decided against the claim of the United States and the right of our citizens to the possession of Alta Vela. The record shows the exact contrary to be true. His assertion to you that I decided the case in favor of his party is as false as the allegation he made to me that you had decided it in the same way. . . . When Mr. Seward's unfaithfulness to his duty became clear there was no remedy left but an appeal to you. It was then that he played his cunningest card. We were to be silenced forever by being informed that you had adjudicated the cause against us. . . . It was all false. You knew nothing of the case until afterwards; you had read no report on the subject nor was any report read to you, and of course you had accepted no conclusion about it. This you averred at the time, and my written exposure of the attempted deception immediately afterwards was placed on record by your own order. It is impossible to understand how you could sleep one night without turning the perpetrator of this scurvy trick out of office." *Black Papers.*

could intervene effectively and restore the island of Alta Vela to Patterson and Murguiendo. It was purely an executive function, and it seems remarkable that none of the Radical members who wrote the endorsements on the Butler letter could have harbored even a slight suspicion that by means of this document the President, who had been impeached by these same Radicals, could be finally forced to take favorable action.

In the press of that day there were many observers who pointed out the weakness in the defense of the Radical members in this regard, and some editorials gave high praise to President Johnson for his resolute stand in this matter. Thus, the Baltimore *Sun* thought it "would be difficult to find on record a more admirable example of lofty and uncompromising devotion to principle, and there is no true man in all the land whose respect for the President will not be increased by it." [89] The Philadelphia *Daily News* was unsparing in its denunciation of the Radical members of Congress who endorsed the Butler letter, and expressed the opinion that

the ranting of Ben. Butler proclaims the iniquity of the mercenary scheme with as much certainty as if he had openly confessed it. . . . The depth of turpitude exhibited in this attempt to make money by operating upon the fears of the President of the United States, and threatening him with expulsion from his office, it is difficult to conceive.[90]

The New York *Times* could not help harboring some suspicions that the Radicals were not as innocent as they claimed to be. Their attempts to explain the Alta Vela letter had only been

partially successful. The bad temper and worse language in which some of them indulged, neither vindicated the purity of their motives nor the propriety of their conduct.[91]

[89] April 27, 1868.
[90] May 1, 1868. See also the *Nation*, VI (1868), 362. The Philadelphia *Evening Star* of March 26, 1868, in commenting upon the retirement of Judge Black as one of the counsel for President Johnson, remarks: "This is a curious case and evidently a big job, or Thurlow Weed would not be in it."
[91] May 4, 1868.

The Radical press, on the other hand, was filled with editorials and articles which belabored the President and Secretary Seward for their dubious conduct in regard to Alta Vela. In this connection the following excerpt from the New York *Tribune* is typical. After discussing the history of the discovery and occupation of the island, and the refusal of Seward to restore the American claimants to all their rights, the *Tribune* then fulminated:

> The history of politics the world over may be searched in vain for a parallel to this imbecility. Think of it! Territory wrested from our ownership—our flag torn down and trampled on by ragged-breeched Spanish half-breeds—our citizens robbed of their property and flung into prison for pursuing a useful business under the authority and guarantees of an act of Congress.[92]

These virulent newspaper attacks and counter-attacks were lightly estimated by many competent observers who could recognize such propaganda for what it was worth, but these same observers could not help recognizing the fact that the cause of Judge Black had not been greatly helped by being associated with certain Radicals like Stevens, Logan, *et al.* This point is well illustrated by the following letter from a distinguished lawyer of Philadelphia, William B. Reed, who wrote to Chauncey Black as follows:

> There are two things, I assume, you will not doubt, one is my sincere friendship for your father, and the other my unmitigated dislike of Mr. Seward. . . . As to Alta Vela, it has come rather unpicturesquely in view just at this moment, and may have exposed your father to unkind comment. . . . I have no doubt Mr. Seward will lie about it. But there is one difficulty which of itself would prevent me from taking part in this: I don't like . . . to have any association or be on the same side with such a gang as Butler, and Stevens, and Logan and Garfield.[93]

There was one thing certain about this Radical " gang " in Congress—they spared no opportunity to confirm the title of

[92] April 29, 1868.
[93] Reed to C. F. Black, May 15, 1868, *Black Papers*, vol. 48.

Judge Black's clients to the island of Alta Vela. Not only did they endorse the Butler letter which caused them no little trouble, but they also had the House Committee on Foreign Affairs investigate the Alta Vela matter and make a report sharply critical of Seward. This report is carefully written and cogently argued, and it is difficult to controvert its conclusions. From the following excerpts it will be possible to ascertain its general tenor:

Assuming that the Dominicans had a title to the island, had they a right to enforce it by sudden violence without notice or warning after acquiescing in the American occupancy for seven months? Your committee would answer this in the negative as a question of natural equity and international law. . . . Had St. Domingo ever a title to Alta Vela? . . . It is a somewhat curious fact that St. Domingo never asserted a title to the island in question. Neither before the expulsion nor afterwards did that Government exhibit any ground of claim, or allege any fact upon which any title adverse to the Americans could be based.

In the case under consideration there was no occupancy previous to that of the American claimants. All the proofs place this fact beyond a possible doubt. The Dominicans and everybody else regarded Alta Vela as utterly worthless until American skill, science, capital and industry had demonstrated its value.

. . . It is also suggested that Alta Vela belongs to the Dominican government or people by reason of its situation relatively to the other territory of that nation. . . . Your committee can find no reasonable grounds upon which this proposition is sustained. The right of a nation to the territory she occupies extends to her natural boundaries or to the line agreed upon between her and her adjoining neighbor. When the sea is a boundary the jurisdiction goes one marine league or three English miles beyond the coast line. . . . The part of St. Domingo which lies nearest to Alta Vela is a cape. From that cape or promontory the distance to Alta Vela . . . is fifteen and a half miles.

In the case of Navassa and Aves, disputes were raised with us by Hayti and Venezuela on precisely the grounds here suggested for St. Domingo. But our government overruled them as promptly, and upon reasoning so satisfactory that the opposing governments in each case yielded all claims, and made immediate atonement for the wrong committed in settling it up. These two cases are conclusive and authoritative precedents for this one. . . . We are compelled to say that the case is too clear to allow of the least hesitation. St. Domingo was guilty of an inexcusable outrage upon the rights of the memorialists and a gross insult to the United States.[94]

This report encouraged Jeremiah Black to hope that when the Grant Administration came into office he would be able to secure that justice for which he and his clients had so long waited. Therefore on May 18, 1869 he wrote to Hamilton Fish, the new Secretary of State, and placed the matter before him as follows:

Under the " guano act " of 1856, Messrs. Patterson and Murguiondo of Baltimore are the owners of the Island of Alta Vela in the Caribbean Sea. Their right to the possession of it is clear and unquestionable. I say this, not because it seems to me alone, but because no conscientious man has ever examined the case, officially or otherwise, without coming to the same conclusion. It is so perfectly plain and simple that it admits of absolutely no doubt.

For some reason which I shall not attempt to explain, your predecessor in office, used all his power to prevent the government from doing justice to these parties, and had influence enough of his own peculiar sort to prevail against the honest convictions of the President. The last administration, therefore, left the case undisposed of one way or the other, the President flatly declining to decide either for or against the right of the United States and of these petitioners to the island in question. Under such circumstances the plundered owners of the property had nothing left but to wait until the Department of State should fall into honest hands.

After this arraignment of Seward, Black tried to insinuate himself into the good favor of Hamilton Fish by a few words of judicious flattery:

If the records of your office were whole and unmutilated when Mr. Seward left it, the case of Patterson and Murguiondo requires no new presentation. It is perfectly satisfactory to me as it stands, as I have no doubt it will be to you. . . . I cannot forbear to add that the President's selection of yourself for the Department of State increased not a little their confident expectation of securing at last that justice

---

[94] The complete text of this report of the House Committee that investigated the Alta Vela matter is available in the collection *Guano Papers*, Dept. of State.

which the government owes them and for which they had waited so long in vain.[95]

Black and his clients, however, were doomed to disappointment, for President Grant became deeply interested in the annexation of the Dominican Republic and refused to take any action that might give umbrage to that nation's government. In the Department of State there is a memorandum signed by Fish on May 10, 1870, the substance of which was later communicated to Jeremiah Black. It indicates how all the documents and pertinent correspondence had been placed before President Grant, who, after " due consideration," determined that " no sufficient reason appeared for reconsidering the conclusions heretofore reached." [96] So ended the question of Alta Vela.

[95] J. S. Black to Fish, May 18, 1869, *Guano Papers*, MS. Dept. of State.

[96] *Guano Papers.* For a colorful but dubious reminiscence of the disagreement between Black and Johnson relative to the Alta Vela affair see E. C. Reeves, *The Real Andrew Johnson*, quoted in L. P. Stryker, *Andrew Johnson* (N. Y. 1929), pp. 829 ff.

CHAPTER IX

IMPERIALISM BECKONS TO PRESIDENT GRANT

Some of the most interesting chapters in world history reveal how certain "men on horseback" conquered adversity and founded empires. These men of destiny, however, were not mere military leaders who were familiar only with the arts of war; they were also constructive statesmen who regarded war as a necessary prelude to national expansion. To them the call of imperialism was a long-awaited summons to creative effort, and their methods of procedure indicated their genius. With Ulysses Grant this was definitely not the case. Although he possessed military skill of a high order, he was singularly ill-cast for the rôle of statesman. In the America of his day there was sore need for a master craftsman who could fashion a new nation from the wreck of the old, but Grant as President never glimpsed the supreme task that lay ahead. To him it seemed as though the imperative need of America was colonial expansion, and his first, fumbling effort at statesmanship was a futile attempt to annex the Dominican Republic.

In the preceding chapters of this book the background of this policy of expansion has been briefly sketched. Seward's conspicuous failures did not daunt the confident spirit of President Grant, who prepared his approaches to the problem of Dominican annexation with the same assurance that always marked his investment of a military stronghold of the enemy. In his case it was the valor of ignorance, for he had neglected to make even the most cursory estimate of the difficulties that lay ahead. These difficulties he soon discovered to be legion, and in seeking a way through them he trod a path that was marked for him by an unscrupulous clique which desired pecuniary profit at the expense of the honor of the national executive.

One of the first items in Grant's program for national expansion was the appointment of a Secretary of State who either leaned towards imperialism or at least had an open mind with reference to a policy of colonial acquisition. After an inclination towards James F. Wilson, and a graceful gesture in the direction of Elihu Washburne (who held office only a few days), the President finally selected for the head of his Cabinet Hamilton Fish, of New York. The choice is somewhat puzzling because in former years Fish had evinced a determined opposition to American expansion.

It is probable that the appointment of Fish to the office of Secretary of State was due to social rather than political considerations. During his campaign for the presidency Grant had been entertained at the home of Fish, and, with that deference to wealth and social distinction that is so characteristic of many persons of humble background, he decided to invite this urbane New Yorker into his official family. On March 11, 1869 Grant received a telegram from Fish refusing to accept the nomination as Secretary of State. The reply from the White House was unyielding. It was " too late " to withdraw the nomination from the Senate. Fish should accept the office that had been tendered to him, and if later on he desired to return to private life he could " withdraw after the adjournment of Congress." [1] With a " heavy heart " and with " unnumbered misgivings," Fish yielded to this strong official pressure and came to Washington to undertake duties for which, he assured his friends, he had " little taste and less fitness." [2]

Grant was fortunate in securing a Secretary of State who stood as a beacon of light during the dark days of party corruption so characteristic of the Grant administration. And Fish was not only a man of unimpeachable character but a far-seeing statesman whose record of achievement in office has seldom been equalled. Before entering Grant's Cabinet, he had represented the state of New York in the national Congress both as a Representative and as a Senator, and had also served a term as Governor of New York. This important political experience, together with the broad horizons that had

[1] Grant to Fish, March 11, 1869; Washburne to Fish, March 11, 1869, *Grant Letter Book*, MS. Library of Congress.

[2] Edward L. Pierce, *Memoir and Letters of Charles Sumner* (4 vols., Boston, 1877-1893), IV, 379.

been established through wide travel and extensive reading, made him an outstanding figure in official circles.[3]

The personal relations that existed between Grant and Fish must at times have been greatly strained. Socially a gulf yawned between them, and intellectually they had very little in common. The coterie of doubtful persons with which Grant surrounded himself in the White House must have aroused in Fish's mind many suspicions as to the fitness of the General for the high office that he held.[4] Upon several occasions he was on the point of resigning as Secretary of State,[5] but he realized that the President might appoint a successor who would court popular favor by adopting a hostile manner towards England and Spain. To keep America out of needless wars and to secure national ends through arbitration rather than through a show of force were the chief reasons why Fish remained in office throughout both administrations of President Grant.

The rôle that Secretary Fish played with reference to the annexation of the Dominican Republic was a far more astute one than most students of history realize. He had early recognized the President's passionate desire for annexation, and he reluctantly acquiesced in a policy which he regarded as ill-starred. But he was keen enough to see that the question of Dominican annexation would result in a feeling of sharp antagonism between Grant and Senator Sumner. These two powerful personalities were openly in favor of employing a belligerent tone towards England with reference to the so-called "Alabama Claims," and this unfriendly attitude might lead to open hostilities. If through a personal quarrel over the merits of Dominican annexation the President and the arrogant Senator from Massachusetts would no longer work together, such a consummation would greatly help the plans of Secretary Fish. Sumner's influence in the conduct of foreign

---

[3] Allan Nevins, *Hamilton Fish* (N. Y., 1937), chaps. ii-v.

[4] In an editorial of February 21, 1876, the New York *Tribune* recounts the different scandals that had marked the administration of President Grant and then concludes with the following observation: "He is better fitted to rule an Asiatic kingdom than a free American republic."

[5] Fish threatened to resign at least five times.

relations would abruptly end and Fish could successfully pursue his policy of peaceful settlement of the most pressing problems in foreign policy.[6] Although Fish was not responsible for the rift between Sumner and Grant it is certain that he profited by it.

With regard to the influence of Senator Sumner in the fight against the annexation of the Dominican Republic, it is now evident that it was not nearly so important as many believed it to be.[7] Even so shrewd an observer as Henry Adams was misled in this regard and was inclined towards the view that in the Senate chamber in 1870 Sumner " issued his orders with almost the authority of a Roman triumvir." [8] The truth is that the treaty for Dominican annexation was not popular in the Senate, and the negative votes in that body were not secured through Sumner's insistence that the President's policy be defeated.[9]

There was a strange fatality about the Grant-Sumner quarrel over American expansion in the Caribbean. It would appear that Grant, during the early months of his administration, was exceedingly anxious not to have any trouble with Sumner, and in 1878 he remarked to James Russell Lowell:

Sumner is the only man I was ever anything but my real self to; the only man I ever tried to conciliate by artificial means.[10]

[6] In a letter from Professor Allan Nevins to the author there is the following observation: " My conviction is that the Santo Domingo enterprise was a blessing to the nation in disguise. It drove a wedge between Grant and Sumner, and so removed the great danger of war with Great Britain. Had those two men, each with his special kind of folly, stuck together in an intransigent attitude towards England, peace would have become impossible."

[7] For statements expressive of the viewpoint that Sumner was the decisive figure in the Senate fight against the Dominican treaty, see Horace White, *Life of Lyman Trumbull* (N. Y. 1913), p. 342; John Sherman, *Recollections of Forty Years in the House, Senate and Cabinet* (2 vols., N. Y., 1895), pp. 398-399; Hugh McCulloch, *Men and Measures of Half a Century* (N. Y., 1888), p. 354; James G. Blaine, *Twenty Years of Congress* (2 vols, Norwich, Conn., 1884-1886), I, 461.

[8] *Historical Essays* (N. Y., 1891), p. 406.

[9] W. Stull Holt, *Treaties Defeated by the Senate* (Balto., 1933), p. 127.

[10] James Russell Lowell, *Letters* (2 vols., N. Y., 1894), II, 233. In a letter to Carl Schurz on April 2, 1888, Edward L. Pierce remarks: " I am disposed to think that Sumner's break with Grant on S. Domingo was already prepared by general want of sympathy—dissatisfaction with appointments as a whole—

It is easy today to recognize the fact that a break between Sumner and Grant was inevitable. Sumner was a man who was quick to take offense at the slightest criticism of his viewpoints, and his urgency of spirit led to an ardor of conviction that strongly resented contradiction. As one looks down the long vista of the eventful but somewhat arid years of the political career of Sumner, it is hard to escape the thought that the sensitive Senator from Massachusetts gave early heed to the stern injunction of Ignatius Loyola to his eager followers: "Develop yourself, not for enjoyment, but for action."

Even before the outbreak of the Civil War, Sumner's overbearing manner aroused the resentment of his friends. Seward once told Sumner to his face that he was a "damned fool," and in February, 1861 Henry Adams cordially subscribed to this opinion:

> Let Sumner get the idea that his dignity is hurt, and he *is* a damned fool.[11]

Many years later another member of the Adams family expressed himself in a similar fashion:

> The difficulty with Mr. Sumner was his intense and overwhelming egoism. As is the custom with all persons, especially those who lead a sort of isolated life, this peculiarity grew upon him as he advanced in years. Finally, he identified his cause with himself, and any person who declined to follow his lead, or to accept his guidance in a matter in which he was interested, incurred his personal displeasure; and he could not help showing it. . . . He required from those about him acquiescence.[12]

---

and disgust at some." Schurz replied on April 4: "You are right in thinking that Sumner entertained an unfavorable opinion of Grant long before the breach on the San Domingo business. I know that the composition of the Cabinet and the manner in which Grant treated the A. T. Stewart case, gave him a severe shock. You know how ideal Sumner's conception of the dignity of the Government was. Grant's way of treating things disturbed and alarmed him constantly." *Schurz Papers*, MS. Library of Congress.

[11] *Letters of Henry Adams* (N. Y., 1930), p. 87.

[12] Charles Francis Adams, 2d, to E. L. Pierce, December 20, 1890, *E. L. Pierce Papers*, MS. Harvard College Library. See also W. M. Stewart, *Reminiscences* (Wash., 1908), p. 239; Hugh McCulloch, *Men and Measures of Half a Century*, p. 234; G. S. Boutwell (2 vols., N. Y., 1902), *Reminiscences of Sixty Years in Public Affairs*, II, 218.

It was not in Grant's nature to render homage to any man, least of all to one who never could be fitted into any of his categories of thought. Neither he nor Sumner could ever understand the other, and this fact made their quarrel all the more bitter. It has been the boast of Sumner's biographers that he never harbored a resentment, but this was not true with regard to Grant. After Sumner's death there appeared certain statements in the press to the effect that just before his demise he had remarked to one of his friends: " I have changed my opinion about Grant." But this little exercise in wishful thinking had no basis in fact. Sumner's hostility to Grant was so deep-seated that there was no possibility of a compromise, and the real situation is described by a close confidant of the Senator from Massachusetts:

I lived in Washington during the last three months of Mr. Sumner's life, and saw him almost daily, either in the Senate Chamber or at his home. . . . I repeat, that he never uttered one word which indicated that he had in the slightest degree changed his opinion of President Grant and his administration. . . . On the contrary, his hostility to President Grant and his administration was as uncompromising at the end as it was at the beginning.[13]

This intense dislike of Sumner for Grant and his intimate associates was in part inspired by the belief that American expansion was being furthered by those who saw a chance for profit in colonial ventures. There is little doubt that the " big business " men of that day were deeply interested in exploiting the highly advertised resources of the Dominican Republic, and their anxiety for the Grant Administration to respond favorably to the call of the Caribbean was a fact which attracted the thoughtful attention of Sumner. The chief representatives of this group of business men who were eager to realize profits from dubious speculations in Dominican projects were General William L. Cazneau and Colonel Joseph W. Fabens. Cazneau, as we have already seen, was an ardent promoter of many unsavory schemes to attract American capital to the Dominican Republic, and Colonel Fabens was his closest

---

[13] Henry L. Pierce to E. L. Pierce, February 4, 1893, MS. *Pierce Papers.*

associate in these nefarious operations. Both were natives of Boston, Massachusetts who had sought fame and fortune in Texas in the stormy days of the struggle for independence, and who had emerged with little more than the military titles which they prefixed to their names. Both had been chosen by Secretary Marcy to serve as special agents for the Department of State: Cazneau was sent to the Dominican Republic to canvass the situation with respect to the acquisition of Samaná Bay, and Fabens was commissioned to investigate the claims arising out of the bombardment of Greytown by Captain Hollis.

In 1859 they made a joint effort to secure a grant of land from President Santana in order to launch a project for the encouragement of emigration from the United States to the Dominican Republic. The annexation of that republic to Spain in 1861 delayed their plans, but in the following year they organized the ill-fated American West India Company whose colorful advertising circulars drew numerous Americans to the border lands between Haiti and the Dominican Republic. Although this venture in induced emigration soon proved a failure, both Cazneau and Fabens seem to have made some profits out of it. Next we find them engaged in a visionary scheme to provide transportation facilities in Santo Domingo through the use of camel caravans.[14]

But this precious pair of unscrupulous adventurers was not always led astray by wild schemes that could never be realized. In 1868 Fabens secured from President Baez a concession for a " geological examination and a general mineralogical exploration of all the provinces and districts of the republic." As a compensation " for the labors and expenses " of this geological survey, Fabens and Cazneau were to receive from the Baez Government, in fee simple, " one fifth part of the lands that may have undergone the . . . examination in the manner above set forth," with the right to " select and set it apart." [15]

---

[14] Fabens to Cazneau, July 8, 1867, *Fabens Papers*, MS. in the possession of Mr. G. C. Lovejoy.

[15] *Report of the Commission of Inquiry to Santo Domingo, 1871*, Sen. Ex. Doc. No. 9, 42 Cong., 1 sess., pp. 185-187. This concession to Colonel Fabens for a geological survey of the public lands of the Dominican Republic was dated July

Such a concession would be subject to the most liberal interpretation by those who enjoyed its privileges, and Cazneau and Fabens soon decided that both mineral and agricultural public lands were included in the grant. In the case of minerals found beneath the surface of lands outside the public domain, the concessionaires would have the right " to come to an understanding with the owner of the surface."

In order to finance this ambitious project, Cazneau and Fabens launched the Santo Domingo Company, with certain well-known business men of New York named as its sponsors. In this scheme we have listed such prominent financiers as William L. Halsey, Cyrus McCormick, Ben Holliday, John Young, and Samuel L. Barlow. As geologist to conduct the surveys of the mineral lands in the Dominican Republic a certain " Professor " William L. Gabb was appointed, and in March, 1869 the professor and seven assistants began their appointed task. At least one-half of the lands in the Republic belonged to the public domain, and according to some estimates this fraction was even larger. Therefore, when Professor Gabb completed his survey at least one-tenth of all the territory of the Dominican Republic would be under the control of Cazneau and Fabens.[16] The annexation of the Republic to the United States would greatly increase the value of this concession by introducing a stable government that would protect the investments of "big business."

In addition to this vast domain that was granted to them for exploitation, Cazneau and Fabens had other concessions from the Dominican Government. Cazneau had claims to copper mines at Monte Mateo, at Maño Matuey, and at Loma

---

3, 1868. Seward, who was Secretary of State at this time, was enthusiastically in favor of this grant to Colonel Fabens, and on August 19, 1868 he wrote to the Colonel to express his favorable opinion of it. It seemed to him that the contract was " a fair one and yet one which is marked with sagacious liberality on the part of the Dominican Government. If its provisions should be executed it cannot be doubted that the results would be useful, not only to the Dominican Government, but also to commerce and civilization generally. It is especially gratifying to see the citizens of the United States take so deep an interest in developing the resources of a sister Republic." *Domestic Letters*, vol. 79, MS. Dept. of State.

[16] *Sen. Ex. Doc.* No. 9, 42 Cong., 1 sess., pp. 232-239.

de la Boca de Diamarte, and he had secured from the municipal government of the city of Santo Domingo a lease of a large part of the wharf front. Fabens, not to be outdone by Cazneau, had managed to get a grant, "in perpetuity," of 1,683 feet fronting on the most valuable part of Samaná Bay,[17] and then, in association with Spofford, Tileston and Company, he had gained title to a thirty-acre tract on the same body of water.

After securing control of the mining lands and the wharf fronts in two Dominican ports, Cazneau and Fabens made a strong bid for the participation of "big business" in their enterprises by securing a charter for a National Bank of Santo Domingo.[18] As associates in this banking venture they enlisted the active support of the large investment and mercantile house of Spofford, Tileston and Company, and they secured the co-operation of Edward P. Hollister and Edward Prime, who were familiar figures in the New York business world. The bank began operations in Santo Domingo City in 1870, with Edward Prime, Jr., as the resident manager. Although it functioned in a very modest way it had great possibilities if the project for the annexation of the Dominican Republic to the United States should be successful.

These concessions which had been secured by Cazneau and Fabens seemed ample to insure their prosperity in the event that the Dominican Republic entered the American Union, but their activities did not stop there. Fabens was the agent for the investment house of Spofford, Tileston and Company, which had obtained a concession (June 15, 1869) for the right to establish a steamship line between New York and the

[17] *Ibid.*, p. 30.

[18] This charter for a National Bank of Santo Domingo was officially granted on July 4, 1869 to Edward Prime and Edward P. Hollister. The prime agent in the movement for a charter was Colonel Fabens himself, and on February 24, 1869 Hollister wrote to that promoter as follows: " A draft of the proposed Bank Charter was enclosed in the package sent to Genl. Cazneau. It will need, doubtless, many alterations, so as to cover every advantage. The superior judgment of yourself and Genl. C. will readily suggest and effect such amendments. I feel confident upon your returning with such a privilege that we can accomplish much to our mutual profit, and at the same time be of no small service to the Dominican Government. *Let it be broad in its provisions and exclusive in its grants.* To you is committed the destinies of us all." MS. *Fabens Papers.*

ports of the Dominican Republic.[19] He was also closely associated with Edward H. Hartmont, whose fiscal relations with the Dominican Government were both complicated and dubious.

Hartmont was a sinister character who changed his name each time that the law caught up with him. Rumor had it that he was a native of Luxembourg whose real name was Edmond Hertzberg. For a while he was connected with the firm of Armand and Company, of Bordeaux, but he forged a bill of exchange in the name of his employers and was sentenced to five years of penal servitude. He fled to England and began a business career as a merchant in London. In March, 1867 he was declared a bankrupt, but in the following year he was able to re-establish himself in business under the title of Hartmont and Company. He next translated his name of Edmond Hertzberg into Edward Hartmont and, lured by the attraction of large profits in Dominican investments, he visited Santo Domingo and secured a concession (on May 8, 1869) to remove and sell guano from the island of Alta Vela.[20]

Hartmont returned to London with a commission to serve as the Consul-General of the Dominican Republic. He also brought back a contract (dated May 1, 1869) which provided that a loan should be floated for the sum of £420,000, of which £50,000 was to be paid to the Dominican Government on the day the contract was signed. As compensation for his " outlays, risks, and commission," Hartmont was given permission to deduct £100,000 from the £420,000. This made him liable for a total loan to the Dominican Government of only £320,-

[19] In a copy of a letter from Santo Domingo City, December 19, 1868, published in the New York *Herald* on January 10, 1869, there are some remarks concerning the activities of Colonel Fabens: " The government continues pressed for money. . . . Latterly other parties have come into the field of Dominican finances. Certain ' steam kings' of New York have sent down propositions to establish various lines of steamers to Samana as soon as it is declared a free and neutral port, and still later Mr. J. W. Fabens . . . has been on here with the representative of several rich and well known capitalists of your city [New York]."

[20] For the year 1869 there is some pertinent material in the British Foreign Office (F. O. 23/60) with reference to the dubious background of Hartmont. For further details see the New York *Tribune*, January 10, 1870, and the *Special Report from the Select Committee on Loans to Foreign States*, British Parliamentary Papers, 1875, XI, 125-142, App., 130-136.

000, and all of this amount was to be paid before December 31, 1869.[21]

On May 1, 1869 Hartmont paid over to the Baez Government the stipulated sum of £50,000, but he failed to fulfil the terms of the contract by neglecting to pay the remainder of the loan during the year 1869. In February, 1870, Hartmont made a visit to the Dominican Republic and offered to pay over to President Baez the sum of £211,110. This figure represented the remainder of the Dominican loan minus the first year's annuity payment of £58,900. In reply to this offer, President Baez told Hartmont of the treaty with the United States which provided for Dominican annexation. This treaty was to be ratified by March 29, 1870, and Hartmont could either stay in Santo Domingo City until ratifications were exchanged or he could " go to Washington and work with his agents for annexation, and pay the balance of the loan over to the United States Government, because it would belong to them as soon as they were annexed." [22]

When the treaty for annexation failed to pass through the Senate of the United States Hartmont returned to London, where for the next two years he continued to deduct from the £211,110 due the Dominican Government the yearly an-

[21] As a guarantee for this loan of £320,000 the Dominican Government pledged its entire assets, " its customs, its revenue, and its domains." It also pledged the import and export duties of the ports of Santo Domingo City and Puerto Plata, and, in addition, the bondholders were granted a first mortgage on the " coal and other mines, and the forests belonging to the Government in the Peninsula of Samana, to the east of Grand Estero, as also on the revenues accruing to the Treasury from the export of guano or guanitos from the island of Alta Velo." On May 1, 1869 Hartmont paid to the Dominican Government the first instalment of this loan. He said that President Baez had received the stipulated figure of £50,000, but the Dominican Government denied having received more than £38,000. Hartmont then had the loan for the Dominican Government placed upon the British market to the amount of £757,700. The total receipts realized from subscriptions were only £372, 009, and the Dominican Government never received any more than the initial payment of £50,000 (or possibly £38,000). For this stipulated loan of £320,000, the Dominican Government agreed to pay an annuity of £58,000 in semi-annual instalments for a period of twenty-five years, amounting in all to a total sum of £1,472,500. At this rate the loan would be placed at more than eighteen per cent. per annum. See *British Parliamentary Papers,* 1875, XI, lxxxi-lxxxiii, 125-142, App., pp. 130-136.

[22] *British Parliamentary Papers*, 1875, XI, 134 ff.

nuities of £58,900. As the years passed on, Hartmont refused to pay to the Dominican Government a single penny of the remainder of the loan which he had floated in their behalf, and in May, 1875 he astounded the " Select Committee of the House of Commons on Loans to Foreign States " by filing a statement which indicated that the Dominican Republic owed him some $450,000.[23]

On their part the Dominican Government claimed that Hartmont had not fulfilled his contract by paying over the entire loan of £320,000 in 1869. In July, 1870 the Senate of the Dominican Republic passed a resolution which repudiated the Hartmont loan, but Hartmont claimed that he had not been informed of such official action until some time in 1872. In this regard we know from the manuscript papers of Colonel Fabens that Hartmont was advised as early as August 16, 1870 that the Dominican Senate had declared his contract invalid.[24] His mendacious statements before the Select Committee of the House of Commons carried little weight in England, where many suspicions of his character were widely circulated.[25]

These details about the Hartmont loan to the Dominican Republic are significant because they are closely connected with the movement for American annexation. Fabens, the indefatigable and astute lobbyist for Dominican annexation to the United States, was an agent for Hartmont and was paid £1,000 for his services. Hartmont himself was in favor of annexation for the simple reason that he believed that the American Government would be responsible for the repayment of his loan to the Dominican Republic, and he had no doubts about the good faith of the United States with respect to its financial obligations.[26] It should also be kept in mind that this Hartmont loan was handled through the London firm of Peter

[23] *Ibid.*, pp. 135-136.

[24] Fabens to Hartmont, August 16, 1870, MS. *Fabens Papers*. See also *British Parliamentary Papers*, 1875, XI, 135 ff.

[25] Secretary Fish heard of the Hartmont loan through Motley, the American Minister at London. See Motley's private and confidential despatch to Secretary Fish of October 6, 1869, MS. *Fish Papers*. It is probable that Fish was also familiar with the items in the London *Times*, July 27, 30, 31, August 2-4, 14, 1869.

[26] *British Parliamentary Papers*, 1875, XI, 133-135.

Lawson and Company. The American agent for Lawson and Company was the New York investment house of Spofford, Tileston and Company, which had already acquired an important concession for the establishment of a steamship line running from New York City to Dominican ports. Closely connected with Spofford, Tileston and Company, and also with Edward H. Hartmont, was the active and versatile Fabens, and thus it is apparent that no matter where one looked in this matter of investment opportunities in the Dominican Republic there were two figures who were always present—Joseph Warren Fabens and William L. Cazneau.

There was one more business man who played an important rôle in this Dominican drama—" Judge " Peter J. O'Sullivan.[27] The " Judge " had a valuable concession on Samaná Bay and was also interested in a steamship line between New Orleans and Dominican ports. He was a smooth, fluent individual who spent considerable time in the Dominican Republic during 1867-1869, and he not only had great influence with President Baez but, according to Senator Cornelius Cole, he was probably the first person to arouse the interest of President Grant in Dominican annexation.[28]

Senator Cole himself was interested in the annexation movement as a stepping-stone to his favorite project of an isthmian canal. This waterway connecting the Atlantic and Pacific Oceans would be of tremendous importance to the western

---

[27] New York *Tribune*, November 26, 1869. See also New York *Tribune*, January 13, 1870, in which the following remarks are made about Judge O'Sullivan: " Rumor links his name with uncertain speculations, as the owner of all sorts of franchises for all sorts of projects, as sure to turn up here when Darien or other tropical schemes for canal or railroad are discussed. If I am not misinformed, no matter what the scheme may be, the ex-Minister to Bogota is sure to control some land or place necessary to be secured before the projects can be carried out. He is said to be, after General Cazneau, well known here [Santo Domingo City] for the past 25 years, the chief if not the only banker of Santo Domingo." Another item concerning Judge O'Sullivan is given in the New York *Herald* of January 22, 1869: " Puerto Plata, Dominican Republic, January 4, 1869. Judge O'Sullivan, the agent for the New York line of steamers latterly established, leaves in the steamer *Pelayo*, on his way back to the United States. The object of his visit is also connected with matters of the greatest interest to this Island, the character of which has not yet transpired."

[28] Cornelius Cole, *Memoirs* (N. Y., 1908), p. 324.

coast of the United States, and Senator Cole did not overlook the benefits that it would bring to his California constituents. His efforts in this regard were ably seconded by Admiral Daniel Ammen, who was an enthusiastic advocate of an isthmian canal. Ammen was an intimate friend of President Grant, and it is quite likely that his ardor for an inter-ocean waterway made some impression upon the plastic mind of the Chief Executive.[29] In the public mind of that day the project of an isthmian canal and the annexation of the Dominican Republic were closely linked together. This American acquisition in the Caribbean would serve as a defensive outpost of the canal in time of war.

There were many other friends and political associates of President Grant who were in favor of Dominican annexation. Secretary Rawlins, Admiral Porter, and Congressmen like John A. Logan, Ben Butler, and Nathaniel P. Banks were ardent imperialists. Moreover, in the White House there was a certain buoyant personality whose views often influenced the President —General Orville E. Babcock. As a military secretary to the Chief Executive he was in a position where his advice could be freely and confidentially tendered, and his persuasive manners often helped to brush away any doubts that may have lingered in the President's mind. Babcock was married to a Galena girl, and he was also a nephew of Grant's old friend, J. Russell Jones. These friendly ties strengthened his position in the White House and made his counsel all the more palatable to a President who was intensely loyal and devoted to his intimate circle of associates. In the matter of Dominican annexation, Babcock was the most assiduous promoter of a project that promised alluring financial rewards, and Fabens soon found that he could safely count upon the General's warm support.[30] With all these individuals representing many di-

[29] Admiral Daniel Ammen, *The Old Navy and the New* (Philadelphia, 1891), pp. 506-510, 527-553.

[30] Although General Babcock was later shown to be a thorough scoundrel, it is certain that in 1869 no serious charges had been brought against his character. It is a grave reflection upon President Grant that he refused to concede the truth of the sweeping accusations that were made against Babcock in connection with the frauds perpetrated by the Whiskey Ring and with reference to other

verse interests, both political and economic, it is no wonder that as soon as President Grant was installed in the White House the movement for American expansion in the Caribbean began to gather momentum.

In order to perfect these plans for Dominican annexation it was necessary for Secretary Fish to resume the negotiations that had been fruitlessly carried on by Secretary Seward. As early as February 15, 1869 Seward had written to J. Somers Smith, the American Commercial Agent at Santo Domingo City, to acquaint him with the fact that General Banks, chairman of the House Committee on Foreign Affairs, was very desirous of securing exact information concerning conditions in the Dominican Republic. Upon the suggestion of Banks it had been decided to send Colonel Fabens upon a special mission for the purpose of collecting these pertinent data, and the Colonel hurriedly departed for Santo Domingo City.[31]

On March 9, J. Somers Smith wrote to Seward to acknowledge receipt of the instruction of February 15. With regard to the character and the diplomatic status of Fabens it was evident that something was amiss. President Baez had indicated to Smith that he was

very much displeased at Mr. Fabens representing himself as an accredited Agent of this Republic. . . . Mr. Fabens sometime since, was instructed by this government to endeavour to find out the doings of the Cabral Administration . . . and what were the actual proposals made by our Government for the purchase of Samana, but nothing more: No Powers whatever to make a negotiation.[32]

oblique actions. The unvarying attitude of Grant towards Babcock is well illustrated in the following excerpt from Jesse R. Grant's book, *In the Days of My Father, General Grant* (N. Y., 1925), pp. 119-120: "Never for a moment did father question Colonel Babcock's honesty. We all knew and loved him. He fought under father, he was a member of the family on I Street. Not only would it have been impossible for Colonel Babcock to have been guilty as charged, but father appreciated just what had happened. . . . He was an able man, a man full of friendliness, and a man without guile." For adverse comments upon General Babcock, see New York *Tribune*, February 14, 17, 22, 23, 24, 1876.

[31] Seward to Smith, February 15, 1869, *Special Missions*, MS. Dept. of State.

[32] Smith to Seward, March 9, 1869, *Santo Domingo, Consular Desp.*, vol. 6, MS. Dept. of State.

On March 19 Smith sent to the Secretary of State a report prepared by Felix Delmonte, the Dominican Minister of Justice, with regard to conditions in the Dominican Republic.[33] Apparently Smith did not care to work in conjunction with Fabens, and for this reason he hastened to send a separate report to the Department of State. Fabens, however, was not dismayed by this lack of official co-operation, and after securing certain data he returned to New York, where he tarried long enough to telegraph to General Banks that matters were " fully arranged." [34]

On April 1, Fabens wrote to Secretary Fish and enclosed a report on the situation in the Dominican Republic. It was a report that reflected his usual optimism and it very closely resembled one of his advertising efforts of former years. Under the benign administration of President Baez

confidence and hope smile upon every citizen and agriculture and commerce arise again from their inactivity. . . . The interior debt and what is owed to Mr. Jeserun and others is of small importance for it does not reach the amount of $700,000. Not a perpetual concession of territory has been granted to an individual or corporation. Some temporary ones conceded by Cabral's government have terminated as the concessionists have not fulfilled their obligations. . . . With regard to Samana Bay it is no doubt the first one in the world, and one that would be very soon the Gibraltar of the New World. . . . The annexation of this country to the United States should be an acquisition of great value. . . . The whole population is ready to do it provided

---

[33] Smith to Seward, March 19, 1869, *ibid.*

[34] Fabens to Banks, March 24, 1869, *Banks Papers*, MS. Essex Institute. In his testimony before the Select Committee of the Senate on the memorial of Davis Hatch, *Sen. Rep.* No. 234, 41 Cong., 2 sess., p. 159, Smith gives the following evidence relative to the opinion entertained in the Dominican Republic with reference to the activities of Colonel Fabens: " After Mr. Seward went out, I commenced my correspondence with Mr. Fish, and reiterated what I had said to Mr. Seward, and told him that Baez wanted $200,000 or $300,000, and one or two men-of-war to protect him. I said to Baez one day, ' What is the use of my doing all this for you when you are employing that go-between Fabens who runs backward and forward? ' ' Sir,' said he, ' he is not my agent,' and he lifted his hand under the very arch of the cathedral and said, ' By Jesus Christ, he is not.' Delmonte said, ' He is not; no one but yourself.' . . . Mr. Baez told me to write at once to the Secretary of State and tell him ' Mr. Fabens has not got that much authority ' (snapping his fingers), ' from me to do anything of the kind.' "

that the United States Government previously declare that they would not refuse it.[35]

These glowing statements of Fabens were soon confirmed by Edward Prime, Jr., who wrote to Secretary Fish that

the People of Santo Domingo are almost unanimously in favor of the proposed plan [annexation] and in return for which we come in possession of a continent unequalled in point of soil and climate and whose commercial advantages are beyond comparison.[36]

From the American Commercial Agent in Santo Domingo City there came further reports that throughout the Dominican Republic it was the " general wish of all parties (with but few exceptions) to be taken into the American Union." [37]

On April 21, Fabens wrote to Secretary Fish to " suggest a lease of such portion of the Bay and Peninsula of Samaná . . . as may be required for the purpose." He was certain that such a lease could be secured from the Dominican Government for an annual rent of $100,000.[38]

[35] Fabens to Fish, April 1, 1869, *Dominican Republic, Notes*, vol. 2, MS. Dept. of State.

[36] Prime to Fish, April 7, 1869, *ibid*.

[37] Smith to Fish, April 9, 1869, *Santo Domingo, Consular Desp.*, vol. 6, MS. Dept. of State.

[38] Fabens to Fish, April 21, 1869, *Dominican Republic, Notes*, vol. 2, MS. Dept. of State. On April 5 Colonel Fabens visited the office of Secretary Fish and showed him a memorandum from the Dominican Government proposing annexation to the United States. Fish was frigid in his attitude towards Fabens and assured him that he was " not inclined to entertain this scheme favorably." MS. *Diary of Hamilton Fish*, April 5, 1869. But despite this rebuff, Fabens was so disingenuous as to write to General Cazneau on April 22, 1869 and inform him that President Grant was " very favorably disposed " towards the annexation project, and that Congressmen Logan and Banks and Secretary Rawlins would co-operate in a movement to push the scheme through Congress. He also said that he had seen Secretary Fish, who was " much interested " and would also co-operate. Fabens to Cazneau, April 22, 1869, MS. *Fabens Papers*. It is interesting to note that Secretary Fish was willing at this time to establish friendly relations with some members of this Santo Domingo group of speculators like Ben Butler. In a letter to Butler, on March 19, 1869, Fish expresses the wish that Butler would do him the favor of calling at the Department of State in order that he might have the " pleasure " of Butler's " personal acquaintance." *Butler Papers*, MS. Library of Congress. This, of course, is no reflection on Secretary Fish, but it does indicate that he was fast learning the arts of diplomacy.

Secretary Fish was not the only one in the Department of State who had suspicions of Colonel Fabens. J. C. Bancroft Davis, the Assistant Secretary of

Some weeks later the matter of annexation was somewhat complicated by a report from J. Somers Smith, the American Commercial Agent at Santo Domingo City, to the effect that President Baez had completed arrangements for a loan from an English banking house. This loan amounted to £420,000 and was to be guaranteed by a portion of the customs receipts at Santo Domingo City and at Puerto Plata. There were other concessions given to this English banking house, the details of which had not yet been made public.

As soon as Smith heard a report of this Hartmont deal he called upon President Baez and questioned him concerning the effect of such a loan upon the proposed negotiations for the annexation of the Dominican Republic to the United States. Baez assured him that only a small portion of the loan had been advanced to the Dominican Government and that it was only a " temporary measure which would probably enable the present administration to maintain itself." The Dominican Administration was still strongly of the opinion that annexation to the United States was the only means of rescuing their country from impending disaster.[39]

The next step on the part of the advocates of annexation was taken by Colonel Fabens, who persuaded the investment house of Spofford, Tileston and Company to extend to General Banks and the other members of the House Committee on Foreign Affairs a cordial invitation to take a trip to the Dominican Republic on one of the company's steamers.[40] The purpose

State, in a letter to John Bigelow makes the following comment: " We are beset by a parcel of speculators, among whom is Fabens,—to take steps for annexing St. Domingo." John Bigelow, *Retrospections of an Active Life,* IV, 306.

[39] Smith to Fish, May 18, 1869, *Dominican Republic, Notes,* vol 2, MS. Dept. of State.

[40] Spofford, Tileston and Company to Banks, May 22, 1869, *Banks Papers,* MS. Essex Institute. See also the letter from Fabens to Banks, May 22, 1869, *ibid.,* in which he warmly urges the visit of the entire Committee on Foreign Affairs to Santo Domingo. As early as April 9, 1869, David Leon, the British consul at Santo Domingo City, informed Lord Stanley that negotiations between the United States and the Dominican Republic looking toward annexation had already been initiated. Although President Baez was " very reserved on the whole affair," there was little doubt in the consul's mind that annexation was on the way. David Leon to Lord Stanley, April 9, 1869, F. O. 23/59, No. 4. On April

of such a trip was to acquaint these important members of the House of Representatives with the unrivalled natural resources of the island of Santo Domingo. They would see, of course, only what Fabens and his clique would arrange for them to see, and there was always the possibility that some members of the committee might find it to their material advantage to espouse the cause of annexation.[41]

For reasons best known to themselves the members of the Foreign Affairs Committee did not accept this cordial invitation to cruise in southern waters, even though Fabens had Messrs. Spofford, Tileston and Company defer for several days the sailing of their steamer.[42]

30, Lord Clarendon wrote to Mr. Thornton, the British Minister at Washington, and requested that he furnish the Foreign Office with "any information which you may, using due caution, be able to obtain on this subject." Clarendon to Thornton, April 30, 1869, *Confidential*, F. O. 115/486, No. 115. On May 17, 1869, Mr. Thornton endeavored to quiet the fears of the Foreign Office with regard to American designs in the Dominican Republic. He had been told by Secretary Fish that "certain persons of high position . . . have implored the United States to take charge of it [Dominican Republic] and to admit it into the number of their States; but that they had no intention whatever of yielding to these intercessions. . . . With regard to the Bay of Samana, I doubt whether General Grant is disposed to favour any purchase of that nature." Thornton to Lord Clarendon, May 17, 1869, F. O. 5/1160, No. 117.

In the New York *Herald*, April 26, 1869, there were published some letters from Santo Domingo City showing the possibility of an effort being made by certain European powers to block annexation by offering to support a "confederation of the Antilles on free trade principles." On April 29 the New York *Herald* printed a letter from Kingston, Jamaica, of April 9, 1869, setting forth in detail the pressure exerted by the British navy in compelling the Haitian Government to make an "abject apology" for certain "insults" offered to "Her Majesty's mails." On May 3 a *Herald* correspondent at Aux Cayes, Haiti, remarked that Haiti is "all ready to fall into the lap of the United States. Why don't they take it?"

[41] With reference to General Banks, the chairman of the House Committee on Foreign Affairs, it should be remembered that in the memorandum written in September, 1869 by President Johnson after a conversation with Secretary of State Seward, General Banks is accused of having received a bribe of $8,000 from the funds of the Russian Minister at Washington for the purpose of expediting the bill which appropriated the money necessary to carry out the treaty for the purchase of Alaska. Apparently General Banks was deeply interested in American imperialism, especially when it served to line his pockets. See W. A. Dunning, "Paying for Alaska," *Political Science Quarterly*, XXVII (1912), 385 ff.

[42] Fabens to Banks, June 1, 1869, *Banks Papers*, MS. Essex Institute.

In the meantime Secretary Fish had decided to send a special agent to the Dominican Republic to report on conditions there, and on June 2, 1869 he sent detailed instructions to Benjamin Hunt, of Philadelphia. Hunt was to make inquiries as to the character of the population, the natural resources, the commerce, and the extent of the public debt of the Dominican Republic. He was also to ascertain whether there was any real disposition on the part of the Dominican people for annexation to the United States.[43]

When, on account of poor health, Hunt had to decline the appointment as special agent to the Dominican Republic,[44] Fabens decided unofficially to serve in his place and thereupon hastened to catch the boat that had been detained several days for the purpose of transporting the members of the House Committee on Foreign Affairs to Santo Domingo City. It was well that Fabens made this hurried visit to see President Baez, for that impatient individual was getting very weary of the lack of response on the part of the American Government to his many attempts to effect annexation of the Dominican Republic to the United States. On June 21 Smith, the American Commercial Agent, called on President Baez and expressed the opinion that the matter of annexation had been delayed because of the maladroit policy pursued by such Dominican

[43] Fish to Hunt, June 2, 1869, *Special Missions*, vol. 2, MS. Dept. of State.

[44] Hunt to Fish, June 10, 1869, *Santo Domingo, Consular Desp.*, vol. 6, MS. Dept. of State. It would appear that Hunt actually embarked for Santo Domingo City but refused to serve as special agent to the Dominican Republic. In the New York *Herald* of June 9, 1869 there is a paragraph of interest on this point: " The steamship *Tybee*, which left our port yesterday as the pioneer of a line of steamers to St. Domingo, carried among her passengers a special commissioner from the government, with orders to proceed to the Dominican republic and report upon its conditions at an early day. Whether Mr. Hunt has higher secret instructions we are not informed."

It is possible, of course, that the New York *Herald* was mistaken in supposing that Mr. Hunt actually sailed for the Dominican Republic. On July 4, 1869, the *Herald* published some letters from Santo Domingo City describing the visit of the *Tybee* to that port. There is no mention of Hunt but there is adequate mention of Colonel Fabens who, at a Government breakfast in honor of some American visitors, offered a toast to President Baez. In these letters, Baez is described as a " man of true principle and extraordinary ability." It is said further that his face " beams with intelligence, and from his eyes flash the fire of an active brain."

agents as Augenard and Fabens. President Baez immediately declared that neither Augenard nor Fabens had been authorized to carry on negotiations leading to annexation. The publicity which had attended their efforts to interest the American Government in the annexation of the Dominican Republic had been highly detrimental to the successful conclusion of this project. In the opinion of President Baez it was necessary to carry on diplomatic negotiations in a " confidential " manner, and if the

United States would give him an assurance of their co-operation, and if they could now meet his proposal and send two vessels of war with the amount of, say 'two hundred thousand dollars,' they could take possession of Samana, and the arrangements for annexation would be immediately inaugurated.[45]

If Fabens had not actually been authorized to carry on negotiations leading to the annexation of the Dominican Republic to the United States it is very apparent that he had for a long time been empowered to prepare the way for such negotiations. Although on June 21, in their conversations with the American Commercial Agent, the Dominican officials distinctly disavowed the activities of Fabens, yet on the following day they secretly urged Fabens to return at once to the United States in order to push forward plans for annexation. On October 8, 1868, a request had been forwarded to the American Government for two vessels of war and a commissioner who would report on conditions in the Dominican Republic. This request had been ignored and now it was imperative that Fabens return immediately to Washington and " seek a method of conferring with President Grant and with his influential friends there and explain these views." [46]

Upon his return to the United States Fabens first addressed a letter to Charles Sumner, chairman of the Senate Committee on Foreign Relations, in which he tried to convince him that the prompt annexation of the Dominican Republic would

[45] Smith to Fish, June 22, 1869, *Santo Domingo, Consular Desp.*, vol. 6, MS. Dept. of State.

[46] Gautier to Fabens, June 22, 1869, *Dominican Republic, Notes*, vol. 2, MS. Dept. of State.

save much bloodshed, and, by inspiring confidence in the law-abiding and industrious portion of the community, will relieve the country from the danger of lapsing into anarchy.[47]

Fabens next wrote to Secretary Fish and informed him of the ardent desire of the Dominican Government for annexation to the United States. He then requested that some "suitable person" be sent at once to the Dominican Republic to study conditions and make "a true and accurate report of the present political situation of that island." [48]

Under pressure from President Grant, Secretary Fish adopted the suggestion of Colonel Fabens, and on July 13 he addressed the following instructions to General Orville E. Babcock:

The President, deeming it advisable to employ a special agent to obtain information in regard to the Dominican Republic, has selected you for that purpose. The points to which your inquiries will be directed are: the population of that republic, in towns and in the country. . . . You will likewise endeavor to obtain full and accurate information in regard to the disposition of the government and people of that republic toward the United States, the character of the government, whether it be military or civil, whether it be stable or liable to be overthrown.

. . . It is also desirable to know what the revenues of that country may be, and whence derived, and the tonnage. . . . Inquiry should also be made as to whether any other foreign power may be seeking to obtain possession of any part of that country. Generally, any information tending to illustrate the condition and resources of that republic . . . would be acceptable.[49]

General Babcock was also given a letter of credence from President Grant to President Baez in which the American Executive spoke in glowing terms of his special agent. When President Grant "commanded the armies of the United States" he had employed General Babcock as one of his aides-de-camp, and since that time he had entrusted him "with confidential

[47] Fabens to Sumner, July 1, 1869, *Sumner Papers*, MS. Harvard College Library.
[48] Fabens to Fish, July 9, 1869, *Dominican Republic, Notes*, vol. 2, MS. Dept. of State.
[49] Fish to Babcock, July 13, 1869, *Special Missions,* vol. 3, MS. Dept. of State.

business of importance." The efficient manner in which these commissions had been handled by General Babcock earned for him the " entire confidence " of the President.[50]

In the meantime President Grant had decided to extend his support to the Baez Administration in the Dominican Republic by employing the armed forces of the United States against certain revolutionary leaders who were disposed to drive President Baez into exile. The most formidable of these revolutionists was General Luperón, who in June, 1869 began to harry the Dominican coast in a small steamer named the *Telégrafo*. The Baez Administration promptly declared such activities to be " piratical " and sent two schooners in pursuit of the *Telégrafo*. They soon overhauled this steamer, and in the engagement that followed several shots from the *Telégrafo* happened to graze the steamer *Tybee*, an American vessel belonging to the New York firm of Spofford, Tileston and Company. Such a grave indignity to the American flag was warmly resented by President Grant, who directed George M. Robeson, the Secretary of the Navy, to issue orders for the immediate capture of Luperón's ship. On July 10, 1869, Commander E. K. Owen was instructed to proceed " without delay " to Dominican waters and begin an intensive search for the *Telégrafo*. This vessel had been " interfering with American commerce and sailing upon the high seas without legal authority." Commander Owen, therefore, was directed to " bring her into the port of Baltimore," and he was expressly cautioned

---

[50] *Hatch Report*, p. 137. It is apparent that General Babcock had discussed the project of Dominican annexation with President Grant many times and had received verbal instructions with reference to his mission. See *Hatch Report*, pp. 35, 138 ff., and C. H. Van Tyne and Waldo G. Leland, *Guide to the Archives of the United States* (Wash., 1907), p. 1.

The views of President Grant upon annexation were familiar to the American public through the attention given to that subject in the press. On June 1, 1869 the New York *Herald's* Washington correspondent reported the following interview between the President and E. D. Bassett, the new Minister to Haiti. According to Bassett his conversation with the Chief Executive was " free and cordial." He further stated: " The President was very emphatic, and at the same time very cautious in expressing himself about the policy of annexation. He said his own views were in favor of such a policy, but that he thought in all cases the people of a country to be annexed should first show themselves anxious for union with us."

to " keep the captured steamer in sight " and " under your guns, on the way home." [51]

On July 13 Commander Owen was given additional orders relative to the Dominican situation. He was to remain at Samaná, " or on the coast of San Domingo, while General Babcock is there, and give him the moral support of your guns." [52]

It is apparent that President Grant feared that Dominican revolutionists like Luperón and Cabral would bitterly oppose his plans for the annexation of the Dominican Republic, and this fact partly explains why he chose as his special agent an experienced soldier like General Babcock. It is probable that Grant had discussed with Secretary Fish the legal aspects of the Babcock appointment, and it is quite likely that his attention had been called to the law of March 30, 1868, which provided that " any officer of the Army who accepts or holds any appointment in the diplomatic or consular service of the Government shall be considered as having resigned his place in the Army and it shall be filled as a vacancy." [53] Indeed, Babcock himself informed Senator Sumner that the reason why he had not been empowered to sign a treaty providing for the annexation of the Dominican Republic was the existence of a law which forbade " officers of the Army and Navy accepting any diplomatic appointments." [54]

---

[51] *Hatch Report*, p. 38. In a note to Secretary Fish of July 9, 1869, Manuel Gautier, the Dominican Secretary of Foreign Relations, strongly complained of the " piratical " activities of General Luperón, whom he designated as a " man of rancorous spirit, and of ideas very much behind the times." In order to capture General Luperón and destroy his steamer, M. Gautier requested that the American Government furnish the Dominican Government with a small steamer well supplied with munitions and coal. Of course it could not be expected that the Dominican Government would make immediate payment for such a steamer. The American Government could afford to be generous, and should await the time when the Dominican Government was in " better circumstances, which perhaps was not far off." *Dominican Republic, Notes,* vol. 2, MS. Dept. of State.

[52] *Hatch Report*, pp. 38-39. For several accounts of the operations of the *Telégrafo* see the New York *Herald*, July 2-22, 1869.

[53] *Revised Statutes of the United States*, sec. 1223.

[54] *Cong. Globe*, 41 Cong., 3 sess., p. 242. See also the letter which Secretary Fish wrote on November 6, 1869 to the Dominican Minister of Foreign Affairs, in which these remarks appear: " Although the laws of the United States

On July 17, 1869 General Babcock left New York in the steamer *Tybee,* which was owned and operated by the well-known investment house of Spofford, Tileston and Company. General Babcock had as his companions on this voyage the ever-present Colonel Fabens, Senator Cornelius Cole, of California, and "Judge" Peter J. O'Sullivan. It was, of course, inevitable that General Cazneau should meet General Babcock and his little party the moment they landed in the Dominican Republic. It happened that General Babcock knew only a little French and less Spanish, and thus it was very natural for President Baez to suggest the General's employment of Cazneau as an interpreter. His appointment immediately followed, and it was not long before Baez, Fabens, and Cazneau had initiated General Babcock into all the mysteries of Dominican politics.[55]

Babcock lost no time in informing Baez of the purpose of his mission, and he also confided to him that "he had no authority whatever to make a treaty," nor could he "bind President Grant in any respect as to a treaty." The most that could be accomplished was to draw up an informal outline or *projet* of a treaty which, if it met with the approval of President Grant and Secretary Fish, could later on be formally negotiated and signed. This clear statement from General Babcock relative to his limited powers as special agent prepared the way for a series of conversations that he held with President Baez and Manuel Gautier, who was commissioned by Baez to assist in the negotiations. Finally, on September 4, 1869, a *projet* was signed by both Babcock and Gautier, and its informal character was indicated by the following preamble:

> The following bases, which shall serve for framing a definitive treaty between the United States and the Dominican Republic, have been reduced to writing and agreed upon by General Orville E. Babcock, aide-de-camp to his Excellency General Ulysses S. Grant, President of

have prevented the President from giving an official position to General Babcock, it is hoped that your excellency will confer freely with him in these negotiations." *Hatch Report,* p. 193, and H. M. Wriston, *Executive Agents in American Foreign Relations,* pp. 164-165.

[55] *Hatch Report,* pp. 35-36, 138-139.

the United States of America, and his special agent to the Dominican Republic, and Mr. Manuel Maria Gautier, secretary of state of the departments of the interior and of police, charged with the foreign relations of the said Dominican Republic.[56]

These "bases" provided first for a treaty of annexation between the United States and the Dominican Republic. The acceptance of annexation on the part of the Dominican Republic would oblige the American Government to advance the sum of $1,500,000 in order to liquidate the Dominican public debt.

The first article of these "treaty bases" also included a remarkable pledge with reference to the rôle that would be played by President Grant in the matter of Dominican annexation. It definitely promised that the American Executive would

use all his influence, in order that the idea of annexing the Dominican Republic to the United States may acquire such a degree of popularity among members of Congress as will be necessary for its accomplishment; and he offers to make no communication to that body on the subject until he shall be certain that it will be approved by a majority.

In the event that the Senate of the United States should prove hostile to the idea of annexation, then the

Dominican Government would accept, as the price of the sale of Samaná, the two millions of dollars in coin ($2,000,000) which the same government of the United States offered it under the administration of President Johnson.

In the third article of the "bases" President Grant assumed

the obligation to remit forthwith to the Dominican Government the sum of one hundred and fifty thousand dollars in coin ($150,000), one hundred thousand dollars to be in cash, and fifty thousand in arms, for the purpose of defraying the unavoidable expenses of the State.

On September 6 Babcock left the Dominican Republic, and

---

[56] *Ibid.*, pp. 188-189. In Article IV of the "bases" the American Government guaranteed "the safety of the country and of the government against every foreign aggression or machination" during the pendency of the treaty.

was soon back in Washington where his arrival with a *projet* of a definitive treaty is generally supposed to have caused an explosion in the office of the dignified Secretary of State. About the same time that Babcock arrived in Washington two reports concerning his mission reached the Department of State. Manuel Gautier, the Dominican Minister in charge of the informal negotiations, had written to assure Fish that General Babcock had revealed " the high qualities " that had " merited the distinction shown him by his Government," [57] while J. Somers Smith, the American Commercial Agent at Santo Domingo City, had expressed definite doubts relative to Babcock's actions. It appeared that the American special agent had refrained from applying to Smith for advice of any kind, and, moreover, he had consorted constantly with Fabens and General Cazneau whom Smith regarded as mere " speculators who stand at nothing to bring about their selfish ends." [58]

The classic account of the Babcock mission and the effect it is alleged to have had upon Secretary Fish was written many years ago by Jacob Dolson Cox, who was Secretary of the Interior in the Cabinet of President Grant. His narrative has a definite note of authority that carried conviction to his readers, and its mordant criticism of Grant's policy left an indelible impression of the President as a most maladroit person who schemed behind the back of his Secretary of State in order to achieve an unworthy end. His account has such an authentic and intimate air that few have doubted its validity. For this very reason it is important to reproduce the following excerpts:

One day . . . the President casually remarked that the navy people seemed so anxious to have the bay of Samana as a coaling station that he thought he would send Colonel Babcock down to examine it and

[57] Gautier to Fish, September 4, 1869, *Dominican Republic, Notes,* vol 2, MS. Dept. of State.

[58] Smith to Fish, September 2, 1869, *Santo Domingo, Consular Desp.*, vol. 6, MS. Dept. of State. There is little doubt that the suspicions of Smith concerning Babcock's relations with Colonel Fabens and General Cazneau were quite justified. In this regard the following excerpt from a letter from Fabens to Babcock of September 12, 1869 is significant: " The country will applaud the action of Genl. Grant as a brilliant manouver, and I trust and believe it will prove the bright beginning of a prosperous career for yourself in business life." MS. *Fabens Papers.*

report upon it as an engineer. . . . A day or two later, it was said that, as Babcock did not speak Spanish, a well-known officer of the Inspector-General's department would accompany him. Lastly, it appeared that Mr. Columbus Cole, then a Senator from California, was to be of the party on this new voyage of discovery to Hispaniola.

. . . After some weeks' absence, Babcock's return was announced by the New York newspapers, with suggestions of interesting results. On seeing this, I called upon Mr. Fish at the State Department the same afternoon. He sent his private secretary from the room and closed the door; then coming toward me with manifest feeling, he said, "What do you think! Babcock is back, and has actually brought a treaty for the cession of San Domingo; yet I pledge you my word that he had no more diplomatic authority than any other casual visitor to that island!" An earnest discussion of the situation followed, in which we agreed that the proper course was to treat Babcock's action as null, and to insist upon burying the whole in oblivion as a state secret. . . . It did not occur to either of us, in view of the past history of the matter, that the President would assume the responsibility for the illegal act of his messenger.

In the informal discussion of the subject which incidentally occurred before the next Cabinet meeting, the view Mr. Fish had taken seemed to be the general one, and it was expected that he would present it when we should be assembled. . . . It had been the President's habit, at such meetings, to call upon the members of the Cabinet to bring forward the business contained in their portfolios, beginning with the Secretary of State. This would at once have brought the action of Babcock up by Mr. Fish's disclaimer of all part in the matter, and his statement of its utter illegality. On this occasion, however, General Grant departed from his uniform custom, and took the initiative. "Babcock has returned, as you see," said he, "and he has brought a treaty of annexation. I suppose it is not formal, as he had no diplomatic powers; but we can easily cure that. We can send back the treaty, and have Perry, the consular agent, sign it; and as he is an officer of the State Department it would make it all right."

This took everybody so completely by surprise that they seemed dumbfounded. After an awkward interval, as nobody else broke the silence, I said, "But, Mr. President, has it been settled, then, that we *want* to annex San Domingo?" The direct question evidently embarrassed General Grant. He colored and smoked hard at his cigar. He glanced at Mr. Fish on his right, but the face of the Secretary was impassive, and his eyes were fixed on the portfolio before him. He turned to Mr.

Boutwell on his left, but no response met him there. As the silence became painful, the President called for another item of business, and left the question unanswered

. . . The position of Mr. Fish was the most difficult one. He was on terms of intimate friendship with Charles Sumner, the chairman of the Committee on Foreign Relations in the Senate, and both official propriety and personal feeling had made him frankly open in discussing diplomatic affairs with the Senator. He had honestly treated the talk of Dominican annexation as mere gossip . . . and now he suddenly found his sincerity in question, under circumstances which forbade him to say how gravely the State Department had been compromised. The situation seemed so intolerable that he took the very natural course of tendering his resignation.[59]

It is strange that no historian has ever taken the trouble to subject to a critical examination the above account by Secretary Cox, for it is obvious that it contains many errors that are quite easy to detect. First of all he would give the impression that Babcock went to the Dominican Republic in an informal manner with instructions from Grant alone. This, of course, is entirely incorrect because Babcock not only carried a letter of credence from the President but was also given definite instructions by Secretary Fish.[60] From the Cox nar-

[59] Jacob D. Cox, "How Judge Hoar Ceased to Be Attorney-General," *Atlantic Monthly*, LXXVI (1895), 165-167. In commenting upon the Cabinet meeting at which Grant brought up the matter of the Babcock protocol, Charles Francis Adams, in his *Lee at Appomattox and Other Papers*, p. 131, accepts without question the Cox version of the refusal of every member of that body to sustain the President in his desire to push through at any cost the annexation of the Dominican Republic. He said: "To say that never before in the whole history of government had any President made such a naive exhibition is quite within safe bounds. Ignorance of law and usage and an utter absence of the sense of propriety were about equally pronounced." Of the same tenor is the following excerpt from Hugh McCulloch, *Men and Measures of Half a Century*, p. 353: "One of the strangest, not to say most astounding things that ever occurred in the history of the country."

[60] *Hatch Report*, pp. 46-47. The doubtful authenticity of the Cox narrative was at once apparent to George S. Boutwell who, as Secretary of the Treasury, sat in the Grant Cabinet. On June 1, 1896 Boutwell wrote a letter of protest to Edward L. Pierce with reference to the article in the *Atlantic Monthly* by Judge Cox. In the last paragraph of this letter he wrote the following: "I cannot endorse your endorsement of Cox's article in the Atlantic. Cox's article is not favorable to Judge Hoar. He errs as to the cause of his departure from the cabinet." *Pierce Papers*, MS. Harvard College Library.

rative it would also appear that on his first visit to the Dominican Republic General Babcock was accompanied by a "well-known officer of the Inspector-General's department." Such a statement indicates a distinct confusion in the mind of Secretary Cox. The "well-known officer" to whom he refers was Delos B. Sackett, the Inspector-General of the American Army, who went with Babcock on his *second* and not on his *first* trip to the Dominican Republic.[61] This confusion is further revealed when Cox refers to Senator Cornelius Cole as Senator Columbus Cole.

The Cox account makes much of the alleged agitation shown by Secretary Fish when he learned of the return of Babcock with an agreement providing for Dominican annexation, and it takes on dramatic color when it describes the Cabinet meeting where Secretary Fish refrained from supporting the Babcock *projet*. It is more than likely that this portion of the Cox narrative is largely fiction. There was little reason for any dramatics on the part of Fish when he heard that Babcock had returned with a protocol for Dominican annexation. Fish was aware of the Act of March 30, 1868, which forbade Army officers from holding appointments in the diplomatic service of the United States, and it was for that very reason that Babcock was not given any diplomatic powers. Also, for this same reason Babcock made no attempt to negotiate a formal treaty for Dominican annexation, and, instead, merely signed a *projet* or outline of a treaty which would have to be approved by President Grant and Secretary Fish, and which later could be formally negotiated by a diplomatic agent under instructions from the Department of State. Babcock did not violate the

[61] Dr. E. P. Oberholtzer, in his *History of the United States since the Civil War* (5 vols., N. Y., 1925), II, 230, evidently relying on the Cox article, gives a lurid account of the Babcock mission and the scene in the Cabinet meeting when the Babcock *projet* came up for consideration. With regard to the attitude of Secretary Fish towards the Babcock negotiations, he makes the following statement: "Having been kept in ignorance of the negotiations the Secretary of State felt he had no recourse but to resign. Twice he did so, once in writing, but later reconsidered his action at Grant's desire and gave his support, however reluctantly, to the enterprise." In view of the actual facts in the case it would be difficult to imagine a more incorrect statement. Louis A. Coolidge, in his *Ulysses S. Grant* (N. Y., 1927), pp. 314 ff., gives close adherence to the Cox account.

instructions that had been given him by Secretary Fish, and in the matter of the signature of the *projet* he merely carried out definite orders. This fact is made very clear by the following letter from President Grant to Senator Nye:

I am pleased to inform you that Gen. Babcock did not exceed my wishes or my verbal instructions to him in connection with the *Confidential Basis*. Gen. Babcock was sent to Sto. Domingo to ascertain so far as he could the wishes of the Dominican people and Government with respect to annexation to the United States. . . . He brought the confidential Basis, which was not binding, or intended to be binding upon either government, unless each saw fit to continue the negotiations.[62]

It is very apparent that Babcock's signature of the *Confidential Basis* for subsequent treaty arrangements with the Dominican Republic could not supply any warrant for an "explosion" of deep-seated indignation on the part of Secretary Fish because of an alleged departure from diplomatic proprieties. Moreover, it should be remembered that Fish was fully aware of Grant's ardent interest in Dominican annexation—an interest which was clearly revealed in the instruction which the Secretary of the Navy issued to Commander Owen to give Babcock the "moral support" of his guns.[63] This instruction was ample evidence that the Babcock mission was not a mere gesture of friendship to a neighboring republic. President Grant anticipated definite difficulties in the matter of Dominican annexation, and that fact explains why a soldier and not a diplomat was sent to open negotiations. Secretary Fish was well acquainted with all these factors in the equation of annexation, and it is hard to believe that he was so taken aback at the news of Babcock's signature of the *projet* that he at once tendered his resignation as Secretary of State.[64]

[62] Grant to James W. Nye, June 27, 1870, *Grant Letter Book*, MS. Library of Congress.

[63] *Hatch Report*, pp. 38-39.

[64] It is evident that Charles Francis Adams, in his interesting paper entitled "The Treaty of Washington," which is contained in his well-known volume *Lee at Appomattox and Other Papers*, pp. 130 ff., accepts unhesitatingly the account given by J. D. Cox in his *Atlantic Monthly* article already referred to. Adams says: " Colonel Babcock, one of the group of young army officers already

Such action is rendered the more improbable when one reads the following item in the *Diary* of Secretary Fish, under the date of June 17, 1870:

I have certainly been loyal to a measure of policy which he inaugurated, [Dominican annexation] and after it was entered upon, have done what I could to sustain it. I might have paused before entering upon it, and think it has been embarrassed unnecessarily by the interference of those who were not properly charged with the management of such negotiations.[65]

With reference to this alleged resignation of Fish as Secretary of State because of the Dominican imbroglio, it is interesting to note that most of our standard historians express the view that Fish was dissuaded from taking such a course by the fervid plea of President Grant that he remain in the Cabinet to serve as a " social guide " to the Administration.[66] If in reality Secretary Fish did remain in the Cabinet because of such an entreaty there would be no better guage as to his

referred to, who, having been members of General Grant's military staff, were retained . . . near his person during his presidency, had been sent down by him to examine, as an engineer, the bay of Samana, and to report upon it as a coaling station. Presently he got back, and, at the next meeting of the Cabinet, the President paralyzed his official advisers by announcing in a casual sort of way, ' Babcock has returned, as you see, and has brought a treaty of annexation.' To say that never before in the whole history of the government had any President made such a naive exhibition is quite within safe bounds. Ignorance of law and usage, and an utter absence of the sense or propriety, were about equally pronounced. . . . Sent to examine a harbor, the President's aide had undertaken to annex a negro republic! " It is patent that this narrative of Adams is as loosely written as that of Cox, but Adams does adduce certain extracts from the *Diary* of Hamilton Fish which indicate that the Secretary of State was anxious to resign from the Grant Cabinet. The entry from which he quotes, however, was made in the *Diary* on June 17, 1870, many months subsequent to the famous Cabinet meeting so graphically described by Judge Cox.

[65] At this point I wish to express my warm appreciation of the unusual kindness of Professor Allan Nevins in permitting me to have access to the manuscript *Diary* of Secretary Hamilton Fish. Further light on the relations between Fish and Grant is cast by the following observation from Adam Badeau's *Grant in Peace*, p. 233: " When Grant determined on a course that Fish would not perhaps have advised, the secretary staunchly supported his chief."

[66] In this regard see the accounts in E. P. Oberholtzer, *A History of the United States since the Civil War*, II, 230-231; C. F. Adams, *Lee at Appomattox and Other Papers*, pp. 222, 247; J. F. Rhodes, *History of the United States* (7 vols., N. Y., 1900-1906), VI, 348.

character. It is extremely doubtful, however, that such was the case.

The scene now shifts from the Department of State to the office of James Gordon Bennett, the editor and owner of the New York *Herald*. Bennett was strongly in favor of Dominican annexation and, in order to further this project, he decided to send one of his reporters, D. R. Keim, to the Dominican Republic to discuss matters with President Baez. Keim was also instructed to send to Bennett letters favoring Dominican annexation. These letters were to be published in the *Herald* and were expected to create a public sentiment friendly to American expansion in the Caribbean.

Keim arrived in the Dominican Republic on June 17, 1869, and he was soon discussing with President Baez the question of annexation to the United States. Baez immediately impressed Keim as " a man of true principles and extraordinary ability." He had " a brunette face, slightly ' off color,' intelligent, and of very agreeable expression." After a few moments of conversation there was no doubt in the mind of Keim as to the " patriotism of Baez and all those associated with him." [67]

As a result of this conversation President Baez decided to entrust to the care of Keim a formal letter addressed to President Grant in which the desire of the Dominican Government for annexation to the United States was clearly expressed. This was delivered to President Grant while he was the guest of Secretary Fish at his estate at Garrison, New York.[68] Its effect upon President Grant was merely to strengthen his resolve to push through without any further hesitation a program for Dominican annexation. With this idea in mind he decided to send General Babcock on a second mission to the Dominican Republic, and, in order that he might have with him a competent interpreter who could also give valuable military counsel if the occasion demanded it, General Delos B. Sackett, the Inspector-General of the American Army, was given instructions to accompany this mission.

General Babcock, flanked by both General Sackett and Gen-

[67] D. R. Keim, *San Domingo* (Phila., 1870), pp. 65-76.
[68] *Keim Papers*, MS. Library of Congress.

eral Rufus Ingalls, arrived at Santo Domingo City on November 18, 1869. Babcock carried with him some lengthy instructions from Secretary Fish, dated November 6, 1869, together with draft treaties which he was authorized to negotiate, and which the new American Commercial Agent to the Dominican Republic, Raymond H. Perry, was to sign. According to these instructions General Babcock was to negotiate two treaties. One treaty was to provide for the annexation of the Dominican Republic as a territory of the United States. In order to liquidate the public debt of the Republic the American Government was to advance the sum of one million five hundred thousand dollars ($1,500,000),[69] while the Dominican Government was to pledge that it would make " no grants or concessions of lands or rights in lands, and to contract no further debts, until Congress shall assume jurisdiction over the territory." In order to take care of the immediate needs of the Dominican Government General Babcock was given the authority to advance to it a draft on New York for $100,000, and an additional amount of fifty thousand dollars' worth of munitions of war.

The other treaty provided for a lease by the American Government of Samaná Bay for a period of ninety-nine years. During this leasing period the American Government would be obligated to pay to the Dominican Republic an annual rental to be fixed by the negotiators, and the American Government would also have the right at any time during the period of the lease to purchase Samaná Bay and its environs for the sum of $2,000,000 in gold.[70]

---

[69] The sum of $1,500,000 was specifically included in the terms of the treaty because, according to an official report of Gautier, the Dominican Minister of the Interior, this amount was approximately the total of the public debt of the Dominican Republic. See *Sen. Ex. Doc.* No. 17, 41 Cong., 3 sess., p. 92. At a meeting of the Cabinet on October 16, 1869, Secretary Fish presented a draft of a treaty with the Dominican Republic. Three days later this draft treaty was discussed by the Cabinet, and Secretary Boutwell was " not much in favor " of annexation but thought that it " must come." Secretary Cox said little but had " no sympathy " with such a project. Secretaries Robeson and Hoar were doubtful about annexation, but Creswell was " thoroughly in favor " of it. MS. *Fish Diary*, October 16, 19, 1869.

[70] *Sen. Ex. Doc.* No. 17, 41 Cong., 3 sess., pp. 80-89. With regard to the

Secretary Fish also sent instructions to Raymond H. Perry, the new American Commercial Agent at Santo Domingo City, with reference to the proposed treaties with the Dominican Republic. It was the desire of President Grant that Perry should " confer with General Babcock in every step of these negotiations, and . . . be governed by his advice." [71] It was evident that Perry's rôle was to be a distinctly subordinate one.

The choice of Raymond H. Perry as American Commercial Agent at Santo Domingo City intrigues one's curiosity. When Grant became President this position of Commercial Agent was held by J. Somers Smith, who occasionally expressed in his despatches to the Secretary of State a sharp suspicion of General Cazneau and Colonel Fabens. In a communication of September 2, 1869, Smith denounced these shady characters as mere " speculators who stand at nothing to bring about their selfish ends." [72] This must have been deeply disturbing to Secretary Fish, who realized that President Grant and General Babcock had reposed great confidence in the integrity of these same adventurous Americans. Cazneau had acted as an interpreter for General Babcock upon his first mission to the Dominican Republic, and both he and Colonel Fabens were regarded by the Grant clique as important factors in the program for Dominican annexation. It is not surprising, therefore, that Grant and Babcock decided to supplant J. Somers Smith by a new Commercial Agent. On October 20, 1869, General Babcock sent a note to Secretary Fish to inform him that the President thought that Major Perry was a " proper person to send to St. Domingo in place of Smith." [73]

Major Perry had achieved nothing worthy of commendation

treaty for the lease or possible purchase of Samaná Bay, Secretary Fish, in a letter to Elihu Washburne of December 24, 1869, remarks as follows: " The Samana treaty was intended as a security for the sum paid on account of the surrender of independent existence [$150,000], and to engage the attention of the People while preparations are making for the election etc." *Washburne Papers*, MS. Library of Congress.

[71] *Sen. Ex. Doc.* No. 17, 41 Cong., 3 sess., p. 95.

[72] Smith to Fish, September 2, 1869, *Santo Domingo, Consular Desp.*, vol 2, MS. Dept. of State.

[73] Babcock to Fish, October 20, 1869, *Grant Letter Book*, MS. Library of Congress.

before being selected for his new post at Santo Domingo City. During his service in the Union army he shot an officer who threatened his life, but he was immediately acquitted by a court-martial. Later, while on duty in New Orleans, he was implicated in the popular pastime of mule stealing and was sentenced to be dismissed from the army. Subsequently he was restored to active duty and after the close of the Civil War was honorably discharged. In 1866 and 1867 he served under General Sheridan in Louisiana and Texas, and on August 7, 1867 Sheridan wrote to Brevet Major-General Charles Griffin that Perry's services as a " special officer " had been " almost indispensable." [74]

Major Perry left for the Dominican Republic on November 3, and, by some strange coincidence, one of the passengers on the *Tybee* was that stormy petrel of Caribbean waters, Colonel Fabens. It was not long before Fabens was indicating the course that Perry should pursue with reference to Dominican annexation, and he endeavored to make his directions all the more attractive by assuring Perry that in the event he proved an apt pupil he would make a " rapid fortune." [75]

On November 16, 1869 Major Perry assumed the duties of Commercial Agent at Santo Domingo City, and he received from J. Somers Smith, the late incumbent of that office, a brief but pungent description of Dominican politics. According to Smith the project for Dominican annexation had been hatched by General Cazneau, who was " running the whole thing." Smith then made his departure for the United States, and after his not unwelcome exit Cazneau and President Baez began to occupy the centre of the stage. Cazneau, concerned to impress Major Perry with his importance, began a conversation by alluding to a correspondence that he had carried on with President Grant on the subject of annexation. Finally he reached the topic he thought would make the most direct appeal to the interest of Major Perry—the opportunity of filling one's pockets with gold. If the American Commercial Agent was

[74] *Hatch Report*, pp. xxxi-xxxiv.
[75] Perry to Fish, June 7, 1870, *Santo Domingo, Consular Desp.,* vol. 6, MS. Dept. of State. Also Perry to Fish, November 16, 1869, *ibid.*

co-operative he would receive a "fine plantation and opportunities to handle money for men in New York City."

Perry, however, had previously been often thrown with adventurers of many types, and he cautiously answered that he was "after a reputation and not money." But Cazneau appeared somewhat suspicious of this fine exhibition of Roman virtue. During the course of his remarks he continued to allude to the mercenary aspects of Dominican annexation until Major Perry found it necessary "several times" to repeat his remark that he was seeking "reputation" and not "money." Cazneau then decided to bide his time until the arrival of General Babcock, who was expected within a few days.[76]

On the morning of November 18, 1869 Perry was having breakfast with Fabens, when the latter suddenly announced that an American war-ship would soon arrive with General Babcock. Some hours later, when this prophecy came true, Perry boarded the war-ship and received the information that Babcock had been instructed by President Grant to negotiate a treaty which Perry was to sign. On the following morning Babcock, together with Generals Delos B. Sackett and Rufus Ingalls, came on shore and formally inaugurated negotiations for two treaties with the Dominican Government: one was to be for the lease of Samaná Bay and the other treaty would provide for the annexation of the Dominican Republic to the United States.[77]

---

[76] Perry to Fish, June 7, 1870, *ibid.*

[77] On November 29, 1869 Thornton, the British Minister at Washington, wrote to Lord Clarendon to acquaint him with the Babcock mission to the Dominican Republic. *Confidential*, F. O. 5/1163, No. 412. On December 9, 1869 David Leon, the British consul at Santo Domingo City, sent to Lord Stanley a similar warning. F. O. 23/59, No. 12. Some weeks later, on December 27, 1869, Thornton wrote to Lord Clarendon to advise him that the mission of General Babcock was not for the purpose of effecting a treaty of Dominican annexation to the United States but in order to acquire Samaná Bay as an American naval station. F. O. 5/1163, No. 451. Thus it would appear that Secretary Fish had been able to keep from Thornton the fact that General Babcock had signed a treaty of annexation. On January 10, 1870, however, Thornton confessed to Lord Clarendon that his "first suspicions that there was a desire on the part of the Government of the United States to effect the annexation of the Republic of Santo Domingo were well founded." F. O. 5/1191, No. 12. A few days later (January 17, 1870) Thornton expressed to Lord Clarendon

Every morning General Babcock, accompanied by Generals Sackett and Ingalls, came ashore and proceeded to the residence of President Baez, where the discussions relative to the two treaties were held. General Sackett acted as an interpreter for General Babcock, while President Baez had the counsel of Gautier, the Minister of Foreign Affairs, and Delmonte, the Minister of Justice. On several occasions General Cazneau was present during these discussions, while Colonel Fabens was invariably present and often assisted General Sackett in his rôle of interpreter.

During the course of these negotiations the part played by

the view that the treaty for Dominican annexation would meet with strong opposition in the American Senate. F. O. 5/1191.

It is important to note that during this same time that the Grant Administration was endeavoring to effect the annexation of the Dominican Republic, it was also casting eager eyes at the Republic of Haiti. On September 16, 1869 E. D. Bassett, the American Minister at Port-au-Prince, sent a despatch to Secretary Fish which indicated that President Salnave had inquired whether it would be expedient for him to send to Washington a special envoy who would suggest to the Department of State a " treaty of alliance." He received some encouragement from Bassett who believed that the Haitian Government wished to procure a loan of several million dollars. In return they would lease or cede to the United States the Môle-Saint-Nicolas. *Haiti, Desp.,* vol. 3, MS. Dept. of State. Without losing any more time, President Salnave sent General Alexander Tate to Washington to make arrangements for this loan and to cede the Môle-Saint-Nicolas. E. D. Bassett to Secretary Fish, November 2, 1869, *Haiti, Desp.,* vol. 3, MS. Dept. of State. In December, 1869, however, President Salnave's Government was overturned by revolution and the President himself was murdered. The feeling in Haiti against Americans was very bitter, and the life of the American Minister was in danger. E. D. Bassett to Secretary Fish, January 15, 1870, Nos. 34-36, *Haiti, Desp.,* vol 3, MS. Dept. of State. It should be remembered that in August, 1868 President Salnave sounded out Secretary Seward with reference to a cession of the Môle-Saint-Nicolas to the United States in return for protection " against internal insurrection and revolution as well as against foreign invasion." Secretary Seward informed President Salnave that the American Government could not consider his proposition. Secretary Seward to Gideon H. Hollister, September 1, 1868, *Hayti-Liberia, Inst.,* vol. 1, No. 12, MS. Dept. of State.

Sir Spenser St. John, the British Minister at Port-au-Prince, was quite disturbed by the turn of events in Haiti, and he wrote to Lord Clarendon on January 20, 1870 and enclosed documents which he thought proved the anxious desire of the American Government to " obtain a footing in the Haitian Republic; these intrigues have been carried on for some time, but Salnave is the first ruler who ever proposed to cede a portion of the territory to the foreigner." *Confidential,* F. O. 115/500, No. 49.

Major Perry was distinctly insignificant.[78] He was several times informed by General Babcock that he

must stand by Cazneau and Fabens and advise with them, that they represented large interests on the Island, that he had interests with them. Cazneau also told me that Babcock and Ingalls had interests in real estate with him, and that he, Fabens, and his friends in New York had originated the idea of annexation.[79]

As the negotiations for the treaty of annexation proceeded there were certain delays occasioned by the evident desire of the Dominican officials to find some means of bribing General Babcock. According to Article 6 of the proposed treaty there should be " no grants or concessions made after the signing of the treaty." This provision embarrassed the Dominican officials, and the reason for their difficulty is clearly described in the following testimony of General Sackett before a committee of the United States Senate:

Just as the sixth article . . . was reached, they [the Dominican officials] objected to it for a long time . . . and General Babcock got very much annoyed at it, and said to me, " There appears to be something wrong here." The conversations ceased, and he got up and passed off to a window, and was looking out of the window when President Baez turned around to me and said: " I will tell you what we want; General Babcock was very kind to us last summer; he sent Captain Queen with the Tuscarora to seize this Telegrafo and run her into a place where she was tied up by the English; and then also Mr. Smith had been very obnoxious to us, and we made certain representations to General Babcock and he investigated them and laid them before the President, and Mr. Smith was dismissed and Mr. Perry sent down in his place; and for these things, showing great kindness on the part of General Babcock, we should like to make him a grant of land in Samana." I told the President in Spanish: " Mr. President, such a thing as that would kill the treaty in a minute." " Well," said he,

---

[78] In a despatch to Secretary Fish on December 10, 1869, Major Perry described his rôle in the following terms: " I signed the papers relating to the lease of Samana Bay etc., under the directions of Gen. Babcock. I had very little to do with the matter, he, Gen. Babcock, deserves all credit for what was done here." *Santo Domingo, Consular Desp.,* vol. 6, MS. Dept. of State.

[79] Perry to Fish, June 7, 1870, *ibid.*

"we want to do it as an act of kindness, and we cannot do it if this is put in the treaty; what we want to do is to have the treaty signed; let it go before our senate tomorrow; they will grant this land, and then we will make the sixth article date two days afterward." I said to him, "Mr. President, it would kill the treaty." I turned around to Babcock and said: "General, do you know what they are after?" He said, "No." Said I, "They want to make you a grant of land at Samana, and want this article dated two days later." Babcock raised his hands and said, "My God! anything of that kind would ruin the treaty; it would not do!" Baez said, "Very well; we only wanted to do it as an act of kindness." Then he signed the treaty immediately, and that was the end of it.[80]

During the course of the negotiations there were certain discussions relative to the most expedient mode of procedure with reference to the drafting of the treaty of annexation and of the treaty for the lease of Samaná Bay. According to the account of Major Perry it would appear that on one occasion General Cazneau

proposed to draw up two separate papers, one to place before the people of St. Domingo to control the elections, the other before the United States Government to keep them quiet. This was approved by Baez and Delmonte, who remarked that it would influence and hasten the election in St. Domingo. I [Major Perry] protested against this to General Babcock, and remarked to him: "We have no right to deceive the Dominican people." Genl. Babcock also protested against this and said it would place Grant in a wrong position. Baez and Delmonte said it was only a fiction and if they did not succeed in the vote for annexation and our Government did not accept them, that it would cost them their lives.[81]

With regard to this same incident General Sackett gave the following testimony:

I know on one occasion we had considerable difficulty, and it looked as though the treaty was going to be a failure; that is, we should not succeed; and on our way home from President Baez's house Mr. Cazneau suggested that we get up a separate treaty, or what he called a secret

[80] *Hatch Report*, p. 49.

[81] Perry to Fish, June 7, 1870, *Santo Domingo, Consular Desp.*, vol. 6, MS. Dept. of State.

treaty, and we all shooed at the idea, and told him that anything that we got up would have to be on the square and aboveboard.[82]

Finally, with reference to General Cazneau's suggestion for a secret treaty we have the following testimony of General Babcock:

The idea of the two treaties was this: A secret treaty that should go before the Senate, and one that should be put before the people. I took down from Washington two draughts—one a treaty for annexation, and the other a convention for the lease of Samana as a security for the money and the arms advanced. This convention contained articles which referred to the subject of annexation; in other words, the two were so constructed as to refer to each other. President Baez said that he did not wish to refer the treaty of annexation to his senate, but he wished to refer the treaty of annexation to his people; but before he could receive any money from our government he must have the approval of the convention for the lease of Samana by his senate. He said that that would go before his senate and be confirmed, and then he would receive the money; and he suggested that that need not appear in Washington with the treaty of annexation. He said it was merely as a security for the money that we advanced, and if annexation took place, as we all believe it would, this convention need never be acted upon by our Senate—might be withheld by President Grant. We explained . . . that that could not be done.[83]

Despite the above testimony of General Babcock it would appear that President Baez went ahead with his program, for on November 28, 1869 he procured from the Dominican Senate the necessary authority to sign the convention for the lease of Samaná Bay.[84] The next day both the treaty for the lease of Samaná Bay and the treaty of annexation were signed. In accordance with instructions, General Babcock immediately

[82] *Hatch Report*, p. 51. When General Sackett was called before the Senate Committee a second time he again told of Cazneau's desire to make a secret treaty. Thus: " I said the other day that one day going home after a stormy debate that we had had, Cazneau, on the way, asked if we could not make a secret treaty. . . . I laughed at the idea, and told him we could not do anything of that kind. He said, ' Sometimes such things are done; sometimes a secret treaty is made to lay before the Senate.' Said I, ' We are not here for any such purpose; anything we do must be open and above-board.' " *Ibid.*, p. 111.

[83] *Ibid.*, p. 110.

[84] *Dominican Republic, Notes*, vol. 2, MS. Dept. of State.

turned over to the Dominican officials approximately the sum of $150,000, and, on December 4, Generals Babcock, Sackett, and Ingalls sailed for Samaná Bay in order to hoist the American flag and to take formal possession of the territory described in the lease.[85]

It is at this point that the question of the Hartmont loan becomes important. On May 18, 1869 the American Commercial Agent at Santo Domingo City wrote to Secretary Fish concerning a loan of £420,000 which had been negotiated with the English banking house of Hartmont and Company. Upon inquiry, the American Commercial Agent was assured by President Baez that only a small portion of the loan had been advanced, and that it was merely a " temporary measure which would probably enable the present administration to maintain itself." [86] As a matter of fact this " small portion " of the loan that had been advanced amounted to £38,095 4s. 9d., which, with interest at six per cent., would reach by December 31, 1869 a total of $260,000.[87]

In the general instructions from Secretary Fish to General Babcock of November 6, 1869, it was clearly indicated that Major Perry was not to sign any treaty with the Dominican Government until the Hartmont loan contract was " duly and legally cancelled." However, in a special instruction of this same date, General Babcock was authorized to disregard the general instructions on this point. In the event he was unable to secure from the Dominican Government the " complete abrogation " of the Hartmont contract, he was then merely to

endeavor to secure the best terms possible in regard to that contract; and if he finds that it is impossible to make any arrangements about it, the President authorizes him, nevertheless, to conclude a convention and treaty in which the Dominican Republic shall assume all future obligations growing out of the contract.[88]

[85] Perry to Fish, Dec. 10, 1869, *Santo Domingo, Consular Desp.*, vol. 6, MS. Dept. of State. See also the long protest signed by Generals Luperón and Cabral against the signature of the lease of Samaná Bay. *Dominican Republic, Notes*, vol. 2, MS. Dept. of State.

[86] Smith to Fish, May 18, 1869, *Santo Domingo, Consular Desp.*, vol. 6, MS. Dept. of State.

[87] *Sen. Ex. Doc.* No. 17, 41 Cong., 3 sess., p. 92.

[88] *Ibid.*, p. 94.

General Babcock was not able to secure the complete abrogation of this Hartmont contract before the signature of the treaties for the lease of Samaná Bay and for the annexation of the Dominican Republic. On December 3, 1869, however, President Baez wrote to General Babcock to assure him that

according to the best information which I have been able to obtain relative to Mr. Hartmont's loan, I am convinced that this gentleman is not in a situation to deliver the balance of the loan at the stipulated time, which is the 31st of this month. If, contrary to the information aforesaid, Mr. Hartmont appears at the proper time with the money to fulfill his contract, we shall receive it, refraining from making any use of it until instructions reach us from Washington with regard to the matter, and until we know whether, in case of our refusing to receive it, the Government of the United States will take upon itself the consequences of such refusal.[89]

On December 21 President Grant called a meeting of his Cabinet, and the matter of the two treaties with the Dominican Republic came up for discussion. The President requested Secretary Fish to read the treaty of annexation, and he then enjoined secrecy with reference to it until after January first. It was permissible, however, to refer to the treaty for the lease of Samaná Bay and to lead the public to suppose that it was the " only treaty." This procedure was advisable because the contract for the Hartmont loan would expire on December 31, and so far its terms had not been fulfilled by the banking house itself. The delay was due to the fact that this English banking house was of the opinion that it need not pay strict attention to the exact letter of the contract. In view of the desperate straits of the Dominican Government it was believed that even though the money due it by the Hartmont contract was not paid within the stipulated time, that government would still be glad to receive it and would waive any technical infraction of the contract. The news of the signature of a treaty for the lease of Samaná Bay would not unduly disturb the directors of this banking house, but it was very possible that if they learned of a proposed treaty of annexation they would hasten to fulfill the terms of the contract and thus would secure valuable concessions that would seriously militate against the advisability of American annexation.[90]

On December 24, 1869 Fish wrote to Elihu Washburne, the American Minister to France, and gave him an outline of the two Dominican treaties. In conclusion he requested Washburne to " observe the utmost confidence " with reference to the terms of these treaties.[91] This admonition, however, was hardly worth while, for the New York press had summarized the probable terms of the treaties in a remarkably accurate manner. It was not long before the American public had a very clear idea of President Grant's objectives in the region of the Caribbean, and special attention was given to the treaty for the lease of Samaná Bay.[92] In this connection the names of General Cazneau and Colonel Fabens were frequently adverted to, and on December 24, 1869 Peter F. Stout wrote to Senator Sumner in order to express his suspicions of these gentlemen:

Gen'l Cazneau and his partner or man Friday, Fabens, have entered into a league with Baez, to conclude certain arrangements with the U. S. whereby they [Cazneau and Fabens] may obtain indemnity from St. Domingo out of any monies paid by the U. S. or any other foreign country for certain *personal* claims they may have against St. Domingo. If the U. S. are to pay $150,000 per annum for 50 years for Samana Bay, it is a swindle. For, at the most one million dollars, the entire Peninsula might have been obtained in fee simple.[93]

It may have been in connection with this letter of Stout's that Senator Sumner, on December 31, called at the White House for a conference with the President about affairs in the Dominican Republic.[94] During the conference President

[90] MS. *Fish Diary*, December 21, 1869.

[91] *Washburne Papers*, MS., Library of Congress.

[92] In the New York *Herald* of December 22, 1869 there is a significant paragraph concerning the Samaná Bay treaty: " The definite and exclusive intelligence in reference to the purchase of the Bay of Samana . . . is awakening the liveliest interest in financial and commercial circles. Wall Street was full of the subject yesterday, and among the business men of Beaver, Water, Pearl, Front, William and other down town streets the new acquisition was variously discussed."

[93] *Sumner Papers*, MS. Harvard College Library.

[94] MS. *Fish Diary*, December 31, 1869.

Grant, if he had desired, could have strengthened Sumner's suspicions concerning Cazneau and Fabens by reading to him a despatch from Major Perry of December 10, 1869. Perry had been advised by General Babcock to " stand by Cazneau and Fabens and advise with them." [95] Perry, however, found this increasingly difficult in the face of direct evidence that both Cazneau and Fabens were largely governed by mercenary motives, and in his despatch to Secretary Fish, on December 10, 1869, he expressed his suspicions in spite of the fact that General Babcock was distinctly friendly to them. It is very probable that he also realized that one of the main reasons why he had been sent to the Dominican Republic to succeed J. Somers Smith, the late Commercial Agent at Santo Domingo City, was that Smith was at odds with Cazneau and Fabens. Throwing caution to the winds, Major Perry, immediately after General Babcock sailed for the United States, wrote to Secretary Fish and remarked as follows:

I am anxious and ready to carry out faithfully all orders that may be sent me. I have no other motive in remaining on this Island. But there are some who are taking a *very active* part in this matter of annexation who are looking only to their own selfish interest and would jeopardise their flag or friends to gain it.[96]

It is extremely unlikely that President Grant, during his conference with Senator Sumner, adverted to this despatch from Major Perry, and it is quite improbable that he subsequently showed the Senator a later despatch from Major Perry in which the American Commercial Agent repeated his suspicions. Thus:

I signed the treaty and followed the orders and advice of Gen. Babcock as I was ordered to do, and am ready to carry out all orders that may be sent me, without personal or selfish motives which I regret to think influence some parties who have acted *here* in connection with this matter.[97]

[95] Perry to Fish, June 7, 1870, *Santo Domingo, Consular Desp.,* vol. 6, MS. Dept. of State.
[96] Perry to Fish, December 10, 1869, *ibid.*
[97] Perry to Fish, December 28, 1869, *ibid.*

It is quite possible that both Secretary Fish and President Grant were much more impressed with a letter from Colonel Fabens, who had been authorized by General Babcock to take charge of American interests at Samaná Bay. Fabens was positive that all Dominicans were

well satisfied with the proposed change in sovereignty, and I believe that if a vote were to be taken today on the question of annexation, it would be decided in the affirmative without a dissenting voice. . . . On the Sunday following the raising of the U. S. flag, I attended service at the American Wesleyan Chapel. . . . The chaplain, Revd. Jacob James, explained in a clear and forcible manner the character of the great political change about to take place. . . . The scene was very touching, for the whole congregation of several hundred were responding with tears and sobs of grateful joy.[98]

It is very apparent that by January, 1870 President Grant and Senator Sumner were regarding the project for the annexation of the Dominican Republic from very different viewpoints. Both Grant and Secretary Fish were deliberately closing their eyes to evidence that was very damaging to the reputations of President Baez, General Cazneau, and Colonel Fabens, while Senator Sumner was daily receiving letters which confirmed his suspicions of these same characters. Moreover, Grant was seemingly unaware of the growing hostility of Sumner to these adventurers who were promoting Dominican annexation only because it appeared to promise large pecuniary profits. Unacquainted with Sumner's attitude in this regard, and ardently wishing to prepare the way for the transmission to the Senate of the two Dominican treaties, Grant decided to pay a visit to the home of the Massachusetts Senator and secure his unquestioned support of the annexation project.

In Washington it has often been the case that a good dinner is a pleasant prelude to a diplomatic bargain. In most instances, however, these dinners are carefully planned and the guests selected with discretion. Perhaps it was because these precautions were not complied with that a certain dinner at Sumner's residence on the evening of the first Sunday in January,

[98] Fabens to Fish, December 30, 1869, *Dominican Republic, Notes,* vol. 2, MS. Dept. of State.

1870 was a dismal failure. Sumner had invited as his guests two well-known newspaper men of that day, Colonel John W. Forney and Ben: Perley Poore. At the close of the dinner Colonel Forney read a letter that he had received from James M. Ashley, who had just been superseded by Colonel Potts as Governor of Montana Territory. Both Sumner and Colonel Forney were friends of Ashley, and they were discussing plans to secure for him another position when the outside door-bell was rung and some one was heard inquiring whether Senator Sumner was at home. Poore at once recognized the voice of President Grant, and Sumner hastened to the door and soon returned with the President whom he placed in a seat opposite to his own. Sumner offered the President a glass of sherry wine, which he declined, and then Colonel Forney resumed the discussion about Ashley. In order that the President might understand the background of the discussion, Colonel Forney handed to Sumner the letter from Ashley and requested that he read it aloud. Sumner immediately began reading in a very sonorous tone of voice, and as he proceeded the face of the President became highly flushed with anger.

As soon as Sumner had concluded his reading of the letter, the President broke through his usual reserve and heatedly denounced Ashley as a " mischief-maker and worthless fellow." He then expressed the hope that Sumner would support the nomination of Colonel Potts when it came before the Committee on the Judiciary.[99] In reply Sumner, in a courteous man-

[99] The removal of Ashley as Governor of Montana Territory was largely dictated by the exigencies of Ohio politics. Colonel B. F. Potts was an important member of the political machine of John Sherman, and he was deeply disappointed when he learned of Ashley's appointment. Writing to Sherman on October 18, 1869, he expressed his surprise at the Ashley appointment and predicted that Ashley would " disgrace the party by his conduct in Montana." *John Sherman Papers*, MS. Library of Congress. When Ashley was removed in December, 1869, he immediately wrote to Sherman to solicit his support. He declared that he had " done no act and uttered no word to which a Republican Administration ought to object." Ashley to Sherman, December 20, 1869, *Sherman Papers*. Ashley, however, had no chance of securing Sherman's support, for Sherman was endeavoring to arrange for the appointment of Colonel Potts as Ashley's successor. On December 20, 1869 Potts wrote to Sherman with regard to the position of Governor of Montana Territory, and he clearly indicated how greatly he depended upon Sherman for political influence: " I shall depend upon you to manage this affair with the President." *Sherman Papers*. It is

ner, informed the President that he was chairman of the Senate Committee on Foreign Relations and not of the Senate Committee on the Judiciary. After this little lesson on the membership of Senate committees had been inflicted upon the uncomprehending President, the dinner party was adjourned to Sumner's library.

It was not long before the question of the annexation of the Dominican Republic was alluded to, and the President made a fervid plea in favor of this measure. At the close of his remarks he turned to Sumner and addressed him as follows:

Now, I am told that you are chairman of the Judiciary Committee, before whom such matters come, and that if you will aid it the thing can be accomplished.

Sumner again quietly corrected the President and informed him that he was chairman of the Senate Committee on Foreign Relations and not of the Committee on the Judiciary. Such a correction, however, was lost upon the President who continually repeated the same mistake during the course of the evening's conversation.

After the President had expressed his views at length, it

evident, therefore, that John Sherman and Grant were working together in close harmony, and that Sherman was receiving a large amount of patronage.

The importance of the Ashley issue to Sumner is told in graphic fashion in a letter from Senator T. O. Howe to Hamilton Fish on November 8, 1877: " I have never doubted that Mr. Sumner then at the interview resolved to make his support of the treaty conditional upon Ashley's restoration. In his speech he dwelt upon the caution with which he selected the words he uttered to Genl. Grant. My conclusion from his narrative was that he did not intend to commit himself, by a distinct promise to support the Treaty. This conclusion was strengthened by two or three other circumstances. 1st. Harlan told me the Treaty had been before the Com. of For. Rel. for weeks before he had the least hint that Sumner wd. oppose it. 2d. When the treaty had been in Com. a long time he asked me what I thought of it. I told him frankly I was very sorry it was ever negotiated. But he did not intimate the slightest objection to it. 3rd. I never saw him so excited as when Potts was confirmed in place of Ashley. I had spoken & voted for confirmation. The day was hot. After the vote I went to a window in the Coat room which opened to the south Corridor. Mrs. Lippincott stopped at the open window to speak to me. While we were speaking Mr. Sumner came out, fanning himself violently, white with excitement & stepping to my side, said to Mrs. L., ' Mrs. Lippincott, the Senate has just done a dreadful thing.' I said, ' Mr. S. is in fun.' He repeated with vehemence ' a most brutal thing! ' " MS. *Fish Papers.*

seemed to Sumner that his chief desire was to secure support for certain expenditures that General Babcock had made with reference to the Dominican negotiations. These expenditures had been made from the secret service funds of the Department of State, and to Sumner it appeared that the President was apprehensive that there might be some criticism of him in the Senate on that point.[100] As a matter of fact the President was not thinking primarily of this expenditure from the secret service fund, and his main purpose in visiting Sumner's residence was to secure his support of the treaty for the annexation of the Dominican Republic. It was very plainly a case of misunderstanding, although it should be recorded that both Colonel Forney and Poore gathered the impression from Grant's conversation that he was endeavoring to enlist Sumner's support of the treaty of annexation, and in this regard their impression was distinctly different from that of Sumner.

When the President was ready to leave he promised to send General Babcock to call on Sumner the following day and leave with him some pertinent correspondence. Sumner then escorted the President to the door, and his farewell words were to the effect that " he was a Republican, a supporter of a Republican Administration, and that he should sustain the Administration in this case if he possibly could, after he had examined the papers." [101]

Grant returned to the White House with the expectation of Sumner's support of the treaty of annexation, and when the

[100] Some months later there was sharp criticism in the public press on this very point that the President had made a misuse of the secret service fund in pushing forward the Dominican treaties. The New York *World*, on March 20, 1870, carried a comment to the effect that the main reason for Grant's insistence upon the ratification of these treaties was the fact that " he has spent already one hundred thousand dollars of the secret service fund in carrying out this scheme, and he hardly likes to face Congress without anything to show for all this money." Ten days later, March 30, 1870, the *World* returned to the attack with the following observation: " Buying Dominicans seems as natural as taking presents or travelling ' free ' in Fisk's steamboats. . . . Presidents do not hesitate to admit that, without stint or scruple, they have secretly used money to induce foreigners to sell us territory for which we shall have to pay publicly a great deal more."

[101] Letter of Ben: Perley Poore to the Boston *Journal*, dated October 21, 1877 and published in the Boston *Journal* on October 24, 1877.

Senator did not fulfill this expectation he denounced him as one who had broken an explicit promise. From the point of view of Grant there was no question but that Sumner had broken faith. On June 8, 1870, in answer to a letter of inquiry from Senator Zachariah Chandler, he gave his version of the affair as follows:

I did call at Senator Sumner's residence during the first week of Jan'y last for the express purpose of consulting with him relative to the treaty which had been negotiated. He seemed to be much interested in the matter and requested me to send Gen. Babcock to see him to inform him more fully of the terms of the treaty, the resources of the island etc. I will not pretend to quote the exact language of the Senator but he did reply to the direct question from Colonel Forney, who was present during the interview, "whether he would support the treaty," in such language as to leave no doubt upon my mind that he would support it. Col. Forney will sustain this statement.[102]

Two days earlier, June 6, 1870, General Babcock had written to Colonel Forney with reference to this interview between Sumner and Grant, and he inquired whether Sumner had not given to Grant the following pledge: "Mr. President, I could not think of doing otherwise than supporting the treaty."[103]

Colonel Forney wrote an immediate answer to this inquiry from General Babcock. It was a very clear-cut confirmation of the Grant version:

I was present at Mr. Sumner's residence when President Grant called and explained the Dominican treaty to the Senator; and, although I cannot recall the exact words of the latter, I understood him to say that he would cheerfully support the treaty.[104]

In his speech on December 21, 1870 Sumner denied that he had given any explicit pledge to Grant concerning the treaty of annexation, and he vehemently asserted that his promise

---

[102] Grant to Chandler, June 8, 1870, *Zachariah Chandler Papers*, MS. Library of Congress. Also, *Grant Letter Book*, MS. Library of Congress, and letter from Chandler to Grant, June 7, 1870, *Chandler Papers*, also in *Misc. Papers*, MS. New York Public Library.

[103] Babcock to Forney, June 6, 1870, *Chandler Papers*.

[104] Forney to Babcock, June 6, 1870, printed in the Washington *National Daily Republican*, December 23, 1870.

to the President was given in the following words: " Mr. President, I am an Administration man, and whatever you do will always find in me the most careful and candid consideration." [105]

It is interesting to note that Colonel Forney, in a letter to the Philadelphia *Press,* October 3, 1877, confirms in a striking manner the Sumner version of the famous pledge to President Grant. According to this Forney letter the promise that Sumner made to Grant was phrased as follows:

Well, Mr. President, I am a Republican and an administration man, and I will do all I can properly to make your administration a success. I will give the subject my best thought, and will do all I can rightly and consistently to aid you.[106]

The task of reconciling the statement that Colonel Forney issued on June 6, 1870 with that which he issued on October 3, 1877 is one that the present writer cheerfully leaves to the reader. It is certainly true, however, that when this dinner party was finally over on that Sunday night in January, 1870, President Grant, Colonel Forney, Poore, and Secretary Boutwell, who also called on this fateful evening, were all of the opinion that Sumner was pledged to support the Dominican treaty. Never was a misunderstanding between a President and a chairman of the Senate Committee on Foreign Relations more fraught with bitterness for both.[107]

---

[105] *Cong. Globe,* 41 Cong., 3 sess., p. 243. With reference to Sumner's statement concerning his ambiguous pledge to Grant, Senator Conkling made the following remark that voiced the feelings of many of his Senatorial colleagues. Thus: " Did that honorable member believe, when the President left his house that night . . . that the President left . . . in doubt? Did he intend the President to leave his house doubting that he would support the treaty, and understanding that the Senator promised only that attention which the oath of every member of this body requires from him? No sir." *Ibid.,* p. 245.

[106] Quoted in the New York *Herald,* October 5, 1877.

[107] Boutwell was Secretary of the Treasury under President Grant, and by some strange coincidence he, on this same Sunday evening, called at Sumner's residence, where he met Grant, Forney, and Poore. He was present when Sumner escorted Grant to the door and gave his pledge of support, which Boutwell remembered as follows: " I expect, Mr. President, to support the measures of your Administration." In this regard see *A Chapter in Diplomatic History* by J. C. Bancroft Davis (N. Y., 1893), p. 51. On the day following this dinner, General Babcock called to see Sumner, and the effect of his visit upon the Senator from Massachu-

On January 7, 1870 President Grant, believing that he had Sumner's support of the treaty for Dominican annexation, signed the vouchers for the " allowance of payments of secret service money " from the funds of the Department of State. General Babcock received $700 in gold to defray the expenses he had incurred, while Spofford, Tileston and Company was given $460 in payment for transportation facilities that had been furnished to the General.[108] Three days later (January 10), Grant sent to the Senate the treaty for the lease of Samaná Bay and the treaty which provided for the annexation of the Dominican Republic to the United States.[109]

On January 9, the New York *Herald* printed a short paragraph that anticipated the despatch of the annexation treaty to the Senate:

Some of our contemporaries have at last made the discovery which we announced to our readers two or three weeks ago, viz., that a treaty for the annexation of the republic of Dominica (about three-fourths of the island of Hayti), agreed upon between the high contracting parties, will very soon be laid before the Senate.

The other New York newspapers were soon filled with comments upon the treaty for Dominican annexation, and their attitude was not as friendly as Grant had hoped.[110] The cue was now given to the friends of the treaty to exert all possible pressure upon the Senate in hopes of securing prompt ratification. Samuel L. Barlow hurriedly wrote to Senator Thomas

setts is well described in the letter from Ben: Perley Poore that was published in the Boston *Journal,* October 24, 1877: "Mr. Sumner told me subsequently that when Gen. Babcock called the next day with a copy of the treaty he read no further than the preamble, in which Babcock was styled ' Aid-de-Camp of His Excellency General Ulysses S. Grant,' before he became prejudiced against it. When he proceeded and read the stipulation that ' His Excellency General Grant, President of the United States, promises privately to use all his influence in order that the idea of annexing the Dominican Republic to the United States may acquire such a degree of popularity among the members of Congress as will be necessary for its accomplishment,' he became the enemy of the whole scheme. He did not believe that the President of the United States should be made a lobbyist to bring about annexation by Congress. I fear, from what Mr. Sumner himself told me, that Gen. Babcock was not very well treated."

[108] MS. *Fish Diary,* January 7, 1870.
[109] J. D. Richardson, *Messages and Papers of the Presidents,* III, 45-46.
[110] MS. *Fish Diary,* January 15, 1870.

F. Bayard to express the hope that he would "examine the whole matter." Barlow himself was warmly in favor of Dominican annexation as well as the additional annexation of

the other Islands on our Coast, in a national point of view. We need them to produce sugar, coffee, indigo, and in fact all of the productions of the Tropics, which we now import. . . . [Santo Domingo was] the best Island of all and can be made to produce as much and export as much as it did before the revolution when its exports exceeded those of *all* the other Islands. . . . Last, but not least, I have already a large investment in land, part of which, when we own it [the Dominican Republic], I mean to use and occupy.[111]

On February 1, Barlow returned to this theme of Dominican annexation and frankly stated that he did not care just what method was used in acquiring Santo Domingo, "whether by Treaty, or under the Admiralty as flotsam or jetsam." The main thing was to secure possession as soon as possible.[112] Some weeks later, Barlow wrote to inquire what was likely to be done about Santo Domingo. He declared: "You know I have a personal interest."[113] Although Bayard did not vote in favor of Dominican annexation,[114] these letters from Barlow give an interesting indication of the personal pressure that was exerted in behalf of that treaty.

At this point there arose a very complicated constitutional question which later received an extended discussion in the Senate of the United States. This question involved the war powers of the President of the United States and, in particular, his power to protect the "inchoate interests" of the American Government. In 1844 a precedent had been established by President Tyler when he signed the treaty providing for the annexation of Texas. The commissioners from Texas had been promised that after this treaty was signed and while ratification by the Senate was pending, the President would employ all the means placed within his power by the Constitution of

[111] Barlow to Bayard, January 25, 1870, *Thomas F. Bayard Papers*, MS. Library of Congress.
[112] Barlow to Bayard, February 1, 1870, *ibid.*
[113] Barlow to Bayard, March 28, 1870, *ibid.*
[114] New York *Herald*, July 1, 1870.

the United States to protect Texas against all foreign invasion.[115] In a special message to the Senate, on May 15, 1844, Tyler strongly defended his power to make this pledge,[116] and in 1869-1870 President Grant based his Dominican policy upon the Tyler precedent.

The constitutional warrant for such a protective policy was clearly outlined in an order from Robeson, the Secretary of the Navy, to Rear-Admiral S. P. Lee on March 21, 1871:

The President of the United States has by the Constitution the right to make treaties, subject to the ratification of the Senate. . . . Thus he had the constitutional power to negotiate treaties for the cession of Samana and the annexation of the Dominican Republic. . . . These treaties were of course inchoate and subject to be confirmed or defeated by the action of the Senate of the United States, and of the people of the Dominican Republic; but by such treaties and pending such final action, the United States acquired an interest in the thing negotiated for, which could not be rightfully disturbed by any other power; and it was the plain duty of the Executive to protect, if need be, the integrity of this constitutionally acquired interest.[117]

In the Dominican Republic there was a strong party of opposition to any plan of annexation to the United States, and this party was vigorously led by General Luperón and by former President Cabral, who, from motives of prudence, directed their campaigns against President Baez from points of vantage outside the Dominican Republic. In carrying out their plans for the overthrow of the Baez Administration these conspirators also supported the pretensions of Nissage Saget to the presidency of Haiti, expecting in the event of his success against President Salnave to receive his assistance against President Baez. The result of these revolutionary conspiracies was to keep both Haiti and the Dominican Republic in a constantly disturbed state, and as early as December, 1869 the Baez Gov-

---

[115] C. C. Tansill, "War Powers of the President of the United States with Special Reference to the Beginning of Hostilities," *Political Science Quarterly*, XLV (1930), 41 ff.

[116] J. D. Richardson, *op. cit.*, IV, 317. See also J. S. Reeves, *American Diplomacy under Tyler and Polk* (Balto., 1907), pp. 145 ff.

[117] *Confidential Letters*, vol. 5, MS. Navy Department Library.

ernment was sending repeated complaints to the United States concerning invasions by Haitian troops.[118] In January, 1870 President Salnave was captured by Cabral, who promptly turned him over to Nissage Saget. After a farcical trial Salnave was placed before a firing squad, and Saget became President of Haiti.[119] With Saget in support of Cabral against the Baez Government in the Dominican Republic, it was inevitable that Baez would quickly solicit the assistance of the American Government. The response of President Grant was immediate and forceful.

On January 29 the President had a conference with the Secretary of the Navy relative to the despatch of war-ships to Dominican waters,[120] and on February 19 Robeson instructed Commodore Joseph F. Green as follows:

You will receive your special instructions hereafter from the Rear Admiral commanding the North Atlantic Fleet, but for the present it is desirable that you should remain with the force under your command in and about the Island of San Domingo, especially the part belonging to the Dominican Government, and the Isthmus of Samana, for the cession of which the United States are now in treaty with the Dominican Government. While the treaty is pending the government of the United States has agreed to afford countenance and assistance to the Dominican people against their enemies now in the Island, and in revolution against the lawfully constituted government, and you will use the force at your command to resist any attempts by enemies of the Dominican

[118] Gautier to Perry, December 27, 1869, January 8, 1870, *Dominican Republic, Notes*, vol. 2, MS. Dept. of State.

[119] Samuel Hazard, *Santo Domingo, Past and Present*, pp. 432 ff. In a long note of January 19, 1870, Secretary Gautier informed Secretary Fish of the capture and execution of Salnave and indicated the connection between Saget and ex-President Cabral: " Nissage being now triumphant, and being indebted to Cabral for the service which the latter has rendered him by his perfidy towards Salnave, it is evident that this protection will assume a more serious character." *Dominican Republic, Notes*, vol. 2, MS. Dept. of State. For descriptions of the defeat and murder of President Salnave see Bassett to Fish, January 15, 1870, *Hayti, Desp.*, vol. 3, MS. Dept. of State, and New York *Herald*, January 28, 1870.

[120] MS. *Fish Diary*. In a letter of January 18, 1870, Commander E. K. Owen gave Secretary Robeson a colorful picture of conditions in Haiti. Americans were greatly disliked in Haiti, but " no violence has yet been offered to their persons. The American Minister has been occasionally insulted by the people and our flag hooted." *Dominican Republic, Notes*, vol. 2, MS. Dept. of State.

Republic to invade the Dominican territory by land or sea, so far as your power can reach them.[121]

The despatch of war-ships to West Indian waters raised serious constitutional questions in the mind of Senator Sumner, who soon became strongly antagonistic to the whole Dominican policy of President Grant. Soon after this opposition became manifest, Colonel Fabens decided to call on the Senator from Massachusetts for the purpose of explaining to him the obvious advantages of Dominican annexation. The result of such a meeting could easily have been forecast by anyone familiar with Sumner's disposition. He promptly assured Colonel Fabens that it would be impossible for him to advocate the treaty, and then Fabens proposed that the Senator sit down and write a treaty which he could support, asserting at the same time that it would be agreed to by Baez. Mr. Sumner was unwilling, however, to consent to annexation on any terms, and gave Fabens his reasons.

During the conversation, Mr. Sumner asked Fabens if he thought that annexation would stop with Santo Domingo.

---

[121] *Confidential Letters*, vol. 5, MS. Navy Department Library. It should be remembered that as early as July 10 and July 13, 1869, Commander Owen had received instructions to assist the Baez Government against attacks of revolutionists. See *ante*, pp. 360-361. It is also important to note that in December, 1869 Captain Bunce, of the U. S. Steamer *Nantucket*, had visited Jacmel on the south coast of Haiti and had informed the authorities there that " any hostile steps taken against the Dominican Republic would be considered as an unfriendly act against the United States Government." Perry to Fish, December 28, 1869, *Santo Domingo, Consular Desp.*, vol. 6, MS. Dept. of State. On February 4, 1870, Secretary Fish instructed E. D. Bassett, the American Minister to Haiti, to notify the Haitian Government that he would be compelled to terminate all relations with it in the event that Haitian troops were not immediately " withdrawn from the Dominican territory." *Hayti, Inst.*, vol. 1, MS. Dept. of State. Bassett hastened to carry out these instructions, and on February 9 he arranged to have Rear-Admiral C. H. Poor call upon the members of the Provisional Government of Haiti and tell them " quite pointedly " that the United States would not brook any interference with its plans in the Dominican Republic. E. D. Bassett to Fish, February 17, 1870, *Hayti, Desp.*, vol. 3, MS. Dept. of State. On February 10 Admiral Poor sent a note to Nissage Saget, the Provisional President of Haiti, informing him of the pending negotiations between the Dominican Republic and the United States. Any " interference or attack therefore by vessels under the Haytien or any other Flag upon Dominicans during the pendency of said negotiations, will be considered an act of hostility to the Flag of the United States, and will provoke hostility in return." *Ibid.*

"Oh, no!" replied the Dominican Envoy, "you must have Hayti too."

"And is that all?" continued the Senator.

Fabens thought that we could not stop with Hayti, but must, in the nature of things finally absorb Porto Rico, Jamaica, Cuba, the Windward Islands, and, indeed, all of the West Indies.[122]

After having dismally failed to convert Sumner into an advocate for Dominican annexation, Fabens next called on Secretary Fish from whom he received another cool reception. During the course of his conversation with the Secretary he indicated that he had been appointed by President Baez as an Envoy Extraordinary of the Dominican Republic for the special purpose of expediting annexation to the United States. When Secretary Fish inquired as to his credentials, Fabens replied that he had "already presented them to the President." Fish bridled at this and administered a sharp rebuke to Fabens for following such an "extremely irregular" procedure. He next informed him that "he had no right to present himself to the President except through the Secretary of State."

Fabens hurriedly explained that he had called on the President only through the earnest solicitation of General Babcock, but Fish refused to be placated and warned him that he had laid the basis for the charge that the Dominican treaties had been negotiated "outside of the regular channels." Fabens next anxiously sought General Babcock who placed the matter before President Grant. In the eyes of the President the question of Dominican annexation was of such paramount importance as to justify any irregularities in the usual diplomatic procedure. It was several days, however, before Grant summoned Fish to the White House and in his characteristic manner assumed the entire responsibility for the conduct of Fabens. Such a gesture on the part of the President clearly revealed to Fish the warmth of the President's conviction that the annexation of the Dominican Republic must be consummated at all costs.[123]

While Fabens was having his troubles in the United States,

[122] New York *Tribune*, April 5, 1871.
[123] MS. *Fish Diary*, April 29, May 3, 1870.

his confederates in the Dominican Republic were making every effort to assure an affirmative plebiscite on the question of annexation to the United States. They even went so far as to secure the imprisonment of an influential American citizen, Davis Hatch, who, they feared, would attempt to defeat the treaties. The prolonged detention of Hatch in a Dominican jail eventually raised a storm of protest in the United States and caused the Senate to appoint a committee to investigate the whole matter. The majority report of this committee practically justified the imprisonment of Hatch for revolutionary activities, while the minority report denounced his detention as clearly illegal and called upon the President to demand of the Government of the Dominican Republic " full reparation for the sufferings and losses of Davis Hatch." [124]

The evidence in the case of the imprisonment of Davis Hatch is very voluminous, and a large portion of it would seem to indicate that Baez, Gautier, Babcock, Cazneau, and Fabens were determined to effect the annexation of the Dominican Republic by fair means or foul. Each member of this little

---

[124] *Sen. Rep.* No. 234, 41 Cong., 2 sess., previously referred to as the *Hatch Report*. On the imprisonment of Hatch there is additional material in the archives of the Department of State, in the *Sumner Papers* in the Harvard College Library, in the *Banks Papers* in the Essex Institute, and in the *Schurz Papers* in the Library of Congress. According to Perry, the American Commercial Agent at Santo Domingo City, General Babcock, General Cazneau, and Colonel Fabens were all privy to the plot to keep Hatch in prison until annexation had been effected. Indeed, Babcock told Perry to make no attempt to secure the release of Hatch because it was feared that he " would work against the Treaty." Perry to Fish, June 7, 1870, *Santo Domingo, Consular Desp.,* vol. 6, MS. Dept. of State. In the *Fish Diary*, on December 5, 1870, there is a notation to the effect that President Grant informed Fish that Hatch was naturalized as a Spanish subject, and that General Babcock had a copy of this naturalization paper in which Hatch renounced his allegiance to the United States. With reference to this charge, Hatch wrote to Senator William A. Buckingham, of Connecticut, on December 13, 1870, and strongly denied that he had ever been naturalized as a Dominican subject. In regard to the existence of a naturalization certificate proving this transfer of allegiance, Hatch remarks as follows: " It is scarcely necessary, I presume, for me to say to you that no such document can exist. All foreigners engaging in business in the Spanish Colonies are obliged to become ' domiciled.' I forward the ' Carta de Domicilio ' given me some months after I took up my residence there, which is the only engagement entered into with the Spanish Government regarding my personal status." *Schurz Papers,* MS. Library of Congress.

group played an important rôle in preparing the way for annexation, but the mantle of leadership really rested upon the ample shoulders of General Cazneau. Since 1854 he had been carefully maturing plans for exploiting the natural resources of the Dominican Republic, and these plans necessarily involved some form of American political control. The General would have been satisfied either with the outright annexation of the Dominican Republic to the United States or with the establishment of an American protectorate over it. In 1870 it appeared to him that annexation could be accomplished if President Grant controlled the American Senate, and he reposed great confidence in the fact that the President was the idol of millions of Americans who regarded him as the military genius who had saved the American Union. Apparently Cazneau had little doubt that Grant would be successful, and he bestirred himself to ensure a favorable plebiscite in the Dominican Republic.

On December 28, 1869, Perry reported that he had been assured by President Baez that " everything relating to the election for annexation is working very favorably." [125] Some weeks later Perry wrote again to Secretary Fish to indicate the growing sentiment in favor of annexation to the United States. So fast was this favorable opinion developing that President Baez believed that it would be " almost impossible to prevent the people pronouncing for annexation before the proper time." [126]

Baez and Gautier, however, were distinctly cautious about taking any premature steps relative to securing a favorable plebiscite on the annexation treaty, and they admitted to Perry their fears that if they did " not succeed in the vote for annexation and our Government did not accept them, . . . it would cost them their lives." [127] The Dominican Presi-

---

[125] Perry to Fish, December 28, 1869, *Santo Domingo, Consular Desp.*, vol. 6, MS. Dept. of State.

[126] Perry to Fish, January 20, 1870, *ibid.* For opinion hostile to the annexation treaty see the petition presented to the United States Senate on February 7, 1870 by a group of Dominican revolutionists residing in Curaçao. See *Dominican Republic, Notes,* vol. 3, MS. Dept. of State.

[127] Perry to Fish, June 7, 1870, *Santo Domingo, Consular Desp.*, vol. 6, MS. Dept. of State.

dent wished to have American war-ships in Dominican waters before the plebiscite was taken, and he strongly preferred to have the United States Senate consent to the ratification of the annexation treaty before any final action should be taken by the Dominican Government.[128] This display of caution on the part of Baez made a deep impression on Major Perry, the American Commercial Agent, who went immediately to see General Cazneau to communicate his doubts about any plebiscite being held in the near future. No sooner had Major Perry broached this subject of an indefinite postponement of the plebiscite when General Cazneau became "very much excited," and boasted to the Commercial Agent that he held President Baez "between his thumb and finger," and that he would "compel him to have the vote at once." [129]

As a result of this pressure exerted by General Cazneau, a decree was issued on February 16, 1870 providing for the holding of a plebiscite on February 19 with reference to annexation to the United States. On the day following the plebiscite Major Perry was able to report that the vote in Santo Domingo City was "unanimous for annexation" and that everything seemed "quiet and favorable." [130] At the end of a week it was apparent that the vote on the question of annexation to the United States was overwhelmingly favorable, and on March 17, 1870 Secretary Gautier wrote to one of the Dominican officials and announced that more than sixteen thousand votes had been cast, "with an opposition not amounting to two per cent." [131] Two days later Gautier wrote to the American Secretary of State and gave a distinctly different estimate of the adverse vote. After commenting on the large number of votes that had been cast in the plebiscite, he declared:

For the first time in the history of this country, an almost unanimous vote has been obtained with more than *ninety* per cent. in favor of the measure.[132]

[128] Perry to Fish, February 8, 1870, *ibid.*

[129] Perry to Fish, June 7, 1870, *ibid.*

[130] Perry to Fish, February 20, 1870, *ibid.*

[131] Gautier to David Coën, March 17, 1870, *Dominican Republic, Notes,* vol. 2, MS. Dept. of State.

[132] Gautier to Fish, March 19, 1870, *ibid.* The italics are the author's. For

Secretary Gautier also assured Fish that the plebiscite had been conducted in a legal and peaceful manner. Major Perry, the American Commercial Agent, gives a different picture of the manner of holding this plebiscite, and it is possible that his statement is slightly more accurate. After General Cazneau began to exert pressure upon President Baez in favor of an immediate plebiscite, Major Perry noticed that a band of musicians paraded the streets of Santo Domingo City, and that along with this musical feast there were certain vocal demonstrations in favor of annexation. Next a list was opened in the headquarters of the municipal police for citizens to register their names. According to Major Perry, however, the actual voting was not without some effective restraint:

Baez and Delmonte have told me several times that any man who opposed annexation, they would either shoot him or send him his passport; they have also told me that it should be a free vote of the people, but such was not the case. . . . I have seen Baez . . . shake his fist in the face of some of his nearest friends . . . and tell them he would banish them from the Island if they opposed annexation.[133]

After this favorable plebiscite had been secured relative to annexation to the United States, an effort was made by General Cazneau and his associates to induce immigrants from the United States to settle in the Dominican Republic. On March 24, there was published in the New York press a statement by General Cazneau relative to the plentiful labor supply that was ready to till the fertile fields or work the rich mines of the Dominican Republic. He said in part:

further information relative to the plebiscite see the *Boletin Oficial*, February 19 and March 5, 1870. See also the New York *Herald*, March 24, 1870. In a note to Secretary Fish, on May 14, 1870, Colonel Fabens stated that the result of the plebiscite was " fifteen thousand one hundred and sixty nine votes in favor of the measure and eleven in opposition." *Dominican Republic, Notes,* vol. 2, MS. Dept. of State. In the New York *Tribune* of May 3, 1870, there is the following paragraph: " The complete elections returns of San Domingo on the Annexation question have just been received here in official form. The act contains over 15,000 signatures in favor of annexation to the United States, and but 110 against it."

[133] Perry to Fish, June 7, 1870, *Santo Domingo, Consular Desp.,* vol. 6, MS. Dept. of State.

As an economical, acclimated and perfectly manageable industrial power, already on the field where it is needed, and which can instantly be made highly remunerative to American capital and enterprise, I consider the colored working population of this island one of its most valuable features in view of annexation. There is not a man too many of this class, and their presence near the coffee and sugar lands, . . . will treble the price and productive value of those fine regions from the first year in which systematic farming is introduced in them.[134]

General Cazneau was also instrumental in having published in American newspapers certain extracts from a letter written by a credulous American who was making a canvass of investment opportunities for his fellow-countrymen. This letter paid a warm tribute to the ample opportunities that awaited the investment of American capital. The gold fields of the Dominican Republic were of astonishing richness, but the easy road to the rapid accumulation of great wealth lay in the development of the agricultural resources of the island. It was apparent that an industrious immigrant would need only the small sum required to buy a " few acres of land and a small outfit to be certain of a fortune in a few years." [135]

It was obvious that Cazneau and his clique had done everything they could to pave the way for annexation. It was now up to the President to exert all possible pressure upon the Senate in order to insure a favorable vote on the pending treaty of annexation. Grant was not one to shirk a responsibility and he bent every effort to shatter Senate opposition. Antiimperialism, however, was a fast-rising tide, and if Grant had read history instead of merely making it he might have given heed to that pertinent and familiar lesson which in another age had been inflicted upon the tide-defying King Canute.

[134] New York *Herald*, March 24, 1870.
[135] *Ibid.*

CHAPTER X

SENATOR SUMNER PLAYS THE PART
OF PYRRHUS

While President Grant was quietly preparing plans to exert pressure upon Republican members of the Senate for the purpose of securing the ratification of the treaty providing for Dominican annexation, certain rumors reached Washington that General Cazneau and his clique were facing unexpected difficulties with reference to their schemes for exploiting the alleged rich resources of the Dominican Republic. In 1869 J. Somers Smith, the American Commercial Agent, had been removed by Grant because he evinced sharp hostility towards Cazneau, Babcock, and Fabens. In his place there had been sent Major Raymond Perry, whose dubious background seemed to promise that he would work in harmony with men who cared more for personal profit than for principle. But even Perry's blunted sensibilities revolted at the schemes of Cazneau and Company, and soon he began to voice to Secretary Fish his suspicions of their motives. By the spring of 1870 his complaints to the Secretary of State concerning Cazneau, Fabens, and Babcock gathered volume and took on a higher note. With regard to the imprisonment of Davis Hatch it was his opinion that

Cazneau and Fabens have used their influence to keep him [Hatch] where he is, for certain selfish and financial reasons known to themselves.[1]

Nearly two weeks later Perry sent to Secretary Fish a sharper denunciation of Cazneau and Fabens:

During my official duties at this place I have come in contact with a Mr. Cazneau and Fabens who are corresponding with General Bab-

[1] Perry to Fish, February 8, 1870, *Santo Domingo, Consular Desp.*, vol. 6, MS. Dept. of State. It is significant that Secretary Fish did not print this sentence in the correspondence he sent to Congress. See *Sen. Ex. Doc.* No. 54, 41 Cong., 2 sess.

cock. The former represents himself as the special and confidential agent of my Government and makes his boast that he is in direct communication with the President of the United States etc. . . . I found it necessary to tell this man in the presence of President Baez and his Cabinet that he was a "trickster and a dishonest man." [2]

At this same time Perry was exerting all his influence to bring to an end the imprisonment of Davis Hatch. On March 8, he addressed to Secretary Gautier a note in which he abruptly demanded the immediate release of Hatch.[3] On the following day he sent to Secretary Gautier a second note, of similar tenor, which elicited a prompt reply from that official. Gautier had read Major Perry's note with "astonishment," and it had served to increase the "painful impression" which the note of March 8 had created. Gautier wished to assure Major Perry that in this matter of the detention of Hatch the Dominican Government had been guided only by the "best principles of equity and justice," and that his government would give the whole question further consideration.[4] On March 17 Hatch was released in care of Major Perry, who lost no time in sending him to Havana, thus closing an incident which threatened serious complications and led to an investigation by a committee of the United States Senate.

This "Hatch incident" had many aspects and all of them were related to the plans of General Cazneau. The General would permit no opposition to his schemes for making money out of Dominican annexation, and when Major Perry espoused the cause of Davis Hatch he earned the bitter enmity of Cazneau. It was not long before there was an open quarrel between Cazneau and Perry, and the latter boldly branded the General as a "trickster and a dishonest man." This serious charge against Cazneau resulted not only from his doubtful dealings with Baez and Babcock but also from the fact that, while the treaty of annexation was pending, Cazneau endeavored to secure from the Dominican Government large grants

[2] Perry to Fish, February 20, 1870, *Unofficial, Santo Domingo, Consular Desp.*, vol. 6, MS. Dept. of State.
[3] Perry to Gautier, March 8, 1870, *ibid.*
[4] Gautier to Perry, March 9, 1870, *ibid.*

of public lands and special privileges relative to the introduction of immigrants. As soon as Perry became acquainted with these designs of Cazneau he addressed a letter to the Dominican Senate, on April 30, 1870, in which he protested against any such grants as a violation of Article 6 of the pending treaty of annexation.[5]

On May 3, Secretary Gautier wrote to Perry to complain against the action of the American Commercial Agent in addressing a note to the Dominican Senate relative to the alleged grants to General Cazneau,[6] and on the following day General Cazneau briefly informed Major Perry that he had "altogether misapprehended the case," which in "no wise" fell within the sphere of the duties of Commercial Agent.[7]

While this tempest in a teapot was disturbing the placid quiet of the long Dominican afternoons, the Baez Government, fearful that Senate opposition would defeat the ratification of the treaty of annexation within the time prescribed by that convention, decided to send an envoy to Washington for the purpose of arranging for an extension of time and also for any other necessary modifications of the treaty. On April 16, 1870, credentials were given to Colonel Fabens authorizing him to go to Washington as the Dominican Envoy Extraordinary and Minister Plenipotentiary with "full powers to arrange . . . whatever shall be best suited to the common in-

---

[5] Cazneau had petitioned not only for a grant of 200,000 acres of the public lands of the Dominican Repubic but also for the privilege of introducing for the next two years 2,000 immigrants, 500 of them for the province of Santo Domingo and the balance for the frontier. Each of these immigrants was to receive 100 acres of land. Cazneau reserved to himself the right to control the administration of these lands granted to immigrants, and he was to be the owner of any mines discovered on this same property. Perry to Fish, June 6, 1870, *ibid.*

[6] Gautier to Perry, May 3, 1870, *ibid.*

[7] Cazneau to Perry, May 4, 1870, *ibid.* In a second letter to Major Perry, on May 6, 1870, General Cazneau informed the Commercial Agent that a "proper sense of self-respect" prevented him from answering any of the questions that had been asked him. He does make, however, a revealing statement which is distinctly pertinent: "I now close this correspondence by informing you that your neglect of due official reticence has brought on a premature disclosure of facts that for the public interest should have been held strictly confidential for the present." *Ibid.* In a letter to Secretary Gautier of May 5, 1870, Major Perry discusses the attitude of the Secretary of Foreign Affairs towards the grants of lands to Cazneau and convicts the Secretary of a downright lie. *Ibid.*

terest of both countries."[8]   On April 29 Fabens called at the Department of State for a short conference with Secretary Fish, and when the Secretary of State learned that the Dominican envoy had already presented his credentials to President Grant he administered to him a crushing rebuke. This difficulty was quickly smoothed over by Grant who absolved Fabens from any responsibility for a breach of diplomatic etiquette, and on May 14 Secretary Fish signed an article extending until July 1 the time for the exchange of ratifications.[9]

It was advisable for Fish to sign this article extending the time for the exchange of ratifications because it was now apparent that Senatorial opposition to the treaty of annexation was rapidly developing. On February 21 the Senate had passed a resolution calling upon the Secretary of State to furnish all the correspondence relating to the imprisonment of Davis Hatch, and three days later Grant complied with this request by sending to the Senate a report prepared by the Secretary of State.[10]   On March 14 Grant sent another special message to the Senate, in which he adverted to the fact that a treaty for the annexation of the Dominican Republic had been signed on November 29, 1869, and that the time for the exchange of the ratifications would expire on March 29, 1870.[11]   He then expressed his " earnest wish " that the Senate would not permit the treaty to " expire by limitation." [12]

On the following day the Senate Committee on Foreign Relations reported adversely upon the Dominican treaty,[13] and Grant, now thoroughly aroused, descended upon the Capitol

---

[8] *Dominican Republic, Notes,* vol. 2, MS. Dept. of State.

[9] See *ante* p. 394. Also MS. *Fish Diary,* May 14, 1870.

[10] J. D. Richardson, *Messages and Papers of the Presidents*, VII, 50.

[11] Grant sent this special message to the Senate without first consulting Secretary Fish. At the Cabinet meeting on March 15 Fish remarked: " Well, Mr. President, I suppose I am to regard the sending of a message on such a subject, peculiarly belonging to my Department, without notice to or a consultation with me, as a want of confidence in the administration of my Department." Grant immediately apologized for his action and blamed his secretary, General Porter, who had told him that it was not necessary to send it to Secretary Fish. MS. *Fish Diary*, March 15, 1870.

[12] J. D. Richardson, *op. cit.*, VII, 52-53.

[13] New York *Herald*, March 16, 1870. Apparently the vote in the committee was five nays and two yeas.

to issue peremptory orders to his Senatorial henchmen. Along with him went General Babcock with maps and data to convince doubtful Senators. That any Republican Senators should have doubts about the propriety of Dominican annexation seemed incomprehensible to Grant, and he had little patience with their scruples. According to the New York *World* he visited the Capitol much in the manner of Oliver Cromwell. Upon arriving at the President's room he handed a list of Senators to a messenger with the abrupt command: " Send these men to me immediately." [14]

Because of his solicitude for the fate of the Dominican treaty, Grant also summoned to the White House, on March 22, Senators Carpenter, Patterson, Ferry, Ross, Sprague, Morrill, Pratt, Tipton, Gilbert, Cragin, Revels, Rice, Abbott, Howe, and Harris in order to canvass all possible means of securing a sufficient affirmative vote in the Senate.[15] On other occasions Grant invited certain Senators to the White House for a private conference upon Dominican matters. Senator Carl Schurz, in his *Reminiscences*, gives an interesting account of an audience with Grant which must have been typical of many other conferences between the President and Senators. After Schurz had been seated in the White House library, Grant immediately plunged

into the subject he had at heart. "I hear you are a member of the Senate Committee that has the San Domingo treaty under consideration," he said, "and I wish you would support that treaty. Won't you do

[14] March 20, 1870. On March 26, the *World* again called attention to Grant's visits to the Capitol and repeated its criticism as follows: " He [Grant] does not enter the Senate Chamber. On the contrary, he calls Senators from their duties, like any other vulgar lobbyist, and taking them into the committee-rooms or into out-of-the-way corners, buttonholes them to vote for the Grant-Baez treaty. It is what country lawyers call *horse-shed* practice with jurymen, and is quite as undignified, dishonorable and disgraceful."

[15] New York *Herald*, March 24, 1870. With reference to this presidential pressure exerted upon Senators, Sumner, in his speech of March 27, 1871, commented as follows: "Never before has there been such Presidential intervention in the Senate as we have been constrained to witness. Presidential visits to the Capitol, with appeals to Senators, have been followed by assemblies at the Executive Mansion, also with appeals to Senators; and who can measure the pressure of all kinds by himself or agents, especially through the appointing power, all to secure the consummation of this scheme?" *Cong. Globe*, 42 Cong., 1 sess., p. 304.

that?" I thought it would be best not to resort to any circumlocution in answering so point-blank a summons, but to be perfectly frank. I said I would be sincerely happy to act with his administration whenever and wherever I conscientiously could, but in this case, I was sorry to confess, I was not able to do as he wished, because I was profoundly convinced that it would be against the best interests of the Republic. . . . I spoke with the verve of sincere conviction, and at first the President listened to me with evident interest, looking at me as if the objections to the treaty which I expressed were quite new to him and made an impression upon his mind. But after a little while I noticed that his eyes wandered about the room, and I became doubtful whether he listened to me at all. When I had stopped, he sat silent for a minute or two. I, of course, sat silent too, waiting for him to speak. At last he said in a perfectly calm tone as if nothing had happened: "Well, I hope you will at least vote for the confirmation of Mr. Jones, whom I have selected for a foreign mission." [16]

The debate in the Senate on the treaty of annexation began on March 24, after Sumner delivered a speech in which he opposed the treaty but was careful always to allude to the

---

[16] (3 vols., N. Y., 1908), III, 307. Apparently, Schurz's opposition to the Dominican treaty did not at once awaken Grant's hostility to him. In a letter to Grosvenor of March 31, 1870, Schurz remarks: "Your apprehension of a breach between the Administration and myself has been verified in a less degree than I myself expected. I told Gen. Grant my opinion about the treaty weeks ago with the utmost frankness, while, as I understand, others made him hope that they would support it and then opposed it. I am told that he speaks very highly of my candor. I have met him since I made my speech, and we met and parted very cordially. . . . Of course, the treaty can never be ratified in the Senate by a two thirds majority." *Schurz Papers,* MS. Library of Congress. Because of the liberal use of presidential pressure with reference to Dominican annexation, some newspapers expressed the belief that the President's policy might succeed. The New York *World,* March 25, 1870, hinted that "big business" was behind the annexation movement: "Twenty millions of dollars, backed by the executive patronage, are hard to beat in this rich and balmy metropolitan atmosphere [of Washington]. The Samana Bay treaty ring are reported to consist of about twenty persons, as follows: President Baez, Felix Del Monte, Hollister, Cazneau, Gautier, Curiel, O'Sullivan, Cole, and last, not least, General Babcock. These are to divide the profits which may arise from the enhancement of the St. Domingo property now held and being daily bought by the above parties and their agents. It is said that there is a written paper now in existence in Wall Street, New York City, by virtue of which General Babcock is to have one-twentieth part of all the profits which may arise from the success of the treaty and its correlative speculations."

President with "great courtesy."[17] According to Senator Stewart, the speech by Sumner was "magnificent," and the chief points he developed were as follows:

a. The proposed annexation would probably encourage further American acquisitions of Caribbean territory and would thus involve the United States in serious complications with other powers.

b. There was little likelihood of further intervention by European powers in the affairs of the Dominican Republic.

c. The United States, in the event of annexation, would probably be saddled with a public debt much larger than had been anticipated.

d. Continued civil war and rebellions would be an aftermath of annexation.

e. Annexation would impair the predominance of the colored race in the West Indies and therefore would be unjust to it.[18]

Senator Morton, of Indiana, replied to Sumner in a speech which stressed the opportunity that Dominican annexation presented to America—a "vast territory open to the hand of art and science and industry, and almost without inhabitants." It was difficult, he thought, to estimate "the immense territorial and geographical value of the island."[19]

[17] Washington *Morning Chronicle*, March 26, 1870. These debates on the treaty of annexation were held in executive session, and the only knowledge we have of the speeches that were made is through "leaks" to newspaper correspondents. The very close watch that Grant was keeping on developments in the Senate is partly illustrated by his correspondence with certain members of that body. His following note to Senator John Sherman, of March 30, 1870, is typical: "Your note of this date just received. Presuming that no vote will be reached today on the Dominican treaty, I will take no steps in the matter before tomorrow unless further advised of the necessity of so doing." *Sherman Papers*, MS. Library of Congress.

[18] E. L. Pierce, *Memoir and Letters of Charles Sumner*, IV, 440-441. Sumner had long been friendly to the administration of President Salnave in Haiti, and he had been interested in the political fortunes of the negro republic. This interest was well known and led Mary Hollister, the wife of the American Minister to Haiti, to write the following letter to Sumner on August 7, 1868: "In a recent interview with President Salnave, His Excellency remarked to Mr. Hollister that ' he wished he had a photograph of Senator Sumner, that he would rather see him than any man in America, for he had always been the friend of his race.' Thinking you would be pleased with a likeness of this remarkable man I send you one lately given to my husband." *Sumner Papers*, MS. Harvard College Library.

[19] New York *Herald*, March 26, 1870.

Morton's speech was able and he spoke with a conviction that was impressive. But he did not rely upon his gift of eloquence alone. General Babcock had brought to the Senate many samples of the products of the Dominican Republic, and these were prominently displayed on Morton's desk. The prize exhibit was a giant block of salt from the salt mountains of Neyba. This block was as clear as crystal, and Morton held it aloft as though he were a country auctioneer showing off his wares. The sight of the distinguished Senator from Indiana playing the part of a petty salesman seemed to evoke a spirit of revelry in the Senate, and soon numerous members of that august body crowded around Morton's desk. Forming a line they each took a turn in licking the block of salt as if to test the verity of the Senator's statements. Then like boys at play they staged a tug-of-war with a quantity of Dominican hemp whose great strength alone prevented them from testing " their own extremities." [20]

After this little horse-play was over, the Senators resumed their gravity, and Schurz, Patterson, and Casserly spoke for the opposition, while Cole, Nye, and Stewart supported the Administration.[21] On March 29 the treaty expired by limitation, and after several weeks of desultory debate it was laid aside and no further action was taken on it until late in June. There was little popular sentiment in favor of such a measure, and only a few newspapers came to its defense.[22] In New York City, however, a mass-meeting was called in the Cooper Institute for the evening of May 12, the object being to impress the public with the advantages that would result from Domini-

[20] *Ibid.*

[21] Despite the able opposition of Sumner and his coterie of friends to the treaty of annexation, the New York *Herald,* of March 26, 1870, was of the opinion that " a majority of the Senate will support the measure."

[22] *Nation*, XII (1871), 172-173. The New York *Herald*, the New York *Times*, and the Washington *Morning Chronicle* were three of the newspapers that were fervid in their support of annexation. On March 24, 1870, the New York *Herald* published an editorial which favored annexation and critized Sumner as the " Old Man of the Sea " who had no idea of the destiny of his country. ". . . Mr. Sumner is a croaker, an obstacle and a dead weight in our noble ship of state, and the best thing his colleagues can do is to throw him overboard." See also the *Herald* for March 28 and 29, 1870, and the New York *Times,* March 21, and 23, 1870.

can annexation. General John A. Dix was invited to preside
over this meeting, and General Banks wrote to him on May 7
and warmly urged him to accept the invitation. It seemed to
General Banks that the question of Dominican annexation was a

national not a party question, and will lead I hope to a broader foundation for our govt. policy than now exists in this administration. . . .
I have a deep and strong conviction that the subject will lead to new
and great results in our political affairs.[23]

General Dix, however, remained deaf to this entreaty from
his old friend, and it was finally arranged that Charles H.
Russell, a prominent banker, should be chairman of the meeting. After Russell had thanked the audience for the honor thus
conferred upon him, Moses H. Grinnell, the Collector of the
Port of New York, made a short speech in which he indicated
the obvious advantages that would attend Dominican annexation. General Banks followed with a short address in which
he attempted to show how Dominican annexation would so
strengthen the Monroe Doctrine that the name of President
Grant would be " worthy of being preserved by the side of
Washington as having completed the work Washington commenced, in leaving the American Continent to the American
people."

John Fitch was the last speaker and he rose to lyric heights
in giving praise to the project of Dominican annexation. By

[23] Banks to Dix, May 7, 1870, *Banks Papers*, MS. Essex Institute. This
meeting in New York on May 12 was the result of strenuous efforts on the part
of Colonel Fabens to stimulate public interest in the question of Dominican
annexation. Fabens had returned to New York on April 27, and soon after
went to Washington where he had a long conference with President Grant. On
May 4, 1870 Fabens wrote to Gautier, the Dominican Secretary of Foreign
Affairs, to assure him that the President was " *almost certain* of carrying the
annexation treaty by a 2/3 vote. We went over the list of Senators and counted
40 clearly in favor." MS. *Fabens Papers*. On this same day (May 4), Colonel
Fabens also wrote to his friend General Cazneau to acquaint him with the
situation in Washington: " President Grant is fully determined on the annexation of Santo Domingo, *and he will succeed*. . . . I have had a four hours
interview with Sumner and have good grounds for hoping that he will come
around. He evidently sees his mistake and laments it. Prest. Grant proposes
next week to meet him with me, and I think we have an argument that will
convert him. But *with or without him* we intend to succeed, and if the situation remains unchanged in Santo Domingo we shall succeed." *Fabens Papers*.

some commercial alchemy not clearly indicated, the Dominican Republic would be able to absorb great quantities of wheat from the Mississippi Valley and large amounts of iron for prospective railroads. Her rich gold fields would require an abundance of American machinery for proper development, while the Dominican demand for cotton goods would cause the spindles of New England to " whirl with increased activity." [24]

As a popular demonstration in favor of Dominican annexation this meeting was of questionable value, but Cazneau and his confederates could overlook no factor that might strengthen their cause. And this was particularly true in May, 1870, for not only was the opposition in the Senate standing firm against pressure from the White House, but their arguments against annexation were about to receive significant reinforcement from Major Perry, who had sharply quarreled with Cazneau and Baez and was about to arrive in Washington. On May 9, Secretary Gautier had written to Perry in order to suspend all diplomatic intercourse between the Commercial Agent and the Dominican Government.[25] On May 16 he addressed a note to Secretary Fish and, after offering a very lame defence of the action of General Cazneau in presenting

---

[24] New York *Tribune*, May 13, 1870. During the spring of 1870, while the treaty of annexation was pending in the Senate, the New York press was filled with propaganda in favor of the President's policy. Some of the statements concerning the alleged vast wealth of the Dominican Republic were manifestly ridiculous, but there were many credulous persons who were influenced by them. A good example of this type of propaganda is the letter written by Dr. W. L. Judd, a missionary in the Dominican Republic. According to Dr. Judd, the Dominican Republic was not only extremely fertile but it was also " exceedingly rich in mines, having apparently as great a variety as is found on the western continent." These gold fields were " richer than those of California," and there were in addition mines of " silver, copper, quick-silver, iron and coal." But the most extraordinary attraction in the Dominican Republic was " the *musicien de arada*," a bird whose singing was so marvelous in " tone and in the more than scientific order of its passages by thirds and fifths, running with the greatest accuracy over several octaves in a single strain, and finally trilling a bass that would cause every nerve in a musician's body to vibrate with delight, that any good musician or person of musical taste would be amply repaid for a journey across the Atlantic simply to hear its tones for the space of fifteen minutes." Washington *Morning Chronicle*, June 8, 1870.

[25] Gautier to Perry, May 9, 1870, *Santo Domingo, Consular Desp.*, vol. 6, MS. Dept. of State.

petitions to the Dominican Senate for special concessions while the treaty of annexation was still pending, he adverted to his recent correspondence with Major Perry. It appeared that the Major's notes had caused the Dominican Government to experience the "most profound grief" and had placed it in a "very critical position." He was obviously not the proper person to represent the United States in the Dominican Republic, and inasmuch as Major Perry was about to visit Washington on a leave of absence, Secretary Gautier expressed the hope that Secretary Fish would "find means to prevent his return to this city."[26]

On the following day General Cazneau wrote a note to Secretary Fish in which he endeavored to explain his position with reference to the concessions he had requested from the Dominican Senate. He protested all too vehemently that his plan to secure these concessions was to have been submitted to President Grant for approval, and he concluded with an acrimonious attack upon Major Perry. The Major was a man of "reckless and violent impulses," with a "rough contempt for the colored citizens" which was bound to lead to the most serious difficulties between the United States and the Dominican Republic. Such a man should never be sent back to Santo Domingo City.[27]

It was evident that Major Perry would have a great deal of colorful information to convey to Secretary Fish when he arrived in Washington, and on June 1 he called at the Department of State to deliver his report in person. He wasted no time in assuring Fish that Cazneau and Fabens were reckless speculators who were interested in annexation merely for pecuniary gain. General Babcock was a "damned rascal," who was intimately connected with the schemes of Fabens and Cazneau and was unworthy of the President's confidence.[28] On June 6, Major Perry wrote a note to Secretary Fish in which he again denounced Cazneau and his clique for their attempts to "monopo-

[26] Gautier to Fish, May 16, 1870, *Dominican Republic, Notes*, vol. 2, MS. Dept. of State.

[27] Cazneau to Fish, May 17, 1870, *Santo Domingo, Consular Desp.*, vol. 6, MS. Dept. of State.

[28] MS. *Fish Diary*, June 1, 1870.

lize all the valuable lands, mining and railroad concessions, emigration grants etc." in the Dominican Republic. He was especially anxious that the

parties concerned in these schemes who have today (I think) the confidence of the President and are using his name as a cover for their financial ring, should, it seems to me, be shown to the public in their true light not only in justice to the people of the United States who pay for the Island and to the people of St. Domingo, but also to President Grant who has taken a personal interest in this question.[29]

Perry followed this note with another letter to Secretary Fish, in which he gave a detailed picture of the operations and schemes of Cazneau, Fabens, Baez, and Babcock, and it was very apparent to Secretary Fish that President Grant would either have to denounce the Cazneau clique or sustain them and terminate Perry's appointment as Commercial Agent.[30] The President's decision was immediately given in favor of Cazneau, and on July 11 Major Perry tendered his resignation as Commercial Agent to the Dominican Republic.[31]

What Secretary Fish thought of Grant's decision to sustain Cazneau and dismiss Perry is not contained in the Fish *Diary,* but it is quite reasonable to assume that he was not favorably disposed towards Cazneau, and it is a matter of record that he was distinctly suspicious of Fabens. He fully realized,

[29] Perry to Fish, June 6, 1870, *Santo Domingo, Consular Desp.,* vol. 6, MS. Dept. of State.

[30] On May 17, 1870, Secretary Gautier wrote a note to Secretary Fish in sharp complaint about the action of Major Perry in a Dominican court-room scene in which the American Commercial Agent slapped the plaintiff's face and then retired to his office and claimed diplomatic immunity. *Dominican Republic, Notes,* vol. 2, MS. Dept. of State.

[31] Perry to Fish, July 11, 1870, *Santo Domingo, Consular Desp.,* vol. 6, MS. Dept. of State On June 13, 1870, at a hearing before the Senate Committee on Foreign Relations, General Babcock denied that he had prevented the release of David Hatch because of a fear that Hatch would oppose the annexation treaty. When General Babcock made this statement Perry, who was present, jumped to his feet and called Babcock a "liar." After some little excitement, quiet was resumed and the hearing continued. New York *Herald,* June 14, 1870. At these same "hearings" before the Senate Committee on Foreign Relations, the speculations and activities of Colonel Fabens were examined. According to the New York *Herald* of June 21, 1870, there was considerable suspicion that the Dominican negotiations were part of a big "job" for certain shrewd adventurers.

however, that Grant was determined to push through the matter of annexation despite every indication that Cazneau, Fabens, and Babcock were supporting this measure only because of an opportunity to make money. Apparently, Fish was so anxious to settle the diplomatic dispute with England concerning the Alabama Claims that he was willing to give at least lip service in the matter of Dominican annexation and help carry out a policy which he felt to be unwise and perhaps corrupt. Of course it is possible that his loyalty to Grant made him ready to believe in projects against which his common sense should have warned him.[32] If he had any real misgivings concerning Dominican annexation he was able during certain periods to overcome them, and so strong did his favorable convictions grow that he found time repeatedly to seek out Senator Sumner for the purpose of impressing upon him the importance of the ratification of the treaty.[33]

This growing belief on the part of the Secretary of State in the importance of Dominican annexation must sometimes have been sharply tested when he came into contact with Colonel Fabens and watched his methods. In April, 1870, Fabens had been commissioned as Envoy Extraordinary and Minister Plenipotentiary of the Dominican Republic for the purpose of visiting Washington and arranging " whatever shall be best suited to the common interest of both countries." [34] This appointment had been effected through the influence of General Cazneau and General Babcock, who wished Colonel Fabens to negotiate some arrangement with Secretary Fish whereby certain funds could be advanced to the bankrupt Dominican Government.[35] On May 28, Fabens wrote to Fish to

[32] Adam Badeau, in his *Grant in Peace*, p. 233, makes the following observation which is distinctly pertinent at this point: " Even when Grant determined on a course that Fish would not perhaps have advised, the secretary stanchly supported his chief."

[33] Secretary Fish, in a letter to Zachariah Chandler on June 8, 1870, tells of his relations with Senator Sumner with reference to the Dominican treaty and states that he had " held several conversations with that gentleman in regard to the Treaty: & I have very earnestly pressed upon him the importance of its ratification." *Chandler Papers*, MS. Library of Congress.

[34] See *ante*, pp. 402-403.

[35] Perry to Fish, May 14, 1870, *Santo Domingo, Consular Desp.*, vol. 6, MS. Dept. of State.

inform him that he had been instructed to communicate " certain facts bearing upon the financial situation " of the Dominican Republic, and asked for an appointment on June 1.[36]

On this day, before the arrival of Fabens, Senator Cornelius Cole and " Judge " O'Sullivan called to see Secretary Fish and indicated the embarrassment of the Dominican Government because of its inability to borrow money. " Judge " O'Sullivan wished to have the American Government extend some authority " to allow Baez to borrow money." Secretary Fish, however, immediately pointed out to O'Sullivan that such an arrangement would be a violation of the terms of the annexation treaty and therefore could not be effected. Senator Cole and " Judge " O'Sullivan thereupon departed, and no sooner had they been ushered out when Colonel Fabens presented himself. The Colonel repeated the same story that had been told by the Senator and his companion, and received from Secretary Fish the " same reply." He then exhibited a letter from Hartmont and Company which asserted that their loan contract with the Dominican Government was entirely valid and would have to be carried out. It indicated, however, a willingness to " accept an annuity of the rent of Samaná for fifty years." When Secretary Fish showed no interest in these proposed financial arrangements, Colonel Fabens withdrew.[37]

The following day he wrote a letter to Fish and frankly confessed that the Dominican Republic was in a very " embarrassing financial situation " and thus looked to the United States for " pecuniary relief." The delay in the action of the American Senate with reference to the annexation treaty was causing serious difficulties, and further delay might " be fatal unless the Dominican Government can obtain the means from abroad to relieve this impatience and thus maintain the present favorable situation." Colonel Fabens then inquired whether some arrangement could be effected whereby this pressing financial emergency might be successfully met.[38]

[36] Fabens to Fish, May 28, 1870, *Dominican Republic, Notes,* vol. 2, MS. Dept. of State.

[37] MS. *Fish Diary,* June 1, 1870.

[38] Fabens to Fish, June 2, 1870, *Dominican Republic, Notes,* vol. 2, MS. Dept. of State.

Although the note of Colonel Fabens was addressed to Secretary Fish the answer was given that same afternoon by General Babcock, who wrote to Fabens as follows:

In reply to your letter of today asking whether the Government has any objection to a change in the plan of payment of the money specified in the Dominican treaty, I have the honor to inform you that the President has no objection to any such change that the Senate may see fit to make, provided the true spirit of the treaty is maintained.[39]

There was little likelihood, however, that the Senate would take any favorable action in this regard, for the opposition in the Senate had not perceptibly abated since the debates in March and April. President Grant was conscious of this fact and endeavored in every way to overcome it, but with little result. On May 14 Senator Schurz had shown Secretary Fish a canvass of the Senate with regard to the treaty of annexation, and this survey estimated that thirty-two Senators would vote adversely. Secretary Fish immediately suggested to J. C. Bancroft Davis, the Assistant Secretary of State, that he see President Grant and suggest that the annexation treaty be modified so as to give Congress the option in the future either " to admit San Domingo as a state or remit it to a state of either separate, or confederated Independence and nationality, with other of the West India Islands." [40]

Davis saw President Grant and communicated to him this suggestion of Secretary Fish. Grant, however, was suspicious of this proposed amendment and regarded it as the handiwork of Senator Schurz. He refused to accept the idea of an American protectorate over the Dominican Republic and resolutely clung to his view that annexation was the only course to follow.[41] On May 28 Grant read to Fish the draft of a proposed

[39] Babcock to Fabens, June 2, 1870, *Grant Letter Book*, MS. Library of Congress.

[40] MS. *Fish Diary*, May 14, 1870. This scheme to substitute the idea of an American protectorate over the Dominican Republic for that of outright annexation was one intended to attract the support of Senator Sumner. According to a letter written to Secretary Fish by Colonel Fabens, June 7, 1870, Sumner was in favor of an American protectorate over the Dominican Republic, and had tried to win the support of Fabens for such a project. MS. *Fabens Papers*.

[41] MS. *Fish Diary*, May 21, 1870.

message to the Senate concerning the annexation of the Dominican Republic, and three days later he transmitted to that body a special message that was a fervid plea for Senatorial support of his policy of expansion. The many far-reaching benefits resulting from annexation he duly catalogued as follows:

The acquisition of San Domingo is an adherence to the "Monroe Doctrine"; it is a measure of national protection; it is asserting our just claim to a controlling influence over the great commercial traffic soon to flow from east to west by way of the Isthmus of Darien; it is to build up our merchant marine; it is to furnish new markets for the products of our farms, shops, and manufactories; it is to make slavery insupportable in Cuba and Porto Rico at once and ultimately so in Brazil; it is to settle the unhappy condition of Cuba, and end an exterminating conflict; it is to provide honest means of paying our honest debts, without overtaxing the people; it is to furnish our citizens with the necessaries of everyday life at cheaper rates than ever before; and it is, in fine, a rapid stride toward that greatness which the intelligence, industry, and enterprise of the citizens of the United States entitle this country to assume among nations.[42]

---

[42] J. D. Richardson, *Messages and Papers of the Presidents*, VII, 61-63. There is a close resemblance between an editorial in the Washington *Morning Chronicle* of March 23, 1870 and Grant's message to Congress of May 21, 1870. It seems more than likely that Grant took many of his ideas from this effusion of Colonel John W. Forney. This identity is easily established by the following parallel columns:

Morning Chronicle, March 23, 1870

"We now import these articles [sugar, coffee, and tobacco] at a cost of one hundred million dollars annually. One hundred million dollars would thus in a few years be annually saved to the country; one hundred million dollars annually added to our favor in the balance of trade. There would be one hundred million dollars more annually to aid in paying off the national debt."

Grant's Message, May 21

"The production of our own supply of these articles [sugar, coffee, and tobacco] will cut off more than one hundred millions of our annual imports, besides largely increasing our exports. With such a picture it is easy to see how our large debt abroad is ultimately to be extinguished."

The reference of President Grant to the Monroe Doctrine in his special message to the Senate of May 31, 1870 elicited the following instruction from Lord Granville to Thornton, the British Minister at Washington: "With reference to . . . the President's Message to the Senate . . . in which he refers to the line of policy known as the Monroe Doctrine, in terms which might be construed as applicable in certain cases to the British West India

Somewhat to Grant's surprise his opponents in the Senate were not greatly impressed by his glowing picture of the flood of prosperity that would pour from the plenteous horn of Dominican annexation.[43] Their failure to respond to his promptings deeply angered him, and with his military cast of mind he began to ponder upon the best mode of disciplining insubordinate Republicans. It was important, of course, to crack the party whip over the shoulders of all who were reluctant to follow his lead no matter what their official position. He had best begin with his own Cabinet members, and on June 13 he complained to Secretary Fish that the Cabinet

Islands, I have to state to you that, as such doctrines can only be dealt with by foreign Countries when some practical proceeding shall be adopted in pursuance of them and as no practical question connected with them is likely to arise in which this Country is concerned, Her Majesty's Government do not think it advisable to enter into any controversy with the Government of the United States on the matter." Lord Granville to Thornton, July 9, 1870, F. O. 115/503, No. 8.

[43] Grant also tried to force the Senate into a more compliant mood by stating that he had " reliable evidence " that a European nation was ready to pay " two million dollars for Samana Bay alone." Message of May 31, 1870, J. D. Richardson, *op. cit.*, VII, 61-63. Although the President did not name the nation that was supposed to be eager for the purchase of Samaná Bay, the Washington *Daily Morning Chronicle* of June 3, 1870 assured its readers that " certain indications point to Prussia . . . as making this offer, as that country is deficient in naval strength, and the wily Bismarck is anxious to further increase the advantages of his nation by every possible means." It is apparent, however, from a survey that I made of the correspondence in the German Foreign Office that this rumor had no foundation in fact as far as Prussia was concerned. As soon as Baron Gerolt, the Minister of the North German Confederation at Washington, read this statement in the *Morning Chronicle*, he called upon certain members of the United States Senate in order to inquire about the basis for such an assertion. He quickly discovered that it was the work of the indefatigable Colonel Fabens, who wished in this way to awaken popular support of the project for the annexation of the Dominican Republic to the United States. Senator Sumner frankly stated to Baron Gerolt that he regarded the whole thing as a " humbug " that had been framed up " between Hartmont and Fabens . . . for the purpose of exerting pressure upon the Senate." The same assurance was given to Baron Gerolt by Senator Carl Schurz. See Baron Gerolt to Chancellor Bismarck, June 3, 1870, MS. Auswärtiges Amt.

It is possible that President Grant's statement was somewhat influenced by the following report from George Bancroft, American Minister at Berlin, of a recent conversation with Chancellor Bismarck: " Having a good chance to speak a private word with Count Bismarck, I said to him: ' See how moderate are the desires of our people; they even hesitate about accepting San Domingo, an island not inferior to Cuba.' He kindled like a fire that blazes up, and said: ' I wish you would give the island to me; I will take it and make of it a king-was not a unit in supporting the treaty for Dominican annexation. He indicated that he found no fault with the actions of his Secretary of State, but was distinctly displeased with the conduct of the Secretary of the Treasury, the Attorney-General, and the Secretary of the Interior. Fish admitted that the Secretary of the Treasury had spoken adversely of the treaty, but he was not aware that the other two Cabinet members had signified any opposition to it. Grant, however, was not to be placated, and he heatedly exclaimed that the Attorney-General " sneered " at the treaty, while the Secretary of the Interior would say nothing in favor of it.[44]

Before long, the President again opened his heart to Secretary Fish concerning the Dominican treaty. He strongly indicated

his desire for its ratification; that he wishes all the members of his Cabinet and all his friends to use all proper efforts to aid him; that he will not consider those who oppose his policy as entitled to influence in obtaining positions under him; that he will not let those who oppose him " name Ministers to London."

dom.' " Bancroft to Fish, February 16, 1870, *Bancroft Papers*, MS. New York Public Library.

In a despatch to Lord Clarendon on June 6, 1870, Thornton, the British Minister at Washington, makes the following observation: " The European Power which the President alludes to as being ready to purchase Santo Domingo, should the United States refuse it, is understood here to signify the North German Confederation; although my Prussian Colleague professes his ignorance of any such desire on the part of the Confederation." F. O. 5/1193, No. 248. In a second despatch to Lord Clarendon, on June 13, 1870, Thornton adds an interesting detail relative to the European power that was supposed to be interested in the purchase of Samaná Bay: " With reference to the assertion made by the President in his message to the Senate . . . that in case the Treaty should not be ratified, a European Power was ready to pay two millions of dollars for the possession of the Bay of Samana alone, I understand that the Committee on Foreign Relations called for any correspondence which might exist in support of this statement. The result was that the President sent a letter purporting to have been addressed by one Herzog Hartmann [E. H. Hartmont?], a Jew residing at New York, to Señor Fabens, a Dominican who took part in the negotiation of the Treaty. . . . In this letter Hartmann states that during a visit he paid to Prussia in the Course of last year, he was told by persons high in authority that the North German Confederation would willingly give two millions of Dollars for the Bay of Samana. It is generally supposed that the contents of the letter are not entitled to the slightest credit." F. O. 5/1193, No. 264.

[44] MS. *Fish Diary*, June 13, 1870.

After warmly stating his desires with reference to the treaty of annexation, he expressed his confidence in the integrity of General Babcock and sharply criticized Major Perry for his actions in the Dominican Republic. His indictment of Perry was based partly upon the Major's army record, which, according to Grant, went through the entire octave of villainy from swindling to rape.[45]

It was easy for Grant to fulminate against Perry and to insist upon his resignation as Commercial Agent to the Dominican Republic. It was distinctly more delicate, however, to compel Cabinet members to resign because they would not support his Dominican policy. At this Cabinet meeting on June 14, Grant announced that he expected all the members of his Cabinet to " sustain the San Domingo Treaty," and it would appear that this announcement met with the " general approval " of that group.[46] But there were certain Cabinet members who, despite presidential pressure, refused to abandon their opposition to the treaty of annexation, and the most persistent of these recalcitrants was Judge Hoar.[47] Realizing that it was difficult for him to be in opposition to the President and still remain in the Cabinet, Judge Hoar must have been thinking of resigning when a letter came from the President on June 15 requesting his resignation. He immediately complied with this request, and the President, on the same day, accepted it with the usual expressions of regret.[48]

---

[45] *Ibid.*, June 14, 1870. There are long excerpts from the *Fish Diary* published in Appendix E of the excellent study by Charles Francis Adams, " The Treaty of Washington," in *Lee at Appomattox and Other Papers*, pp. 216 ff.

[46] *Ibid.*, June 14, 1870, and C. F. Adams, *Lee at Appomattox and Other Papers*, p. 218.

[47] As early as March 29, 1870 there were strong rumors that Judge Hoar would leave the Grant Cabinet. In the New York *World* of this date there is the following pertinent comment: " There are various reports in circulation touching a reorganization of the Cabinet. . . . [One] is that Judge Hoar is to be turned out to make room for Noah Davis—a report started probably by the carpet-baggers, to whom Hoar is very obnoxious." In the New York *Herald* of April 13, 1870 there is another rumor about the impending resignation of Judge Hoar: " It is now said positively that Attorney General Hoar is to retire from the Cabinet, but that he will not do so till next September."

[48] Grant's letter of acceptance of Judge Hoar's resignation is contained in the *Grant Letter Book*, MS. Library of Congress. In 1895 a controversy arose between E. L. Pierce and Senator George F. Hoar with regard to the background

On June 17, Grant had a long conversation with Secretary Fish in which the Dominican treaty again came up for discussion. He expressed his appreciation of the support Fish had given to this measure and also his gratitude for the assistance of other members of his Cabinet like Belknap, Robeson, and Creswell. He was deeply disappointed, however, with the attitude of Boutwell and Cox.

At this point Secretary Fish referred to the fact that several newspapers had published rumors to the effect that the Secretary of State was about to resign. He then expressed to Grant his desire to withdraw from the Cabinet and, when Grant offered strong objections to such a course, he consented to remain for a while as Secretary of State but frankly admitted to the President that he " could not stand it much longer." [49]

---

of the resignation of Judge Hoar. Pierce had received most of his information from Jacob D. Cox, who was Secretary of the Interior in Grant's Cabinet, and on April 18, 1895 Cox wrote a letter to Pierce in which he made the following comments: " I am glad to know of your further correspondence with Senator Hoar. I agree with you that he is in error as to relative dates of some events, and as to the substance of some others. There is no room for doubt in my mind as to the fact that Grant's demand of Judge Hoar's resignation was in writing and was the utter surprise to the Judge which he declared it to be. That he so declared it, *I know*." *Pierce Papers*, MS. Harvard College Library. Cox then went ahead and wrote for the *Atlantic Monthly*, LXXVI (1895), 162 ff., under the title " How Judge Hoar Ceased to be Attorney-General," the " inside " story of this event. According to this version, President Grant suddenly called for Hoar's resignation without any preliminary warning, and Hoar, greatly surprised at this abrupt demand, responded with a brief note which Grant immediately accepted. The Cox article did not stop the controversy concerning the facts leading to Judge Hoar's resignation, and George S. Boutwell, Secretary of the Treasury in the Grant Cabinet, wrote to E. L. Pierce on June 1, 1896 and frankly disagreed with the Cox interpretation. Thus Boutwell wrote: " Cox's article is not favorable to Judge Hoar. He errs as to the cause of his departure from the Cabinet." *Pierce Papers*. One of the points raised by the opponents of the Cox version is that Judge Hoar did not receive any note from President Grant requesting his resignation: the resignation is supposed to have been voluntary. On the basis of materials in the *Fish Diary*, this viewpoint can hardly be sustained.

[49] C. F. Adams, *Lee at Appomattox and Other Papers*, pp. 222-223. Fish's desire to resign was hinted at in press reports soon after this conference between the President and the Secretary of State. In the New York *Tribune* of July 6, 1870 the following item appears: " It is rumored to-night, and credited in official circles, that Mr. Hamilton Fish has tendered his resignation. Mr. Fish has been urging the President to accept his resignation, as he desires to retire from official life in this country. The President has said that he would not permit

This admission did not mean, however, that Fish would no longer advocate the ratification of the Dominican treaty. As long as he remained in the Cabinet he was determined to support the President's policy of annexation, and as an indication of this resolve he made a visit to Sumner's home one night toward the middle of June in a vain endeavor to effect a change in the Senator's attitude concerning the treaty. He found Sumner in a very depressed mood. Certain domestic troubles were giving the Senator deep concern, and in the intervals between spells of weeping he compared his unhappy lot with the marital happiness of the Secretary of State. Fish, of course, felt an instant sympathy for his old friend, and was fearful of mental derangement if some diversion were not found. He first suggested a trip to Europe. When Sumner pleaded his inability to go, Fish then " incautiously " asked the Senator if he " would like to be minister to England." Sumner at once replied that he would not like to " interfere with Motley," who was his friend, and Fish agreed with him

him to retire, if he could by any means keep him in the State Department." There were, of course, earlier rumors of Fish's probable resignation. In March, 1870 some newspapers carried an item that Ben Butler might succeed Fish as Secretary of State. New York *World*, March 24, 26, 1870. At this same time the New York *Herald* openly called for the resignation of Fish because of his alleged indifference to the fate of the Dominican treaty: " It is evident the President is not assisted by his Cabinet as he ought to be in the public policy he has marked out for his administration. This is particularly the case in his policy with regard to St. Domingo. . . . The Secretary of State, whose business it is especially to attend to such matters, does not sympathize with the President nor enter into his views. . . . He is too conservative and timid. . . . Besides, he is under the influence of Mr. Sumner. . . . The Secretary must see that he is in the way. Will he not gracefully retire? " New York *Herald*, March 29, 1870. On June 25, 1870 the Washington *Morning Chronicle* contained an editorial which warmly praised Secretary Fish and in a vein of irony castigated his opponents: " When we have swashbucklers who would fight in a month, and politicians who would cover blue books with florid rhetoric, and feathered statesmen who would roar like Bulls of Bashan and keep the country in constant clamor, all anxious to enter the State Department, we are surprised that the President retains him [Fish]." When the rumors of resignation continued to persist, Representative L. P. Poland wrote to Fish on July 16, 1870 and expressed his anxiety concerning them: " I have felt somewhat disturbed by the rumors that you contemplated surrendering the *Premiership*. I hope not—the sober men of the country want you there for the same reason that wild buccaneers and filibusters do not." *Misc. Letters, July, 1870*, MS. Dept. of State.

that it would be better to take a trip "without any official cares or duties." [50]

In a letter published in the Boston *Transcript* of October 31, 1877, Fish vehemently denies that his "incautious" offer to Sumner of the post of Minister to the Court of St. James had any connection with the Dominican treaty of annexation. This might very well be true,[51] but it is apparent that many of Grant's friends thought that the best way of securing Senate approval of the treaty of annexation was to get Sumner out of the country on a diplomatic mission. With this end in view Senator Simon Cameron and Ben Butler called to see Secretary Fish for the purpose of suggesting that Sumner be sent to London to supersede Motley. They believed that it would be impossible for the Dominican treaty to pass the Senate with Sumner as chairman of the Senate Committee on Foreign Relations. It would be good political tactics to send Sumner to England with definitely limited powers, and in order to snub him for his arrogance it would be possible to send over a special envoy to settle all important diplomatic questions.[52]

On June 29, Secretary Boutwell had a conversation with Fish during which he expressed his concern over the "estrangement" that was developing between the President and certain members of the Senate. He recognized that Sumner was "peculiar and arrogant," but he felt that the Senator had a powerful hold on the "public confidence" and was "all potential" in Massachusetts. For party reasons it would be expedient to observe great caution in dealing with him.[53]

On the day that this conversation took place the debate in the Senate on the Dominican treaty was resumed. Sumner was studiously silent upon this occasion, and on June 30 the vote was taken in the Senate and resulted in a tie—twenty-

[50] Fish to George W. Curtis, May 14, 1874, MS. *Fish Diary.*

[51] In the New York *Tribune* of April 6, 1874 Sumner gives a very different version from that of Hamilton Fish, and he makes the specific statement that Fish did connect the offer of a London mission with the requirement that Sumner cease his opposition to the Dominican treaty.

[52] MS. *Fish Diary,* June 27, 1870.

[53] *Ibid.,* June 29, 1870.

eight to twenty-eight. Inasmuch as a two-thirds vote is required for ratification this meant that the treaty was defeated.[54]

Grant, now thoroughly enraged, lost no time in striking back at Sumner, whom he regarded as the chief factor in the defeat of the treaty. On the day following the vote in the Senate he ordered the immediate removal of Motley as the American Minister to England, and when Motley refused to retire he later had Secretary Fish send him a letter of recall.[55]

This summary removal of Motley opened wider the rift between Sumner and Grant, and it had considerable influence on the growing coolness between Sumner and Fish. The appointment of Motley as Minister to England had been due largely to the insistence of Sumner,[56] and consequently he

[54] *Sen. Ex. Jour.*, XVII, 502. The large adverse vote in the Senate clearly indicated the lack of popular support of the treaty. This fact is made the subject of comment by the New York *Evening Post* on July 1, 1870: "That the San Domingo scheme broke down yesterday in the Senate is due largely to the fact that it had no sympathy or favor among the people. The few journals which favored it were not able to give good or even plausible reasons for the annexation of half an island; and the desire for economy . . . increased the feeling of opposition to a scheme, the weakness of which was most glaringly shown by the President's own defence of it."

[55] Oliver Wendell Holmes, *John Lothrop Motley* (Boston, 1897), chap. xxi. Fish strongly remonstrated with President Grant against the removal of Motley: "I urge you to let him remain until next winter." "That," said Grant, "I will not do. I will not allow Mr. Sumner to ride over me." When Fish explained that it was not Sumner but Motley at whom the President was striking, Grant replied: "It is the same thing." MS. *Fish Diary,* July 1, 1870.

Grant also sharply denounced Sumner and Schurz to General Rutherford B. Hayes. C. R. Williams, *Diary and Letters of Rutherford B. Hayes* (2 vols., N. Y., 1914), III, 110-112. Schurz soon got wind of these denunciations and wrote to Grant on July 17, 1870 in defense of his position: "I am painfully sensible of the change which our personal relations have suffered in consequence of our differences on the San Domingo treaty. I have reasons to believe that there has been much mischievous tale-bearing connected with this matter. You have been informed as I understand, that I attacked you personally in the secret deliberations of the Senate. Whoever may have carried that story to you, I pronounce it unqualifiedly untrue. I desire now to remove this erroneous impression, not as a man who has favors to seek, for that is not my condition, but as one who has great interests to serve." Schurz to President Grant, July 17, 1870, *Schurz Papers,* MS. Library of Congress. Grant gave Schurz an audience and a truce was established for that summer.

[56] J. C. Bancroft Davis, *Mr. Fish and the Alabama Claims* (N. Y., 1893), pp. 23 ff. See also MS. *Fish Diary,* June 25, 1870, for Grant's comment in this regard. In the *Moran Diary,* MS. Library of Congress, under date of August 22,

interpreted Motley's removal as an illustration of presidential displeasure at his attitude toward the Dominican treaty. In this assumption he was undoubtedly correct, but it should be noted that President Grant had evidenced strong distaste for Motley as far back as June, 1869, when he urged Secretary Fish to "dismiss Motley at once." [57] In the early summer of 1870, as friction between Sumner and Grant relative to the Dominican treaty grew in volume, there were many occasions when Grant seriously thought of removing Motley. On June 25, he spoke to Secretary Fish of a recent conversation he had had with Senators Chandler, Morton, and Carpenter, who complained to him that the Senators who were opposing the Dominican treaty had received more patronage than those who were in support of it. Grant then assured them that this would no longer be true, and he referred specifically to Sumner, who "had got Motley appointed to England." With reference to Motley, Grant informed the Senators that he intended "to recall him as soon as he could find the right man," and he indicated his readiness to receive suggestions as to the proper person to send to London.[58]

On June 28 Grant discussed with several of his Cabinet members the question of Motley's removal, and Secretary Fish in his *Diary* refers to many occasions when the President announced "his intention to make the removal." [59] It is obvious, therefore, that there was a distinct possibility that Motley

---

1870, there is an entry concerning a conversation with George Jones at the Alexandra Hotel, London. Jones assured Moran that President Grant had informed him that "he had appointed Motley to please Sumner and at Sumner's earnest solicitation—as he knew nothing about him, himself, and never saw him until after his own election—and now that Sumner behaved so badly in the San Domingo business he would remove him to please himself."

[57] Grant's interview at Edinburgh, Scotland, published in the New York *Herald,* September 25, 1877. This expression of Grant's desire to dismiss Motley in June, 1869 grew out of Motley's report of a conversation with Lord Clarendon in which Motley over-emphasized the importance of the British Proclamation of May, 1861 as a constant irritant in Anglo-American relations. Grant was then intent upon issuing a proclamation recognizing Cuban belligerency, and he did not relish Motley's insistence upon the illegality of such proclamations. See C. F. Adams, *Lee at Appomattox and Other Papers,* pp. 117 ff.

[58] MS. *Fish Diary*, June 25, 1870.

[59] *Ibid.,* June 29, 1870.

might have been removed before July 1, 1870, but it is never-theless true that there was a definite connection between the defeat of the treaty on June 30 and the removal of Motley the next day. That there was no immediate necessity for such action is proved by the fact that when Motley refused to retire he was allowed to remain in London until his recall in De-cember, and it is apparent that Fish did not regard Motley's presence in London as a serious obstacle to his policy of re-conciling the major differences between England and the United States.[60]

Whether necessary or not, it is certain that Motley's removal deeply stirred Sumner's anger against Grant, and during the summer of 1870 he freely gave vent to his feelings. He still maintained friendly relations with Secretary Fish but his constant denunciations of President Grant were tending rapidly to dissolve that friendship. Thus we find Fish writing to Senator Howe, of Wisconsin, on August 6, 1870 with reference to Sumner's attitude:

Mr. Sumner, I fear, is implacable. I passed an hour in his study the evening before I left Washington. . . . He was very severe towards the President. . . . I am quite convinced that on such occasions, he is not conscious of the extent and violence of his expressions.[61]

On September 6 Fish wrote to Senator Justin Morrill, of Vermont, and described Sumner's outbursts against the President.[62] A few days later Senator Morrill received from Sumner himself a letter which confirmed the statements of Secretary Fish, whereupon Morrill wrote to Sumner and admonished him to be silent. It was apparent, said Morrill, that Motley could not be retained in London

[60] With reference to Motley's removal Charles Francis Adams makes the fol-lowing pertinent comment: " It is sufficient here to say that whatever was then done, was done by General Grant's imperative order, and solely because of Mr. Motley's relations with Mr. Sumner, and the latter's opposition to the President's Dominican policy." *Lee at Appomattox and Other Papers*, p. 138. For a dif-ferent opinion see J. C. Bancroft Davis, *Mr. Fish and the Alabama Claims*, p. 145.
[61] C. F. Adams, *Lee at Appomattox and Other Papers*, p. 249.
[62] *Ibid.*, pp. 250-251.

after what has occurred, but I think the President might be quite willing to keep silent if you would. . . . Your words must leap out in your conversation, and they will inevitably reach the ears of the President. " Brutality," " indignity," " offensive," " utterly indefensible conduct," . . . would make any man's ears tingle. It may be too much to ask you to forget and forgive but I think it might be wise to let the subject " alone severely." [63]

Sumner, however, would not accept such good advice, and throughout the summer and fall of 1870 echoes of his sharp criticism of the President continued to reach the White House.

The following statements made by Sumner to a reporter from the Chicago *Republican* with reference to the Dominican policy of President Grant are typical:

Those young military men whom the President had gathered around him or in his actual Cabinet . . . had taken a notion that there was a good speculation in that quarter [Dominican Republic] and Grant, had, honestly enough, been persuaded into their scheme. Why, a friend of mine, who has been down there, says that the whole coast of the Bay of Samana is staked off into lots and marked " Cazneau," and " Babcock," and " Baez," and that one or two particularly large ones are marked " Grant." [64]

While Sumner was busily feathering shafts for the President's discomfort, Motley, in London, was giving unmistakable evidence that a literary lion can growl if not bite. He was deeply incensed because a cablegram from the Department

[63] Morrill to Sumner, September 10, 1870, *Sumner Papers*, MS. Harvard College Library.   Also Justin S. Morrill, " Notable Letters from My Political Friends," *Forum*, XXIV (1897), 409.

[64] Quoted in the New York *Herald*, November 21, 1870. On November 30, 1870, Colonel Fabens wrote to Secretary Fish and insisted that Senator Sumner's statement concerning the staking out of lots on Samaná Bay was entirely false. *Dominican Republic, Notes,* vol. 2, MS. Dept. of State. Moreover, in speaking of the statements attributed to him during this interview in Chicago, Sumner himself declared during the Senate debate, on December 21, 1870, that they were false and had been contradicted in the newspapers. The account of this interview, which was first published in the Chicago *Republican,* on November 19, 1870, was criticized by Sumner as " a stolen, surreptitious, and false report of a conversation, or what purported to be a conversation of mine at Chicago. . . . It was a stolen thing, with a mixture of truth, of falsehood, and of exaggeration, producing in the main the effect of falsehood." *Cong. Globe,* 41 Cong., 3 sess., p. 247.

of State demanding a reply was received at the London Legation before the formal letter of July 1, requesting his resignation, had arrived.[65] This letter, however, had been expected
many days before it actually reached London, and as early
as June, 1870 it was an open secret in England that Motley
would be recalled. Even Adam Badeau, who had little affection
for Motley, felt that the matter had not been properly handled,
and on July 14 he wrote to J. C. Bancroft Davis that

telegraphic reports of Mr. Motley's recall have abounded here for
several weeks and caused him great annoyance. It is a pity that they
should have preceded any notice to him.[66]

On July 14 Motley cabled to Washington that he would not
resign, and thereafter he devoted himself to the congenial
task of damning Grant in particular and cursing his countrymen in general. On this same day Moran reported that Motley
was in a " great rage," and on the following day he " went
on like a madman." He " swore at the President, damned his
countrymen as vulgar and brutal, and wished the damned
Govt. might be destroyed." After a week he was still so angry
that he classed his American callers as " vulgar brutes," and
he openly declared that General Nathaniel Banks was both
a " sneak and a brute." [67]

[65] Motley received the cablegram from the Department of State on the evening
of July 12, and the letter requesting him to resign arrived on July 13. *Moran
Diary*, MS. Library of Congress, July 13, 1870. See also *Sen. Doc.* No. 11, 41
Cong., 3 sess., pp. 15-16.

[66] Badeau to Davis, July 14, 1870, *J. C. Bancroft Davis Papers*, MS. Library
of Congress. See also the MS. *Moran Diary*, July 11, 1870, for the following comment: " Private letters from home today confirm the news that Mr. Motley is
to be removed."

[67] MS. *Moran Diary*, July 14, 15, and 20. With reference to the request of the
President for the resignation of Motley, Francis G. Young wrote to Grant as
follows: " I recall no act of the Executive which has met with such unanimous
assent. Mr. Motley has the misfortune to disappoint and displease most persons
who wait upon him and all are impressed with his unfitness for the post."
Misc. Letters, July, 1870, MS. Dept. of State. Sumner's attitude toward the recall
of Motley is indicated in his letter to Carl Schurz on September 15, 1870:
" Every reason assigned makes it [Motley's recall] worse. One after the other
a new reason is put forth. Yesterday I had a long letter from Fish showing
great nervousness. I told him plainly all my regret, that he allowed himself
to be a party to such a transaction being the most grievous personal wrong &

While Motley was daily fulminating at Grant, the President was endeavoring to select, with the utmost despatch, a new Minister to England. He first nominated Senator F. T. Frelinghuysen for that post,[68] and when he declined to accept this honor Grant then offered it to Lyman Trumbull, who likewise refused to enter the diplomatic service.[69] In September Samuel G. Howe was approached with negative results, and then Senator Oliver P. Morton was selected because Grant believed that the United States needed in London " something more than a ' figure-head.' " [70] Local politics in Indiana compelled Morton to remain at home,[71] and the President finally had to be satisfied with Robert C. Schenck, who had long been an active figure in the House of Representatives but whose chief literary effort had been a treatise on " draw poker." [72]

While the President was anxiously seeking for a successor to Motley the question of Dominican annexation again came before him. On August 29 he received a letter of inquiry from President Baez relative to the attitude of the American Government in regard to this question. After a delay of several weeks Grant finally prepared an answer, which he read to Secretary Fish. In this answer he assured President Baez of his " unabated " interest in this matter and promised that when

---

irrational thing in the history of the Dept. of State—that it was painful to his friends, that his name was in it—that rather than do it, he should have resigned. Of course he should—as he should have resigned rather than allow the St. Domingo business to proceed. Meanwhile Motley remains in London, surprized & utterly ignorant why he has been struck; but making no complaints, & writes to nobody here." *Schurz Papers*, MS. Library of Congress.

[68] *Sen. Ex. Jour.*, XVII, 545-547.

[69] Horace White, *Life of Lyman Trumbull*, pp. 347-348.

[70] Grant to Chandler, September 22, 1870, *Chandler Papers*, MS. Library of Congress.

[71] Grant's letter of October 21, 1870 to Governor Morton, in which he accepts Morton's declination of the London mission (October 19), is in the *Grant Letter Book*, MS. Library of Congress. Horace Greeley was also thought of in connection with this English mission, and again it was local politics that excluded any chance for his nomination. See Whitelaw Reid to J. C. B. Davis, August 26, 1870, *Davis Papers*, MS. Library of Congress.

[72] W. E. Woodward, *Meet General Grant* (N. Y., 1928), p. 448. For some interesting evidence that General Schenck was a member of the notorious Whiskey Ring in the Miami Valley see the letter from Giles Whiting to Ben Butler, March 19, 1869, *Butler Papers*, MS. Library of Congress.

Congress convened he would send another message recommending annexation. Fish advised against including in the answering letter any mention of a promise to send a message to Congress recommending annexation, but Grant refused to heed this advice and the letter was sent without amendment.[73]

On December 5, President Grant carried out this promise by including in his annual message to Congress a long statement in which he rehearsed the many advantages that would accrue to the United States from the annexation of the Dominican Republic. He also recommended that Congress pass a joint resolution authorizing the President to appoint a commission to negotiate a treaty with " the authorities of San Domingo for the acquisition of that island." [74]

While the President was thus exerting all his power to help consummate the annexation of the Dominican Republic, Secretary Fish was engaged in giving Colonel Fabens a lesson in diplomatic procedure. On December 2, Fabens had written a letter to Secretary Fish advising him of the appointment of William M. Ringwood as the Consul-General of the Dominican Republic at the Port of New York. On the following day Secretary Fish wrote to Colonel Fabens and informed him that he had no authority to make such an appointment.[75] Fabens quickly replied that he had received full powers " as Minister Plenipotentiary, from the President of the Dominican Republic, to make a new treaty of annexation," and that the Dominican Government relied upon him " to look after its interests generally in this country." [76]

Fabens then rushed to Washington to have a conference with Secretary Fish, and on December 8 he was informed by

[73] MS. *Fish Diary*, October 15, 1870, and *Grant Letter Book*, October 17, 1870, MS. Library of Congress.

[74] J. D. Richardson, *Messages and Papers of the Presidents*, VII, 99-101. It is significant that Grant refused to accept the draft of the annual message prepared by Secretary Fish with reference to Dominican annexation. He frankly informed the Secretary that " he had written something about San Domingo" which he preferred to that which the Secretary had prepared. MS. *Fish Diary*, Nov. 21, 1870.

[75] Fish to Fabens, December 3, 1870, *Dominican Republic, Notes to*, vol. 1, MS. Dept. of State.

[76] Fabens to Fish, December 6, 1870, *Dominican Republic, Notes*, vol. 2, MS. Dept. of State.

the Secretary that his credentials merely gave him power to negotiate a treaty of annexation, and that as no treaty was at that time in the process of negotiation his credentials were of no " immediate value." Fish flatly refused to recognize that Colonel Fabens had any authority to appoint Ringwood as the Dominican Consul-General at the Port of New York.[77] After this sharp rebuff Colonel Fabens must have realized that President Grant's unbounded enthusiasm for Dominican annexation had little effect upon the cool judgment of the American Secretary of State.

While Secretary Fish was having this little brush with Colonel Fabens, the recommendations in the President's message to Congress with reference to Dominican annexation were the subject of discussion by many of the friends of the Administration, who were anxious that no political defeat be recorded against the President. They were distinctly disturbed when Sumner, on December 9, 1870, introduced into the Senate a resolution calling upon the President to send to that body all " papers and correspondence relating to the proposed annexation of the Dominican portion of the island of San Domingo." [78]

Three days later Senator Morton, of Indiana, introduced a resolution authorizing the President to appoint three commissioners to proceed to the Dominican Republic for the purpose of making a careful survey of the political, economic, and social conditions existing there. In their report they were also to indicate whether the inhabitants of that republic were desirous of being annexed to the United States.[79]

[77] MS. *Fish Diary,* December 8, 1870. W. M. Ringwood was a member of the firm of Spofford, Tileston and Company, and on December 9 he wrote to Colonel Fabens to assure him that he could have plenty of money for the Santo Domingo lobby. If money had been able to buy the number of votes necessary to approve the Alaskan Treaty, why could not the same procedure be followed now: " Mr. J. L. Spofford, knowing that I was writing to you, desires me to say that he and Mr. Lawson upon reading the state of affairs in the Senatorial caucus, concluded that it might not be injudicious to make an investment among some of them to attain the object in view. He would like you to ' sound ' Genl. Babcock, and others on this point so that you will be able to tell them on Monday next, just what can be done and about the size the investment required would be." MS. *Fabens Papers.*

[78] *Cong. Globe,* 41 Cong., 3 sess., p. 51.   [79] *Ibid.,* p. 53.

On December 20 these resolutions were discussed, and a motion was made by Senator Buckingham to refer the Morton resolution to the Senate Committee on Foreign Relations. This motion was immediately opposed by Morton because he realized that the majority of that committee was opposed to Dominican annexation and therefore would return an unfavorable report. In the ensuing debate on the merits of the Morton resolution every aspect of the question of Dominican annexation was discussed, and Sumner openly charged that President Grant had been endeavoring to displace certain members of the Senate Committee on Foreign Relations in order to secure control over that committee. He had been informed that the President

was not satisfied with the Committee on Foreign Relations as constituted for years. He wished a change. He asked first for the removal of the chairman. Somebody told him that this would not be convenient. He then asked for the removal of the Senator from Missouri [Mr. Schurz], and he was told that this could not be done without affecting the German vote.[80]

When Senator Chandler challenged Sumner to produce evidence that the President had desired to change the membership of the Senate Committee on Foreign Relations, Sumner replied that he had

understood that the President, in conversation with a Senator, expressed a desire for the removal of the chairman.[81]

[80] *Cong. Globe,* 41 Cong., 3 sess., p. 230.

[81] *Ibid.,* p. 241. In an editorial of December 24, 1870, the Boston *Journal* deprecated any idea of removing Sumner as chairman of the Senate Committee on Foreign Relations. Thus: " The general response of the press and of public opinion otherwise manifested will . . . convince Senators of the great mistake they have made. . . . Among other good effects, also, we hope will be the abandonment of the alleged design to depose Mr. Sumner from the chairmanship of the Committee on Foreign Relations. The mere mention of such a thing was unworthy of men like Senators Morton and Conkling. . . . Mr. Sumner has served in that high position for seven years, and with an efficiency that is beyond all praise." In the New York *Herald* of December 31, 1870 Senator Wilson, of Massachusetts, is quoted as follows concerning the rumor about the removal of Sumner as chairman of the Senate Committee on Foreign Relations: " I am opposed to the removal of my colleague from the Committee on Foreign Affairs, and I will fight such a proposition with my utmost strength. . . . Mr. Sumner is entitled to the place and has done nothing which merits such punishment."

Sumner refused, however, to give the name of the Senator who had given him this information, and Chandler, who as chairman of the caucus committee was supposed to be familiar with every phase of party intrigue concerning the membership of Senatorial committees, assured the Senate that

so far as my knowledge goes those charges against the President are false.[82]

In his indignation Sumner did not stop with charges against President Grant relative to attempts to control the Senate Committee on Foreign Relations. No sooner had the debate started on December 21 than he delivered a lengthy speech in which his unrestrained criticism of the President's Dominican policy reached a definite degree of hysteria. The Morton resolution providing for a commission of inquiry into conditions existing in the Dominican Republic would commit Congress

to a dance of blood. It is a new step in a measure of violence. Several steps have already been taken, and Congress is now summoned to take another.[83]

During the course of this speech of December 21, 1870

---

[82] *Cong. Globe,* 41 Cong., 3 sess., p. 242. Senator Conkling agreed with Senator Chandler on the falsity of Sumner's statement that Grant attempted to change the membership of the Senate Committee on Foreign Relations. After making this denial of the President's alleged effort in this regard, Conkling stated that he believed the time had come when " the Republican majority here owes it to itself to see that the Committee on Foreign Relations is reorganized and no longer led by a Senator who has launched against the Administration an assault more bitter than had proceeded from any Democratic member of this body." *Cong. Globe,* 41 Cong., 3 sess., p. 246. Despite these denials of Senators Chandler and Conkling there persisted rumors that the way was being prepared to remove Sumner from the position of chairman of the Senate Committee on Foreign Relations. The New York *Herald* of December 24, 1870 prints a despatch from its Washington correspondent which is distinctly pertinent. The following excerpt indicates the strength of these rumors: " The effort to remove Senator Sumner from the chairmanship of the Senate Committee on Foreign Relations seems, on inquiry, to be more strong and determined than was at first supposed. Mr. Sumner, himself, has had hints about it from various quarters, and he is not quite sure whether it will be done or not." The active parties in this move to oust Sumner were " Zach Chandler and Senator Conkling. Chandler, who was clamorous in favor of removing Schurz from the committee . . . , is now going around calling for blood."

[83] *Ibid.,* pp. 226-227.

Sumner showed an intimate knowledge of the practice of American diplomacy, and he clearly demonstrated that the Morton resolution was " entirely unnecessary " because the President already had " all the power it pretends to give." [84] He was not equally convincing, however, in his argument that, while Grant had ample authority to send General Babcock to the Dominican Republic as a " special agent," he did not have power to designate him as an " aid-de-camp to his Excellency Ulysses S. Grant, President of the United States." This title, which was used in the Gautier-Babcock protocol, was, according to Sumner, unknown in American practice, and Babcock's use of it stood " alone in the history of free Government." [85]

Senator Nye, in a bantering vein which must have greatly annoyed Sumner, showed that the Gautier-Babcock protocol was probably drawn up by Gautier and that the designation of Babcock as an " aid-de-camp " to President Grant was quite harmless because " when Mr. Babcock comes to sign his name, he signs it plain ' Orville E. Babcock.' " [86]

Sumner's speech, however, was not devoted merely to legal quibbles. He vehemently attacked the President for his policy of expansion, and warmly asserted that the

island of San Domingo, situated in tropical waters and occupied by another race, never can become a permanent possession of the United States. You may seize it by force of arms or by diplomacy, . . . but the enforced jurisdiction cannot endure. Already by a higher statute is that island set apart to the colored race. It is theirs by right of possession; by their sweat and blood mingling with the soil; by tropical position; by its burning sun, and by unalterable laws of climate.

He also bitterly criticized the President for the use of the Navy in promoting his policy of acquisition, and he launched a sharp invective against President Baez, General Cazneau, and Colonel Fabens, whom he termed " political jockeys " who

[84] *Cong. Globe,* 41 Cong., 3 sess., p. 227.

[85] *Ibid.,* p. 227. See also H. M. Wriston, *Executive Agents in American Foreign Relations,* p. 269.

[86] *Cong. Globe,* 41 Cong., 3 sess., p. 240.

had " seduced into their firm " the President's special agent, General Babcock.[87]

It was only to be expected that such a speech would evoke the virulent hostility of the friends of the Administration, and then to make their hostility even more pointed Sumner had the Chief Clerk of the Senate read excerpts from the press which dealt in detail with the quarrel between Sumner and Grant. According to these excerpts the President was deeply disturbed about the aspersions which Sumner had cast upon his motives in supporting the policy of Dominican annexation. In the course of a conversation with a " distinguished New England Senator " who had attempted a reconciliation between Sumner and the President, it was alleged that Grant had referred to the newspaper reports which recounted how the Senator had spoken " bitterly of him publicly in street cars and other public conveyances " and had also " attributed dishonest motives to him." It was further stated that Grant then informed the would-be peacemaker that if it were not for the fact that he was President of the United States he would " hold Mr. Sumner personally responsible for his language, and demand satisfaction of him." [88]

[87] *Ibid.*, pp. 226-231, 244-245. According to a special despatch from Washington to the Boston *Journal* of December 30, 1870, Sumner's speech was " severely criticized by nearly all the leading Republican newspapers, and by a large majority of the prominent Republican politicians in the Atlantic States." In a summary of editorial comments, the *Daily National Republican*, of December 24, 1870, shows that the following papers advocated the passage of the Morton resolution and condemned Sumner's opposition: New York *Tribune*; New York *Times*; New York *Herald*; New York *Standard*; New York *Commercial Advertiser*; Boston *Evening Traveller*; Philadelphia *North American*; and the Philadelphia *Morning Post*. At the same time that these newspapers were critical of Sumner's course in opposing the passage of the Morton resolution as a step towards Dominican annexation, Sumner was receiving from many of his friends personal letters strongly approving his course. Not only did friends like W. L. Garrison, Moorfield Storey, and Gerrit Smith warmly praise his stand, but other friends who were able politicians wrote to say that thousands of Republicans in every part of the North approved his opposition to the President's course. Neal Dow wrote on January 3, 1871 to assure him that in Maine his " whole course on San Domingo is approved by Republicans," while Jacob Brinkerhoff expressed the view that there were " not a thousand men in Ohio who are in favor of this project of annexation." *Sumner Papers*, MS. Harvard College Library.

[88] *Cong. Globe*, 41 Cong., 3 sess., pp. 217-218. See also the Boston *Journal,*

These newspaper reports thoroughly infuriated the friends of Grant, who heatedly denounced Sumner for introducing into a Senate debate mere rumors which had no foundation. But whether these rumors were facts or falsehoods it was certain that the differences between Grant and Sumner were beyond all possibility of reconcilement, and as the Senate debate on the Morton resolution proceeded it was apparent from the personal quality of the attacks upon Sumner that his foes were preparing a swift and certain political doom for the Senator.

Sumner, however, was not without his supporters in this matter of opposition to Dominican annexation. Senator Schurz made a learned and cogent speech against American expansion in the tropics,[89] while Senators Casserly, Thurman, Morrill, Patterson, Bayard, and Davis indicated the many dangers that would accompany any American venture in imperialism. Bayard led the Democratic opposition to the Morton resolution, and he not only held that an imperialistic policy was lacking in wisdom but also insisted that it was incumbent upon the President to send to the Senate for confirmation the names of

December 21, 1870. In the New York *Herald,* on December 22, 1870, there was a long account of this quarrel between Sumner and Grant. Pertinent excerpts from this account are as follows: " Today [December 21] Senator Sumner is reported with having said to Lieutenant Governor Dunn, of Louisiana, now on a visit to Washington, ' Did you know, Mr. Dunn, that I stand in fear of personal violence from the Executive Mansion? ', and to a Senator, that he had been threatened with personal chastisement by one of the President's private secretaries (alluding to General Babcock). . . . A gentleman with whom General Babcock talked since the opening of the present session, represents him as saying that if Sumner was not a Senator and he [Babcock] an officer of the army, he would have pulled the Senator's nose; and, further, that he would do it as it was if Sumner was not a ' damned coward.' "

[89] *Cong. Globe,* 41 Cong., 3 sess., pp. 430 ff. On February 14, 1871 Jacob Dolson Cox, former Secretary of the Interior in the Grant Cabinet, wrote to express his approval of the stand Schurz had taken against imperialism. He was glad that Schurz had placed " squarely before the country the fact that the extension into tropical regions is proven by all experience to be dangerous to republican institutions. . . . I have no patience with any attempt to dilute our republicanism with an admixture of West Indian, of Mexican or of South American turbulence. . . . That the Navy wants St. Domingo I can understand, because it would be sticking out into the air like a sore thumb, and would at once make us vulnerable to the naval powers of Europe. We should have *invented* a weak place for them to attack us on equal terms in case of a quarrel, and to be ready for its preservation we should need a navy ready at all times to cope with the strongest in Europe." *Schurz Papers,* MS. Library of Congress.

the commissioners who were to be sent to the Dominican Republic.[90] In this he was seconded by Senator Thurman who argued that if

the President cannot appoint a foreign minister of the lowest grade to make the most insignificant treaty in the world without the advice and consent of the Senate, . . . will you say that he shall appoint, without the advice and consent of the Senate, three commissioners to inaugurate this question of the annexation of Dominica to this Government? [91]

In support of the Morton resolution there were speeches by Senator Morton himself, and by other Republican Senators like Nye, Conkling, Howe, Edmunds, Chandler, Williams, Carpenter, Harlan, Stewart, and Yates. The personal attacks upon Sumner were made by Senators Conkling, Edmunds, and Chandler, and they did not try to conceal their contempt for the Senator from Massachusetts.[92]

After an all-night debate the Morton resolution passed the Senate in the early morning of December 22, 1870, by a vote of 32 yeas and 9 nays.[93] Some two weeks later, on January 9, 1871, the Morton resolution was taken up and debated in the House of Representatives under a suspension of the rules. Representatives Fernando Wood, Willard, Cox, Potter, and Farnsworth spoke in opposition to the passage of the resolution, while Butler, Bingham, Poland, Kellogg, and Orth made speeches in its favor. During this debate in the House Representative Garfield moved that fifteen minutes be added to the time agreed upon for debate. Such a motion required unanimous consent and Ben Butler promptly objected. Garfield, much annoyed, remarked: " Listen to the man who cracks the whip! " Butler, with evident relish, quickly replied: " Listen to the man whose back smarts! " [94]

[90] *Cong. Globe*, 41 Cong., 3 sess., p. 256.
[91] *Ibid.*, p. 257.
[92] *Ibid.*, pp. 222-231, 236-271, 427-431.
[93] *Cong. Globe*, 41 Cong., 3 sess., p. 271. With reference to the passage of the Morton resolution in the Senate the New York *Herald,* on December 23, 1870, expressed the opinion that " General Grant has gained in the Senate a victory on St. Domingo; but he may well say, as Pyrrhus said on a memorable occasion: ' One more such victory will undo us.' "
[94] *Cong. Globe,* 41 Cong., 3 sess., p. 414.

With Butler in control of the situation there was little chance for the opposition to air its opinions, although Ambler was allowed to introduce the following amendment to the Morton resolution:

Provided, that nothing in these resolutions contained shall be held, understood, or construed as committing Congress to the policy of annexing the territory of said republic of Dominica.

That this resolution expressed the sentiment of the majority in the House of Representatives was evident when the vote was taken upon it—108 yeas, 76 nays.[95]

On January 10 the Morton resolution with the Ambler amendment was passed by a vote of 123 yeas and 63 nays,[96] and on the following day the Senate concurred in the Ambler amendment by a unanimous vote.[97] Grant approved the joint resolution on January 12, and forthwith appointed as members of the Dominican commission of inquiry Dr. Samuel G. Howe, a noted philanthropist, former Senator Benjamin F. Wade, and Andrew D. White, President of Cornell University.[98] This commission left New York on January 17, 1871, arrived at Samaná Bay on January 24, and returned to the United States on March 26, having been absent just seventy days. In their report which Grant submitted to Congress in a special message, on April 5, 1871, the commissioners dealt exhaustively with conditions in the Dominican Republic and sustained all that the President had strongly affirmed of the " productiveness and healthfulness of the republic of San Domingo, of the unanimity of the people for annexation to the United States, and of their peaceable character." [99] There was no question but that the

[95] *Ibid.*, p. 416.   [96] *Ibid.*

[97] *Ibid.*, p. 431. The vote in the Senate was 57 yeas and 0 nays.

[98] Grant's letter of January 10, 1871 to Andrew D. White, inquiring if he would accept an appointment on the commission; his telegram to S. G. Howe of January 13; his letter to General Franz Siegel of January 10, offering him the post of secretary to the commission (which he declined); and his letter to President Baez of January 15, introducing the American commissioners, are all in the *Grant Letter Book*, MS. Library of Congress. The instructions from Secretary Fish to the three members of the commission are to be found in *Special Missions, American Hemisphere*, vol. 2, MS. Dept. of State. See also Julia Ward Howe, *Reminiscences* (N. Y., 1899), pp. 280 ff.

[99] *Sen. Ex. Doc.* No. 9, 42 Cong., 1 sess., p. 1.

people of the Dominican Republic were eager for annexation to the United States as the only means of preserving their liberties. The physical, mental, and moral condition of the inhabitants of the republic was found to be " much more advanced than had been anticipated." Although the mass of the people were without educational advantages, yet it was believed that there were definite indications of " general political capacity." From an agricultural point of view there was every opportunity for significant development, for it was " one of the most fertile regions on the face of the earth." With regard to conditions of health the commission reported that the " average general health and longevity is quite equal to and probably greater than that of the United States, as a whole." The total public debt was only $1,334,487.59.[100]

There is one portion of the commission's report that is of particular interest. Before the departure of the commission from the United States President Grant had indicated his desire that the members examine most carefully the town records in the Dominican Republic for any evidence that he or any

---

[100] *Sen. Ex. Doc.* No. 9, 42 Cong., 1 sess., pp. 1-34. General Cazneau and his confederates had long been stressing the richness of the gold deposits in the Dominican Republic. The report of the commission is very guarded on this point, and merely says that " the gold region is extensive, and, though worked anciently, is at present but little known. It invites patient exploration by practical miners." *Ibid.*, p. 15. The geologist who accompanied the commission is much more discouraging in his report: " I deem it my duty to add that the impression produced upon me by what I have seen and heard of the mineral riches of Santo Domingo does not justify any enthusiastic expectation of wealth to the island from its mines." *Ibid.*, p. 145.

It was largely due to Professor Gabb that the commission made as favorable a report as it did on the resources of the Dominican Republic. In a letter that he wrote to Colonel Fabens on February 11, 1871, he revealed just how he worked upon the members of the commission: " Everything is serene here [Santo Domingo City]. . . . The commission & all the attachees except the editor of the ' Sun ' . . . are committed to annexation without ifs or buts. They are all very agreeably disappointed & old Ben says ' I think that the Devil must have got into Brother Sumner.' . . . My annual reports to the Govt., which were very guardedly written with a view to the present contingency, will be quoted at length and endorsed as reliable. . . . The Commissioners are all three ' down on ' their own geologist. . . . In 2 days I'm off for the field again, thank God. I'll get rid of the slavery of interviewing and dictating the same old story about the value of the country, resources, opinions of the people, absurdity of Cabral etc. *ad infinitum.*" MS. *Fabens Papers.*

other American official had received any concessions of any kind from the Dominican Government. In this regard the commissioners reported that they had not been unmindful of

various rumors . . . that concessions or grants of land were made to officials of the Government of the United States when the treaty of annexation was negotiated in 1869. No pains were spared to ascertain the exact truth on this subject. In addition to an examination of all grants from the government of the republic, the commission further carried their researches to all municipal grants by the town of Samana, where rumor located the supposed grants. . . . After this investigation the commission can declare, without hesitation, that there was no particle of evidence or color of evidence for these charges.[101]

Not only did the American commissioners fail to find any

[101] *Sen. Ex. Doc.* No. 9, 42 Cong., 1 sess., p. 31. In this same regard there is an interesting passage in the *Autobiography* of Andrew D. White (2 vols., N. Y., 1905), I, 487-488: " At various times I talked with the President on this and other subjects . . . and as I took leave of him, he gave me one charge for which I shall always revere his memory. He said: ' Your duties are, of course, imposed upon you by Congress; I have no right as *President* to give you instructions, but as a *man* I have a right in this matter. You have doubtless noticed hints in Congress, and charges in various newspapers, that I am financially interested in the acquisition of Santo Domingo. Now, as a man, as your fellow citizen, I demand that on your arrival in the island, you examine thoroughly into all American interests there; that you study land titles and contracts with the utmost care; and that if you find anything whatever which connects me or any of my family with any of them, you expose me to the American people.' The President uttered these words in a tone of deep earnestness. I left him, feeling that he was an honest man; and I may add that the closest examination of men and documents relating to titles and concessions in the island failed to reveal any personal interest of his whatsoever." It is doubtless true that Grant did not have any personal interest in concessions in the Dominican Republic. This does not mean, however, that General Babcock, General Cazneau, and Colonel Fabens were not involved in a plot with Dominican officials to " clean up big " if annexation went through. It should also be remembered that under a dictatorship like that of Baez it would be possible to " fix " town records in any manner desired. In the latter part of January, 1871 C. A. Poizat, who owned large tracts of land in the Dominican Republic, left with Robeson, the Secretary of the Navy, a letter he had received on January 11, 1871 from his agent in the republic, Waldmayer. According to this letter of Waldmayer the movement for Dominican annexation was " one tremendous job, one grand swindle in which Baez, Fabens, Cazneau, Spofford and Tyleston and a few more have the largest and most important shares. The Bay of Samana is now literally held by Spofford, Baez, Fabens, and Cazneau; it having been surveyed and staked out for them and they have put up sign boards with their names on, on the different grounds." MS. *Fish Diary*, January 27, 1871.

evidence implicating American officials in unworthy schemes to secure Dominican concessions, but they also discovered that President Baez was apparently a gentleman of culture and rectitude. Andrew D. White, a college president with a wide knowledge of men and affairs, was very favorably impressed with Baez, whom he describes as follows:

The president, Baez, was a man of force and ability, and, though a light mulatto, he had none of the characteristics generally attributed in the United States to men of mixed blood. He had rather the appearance of a swarthy Spaniard, and in all his conduct he showed quiet self-reliance, independence, and the tone of a high-spirited gentleman. . . . There was a quiet elegance in his manners and conversation which would have done credit to any statesman in any country, and he had gathered about him as his cabinet two or three really superior men who appeared devoted to his fortunes. I have never doubted that his overtures to General Grant were patriotic.[102]

Another American commissioner, Dr. Samuel G. Howe, was equally attracted by the personality of President Baez. In a letter to the editor of the New York *Independent*, of September 13, 1871, Dr. Howe gave the following pen picture of the Dominican President:

He is simple and courteous in manners; has considerable culture; and is familiar with European countries and languages. He is respected and beloved by his neighbors, who are very proud of him, as I can testify. He has been much abroad, and is there regarded as an able diplomat.[103]

These favorable opinions of the American commissioners concerning Baez and Dominican annexation had little weight with the opposition in the Senate, and no further legislative action was taken with reference to the treaties that had been

---

[102] *Autobiography*, I, 490.

[103] *Letters on the Proposed Annexation of Santo Domingo* (Boston, 1871), pp. 14-15. Ramsdell, the correspondent for the New York *Tribune*, gives a very different picture of Baez: " The fact is Sumner spoke nothing but the truth when he called Baez a ' political jockey.' He jockeys his people, and he has done his best to jockey the Commissioners. . . . He has no wife, but scores of children. He has no salary, but lives in luxury while his soldiers starve. He has neither character nor courage." New York *Tribune*, March 17, 1871.

negotiated with the Dominican Government. In the meantime, however, there were other complications in this long and involved story of American diplomatic relations with the Dominican Republic. The most disturbing factor in the situation was the attitude of Sumner towards any settlement with England relative to the " Alabama Claims." One of the main reasons why Secretary Fish retained office under Grant was his strong desire to improve the relations between England and the United States through a settlement of these claims. We have already alluded to the defeat on June 30, 1870 of the treaty providing for annexation of the Dominican Republic, and to the telegram which Secretary Fish sent to Minister Motley, at London, on the following day requesting his resignation.[104] When Motley refused to resign he was permitted to hold his post until he received, on November 22, a letter of recall from Secretary Fish (November 10, 1870).[105] He retired from his mission on December 7, upon which day he wrote to Secretary Fish a long *apologia* which reviewed at great length his services as Minister. It concluded with an acid reference to the alleged connection between his recall and Sumner's opposition to the Dominican treaty of annexation:

It has been rumored . . . that I have been removed from the post of minister to England because of the opposition made by an eminent Senator who honors me with his friendship to the ratification of the San Domingo treaty. . . . I know not whether the rejection of that treaty by the Senate was the cause of my removal, but this I do know: that the Senate rejected the treaty on the 30th of June of this year, and that the letter requesting my resignation was written the next day, namely, on the 1st of July. I here place it on record as an historical fact. I have thus recorded in my last official act a solemn protest against the outrage, as I believe entirely without precedent, of my peremptory removal.[106]

While Motley was expressing his pent-up wrath against the Secretary of State, Fish was anxiously striving to effect an agreement with England relative to the Alabama Claims. One

---

[104] See *ante,* pp. 421-422.
[105] Fish to Motley, November 10, 1870, *Credences,* vol. 3, MS. Dept. of State.
[106] *Sen. Doc.* No. 11, 41 Cong., 3 sess., pp. 25-26.

of the chief difficulties that had long stood in the way of such an agreement was the desire of certain prominent Americans to secure Canada in payment for these claims. At the beginning of his administration Grant himself had looked upon " the accession of the British Dominion to the American Union as both inevitable and highly desirable." [107] Many influential members of the Republican party reflected this same viewpoint, and Senator Chandler, of Michigan, openly declared that if England would not cede " all her interests in the Canadas " America would have to fight for them.[108] Sumner was warmly desirous that Canada be added to the American Union, but he was of the opinion that such a consolidation could best be effected through peaceful means.

It is interesting to note that this desire on the part of many Americans to bring Canada within the American federal fold was met with a definite readiness on the part of certain British officials to satisfy American wishes. In the two decades just preceding 1870, the wave of anti-imperialistic sentiment in England reached its crest.[109] Important publicists, like Goldwin Smith,[110] Henry Thring, Viscount Bury,[111] Sir George Cornewall Lewis,[112] Lord Granville,[113] Sir Frederic Rogers, and Sir

[107] C. F. Adams, *Lee at Appomattox and Other Papers,* p. 153. For a scholarly and interesting account of the diplomacy of Secretary Fish with reference to the " Alabama Claims " see Allan Nevins, *Hamilton Fish,* pp. 142-175, 201-230, 296-301, 384-399, 423-448.

[108] C. F. Adams, *op. cit.,* pp. 152-153. In his letter to Sumner of December 2, 1868, Joseph Medill gives expression to a sentiment that was common throughout the North: " There is only one adequate atonement for the injury she [England] inflicted on us in the hour of our adversity: the surrender of her North American colonial possessions to our Government." *Sumner Papers,* MS. Harvard College Library.

[109] R. L. Schuyler, " The Climax of Anti-Imperialism in England," *Political Science Quarterly,* XXXVI (1921), 538 ff.; *ibid.,* " The Recall of the Legions," *American Historical Review,* XXVI (1920), 32 ff. Also C. A. Bodelsen, *Studies in Mid-Victorian Imperialism* (London, 1924).

[110] *The Political Destiny of Canada* (London, 1878), pp. 7-114.

[111] G. B. Adams, " The Origin and Results of the Imperial Federation Movement in England," in *Proceedings of the State Historical Society of Wisconsin, 1899* (Madison, 1899).

[112] *An Essay on the Government of Dependencies* (London, 1841), pp. 334 ff.

[113] Lord Edmond Fitzmaurice, *The Life of George Levenson Gower, Second Earl Granville* (2 vols., N. Y., 1905), II, 22 ff.

Henry Taylor,[114] all inclined towards the belief that the importance to England of a vast colonial empire had been grossly exaggerated, and they shared a common opinion that these colonies would eventually proclaim their independence. On July 14, 1870 Adam Badeau, the American Consul-General at London, wrote to J. C. Bancroft Davis, the Assistant Secretary of State, with regard to British sentiment towards the United States, and in conclusion he reported as follows:

Lord Granville is strong for letting Canada go whenever she wants to.[115]

Some six months later Benjamin Moran, the American chargé d'affaires at London, wrote to Davis in a similar vein:

You will have no trouble in arranging the Fishery question at Washington and in bringing those impenitent Canadians to reason. People don't care much about retaining them and if they were to ask their independence I believe it would be granted with but little regret. . . . Ours the province must be sooner or later, and this idea is generally accepted here.[116]

The chief difficulty, however, about ceding Canada to the United States was the fact that the Canadians themselves did not look with favor upon such a transaction.[117] The British Government was forced to give careful consideration to this Canadian sentiment for a dominion status, and all talk of a possible cession to the United States was quickly abandoned.

---

[114] *Autobiography* (2 vols., N. Y., 1885), II, 194 ff.

[115] *Bancroft Davis Papers,* MS. Library of Congress.

[116] Moran to Davis, January 11, 1871, *ibid.*

[117] When Fish pressed upon Sir Edward Thornton, the British Minister, the advisability of ceding Canada to the United States, he received the following answer: " Oh, you know that we cannot do. The Canadians find fault with me for saying so openly as I do that we are ready to let them go whenever they shall wish; but they do not desire it." C. F. Adams, *Before and after the Treaty of Washington* (N. Y., 1902), p. 109. Even as late as September, 1870 Secretary Fish again pressed the matter of the cession of Canada, and again Mr. Thornton replied: " It is impossible to connect the question of Canadian independence with the Alabama claims; not even to the extent of providing for the reference of the question of independence to a popular vote of the people of the Dominion." *Ibid.,* p 112.

Secretary Fish soon realized that British policy could not run counter to such strong Canadian desires, and by December, 1870 he was entirely willing to arrange a settlement with Great Britain on terms other than those providing for a territorial cession. Sumner, however, was not willing to give up hope of securing Canada, and he was not aware of the fact that President Grant and Secretary Fish had completely reversed their former stand on this matter and were now willing to abandon all thought of acquiring Canada. He certainly had no idea that Fish would regard this adherence to an old conviction as an indication of inveterate hostility to the policy of the Administration, or that he would seize upon this as a pretext for a rupture of long-established friendly relations. The truth is that Fish was ready for an open break with Sumner. For several months prior to December, 1870 he had been growing more and more critical of Sumner, and on December 23 he expressed to Boutwell, the Secretary of the Treasury, the opinion that Sumner was " crazy," and a " monomaniac upon all matters relating to his own importance." After expressing the same opinion to Senator Conkling,[118] he sat down and wrote the well-known instruction of December 30, 1870 to Benjamin Moran, the American chargé d'affaires at London. This instruction was in answer to Motley's acrid despatch of December 7, and Fish did not mince words. With reference to Motley's insinuation that he was removed because of Sumner's hostility to the Dominican treaty of annexation, Secretary Fish remarked as follows:

Mr. Motley must know, or if he does not know it he stands alone in his ignorance of the fact, that many Senators opposed the San Domingo treaty openly, generously, and with as much efficiency as did the distinguished Senator to whom he refers, and have nevertheless continued to enjoy the undiminished confidence and the friendship of the President—than whom no man living is more tolerant of honest and manly differences of opinion, is more single or sincere in his desire for the public welfare, is more disinterested or regardless of what concerns himself, is more frank and confiding in his own dealings, is more

[118] C. F. Adams, *Lee at Appomattox and Other Papers,* pp. 251-252. Also MS. *Fish Diary,* December 23, 1870.

sensitive to a betrayal of confidence, or would look with more scorn and contempt upon one who uses the words and the assurances of friendship to cover a secret and determined purpose of hostility.[119]

It is very difficult to defend this ill-tempered instruction, and Professor Nevins frankly states that Fish must be " severely censured " for it.[120] It is hardly likely that many other Senators opposed the Dominican treaty with as " much efficiency as did the distinguished Senator " from Massachusetts, and it would appear that the warm adulation of Grant, coupled with the studied insult to Sumner, must have been written with an eye to presidential favor.[121]

On January 9, 1871, President Grant sent to the Senate the correspondence relative to the recall of Motley as Minister to England. It was not long before Sumner was apprised of the fact that Secretary Fish had made a sharp attack upon his character, and to Sumner this thrust came as a distinct surprise. Although his relations with the Secretary of State had not been as intimate as they had been during the early months of the Grant administration, yet there had never been any rupture

[119] *Sen. Doc.* No. 11, 41 Cong., 3 sess., pp. 36-37.

[120] Allan Nevins, *Hamilton Fish,* p. 455.

[121] In later years Fish indicated that he had long believed that Sumner had really promised Grant at the dinner in January, 1870 to support the Dominican treaty. On the day following this dinner at Sumner's residence, Grant told Secretary Fish " the purport of Mr. Sumner's assurances," and a few days later when Fish was discussing the matter with Sumner he was " not made aware of any difference with regard to it between the two gentlemen." See letter from Fish to the editor of the Boston *Evening Transcript,* dated October 29, 1877, published in the issue of October 31, 1877. With reference to this insult to Sumner in the instruction to Moran of December 30, 1870, Professor George H. Haynes, in his volume, *Charles Sumner* (Phila., 1909), pp. 361-362, makes the following comment: " How Fish could have allowed a not unnatural irritation to betray him into so gross an injustice to a friend of many years is as incomprehensible as his later declaration that he was ' not conscious of any just cause for the discontinuing of the relations which had existed between us.' " Sumner himself, in discussing this insult by Fish, made the following observation: " Nothing like it can be shown in the history of our government. It stands alone. . . . For years I have known secretaries of state, and often differed from them; but never before did I receive from one anything but kindness. Never before did a secretary of state sign a document libelling an associate in the public service, and publish it to the world. Never before did a secretary of state so entirely set at defiance every sentiment of friendship." *Works* (20 vols., Boston, 1899-1900), XIV, 265-266.

in their personal relations, and on December 23 he had dined at the home of Fish in company with Senator Morton. He had also assisted in the confirmation of Schenck as Motley's successor at the Court of St. James, and after this gesture of friendship he had called at the Department of State for a conference with Secretary Fish. He had no idea that Fish could use an appearance of friendship to cover a secret enmity that had long been clamoring for acidulous expression.[122]

Despite this unwarranted insult inflicted upon him by a supposed friend, Sumner was still willing to confer with Fish upon official matters. When Sir John Rose returned to Washington in the second week of January, 1871, Fish was very anxious to consult with Sumner concerning the proposed arrangement with England relative to the Alabama Claims. Since his treatment of Sumner made him somewhat fearful of the reception which would be accorded in the event that he called at the home of the Senator from Massachusetts, he commissioned Senator Patterson to inquire of Sumner whether he would be willing to receive the Secretary of State. Sumner immediately informed Patterson that " he would receive Mr. Fish as an old friend, and would be not only willing but would be glad to discuss such matters and to transact such business with him as might happen to be up for consideration." [123]

[122] E. L. Pierce, *Memoir and Letters of Charles Sumner,* IV, 465-469.

[123] *Cong. Globe,* 42 Cong., 1 sess., p. 36. With regard to his answer to Senator Patterson, Sumner gave the following version in a letter to Edward Eggleston on March 10, 1871: " The Secretary of State sent to me through Senator Patterson to know if I would receive him if he came to my house on business. I replied that I had a deep sense of wrong from him, but that I should receive him at any time, or confer with him, on public business. Accordingly, he came to my house, and I received him kindly." E. L. Pierce, *op. cit.,* IV, 468. Senator Patterson, in a letter to Secretary Fish of January 12, 1871, makes the following statement: " Mr. Sumner said he could never feel or say anything unkindly of you, as your friendship had a standing of twenty years. . . . He will receive you kindly, should you call on him." J. C. Bancroft Davis, *Mr. Fish and the Alabama Claims,* p. 134.

The anxiety of Secretary Fish with reference to Sumner's opposition to the Dominican Treaty and his desire to separate Sumner and Schurz are shown in the letter that Fish sent to Schurz, January 23, 1871: " I stated this morning to the President, the substance of your statement & arguments, . . . with regard to the sale of arms [to France], & the President sent an order to the Secretary of War, to suspend all sales. Now my dear General, you may see here an evidence

This conference between Fish and Sumner was held on January 15, and, after the whole subject of the Alabama Claims had been exhaustively discussed, Sumner promised to send to the Secretary of State a memorandum which would embody his views. In this memorandum of January 17, Sumner still adhered to his belief that the cession of Canada to the United States was the only means of effecting a permanent settlement of Anglo-American differences, and he also indicated his conviction that this cession should be merely a prelude to the complete withdrawal of the British flag from " this hemisphere, including provinces and islands."[124]

Secretary Fish gave scant heed to the recommendations contained in this Sumner memorandum, and he went ahead and made an arrangement with England which completely disregarded them. There was no reason, however, why Fish should have been deeply disturbed by these recommendations, for they clearly expressed the very viewpoints that both he and President Grant had entertained until the late autumn of 1870.[125] It is difficult, therefore, to understand why Fish should have been so " astonished " when he received Sumner's memorandum, and why Administration leaders should have immediately agreed that the opinions expressed in this memorandum were so outrageous as to justify severe party discipline being meted out to Sumner.[126]

---

of the desire on the part of the Prest. to consult your wishes, & accept your suggestions. Let me add (in confidence) that the President expressed a wish that you would call upon him." *Schurz Papers,* MS. Library of Congress.

[124] C. F. Adams, *Lee at Appomattox and Other Papers,* pp. 145-147. Sumner's attitude in the matter of the Alabama Claims is clearly expressed in his letter to Caleb Cushing of September 8, 1870: " Bemis has returned satisfied that the recent change in the English neutrality law will be set up as a bar to us in our debate, & that they are determined to . confine the question between us to the *Alabama* alone & even on this ship, to the one point of diligence in preventing the escape. Will our excellent Sec. of State play into their hands? The best part of our case is on the belligerent question. This is applicable to *all the escaped ships,* & its pressure upon England will make her more than anything else see the policy of withdrawal from our hemisphere. I take it our great object now should be the retreat of the English flag." *Caleb Cushing Papers,* MS. Library of Congress.

[125] C. F. Adams, *Before and after the Treaty of Washington,* pp. 111-114.

[126] J. C. Bancroft Davis, *Mr. Fish and the Alabama Claims,* pp. 137-139.

The infliction of party discipline upon Sumner could not be carried out until the meeting of the new Congress (the Forty-second) on March 4, 1871. In the meantime the relations between the President and Sumner continued to be as colorful as they were unpleasant. In the *Autobiography* of George F. Hoar there is to be found an interesting account of how Hoar, then a Representative from Massachusetts, met President Grant as he was walking by Lafayette Square in the direction of the residence of Senator Sumner. Hoar joined step with the President and alluded to the recent nomination of William A. Simmons for the position of Collector of the Port of Boston. Hoar drew the President's attention to the opposition that would be aroused in Massachusetts by such a nomination, and the conversation was

exceedingly quiet and friendly on both sides until we turned the corner by Mr. Sumner's house, when the President, with great emphasis, and shaking his closed fist towards Sumner's house, said: " I shall not withdraw the nomination. The man who lives up there has abused me in a way which I never suffered from any other man living." I did not, of course, press the President further. But I told him I regretted very much the misunderstanding between him and Mr. Sumner, and took my leave.[127]

While Grant was shaking his fist at Sumner's house and denouncing the Senator from Massachusetts, the Senator himself would often come to the door of his house, which faced the White House across Lafayette Square, and would proclaim in stentorian tones his bitter dislike of the President. According to Judge E. Rockwood Hoar, who often heard him, Sumner would raise his voice until he " roared like the Bull of Bashan," and it would seem that " all Washington, including Mrs. Grant, must hear and the police would have to interfere." [128]

In a bitter personal quarrel of this type it was inevitable that Grant, with all the power and prestige of his office, would be able to inflict some deep humiliation upon Sumner. The first

[127] G. F. Hoar, *Autobiography of Seventy Years* (2 vols., N. Y., 1903), I, 210-211.

[128] G. H. Haynes, *Charles Sumner*, p. 359.

manifestation of Grant's power in this regard came in the early part of February, 1871. Grant had sent to the Senate the nomination of M. J. Cramer as Minister to Denmark. Cramer was a brother-in-law of the President, and his main qualification for office was the fact that he was a Methodist preacher with a certain eloquence as an exhorter. Sumner was not impressed with this somewhat dubious qualification and immediately opposed the confirmation of Cramer's nomination. Senator Chandler promptly moved that the Senate Committee on Foreign Relations be discharged from any further consideration of Cramer's nomination, and during three long executive sessions this motion was warmly debated. Finally Sumner, sensing defeat, left the Senate Chamber, and Cramer was confirmed " without a division of the Senators." [129]

The New York *Herald,* in commenting upon this defeat of Sumner, called attention to Chandler's desire further to humble Sumner:

Chandler is greatly elated at his success. He may now attempt to carry out his original idea of reconstructing the Foreign Relations Committee and leaving Sumner out in the cold.[130]

The accuracy of this premonition was proved by the actions of Chandler and his coterie. In their attack upon Sumner they were greatly aided by the intemperate utterances of the Senator himself. At a dinner given by one of the British members of the Joint High Commission, an illusion was made to the evident popularity of President Grant and the likelihood of his being elected a second time. Upon hearing this remark, Sumner is said to have exclaimed in great excitement:

No, he'll be impeached for high crimes and misdemeanors. I tell you, he will be impeached for high crimes and misdemeanors.[131]

Senator Dickson, of Connecticut, was present at this dinner, and on the following morning he related to Senator William M. Stewart, of Nevada, the story of Sumner's heated remarks about the President. Senator Anthony, of Rhode Island, the

---

[129] New York *Herald,* February 6, 1871.
[130] *Ibid.*   [131] W. M. Stewart, *Reminiscences,* p. 247.

chairman of the Senate Republican caucus, was next consulted, and he at once invited Secretary Fish to come to the Capitol to confer with the Republican Senators. Fish accepted this invitation and confirmed the account given by Senator Dickson, whereupon Senator Anthony called for a meeting of the Republican caucus.[132] At this meeting some of the Senators, like John Sherman, deprecated any move to depose Sumner as chairman of the Senate Committee on Foreign Relations and preferred merely to have the membership of the committee fixed so that the Administration would safely control a majority.[133] The opponents of Sumner, however, were not satisfied with such a tame solution of the quarrel between Sumner and Grant, and they insisted upon Sumner's deposition as chairman and his transference to a new committee which was to be designated the Committee on Privileges and Elections.

It happened that Horace White was then in town, and at a dinner given by Representative William B. Allison he heard the full story of the meeting of the Republican caucus and the action that had been taken with reference to the deposition of Sumner. Fearful that such a step would be a fatal blow to the Republican party, he persuaded Allison to accompany him to the apartment of Senator Howe in order that they might convince the Senator of the inexpediency of deposing Sumner.[134] Many years later he related to E. L. Pierce, who was writing the definitive biography of Sumner, the failure of his efforts:

My interview with Senator Howe in March, 1871, was sought for the purpose of persuading him to reconsider his purpose of displacing Mr. Sumner from the Chairmanship of the Committee on Foreign Relations. Mr. Howe was, as you know, the Chairman of the Senate Caucus Committee. . . . I sought the interview not from any desire to be serviceable to Mr. Sumner, but in order to prevent . . . a schism in the Republican party, which I thought would be most likely to follow an attempt to punish a Senator of Mr. Sumner's standing for exercising

---

[132] *Ibid.*, p. 248.
[133] John Sherman, *Recollections of Forty Years in the House, Senate and Cabinet*, I, 472-473.
[134] Horace White, *Life of Lyman Trumbull*, pp. 346-347.

his right to oppose the annexation of Santo Domingo. He [Mr. Howe] considered it of the first importance that the Chairman of the Foreign Committee should be a person not obnoxious to the President. . . . All this harmonizes with what Mr. Howe subsequently said in public debate except that in the debate he put Secretary Fish in the forefront instead of the President. . . . If Mr. Fish alone had been concerned not one Senator in the whole number would have dreamed of doing such a thing.[135]

All the admonitions of Horace White and Allison were in vain, and on the following day the caucus list of Senate committees was formally presented to that body. It was evident at once that the enemies of Sumner had been busy, for he was no longer listed as a member of the Committee on Foreign Relations but was named as chairman of the Committee on Privileges and Elections. His deposition as chairman of the Committee on Foreign Relations aroused a bitter and lengthy debate. Sumner quickly informed the Senate that he did not care to serve as chairman of the Committee on Privileges and Elections, and permission was given him to withdraw his name.[136]   Senator Schurz then inquired into the reasons for Sumner's deposition. He was confident that both the Senate and the country at large realized that

the duties connected with the chairmanship of the Committee on Foreign Relations have been discharged by the Senator from Massachusetts with great credit to himself and to the committee, and I have no doubt with great satisfaction to the American people.

Schurz next expressed serious doubts that the new chairman of the Committee on Foreign Relations, Simon Cameron, possessed qualifications superior to those of Sumner, and turning to Senator Howe he demanded that the real reasons for Sumner's deposition be made public.[137] As he stood on the Senate floor waiting for Howe's reply, several of the Administration leaders in the Senate advised Howe in a stage whisper—" Don't

---

[135] White to Pierce, October 9, 1888, *Pierce Papers*, MS. Harvard College Library.

[136] *Cong. Globe*, 42 Cong., 1 sess., p. 34.

[137] *Ibid.*, pp. 34-35.

answer him." [138] Senator Stewart, in particular, seemed especially anxious that no answer be given to Schurz, and he openly admonished Howe not to " say a word." [139]

It was an awkward moment for Administration leaders. Senator Morton could not sit still and kept twisting around in his chair as though he were wearing a Nessus shirt. Senator Sherman was equally uneasy, and, after making a pretense of reading a newspaper, he began tearing up small strips of paper and finally paced the Senate chamber with a nervous tread.[140] But Senator Howe, who " appeared throughout like a gentleman engaged in a dirty piece of work," [141] was willing to assume the task of speaking for the Administration forces, and he advanced as the reason for Sumner's deposition the alleged fact that the " personal relations existing between the Senator from Massachusetts and the President of the United States and the head of the State Department are such as preclude . . . all social intercourse between them." He had understood that the Senator from Massachusetts

refused to hold personal intercourse with the Secretary of State and that he has not had any personal intercourse with the President of the United States, and it was deemed best that the head of that committee should be on speaking terms, at all events, with those officers, in order to discharge all his duties to the people of the United States.[142]

When Senator Schurz asserted that Sumner had been entirely willing at all times to enter into " official relations " with either the President or the Secretary of State, Senator Howe replied that he had not spoken of " official relations " but of " personal relations." [143]

Senator Wilson, of Massachusetts, in defense of his colleague expressed the opinion that it was not the business of the Senate to concern itself with the personal or social relations between the chairman of the Committee on Foreign Relations and the President and the Secretary of State.[144]   The

[138] *Nation*, XII (1871), 175.
[139] *Cong. Globe*, 42 Cong., 1 sess., p. 35.
[140] New York *World*, March 11, 1871.
[141] *Nation*, XII (1871), 175.
[142] *Cong. Globe*, 42 Cong., 1 sess., p. 35.
[143] *Ibid.*, p. 35.   [144] *Ibid.*

position taken by Senator Wilson was strongly supported by Senator Schurz, who came to the concluson that the real reason for Sumner's deposition was the " San Domingo scheme." [145]

Senator Howe now returned to the attack with a new charge against Sumner. It was only something that he had " heard " about the Senator from Massachusetts, but it was a very grave indictment. He had heard

from the lips of a Secretary and the lips of a Senator, that the Secretary of State addressed a question to the Senator from Massachusetts, in a public place before official characters, which the Senator refused to answer.[146]

The position taken by Senator Howe was so ridiculous that Senator Bayard, of Delaware, lost no time in introducing a resolution which seemed to fit the situation:

That the title of the committee heretofore known as the Committee on Foreign Relations be changed to the Committee on Personal Relations.[147]

The comic-opera quality of the discussion was clearly indicated by Senator Trumbull, who was opposed to Sumner's deposition. He thought things had come to a sorry pass when the Senate would stoop to an inquiry into the " personal relations " between the members of its body and " any man under Heaven." For several hours the Senate had been discussing this trivial point, and

what had this discussion disclosed? Let it go out to the American people that the Senate of the United States has occupied a whole day in inquiring upon the doubtful question as to whether one of its members answered an inquiry on some social occasion, not in discharge of official duty; for it is distinctly avowed that there is no pretense that there has been any discourtesy, so far as official intercourse is concerned, between the chairman of the Committee on Foreign Relations and either the President of the United States or the head of any of its Executive Departments. Whatever there is of it is a personal matter; and we are to investigate that! Why, sir, I have no patience to talk about it, to spend a moment's time in regard to it.[148]

[145] *Ibid.*, pp. 36-37. See also C. M. Fuess, *Carl Schurz* (N. Y., 1935), pp. 174 ff.

[146] *Ibid.*, p. 41.   [147] *Ibid.*, p. 53.   [148] *Ibid.*, p. 50.

Although the friends of Sumner had reduced to an absurdity the chief argument presented by Administration leaders with reference to Sumner's deposition, the Republican majority in the Senate followed directions from the White House and the caucus list of Senate committees was adopted by the large vote of 33 yeas to only 9 nays.[149]

The " hero of Appomattox " had won another victory but he had not counted the cost. On the day following the deposition of Sumner there was an outburst of indignation throughout the country against such an action. The New York *World* thought that the " exchange " of Cameron for Sumner as chairman of the Senate Committee on Foreign Relations was like " swapping an eagle for a toad," and that the " Republican party is no longer a party of ideas and principles, but the personal party of President Grant, held together by ' the cohesive force of public plunder.' " [150]

A large number of newspapers, both Republican and Democratic, were unsparing in their criticism of the Senate caucus committee for deposing Sumner. The following excerpt from the Philadelphia *Press* indicates the tenor of these newspaper attacks:

Every Republican paper that comes to us, with but one or two exceptions, denounces the removal of Senator Sumner from the chairman-

[149] *Ibid.*, p. 53. With regard to Grant's insistence on the deposition of Sumner there is a pertinent passage in a letter from Horace White to E. L. Pierce on October 14, 1888: " One of the stories going around Washington by word of mouth at that time was that Grant had said that if Sumner was not removed from the chairmanship of the Foreign Committee he (Grant) would resign the Presidency. This story has some verisimilitude in Grant's terrible earnestness about anything that he had set his mind on." *E. L. Pierce Papers,* MS. Harvard College Library. In a letter to A. G. Cattell, on March 21, 1871, President Grant denied that at the opening of the Forty-second Congress he had " desired a reconstruction of the Senate Committee on Foreign Relations for the purpose of securing favorable action upon the question of annexation." He then stated that he had " never asked to have any particular person put upon any one of the Senate Standing Committees. All that I have asked is that the Chairman of the Committee on Foreign Relations might be some one with whom the Secretary of State and myself might confer and advise. This I deemed due to the Country in view of the very important questions, which, of necessity, must come before it." *Grant Letter Book,* MS. Library of Congress.

[150] March 14, 1871.

ship of the Foreign Relations Committee, and protests against the un-justifiable and insane action of the Senate caucus.[151]

Indignation at Sumner's deposition was not confined to the public press. Many outstanding leaders in the Republican party deeply regretted the action of the caucus committee. James A. Garfield wrote to T. J. McLain that he regarded Sumner's humiliation as " an act of the most stupendous folly." He added: " It will remind the country of Buchanan's removal of Douglas from the Chairmanship of the Committee on Territories in 1858." [152] Horace Greeley expressed the opinion that the discipline enforced upon Sumner was " a mistake," [153] while Speaker James G. Blaine in later years denounced Sumner's deposition as " an act of grave in-justice."[154]

The manifest absurdity of deposing Sumner because he no longer had " personal relations " with the President and the Secretary of State soon became so increasingly apparent even to " stalwart " Republicans that both Grant and Fish endeav-ored to find other arguments that would have more weight with the intelligent public. After much careful consideration they finally adduced the following:

1. Summer was negligent in not reporting treaties referred to the Senate Committee on Foreign Relations.

2. He was seriously at fault in not " moving forward " the treaties in the Senate and " securing its action upon them."

3. He would have impeded the negotiation and ratification of the Treaty of Washington.

The first two of these charges against Sumner have been

---

[151] New York *World*, March 13, 1871, publishes a symposium of press opinions hostile to the deposition of Sumner. Among the papers quoted are the Chicago *Tribune*, Toledo *Blade*, Boston *Transcript*, Hartford *Post*, Philadelphia *Bulletin*, Boston *Journal*, Springfield *Republican,* Rochester *Democrat*, and the Providence *Press*.

[152] Theodore C. Smith, *Life and Letters of James A. Garfield* (2 vols., New Haven, 1925), I, 469.

[153] New York *Tribune*, March 13, 1871.

[154] *Twenty Years of Congress*, II, 503. Vol. 106 of the *Sumner Papers* in Harvard College Library is filled with letters of indignation from Sumner's friends with regard to his deposition.

completely broken down by Edward L. Pierce, in his monu-mental biography of Sumner.[155] The last charge has been echoed by certain historians, and was given the most scholarly support by Charles Francis Adams in his able monograph, *Before and after the Treaty of Washington*. After a pains-taking examination of all the factors in the situation and es-pecially of Sumner's insistence upon the withdrawal of the British flag from the North American continent, Adams comes to the conclusion that

under these circumstances the course now pursued [the removal of Sumner] was more than justifiable; it was necessary, as well as right.

---

[155] *Memoir and Letters of Charles Sumner,* IV, 479-480, 625-638. The fol-lowing statement of Ben: Perley Poore, in his letter published in the Boston *Journal* on October 24, 1877, is quite significant: "I must add, in justice to the memory of Mr. Sumner, that in my long experience at Washington, as a journalist and as an officer of the Senate, I have never known a chairman of a committee who was more diligent and painstaking with regard to the business referred to his committee than Mr. Sumner was in 1861-63, when I had the honor to serve as clerk of the Committee on Foreign Relations of the Senate, of which he was the Chairman. Every bill, resolution, nomination or treaty referred to the committee was immediately examined, references bearing on it were hunted up and briefed, and when the committee met, Mr. Sumner was able to answer all inquiries as he pushed the business, invariably clearing the committee docket."

As an evidence of the care and punctuality with which Sumner conducted the duties of chairman of the Committee on Foreign Relations the following letter has some value: "I hope you will pardon me if I call your attention to my communication two weeks ago inviting you to furnish the draft of a bill to carry out the recommendation of the President in his annual message with regard to the claims on England." Sumner to Fish, January 28, 1871, *Misc. Letters, January, 1871,* MS. Dept. of State.

With regard to the alleged fault of Sumner in delaying the consideration of treaties, the following letter from Secretary Fish to Senator Cameron, the new chairman of the Senate Committee on Foreign Relations, is pertinent: "I beg to tender to you my very sincere and earnest thanks for the generous and very efficient and effective aid and support you have rendered to the various subjects which have gone from the Department of State to the Senate since you have been at the head of the Committee on Foreign Relations, and particularly to the Treaty with Great Britain. Since you took charge in the Senate of the business from this Department I have felt that important measures and Treaties negotiated were no longer to be smothered or pigeon-holed in the Committee Room, and the Country owes to you that a number of Treaties which had thus laid buried for weeks and months were readily and easily passed and the nation saved the discredit of negotiating and then neglecting to act upon solemn conventions with other Powers. Personally I desire to make my thanks for your warm support of the Treaty with Great Britain." Fish to Cameron, May 30, 1871, *Simon Came-ron Papers,* MS. Library of Congress.

For the Administration, in the face of the notice thus given, to have permitted the continuance of Mr. Sumner in his chairmanship, if to prevent was in its power, would have been worse than childish; it would have distinctly savored of bad faith.[156]

This conclusion of Adams is based upon the idea that if Sumner had remained in his position as chairman of the Committee on Foreign Relations it would " almost unquestionably have been in his power to secure the defeat of the Treaty through the adoption of plausible amendments." [157]

Such a statement hardly does credit to the ability of the astute Administration supporters in the Senate, and one should keep well in mind the fact that, aside from his memorandum of January 17, Sumner had at the time of his deposition given no sign of obstructing, or wishing to obstruct, the progress of negotiations for a treaty which were then under full headway.[158]

But if Sumner showed no disposition to obstruct the ratification of the Treaty of Washington, he indicated very positively that he was still actively opposed to the Administration in the matter of Dominican annexation. On February 18, 1871 he suffered a severe attack of angina pectoris, but this did not prevent him from gathering materials for a last attack upon the Dominican policy of the President. On February 23, Ben: Perley Poore wrote to E. L. Pierce that Sumner's " whole heart and soul " were bent upon making a speech about the Dominican Republic which would be " virtually an impeachment of Grant before humanity for having used our forces to maintain peace on the island pending negotiations." [159]

---

[156] *Op. cit.*, pp. 128-129. In this same regard see the comments of Allan Nevins in his *Hamilton Fish*, p. 463: " By a few fiery speeches, Sumner might easily have excited public opinion again; by adroit amendments, he might have played the rôle that Lodge played with reservations in 1919. From this point of view, the displacement of Sumner was the Administration's practical answer to the ' hemispheric withdrawal ' letter of January 17."

[157] *Ibid.*, p. 131.

[158] Daniel H. Chamberlain, *Charles Sumner and the Treaty of Washington* (Worcester, 1902), p. 24.

[159] *Pierce Papers*, MS. Harvard College Library. On March 19, 1871, Fish was informed by a friend that Sumner was threatening to make a speech in which he intended to attack the Secretary of State " violently." It was said that Sumner

On March 27 Sumner finished his feverish preparations for a final assault upon the President's position, and the élite of Washington society crowded the Senate gallery and over-flowed into the lobbies and cloak-rooms in their anxiety to hear the Senator from Massachusetts deliver his long-heralded attack on executive usurpation. The House of Representatives adjourned for the occasion, and Speaker James G. Blaine occupied a seat beside the Vice-President. As Sumner entered the Senate chamber there was a burst of applause from the galleries,[160] and encouraged by this manifestation of cordial popular support he began a speech which has long been a classic in the literature on presidential powers.

In this speech Sumner echoed a note which he first sounded in June, 1862, in a debate in the Senate on the Confiscation Acts. At that time Sumner attacked President Lincoln for exercising powers that rightly belonged to Congress, and he warmly asserted that "Congress is the arbiter and regulator of the War Powers." Any "pretension" that these enormous powers belonged to the President was regarded by him as "absurd and tyrannical" and not "entitled to respect."[161] In 1871 Sumner still believed in a narrow construction of the war powers of the President, and he now marshalled a vast amount of material to show how Grant had exceeded these powers. On the basis of the evidence that was before the Senate it was

plain that the Navy of the United States, acting under orders from Washington, has been engaged in measures of violence, and of bel-ligerent intervention, being war, without the authority of Congress. . . . Such a case cannot pass without inquiry. It is too grave for silence.[162]

Along with this speech against the President for his alleged exercise of war powers that belonged only to Congress, Sumner also introduced resolutions which declared that the President

had remarked that "he excused Grant for his ignorance, but that Fish was the Mephistopheles who entrapped, and led him astray." MS. *Fish Diary.*

[160] New York *Herald*, March 28, 1871.

[161] Charles Sumner, *Works*, IX, 138-139.

[162] *Cong. Globe*, 42 Cong., 1 sess., p. 294.

could not, by the mere negotiation of an unratified treaty, acquire the right to make war upon another nation. Therefore, the

employment of the Navy without the authority of Congress in act of hostility against a friendly foreign nation, or in belligerent intervention in the affairs of a foreign nation, is an infraction of the Constitution of the United States and a usurpation of power not conferred upon the President.[163]

On March 28, Senator Schurz made a speech in which he gave strong support to Sumner's resolutions. In criticizing the President's action relative to the employment of the Navy for the protection of the territory of the Dominican Republic during the pendency of the treaty for annexation, Schurz made the following remarks:

The Constitution of the United States provides that the Congress shall have power to declare war; but my eloquent friend from Wisconsin [Senator Howe], steps in and says, as I understood him, although Congress may have the sole power, with the approval of the President, to declare war, yet war can be made, acts of war can be committed without the authority of Congress. . . . What is that great safeguard of our peace and security, as it is written in the Constitution, that Congress, and not the President alone, shall have the power to declare war—what is it worth if an executive officer of the Government can initiate or make war

[163] *Ibid.*, p. 294. The New York *Herald*, which in 1870 had been hostile to Sumner, in March, 1871 was distinctly friendly. With reference to his speech on March 27, the *Herald* of March 28, 1871 remarked as follows: "Rarely has there been delivered in the halls of Congress a speech marked with as much ability or carrying more important political consequences in its train. Though a long one, it is terse, argumentative, statesmanlike and confined to the subject embraced in the resolution submitted by the Senator. . . . In fact, Mr. Sumner makes out a case for impeachment of a much more serious nature than that worked up against President Johnson." Of like tenor is the following excerpt from an editorial in the New York *World* of March 30, 1871: "Grant's use of the military power, as he employed it in the West Indies, is clearly an impeachable offense. Sumner uncovered the crime, and for *that* he was ejected from his place on the Foreign Affairs Committee of the Senate." There were some opponents of annexation who did not think that Sumner's speech was any too effective. Edward G. Holden in writing to Schurz, March 31, 1871, observed: "I hope the San Domingo Humbug is dead and that it will be kicked out of politics, but I don't think Sumner's last speech a very strong one." *Schurz Papers*, MS. Library of Congress.

without congressional authority? . . . Sir, that simple provision of the Constitution that Congress shall have power to declare war cannot by any rule of construction be interpreted to mean anything else but that Congress, and not the President alone, shall define the contingencies in which the belligerent power of the United States is to be used. I therefore affirm that the President in ordering the naval commanders of the United States to capture and destroy by force of arms the vessels of a nation with whom the United States were at peace, in a contingency arbitrarily defined by himself other than self defense, did usurp the war-making power of Congress.[164]

On the following day (March 29), Senator Harlan delivered a speech in answer to the attacks of both Senators Sumner and Schurz upon the Dominican policy of the Administration. It was an able and cogent defense of the actions of President Grant, and it brought to a close the debate on Sumner's resolution. With reference to the power to protect the " inchoate interests " of the United States in a territory during the pendency of a treaty, Senator Harlan observed:

When we were disputing with Great Britain about our northeastern boundary, I remember we arrayed some military forces in that vicinity. When we were engaged in a controversy with the same Government on the northwestern boundary, I remember that the disputed territory was taken possession of by the troops of the United States without any formal declaration of war. I have heard something of the bombardment of Greytown by the Navy of the United States, and I have never seen any declaration of war to justify that act of hostility. . . . I have heard something of the bombardment of the ports of Japan by the combined Navy of the United States, France, and England, which . . . was not condemned, and we took our share of the indemnity thus secured from the Government of Japan, . . . yet there was no formal declaration of war to justify it.

. . . Now, how do you account for all these acts of hostility, not threats, not diplomatic despatches merely, not a declaration if our rights shall be invaded we would defend them, but actual war; not a war of words, but a war made with armies and navies, taking possession of disputed and hostile territory, fighting pitched battles and bombarding cities; war made with guns and solid shot and shell, where we compelled

[164] *Cong. Globe*, 42 Cong., 1 sess., App., pp. 51-52.

the vanquished to pay indemnity and put it into our Treasury, and yet no declaration of war? How does it happen that these two Senators, in their zeal to defend the Constitution of the United States, can find but one case worthy of their logic, their great learning, and their eloquence? [165]

In this speech in defense of the President's Dominican policy Senator Harlan showed that he could be adroit as well as direct. There was a definite weakness in the President's position which the opponents of annexation overlooked, and which the supporters of the Administration ignored. According to Article IV of the treaty of annexation (November 29, 1869) it was expressly provided that

the people of the Dominican Republic, shall, in the shortest possible time, express, in a manner conformable to their laws, their will concerning the cession herein provided for; and the United States shall, until such expression shall be had, protect the Dominican Republic against foreign interposition, in order that the national expression may be free.

The phraseology of this article was very clear and could bear but one interpretation—that the American Government would afford protection to the Dominican Government only during the period necessary for securing from the Dominican people an expression of their sentiment relative to annexation. This expression was secured through means of a plebiscite which was held on February 19, and the results of this plebiscite were communicated by the Dominican Secretary of Foreign Affairs to the American Secretary of State on March 19, 1870.[166] It may well have been that President Grant and Secretary Fish were of the opinion that, after the people of the Dominican Republic had voted in favor of American annexation, such a pledge of protection was no longer needed because no nation would dare to oppose American desires. However that may be, it is certain that Secretary Fish had qualms about the right of the American Government formally to extend protection to the Dominican Government after the results of the plebiscite had been communicated to it on March 19. But these qualms

[165] *Ibid.*, p. 65.   [166] See *ante*, pp. 396-397.

did not extend to President Grant, who, long after March, 1870, continued to send orders (through Secretary Robeson) to the commanders of American squadrons in the West Indies to repel any attacks upon Dominican territory.

Throughout the summer of 1870, after the defeat of the annexation treaty in the Senate on June 30, this policy of protection was adhered to, and on July 21 Commodore J. F. Green informed the Secretary of the Navy that a reversal of this policy would "instantly lead to a revolution, headed by Cabral." [167]   In January, 1871 Rear-Admiral S. P. Lee was still carrying out orders for Dominican protection,[168] and on February 8 the President himself ordered the Secretary of the Navy to send a vessel to Haitian waters for the purpose of watching the movements of General Luperón, a Dominican revolutionist.[169]

On March 20, 1871 the Dominican Secretary of Foreign Affairs, Manuel Gautier, addressed a letter to Secretary Fish in which he complained of the assistance being given by the Haitian Government to Dominican revolutionists. In concluding his letter he asked for American protection against these attacks from Haitian territory, and on April 14 the whole matter was discussed in a Cabinet meeting.[170] The President was inclined to let the letter remain unanswered, but Secretary Fish expressed strong opposition to such a course and finally it was decided that a very "guarded" answer should be sent to Gautier.

During the discussion as to the action to be taken in regard to this letter from M. Gautier, the question of American protection of Dominican territory inevitably arose. Secretary Robeson, through whom the President's orders were being executed, thought that it was "important" to have this question of protection properly understood, and the other members of the Cabinet waited for the Secretary of State to express himself. Fish immediately informed them that he believed that the pledge of protection in the treaty of annexation referred only

---

[167] *Sen. Ex. Doc.* No. 34, 41 Cong., 3 sess., p. 23.

[168] *Ibid.*, p. 29.

[169] MS. *Fish Diary*, February 8, 1871.   [170] *Ibid.*, April 14, 1871.

to the period during which the plebiscite was to be held, and was for the purpose of securing " a free and uncontrolled expression of the popular will." He also believed that when this plebiscite had been taken the pledge of protection was no longer operative.

President Grant was dubious about this interpretation of Secretary Fish, and he inquired about the relationship between the treaty for the lease of Samaná Bay and the pledge of protection. Fish promptly answered that the time for the exchange of the ratifications of this treaty had expired without affirmative action, and Grant then remarked that at any rate the United States was still in possession of Samaná. Fish closed the discussion by expressing the view that the possession of Samaná Bay did " not renew or extend " the obligation of American protection of Dominican territory.[171]

Some two months later another Cabinet meeting was held with reference to the Dominican situation, and the President read a letter from Dr. S. G. Howe in which a strong plea was made for a renewal of the lease of Samaná Bay and the continuance of American protection over the Dominican Republic.[172] Secretary Robeson then referred to the orders that had been given to the commanding officers of American war-ships

---

[171] *Ibid.*

[172] In a letter to Andrew D. White, on June 5, 1871, Dr. S. G. Howe enclosed a copy of his letter to President Grant. The tenor of this communication to the President is clearly shown by the following excerpts: " I believe that you can, at this moment, do more than any human being, to avert a civil war which with all the usual train of blood and misery, impends over a neighboring people. . . . The Dominicans perish while our politicians squabble and insist that they shall not be saved, except by their special prescriptions. . . . A fearful crisis has arrived in the island. The treasury is depleted. The general hope and belief so fondly entertained by the masses that annexation would come to give them peace and security is turning to bitter disappointment and despair. The only thing which feeds hope is the fact that our flag still floats over Samana. . . . If I understand right, we hold Samana in virtue of an article extending the time for ratification of the treaty of 1870, to July, 1871. Now even if the whole project of a treaty was not annulled by the failure of the Senate to ratify it, still it must expire with this month of June. For the honor of our country, the rent now justly due for our use and occupation of Samana Bay ought to be paid to the government of Santo Domingo. . . . But if this cannot be, then for the sake of humanity, I hope that a new treaty may be immediately initiated." *Andrew D. White Papers*, MS. Cornell University Library.

in Dominican waters relative to protection of Dominican territory. Secretary Fish remarked that all obligations of American protection had long since expired and suggested that these orders be immediately revoked.[173]

On the following day Secretary Boutwell called at the home of Secretary Fish to discuss the matter of American protection of Dominican territory. Boutwell was fearful that the orders from the Secretary of the Navy to the naval officers in Dominican waters would involve the Administration in an " active complication," and he was in favor of their revocation. Secretary Fish concurred in this view inasmuch as the pledge of protection in the treaty of annexation had referred only to the period preceding the plebiscite. Even if it were held that the treaty for the lease of Samaná Bay implied a promise of American protection, it was now apparent that this pledge had expired in July, 1870.[174]

These references to the manuscript *Diary* of Secretary Fish shed new light on this Senate debate in March, 1871. They clearly indicate that Senators supporting the Administration were visiting the Department of State in order to secure information concerning American pledges of protection to the Dominican Government.[175] They also reveal the fact that Secretary Fish himself realized that President Grant had exceeded his authority in giving orders for the protection of Dominican territory after the expiration of the treaties which gave the basis for this authority. Fish had gladly supplied Senator Morton with information concerning the pledge of protection that had been given by President Tyler and Secretary Calhoun to the Government of Texas in 1844, upon the signature of the treaty of annexation.[176] He had supplied simi-

---

[173] MS. *Fish Diary*, June 16, 1871.

[174] It had been the purpose of President Grant to have the treaty for the lease of Samaná Bay extended for one year in order to permit the exchange of ratifications as late as July 1, 1871. On July 7, 1870 Secretary Fish and Colonel Fabens signed an article extending the time for the exchange of ratifications to July 1, 1871, but President Grant, through an oversight, forgot to transmit this article to the Senate and it was never voted upon. MS. *Fish Diary*, June 17, 21, 1871.

[175] *Ibid.*, March 24, 1871.

[176] *Ibid.*, March 24, 1871, and *Cong. Globe*, 42 Cong., 1 sess., pp. 327 ff.

lar information to Senator Harlan for the purpose of defending the Administration against the attacks of Sumner and Schurz, but he well realized that the Texas precedent had little relation to the Dominican situation. The pledge given to the Government of Texas had reference only to the pending treaty of April 12, 1844, and was to be in force merely while this treaty was pending in the American Senate.[177] The pledge given to the Dominican Government had certainly lapsed in July, 1870, upon the expiration of the treaty for the lease of Samaná Bay, and the orders given by President Grant after that date for the protection of Dominican territory were undoubtedly without any authority whatever. Sumner was on much firmer ground than even he realized, and it is a curious circumstance that the best justification of his position is now revealed in the manuscript *Diary* of Hamilton Fish.

---

[177] C. C. Tansill, " War Powers of the President of the United States with Special Reference to the Beginning of Hostilities," *Political Science Quarterly*, XLV (1930), 41 ff. The inapplicability of the Texas precedent to the Dominican situation was clearly recognized by many leading Republican periodicals. The following excerpt is typical of this attitude: " The precedents of Texas and of Florida, which were quoted, are wholly inapplicable. There has, unquestionably, been a misconception of the limits of executive power, and a consequent action which is constitutionally indefensible." *Harper's Weekly*, XV (1871), p. 331.

INDEX

Abbott, Senator Joseph C., 404.

Adams, Charles Francis, justifies deposition of Sumner as chairman of Senate Committee on Foreign Relations, 455-456.

Adams, Henry, exaggerates importance of Sumner's rôle in fight against Dominican treaty, 341.

Adams, John, emphasizes importance of American trade with French islands, 3; favors Haitian independence, 34; makes no response to British offers of naval protection, 32; is not ready for alliance with England, 35; opposes Haitian independence, 53; believes Anglo-American harmony essential, 68-69; lifts embargo on trade with Haiti, 70; favors strong measures against Rigaud, 73.

Adams, John Quincy, favors independence of French islands, 13; believes Jefferson anxious to restrain trade with Haiti, 104; supports appointment of American consul to Haiti, 123.

Allison, William B., 449.

Alta Vela, guano island, is discovered by Captain Kimball, 290; taken possession of in names of Patterson and Murguiendo, 290-291; Americans ejected from, 292; discussions in regard to, 287-337.

Ambler, Senator Jacob A., introduces amendment to Morton resolution, 436; amendment agreed to, 436.

American West India Company, is organized by General Cazneau, 216-217; issues circulars to induce immigration, 218; its project fails, 220.

Ammen, Admiral Daniel, advocates annexation of Dominican Republic, 351.

Anthony, Senator Henry B., chairman of Senate caucus, invites Fish to Senatorial conference, 449.

Armstrong, Andrew, is received by President Boyer as Commercial Agent, 119.

Armstrong, General John, American Minister at Paris, 106-108.

Ashley, James M., is removed as Governor of Montana Territory, 384; effect of removal upon Ohio politics, 384-385; anger of Sumner at removal of, 384-385.

Augenard, Louis P., agent of Dominican Government, works for annexation, 272; supplies Seward with information, 277-278.

Aves Island, 305.

Babcock, General Orville E., background and character of, 351-353; sent to Dominican Republic, 359; without diplomatic status, 361; arrives at Santo Domingo City, 362; concludes treaties, 362-363; returns to Dominican Republic, 371; urges Major Perry to be friendly with Cazneau, 376; has Perry sign treaties of annexation and lease of Samaná Bay, 378; hoists American flag over Samaná Bay, 379; advises Fabens on Dominican finances, 414.

Badeau, General Adam, believes Lord Granville favors cession of Canada to United States, 442.

Baez, Buenaventura, President of Dominican Republic, is ready to accept French protectorate, 124; accedes to presidential office, 134; character of, 134; becomes President second time, 206; hostile to United States, 206; retires from presidency, 207; criticism of, 223-224; returns to presidential office, 224; requests Johnson to recognize Dominican Republic, 228; is praised by Mrs. Cazneau, 229-230; invites American investments, 229-230; is forced to vacate presidency, 231; reinstalled as Presi-

public, 206-207; urges Cass to negotiate for naval base, 208.

Eppes, John W., is opposed to American trade with Haiti, 105.

Everett, Edward, Secretary of State, fears French intrigue in Dominican Republic, 172; requests Secretary of Navy to have survey made of Dominican situation, 173; is informed France harbors no designs upon Dominican Republic, 173.

Ewing, Thomas, urges President Johnson not to select Jeremiah Black as one of his counsel, 313.

Fabens, Colonel Joseph W., tries to secure concessions from Spanish Government, 216-217; appointed secretary of American West India Company, 217; writes pamphlet on resources of Santo Domingo, 218-219; publishes travel-book on Dominican Republic, 219-220; believes Samaná Bay can be secured, 246; suggests naval base at Monte Christo, 247; tells Seward of opportunities for American capitalists, 260; wins support of Thaddeus Stevens, 265; informs Seward of mining concession, 266; inquires of General Butler about payment for Samaná Bay, 273; gives estimate of Dominican public debt, 282; early life of, 343-344; tries to secure concessions from President Santana, 344; helps to organize American West India Company, 344; persuades Dominican Government to grant concession for geological survey, 344-345; launches Santo Domingo Company, 345; has close association with Spofford, Tileston and Company, 346; incorporates National Bank of Santo Domingo, 346; is employed by Edward H. Hartmont, 349; sends Fish report on conditions in Dominican Republic, 353-354; assures State Department Samaná Bay can be leased, 354; informs Cazneau that Fish favors Dominican annexation, 354; visits Dominican Republic, 357-358;

is sent back to United States as Dominican agent, 358; writes to Sumner about Dominican annexation, 359-360; urges Fish to send agent to Dominican Republic, 359; accompanies General Babcock on first trip to Dominican Republic, 362; assists in negotiations for annexation, 375; assures Fish Dominican people desire annexation, 383; tries to enlist support of Sumner, 393-394; is snubbed by Fish, 394; commissioned by Dominican Government to expedite annexation treaty, 402-403; is rebuked by Fish, 403; assures Cazneau annexation program will succeed, 408; urges financial assistance be extended to Dominican Republic, 413; is given lesson in diplomatic procedure by Fish, 428-429.

Farrington, Theodore, British vice-consul at Porto Plata, informs Lord Stanley Samaná Bay can be acquired, 242.

Faustin, Emperor of Haiti, refuses to agree to policy of peace, 168; is warned by Sir Henry Bulwer, 168; prepares to wage war, 169-170.

Ferrand, General Louis, issues decree against armed American trade with Haiti, 107.

Ferriss, Orange, 276.

Ferry, Senator Thomas W., 404.

Fessenden, Senator William P., favors purchase of Samaná Bay, 237.

Fiallo, Ramon, inquires concerning American support of Dominican Republic in event of sale of Samaná Bay, 248.

Fillmore, Millard, refers in annual message to Dominican situation, 154.

Fish, Hamilton, Secretary of State, refuses to act in Alta Vela case, 337; political background of, 339; character of, 339-340; relations with Grant, 340; attitude towards Dominican annexation, 340; sends General Babcock to Dominican Republic, 359; gives Babcock instructions on Hartmont loan, 379-380; instructs Wash-

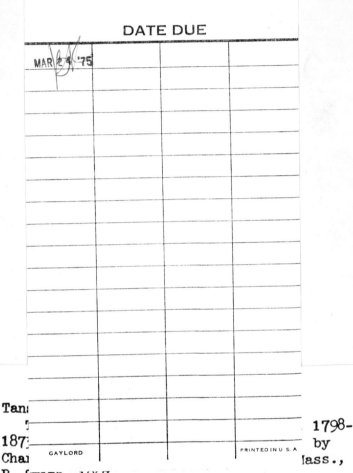

E
183.8   Tan
D6   1798-
T16   187   by
       Cha   lass.,
       P. Smith, 1967.
282463 487p.   21cm.
         At head of title: The Walter Hines Page school
      of international relations, the Johns Hopkins
      University.
         Bibliographical foot-notes.
1.U.S.-For. rel.-Dominican republic.   2.Dominican repub-
lic-For. rel.-U.S.   I.Johns Hopkins University.   Walter
Hines Page school of in-   ternational relations.
II.Title.